THE FED

A History of the South Wales Miners

in the

Twentieth Century

Emblem of the South Wales Miners' Federation, also used by the National Union of Mineworkers (South Wales Area), suitably modified.

THE FED

A History of the South Wales Miners

in the

Twentieth Century

HYWEL FRANCIS
and
DAI SMITH

UNIVERSITY OF WALES PRESS
CARDIFF
1998

First published in 1980 by Lawrence and Wishart Ltd., London
Reprinted in 1981 by Lawrence and Wishart Ltd.

New edition in paperback with new preface by University of Wales Press,
1998

ISBN 0-7083-1422-8

Published with the financial support of the Arts Council of Wales

Printed in Great Britain by Dinefwr Press, Llandybïe

Contents

Illustrations

TEXT ILLUSTRATIONS

Acknowledgements

We would like to thank the following for all their help in making this book possible: Geoff Davies and Guy Lewis of University College Swansea for photographic and mapwork respectively; Margot Jenkins, Mona Robinson and Margaret Sterne for typing the manuscript; Nan Campbell and the South Wales Miners' Library for endless help, particularly in providing most of the photographs; T. J. Davies (Ystradgynlais) for permission to reproduce the photograph of the Abercrave miners (1967); Wynford Emmanuel and Dick Marks of the National Coal Board for help with text illustrations and statistics; John Thomas for permission to reproduce the photograph of underground Markham; the *Western Mail* for permission to reproduce the 1906 cartoon; and David Bevan, the Archivist at the University College Swansea Library, for constant assistance with the NUM collection.

For the loan and identification of photographs the following were particularly helpful: George Baker (Gelli), Cyril Batstone (Pentre), Alun Burge (Blackwood), J. G. Davies (Pontypridd), Clive Edwards (Maesteg), Velinda and John Evans (Mardy), the late Dai Dan Evans (Cardiff), Edgar Evans (Broad Haven), Dai Francis (Cardiff), Kim Howells (Aberdare), Archie James (Treherbert), Evan John (Glais), Andrew Reeves (Melbourne, Australia) and George Thomas (Porthcawl).

For

Jack Wyson
(1915–1997)

and

Sam Francis
(1980–1997)

Foreword

The South Wales Area of the National Union of Mineworkers is delighted to present this history, which complements the earlier volumes by the veteran historian Robin Page Arnot, to its members and their families. We also hope that it will be read in other coalfields and by those throughout the world who wish to learn about the struggles of the South Wales miners in the twentieth century.

This union has always been conscious of recording not only its own history but also the history of the industry and the communities which so decisively shaped our organisation and which in time, and in turn, were shaped by what is still sometimes called 'The Fed'. It is our view that, without a critical appraisal of the whole of our society's past, our lodge, area and national leadership cannot adequately equip itself for the problems which confront us today. For this reason, we believe that this work by these two young historians, both of whom were born and raised in this coalfield and who are now intimately associated with the union's present educational programme, is of particular importance to our newest members.

The problems of non-unionism, scab unionism and of pit closures; the struggle for and in defence of both nationalisation and unity at every level of the union; the concern with wider social and political issues at home and abroad are all detailed and scrutinised as is the dynamic role of the union and its members in the cultural life of the coalfield.

We trust that this volume will assist our members in gaining a better understanding and appreciation of past sacrifices so that they, and succeeding generations, may strive more vigorously for the socialist society our forebears struggled valiantly to attain.

EMLYN WILLIAMS, President
WILL HAYDN THOMAS, Vice-president
Pontypridd,   GEORGE REES, General Secretary
November 1979   South Wales Area, National Union of Mineworkers

Preface to the First Edition

This is not the book we intended to write. It is not the complete, rounded social history of South Wales we plotted and carried in our heads for years. Perhaps that was always an unrealisable ideal though one, even in this book, we have not entirely forsaken. It is for others, and principally the men and women of our community, to say whether we have succeeded in some part of our purpose. Anyway, before the drama unfolds we attach this programme note by way of explanation of its ultimate shape.

The book, although it follows on from Robin Page Arnot's two volumes on the South Wales miners and acknowledges, as must all historians of the British miners, its debt of gratitude to him, stands also on its own. We have attempted to write about the principal institutions used and devised by the South Wales miners within, and for, their society. This is then a trade union history as our title implies: 'the Fed' was the popular name for the South Wales Miners' Federation from 1898 and, although the union became the South Wales Area of the NUM from 1945, it continued to be known by its early abbreviation. What has surprised us is that large numbers of young miners still refer to their organisation as 'the Fed' and we would like to think that this history, officially commissioned as it was by the NUM in South Wales, will stand as a record of struggle that may act as a link for those younger members and their families with their own past. Professional historians have, over the last decade or so, made sterling efforts to break away from the chains that bound labour history exclusively to the study of leadership or of bureaucracy or even politics. Instead there has been fresh, welcome emphasis on the structure of individual communities, on the role of the 'rank and file', of the pressing urgency of work itself and the variety of working-class response beyond the orthodoxies of official pronouncements. With none of this would we quarrel. Hopefully much of the above approach has been incorporated but in a study of this length, with its concentration on the union itself, there are inevitable omissions. Thus, although we do refer, from time to time, to working conditions, we have been reticent, not being miners, to write with the authority needed on such a subject (fortunately the coalfield has an excellent guide in the works of B. L. Coombes; supplemented now by oral testimony). Similarly, we have, apart from lengthy forays into particular examples, not attempted an analysis of those aspects of South Wales' society that do not impinge directly on our subject.

However, it is our argument, too, that the dismissal of histories about trade unionism as 'old hat' can be as crippling as making them the sole purpose of labour history. We are, of course, fortunate in that *our* chosen union was, as we show, intimately associated with its society so that to write a history of the one without the other would be to divorce Adam from Eve by academic decree. It is not a divorce that the people, both leaders *and* led, of whom we write would have approved, or understood. The making of, and struggle for, trade union organisation (within and without) is for us one of the great creative acts of working people. More than this, the trade union movement was the focus for debate on the strengths and weaknesses of the political thrust of the class. Despair could lead many to give up the struggle, but despair never alters the shape of the reality within which the struggle will anyway occur: this is what marks out the critical years 1926 to 1939 when the very existence of the union and its society were directly threatened. Our work is therefore principally focused upon this period whose legacy deeply affects the South Wales in which we have lived.

'Relationship' (often stormily dialectical!) is what has characterised its writing throughout. We came together in the late summer of 1968 outside the leafy, bulbous frontage of Cardiff's Central Library. One of us, the shorter of the two, had made an exile's return (from New York) the previous year to find out, at University College, Swansea, why he knew so little of the inter-war history of Wales; the taller of us had graduated from Swansea in the summer of 1968 intent on discovering the detail of those from Wales who had fought in the Spanish Civil War. From then until the scintillating victories of 1972 and 1974 we worked and thought in a heady atmosphere. Maturity, as well as subsequent setbacks, have induced more tempered opinion but not altered either the memory or the reality of those advances. Even tyro historians could share in that. Indeed we soon discovered that we had literally to make our own past as well as the future.

Looking at material on the Welsh working class that has appeared since the early 1970s with ever-increasing momentum it is salutary to recall the position in 1968. There had been exciting developments in the writing of history about nineteenth- and early twentieth-century Wales by David Williams, and Gwyn A. Williams of Aberystwyth, and by Ieuan Gwynedd Jones and Kenneth O. Morgan of Swansea but there were no secondary works of any real value on post-1918 Wales. Shortly afterwards Michael Woodhouse's pioneering thesis *Rank and File Movements Amongst the Miners of South Wales*, 1910–26 (Oxford D. Phil., 1969) would appear, and we would not feel quite so isolated. Still, worse than this lack of any guide to an uncharted land was to be our discovery that there was no central archival provision for such a major historical experience. Where could we go for primary sources? There were the newspapers of course but, that apart, except on a haphazard basis, there had been no systematic gathering-in of the materials for working-class history in South Wales.

At that time the miners' headquarters was still in Cardiff in 2 St Andrew's Crescent where a kindly executive council provided a desk in a basement room for perusal of their minute books. This only added to the growing sense of frustration since they were, for this period, thin and uninformative. We worried away at the problem, sure there must be more material than we had yet seen. On a gloomy Christmas Eve in 1968, with rain washing drearily down the basement window outside, we, fortified by Christmas sherry inside, put the question to the General Secretary, Dai Francis, yet again. The taller of us asked about the concrete, rectangular annexe attached to the building and used as a store-room for all sorts of things. The key was produced. In the middle of the afternoon we walked into that damp vault and started pulling down file boxes from the shelves. They were mixed up, they were without order of any kind, they were fragmentary: they were also one of the voices we had been waiting for. This was the correspondence, on any and every subject, from the coalfield to the central office. They dated entirely from 1934, the year of reorganisation. Before that, nothing. Later there would be other memoranda, circulars, letters, leaflets and a host of other material, but this was the best Christmas present we could have had. Two days later we were back, squatting on the stone floor for hours, cataloguing with pencil stumps on torn paper (with great crudity no doubt) our 'treasures'.

The NUM could not be blamed for its failure to provide an archive where so many public bodies had faltered; but what, then, of the situation in the coalfield where a Labour government's 'enlightened' fuel policy was shutting pits at a startling rate? We began talking to people, only too acutely aware now that Arthur Horner had died the month we met. Will Paynter and Dai Dan Evans, along with many others, proved invaluable for information, advice and contacts; in miners' fortnight in 1969 we travelled up to Bedlinog and learned that you sometimes had to drink in order to listen. The real pressure came from the crushing realisation that irreplaceable local material was being destroyed, by neglect or accident or, more often, sheer frustration at not knowing how to keep acres of musty books in an upstairs bedroom. As the last lodge secretary died or moved, a hundred years of men's history in a pit or a village could go with him. Fast as we moved, and no matter how much we neglected our ostensible research projects, we could not keep up.

In September 1969 David Smith went to teach in Lancaster University; Hywel Francis, still in South Wales, kept in touch, and grew more anxious. At Bedlinog in the summer we had talked of the need for a Welsh Labour History society, to institutionalise our anguished, but feeble, efforts. In the summer of 1970, with the keen support of the NUM, a few historians met in the Bay View Hotel, Swansea, and so constituted themselves. At last matters moved quickly. Before he was whisked away to the TUC in London Hywel Francis drew up a one-year salvage operation to put before the Social Science Research Council. This had the backing of Professor Glanmor Williams of University College, Swansea, who arranged, in spring 1971, a Colloquium on Welsh Labour History that widened the personnel and concept of the new Society. From September there were three research officers (Merfyn Jones, David Egan and Alun Morgan) in Swansea on the Coalfield History Project and David Smith, now teaching at Swansea, complemented their efforts on the spot.

The Project, extended for a further two years, and with Hywel Francis drafted in, succeeded beyond expectations. It not only established an archive at Swansea for all future research and so saved coalfield history, it also initiated an oral history of industrial workers in South Wales and established in October 1973, on the wreck of the old Institute Libraries, the South Wales Miners' Library. The latter has inaugurated further programmes of salvage and research. More importantly it has, through the Extra-Mural Department at Swansea and the NUM, become a centre for both day-release and residential schools for miners and other industrial workers. In tandem, and in relationship with these foundations for work, the writing of the history began to blossom. In summer 1973 the *Welsh History Review* generously devoted a whole number to Labour History – the

Colloquium Lectures of 1971; then, in May 1972, the journal *Llafur* was launched. At first articles and lectures had to be specially commissioned or cajoled but, via day and then weekend-schools, the impetus has proved irresistible. There is now an audience for serious history in Wales, beyond any narrow circles, that was not tapped before; there is now a written body of their own history that did not exist before. Already there are welcome voices that criticise what has been achieved as not 'enough' in one way or the other. They are right, but *Llafur* is theirs to support and to change, whilst at University College, Cardiff, since 1978 a permanent Research Unit has been established to probe the framework of this history and the unchallenged conceptualisation of modern Welsh historiography. There can be no retreat from this.

We are indebted to many of those younger historians whose articles, theses and, soon, books will take the social history of South Wales beyond present limits. In particular, with this book in mind, we would thank Stuart Broomfield whose valuable Ph.D. (University of Wales), *South Wales in the Second World War: The Coal Industry and its Community* we consulted, and Kim Howells who has given us the benefit of his own experience as both an underground and open-cast ('sunshine') miner, his researches for his Warwick Ph.D. on the miners of the upper Aberdare and Neath valleys from 1937 to 1957, and, stretching friendship beyond reason, even read our entire manuscript before publication.

Our list of debts is truly endless so that we must hope that those who have contributed in many ways to our joint endeavour will find our grateful thanks in this book's appearance. It is our hope that it will contribute, by way of a temporary summation, to the co-operative work in train on the writing of Welsh working-class history and that it will enrich, and so strengthen, by its detail, that collective memory which must possess its own past for itself if it is ever to possess the future for its sons and daughters. Finally, it would be remiss not to single out, for their ceaseless support, the officials and members past and present, of the NUM in South Wales, the Chairman of Llafur, L. J. Williams, whose labours in Labour history have been as selfless as they have been herculean, and our wives, Mair and Norette, who also met in 1968 and have since produced a great deal that was, like this book, entirely unexpected, then, by all parties concerned.

Hywel Francis
David Smith

May 1979

Abbreviations

(in text and notes)

AACC	Amalgamated Anthracite Combine Committee
CI	Communist International
CP	Communist Party
DW	*Daily Worker*
EC	Executive Council
GLRO	Glamorgan Record Office
GRO	Gwent Record Office
ICWPA	International Class War Prisoners' Aid
IFTU	International Federation of Trade Unions
ILP	Independent Labour Party
MFGB	Miners' Federation of Great Britain
MM	Minority Movement
MMM	Miners' Minority Movement
NCB	National Coal Board
NCLC	National Council of Labour Colleges
NUM	National Union of Mineworkers
NUWM	National Unemployed Workers' Movement
PAC	Public Assistance Committee
POUM	Partido Obrero de Unificacion Marxista
PRO	Public Record Office
PD	Powell Duffryn Associated Collieries
RILU	Red International of Labour Unions
SW	*Sunday Worker*
SW(D)N	*South Wales (Daily) News*
SWMF	South Wales Miners' Federation
SWMIU	South Wales Miners' Industrial Union
SWML	South Wales Miners' Library
TUC	Trades Union Congress
UAB	Unemployment Assistance Board
UCS	University College, Swansea
WHR	*Welsh History Review*
WM	*Western Mail*

A Centenary Foreword

> When we were kids we wrote essays on what the valleys must have
> looked like before there were any pits here . . . We're not kids any more
> . . . (soon) . . . we'll be setting essays for kids to write: what'll we we
> give them? 'What did this valley look like when there were pits?'
>
> Gwyn Thomas, *Sorrow For Thy Sons* (1937)

There was nothing that occurred, in general, in South Wales in the
1980s that had not been anticipated; but expecting an outcome one
day is not quite like meeting your fate today. The Welsh coal industry
had been in a long-term, if sporadic, decline since the 1920s; and, at
least since then, the easy assumption that the 'management' of
economic change could be wantonly separated from the attendant
social and cultural structures which had evolved had met with fierce
opposition, in word and deed, from the people most affected. That
was our starting-point.

We began our separate but connected research in the late 1960s
with the conviction that the story we were trying to uncover had not
been fully told; indeed that, in some respects, it had been 'hidden
from history' even within Wales. Our generation of historians was
riding a wave of social and labour history across Europe and
America but it was one which, surprisingly, had relegated the
significant case of the South Wales coalfield to an occasional
illustrative point. Partly that was because no rigorous or committed
archival undertaking, or even work of simple retrieval of materials
in a palpably diminishing industry, had been or was being done. A
great deal of our untutored effort went, down to 1971, into
addressing that situation. The Social Science Research Council
project subsequently established a team of workers who succeeded in
that primary task of assembling the materials at risk. All this, and
the ongoing educational developments at the University of Wales,
Swansea, including the foundation of an Archive and the South
Wales Miners' Library, was, of course, a scholarly and academic

pursuit. No project which had Professor Glanmor Williams to support and inspire it could have been anything else. However, it would be disingenuous not to alert new readers of this book to the overt intention of its authors to help inform the stormy politics and industrial disputes of the 1970s with a knowledge of their antecedents. We looked for a wider audience and we offered our work for publication via the South Wales Area of the National Union of Mineworkers who, in turn, distributed many copies of the published work through their lodges. It was equally clear to us that the often provocative and challenging material – to an existing historical consensus and a homogenising Welsh politics – which we were narrating had, for that very reason, to be buttressed scrupulously and exhaustively by citation of the evidence at each and every step.

Even so, the leap from recorded (and hitherto forgotten) event to action replay was occasionally astonishing. On more than one occasion, we were 'blamed' for the rash of strikes in the early 1980s, when younger miners drew sustenance from *The Fed*: it was even alleged to have been the origin of the Lewis Merthyr stay-in strike of 1983. This was to exaggerate our direct influence as historians. Nevertheless, the frequency with which *The Fed* was quoted by rank-and-file miners and presented to public supporters of the struggle all over Europe, especially in 1984–5, was testimony to its catalytic purpose.

Over the years, *The Fed* has, largely, received a good press and where our interpretation or analysis has been here and there questioned or corrected the overall thrust of the argument seems to us to have stood the test of time. The current volume is, therefore, republished in an unchanged format since it was, in its own time, as historicised by its time as it was itself about a time past. At the bar of historical scholarship we would still plead our footnotes.

By the end of the 1970s and with the advent of a Conservative administration for whom the post-1945 settlement of the economy and society was no longer desirable politics, the kind of educational and intellectual venture on which we had been engaged looked, to us, just as desirable but rather less assured of the 'long revolution's' time-scale which we had imbibed in the 1960s. Some of our own disputatious energy had been poured into scornful dismissal of the tactical opportunism of those who postured and postulated on the left; the danger now was of being wrongfooted by a right-wing politics which might successfully tantalise and enrage until it turned a defensive upheaval to its own advantage. The first edition of this book was published in 1980 at the start of that climactic decade in the history of Wales. A governmental change in 1979 had been preceded by the overwhelming rejection of an elected assembly whilst the collective institutions which had shaped the industrial and urban culture of our country (trade unions, local politics, county councils and the myriad of domestic voluntarist bodies associated with them) were already, and in advance of any concerted dismantling, obviously in terminal decline or smug disarray. Despite the accumulative detail we had garnered to prove that the unsung heroes of our epic story were part of a conscious attempt by the Welsh working class to forge and sustain a differently designed world, not just some emotional thrashing about in the margins but a concerted, institutionalised threat to political power elsewhere and the redirection of culture at home, writing at that cusp time often felt as if we were delivering public history as national elegy. Our closing paragraph weaved cautious hope with pessimistic prophecy.

Then, it was as if the elongated process of a slowly unravelling history and its recording, went into a fast-forward tempo which whirred on relentlessly until the spool shuddered to a halt and the film spiralled off the machine. Aneurin Bevan had written in 1952 that to experience 1926 was 'like watching a film unfold that I had already seen made'. That was certainly the feeling of miners from Brynlliw and Maerdy who, at this time, visited the US coalfields of Appalachia. What they saw was a rampant capitalism, a virulently anti-union state and the decimation of their communities: it was their parents' past and indeed at the same time their own, and their children's future.

To live through the early 1980s, after years bent over yellowing newsprint or burrowing amongst fragmentary documentation, was like watching a series of overlapping images collide and blur into myth until reality re-focused them. In 1981, Emlyn Williams, the president of the South Wales NUM, invoked the power of direct action and the syndicalist tradition of industrial democracy:

> I won't call it a strike. I would call it a demonstration for existence . . . The miners in South Wales are saying 'we are not accepting the dereliction of our mining valleys, we are not allowing our children to go immediately from school into the dole queue. It is time we fought.'

This time Emlyn Williams wobbled a government which, peeved and perturbed by the unresolved problem of the miners across Britain, halted and waited until, in recoil and with increased determination, it organised itself for the bruising, crushing conflict to come. In the early 1980s the Conservative Government, having learned the lessons of defeat in 1972 and 1974, decided to wait. They now prepared for battle as the secret Ridley Report subsequently revealed.

There had been serious skirmishes, virtually on an annual basis, from the moment the Conservative Government came to power. Beginning with the Deep Duffryn campaign of 1979, however, resistance began to take on a qualitatively different form which reached a high-water mark in the fraught conflict of 1984–5. The linking of pit jobs to community survival and indeed to the national survival of Wales was a phenomenon with echoes of the past, yet now on a different scale. Using what was originally a slogan inspired by Cymdeithas yr Iaith Gymraeg (the Welsh Language Society) the NUM in South Wales turned a slogan into a nation-wide strategy: 'Cae pwll, lladd cymuned' ('Close a pit, kill a community'). The writer Raymond Williams wrote memorably of the nature and intensity of this resistance:

> The miners' strike is being represented as the last kick of an old order. Properly understood, it is one of the first steps towards a new order. This is especially the case in the emphasis they have put on protecting their *communities*. Here is another keyword which needs to be understood.
>
> What the miners, like most of us, mean by their communities, is the places where they have lived and want to go on living, where generations not only of economic but of social effort and human care have been invested, and which new generations will inherit. Without that kind of strong whole attachment, there can be no meaningful community.

Much was claimed, then and later, for the sense that a new kind of politics – pluralist and participatory – was emerging around the miners' struggle. Doubtless the Wales Congress in Support of Mining Communities was a unique, albeit temporary, coalition which embraced unions and political parties but also women's support groups, churches and gay and lesbian groups. In particular, the women's groups, initially simply, as their name implied, a support of an old patriarchal society, did begin to raise fundamental questions about the place of women in a still largely 'male chauvinist' valleys' world: individually and collectively women used the strike to create new spaces and opportunities for themselves.

The depth of the resistance in South Wales (it was the only coalfield where any pit was 'scab-free' – six in all) meant that it had the moral authority to call for a national return to work when all was clearly lost. That return, dignified as it was, was a recognition that a *nationalised* coal industry and a *National* Union of Mineworkers were perilously close to extinction. The death of Will Paynter (to whom we dedicated the first edition of this book) in the December of the strike seemed to symbolise the passing of an era. His funeral, however, provided the opportunity for an oration which reaffirmed community and internationalist values which were to endure long after the strike in what were subsequently to become known as 'post-coal communities'.

In the ensuing years, family debts, low morale, redundancy payments, wave after wave of closures and two further Conservative victories in 1987 and 1992, spelt the end of the South Wales coalfield as a major employer. By the autumn of 1992, when the Secretary of State for Energy, Michael Heseltine, announced what seemed then to be the final round of major pit closures, it was already all but over in South Wales, with Betws, Taff Merthyr and Tower the only pits remaining. The massive national demonstration in London in support of mining communities appeared to herald a brief revival of hope. Nevertheless the government was still able to pick off pits individually throughout 1993–4 in readiness for their real long-term goal, the privatisation of the industry, which they were able to achieve by 1 January 1995. Communities had been laid to waste because 'society' seemingly no longer existed.

If indeed there was 'no such thing as Society', it had required a surprising amount of smashing up by the indisputably existing power of the State. Twinned images of 1984–5 illustrate graphically the tension and its temporary resolution. The first is of a lengthy, repeated journey across the Severn Bridge and along the M4 corridor, here more a means of tightening the noose than a conduit for hi-tech prosperity, by juggernaut lorries led and flanked by police cars and motorcycles which closed the slip roads to let the wagons, nose to tailgate in convoy, accelerator pedals to the floor, roar through unimpeded, night and day, empty then full, to blitzkrieg the rebellion into submission. It was as brutal, as mechanical and as anonymous as a gang rape. At the very end, the unblinking cameras swung back to the places where people lived, where food parcels had been assembled and hopes nurtured until they broke. The second set of unforgettable images in South Wales was that of the men and women who had tried, unavailingly after all, to stem such an armoured assault, assembling in the cold March dawn to walk back, in order, to the pitheads that now tugged at them like impatient mausoleums. At Maerdy, solidly resolute to the last at the top of the Rhondda Fach, behind a fading banner and to the brave, plaintive beat of a band, the strikers and their families walked from the 1905 Institute the long final half-mile to Maerdy colliery and the pit cage. That procession was flanked all the way by the applause, the helpless plaudits of supporters and, you sensed all too readily, by the ghosts of an industrial history that was over.

The obituaries of the remaining pits had already been written. And before the centenary of the Fed could be celebrated by its members the living organism atrophied into a winding-up service. The optimistic historiography of the South Wales miners remained resilient in academe but in popularising work was either sentimentalised or translated, sometimes uneasily, into the growth industry of heritage centres and industrial museums. By the 1990s, with a working-class world in shards in Wales more than anywhere else, there was a whole-scale degeneration into a mythology blurring together national identity and class struggle to make the past acceptable for a self-selective Wales temporarily in possession of an ideologically defined present. This shining morning-face of the nation fed itself and concealed the bare arse of the Welsh people as best it could.

And more than all of this, the industrial defeat of 1984–5 was followed by an ideological assault whose objective it was to wipe out the collectivist culture of the valleys. The Conservative Government's Valleys' Initiative in 1988 was, behind the greening of the slagheaps and the planting of daffodils in every conceivable open space, a serious attempt at destroying the inheritance of solidarity and struggle by turning the valleys into a 'Greater Cardiff'. This was to be achieved through a single economic strategy: a market-led approach of inward investment for a 'screw-driver' economy, based on low-paid employment and the creation of a new individualistic entrepreneurial culture.

Myths, as functions in the historical development of marginalised groups led by deracinated politicos, serve the interests of those who would wish for equal validity or weight for all the narratives of modern Wales. A future without the overlordship represented by the Fed and all its offshoots was balm alike to the deferentially compromised and to the *bien-pensants* who had long wished that the bulk of their compatriots would think other thoughts. Physical disappearance allied to historical amnesia might yet do the trick and so create a Wales plc as palatable to potential buyers as the worthies who had clung to the wreck of twentieth-century Wales since, after all, it was the only wreck they had. Yet, the narrative had a twist left.

For sure, a particular 'degenerate syndicalist' style of leadership had been discredited. Pits were shut down. Despair followed on agony and some communities literally fell apart in its wake. Odd alliances were sought and made in deals and compromises that are still to hatch. Political concepts were summarily discarded by some, along with values and principles in other cases. Not every truth was faced or digested, not every mistake confessed or hypocrisy dissected. No victory, except in the fevered recess of some activists' dreams, could possibly be claimed. A way of life had, by the mid-1990s, to all intents and purposes passed out of viable historical existence. But if this was no claimable victory, nor was it the nightmare of defeat which 1926 had brought to an as yet socially unformed people. History, with a sense of the mutual obligations and strengths across future and past generations, had more than whispered through the 1984–5 conflict and would not be silenced for, in the considered surrender of that strike's closure, no cultural weapons of identity were shouldered, no pride was taken away by what had occurred and no promises made. The achieved history, now brought to a point of action, now diffused into yearning or reminiscence, was too powerful to suppress. The narrative line had not petered out. The spool would take the re-threaded, mended and adjusted film. It was, more than mere economic survival, an historically induced self-belief in their own worth as themselves in their own communities, which had made the duration of the strike, against all the odds, unimaginable to the logic which enumerates societies by shareholders and mortgages. What had been inherited had been reaffirmed and so in its contemporary context altered. Tower Colliery proved to be more than emblematic. It was a new chapter heading.

In the government's unseemly rush towards coal privatisation, Tower, the last deep mine left in South Wales, became the final sacrifice in April 1994, or so it seemed. A massive political and fund-raising public campaign ensued, including a stay-down strike, a march to London and an art auction. The Tower Employees' Buy-Out (TEBO) won the tender to own the pit, in a genuine workers' co-operative initiative. All this was achieved through the sacrifices of supporters and most of all through the £2 million raised by the 239 miners who pledged £8,000 each from their redundancy money.

On 2 January 1995 the Tower miners, their families and their supporters took over the control of the pit as they marched triumphantly back to work: it was a historic moment which gladdened the hearts of all those who had always judged nationalisation to be a political error, as indeed predicted by *The Miners' Next Step* in 1912.

There was, of course, a certain poetic justice in all of this. Tower had received transferred miners from many pits: it was in many ways a microcosm of the best of the coalfield, and symbolised the communal aspirations of Wales itself. As such it was uncompromisingly socialist in ethos and aspiration. Elaine Morgan, writer and daughter of a miner 'summed it up' in the award-winning BBC Wales documentary *Walking Towards the Light*:

> Nearly everyone in Wales was keeping their fingers crossed for them. It seemed to me a kind of socialism . . . and it seemed to me that Tower was pulling a very good trick. If you want to get rid of capitalists, one way is to bypass them, making them redundant.

The story of Tower Colliery reverberated. No single piece of industrial history lifted so many hearts and minds in 1990s Wales. Far from being a moment that would pass, it has proved to be an example that resounds. The clearest indication of its fertile power resides in the documentaries, plays, films and even opera which are spinning off its axis. When this last deep mine in Wales eventually closes sometime in the next century, it will, therefore, only be after it has opened up, in the most practical sense possible, the social potential latent in co-operative self-direction and communal self-help. In the penultimate year of the century since the foundation of the Fed the concentric ripple effect from Tower moved outwards to the astounding electoral victory of the Labour Party and then the narrow delivery, ensured basically by the votes at the epicentre of the old coalfield, of an elected National Assembly for Wales. If the most vitally significant Welsh institution this century, as our book demonstrates, is the Fed, then it will be up to the people of Wales to see if they can and will breathe as much citizenship and democratic life into the new institution which they have now willed into being. They have their example. They have their chance.

Hywel Francis   Dai Smith
1998

I would like to restore to . . . the poor of the past, the gift of theory. Like the hero of Molière, they have been talking prose all the time. Only whereas the man in Molière didn't know it himself, I think they have always known it, but we have not. And I think we ought to.

Eric Hobsbawm, *On History* (1997)

CHAPTER ONE

The Union in its Society

The South Wales miners entered the twentieth century with a history of compromise as well as of defiance, with a string of defeats and precious few victories, with a culture in as much flux as the population was fluid. They also entered it with a union that was, for the first time, coalfield-wide, operating from Carmarthenshire through Glamorgan to Monmouthshire in an industrial belt that would before 1914 hold two-thirds of the population of Wales. Like so many of the miners' responses to the realities of struggle in capitalist society the union was born from despair more than from hope. None the less, the mixture of ethnic and cultural factors that was busy acting as a yeast in this impersonal world would soon claim the union too as a focus for thought and action within, and beyond, the mining communities that were now taking permanent shape in the folds of those steep valleys whose upper slopes were buried by waste-tips that replaced the forests in an inverted, deadly reminder of the coal below. It was a swift process of change that left a sour legacy. The buzz and hum of South Welsh life in its prosperous heyday can be as easily over-romanticised as the later grey days of economic misery can be made to lose their human vitality, but what both these delivered worlds had in common was a reliance upon and a growing con-sciousness of the need for organisations that could be controlled. The miners found them sometimes in rugby clubs, frequently in the societies spawned by chapels; they sang in them and played in them from choral groups to comic jazz bands; they worked through political parties and in their unions. Knowing the fragmented nature of their own lives, whether at work or in their sprawling villages, they did not despise the hard virtues of institutional continuity though they readily questioned their own creations. None of this was unique to South Wales, yet all of it was quick with the particular life that had come into being there. The history of the South Wales miners did not begin in 1898 but that year did signal the start of what would be a profound shift of emphasis in their own lives of continuing struggle.

The foundation of the SWMF in October 1898 was effective recognition by the leadership of the seven District Unions in the Coalfield that the stage in economic development which had seen the opening up of virgin seams of coal by family concerns was now over.[1] The six-month strike which preceded the Federation's formation, and which finally weaned even traditionalists like Mabon away from the sliding scale, was the result of the coalowners' determination to preserve their rate of profit. They were prepared, in a rising market, to sustain a temporary loss in order to defeat the men's proposals for a more favourable scale or a Conciliation Board. For the miners' leader, Mabon, that epitome of late Victorian compromise, the dispute came as a profound shock, whilst he found in its ending only humiliation at the hands of the men whom he regarded as, in a sense, partners in the great enterprise of developing South Wales:

> Surely our services to the community and to the coal trade deserve some better treatment at your hands than that which you now offer us. I entreat you . . . to give us something to go back to the men which we can . . . advocate.[2]

It seemed that a new form of organisation would be necessary before the owners would again accord a respect to reasonable demands. The new Union, and its affiliation to the MFGB, would make more effective any coalfield-wide strategy that the men might adopt. Nevertheless, the leadership of the SWMF was concerned, above all, with a stabilisation of what it regarded as its legitimate role in South Wales society, a role which implied inclusion in the social fold. The eventual acceptance, by the owners, of a Conciliation Board, in March 1903, allowed the workmen's representatives to see themselves as an accepted side of the equation in labour relations which, it had long been their contention, was a necessary factor in a maturing economy. The President (Mabon), Vice-President (William Brace), and General Secretary (Thomas Richards), were entitled to view their stance in the Union, and later in Parliament as Lib.-Lab. MPs, as being a more sophisticated, not to say progressive, approach to the problems of their society. Indeed, the second object of the SWMF's first set of rules was:

> To take into consideration the question of trade and wages, and to protect workmen generally and regulate the relations between them and employers.[3]

Certainly, this desire for accommodation was neither sinister nor defeatist. It was rather symptomatic of a vibrant optimism. South Wales had literally been giving a shape, architectural and cultural, to the economic and industrial power produced from its coal and iron and shipping. The turbulence that surged beneath its surface was mostly checked by the outward signs of success whilst the population, at large, was imbued with the same values that its leaders represented. Labour was dignified and virtuous; sobriety and self-help, allied to organisation, would win for Labour a rightful place. In most areas of the coalfield, communities – and their attendant services – had been created out of mere aggregations of colliers by men who soon organised their local politics as effectively as they had their religion and their Union. Perhaps nothing is more revealing of the unity behind the life of these communities than the inter-relationship of activities in one man's career. This was true consensus politics for it was not just about meeting those of different interests on a common ground, it was expressive of a real satisfaction with the possibilities of life.[4] The satisfaction was fed by future promise.

South Wales was full of markets and market-days but not the cattle-marts and fairs of its rural past; these were consumers' markets, as were the horse-and-carts that trundled around selling cockles or fish and chips. Even neighbours, especially the widowed, could find a ready market for their wares – hot faggots or small beer on Sunday mornings for the hung-over. And in most valley towns there existed embryonic chain-stores, cavernous emporia positively dripping with hardware of one sort or another. This was a society concerned about its appearance, anxious about its watch-chains and fobs, queueing for haircuts and shaves on Saturday nights, reeking of mothballs and boot polish on Sundays; and inside the houses ornaments of china or brass were three-dimensional proof of money and concern for the 'higher' things of life, whilst a framed photograph on a piano was conclusive testimony of hard work, thrift and status. Meanwhile the coal-dirt could be kept at bay by an army of women trained to wash and scrub and polish as men trooped in and out on alternate shifts. The shops dutifully supplied tons of buckets, acres of linoleum and miles of coconut matting.[5]

If the chapels were full, so were the music halls, the boxing booths and the football matches. Building of workmen's houses may have been hasty and inadequate (though by no means always so) yet great care was lavished on monumental places of worship, intricate design grafted on to town halls and hotels, and architectural *gravitas* invested in the mercantile offices and streets of the ports. A society, then, intent on bolstering its much-professed spirituality with a strong dose of the materialism that was its *raison d'être*.[6]

The nature and structure of the SWMF were inseparable from its social base. To an extent the federal basis that gave its twenty constituent Districts great powers of autonomy was a product of the geographical configuration of the area. Inter-valley communication was poor, so that opinion tended to flow up and down a particular valley instead of being exchanged and altered at a common meeting-place. There was more to it than this, however. Geological conditions might vary considerably in South Wales, not just from area to area or pit to pit but even within a pit itself. Since the collier's wages depended heavily on the local customs and price lists that his local leadership negotiated, his first defence, he felt, had to be at this level. Only half of the monthly contribution of 1s. went to the new Central Executive. Those whose voices were soon raised in demands for stronger centralisation could be characterised as men with a grudge (sometimes temporary) against the workings of a system which looked continually for accommodation; the more independent the District organisation was, the more likelihood of keeping any dispute a local one. In all of this, the miners' agents and sub-agents, men appointed and paid by their own Districts, were key figures.[7]

They were, of course, much more than mere industrial experts. Their style of life was more that of a professional man, a white-collar worker, than it was that of tne collier. The position was one of considerable responsibility and had commensurate power and influence. Mabon's career was a shining example of the potential in a miners' agent's life; the message was not lost on younger men like Frank Hodges or Vernon Hartshorn, whose espousal of different methods and more radical language cannot conceal their kinship to the older men. It would be wrong, too, to characterise this as self-seeking. On the contrary, it was considered a correct pursuit of an advantage that was mutually beneficial to men and leaders. It was Social Darwinism in practice, tempered by humanity and tenderised by the collier's self-esteem. His leaders were talented but not above him in the sense that those other sociological products of the time, the Captains of Industry, were. The careers of the miners' agents were dependent, to a considerable degree, on the extent to which they impressed their abilities on a wider public. Only with this kind of base could Hartshorn rise to political victory in Maesteg; only with this sort of philosophy could the press take pride in the leaders of all sections of South Walian society. The maverick figure was much more the exotic, revolver-shooting C. B. Stanton, whose dramatic career corkscrewed in and out of prominence at precisely the time when the pre-1914 certainties were being remoulded.[8]

Leadership by the agents could affect the whole industrial and political tenor of their Districts. The latter acted as power bases for the agents whose own political ambitions invariably gave them the look of American political bosses. Their removal from office was not easy nor could their right to take unilateral decisions be challenged to much effect. That a strong trade union, imbued with a 'responsible' philosophy, like the SWMF, could act for the good of society as a whole was a viewpoint not in dispute in the first decade of this century, in South Wales. The District system, then, reinforced the existing desires to negotiate rather than confront by allowing each District considerable autonomy over its funds and local disputes. The agent was the lightning rod. The qualities required by these men were, according to the press, those of moderation, of financial acumen, pragmatism and administrative skill; not a recipe for a zealot. Even as sympathetic an observer as H. S. Jevons, writing in 1915, took exactly this view:

> Under present conditions very much depends upon the personality of the Agent. If he is a good organiser, energetic and firm in negotiations, he secures good terms for his men in all disputes, and keeps them loyal to the Union, whilst strikes are rare and never unofficial, because he has the men well in hand. On the contrary, an agent who is a poor organiser, and slack or weak in negotiations, does not keep the confidence of his men, and a state of industrial unrest ensues which is bad for all concerned. Unofficial strikes of a few days' duration become frequent, whilst the membership of the Union dwindles away. It would seem that the system of electing agents is partly at fault, for a fluent speaker may capture his audiences with oratory, but have few of the business qualities required for his work.[9]

Jevons was able to write in this tone in 1915 because the duality he mentions had become more worrying to those who had seen trade unions as instruments of control by which the working masses could be both appeased and brought, voluntarily, within the social compact. What was disturbing was the willingness of the men to break that compact and, of course, South Wales had been a violent indicator of this willingness after 1908. The duality was one that ran through the entire society.

The ethos of 'respectability', much vaunted and well fostered by South Walian communities, could survive only fitfully if economic well-being diminished. The difficult geological conditions under which the

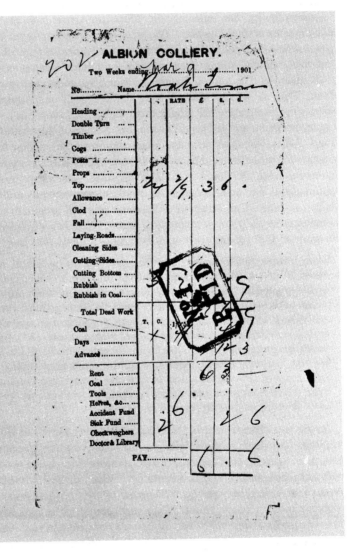

Albion (Cilfynydd) miner's docket, 1901.

colliers worked could cause a fall in the rate of profit; almost inevitably this would be the signal for a loss in the rate of wages. Wages, in their turn, were the foundation stone of the general prosperity of South Wales, not just that of the colliers. This, allied to the rise in living costs since the mid-1890s, the operation of the Eight Hours Act and the consequent further decline in productivity, led to a clustering of bitter grievances around the issue of abnormal places and a minimum wage.[10]

When the basic material existence of this society suffered, for whatever reason, its hidden fissures were revealed. Then the mushroom growth of the coalfield from the 1870s was not indicated by the pretensions of its chief city or the size of its town halls with their insistent clock-faces but in spasms of feeling that denied the ordered, machine-run society. The revival of 1904–5 is, in part, the expression of the anguish that a first-generation industrial population feels at its own implicit denial of a previous pattern of life; the sobriety of the established nonconformity, at times, proved inadequate as a salve for the new miseries.[11] South Wales for two decades (1890–1910) absorbed immigrants at an almost identical rate to that of the USA with the consequent overcrowding and inadequate urban facilities.[12] Coal was hand-cut, so that productivity was in direct proportion to male population. Fluidity led on to fertilisation of the people with ideas and expectations. If this was not yet a throw-away society, neither was it a static one.

The social philosophy that was dominant extended its grip into the work-place even though it was there that its contradictory nature was often revealed; the men's discontent was, still, often expressed in its form, oftener tempered by it. Conciliation was more than an industrial policy, it was a manner of life. If there were disagreements between the generations of Lib.-Labs. and ILPers, the gap widened still more between both of the former and those who saw and felt their industrial power all around them and looked for bolder remedies to discontent. The immigrants were mostly young men; they were joined to those colliers whose youth and skill were the pre-1914 substitutes for machine-mining. The historical differences between pit villages and the contemporary sociological and economic variety of South Wales seemed to pale into insignificance beside the commonalty induced by similar labour, similar living conditions and similar work. For all that, the demands for a greater degree of centralisation in the affairs of the federated Union foundered on the rocks of local pride. The Rhondda No. 1 District, in its debate on the centralisation of funds that had been

tabled on the SWMF Conference Agenda, spoke with a single voice
against any change at all until, in the words of the agent, Watts-
Morgan, all districts had first attained the power and organisation that it
already possessed. Delegates spoke against any loss of 'Home Rule of
the District' and of their fears that centralisation might put them under
'some Czar or other' whilst Mabon administered the kiss of death:

> The physical peculiarity of the country in the South Wales Coalfield
> rendered the centralisation of funds far more unworkable than it was in
> England. Mabon remarked 'that it was the thirtieth year that he had been
> serving the Rhondda men. He was glad to see the number of young men
> around them that day (*applause*). It was not the first time they had this
> question put before them. It had a kind of resurrection about every five years
> (*laughter*). It was one of the weaknesses that did happen, unfortunately. The
> gentleman who first raised this question was now a manager of a colliery in
> China, he thought – (*laughter*) – who stated that he believed none of the men
> on the Central should be paid two or three days' pay for one day's work but
> he [Mabon] could assure them there was no two day's pay for one day's
> work for any official from the top to the bottom.

With pious resolutions to help poorer districts and weaker lodges,
Rhondda voted against (only two delegates were for) centralisation.[13]
The scheme was duly rejected and in 1908 a special conference, tired of
the resurrectionary habits of the centralisers, voted against 'the
principle of Centralisation'.[14] Behind these insistent demands was the
notion that a Union could be organised whose integrated nature might
belie the atomistic conditions of the men's lives rather better than did
their self-confident societies, since the imposing structure of the latter
had weak foundations.

   The SWMF's task of convincing a tempestuous workforce of the
need for organisation was ultimately made easier by the speed of
economic development and the rapidity of company amalgamations
into combines which flowed from it. The most industrially and
politically conscious section of the South Wales miners before 1914
were those employed by the first Welsh coal trust, the Cambrian
Combine.[15] This forging of a consciousness was hastened by the social
geography of the narrow steep-sided valleys. Housing tended to be
cramped and terraced and the ribbon development prevented the
establishing of a physical civic centre to the communities, a feature
which could have countered the hardening class identity. On the
contrary, the few social amenities, particularly the institutes and their
libraries, were overwhelmingly proletarian in origin and patronage.[16]

Peaceful Persuasion:

or, Strengthening the numbers of the Federation at Maesteg.

Western Mail cartoon which manages to be both anti-woman and anti-Federation (4 September 1906).

Even the Nonconformist chapels, traditionally seen as one of the more effective agencies of social control, were in certain circumstances interpreted as being breeding grounds for young militant miners. Aneurin Bevan considered that their Sunday schools helped mould the character of the miners by cultivating the gift of expression.[17] In the mining village of Cwmgiedd in the Swansea Valley the Congregational Minister ensured that no one volunteered for the Great War by constantly delivering pacifist sermons from his pulpit.[18]

The evolving out of this of what can be called a political consciousness did not end by any means with the SWMF's affiliation to the Labour Party in 1908.[19] The South Wales miners indicated in the following year both their political and educational independence by their support of the Ruskin College Strike which led to those pre-eminently Marxist institutions, the Central Labour College and the Plebs' League, becoming so much part of the future of the coalfield.[20] The role the College and the League were to play and the influence they exercised over the educational and political development of the institutes and their libraries cannot be overemphasised.[21] The first tangible expression of this influence was the publication in 1912 of *The Miners' Next Step* by the largely Mid-Rhondda based Unofficial Reform Committee whose links with the Labour College and the Plebs' League were close and vital.[22] By the spurning of conventional Labour parliamentary politics and in lauding the syndicalist virtues of direct industrial action, it obviously drew on the experiences of its own locality during the Cambrian Combine Dispute of 1910–11. It can be argued that serious industrial disturbances were a form of direct action; there had been unrest of this kind in 1898, 1893 and in the 1870s, but with nothing like the magnitude, drama and lasting effects of those of 1910–11.

The evolution of this class/trade union/political consciousness towards proletarian *internationalism* was accelerated both by the cosmopolitan nature of parts of the coalfield and later by the radicalising effect of the Great War. But there were serious initial difficulties. One miner recalled the problems associated with a racially mixed workforce in the Neath Valley in the early years of the Federation:

> What a mixture of languages and dialects were there sometimes! Yorkshire and Durham men, Londoners, men from the Forest of Dean, North Welshmen – whose language is much deeper and more pure than the others from South Wales – two Australians, four Frenchmen and several

coloured gentlemen. Of course, the Welshmen were at a disadvantage when they tried to convey their thoughts in the mixture of languages that is called English. The meetings had to be in English because most of the Welshmen could express themselves to some extent in English, while the majority of the English maintained a frightened silence whenever Welsh was spoken.[23]

Probably the most telling wave of immigration (and possibly the largest single ethnic injection since the Irish of the 1840s) to break down the parochialism of the Welsh miner was that which came from Northern Spain from 1907 onwards.[24] The Spanish Orconero Iron Ore Company had since 1873 been a subsidiary of the Dowlais Iron Company which entailed that the former guaranteed to supply a regular, fixed quantity of ore to the latter.[25] This close working arrangement took on a new dimension in 1907 when several hundred Spanish workers and their families were imported into the Dowlais Iron Works for the allegedly explicit purpose of undercutting wages. In order to help them to settle, a street was built specifically for them and given the name King Alphonso Street after the reigning monarch of the time. But the whole exercise was ill-conceived, for the most influential members of this new community were strongly republican and either socialist or anarcho-syndicalist in political outlook. By 1911 there were two hundred and sixty-four Spaniards living in the Merthyr Tydfil County Borough, within which Dowlais was located.[26]

Shortly after arriving in Dowlais, several of the families moved to the almost wholly Welsh-speaking mining community of Abercrave in the upper Swansea Valley, some twenty-five miles to the west of Dowlais. A French mining company had opened up what became appropriately named International Colliery and in the years before the Great War a large influx of Portuguese, Germans, Frenchmen, Belgians and Spaniards, along with the native Welshmen, worked there. The largest group of immigrants were some two hundred Spaniards who eventually settled as a homogeneous community in Davies Street and the Brooklands which was a single-tiered terrace of dwellings. The Brooklands soon became known to the native Welsh as 'Spanish Row' or more exotically 'Espaniardos Row'.[27]

But by the summer of 1914, the Spaniards were accused by many of the older Welsh colliers of not being given abnormal places, of untrustworthiness and living in 'disgusting conditions'. Several meetings were held, a demonstration was organised and a strike only narrowly averted. But all these 'foreigners' were known to be members of the SWMF and the Spaniards in particular were strong trade unionists. At the height of the crisis, Esteban, one of the leaders of the Spanish community, whose son twenty years later was to return to Spain as a volunteer in the International Brigades, made an appeal for international working-class solidarity:

> Fellow workers of Abercrave do not besmirch the fair reputation of the Welsh collier for love of freedom and chivalrous readiness to succour the weak and harbour the oppressed.[28]

It is significant that the miners who tended to support the immigrants were also recent arrivals in the village. One was the Irish born father of Dick Beamish who had been a merchant seaman in Cardiganshire in his early life. His championing of the immigrants led him to be elected on to the lodge committee, backed mainly by Spanish votes.[29]

The Spaniards were feared because their very arrival challenged the stable paternalistic social order in a hitherto closed semi-rural Welsh community. It was their life-style and culture which seemed most of all to transgress the norms of a Welsh Nonconformist village. The chapel deacons were horrified by the garlic-smelling Spaniards who drank, sang and danced to the accordion outside their homes on Saturday and Sunday nights. The fact that they were Catholics, lapsed Catholics or, even worse, militant atheists did not help matters. This hostility translated itself into the industrial conflict which erupted in 1914.[30]

The influence of the village elders, whether as lodge officials or deacons (or both) was however seriously undermined by a younger generation who welcomed this transgression of the old order. The process of acceptance was accelerated by their trade union consciousness for, as we have seen, many of them were socialists or anarcho-syndicalists. In Dowlais a branch was actually established of the PSOE (the Spanish Socialist Workers Party). It was never known of a Spaniard to be in arrears with his Federation dues and some became active lodge committeemen. They were also noted for their skill and for being 'good workmen'.[31] An indication of their assimilation was that Welsh colliers learnt Spanish words and phrases in order to work with them more easily and many of the Spaniards spoke Welsh fluently. Some of their closest Welsh working friends could converse in Spanish quite fluently. Colliery districts acquired Spanish names and it was not uncommon to hear a Welsh collier shout from the coalface to a Spanish haulier: '*Caballista! Uno caballo!*' ('Haulier! One horse!') The reply was likely to have been in Welsh or Spanish but not in English.[32]

Perhaps even more importantly, the younger generation of Welsh colliers grew to respect this new immigrant community all the more when many of its sons excelled on the rugby field, some of whom graduated to first-class clubs where they had distinguished footballing careers.[33]

The young militant miners' leaders in Abercrave who emerged in the 1920s acknowledged that they primarily acquired much of their sharpened trade union consciousness and internationalist outlook from the presence of the Spaniards in their midst. The more 'advanced' ideas of socialism and particularly syndicalism did not arrive in the upper Swansea Valley with the publication of *The Miners' Next Step* but with the coming of the Spaniards.[34]

The famed dispute at the Cambrian Combine Collieries was an industrial struggle whose origins lay deeper than in the immediate issue of cutting prices. The simultaneous, and almost equally intense, strike and riots in the Aberdare Valley had as their immediate cause the ending of the men's customary privilege of having blocks for firewood from the colliery's timber-yard.[35] The issue of control, albeit on a small scale and about 'work' matters, was at stake; certainly the question of control, in the wider social sense, was in the minds of the most ardent opponents and proponents of the men. However, the strikers in mid-Rhondda in 1910 were asking for all-out coalfield-wide support of a sort that could not (and some thought should not) be given so long as the Union retained a structure in which geographical districts governed like autonomous units by powerful local Union bosses – the miners' agent – remained the norm. There was, in 1910–11, no organisational means, apart from the men's local unofficial committee, to give vent to the aggression that gathered like a boil. This aggression was not reflected by the established leadership because it was a symptom which the whole striving for 'Respectability' was designed to ignore. The inevitable result was that the social controls which could be exercised by allowing organised labour a recognised position within the fold would snap at times of crisis.

Although the mid-Rhondda dispute ended in the men's defeat, it gave fresh impetus to the demands for more effective control, by the men, of their own Union, and it added to the audience ready to listen to the ideas brought into the coalfield via Ruskin College, the new Central Labour College and its literary and scholastic offshoots, the *Plebs Magazine* and classes. Again it is no coincidence, but the very nub of the matter, that the issue of *The Miners' Next Step* from Tonypandy, in early 1912, should occur after men had been radicalised by the Cambrian strife, should have come after the Executive Council had been harried over centralisation again, in 1911, but before, in 1912, the greatest pre-war debate on the matter was to take place. That the pamphlet's sub-title was 'being a Suggested Scheme for the Reorganisation of the Federation', is the clearest sign that the most 'advanced' thinkers in the coalfield clearly tied together the restructuring of their Union with that reshaping of society they so desired. These men had met in Cardiff in the summer of 1911 to discuss the furtherance of 'a militant policy' and had resolved to form themselves 'into a party for the purpose of propagating advanced thought'. At their next meeting, held in Tonypandy in August, their ideas were brought into focus by the organisation of a programme for discussion in the separate areas of the coalfield. Finally, the programme was turned into a pamphlet and, at its first full reading on 18 November 1911, entitled *The Miners' Next Step*.[36]

The pamphlet's reputation as syndicalist and the concentration on its more blood-curdling pronouncements has tended to obscure the main contents. It is symptomatic of this style of thought that A. J. Cook who made no contribution to it, has been regarded, for over half a century, as one of its authors.[37] What is really important about the question of authorship was the belief of the principals involved that contributions had been made from lodges all over the coalfield. However disingenuous this was in the light of the organisation of those views, it remains true that there was a large catchment area of support to be tapped. Hence the meticulous detailing of the policies adopted and results obtained by the 'Conciliation policy' since 1900.

Since these were men fully attuned to the peculiar development of the coalfield, one might expect the burden of their attack to be precisely that localism and type of leadership which they saw as the deadweights of their communities. Throughout, the critique must be seen as one in which the methods of industrial bargaining complement the social aspirations of the many but make attainment possible only for a few, i.e. the leaders. Its analysis of the donation and receipt of power is consistently harsh in its insistence that delegated power is necessarily an evil, and that for both sides of the power equation.

It asks why the leaders of the Federation are respected by the Owners, and answers:

> Because they have the men – the real power – in the hollow of their hands. They, the leaders, become 'gentlemen'; they become MPs, and have

considerable social prestige because of this power. Now when any man or men assume power of this description, we have a right to ask them to be infallible. That is the penalty, a just one too, of autocracy.[38]

Worse than this duping of the leaders is the further contention that the leaders, of necessity, connive at this state of affairs:

> For a moment let us look at the question from the leaders' standpoint. First, they are Trade Unionists by trade and their profession demands certain privileges. The greatest of these are plenary powers. Now, every inroad the rank and file make on this privilege lessens the power and prestige of the leader. Can we wonder then that leaders are averse to change? Can we wonder that they try and prevent progress? Progress may arrive at such a point that they would not be able to retain their 'jobs', or their 'jobs' would become so unimportant that from this point of view they would not be worth retaining. The leader then has an interest – a vested interest – in stopping progress. The condition of things in South Wales has reached the point when this difference of interest, this antagonism, has become manifest. Hence the men criticise and are discontent with their leaders. But the remedy is not new leaders.[39]

So the remedy has to be found in a new system of administration. The men must retain control by having the final say in all negotiations via the ballot box, and leaders are to be reduced to ambassadors from the men to their employers. And here the argument takes off into different realms, for the Unofficial Reform Committee are not concerned with only changing the structure of the Federation; that is merely the eventual precondition to wider societal change. South Wales had become, by 1910, synonymous with the coal industry and in direct relation to the manner in which this affected the population of the coalfield (even those who were not miners, even those who worked on the coast or on the land) was the conviction that the SWMF was not only in a position to dictate the men's conditions of work, but further, in a society in which its members served, as drones, various Queen Bees, it presented the most direct and desirable route towards total control. Industrial unionism as a path to workers' control did not seem, to many, impossibly utopian in these conditions.

Supreme control of the organisation must, then, be in the hands of the men since anything else would be a denial, at the outset, of the power for good that lies in the Union. The Federation is seen as a vehicle by which the men organise institutionally the fraternity that their working lives give them; it is the material expression of their collectivity and much too precious to be resigned away:

The order and system (a leader) maintains is based upon the suppression of the men, from being independent thinkers into being 'the men' or 'the mob'. . . . In order to be effective, the leader *must* keep the men in order or he forfeits the respect of the employers and 'the public', and thus becomes ineffective as a leader.[40]

So the leader becomes a distillation of the men's collective initiative and self-respect (their 'expressed manhood' in the pamphlet's words), leaving them, by implication, castrated in their valleys while their virility symbol struts abroad. Again the analysis is rooted in their contemporary South Wales, for they are concerned with rejecting the reality of the consensus society that had developed and with replacing it by more divisive, combative tendencies. Community must give way to solidarity, become thus the expression of a self-conscious working class:

Sheep cannot be said to have solidarity. In obedience to a shepherd, they will go up or down, backwards or forwards as they are driven by him, and his dogs. But they have no solidarity, for that means unity and loyalty. Unity and loyalty, not to an individual, or the policy of an individual, but to an interest and a policy which is understood and worked for by all.[41]

After 1910 there was, in fact, a change in the old policies and in the old leadership. Neither the attacks, however, nor the new personnel elected were necessarily connected with the militants of the Unofficial Reform Committee. In 1911, for instance, Mark Harcombe, a man who was to dominate Rhondda Labour Party politics for decades, could write, after his experience in the Cambrian Combine struggle:

It is simply sickening to read of the half-hearted way the leaders are taking up the question of a minimum wage in abnormal places, and if the worker is to come into his own he must get rid of this present-day 'oligarchy' manifested by his accredited leaders.[42]

It was this wider support that gave the Conference in 1912 on reorganisation such significance. However, the debate also stimulated the majority tendencies in coalfield society into a defence of their views that effectively isolated the militants by revealing their own social outlook to be more visionary than practicable in pre-1914 Wales.

The Annual Conference in June 1912 saw the departure of the preeminent figure in Welsh Trade Unionism, Mabon, and the same assembly voted, once more, to consider the question of centralisation. A committee of 12 (six EC Members and six elected by Conference) was delegated to draft a scheme. However, when the reorganisation scheme was presented to a Special Conference in July the division of feeling became all too apparent; the motion to reject the scheme was defeated by a small majority but a similar majority voted for retention of the present districts, thus effectively quashing the proposals. It was not possible, in the view both of the Executive Council and of the drafting Committee, to have financial and administrative centralisation so long as the existing districts remained. It was decided, therefore, to ballot the men who, in September, voted by a majority of 10,340 for abolition of the districts in favour of centralisation.[43]

At no point did the Executive Council show any enthusiasm for these proposals; the Anthracite District, the most remote and distinct of the Areas, even threatened to use the centralisation issue as a means of seceding from the SWMF. Meetings were held designed to discredit the scheme before Conference. At Cross Keys, Onions, the SWMF Treasurer and Agent for Tredegar pointed out that under the old system there were 22 agents and 3 advisory ones; under the new scheme there were to be only 8, and these would be under the central EC rather than under the guidance of the Districts. He analysed the costs and the efficiency of the new scheme and, as SWMF Treasurer, found both wanting. The burden of the argument was the value of maturity, stability and local control. At Question time the point was pressed:

A miner in the body of the hall said: 'I think it is an absolutely rotten scheme. There are too many going to Cardiff now, and they sit there too long already. We are not going to vote to keep them there every day of the week – 28 of them', and Charles Edwards JP (then agent for the district), added that 'the scheme was the most impracticable and impossible ever discussed. . . . It would be news to them to know that it was advocated in the Council by four men who were not Miners' Agents. It was they who were pushing it forward'. And that particular meeting ended by urging their delegates to vote for a more workable scheme.[44]

The details of the reorganisation scheme to be discussed were simple and radical. The Districts, of course, were to go and power was to be shared between an Executive Council, composed of twenty-four ordinary, or rank-and-file, members, and a Conference of delegates that would meet, in addition to an Annual Meeting, at quarterly intervals. Salaries, expenses and the share of finance to go to the lodges were all set out before the 200 delegates present. These, in fact, represented only 89,150 members – a sign of the extreme fluctuation in Union membership, and of the abstention of the 13,000 strong Anthracite District.

The decisions now taken, and their consequence, comment graphically on the confusion of the men. They were not helped in this by the Executive's obvious distaste for the scheme that they were bound, by the ballot vote, to propose. It became, finally, a protest vote only.

The protest was directed against paid officialdom and its powers. Thus there was such strong opposition to the proposal that all negotiations for a settlement of strikes 'must either be conducted or sanctioned by the Executive Council and any terms arranged for resumption of work must receive approval of Council or Conference', that the words 'or by a ballot vote of the workmen affected' had to be tacked on. Although the power of the EC to remedy grievances itself without the aid of the proposed Quarterly Conferences was defeated, the words 'and their decision to be final' was deleted. The EC was to be able to retain services of advisory agents even if elected to Parliament but their long-desired wish for an increase in contribution to 2s. a lunar month was lost. The EC's argument was that the scheme could not function without an increase in contributions to the Central fund; the men were reluctant to pay any more to a 'generalised' fund.

As the Conference moved into its second and third days, the dissensions deepened. The proposal that agents be re-elected every three years was defeated, but when the vote to confirm their salaries at £4 per week and travelling expenses was taken, a delegate rose to move his lodge's amendment to lower the salaries to £3 per week. He said 'most of the miners who worked far harder than did the agents, received far less money, and they thought that £3 a week was quite enough for those who did not take their coats off (*laughter and hear, hear*)'.

Others came to his support pointing out that by means of writing newspaper articles and other 'extras' given for attendance at meetings in Cardiff, many received in excess of £4. A card vote gave a majority for the amendment. This episode proved the high point of the Conference; certainly it reveals the nature of the support that had crystallised around the more theoretical schemes for reorganisation of the 'unofficial' ginger groups in the coalfield and, at the same time, it was to show the hold on the coalfield community of rather different ideological values.

Immediately after the lunch-time session a counter-attack was under way – the motion to reduce the General Secretary's salary met with defeat, and the old bugbear of the Districts came up again with a 2-to-1 majority in favour of their retention with the same number of agents as before. Altogether there were some 45 amendments; obviously no consensus had arisen in agreement with the scheme. There was to be a ballot decision on it in January 1913.[45]

In no sense can it be said that the issue of centralisation was being presented in the most favourable light. It was tarred with the brush of new-fangled theory, attributed to immaturity and impetuosity, described as the product of jealousy; just to be sure that this message went out to all, 'for the first time for many years the agenda [to the Conference] had been set out both in English and Welsh, the usual practice being to issue the agenda in the English language only', and, after the Conference, each member was to receive a copy of the scheme of which 10,000 would be in Welsh. The inescapable conclusion must be that Welsh was seen as a guarantor of conservatism.[46]

It had not been centralisation as such to which the EC had objected; far from it, for a further degree of administrative and financial control was much desired. H. S. Jevons chided the Welsh miner, shortly afterwards, for his unwillingness to pay more to his Union, despite the effort of the men's leaders to improve the organisation:

> The Federation employs a whole-time Secretary, Assistant Secretary, and some clerks, and the business is now all conducted from Cardiff. This, however, is a recent innovation, the Secretary and Treasurer having previously lived in different remote valleys from which the business was conducted, there being merely a small office in Cardiff for the Executive Council to meet in. Great efforts are being made by the Officers and Council to carry out a policy of centralisation, but they receive little encouragement from the workmen, who manifest some degree of suspicion of paid officials.

And Jevons goes on to encapsulate the reasons for this desired centralisation, in a manner that links up with his earlier recommendation of agents who are 'strong men' in their districts. It is a familiar litany – talent, sobriety, maturity and, therefore, responsible leadership:

> A proposal of the Executive Council to increase the contribution to the Federation was recently 'negatived' in a general ballot vote, and there seems little prospect of a strong centralised Union for the whole coalfield coming into being at an early date. Such a strong central body, supervising and controlling the whole business and negotiations from Cardiff, could not only be a great benefit to the workmen but in many ways also to the Trade as a whole. Inconsistent action in neighbouring districts, vacillating policy, and divided counsels on the Executive of the Federation have been features of the Miners' Trade Unionism for many years, and the important strikes of

1893, 1898 and 1910 were largely brought about or intensified by differences of opinion between the Miners and their Leaders and among the Leaders themselves.[47]

Here was the root difference between those who welcomed either local control or centralisation because it removed power from paid officials and those who hailed the same concepts (though in different form) because of the very power thereby given to a leadership which had proved its superiority by its own evolution. It is a point on which Noah Ablett elaborated in July 1913 at a Conference organised by Beatrice Webb. Ablett was at pains to separate the nobler element of the parochial spirit ('its horror of bureaucracy and uniformity', 'the desire to govern as much as possible the conditions under which one has to live') from the miseries that a local fixation could entail in the form of petty leadership. He recognised clearly the increased influence and importance that centralisation might give to a leadership intent on power and social prestige but, nevertheless, he advocated it as the only means of transferring individual power into the organisation, and hence extend democracy – 'and thus to find oneself in a still larger sense by synthesising the differences between autonomy and centralisation'.[48]

Social Darwinism had many willing advocates in South Wales; it was a creed that could accept the coal owner, D. A. Thomas, and the miners' leader, William Brace. Its enemy was any levelling tendency, any notion that the men's leadership was anything more than the talent that had flown down that particular channel. Therefore any attack on this leadership's right to a good recompense for its services, its social duties, could only be a 'vulgar envy', for 'cheap leaders' were of no use:

This jealousy in which the rank and file hold their leaders is the curse of democracy. And this talk about one man being as good as another, and about the importance of taking off one's coat to work is simply moonshine. Every disgruntled Trade Unionist, even one whose mental equipment will not allow him to say with certainty how many beans make five, can rail against his leaders for not taking off their coats. When he has lost the power of thought altogether he can still chatter that he is as good as his leaders, he can still snarl enviously.[49]

The virulence of editorial comment like this was not empty ranting but rather an essential piece of the philosophy of social accommodation on which public men based their lives. It was just as much the philosophy of ILP supporters, like Vernon Hartshorn, as it was of the Lib.-Labs.; in some ways more so, since the claim for independent action by Labour was often stated in terms of that dominant social philosophy (that is, its common sense, maturity and responsibility). Hartshorn wrote a column for a South Wales' Liberal newspaper. His attack on reorganisation is a classic example of the terminology used to refute radical change, it is a case of judgement by epithet – the reformers are 'arrogant and blundering', 'inexperienced reformers on the rampage', 'a caucus of young enthusiasts who have had little or no experience of the immense practical difficulties of building up and administering a huge and rather cumbersome organisation like the Federation'.[50] A centralisation of funds and a uniformity in wage standards he could agree with but not in all matters because this would destroy the fragile unity achieved:

> We must recognise that districts with strong local patriotism and prejudice, and strong claims to some measure of local autonomy, if their administration is to be practical, are absolutely inevitable in the SWMF.

Hartshorn, with the possible exception of Frank Hodges, was the most able leader of his generation in South Wales; that he stayed within the Labour Movement testifies to his deeply-held political beliefs, for he was no self-seeker but neither was he removed from those attitudes of which he is, in so many ways, emblematic. To succeed for oneself was, in part, to succeed for others; the more he was valued (that is, supported reasonably well by the men), the more valuable he was. His rejection of a wage cut was proud and symptomatic – he could brook no affront to his self-respect nor ignore his family's just needs; his sacrifice was there already in the use to which he was putting his talents for small financial return:

> If it [i.e. the wage cut] is approved by the men, I shall give my service in directions where it may be more kindly appreciated.[51]

Other agents felt the same, from George Barker (an opponent of Hartshorn's moderation), to William Jenkins of Neath and Watts-Morgan of the Rhondda, who told an audience in Penclawdd, in a speech against the 'insincerity and shabbiness brought into the movement by a caucus of young men who were crude and grotesque in their ideas' and 'doing incalculable injury to the Federation', that he worked from 8 a.m. to midnight and that, if he accepted a wage cut – 'an insult' – he 'should be kicked out of any self-respecting community if he did not voluntarily retire if such a thing was brought about (*Applause*)'.[52]

The self-respect of leader and community was, then, to be on both sides and clearly established – the community accepted that it did not want shoddy goods if it could afford better. The campaign against the scheme was fierce and effective. It was rejected by 43,508 against 24,106;[53] the duet between pressing economic and political shifts and an abiding social reality was to continue until the latter could maintain the myth of its perpetual presence no longer.

After 1914 the victories of the militants within the Federation proceeded apace but proved to be more paper than real ones in the sense that the militancy and power of the miners in South Wales, although at times overwhelming in appearance, were not reflected in an organisational framework. Thus the defeat of Mabon, Richards and Onions as representatives on the MFGB by Barker, Hartshorn and Stanton, is a significant but not decisive shift in power since the three latter were miners' agents anyway; similarly too much can be read into Noah Ablett's elevation to the Executive Council, an appointment condemned by other syndicalists.[54]

Shortly after the outbreak of the war, on 1 September 1914, a delegate conference of the SWMF demanded that all men in the Army and Navy should be given higher rates of pay, believing that 'the financial resources of the Government and the leisured class are such that no difficulty would be experienced by doing so'.[55] A growing anti-war feeling, largely at this stage unconscious, found a clear expression in July 1915 when a coalfield conference called a strike for a new wages agreement. The Government proclaimed the coalfield under the Munitions of War Act by which over 200,000 could now have been imprisoned. After five days of strike action, Lloyd George, the Minister of Munitions, came to Cardiff to concede the demands.[56]

Conscious and open hostility to the war, up until 1917, however, tended to be confined to miniscule local Socialist Societies and focused on the actions of individual miners in refusing to be conscripted, or on the outspokenness of some prominent Socialists.[57] Consequently, an explicitly anti-war position, as expounded by W. F. Hay, one of the co-authors of *The Miners' Next Step*, in his pamphlet, *War! and the Welsh Miner*, failed to gather many open supporters before 1917.[58] What did change the situation was the two Revolutions in Russia in 1917, about which there was a lack of detailed information but widespread and enthusiastic support.[59] In August 1917, after proposals made by the Workers' and Soldiers' Council, the SWMF decided to ascertain the views of the British Labour movement on a Peace Settlement so that

such views could be made known to the labour movements of the
Belligerent Powers and on 8 October a coalfield conference refused to
assist in the recruitment of colliery workers into the Army.[60]

A revealing, although by no means generally typical, indication of
this growing internationally orientated proletarian consciousness, was
the sympathy for the independence struggle in Ireland. Irish
communities in such towns as Aberdare, Maesteg and Merthyr made
the issues all the more immediate: some Irish exiles in Wales were not
unknown to steal colliery explosives and send them in suitcases to the
'old country' via Liverpool.[61] But a handful of Welshmen from the
Rhondda and Abertillery went further than this. They evaded
conscription into the British Army by leaving for Ireland and joining its
Citizen Army. One such volunteer was the Abertillery miner, Tom Gale
who, after spending a short time in Ireland, emigrated to America until
he felt it was safe to return to South Wales. His action anticipated that
of his younger brother who served in Spain with the International
Brigades.[62] Another who served with the Irish Citizen Army was the
young Arthur Horner, who on his return was arrested, court-martialled
and given a six-month, followed by a two-year, sentence, for
'incorrigible misconduct'. But it was not so much his individual action in
fighting in Ireland and refusing to serve in the War of Intervention in
Russia that was so significant: it was the support he received from the
miners of Mardy who elected him one of their checkweighers whilst he
was still in prison, and the high-level representations made by the
SWMF leadership, that was much more revealing.[63] On his release,
he emphasised that he was no pacifist but rather a man who was only
willing to shoulder arms in the interests of his own class.[64]

The conditions of the war allowed the divergent features of South
Wales life to emerge: the mass volunteering, the rise in pacifism and
anti-conscription feeling, the recruitment campaigns and heroism, the
rejection of leadership's plea to moderate wage demands and not to
strike, jingoist mobs, the support given to anti-war feeling and to Plebs
League classes, the decisive shift, in politics, all happening below the
public level, from Liberalism to Independent Labour politics. Certainly
there is no single direction to be traced, though equally (and in imitation
of the wider shifts in British society) the emphasis was on cutting ties
with pre-war opinions and developing industrial strength.[65] After the

victory achieved by the 1915 strike, the pre-war militants regrouped at their old meeting-place the 'Aberystwyth Restaurant' in Tonypandy on 15 August 1915. Significantly, the immediate cause of the meeting was the knowledge that the Ogmore and Gilfach district was intent on proposing abolition of the district form of organisation – 'it was decided that now was an opportune time to re-engage in our propaganda in favour of the principle'. In fact the subsequent 'wider' meetings revealed old differences over the desirable degree and form of centralisation, the dangers of bureaucracy and the necessity (or otherwise) of a cautious approach via a manifesto eliciting 'suggestions' from the lodges. A groundswell there was certainly, but its force was, once again, by no means irresistibly concerted.[66]

These divergent tendencies could be seen together at the Rules Conference called in June 1917 to consider the new rules needed in the light of the adoption of out-of-work and other benefit funds. To the fifty rules drafted by the EC the lodges sent in over 200 amendments, which were debated by 254 delegates representing 145,892 members. There is no doubting the influence of the Plebs League and its associated personnel in the framing of some of these amendments. Thus, the Second Object, Rule 3 of the Federation, was to be to secure 'the complete organisation of all workers employed in and about collieries situated in the South Wales coalfield'. This was amended to read that 'membership of the Federation shall be a condition of employment' and then the amendment from the Cwmaman Lodge was put in a subordinate clause – 'with a view to the complete abolition of capital', and passed. The Great Mountain Lodge wrote in a stage on the way, so that another object should be 'to regulate the relationship existing between the members and their employers, with the view to increasing the members' control of the conditions of employment and generally to protect their interests'.[67]

Already some areas of the coalfield were feeling the impact of the 'combine companies', such as that of the Powell Duffryn Steam Coal Company Ltd, in the Aberdare and Rhymney Valleys which, with 13,611 men on its books in 1915, was the single largest employer among the coalowners.[68] The Coedcae Lodge had a new Rule 48 adopted which declared that:

The formation of Joint Committees representing groups of collieries or collieries owned by the same Company, shall be encouraged by every means possible, the same to be recognised by the District and Executive Council.[69]

These were to become the Combine Committees which were to play such a crucial role in the 1930s, adopted here, in principle, as a step on the road to greater centralisation of action. These were the successful sallies of men who were riding a groundswell of militancy. W. J. Edwards, who was banned from work in the Combine pits in the Aberdare Valley, after 1910, pulled together, in himself, these threads:

> Together once more at Ruskin, those of us who had been home could compare what impressions of our movement's progress we had gained from local trade union meetings. There was an idea being widely discussed whose object was combination of effort in the struggle. Parochial trade unions had their uses when mines were owned and controlled by individuals who were at least human; but now that mining interests were joining up into soulless combines, the small individual unions tended to lose what effect they had had. And these small unions did not represent mining as a whole in an area; there were colliers' unions, surfacemen's unions, hauliers' unions and a general workers' union. Some lodges had been discussing not only reorganisation – one union with one programme, one policy, one agreement and leadership – but also a new object: nothing less than the total abolition of capital in the mining industry. . . . The mine-owners had combined to win more profits and had lost their souls; we would combine to win more justice.

W. J. Edwards, and others like him, were fulfilling the promise of the Ruskin/Central Labour College students to utilise, on their return, their education in formulating new concepts:

> In a few weeks' time I was made a member of the pit committee, and it was a resolution I made which called for a joint meeting of all the colliery committees under the same ownership and thus to begin establishing that unity which is strength. [and then, later:] At the next general meeting in the Workmen's Hall called before the Annual Conference at Cardiff to permit our Branch to prepare resolutions, I moved a resolution that was not only carried unanimously in my valley but enjoyed a similar result at the Cardiff Conference. My resolution, which accompanied a long speech, urged that the objective of the South Wales Miners' Federation should be the abolition of capital in the coalfield.[70]

However, the radicalism of this Conference, in these respects, can be misleading, for the 'abolition of capital' remained a long-term objective and the Joint Committees had to wait many years before receiving any full-hearted encouragement. On matters that counted in any immediate sense there was no wresting of the reins by 'the progressives'.

On the day after the delegates had voted to end capital, they rejected all amendments designed to alter the constitution of the Federation either in respect of the District system or the duties of the officials. There had been an attempt to stop the election of miners' agents on to the EC and to reduce their salaries, along with that of the General Secretary, so that it would be 'the standard rate with the current percentage'. The power of the EC was, in general, confirmed, despite these forays against it:

> One Lodge actually proposed that the Executive 'should be composed of workmen from the working faces' and another that the Executive be elected annually by Conference. All the amendments in favour of electing the Executive from men employed in or about the collieries were defeated by overwhelming majorities.[71]

Whatever the form of organisation, the continuing need was for a more complete control of the men employed. The war provided a temporary settlement of the Federation's perennial, and most intractable problem, that of non-Unionism.

Since the inception of the SWMF in 1898 the problem of organising such a fluid work-force into the Federation had proved daunting in the short term and almost intractable in any final sense.[72] 'Show Cards' campaigns alternated, in the early years, with the more terrifying 'white-sheet' tactics of the women-folk, whilst attempts to merge the Craftsmen's Union into the Federation also foundered on the reefs of suspicion and self-interest.[73] The early years of the war saw the non-unionist situation aggravated by the exit from the coalfield of many SWMF stalwarts. There were a series of local stoppages and a number of attempts by the EC to obtain the owners' agreement to settle this troublesome matter. The latter refused to co-operate even on the grounds of 'helping the war effort'. They were shaken out of their complacency by the successful coalfield strike of July 1915 that forced a government to capitulate; the clauses in that Agreement were to apply only to SWMF members so that craftsmen began to join the Federation, until in September a delegate conference recommended that the 6,000 craftsmen in the South Wales Enginemen and Stokers' Association should merge with the Federation.[74] They had been induced by payment of the 'bonus turn' and now, increasingly, faced a systematic SWMF policy since the EC, faced with a continued refusal by the owners, had to advise its Districts to continue to take action against non-Unionism.[75] In the Rhondda there was a 'quarterly show' of cards at the pit-heads:

> The men display their 'clean cards', i.e. free of arrears, on their caps, and refuse to descend the mine with anyone who cannot 'show a clean card'. The

presence of 'non-unionists' is not tolerated in the collieries, and at some periods the latter have been decorated with a white shirt in order to mark them out. . . . Up to September it has been considered satisfactory if the craftsmen could produce the clean card of their sectional union; but after the September settlement the Rhondda collieries opened a new campaign by deciding to treat the craftsmen as 'non-unionists' unless they joined the Miners' Federation, as the delegates of the sectional union had recommended and the bulk of the latters' members had already done.[76]

Finally, in March 1916, the Board of Trade had to intervene as a mediator with the result that, on 18 April 1916, an agreement was reached to the effect that 'the representatives of the Monmouthshire and South Wales Coalowners' Association, without prejudice to the position after the war, agree that the workmen employed at the Collieries shall be required to become members of one or other of the recognised Trade Unions'. Then, in December 1916, in the face of continuing strife, the Government assumed control of the coalfield; until de-control in 1921 the policy on non-Unionism was to continue.[77]

Its implementation was regarded as a hard-won concession rather than an all-out victory or a change of heart by the owners. Frank Hodges, then miners' agent in Bridgend, pointed out its flaws:

It has been the ambition of the South Wales Miners for many years to impose upon the employers the principle that the condition of employment of any workmen in or about the mines should be membership of the Miners' Federation. The propaganda for the realisation of this ambition had largely been in the nature of strikes at local collieries. There are scores of collieries where it has been realised but the owners as an Association have resisted it tooth and nail. In 1915 they intimated to the men that they would agree to a scheme of compulsory Trade Unionism if the men would allow the 1910 Conciliation Board Agreement to continue for the duration of the war. For years they had said that they would never accede to any request of the men to assist in preventing stoppages on non-Unionism. To them it was a point of principle of first-class importance. But the monetary advantages of the old agreement were so wonderfully attractive as to compel them to set aside their professed unalterable principles in the hope of a golden harvest out of increased prices of coal. When the workmen rejected this altruistic offer, the owners in their anger fell back again upon their fundamental principles, and there they have stuck until the last few days. The lesson to be drawn from this is that the coalowners, like other capitalists, as a class have no unchangeable principles except the all-powerful one of profiteering . . . At last ['the pestilence of non-unionism'] became unbearable . . . the Government intervened. . . . The first principle of importance in the scheme is the fact that every workman employed at the collieries must be a Trade Unionist; not necessarily a member of the Miners' Federation, but a member of one of the recognised Trade Unions, of which there are three in the South Wales Mining Industry. The Government, even when at war, will not permit itself to be used as the propagandist of industrial unionism pure and simple.[78]

This was a salutary warning. Nevertheless, by February 1921, with a membership of over 200,000 and with the South Wales Colliery Enginemen and Mechanics' Union finally within the wider fold, the SWMF had never been larger or stronger, or more militant in pursuit of its demands. The years 1918–21, in retrospect, can be characterised as a final flaring of the power of the Mining Unions and the attendant boom in coal; convinced of the righteousness of their cause and the strength of the MFGB, lulled into waiting by the Sankey Commission and post-war adjustments, the miners were out-manoeuvred and, finally, crushed into submission by the vagaries of world trade, the running-down of the industry, mass unemployment and wage cuts. Their strength, both in 1921 and in 1926, with rare exceptions, was exerted *within* their own Areas, as if in implicit defence of the civilisation built up within their communities. None the less the particular nature of their history did not preclude wider horizons.

The Great War had consequently strengthened the already existing processes which had been at work before 1914. Greater concentration of capitalist ownership and control, increasing industrial militancy, growing hostility to conscription along with the events in Ireland and Russia all in their way now contributed to an internationalist perspective rooted in the direct and indirect experience of the South Wales miners.[79]

In the immediate post-war years, attempts were made to channel this particular kind of outlook into a Communist direction now that a Bolshevik Government had firmly established itself in Russia. One of the few areas in Britain where the Communist Party of Great Britain (CPGB), formed in 1920–1, had substantial roots was the South Wales coalfield where some of the supporters of the Unofficial Reform Committee and what remained of the Rhondda/South Wales Socialist Society had joined the new organisation.[80] The schism in the International trade union and labour movement created by the form- ation of the Third (Communist) International (CI) in 1919 and then its subsidiary, the Red International of Labour Unions, provided the opportunity for the CPGB to encourage a reorientation of allegiance in

D. DAVIS & SONS, Ltd.
FERNDALE COLLIERIES.

NOTICE!

The attention of all workmen is called to the fact that the output obtained from these Pits is so low that the question of continuing working is being seriously considered.

Unless the OUTPUT per man employed is IMMEDIATELY IMPROVED the Pits must stop.

F. LLEWELLIN JACOB,
GENERAL MANAGER.

1st November, 1921.

Threat of pit closure in Rhondda Fach, 1921 (poster).

South Wales. The response, even given the immediate past history of the coalfield, was swift and startling. A coalfield conference in July 1921 representing over 150,000 men voted 120 to 63 to urge the MFGB to affiliate to what it mistakenly called the Third International. This clear intention to join the Red International of Labour Unions (RILU) was one of the very few instances of a British trade union, of any size, indicating its adherence to 'revolutionary' trade unionism, which made the decision all the more remarkable.[81]

The two supporters of the resolution at the ensuing MFGB Annual Conference in 1922 were A. J. Cook of the Rhondda and S. O. Davies of Dowlais, significantly neither of them members of the CPGB. Their arguments emphasised the practical advantages of joining the RILU. They criticised the roles of the Trades Union Congress (TUC) and the International Federation of Trade Unions (IFTU) during the National Miners' lock-out of the previous year and maintained that there was greater hope of gaining wider international solidarity during industrial disputes by supporting the new body. Davies considered that the IFTU's close association with the League of Nations revealed its support of capitalism which the SWMF's constitution since 1917 had vowed to abolish. Without any support from the other coalfields, the resolution was overwhelmingly defeated.[82]

Nevertheless, an indication of the strengthening of feeling on the matter was shown when the issue of affiliation (now of the SWMF itself) continued to be vigorously debated, at least in the Districts represented by Cook and Davies. A conference chaired by S. O. Davies was convened at Cardiff on 21 October in order to build up support for the RILU at every trade union level. The Dowlais district delegate to the conference was J. S. Williams who, fifteen years later, joined the International Brigades. The same District also gave its agent, S. O. Davies, long leave of absence so that he could attend the second world conference of the RILU even though the District itself was currently facing enormous financial and membership problems.[83]

But the most critical discussions occurred in the Rhondda District of the SWMF when CI representative, Borodin, came to Britain to ascertain whether the SWMF would affiliate directly to the RILU. Tradition has it that he consulted the CPGB leadership neither at national nor at district level but went directly to the Unofficial Reform Committee led by Jack and Tom Thomas at Ynyshir. The Committee at that time was very influential in that it controlled the Rhondda District, which in turn largely controlled the SWMF. But the suggestion was rejected because it was feared that the SWMF would be expelled from the MFGB if it went ahead with its decision.[84]

Unlike the United Mineworkers of Scotland, which later did affiliate to the RILU, the SWMF never succeeded in bringing its 1921 decision to fruition. But its allegiance to a 'proletarian internationalist' perspective, which was so out of step with the mainstream of British labour history, did not diminish. The events of 1926 were to harden and deepen the commitment at local level to extra-parliamentary methods (which had re-emerged in the 1921 lock-out) and to its revolutionary international links.[85]

After the SWMF had taken its 1921 decision, Lenin was prompted to speculate whether this meant the 'beginning of the real proletarian mass movement in Great Britain in the communist sense . . . perhaps it is the beginning of a new era'.[86] For Lenin, however, it proved to be a false dawn; but for the South Wales miners it was but one more indication of a particular kind of evolving internationalist consciousness which was to have its highest expression much later, on the battlefields of Spain.

The wheels of progress were reversed sharply from 1921 onwards. In August of that year a breakaway section of enginemen and other craftsmen broke through the unitary structure so recently achieved.[87] The high unemployment, mostly through trade depression causing lay-offs or short-time working, undermined the high returns of membership made by the SWMF, whilst the lock-out imposed by the owners on their resumption of control of the mines in March 1921 effectively ended any lingering hopes of just rewards for war-time endeavour and began the reduction of wage and living standards that was to mark the following two decades.[88]

As the recession in the coal trade bit deeper and the economic misery of the coalfield increased, so did the Federation's ability to defend its active membership and maintain its numbers decline also. For most of 1922 and 1923 the organised membership was reduced to under 100,000. Only a vigorous 'Back to the Union' campaign in 1923 restored the number organised in 1924 to some 148,000. Nevertheless, no matter how keenly non-Unionism was combated, unemployment itself ravaged the work force, as pits closed abruptly.[89]

In these circumstances the leadership of the SWMF was at odds with itself, though all shades of opinion were still concerned with the role of the Union in national and international affairs as the relative merits and demerits of the IFTU and RILU, of the Labour Party and the CP, of

Parliamentary Government or Direct Action, all made their rounds (sometimes in echo of previous years) in speeches and in newspapers.[90] The rebuilding of the Union in 1923 was seen as a precursor to future mass activity on the scale pursued since 1912; and indeed the success at least of the solidarity attained in the General Strike and subsequent seven months' lock-out of 1926 is eloquent testimony to the continuation of the old hopes and spirit. This was the mood invoked by Vernon Hartshorn's Presidential Address in July 1923 when he stated:

> . . . that he had known this coalfield for about 40 years; he had known it during periods of prosperity and adversity, during good times and bad times, he had known it during times when they had an efficient organisation, and also during times when they had practically no organisation, but he had never known a period when the workmen had been more demoralised than they were during the year 1922. It had been a most difficult time for leaders to give an efficient lead. Wages had been low, unemployment had been extensive and the owners had taken advantage of the general position to attack standard wages and customs which had been in existence for many years. He was glad, however, to be able to report that at last the demoralisation that had hung over them like a pall was rapidly disappearing; the membership of the Federation for the last 3 months had been restored almost to the pre-war position, and this was indicative of great improvement in the morale of the workmen generally, and was evidence of a determination on their part to make their Organisation strong and effective.

At the same Conference two resolutions were passed calling for a clause making membership of the Federation a condition of employment in any future Agreement, and another urging that the EC prepare yet another scheme on Centralisation for submission to the coalfield.[91]

It was only after the destruction in 1926 of the mythical properties of a General Strike, and thereafter, the hounding of the MFGB until it retreated from its 'national' position that these 'local' issues were to become, again, as important as they had seemed before 1914. When they were finally settled, this time, in the main, to the liking of progressives in the Federation, it was against a markedly different social 'backdrop' from that of Edwardian South Wales.

For forty years down to World War One population had been sucked into the coalfield from rural hinterlands, as if by a vacuum cleaner; a similar process, but in reverse, could be observed in the inter-war period. The descent from the halcyon days of coalfield expansion had been a steep one. The opulent architecture that had been designed to bring a touch of saving grace to the barrack-like terraces did not receive additions, unless the halls of the Quakers, or the corrugated iron sheds of the unemployed could be seen as such.[92] One or two new cinemas (like Cardiff's Capitol) alone made explicit, now, the unity of public building and social dreams; though the latter were not proclaimed for a community's appreciation any more but rather reduced, in the dark, to individual fantasy. The cinematic opiate nourished as many as did the declining chapels. Local authorities, with rates rocketing and financial sources plummeting, faced bankruptcy; those who looked for deficit financing were disciplined, those who clung to the high status derived from past industrial glories succumbed to present misfortune – the proposal to demote Merthyr from its borough status in 1935 was, perhaps, the most symbolic emblem of the changed fortunes of South Wales.[93] A society that had been assembled, as were the coalfield communities, as a male work-force, had taken pride in the support of its women-folk (themselves not exactly creatures of leisure in an age when the physical presence of the pit was transferred to the house, and often twice a day);[94] mass unemployment added the impulse of necessity to those Welsh girls who wished to leave home, and whose training had been strictly 'domestic'. The press carried unending columns in which people from suburban Cardiff or the South East required Welsh maids.[95] Suicides and murders and cases of the 'missing' followed in this melancholy wake. The Rev. William Bradshaw, a Methodist circuit minister for West Monmouth, suggested that the young unemployed should not marry and increase the burden on the State. Aneurin Bevan asked: 'Were unemployed men to live lives of celibacy and their young girls leave their homes to become the playthings of wealthy people in other parts of the country?'[96] Most left for the more mundane pursuit of seeking work; for, between 1921 and 1936, 241 mines had closed down in South Wales, whilst the work force had decreased from 271,161 in 1920 to 126,233 in 1936 (the latter not a particularly bad year), and the reduction of the wages bill from £65 m. to £14 m. (1920 and 1933s figure), had the effect of sending poverty spiralling through South Wales by means of a *downward* economic multiplier. A number of industrial surveys (by Government, University and Charity Organisations) investigated the area, made sensible recommendations and drew similar pictures of misery. In almost all her industries, and especially in that of coal, the incidence of unemployment, in terms of a percentage of the whole for Britain and in terms of long-term unemployment, was abnormally high.[97] The net result was that the quality of life, and perhaps more importantly, of its expectations, was weakened at root. If the SWMF in its short and stormy career had been an attempt to forge a weapon to defend the men from the worse forms of exploitation, and some would have said to destroy that exploitation itself, then it had also been integrated into the society of the coalfield at every level.

The transformation of the raw mining townships of the late nineteenth century had been made possible by the power of Victorian legislation but effected, for the most part, by the desire of the population to create, for themselves, communities rather than aggregations of work-people. From the chapels to the free libraries, from the Institutes to the sports teams, the control was a popular and a democratic one.[98] The organisation of politics in the localities had a similar intent (diverse ideologies notwithstanding), and in all this the primary organisation was the Union, and from 1898, the SWMF. It could not be otherwise given the nature of the work-force and the pressing realities of work itself: the SWMF was, literally, the fount of control in other spheres as well as that of the industry itself. Ness Edwards could write, with considerable justice, in 1936 that the 'transformation of the coalfield area from an agricultural parish council standard of amenities to a highly urbanised area, catering for the needs of some hundreds of thousands, has on its civic side, been the work of thousands of Local Officials and Committeemen of the Federation'. The Checkweigher, the Lodge Secretary and the Miners' Agent were as powerful as the RC priests in Irish villages and 'this power rested completely upon service'.[99] The sociological ramifications of the mining communities, were, by no means, without complexity but the sociological explanation of the SWMF's hegemonic control was simple:

> The 'Fed' was the single decisive union operating in the pits, the communities existed around the pit, and Union branches were based upon it, hence the integration of pit, people and union into a unified social organism.[100]

In these primary and secondary stages of coalfield development (expansion and decline of the basic industry), all other aspects of life were affected too. Every other major industry also suffered a higher rate of unemployment than the British average, whilst the run-down of the great ports of the coastal strip was absolute. The availability of goods in the shops was limited and all other offshoots of that vibrant, pre-1914 society began to wither.

The year 1928 is perhaps the grimmest in the coalfield's Depression years. There were to be years of heavier unemployment, and a sequence of downward steps to poverty, but 1928 was a harsher blow because it was the start of a long descent. Even after 1921 there had been hope that recession might be temporary or that the exertion of a will by political means or by the use of industrial Direct Action might, at the very least, halt the trend. No such hopes could be entertained realistically in 1928; the very foundations of the society had cracked. In March and April of 1928, *The Times* commissioned three long, fact-finding articles to survey the state of South Wales and its future possibilities. The 'correspondent' was a resident of a Welsh mining valley. His words were liberal, informed, humane and concerned. They were also steeped in the consensus, societal and political, that so many had sought down to 1918. What was missing was the realisation that all the coalfield was Tonypandy now.

That economic and social distress is graver than before he does not question. Some 70,000 unemployed, as compared with four years previously, from the coal industry, and some 100,000 registered as unemployed in Glamorgan and Monmouthshire. The rate of relief is inadequate, savings are gone, the number of wage-earners is reducing all the time. With an acute eye for the inadequacies of statistical evidence, the correspondent pinpoints what was to be a constant in the lives of wage-earners through the 1930s, unemployment would be 'concealed'. There were four main categories of workers:

> . . . those fortunate enough to be working six days a week; those on short-time, whose pits are closed 2, 3 or 4 days a week through lack of orders; those permanently unemployed but receiving unemployment pay; and those who perhaps through their own fault, more probably because of the length of time that they have been without work, have been notified that they are no longer insurable persons, are now wholly dependent on the guardians.[101]

In other words, the third category were those who had exhausted their covenanted benefit and were now on extended benefit which, in its turn, could end; the second group (some 25,507 mineworkers in Wales and Monmouthshire, were temporarily stopped, and some 51,698 permanently, on 20 February 1928) was not adequately represented by the figures since these were taken on one day of the month, and could therefore lay no claim to being a 'typical' day. Indeed, the short-time worker was often worse off since he would receive no benefit for the days when he was not at work, 'unless his pit has been stopped recently for the continuous period of 6 days which enables him to qualify. Further if he incurred debts to tradesmen in 1926, the collector will continue to press him for a weekly instalment, though passing by as hopeless the men permanently unemployed.'[102]

The 'maladministration' of over-generous Boards of Guardians is castigated at the same time as the inadequacy of wages or relief is lamented. The permanent decay is, the correspondent feels, unprecedented, and this is 'unprovided for in our natural arrangements'. These latter had, in the past, beneficial social effects, for though the profits made had not been ploughed back to improve the valley towns, the miners, nevertheless, 'have achieved for themselves an astonishingly high level of cultivation, intellectual and domestic. They have been left to do everything for themselves. No aristocracy of any kind existed to point the way. . . . With this alertness, partly a Welsh characteristic, goes a lack of that balance which would be provided either by old home ties or by a wider knowledge of the world outside.'[103]

A 'lack of balance' is a discreet euphemism for proletarianisation; it is the further encroachment of this rootless existence, no longer eased by some social attainments, that goes through the seeker after consensus like a knife. He insists, for his readers who equate the working class with city slum-dwellers, that this is not the case:

> They are cultivated people with self-respect and an obvious pride in home cleanliness, and sparkling brasses in the chimney-pieces; quietly, for crime is not increasing yet, they feel the degradation of their sudden poverty. Inevitably, as the standard of income falls, slum habits will be forced upon them. That is the tragedy.

Even here there is compensation to be had:

> (Tradespeople) agree . . . that they do less business now than even in the hungry autumn of 1926. Public houses and the dividends of brewery companies repeat the same tale – Money flowed freely once, and the miner will tell you, with a gleam in his eye, how it was risky then to be out alone after dark. The hard times have changed all that. Insolent self-importance has given way after the last seven years to quiet, dull bitterness. Certainly, the financial stringency in every home is purging the valleys of much that was deplorable.[104]

There is almost a relish for the destruction of this Sodom where the miner 'still intensely religious, especially on Sundays, has lost his light heart and taken to politics', and where there has been 'a scramble by everybody, high and low, for quick money'. The projected solution is reminiscent of a Carlylean social philosophy crossed with the humaneness of Mrs Gaskell: more retraining centres, the reintroduction of farming skills so that emigration to the White Dominions overseas might succeed; a more efficient production of what is left and government aid for it; above all, goodwill and the end to this 'tale of misunderstanding'.[105]

This was, although slowly and inadequately, the pattern of aid received in the 1930s as Industrial Transference Boards gave way to Special Areas, and labour camps, away from the local vicinity, turned into Trading Estates. The 1934 Unemployment Act did have the virtue of recognising the existence of permanent, and long-term, mass unemployment and made administrative provision accordingly. Industrial surveys and well-wishers to the Distressed Areas signify the 1930s as clearly as Art-Deco and arterial roads.

This was only to scratch at the problems. At root, the society was not to be rescued. The correspondent of *The Times* rejected the notion of 'moving' the 'curse of capitalism', whose tentacles were gripping harder as amalgamations proceeded, leaving the 'personal touch' the necessary victim of more economy and more efficiency ('Finance has come in, and friendliness has departed'), whilst beyond the valleys lay, for their people, an 'unknown land'. It was the very lack of any intermediate social group able to oil the wheels of envy and bitterness, able to speak for the community as a whole that he regretted most since it implied the isolation of a people and a 'mental atmosphere' of 'intense suspicion and suppressed bitterness.' To his chagrin this left the SWMF, almost alone, as an organisation integrated into every aspect of coalfield life:

> No strangers come to the valleys except with a commercial or a political purpose. . . . It seems as though in the past no one from outside had ever taken a social interest in the miner; this task has fallen wholly on the SWMF which proclaims that it exists for the complete abolition of capitalism, and teaches its members that the upper classes never do anything for nothing. The miner finds that easy to believe. There are no well-to-do people living in the valleys, they choose to avoid the ugliness and the high rates.

In 1932 the Board of Trade commissioned its first Industrial Survey of South Wales. After the description of a decade of pit closures that topped the hundred mark and saw considerable internal migration from more depressed to more prosperous parts of the coalfield, the melancholy conclusion was that South Wales still equalled Coal:

> South Wales owes its existence as an industrial region to its coalfield, and coal mining, in spite of the vicissitudes of recent years, still overshadows in importance all other industries in the area.[106]

There was, of course, to be no diminution of the run-down in the 1930s as another hundred pits were lost through trade depression and the rationalisation brought about by company amalgamations.[107] The most dramatic example of this was, undoubtedly, in the area between the Rhondda and Rhymney valleys in east Glamorgan where 27 companies working 121 collieries and employing 98,000 men had been reduced by 1938 to 1 combine (Powell Duffryn Associated Collieries) working 49 pits and employing 37,000 men. Their further control of selling agencies and by-product plants with a demand for 'sized coal' led to further complaints about 'hidden profits'.[108] Of course the plight of the coal export trade in the 1930s needs no elucidation; the policies of rationalisation and of reorganisation had long been advocated by the MFGB itself, provided it was phased and controlled.

After 1926 the owners had *carte blanche* in their policies, with smaller, uneconomic concerns going to the wall irrespective of social consequences. These were immense.[109] Emigration ensured that the population hardly increased at all over the thirty years from 1935 to 1965, whilst the change in the nature of the economy of South Wales (more diversification, further pit closures, better road communication with England) caused an absolute shift in the relative balance between the population of the coalfield and that of the coastal strip.[110]

From 1957 the increasing pace of run-down in the coal industry appeared to signal the end of the power of the coal industry and its position as a large employer of men (there were only 32,000 miners in the employ of the NCB in South Wales in 1972). The subsequent dramatic victories for the NUM in 1972 and 1974 have, rightly, been seen as the fruits of an unexpected reversal in the fortunes of coal as an energy source. Clearly the decline of the coal industry and the alteration in the nature of 'traditional' coalfield society, a complex of images which is subsumed under that appellation, 'The Valleys', has gone hand in hand. In this sense, the struggles waged by the SWMF were forlorn ones, for their organisation would crumble as surely as any others that had been once supported by the vibrancy of the society.[111]

That society has been, itself, in question since the 1930s. Tom Jones may have been satirically indignant when he suggested turning it all into a vast industrial museum after removing the inhabitants east, but he was gloomily consistent in his belief that there was 'no solution' to the distress, only 'mitigation by relief and recreation'.[112] The meaning of the South Wales experience was mulled over by all sorts of commentators, from sociologists to novelists and poets. What was clear was that the industrial and urban experience of South Wales was a new phenomenon in Welsh life, altered irrevocably the balance of the Welsh pôpulation and its nature with, some argued, wholly detrimental effects upon Welsh culture.[113] Significantly the pessimistic view of the creation of coalfield society, and the fatalistic 'bread and circuses' attitude to its condition in the Depression, was not adopted by those same upholders of 'Welsh values' in the days of expansion. Then the encouragement was in terms of a respectable working class organised for work by social control and by self-control. The former was seen in terms of provision of better social services, cultural pursuits, even the encouragement of 'a national game' played by 'the democracy' and yet amateur in spirit and aristocratic in origin, all developed and run by a disinterested élite, itself patronised by the commercial and industrial concerns who were leading 'Wales' (another term where image and reality are blurred) into a new age of prosperity and dignity.[114] And self-control, encouraged through the agency of Welsh Nonconformist chapels[115] and the University settlement movement, was represented by a responsible leadership. Tom Jones framed it succinctly:

> Democratic institutions must be based on equality, but they can only flourish under leadership. The provision and election of wise leaders is the acid test of democracy.[116]

Now, the problem with the coalfield was twofold. On the one side it periodically gave way to riotous passion (lack of both forms of control), and on the other, and even worse, it spawned a breed of men, rooted in the work of the coalfield, who advocated an intellectual rejection both of controls and of the society that wanted them. In the first case, allied to references to aliens, immigrants, Irish, agitators and drink,[117] the unnatural state of South Wales was stressed ('natural' was Welsh neo-pastoral):

> The coalfield continued through the first quarter of the new century to be the cockpit of many battles, in the course of which it threw up a succession of notable leaders: Mabon, Tom Richards, William Brace, Vernon Hartshorn, A. J. Cook and Frank Hodges became national figures known throughout Great Britain. They had all worked as boys in the mine, were products of Sunday Schools, local preachers, more deeply steeped in the Christian doctrine of the value of human personality than in any economic theory. . . .
>
> These leaders dealt with an inflammable population easily ignited by what they felt to be injustice, and although tamed and civilised by religion and tradition, and upheld and guarded in decent behaviour by social props and

fences, primitive barbaric instincts were never far below the surface and
these could most easily be released by an excess of alcohol. Wild orgies or
violence sometimes disfigured the hymn-singing valleys. . . . In North Wales
the social structure was better balanced between agriculture, industry and
well-to-do visitors from Liverpool, Manchester and the Midlands. Everyone
enjoyed more elbow-room. It had rarely been necessary to order troops into
the area to quell or shoot a turbulent mob.[118]

An imbalanced South Wales could lurch into an unbalanced state.
The infamy of *The Miners' Next Step*, with its 'No leadership'
proposals, becomes more understandable when its resonance is heard
within this particular social context. The concept of leadership was a
key one for a society whose continued progress depended, as its more
progressive spirits saw, on accommodation rather than conflict, for
there were, before the 1914–18 War, 'many who hope . . . that the wage
system may eventually give place to some form of cooperation among
workers, or co-partnership between capital and labour, which may
result in the absolute identification of employer and employed, and the
consequent disappearance of the present . . . antagonism between class
and class'.[119]

The shattering of the other pattern of consensus politics after 1918
led away from this vision as an ideal of partnership but it had its day,
after all, in an enforced 'absolute identification of employer and
employed' in the life of the 'scab union' after 1926. Since the battered
SWMF, despite its internal wrangles, did not lie down and die, between
1934 and 1936 overt struggle gave way to concessions won and
accommodation established on the uneasy tandem a trade union rides.
Outwardly the concessions were paltry enough, and the
accommodation destructive enough of wider options, to make the
sacrifices undergone seem incommensurate with any gains achieved.
After all, enlightened owners like David Davies had long been appealing
for arbitration and conciliation of disputes to avoid unnecessary strife.

Clearly this version of events is, in the light of the actual history,
disingenuous, for the offer, even of conciliation, was always reluctant,
hedged about with safeguards and, generally, extracted by the threat of
disruption. The weaker the threat, the less lip-service need be paid to
union demands. So the rebuilding of Federation strength was of
paramount importance: that was the supreme, and continuing, lesson.
Horner knew what a fragile plant he had to tend:

> I was selling something – labour power, and they had to buy it. I was selling
> a perishable commodity – it had to work or it had to die. And the coalowners

couldn't remain the coalowners unless they bought what I had to sell. That's the real underlying purpose of 100% membership of the Union. It is to prevent the employers being able to buy in a market outside of your control. And labour power is as much a commodity as cabbages or potatoes, and very much of a resemblance to it because if it isn't disposed of it will rot. Well, they used to fight their battle – I never depended on their goodwill. I had no social relations with them at all. I never had anything to do with them outside the meetings, and in the meetings themselves it was a very impersonal matter. And we depended on the outcome of the negotiations and that depended in its turn on the relative strengths. I never had any illusion that we'd get anything out of the owners because of kindness of heart – I knew that we'd get what we were strong enough to take.[120]

With the end of the weak organisational condition of the SWMF in 1934, there was no looking back as the Company Union and then non-Unionism itself were eliminated. The paradox lay in the fact that the institutional vitality of the SWMF was sounder at the end of the 1930s than it had ever been hitherto, despite the appalling economic and social handicaps thrust its way. There could be no clearer indication that it was a social organism. And this was another root cause of the struggle, for the SWMF had become the body and the mind not of an anonymous mass of people conveniently labelled 'the coalfield', or 'the community' or 'the miners', 'the work-force', 'the immigrants' or 'the unemployed', but rather of distinct social beings who maintained their localities, as they established their own dignified individuality, by collective action and collective institutions. The SWMF was either at the source of or deeply involved in all the political and social initiatives of the 1930s. Where it was not so involved, those initiatives were, and remained, the activity of minorities. Their developing political hegemony, despite falling economic power, can be seen in the disputes over parliamentary seats that went to miners in Merthyr, Llanelli, Pontypool and Caerphilly, and over the row in Pontypridd.[121] The union was 'a body' because its existence and its role were fully integrated into local life, and 'a mind' because, in different ways of course, it attempted to give direction:

The South Wales Miners' Federation – the 'Fed' as it was called and is still called in many places – was unique among unions, even among those federated to the Miners' Federation of Great Britain. The Fed was a lot more than a trade union; it was a social institution providing through its local leaders an all-round service of advice and assistance to the mining community on most of the problems that could arise between the cradle and

the grave. Its function became a combination of economic, social and
political leadership in these single industry communities. After all these
communities existed in narrow valley concentrations, were dependent upon
a pit for their existence, and were tightly bound together by this common
interest. The leaders of the local miners' lodges were very much more than
representatives dealing with problems of wages and conditions of
employment in the mines. They were acknowledged social leaders called
upon to help and advise in all kinds of domestic and social problems; they
were indeed the village elders to whom the people went when in any kind of
trouble. . .
    . . . The Fed was a social institution and acted as such without question.
Without doubt, its strength and ties with the communities were based on its
intimate involvement in social and domestic affairs. . . . The Fed, now
integrated into the National Union of Mineworkers, still sees itself in many
situations as giving political leadership and initiating general political
campaigns.[122]

The society whose social characteristics were so varied as to make
any total control impossible without a root alteration might change,
haphazardly, for better or worse, but the SWMF itself was an artifice,
the outward emblem of the organisation of the miners' collective
existence, made by the men themselves. The Federation was the
product of a self-conscious industrial society that developed in places a
sophisticated class-consciousness, and it was, in many ways, the finest
manifestation of that society, because it refused to be bound by that
very parochialism, which in its local, human guise, not its received,
introverted mode, was its greatest strength. Hence the clarity with
which the rebuilding of the SWMF was linked to wider purposes.
Equally, the stinging setbacks received made advocates of radical
change move cautiously in the late 1930s.
    In the post-war world this caution was first encouraged by the hopes
induced by nationalisation and then rooted, after the mid-1950s, in a
defence of the future of the industry itself. Any atrophy of will caused by
pit closures and by the boosting of other energy sources went far deeper
than leadership level. However, by the late 1960s that atrophy, too, was
sloughed off in actions reminiscent of pre-1926 days. The nourishing of
the new militancy of the early 1970s was as much the product of the
retained memories of coalfield society in South Wales as it was the
rejection of hitherto received (and profoundly mistaken) 'expert'
wisdom about energy requirements. This history seeks to sustain that
collective memory.

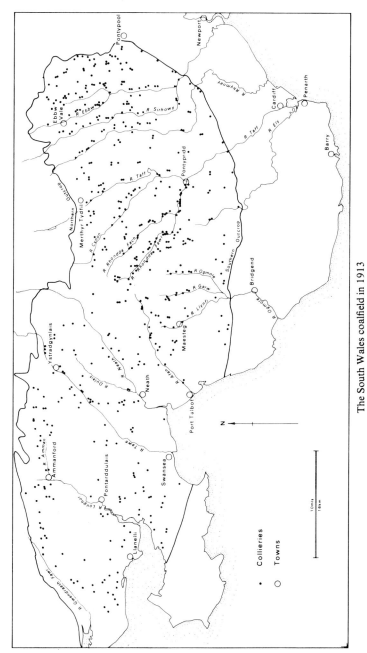

The South Wales coalfield in 1913

Collieries ·
Towns ○

Pontypool
Newport
Pontypridd
Merthyl Tydfil
Ebbw Vale
R Ebbw
R Sirhowy
R Rhymney
R Taff
R Ely
Penarth
Cardiff
Barry
Northern Outcrop
Southern Outcrop
R Taff
R Cynon
R Rhondda Fach
R Rhondda Fawr
R Ogmore
R Garw
R Llynfi
Maesteg
Bridgend
R Ogmore
Ystradgynlais
R Neath
R Dulais
R Afan
Neath
Port Talbot
Swansea
R Tawe
Ammanford
R Amman
Pontarddulais
R Loughor
Llanelli
R Gwendraeth Fawr

N

10 mls
16 km

NOTES

1. J. H. Morris and L. J. Williams, *The South Wales Coal Industry, 1841–1875* (1958), *passim*; E. D. Lewis, *The Rhondda Valleys* (1959).
2. Quoted in L. J. Williams, 'The Strike of 1898' in *Morgannwg*, Vol. IX (1965), p. 77.
3. Quoted in R. P. Arnot *South Wales Miners*, Vol. I, 1898–1914, (1967), p. 99.
4. See Peter Stead 'Working-class Leadership in South Wales, 1900–1920', *Welsh History Review (WHR)*, Vol. 6, June 1973.
5. For a development of this view, consult David Smith 'Leaders and Led', in *Rhondda – Past and Future*, ed. K. S. Hopkins (1975).
6. John B. Hilling, *Cardiff and The Valleys* (1973); Cyril Batstone, *Rhondda in Old Photographs* (1974); David Smith, 'The Camera as Historian' in *W.H.R.*, Vol. 7, 1974.
7. I. G. Jones, 'The South Wales Collier in mid-Nineteenth century' in *Victorian South Wales – 7th Conference Report of the Victorian Society*, p. 35.
8. E. W. Evans, *Mabon* (1959); Peter Stead, 'Vernon Hartshorn' in *Glamorgan Historian* (1969), ed. Stewart Williams; Christopher Howard, 'Reactionary Radicalism' in *Glamorgan Historian* (1973), ed. Stewart Williams.
9. H. S. Jevons, *The British Coal Trade* (1915), p. 131.
10. L. J. Williams, 'The Road to Tonypandy', *Llafur* (Vol. I, No. 2), 1973, *passim*.
11. The 'story' of the Revival can be traced in Awstin's reports for the *Western Mail* (put out in pamphlet form) but its significance awaits its historian. For a suggestive approach see Bryan Wilson, *Religion in a Secular Society* (1966) and especially, pp. 48–9: 'In many ways revivalism represented the attempt to re-establish agrarian values, to restore the advantages of stable community life to people who had lost all community sense. . . . It is not surprising that such revivals had their impact in new urban areas, full of recently transplanted rural populations. . . . Revivalism promises a return to the decencies of the past through a reassertion of fundamental truths.'
12. Brinley Thomas, 'Migration into the Glamorganshire Coalfield 1861–1911', reprinted in *Industrial South Wales* (1969), ed. Minchinton.
13. Rhondda No. 1 District Minutes, 11 March 1907.
14. Page Arnot, *op. cit.*, pp. 145–8.
15. R. Page Arnot, *op. cit.*, pp. 175–273; D. Evans, *Labour Strife in the South Wales Coalfield* (Cardiff, 1911); E. D. Lewis, *The Rhondda Valleys* (Cardiff, 1959) pp. 172–9.
16. Commission of Inquiry into Industrial Unrest: No. 7 Division: *Report of the Commissioners for Wales including Monmouthshire 1917* (Cd., 8668) *passim*.
17. D. J. Davies, *Ninety Years of Endeavour: The History of Tredegar Workmen's Hall*, 1861–1951 (Cardiff, 1951) p. 71.
18. South Wales Miners' Library (SWML), Interview with D. D. Evans, (Ystradgynlais), 5 December 1972.
19. R. Page Arnot, *op. cit.*, p. 149.

20. R. Lewis, 'The South Wales Miners and the Ruskin College Strike of 1909', *Llafur*, Vol. 2, No. 1, Spring 1976.

21. Hywel Francis, 'The Origins of the South Wales Miners' Library' in *History Workshop*, No. 2, Autumn 1976.

22. W. W. Craik, *Central Labour College* (London, 1964) p. 117; Bob Holton, *British Syndicalism* 1900–14 (London, 1976), pp. 80 and 168–70.

23. B. L. Coombes, *These Poor Hands* (London, 1939) p. 88. There were in the Rhondda, for example, in 1911, 929 Irish, 263 Scots, 173 Italians, 285 Americans (USA), 4,057 from Somerset, 2,875 from Gloucester and 1,681 Londoners. *Census of England and Wales, 1911: County of Glamorgan* (HMSO, 1914); E. D. Lewis *op. cit.*, pp. 238–9. The Tonypandy riots were a social fracture for which the 1910–11 dispute served as a catalyst.

24. Interview with Gregorio Esteban (Abercrave) 10 October 1969, who was born in Baracaldo near Bilbao in the Basque Country of Spain in 1897. His father was a steelworker in Bilbao who obtained work in the Dowlais Ironworks in 1907 and shortly afterwards at the International Colliery, Abercrave. He was a strong trade unionist, socialist and atheist.

25. Glamorgan Record Office (GLRO), D/DG Section C.3, Dowlais Iron Company Contracts: Orconero Iron Ore Company Limited.

26. Leandro Macho, 'Growing up in Spanish Abercrave', Transcript of Lecture delivered at SWML, 27 September 1976; *Census of England and Wales, 1911: Counties of Brecknock, Carmarthen, Pembroke and Cardigan* (HMSO, 1914) p. 124.

27. *Ibid.* There had been 72 Spaniards (50 males, 22 females) in the County of Breconshire in 1911. It can be reasonably assumed that all or almost all of these had settled in Abercrave. *Census of England and Wales, 1911, op. cit.*

28. *Western Mail*, 20 July 1914; D. D. Evans interview, *op. cit.*

29. Interview with Dick Beamish (Abercrave) 10 October 1969.

30. Macho, *op. cit.*, D. D. Evans interview, *op. cit.*

31. *Ibid.* Information from Maria Williams (Cardiff), 16 May 1974, who was brought up within the Dowlais Spanish Community and who still possesses her father's PSOB (Dowlais branch) membership card.

32. Interview with Jim Vale (Abercrave) 10 May 1974.

33. *Ibid.*

34. Dick Beamish, D. D. Evans, Jim Vale interviews *op. cit.* The banner of the Abercrave lodge, made in the early 1960s, bearing the slogans 'Workers of the World Unite for Socialism' and 'Mewn Undeb Mae Nerth a Heddwch' ('In Unity there is Strength and Peace') against a background of black and white miners shaking hands.

35. David Evans, *passim*.

36. W. H. Mainwaring MSS., National Library of Wales. 1911 Notebook. W. H. Mainwaring kept minutes of early meetings he attended as an 'Unofficial Reformer.' The records are fragmentary but invaluable in terms of the information they provide, *re* timing, personnel and opinions. In 1911 he records six meetings between 29 July and 18 November 1911.

37. It was, in fact, written by 3 men (and their assistants), i.e. Ablett, Rees, Hay, Dolling, Mainwaring and Gibbon. Although others were 'involved'. See W. H. Mainwaring MSS., *loc. cit.* For a detailed discussion of the authorship, see David

Egan, 'The Unofficial Reform Committee and the Miners' Next Step' in *Llafur*, Vol. 2, No. 3, 1978, pp. 64–80.

38. *The Miners' Next Step* (1912), p. 8.

39. *Ibid.*, pp. 8–9.

40. *Ibid.*, p. 14.

41. *Ibid.*, p. 14.

42. Quoted in M. G. Woodhouse, *Rank and File Movements among the Miners of South Wales, 1910–26* (Oxford D.Phil. 1969).

43. Page Arnot, *op. cit.*., pp. 321–7.

44. *South Wales Daily News*, 9 November 1912.

45. *Ibid.*, 12, 13, 14 November 1912.

46. For a discussion on the importance of dating the effective public decline of the Welsh language in the coalfield, see David Smith 'The Future of Coalfield History' in *Morgannwg*, Vol. XIX, 1975; and Ceri Lewis 'The Welsh Language in the Rhondda', in *Rhondda Past and Future* (1975).

47. Jevons, *op. cit.*, pp. 133–4.

48. Quoted in R. P. Arnot, *South Wales Miners*, Vol. II (1976), p. 13. The views of the Unofficial Reformers were not always as subtle as Ablett's; nor were they as R. Merfyn Jones suggests, in his Introduction to *The Miners' Next Step* (reprinted in 1973), uniformly pro-centralisation (p. 7). See, for example, Nemo's article in *The Rhondda Socialist*, 26 October 1912, just prior to the vital Conference, in which centralisation is attacked because 'it requires more officials at headquarters, and renders proper attention to individual or sectional disputes impossible'.

49. *South Wales Daily News*, 14 November 1912.

50. The argument had been met by the Vice-President of Tynbedw Lodge in the Rhondda who protested 'against the assertion that the proposed £3 per week to Agents has been engineered by the younger members of the Federation to 'freeze out' some of the Agents who are opposed to their policy. The proposal was made at a general meeting of Tynbedw workmen and carried unanimously. It was proposed by one of the oldest members and supported by men whose sincerity and integrity is beyond question – men who have sacrificed everything for the enhancement of the Federation. As Vice-President of the above Lodge, I feel that the public should know the truth.' *Letter* in *South Wales Daily News*, 15 November 1912.

51. *Ibid.*, 16 November 1912.

52. *Ibid.*, 18 November 1912.

53. Page Arnot, *op cit.*, p. 324.

54. *South Wales Worker*, 1913–14, *passim*.

55. SWMF minutes 1 September 1914.

56. Arnot, *op. cit.*, pp. 43–93 *passim*.

57. SWML interviews with D. J. Davies (Ystrad-Rhondda), 14 October 1974, and Tommy Nicholas (Neath), 16 May 1974; Deian Hopkin, 'Patriots and Pacifists in Wales, 1914–1918: The Case of Capt. Lionel Lindsay and the Rev. T. E. Nicholas', *Llafur*, Vol. 1, No. 3, May 1974; Keith Robbins, 'Morgan Jones in 1916', *Llafur*, Vol. 1, No. 4, Summer 1975.

58. W. F. Hay, *War! and the Welsh Miner* (Tonypandy, n.d.)

59. SWML interviews with Max Goldberg (Aberdare), 6 September 1972 and Will Paynter, a Cymmer International Brigade volunteer, 18 April 1969.

60. SWMF minutes, 3 August, 8 October 1917.
61. Goldberg interview *op. cit.*; information from members of the Maesteg Irish community (who wish to remain anonymous), summer 1974.
62. SWML interview with Tom Gale (Abertillery) 1 July 1974; Tom Gale to Hywel Francis 27 October 1976.
63. A. L. Horner, *Incorrigible Rebel* (London, 1960), pp. 34–7.
64. U.C.S. Mardy lodge minutes 14 May 1919 quoted by D. B. Smith, 'The Future of Coalfield History in South Wales' in *Morgannwg*, Vol. XIX, 1975.
65. David Egan, 'The Swansea Conference of the British Council of Soldiers' and Workers' Delegates, July 1917: Reactions to the Russian Revolution of February 1917 and the Anti-War Movement in South Wales', *Llafur*, Vol. 1, No. 4, 1975.
66. W. H. Mainwaring MSS. Notebook for 1915. This records four meetings between 15 August and 31 August 1915. Ablett and Cook chaired the meetings, the last of which, held in Cardiff, drew representatives from Maesteg, Garw, Eastern Valleys, Aberdare, Rhondda and Western Valleys.
67. *South Wales Daily News*, 13 June 1917. The word 'Monmouthshire' was then added!
68. Jevons, *op. cit.*, Appendix III, p. 802.
69. *South Wales Daily News*, 18 June 1917.
70. W. J. Edwards, *From the Valley I Came* (1956), pp. 195–6, pp. 205 and 233.
71. *South Wales Daily News*, 14 and 15 June 1917.
72. For an example of the difficulties of unionising a fluid, immigrant population, see B. L. Coombes *These Poor Hands* (1974), pp. 86–8.
73. Page Arnot, *op. cit.*, pp. 334–5; there were four unions in the coalfield, in addition to the SWMF, i.e. the South Wales Colliery Enginemen and Surface Craftsmen's Association (approximately 6,000 members); the Winding Enginemen's Association; the Colliery Examiners' Association and the South Wales Colliery Officials' Union. (The craft union was variously named, see p. 26.)
74. G. R. Carter, 'The Coal Strike in South Wales' *The Economic Journal*, No. 99, September 1915, Vol. XXV, p. 463.
75. SWMF, EC Minutes, 24 September 1915.
76. Carter, 'The Sequel of the Welsh Coal Strike and its Significance' *The Economic Journal*, No. 100, December 1915, Vol. XXV, pp. 526–7.
77. See John Thomas 'The South Wales Coalfield during Government Control, 1914–21' (University of Wales M.A. thesis, 1925).
78. Frank Hodges, 'The South Wales Non-Unionist Agreement' in *The 'Plebs'*, Vol. VIII, No. 4, May 1916.
79. One indication of the increasing internationalism of individual miners' lodges is revealed by the Ferndale lodge whose general meetings between August 1919 and February 1920 passed resolutions of protest against Intervention in Russia (calling for a Stop Day each month), repression of Industrial Workers' of the World members in the USA and the actions of the British Army in India, UCS, Ferndale lodge general minutes, August 1919–February 1920 *passim*.
80. L. J. Macfarlane, *The British Communist Party: Its Origin and Development until 1929* (London 1966), pp. 44–6.
81. SWMF minutes, 23 July 1921.

82. MFGB minutes, 19 July 1922.

83. UCS Dowlais District minutes, 16 September, 15 October, 9 November 1922.

84. Interview with W. J. Griffiths, a Tonypandy volunteer in the International Brigades, 16 October 1969; L. J. Mcfarlane, *op. cit.*, pp. 130–1. The SWMF did, however, raise the matter of affiliation in 1924 when its Annual Conference decided to call on the TUC to join the RILU: SWMF minutes, 24–8 July 1924.

85. Hywel Francis, 'South Wales', in J. Skelley (ed.), *The General Strike, 1926* (1976), *passim.*

86. *Lenin on Britain* (London, 1934), p. 272.

87. The Federation's rule 3 (b) had been altered in February 1920, to read:

> To secure the entire organisation of all workers *and officials* employed in and about collieries . . . in the South Wales and Monmouthshire Coalfield.

The craftsmen had been brought in by February 1921, though in August, D. B. Jones led a breakaway section of some 6,000 craftsmen into a new Boilermen and Engine-Winders' Union; see SWMF Rules, 1920, and *South Wales Daily News*, 12 August 1921.

88. Page Arnot, Vol. II, p. 200. In February 1921 an estimated 80,000 miners were unemployed through trade depression; and p. 213: 'The SWMF emerged from the lock-out of 1921 battered and beaten. . . . Wages were brought down with a rush. In South Wales the fall (of the average daily wage) was . . . from $21/6\frac{3}{4}d$ per shift in January 1921 to $9/5\frac{1}{2}d$ in October 1922.'

89. From May to December 1924, 35 pits closed in the coalfield. *Ibid.*, p. 250. At the start of 1921 there were 197,668 men within the SWMF; the figure shrank to 117,610 by the end of the year, was reduced to 87,080 by the end of 1922 and only climbed again to 147,611 by the start of 1924. See *Annual Returns of the S.W.M.F. to the Registrar of Friendly Societies, 1912–50*. F.S. 12/137. 1160 T. P.R.O.

90 There were bitter attacks, on one another, made by Hartshorn and Barker, Hartshorn and Cook, Ablett and Hodges between 1918 and 1921.

91. *The Colliery Workers' Magazine*, July 1923, Vol. I, No. 7.

92. There was a spread of 'social religion'. See C. Gwyther *The Valley shall be Exalted: Light Shines in the Rhondda* (1949); R. J. Barker, *Christ in the Valley of Unemployment* (1936).

93. The Bedwellty Board of Guardians received the same treatment as Chester-le-Street and Poplar, i.e. their responsibilities were taken away by Government. See *Western Mail*, 11 March 1927, and June 1935 *(passim)*; Sian Rhiannon Williams, 'The Bedwellty Board of Guardians and the Default Act of 1927' in *Llafur*, Vol. 2, No. 4, Spring 1979, pp. 65–77.

94. B. L. Coombes in *Those Clouded Hills* (1944), and *Miners' Day* (1945) sees the advent of pit-head baths in the Second World War as a tremendous boon, and contrasts this with the hard labour required of women before (for which consult his *These Poor Hands* (1939)).

95. A correspondent in *The Times* wrote, 29 March 1928:

> Formerly girls were discouraged by their parents from going out to domestic service in Cardiff, London, or elsewhere. It was once considered beneath the dignity of a miner's family, and there was no need to supplement the wages of fathers and brothers.

Three domestic training centres had already been set up for girls aged 14 to 20, in 1928, but when S. P. B. Mais broadcast his experiences of the 'distressed areas' in 1933, correspondents from Wiltshire and elsewhere wrote in indignation at their inability to find domestic servants. See Mais, *S.O.S. Talks on Unemployment* (1933), pp. 127–9.

96. *Western Mail*, 4 March 1935.
97. Official figures quoted in the 5th Annual Report of the SWMF EC 1938–9. See also *The Second Industrial Survey of South Wales*, 3 Vols. (1937), ed. H. Marquand.
98 See I. G. Jones 'The Valleys: The Making of a Community' in *Call to the Valleys* (1975); Hywel Francis, 'Survey of Miners' Institute and Welfare Hall Libraries', *Llafur*, Vol. 1, No. 2, 1973. It was this popular control that worried the 1917 Commissioners:

> With the dwellings and other buildings ranged in streets that run along the length of the valleys in monotonous terraces, instead of . . . radiating from a common centre as would be possible on fairly level sites, the civic and corporate life of the community has suffered owing to the absence of 'town centres' and of any conveniently centralised institutions. For instance, dignified municipal buildings are extremely rare; not a single municipally maintained public library is to be found in the central Glamorgan block of the coalfield – it is only on the sea-board and in the older towns of Merthyr, Aberdare and Pontypridd, that any exist. There are many working men's Institutes, most of them with collections of books, attached to different collieries . . . the Rhondda has an abundance of cinemas and music halls, but not a single theatre. Owing to this absence of municipal centres and centralised institutions, the development of the civic spirit and the sense of social solidarity – what we may in short call the community sense – is seriously retarded *(Commission of Enquiry into Industrial Unrest No. 7 Division, 1917* (Cd. 8668).)

99. Ness Edwards, *History of the S.W.M.F.* (1936), Vol. II. Uncorrected proof copy, unpublished, in Nuffield College Library, pp. 225–8.
100. Will Paynter, 'The "Fed"', in *Men of No Property* (1971).
101. *The Times*, 28 March 1928.
102. *Ibid.*, 29 March 1928.
103. *Ibid.*, 28 March 1928.
104. *Ibid.*, 29 March 1928.
105. *Ibid.*, 2 April 1928.
106. *An Industrial Survey of South Wales* (1932), pp. 22–3. And see Brinley Thomas, 'Labour Mobility in the South Wales and Monmouthshire Coal-mining Industry, 1920–30', *The Economic Journal*, Vol. XLI, June 1931.
107. There were 566 pits (large and small in 1920), 472 in 1930 and 370 in 1938. See the *Regional Survey Report, South Wales Coalfield* (1946), Table XXXI.
108. See Anthony-Jones, 'Labour Relations in the South Wales Coal Mining Industry', 1926–39 (Ph.D., University of Wales, 1959), *passim.*
109. For a contemporary invective, mostly drawn from MOH Reports and still attacking 'the influence of the enemy' in 'the movement in South Wales' (p. 52), see Allen Hutt 'The South Wales Coalfield To-day' in *The Condition of the Working Class in Britain* (London, 1933): 'Monopoly has developed in the South

Wales coal industry as an accompaniment, not only of growing unemployed and the impoverishment of the unemployed masses, but of the impoverishment and increased exploitation of the men in the pits. Visit a few mining townships in, for example, what is now the territory of the Powell Duffryn combine; men will tell, with a wry face, of "how the P.D. came" to their areas as if it were a pestilence or a barbarian invasion. The initials of this huge concern are bitterly translated always as "Poverty and 'Dole'"' (p. 22).

110. See Graham Humphrys *Industrial South Wales* (1972), and Graham Rees, 'The Welsh Economy' in *Anatomy of Wales* (ed. R. Brinley Jones, 1972).

111. D. B. Rees, *Chapels in the Valley* (1975), concluded: 'All the Welsh Nonconformist denominations have witnessed a substantial decline in membership figures since the 1926 General Strike', p. 72. This would seem to bear out Sir William Jenkins' address to the Congregational Union in London in 1937 in which he lamented a decline in church membership and authority, declared that over half the churches in South Wales were without ministers and that the total debt of the Nonconformist churches in Glamorgan and Monmouthshire was £402,955. Renovation was ignored and expenses cut, whilst 75 per cent of the debt was owed to private individuals: 'In the little chapel where I attend the debt is £400 for 120 members. We pay our minister £4 a week, and for 3 months in 1935 he had no stipend,' *Western Mail*, 7 May 1937. It was estimated that the chapels in the Rhondda had *c.* 70 per cent reduction in membership between 1921 and 1935. *Men Without Work* (1938), p. 291.

112. Thomas Jones *What's Wrong with South Wales?* (1935) and *The Silver Jubilee* (1935) in *Leeks and Daffodils* (1942).

113. See David Smith, 'Myth and Meaning in the Literature of the South Wales Coalfield – the 1930's' in *Anglo-Welsh Review*, Spring 1976.

114. This is a subject that still requires investigation but we would suggest that a rise of a Welsh bourgeoisie from the mid-nineteenth century, the 'disinterested' educational philanthropy that led, at its summit, to the establishment of the University of Wales, the growth in numbers of Welsh 'public servants' and the 'natural' economic forces that produced, via the coalfield, the money, should not be so readily separated. Consult E. L. Ellis, *The University of Wales, Aberystwyth 1872–1972* (Cardiff, 1972); *Enquiry into Industrial Unrest*, 1917; *The Welsh Outlook*, January 1914 (for a view of rugby as the Welsh social cement); and J. Vyrnwy Morgan *Welsh Political and Educational Leaders in the Victorian Era* (London, 1908).

115. For a view that sees *Welsh* nonconformity as out of step with working-class needs long before 1900 consult W. R. Lambert 'Some Working-class Attitudes Towards Organised Religion in Nineteenth-century Wales' in *Llafur*, Vol. 2, No. 1, Spring 1976.

116. Thomas Jones, 'Workmens' Libraries and Institutes' in *Leeks and Daffodils* (1942).

117. See J. Vyrnwy Morgan, *The Welsh Mind in Evolution* (1925); Rhys Davies, *My Wales* (1937); Richard Llewellyn, *How Green was My Valley* (1939) and again, the 1917 enquiry into Industrial Unrest.

118. Thomas Jones, *Welsh Broth* (1951), p. 143.

119. D. Lleufer Thomas, *Labour Unions in Wales – Their Early Struggle for Existence* (1901), pp. 25–6. Lleufer Thomas was, of course, the principal co-

ordinator of the 1917 Enquiry, as well as being a Stipendiary Magistrate for Pontypridd and Rhondda for 25 years.

120. UCS, Arthur Horner MSS. Transcript of radio broadcast, 'I remember' in 1959 (he was interviewed by John Griffiths).
121. See below, pp. 309–10, 345n.
122. Will Paynter, *My Generation* (1972), pp. 110–11. In 1945, in its membership returns to the Registrar-General, it called itself the South Wales Miners' Federation branch of the NUM instead of the more correct NUM (South Wales Area).

CHAPTER TWO

1926

The period from the outbreak of the Great War to the commencement of the General Strike and miners' lock-out was one which saw a deepening of the radicalisation of the South Wales miners which had been apparent in certain parts of the coalfield since the tumultous years of 1910–11. By 1926 the South Wales miners were the pace-setters within the MFGB.[1] It was from this district more than any other that new leaders and new policies were constantly being produced and in particular focusing on the Miners' Minority Movement which must have considered South Wales to be its spiritual home.[2] Such a dynamic transformation, reflecting as it did the enormous economic and demographic changes of the region, led to the projection of this consciousness on to an international plane. But whether this new development could be maintained in times of adversity with collapsing overseas markets, two prolonged lock-outs and growing mass unemployment, only time could reveal.

There was certainly ample evidence during the 1926 lock-out that proletarian internationalist links were not only enduring but being strengthened at local level. Internationalist organisations closely linked with the Communist International were active in the coalfield and received considerable support. The Workers' International Relief provided funds to such lodges as Mardy which received £50 for its communal kitchen at the end of the lock-out.[3] The International Class War Prisoners' Aid (British section) had already been closely involved in campaigning on behalf of imprisoned miners from the Anthracite Coalfield in West Wales and in presenting them with medals and scrolls.[4] The International Class War Prisoners' Aid (ICWPA) organised a conference in Cardiff on 6 February 1926 presided over by S. O. Davies, vice-president of the SWMF, which set up a South Wales District with a view to collecting funds for 'Class war prisoners', providing legal defence, conducting release campaigns and securing affiliations.[5] During the course of the lock-out individual lodges did affiliate to the ICWPA.[6]

But it was not the activities of these two organisations, significant as they were, that encouraged a more left-wing outlook to internationalist links and resulted in such lodges as Penallta, never one considered to be industrially or politically militant, to demand the MFGB's affiliation to the 'Third or Red International of Labour Unions'.[7] Rather it was the vast support which the Russian trade unions gave to the British miners during their lock-out. The Russian contribution of £1,161,459 2s. 6d. to the British Miners' Relief Fund amounted to 87 per cent of all overseas donations.[8] One simple indication of the appreciation felt for the Russian aid in sustaining the miners' struggle was the occasion when a full area conference stood in silence as a mark of respect to Krassin, the Soviet chargé d'affaires in London, who died in November 1926.[9] Individual lodges also sent their sympathy.[10] There was a widespread and enduring belief that the Russian support had been vital and its significance was recalled fifty years after the lock-out.[11] One lodge, Nine Mile Point, openly and unequivocally referred to the grants dispensed to its members as 'Russian money'.[12]

One other aspect of this particular kind of internationalism was the perverse pride which was felt by many of Mardy's inhabitants when hostile press reporters inflicted what they considered to be a calculated insult by nicknaming Mardy 'Little Moscow' immediately after the General Strike.[13] Mardy was to live up to such a reputation and was rewarded for its faithfulness. Local legend has it that A. J. Cook presented it with a vivid red and gold banner which he had accepted on behalf of the British miners and their wives from the working women of Krasnaya Presna, Moscow. He had been in Moscow during the lock-out to acknowledge their financial support. Cook is reputed to have said that the most appropriate place to keep the banner was Mardy Workmen's Hall. It was likely that the banner was brought back by Dai Lloyd Davies, secretary of the Mardy lodge, who had also been to Russia, towards the end of the lock-out. In any event, the banner was given pride of place with a commemorative photograph being taken of it soon after its arrival. Crowded into the photograph were all the local Communists, their children, and a life-size portrait of Lenin in the background. The banner was to be used only on such special occasions as Communist funerals when it draped the coffins.[14]

Such links with the Soviet Union, strengthened as they were during the lock-out, were personified in Jack Roberts of Abertridwr who spoke so frequently and so forcefully about Russia's support in 1926 that he became known locally as 'Jack Russia'.[15]

Important as these international relationships were, they were not to endure and broaden beyond the end of the lock-out simply out of a sense of gratitude. Other coalfields, Durham in particular, had their 'Little Moscow', their banners and their proletarian internationalism, but their industrial and political militancy along with a revolutionary world view was not to survive 1926 (except in Fife).[16]

What did make the situation different in the mining valleys of South Wales was the nature of their struggle and the manner and intensity of their resistance. It had already been noted in 1917 that hostility to capitalism had become part of the political creed of the majority of SWMF members.[17] One enthusiastic contemporary observer claimed that the writings of Karl Marx had become household words.[18] It was quite evident that a cultural shift was taking place. The phenomenon was labelled 'prolet-cult' by those who were most disturbed by it and who blamed the influence of independent working-class education for its proliferation:

> It seemed at one time that the miner in South Wales was going to replace his old native culture with another – a culture based on his needs as a worker and fostered by means of the classes organised by the National Council of Labour Colleges'.[19]

These indications of a shift in political outlook reflected what can best be described as a change towards an 'alternative culture', where social, political and cultural norms were being increasingly rejected. Aspects of this new behavioural pattern had already been evident in the 1925 Anthracite strike. Indeed the events of 1926 were for a generation of Anthracite miners overshadowed by their localised strike of the previous summer. For them, 1925 was their sobering experience in which new attitudes and new forms of action emerged. There was an unusual aggressive willingness; to escalate their strike; use mass mobile picket lines, a network of spies (which penetrated the police), riots and disturbances. It led to the control of the town of Ammanford for nearly a week. There was a remarkable and widespread acceptance of prison sentences and gaoled leaders were fêted as folk heroes.[20]

The nine days of the General Strike and more especially the seven-month lock-out revealed an alternative cultural pattern which had no comparable equivalent in the other British coalfields. The totality of commitment to the miners' cause was a form of class consciousness which translated itself into a community consciousness, so overwhelming were the miners in numbers and influence. It was a collectivist conception which burnt into the collective memory of the whole region and was most succinctly described by the poet, Idris Davies, in what he called 'The Angry Summer':

We shall remember 1926, until our blood is dry.[21]

The industrial crisis of 1926 precipitated a polarising of class and community forces. During the course of the Nine Days, the Strike appeared to be something of a non-event. The Emergency Powers Regulations and the Organisation for the Maintenance of Supplies were hardly invoked in the mining valleys. It was as if the authorities deliberately stood to one side and seemed temporarily to allow the mining communities to carry on much as they wished. So overwhelming was the support that to contemplate not joining the strike would have been tantamount to committing social suicide. Not one miner is said to have been arrested, although there was much illegal action. It was not so much a question of 'dual power' as almost one of transference of power in some valleys. In such villages as Bedlinog and Mardy, the miners through their strike committees and councils of action virtually ran their communities unchallenged.[22]

The most profound effect the events of 1926 had on the coalfield was the way in which they clarified and then polarised class loyalties. Within a community under seige, the miners and their families armed with their essentially proletarian institutions of the 'Fed', the 'Co-op', the Institute and the Chapel, along with the ILP, CPGB, Labour Party and the remainder of the trade union movement, were ranged against the Government, the coalowners and their officials, the police, the judiciary and the 'blacklegs'. But the new dimension in the situation was the lower middle class made up predominantly of teachers, shopkeepers and ministers of religion who merged 'downwards' and openly took up the cause of the miners or slipped into total passivity.[23]

This social class polarisation deepened considerably during the lock-out. But what characterised the South Wales miners was the scale and degree of their resistance and the way in which they confronted the dual problems of relief and 'blacklegging'.[24] It becomes increasingly clear as the lock-out extended into the summer and autumn that the 'alternative culture' was being diversified and deepened so that it was founded on class discipline, resourceful quasi-political illegality, direct action resulting often in guerrilla and open warfare, collectivist action of various forms, perverse humour and escapism.[25] These communities seemed prepared, in lemming-like fashion, to rise to the challenge of the overwhelming odds against them rather than accept the inevitable defeat with equanimity. The distortions in the traditional society took many forms:

> 'I saw two grown men in their thirties, fighting each other to the point of unconsciousness over two marbles, because we had to get something for currency. . . .'[26]

The response of the miners to the inadequacies of relief was immediate and direct. The first demonstration with contingents headed by bands and bearing banners proclaiming 'Workers of the World Unite' and 'Give Us Our Daily Bread' converged on Pontypool from Blaenavon, Abersychan, Cwmbran and Griffithstown.[27] On 21 May, thousands from Risca, Abercarn, Cross Keys, Cwmfelinfach, Pontymister, Bedwas and Machen responded to the call by Nine Mile Point Lodge to march on Newport Workhouse to obtain relief, only to be halted at Bassaleg by the Chief Constable.[28] On 5 June, 2,000 people confined the relieving officer to his office for several hours in Blaenavon because he refused to pay out relief unless husbands gave signed receipts.[29]

Yet some personified the independent qualities of these communities by being too proud to ask for relief and relying on their own savings which was normally their Co-operative Society dividend.[30] More often, they were sustained by the sporadic Federation strike pay and the communal kitchens in institutes and chapels supported by funds from MFGB, lodge reserves, institute investments and touring choirs and bands.[31] A few maintained, again through their independent attitudes and resourcefulness, that they actually lived better during the lock-out. This was clearly the case in parts of West Wales where lambs and tons of vegetables were presented to communal kitchens by farmers who knew that they would in any event eventually be stolen.[32]

Lenin had been dismissive of the political importance of communal kitchens during the 1921 lock-out.[33] But as in 1921 so also in 1926 the miners were in retreat. The communal kitchen was the cement in holding miners and their families together. James Griffiths, at the time a miners' agent, recalled the situation in the Anthracite district:

... we went through the seven months in our area without a single breakaway . . . due . . . to the Fellowship engendered by that one meal a day.[34]

Conversely, those areas in South Wales which opted for the issuing of food vouchers to individual families in preference to the collectivist approach of the kitchens, tended to be the very areas which suffered the most serious 'blacklegging'.[35]

But the communal kitchens were but one form of collectivist approach adopted during the lock-out. At an institutional level, this took the form of fully utilising those organisations which they influenced or controlled. After the MFGB had failed in its collective submission for unemployment benefit for all its members the onus was now placed on individual miners' lodges to pressurise their local Poor Law Guardians (who could relieve wives and children) and their local education authorities which could invoke the Feeding of Necessitous Children Act. The Boards of Guardians and the Councils, often sympathetic and Labour controlled, were hamstrung by lack of resources and strict Ministry of Health instructions.[36] But some authorities did spend considerable sums in relieving hardship. Rhondda's programme for the whole lock-out cost £57,708 with as many as 18,050 children being fed during the week ending 26 June. The Rhondda Schools' Medical Officer could boast with pride that 5,986,257 meals were provided from public funds from the beginning to the end of the lock-out. But Rhondda was not typical of the coalfield. Rhondda's Schools' Medical Officer provided statistics in his 1926 report which showed that 64 per cent of its children had shown an improvement in their nutritional and health standards by the end of the year, due almost entirely, he claimed, to the blanket school feeding. Such claims could not be made in all valleys.[37]

Another collectivist activity was the co-operative boot centre, usually set-up on lodge initiative, which did so much to keep the humiliation of children and parents alike at bay. The Ynysybwl centre alone repaired seven hundred and eighty-two children's boots and three hundred and forty-seven adults' shoes.[38]

Other similar co-operative enterprises included working outcrops and collecting coal from tips. This was usually under the strict supervision of the miners' lodges, as with the Glynneath Soviet Level[39] but occasionally they became commercial enterprises and developed into serious problems for the strike committees.[40] Desperate miners even lived in rough shanties on the tips so as to preserve their claims.[41]

Local activists, like Aneurin Bevan, dealt with the problem by sabotaging workings and by physical attacks on the transgressors.[42]

If the resilient, collectivist alternative culture was seen anywhere it was in the carnivals of jazz and 'comic' bands which proliferated in particular in the more desperate and proletarianised areas of the Rhondda and Aberdare and were sometimes considered a spiritual threat to the established cultural pattern. An Aberdare Primitive Methodist bitterly complained of:

> 'A most vulgar spectacle – indeed a most indecent spectacle. It was immoral and blasphemous. One jazz-band had the audacity to carry a card upon which was the writing: 'I am the bread of life.'[43]

But the escapism of such bands as the Seven Sisters Black Natives, the Gelli Toreadors and the Cwmparc Gondoliers, with a whole way of life revolving around them, became as important as the Federation in maintaining morale. One Pontypridd banner showing the humour and perhaps even the aspirations of the miners, proclaimed:

> The Graig Miners Perfect Musicians: As Played Before Dai Lossin and other Crowned Heads: $10,001\frac{1}{2}$ Medals and Diplomas.[44]

Such collective humour in adversity helped insulate these communities against the enormous problems of hunger and demoralisation which continuallly threateñed to envelop them.

The focal points of the day-to-day survival and resistance were the Federation Lodge, its strike or distress committee and the secular and religious centres of the village, the Miners' Institute and the Chapels. Regular concerts were held at the Institutes, with local acts such as Ted Lotto the Comedy Cyclist, the Pontypridd Frolics and the Mountain Ash Versatile Five vying with each other to give performances. Raffles at such concerts for trousers and boots became the order of the day.[45] The Institute's library also provided an escape for many. At Cymmer Colliery Workmen's Institute (Porth) lending increased from 29,238 (1925) to 49,161 (1926) although stocks could not be replenished.[46]

Beneath the almost blind defiance revealed by the rejection of the compromise with the Bishops' Proposals in August, cracks in the resistance began to appear.[47] Demoralisation bordering on despair was accelerated by the running down of communal kitchens. By 13 August three parts of the Rhondda were on dry rations of bread and bully beef. Some found relief by emigrating, becoming hotel waiters on the South

Coast or in London, or joining the army. Young girls in particular sought work in the Home Counties as domestic servants.[48]

Others sought the undignified and humiliating escape of returning to work. It was in the treatment of the 'blacklegs' that the alternative culture, with its own morality, code of conduct, and extra-legal actions revealed itself most clearly. In South Wales, unlike the other coalfields, the resistance to the return to work from August onwards turned to guerrilla and even open warfare. Miners actually called a 'Council of War' in the Afan Valley and elsewhere.[49] It was this form of action rather than the official SWMF policies of sending in prominent speakers which really staved off collapse.[50] Apart from innumerable minor, often unreported, skirmishes, there were eighteen serious disturbances, all of which involved protection of blacklegs by imported and local police.[51]

The early minor skirmishes concerned the prevention of outcrop workers from obtaining coal from the mountainside for commercial purposes as at the Race Mountain, Pontypool, on 28 June.[52] The miners also dealt in their own curious way with the occasional early breakaway, as at Pencoed where local people ambushed a cycling blackleg, covered him in a white shirt and conveyed him in a wheelbarrow to his home in Coity to the accompaniment of a concertina.[53] Twelve days later, on 25 August, the *South Wales News* was reporting hostile crowds booing blacklegs at Ton Pentre and New Tredegar. They were confronted at Elliotstown and Phillipstown by women armed with white shirts and a supply of whitewash. In response to such demonstrations, many of which temporarily held up the stampede back to work, the local police were augmented by detachments from other forces.[54]

The Minority Movement Conference of 30 August was called so as to help stem the 'blackleg' tide. It was to be expected that Arthur Horner, the Mardy checkweigher and lodge chairman, would crystallise the mood of the coalfield by calling for the use of extra-legal methods. The returning miners should be stopped 'even by devious means – and the delegates know what I mean by that'.[55] It could be interpreted that he was merely predicting the violence which was about to occur, but in his rallying cry he was accentuating the possibility of it happening.

The decision taken in October by the MFGB, on South Wales' initiative, to withdraw safety men was the occasion for further and heavier police reinforcements.[56] The invasion of the valleys by these outside forces was deeply resented and only succeeded in worsening an already embittered atmosphere.[57] In Glamorganshire alone, some two hundred and forty men of the first police reserve were called up and four hundred and forty-seven from Plymouth, Devonshire, Dorset, Hampshire, Brighton and Portsmouth came to their assistance.[58] The coalfield resembled a battlefield with an 'army of occupation' attempting to break the spirit of a hostile, turbulent population and with local newspapers publishing lists of 'riot' summonses, almost as if they were wartime casualties.[59] Hostility towards the imported police was much in evidence in the Pencoed, Llanharan and Heol-y-Cyw area which led to a hardening of attitudes on the part of the more determined miners and their local leaders. Ted Williams, the local miners' agent, was reported as stating at a public meeting on 20 October:

> Whilst on my way from Bridgend to Llanharan today I saw a policeman on every lane and turning. They of course were there to do their duty as ordered by the state, that is, protect property and not human life, you can make a note of that. I got nothing to say against the police, but the day will come when the position will be reversed and the police will be protecting human life and walking on property.[60]

The eighteen major clashes between striking miners and police occurred mainly during the last eight weeks of the lock-out. By far the most serious were those in the Upper Afan Valley where activities bordered on insurrection.[61] In common with Merthyr, the northern parts of Monmouthshire and the Swansea Dry Steam District, it had suffered a depression before the 1926 lock-out, with the closure of a number of collieries. The area was dominated by the two isolated, single industry, colliery communities of Cymmer and Glyncorrwg where the simple social structure was made up almost entirely of striking miners and their families and where the community belief of sharing poverty and adversity must have been intense. It was all the more significant that the first blacklegs were very much outsiders: a family of Merthyr Pentecostals,[62] and then later a group of eight Port Talbot miners.[63] During the week ending 17 October, when the most serious rioting in the coalfield occurred in the Upper Afan Valley, one hundred and forty-one children in the Glyncorrwg area actually attended school barefooted and ninety-one were absent owing to lack of footwear.[64]

After an initial skirmish on 29 September, a lorry of blacklegs was ambushed in Cymmer Square on 6 October. One of the Cymmer miners involved, David Chappell, threw a stone through the lorry's windscreen for which he was later given a three-month sentence.[65]

The following day, a disturbance occurred one and a half miles from

Cymmer at Nantewlaeth Colliery where eight or nine Port Talbot blacklegs were working. At Heolgwynt, a crowd of five hundred men and women armed with sticks and jam-jars attacked a blackleg's lorry which was being escorted by a police motor-cycle escort. The chief instigator of the protest again seemed to be David Chappell who distinguished himself by repeating his previous day's performance in shattering another windscreen. He urged the crowd to attack the police (who were knocked off their motor-cycles) and the 'blacklegs':

Come on, boys, let's kill the . . . . . . The . . . ought to be burnt out. . . If you go down the pit tomorrow you will never go home alive again[66] (expletives deleted by the reporter).

The 'blacklegs' were rescued by police reinforcements: eleven days later five men and eight women appeared in the Port Talbot Magistrates Court to answer charges of intimidation, unlawful assembly, attempting to cause disaffection among the civilian population, rioting and 'an attempt against the emergency Regulations'. Chappell, almost inevitably, received three months' hard labour; the other men were given sentences of one to two months (some with fine options), and all the women were fined forty shillings.[67] On 1 November a further batch of eighteen miners and eight married women mainly from Abercregan were answering further charges at Port Talbot for their involvement in the events of 6–7 October. All the miners (except one) were fined £15 or one month hard labour and the women fined forty shillings, although one women defiantly preferred 'to do time'.[68]

The persistence of blacklegs in working at another colliery sparked off another more serious disturbance on 14 October. On hearing that a blacklegs' lorry, coming from the Glyncymmer Colliery (known locally as the 'Goodie'), had been attacked and burnt, a detachment of twenty-six police from Port Talbot rushed to the scene in a charabanc. They were met by stone-throwing miners, women and children, on the mountainside above them. Baton-charges at Cymmer and Heolgwynt cleared the area and the blacklegs returned safely to Port Talbot in the charabanc.[69]

But the most intriguing event occurred the following day, again at the Glyncymmer Colliery. The local 'Council of War' must have been responsible for the calling of picket reinforcements from Maesteg and for the spreading of false rumours which resulted in the decoying of police reinforcements to another part of the Afan Valley. With the 'Goodie' left protected by only twenty-one policemen, women and boys were in a strong position to storm the colliery where the blacklegs were working.[70] Provoked by booing and stone-throwing, police reinforcements charged the crowd up the mountainside, only to be halted and forced to retreat by fresh ammunition, taken by the miners from the mountain walls. But Police Inspector Cole of Glynneath failed to escape:

> . . . the boys were going to throw him over the quarry . . . and he was begging, asking them, 'Be British, be British'. Well I did argue with the lads, 'Let him go, let him go' and he was cut and bleeding and the old fellow was crying. And they let him go. But they threw more stones at him as soon as he went . . . .[71]

The quarry symbolised the point to which the miners were prepared to go. The police made only one arrest, which indicated, if nothing else, their difficulties in maintaining order in the Upper Afan Valley (although fifteen others were later summonsed). Yet, despite the overwhelming odds, the miners had either failed to capitalise on their temporary advantage or were not prepared to do so. Joseph Eadie, the Maesteg Communist miner, who was given six months' hard labour for his part in the disturbance which resulted in injuries to twelve policemen, forty-four miners and three women, recognised the dilemma:

> We are not men together boys [sic], we ought to have slaughtered them. I outed the Inspector. . . . They have not enough guts here [Afan Valley] and they have to fetch us over.[72]

The situation had been made all the worse by the issuing of summonses in the locality the previous day (resulting from earlier disturbances) which added the essential element of embittered spontaneity to the 'well-thought-out scheme'.[73]

By the end of October, over two hundred extra police were in the area and sixty-three miners and sixteen women had been summonsed.[74] Open-warfare ended, but groups of young miners, sworn to secrecy, continued a desperate guerrilla action which included terrorising the families of 'blacklegs', window-breaking and threats of arm-breaking 'so [that] they wouldn't work again . . . during the strike . . .'.[75]

In this twilight world which was neither orthodox political activity nor criminal in the normal sense, many South Wales miners delved in an underworld of anonymous intrigue and quasi-illegality. To carry out 'effective picketing', Ystradgynlais miners indulged in historical gymnastics and disguised themselves as 'Scotch Cattle'.[76] The identities of pickets at Ynysybwl were concealed by their lodge secretary who wrote their names in the lodge minute book in his own personal short-hand (although he revealed for posterity the names of the blacklegs).[77] It became a disciplined society where groups were sworn to secrecy and 'nobody named anybody'.[78]

It was also a society which saw the evolving of a morality and a code of conduct which extended beyond the law. Stealing became a morally acceptable act of survival. As one Dulais Valley miner revealingly recalled:

'There was a lot pinched off the railways, but nobody pinched off each other'.[79]

Although the case of breaking and entering by five Pontygwaith miners into the local Co-operative Store was rather exceptional, it was symptomatic of an atmosphere which led to the business of Valley Courts at the end of the lock-out being taken up almost entirely with charges against miners who 'borrowed' material for working their outcrops.[80]

Despair and frustrations at the end of the dispute drove a few young miners to undertake curious and outrageous semi-political actions. Two Pengam miners had eighteen months' hard labour for burning down colliery offices.[81] At Glyncorrwg, miners tried to disrupt the opening of the new Workmen's Memorial Hall because of 'the scandal of glorifying the dead and starving the living' and, above all, because of the presence of the local coalowner, Robert Gibb:

I remember when the blacklegs had just gone past, the police with them, and they were opening the Memorial Hall [and] a plaque to the fallen in the 1914–18 War. . . . We'd run into the Hall, one set would run upstairs and knock out the lights, the rest would get hold of Robert Gibb and Sam would make this statement on the platform. . . . So Sam jumped on the platform . . . and the Bishop was there . . . to unveil this plaque to the fallen . . . and we were . . . trying to get the lights out, but the Legion boys blocked it . . . But Sam had his speech in remember and Sam never had any work after . . . there was such hatred, it was so strong in the valley and Gibb was there see. I think if Gibb wasn't there nothing would have happened . . .[82]

Social class divisions thus became so polarised that there appeared to be no middle ground. In virtually every disturbance, leading and 'respectable' members of colliery communities, particularly lodge officials, were brought before the Courts. Iorwerth Thomas (Chairman

of Parc and Dare lodge and later MP for Rhondda West), William
Parfitt (a Tylorstown checkweigher), Alf Palfreman (an Ogmore Vale
checkweigher) and Thomas Hopkins (Treasurer of the Bryn lodge and
Superintendent of the Bryn Baptist Sunday School) were some of the
local leaders who were summonsed.[83] Even the mild-mannered miners'
agent, Arthur Jenkins, along with his colleague on the Monmouthshire
County Council, William Coldrick, found that they were being treated
in the same way as Alec Geddes, the Clydeside Revolutionary who
delivered seditious speeches in mid-Glamorgan. The heavy sentences
given to all these indicated not only a definite hardening of attitudes on
the part of the police and judiciary, but also a widespread feeling
throughout the coalfield of a miscarriage of justice.

The case of Arthur Jenkins, in particular, clearly revealed the
situation. Relying entirely on police evidence the judge, Mr Justice
Swift, in sentencing him to nine months' imprisonment, seemed, by
implication, to question the 'suitability' and role of the overwhelming
Labour dominance in the public affairs of the valleys:

> Your position is deplorable. You were a man of high position not only in the
> Miners' Federation, but in the County and it was above all things your duty
> as a public man, as a member of the County Council, and as one of the
> Standing Joint Committee, to have assisted the police and maintained
> order. . . . I am satisfied that from the early morning of August 30 until after
> 2 o'clock you were laying plans to intimidate those working men and to
> thwart the police.[84]

That Arthur Jenkins claimed he had tried to pacify the crowd, and
that Will Coldrick considered the police evidence bore no resemblance
to the actual events, gave credence to the view that two prominent union
officials (they were both members of the Executive Council of the
SWMF) had been framed so as to make an example of them.[85]

The episode accentuated the loss of confidence and credibility in the
police throughout the valley communities but particularly within
Labour-controlled local government. The Monmouthshire Standing
Joint Committee had, as early as 20 June, asked its Chief Constable to
resign.[86]

The situation worsened with the continuation of the Emergency
Regulations, the importation of police and the disturbances of October
and November. Allegations made by Labour MPs of police brutality
harassment, drunkenness and bad language led to the unexpected
Home Office decision on 29 November to send Sir Leonard Dunning
down to South Wales to make investigations.[87]

In this embittered polarised atmosphere, an edge was provided by the involvement in the disturbances of married women who inevitably felt the hardships most acutely. Women figured prominently in twelve major prosecutions and from the limited evidence available, on each occasion their average age was always considerably greater than the men being prosecuted: a pattern which was to be repeated in the unrest of the 1930s.[88] The *Western Mail* considered their involvement 'surprising' and 'strange' but in essence it was another indication of the totality of involvement of these communities in extra-legal and extra-parliamentary actions:

A strange feature of the disturbance is the surprisingly prominent part played by the women folk, many of whom loiter persistently in the drizzling rain with babies in arms to witness the wretched spectacle. Their presence considerably hampered the police in their efforts to clear the streets.[89]

Their significance was appreciated by the Courts. On giving Mrs Elvira Bailey of Treorchy a two-month prison sentence, the Stipendiary D. Lleufer Thomas said:

You threw the first stone at the police constable and you set a very bad example to the women of the district. I find that the women have been taking too prominent a part in these disturbances and I must impose a penalty that will be a deterrent to others.[90]

The resourcefulness of these colliery communities extended as far as utilising military experience from the Great War to good effect. Delayed concentrated fire was used in stone-throwing by Ogmore Vale miners,[91] while at Abercwmboi thirty Plymouth police were attacked from the front and rear by stone-throwing miners, women and children.[92] Their shrewdness also included joining a funeral cortège in order to get through a police cordon.[93]

But the most intriguing feature of this adroitness was the thorough 'briefing' of the accused before the mass trials which at Swansea alone took three weeks to complete. One witness was asked to imagine at the trial that she was a Hollywood actress to 'impress' the court. Wearing a borrowed coat, skirt, hat, fur and gloves, she was cross-examined by the Judge:

She drew herself up to her full height and takes off one glove and puts it on the ledge, takes off the other glove and puts it on the ledge, she said, 'Your Honour', she said, 'I am fully aware that I am here in the presence of my God'.[94]

She succeeded in getting a reduced sentence, but the heavy sentences on hundreds of miners and their wives were as inevitable as the final defeat. In Swansea alone, there were three hundred and ninety-five intimidation charges to be heard from 29 November onwards.[95]

With total submission to lower wages, longer hours and district agreements in December, only a skeleton remained of the communities which had sacrificed everything in the 'war between poverty and opulence'.[96] The 'Fed' was shattered for nearly a decade, lodge officials and activists were victimised, blacklists abounded, a rival 'scab' union reared its head, the migration of population out of the valleys accelerated, and Ablett, the most respected militant in the coalfield, had been suspended from the Federation for signing a premature settlement.[97] All the assets painstakingly built up by the mining communities – colliery customs, medical schemes, chapels, football teams, the Institutes and their libraries – dramatically declined.[98] Enormous family debts needed to be repaid to the local shopkeepers and the Poor Law Unions, amounting, according to one estimate, to at least £2,500,000 for South Wales alone.[99]

The lock-out had been a catastrophe, but something could be claimed from the wreckage, for 'it taught us to know our enemies'. The political consciousness which was seemingly lacking among the leaders *and* the led during the Nine Days began to evolve in the coalfield during the lock-out.[100] What emerged was in the manner of an alternative culture with its own moral code and political tradition: it was a society within a society. Although it appears that the defeat in the lock-out was catalytic in turning many miners towards conventional Labour Party politics and away from the quasi-syndicalism of industrial action,[101] something much more subtle occurred. The Labour Party strengthened its support in the valleys so that in the debacle of the 1931 General Election, whilst the party was decimated everywhere else, South Wales was the only big coalfield to hold all its mining seats with four of the candidates returned unopposed.[102]

But a pattern had developed which often ran counter to parliamentary politics and official trade union activities. A semi-guerrilla warfare and an extra-parliamentary tradition involving broad *ad hoc* organisations, often harnessed by the CPGB yet still significantly centred on the Federation, appears for the first time on a universal basis throughout the coalfield during the lock-out. The CPGB had grown in South Wales from 1,500 in September 1926 to 2,300 a year later,[103] so that in some areas such as Maesteg it was claiming 'hundreds' of recruits during the lock-out.[104] A. J. Cook was asserting in Moscow in December (he had not been a member since 1921) that there were 12,000 British Communists, 80 per cent of whom were allegedly miners.[105] In an atmosphere of confrontation, the CPGB was recruiting or attempting to recruit those young miners who were to the fore during the dispute and who could be seen as potential 'political cadres'.[106]

Embittered and steeled by the seven-month ordeal, a generation was now growing up which took a certain pride in challenging the police[107] and which saw the political prisoner as having some significant status and prestige within the community.[108] When nine men and two women were released from prison after serving sentences for their parts in a riot, a meeting was held in their honour at Fochriw's Carmel Congregational Chapel. The chief speakers, Morgan Jones, MP, S. O. Davies (vice-president of the SWMF), Mrs S. O. Davies and the Rev. D. M. Jones presented the men with gold cigarette cases and the women with necklets and gold pendants, all suitably inscribed.[109]

In the face of lodges accepting any settlement terms offered them, it was this almost millenarian spirit which Horner hoped would not be crushed when he suggested the form the resistance should take:

> Where lodges cannot continue the fight in an open manner, they should fight with such means as there are at their disposal. No man must work in another man's job or place. Where any man is victimised, boycott the place where the victimised man worked. Rates of pay and customs must be safeguarded by all the methods known to those who have waged *guerrilla* struggles in the mines before[110] (authors' emphasis).

As if instinctively following such advice, the last acts of open and brazen 'warfare' occurred in the weeks following the settlement. In early January 1927, for example, a thousand South Celynen miners attacked the colliery manager's house in Newbridge[111] and a group of young Mardy miners were imprisoned for smashing a blackleg's window on Christmas night. When given the option of a twenty-shilling fine or three weeks' imprisonment, there was an almost general and defiant chorus from the Mardy defendants of 'three weeks'. The prosecution counsel with noticeable irritation could not understand this passion and confidence:

> With the settlement of this unfortunate industrial dispute one would expect everyone to submit to the inevitable instead of carrying on as at Mardy what is, after all, *a sort of guerrilla warfare*[112] (authors' emphasis).

BADGES, EMBLEMS AND TOKENS

1–5. Membership dues tokens used in early years of SWMF.
6. Picket identity card, 1974 strike.
7. International Class War Prisoners' Aid medal awarded in South Wales (and elsewhere), particularly in 1925 and 1926.
8. Pantyffynnon lamp check, used in 1950s.
9. Seven Sisters beer token used in 1930s.
10. SWMF membership card, 1941.
11. South Wales Area NUM 'Victory' pin, following 1972 strike.
12. Children's badge for institute cinema worn in 1950s.
13. Solidarity badge with Deep Duffryn, June 1979.

When all seemed lost, it was this unquenchable and unorthodox spirit which survived throughout the Depression and which largely explains why the rebuilding of the Miners' Federation in the South Wales coalfield was to have so many unique features.

NOTES

1. R. Page Arnot, *op. cit.*; *Idem., The South Wales Miners Vol. 2 1914–26* (London, 1974); Roy Gregory, *The Miners and British Politics, 1906–14* (Oxford, 1968). One indication of this vanguard position was that two successive South Wales miners became general secretary of the MFGB in these crucial years: Frank Hodges (1918–24 and A. J. Cook (1924–31).
2. M. Woodhouse, *op. cit.*, pp. 316–24; L. J. Macfarlane, *op. cit.*, pp. 158–9.
3. UCS, Mardy Distress Committee minutes, 30 November 1926.
4. George Lansbury, *The ICWPA at Work* (London, 1926), pam. pp. 5, 9, 11.
5. SWML, ICWPA Circular and agenda re Conference on 6 February 1926.
6. See, for example, GRO, Arrael Griffin lodge minutes, 22 June 1926; UCS Nine Mile Point lodge minutes, 19 July 1926.
7. UCS Penallta lodge minutes, 12 October 1926.
8. MFGB bound minutes, General Statement of Receipts and Accounts, 1926.
9. UCS Ferndale lodge minutes, 21 November 1926.
10. See for example UCS Cambrian lodge minutes, 28 November 1926.
11. SWML interview with Will Thomas (Cwmparc), 19 December 1974. At a concert given by Soviet artistes in South Wales in 1976 the Mardy NUM lodge once again acknowledged the support they had received in 1926. 'The Mardy miners and their families will always remember the assistance given to our fathers by the Soviet people during the 1926 lock-out'. International Concert, Pavilion, Porthcawl, *Souvenir Programme*, 5 November 1976.
12. UCS Nine Mile Point lodge minutes, 3, 14, 19 July 1926.
13. See for example *South Wales News (SWN)*, 25–8 May, 1–2 June 1926.
14. SWML interviews with Will Picton (Mardy), 9, 18 May 1973. The banner now hangs in the South Wales Miners' Library. Its two slogans are:
   Front: Proletarians of all countries unite!
                  To the fighting British Miners and the British Miners' Wives
                  From the Working Women of Krasnaya Presna. June 3, 1926 Moscow.
   Reverse: 1905 led to the victory of the Krasnaya Presna working women. Let Your Heroic Struggle Herald your Victory over Capitalism. Long Live The Proletarian Revolution in Great Britain. Long Live its skirmishers, The British Miners [reproduced in photograph section].
15. SWML interview with Jack Roberts (Abertridwr), 27 March 1969.
16. Dave Douglass, 'The Durham Pitman', in Raphael Samuel (ed.), *Miners, Quarrymen and Saltworkers* (London, 1977).
17. *Report of the Commission of Enquiry into Industrial Unrest, op. cit.*, p. 24.

18. John Thomas, 'The Economic Doctrines of Karl Marx and their Influence on the Industrial Areas of South Wales, particularly among the Miners' (unpublished essay submitted to the National Eisteddfod at Ammanford, 1922).

19. Workers Education Association (WEA) (South Wales District) collection, Minutes of the Joint Committee for the promotion of educational facilities in the South Wales and Monmouthshire Coalfield, 1929–30. (The enquiry was financed by the Carnegie Coalfield Distress Fund.)

20. Hywel Francis, 'The Anthracite Strike and Disturbances of 1925', *Llafur*, Vol. 1, No. 2, May 1973.

21. Idris Davies, 'Gwalia Deserta' (1938) quoted in *The Collected Poems of Idris Davies* (Llandysul 1972) (Islwyn Jenkins ed.), p. 30.

22. Hywel Francis, 'South Wales', *op. cit.*, p. 233. We draw extensively on this essay for this particular chapter.

23. *Ibid.*, p. 244.

24. Paul Jeremy, 'Life on Circular 703', *Llafur*, Vol. 2, No. 2, May 1977.

25. This seemingly secret world can now only be penetrated by examining the distorted images provided by the newspaper reports of mass trials and by collecting the fading memories of the veterans of the period.

26. SWML interview with Jim Evans (Abercrave), 29 November 1972.

27. *SWN*, 15 May 1926.

28. UCS Nine Mile Point lodge minutes, 18 May 1926; *SWN*, 22 May 1926.

29. *SWN*, 12 June 1926.

30. SWML interview with Mavis Llewellyn (Nantymoel), 20 May 1974.

31. Paul Jeremy, 'The South Wales Miners and the Lockout of 1926' (MA dissertation, University of Warwick, 1971). Some lodges even went so far as to try to liquidate the investments of the Caerphilly Miners' Hospital, but without success, *WM*, 17 August 1926. Only limited support was given by Co-operative Societies because most of the debts from the 1921 lock-out had not been recouped by 1926 (see Ferndale lodge minutes, 28 April 1926), although they did generously extend credit to thousands of their members, and according to widely held belief wrote much of this off in later years.

32. Interview with Evan John, a Craig-Cefn-Parc volunteer in the International Brigades, 2 June 1975.

33. *Lenin on Britain*, *op. cit.*

34. Interview with James Griffiths (Llanelli), 16 February 1970.

35. See, for example, UCS, Lady Windsor lodge minutes, July–December 1926, *passim*.

36. Paul Jeremy, 'The South Wales Miners and the Lockout of 1926', *op. cit.*; Paul Jeremy, *Llafur*, *op. cit.*

37. Rhondda Urban District Council, *Report of the Medical Officer of Health and School Medical Officer, 1926*, *passim*.

38. UCS Lady Windsor lodge minutes, 5 October–20 November 1926, *passim*.

39. See SWML photographic collection, 'the Glynneath Soviet Level'.

40. See, for example, *SWN*, 30 June 1926.

41. *Western Mail* (*WM*), 19 October 1926.

42. SWML interview with Oliver Powell (Tredegar), 29 November 1973. Powell was later to become a member of the Tredegar Workers' Freedom Group in 1933 (see below, pp. 192–8).

43. *Aberdare Leader*, 24 July 1926.

44. J. G. Davies (Pontypridd) photographic collection (see photograph section).

45. See, for instance, UCS, Mardy lodge minutes, *op. cit.*; Mardy Distress Committee, November 1926, *passim*.

46. SWML, Report on the Condition of Workmen's Libraries in the *Rhondda Urban District Council* (n.d.).

47. SWMF minutes, 7 August 1926. The Conference vote of 165 to 78 exposed the soft underbelly of defiance.

48. Paul Jeremy, 'The South Wales Miners and the Lockout of 1926', *op. cit.*

49. *Sunday Worker (SW)*, 17 October 1926. Similar class war language had been used at the height of the Anthracite Strike of 1925 when S. O. Davies (vice-president of the SWMF) had called for a united army, and a Defence Corps was formed in the Amman Valley, see Hywel Francis, *Llafur, op. cit.*

50. See, for instance, Lady Windsor lodge minutes, August–September 1926; Penallta lodge minutes, November 1926, *passim*.

51. Reports of most of the incidents and the subsequent trials appeared in the *Western Mail*, October 1926–January 1927.

52. *SWN*, 30 June 1926.

53. *SWN*, 13 August 1926.

54. *SWN*, 25 August 1926.

55. UCS, St John's (Cwmdu) lodge minutes, report of lodge delegate to Minority Movement Conference, 30 August 1926.

56. *SWN*, 12 October 1926.

57. The Rhondda Urban District Council passed a resolution protesting against the introduction into the Treorchy and Cwmparc districts of the outside forces, *SWN*, 14 October 1926.

58. *SWN*, 12 October 1926.

59. See, for example, *WM*, 30 October (Fochriw); *SWN*, 2 November (Cymmer and Gilfach); 3 November (Tylorstown); 5 November (Hirwaun); 6 November (New Tredegar); 8 November (Pontypool); 9 November (Ystrad Rhondda and Treorchy); 12 November (Gelli and Cwmparc).

60. GLRO, D/D con. 52. *Llanharan Strike Duty Journal*, 20 October 1926. At an earlier meeting, on 22 September, the miners' agent Sidney Jones of Blackwood encapsulated and sharpened class relationships: 'In 1914 your King and Country need you, in 1926 your King and Country bleed you'.

61. For vivid, even lurid, accounts, see *Western Mail* reports of the period.

62. SWML interview with Glyn Williams (Glyncorrwg), 21 May 1974.

63. *WM*, 14 October 1926.

64. Paul Jeremy, 'The South Wales Miners and the Lockout of 1926', *op. cit.*

65. *WM*, 19 October 1926.

66. *Ibid.*

67. *Ibid.*

68. *SWN*, 2 November 1926.

69. *WM*, 15 October 1926.

70. *SW*, 17 October 1926; *WM*, 16, 18 October 1926; SWML interview with Mel Thomas (Maesteg), 17 May 1973.

71. Glyn Williams interview, *op. cit.*

72. *WM*, 19 October 1926; *SWN*, 6 November 1926.

73. *WM*, 16 October 1926.

74. *WM*, 19 October 1926; *SWN*, 2 November 1926.

75. Conversations in the summer of 1974 with Glyncorrwg miners who prefer to maintain the secrecy of their identities.

76. Conversations in May 1975 with Ystradgynlais miners who prefer to maintain the secrecy of their identities.

77. UCS Lady Windsor lodge minutes, 18 August 1926. The lodge secretary, J. E. Morgan, was the father of Morien Morgan who later joined the International Brigades in Spain.

78. Glyn Williams interview, *op. cit.*

79. R. A. Leeson, *Strike: A Live History* (London, 1973), p. 105.

80. *SWN*, 12 November 1926; *WM*, 28 October 1926.

81. *SW*, 3 December 1926.

82. Glyn Williams interview, *op. cit.*

83. *SWN*, 2 November, 3 December 1926.

84. *WM*, 29 November 1926.

85. SWML interview with Will Coldrick (Bristol), 24 September 1973; SWMF minutes, 30 November 1926.

86. *SWN*, 21 June 1926.

87. *SWN*, 30 November 1926.

88. Younger women had probably already left almost *en masse* to work elsewhere as domestic servants whilst the involvement of younger men might have been precipitated by their failure to get relief from the Poor Law Unions.

89. *WM*, 5 November 1926.

90. *SWN*, 3 November 1926.

91. Interview of Dick Cornelius (Ogmore Vale) by R. Keen and J. Watts Williams, April 1970 (copy of transcript in SWML).

92. *WM*, 11 November 1926.

93. SWML interview with Anne Thomas (Cwmparc), 28 November 1973.

94. *Ibid.*

95. *SWN*, 19 November 1926.

96. A phrase used by Tom Richards, general secretary of the SWMF, UCS SWMF Circular, 17 December 1926. The dictated terms in South Wales included an eight-hour day and such a loose agreement which allowed for the erosion of earnings per man shift from 10s. 0¾d. (1927) to 9s. 2½d. (1929). For details of the national and district positions, see R. Page Arnot. *The Miners* (1954), pp. 527–30; M. W. Kirby, *The British Coalmining Industry 1870–1946* (1977) pp. 102–23. Even the printed *Minutes of Proceedings* (Revision of the Conciliation Board Agreement, 1926) reveal a degree of inhumanity on the part of the owners difficult to describe. For this reason we reproduce extracts in Appendix II (pp. 500–4 below). Victimisation details are to be found in Appendix III (pp. 505–7 below).

97. SWMF minutes, 23 November 1926. For an account of the history of this 'scab' union, see Ch. 3, below (pp. 113–44).

98. For example, the Aberdare AFC, in the Third Division South of the Football League, folded soon after the lock-out. This is confirmed by financial evidence provided by Alistair Wilson whose father was a longstanding official of the club.

99. *Colliery Workers Magazine* (official organ of the SWMF), January 1927.

100. Conversations with Dai Dan Evans during the 1972 miners' strike.

101. This is an argument put forward by many historians and most cogently in Michael Foot, *Aneurin Bevan*, Vol. 1, 1897–1945 (London, 1975), p. 81.

102. R. Page Arnot, *The Miners in Crisis and War* (London, 1960), pp. 100–1; *WM*, 17 October 1931.

103. CPGB, *Report, Theses and Resolutions of the Eighth and Ninth Congresses* (London, 1926 and 1927). These figures are disputed by Idris Cox who became West Wales organiser of the CPGB in 1927. He maintains that the 1926 figure was accurate but the true figure for 1927 was nearer 1,300. The 1927 figures had been 'highly inflated' by J. R. Wilson, the District Secretary. (Interview with Idris Cox, 23 December 1969.)

104. Mel Thomas interview, *op. cit.* Cox puts the figure for Maesteg at 150 to 200 (Idris Cox, 'Story of a Welsh Rebel', unpublished MSS, 1970), p. 24.

105. *WM*, 7 December 1926.

106. Glyn Williams interview, *op. cit.*, who sold the *Young Worker* for the CPGB but preferred to stay within the Labour Party. He had been noticed by the CPGB because of his prominent role in the disturbances.

107. 'I can recall my father being brought home by two policemen . . . who had beaten him up. . . . Set upon by Devon police, with no accusations, nothing said, just beaten up and then frog-marched through the village, to show those young militants exactly what would happen to them if they didn't curtail their activities . . . they'd only just come in there [Pencoed]. I think they were trying to show their own strength. . . . And they brought him home, they dumped him on the couch we had inside the door, and then left . . . he'd been accused of no crime, his only crime was, of course, that he was on strike and not working.' SWML interview with D. C. Davies (Coity), 4 April 1975.

108. Inscribed Medals and Scrolls had been awarded to most of the 1925 Anthracite prisoners by the International Class War Prisoners' Aid Society but only a few were left for the flood at the end of 1926. One of those presented in 1926 was Tommy Nicholas whose medal was donated to the SWML.

109. *SWN*, 24 December 1926. This was a status assumed again in the 1930s when political prisoners and International Brigaders were lionised by their communities.

110. *SW*, 26 December 1926. The socio-political attitudes of the hard core of miners who carried on the guerrilla tactics after 1926 were not unlike those of the millenarian Italian peasant, see E. J. Hobsbawm, *Primitive Rebels* (Manchester, 1958).

111. *WM*, 4 January 1927.

112. *WM*, 7 January 1927.

CHAPTER THREE

Blind Alleys and Some Exits

The MFGB responded to the crisis of the coal industry after 1921 with all the justifiable anger and industrial ineptitude of a whale inexplicably stranded on a tideless shore. It was a prisoner of its own sprawling growth in the past; endowed with formidable strength but lacking the co-ordinated will to exert it. The SWMF, as one of its principal federated areas, was no better equipped to respond, despite the efforts over two decades of the reformers within its ranks. Almost the only concession it had made to the increasing pace of events after the First World War was to alter the position of its General Secretary into that of a full-time office whose holder was barred from sitting in Parliament.[1] Tom Richards retained the office, and was aided in it by the setting up of a statistical department with a full-time secretary, Oliver Harris.[2] It continued to declare the complete abolition of capitalism and 'members' control of the conditions of employment' as two principal aims, in addition to the usual clauses concerning the securing of legislation, the furtherance of trade unionists' education in 'Social Science', the payment of benefits, and so on.[3] However, beyond this small addition to its full-time staff the wider aims were still to be implemented by an organisation akin, in most respects, to its pre-war predecessor.[4]

Thus the President, Vice-President and Treasurer (abolished when, in 1931, Oliver Harris became General Secretary), were to be elected annually by delegate Conference, and to sit as ex-officio members of an executive council composed of members sent by their Districts (to the tune of one representative for 3,000 members, plus an additional representative for every 6,000 members over and above this). The council was the governing body of the Federation, with powers of decision beyond the instructions of conferences; it reflected, in 1926, the hierarchical structure of union affairs, for on the executive council of 28 ordinary members, 20 were miners' agents; of the other 8, one was the secretary of his District (of which the agent was the SWMF President, Enoch Morrell), and two were prominent local councillors.[5]

In this way the leadership offered by the Districts and the Central EC were virtually synonymous. There were, in 1926, twenty districts within the SWMF,[6] governed in their turn by monthly District meetings (one delegate per Lodge) and by a District Executive (a facsimile of the Central Executive, except that the agent was always included, and other members than officers could be appointed from the lodges, in rotation) whose President and Vice-President were to come, for twelve months at a time, from each Lodge in turn, and a Treasurer and General Secretary to be elected, also for twelve months, by a majority of the District membership. The agent, of course, was also elected and his salary determined by the District.[7]

There were glaring differences between the Districts despite these formal requirements. Thus the Anthracite District, in 1926, included 107 lodges and employed three agents who also all sat on the Executive Council; the Maesteg District had 16 lodges and one agent, also its EC member; Merthyr had 8 lodges and one agent, its EC member; Rhondda, with large pits, had 25 lodges, one agent and six EC members. The Afan Valley District retained the services of William Jenkins, MP for Neath, as its chief agent in addition to their regular agent, John Thomas, whilst Monmouth Western Valleys District employed their Secretary as a sub-agent in addition to their agent.[8] Much depended on financial membership and economic health, but some of the government of these Districts represented a heritage of independence.

Similarly, each lodge had a defined constitution (on the previous pattern) but the power and influence of a lodge might rest on the size of its own membership or the persuasive powers of its officials and checkweighers. A lodge well equipped to sort out its own difficulties with the local management could scorn the help of its agent or of the District; a lodge with an active checkweigher might reap the benefits of local negotiating skill and lose those benefits because of the equal skill in politicising the membership.[9]

The defeat of 1926 was overwhelming – 'The rush to the pits in South Wales (in November 1926) became serious. The result of this ballot vote of the men to get authority to negotiate a settlement was made known on 30 November 1926. The result was 50,815 for and 27,291 against. The SWMF had become a ghost. After a strike lasting from 1 May to 30 November, some 70,000 had deserted. . . . The new South Wales Agreement was dictated by the owners, and was signed on 13 December. The SWMF entered the fight as an army and ended it as a rabble. This was not fighting, but a massacre.'[10]

Even though the Monmouthshire and South Wales Coalowners' Association had promised in the Settlement Agreement that there 'was not the slightest intention to victimise any man for the part he had taken in connection with the stoppage', the Agreement was sufficiently loose and vague as to make no obligation on the part of the local coalowners to reinstate anyone (quite apart from re-employing them).[11] The result was widespread victimisation of lodge officials and activists,[12] except in the Anthracite District, where a lower level of unemployment and the continued successful application of the Seniority Rule, ensured a measure of security which did not exist elsewhere in the coalfield[13] (although it happened to a degree here also). The coalowners appeared determined to derive every advantage out of their victory by depriving the SWMF of its real power: its militant lodge leadership, its long established customs and its rebellious rank and file. Even before the Agreement was finally signed, checkweighers were being ordered off colliery premises in the Rhymney Valley and Rhondda managers were putting up obstacles against a general resumption of work by seeking concessions on customs and price lists.[14] Those who refused to work in other men's places were threatened with loss of unemployment benefit; many had been chosen because they had large families so as to 'starve them back'.[15] In some areas, the Garw District in particular, many collieries were filled with strangers long before the general resumption of work.[16]

In the Rhondda District brave words were uttered by the miners' agent, M. H. Mainwaring:

> I shall do all I can to stop the Rhondda and failing that I shall stop the Ocean and Cory's (over the loss of customs). Customs pre-1915 are practically safe. But those since 1915 and during the War can only be retained by our local strength.[17]

By the end of December he was favouring the giving of notices over victimisation.[18] But in reality, the owners, with a few exceptions, had achieved their aim. Even in the Cambrian Combine Collieries (where miners were noted for their advanced industrial and political outlook) managers were refusing to operate any seniority rule, were abusing customs, and were not prepared to make deductions for the miners' benevolent fund. There were cases of the lodge officials being victimised, men being made to do two men's work, and widows no longer being allowed concessionary coal.[19] Outside the Anthracite, only

CAMBRIAN COLLIERIES, Limited

PENTRE SEAM.

MACHINE-CUT AND CONVEYOR PRICE-LIST.

	s.	d.
1.—Breaking Out and Filling Machine-Cut Large Clean Coal on to the Conveyor into Trams, per Ton..	2	3.00

This price includes all conditions of labour, as per Coronation Seam Price-List. The above Price also includes the Cleaning and Gobbing of the stone in the Coal.

2.—CLOD : For taking down and Gobbing the Clod in the Conveyor Face, complete four inches, per Ton	0	1.00
For every complete inch above four inches ..	0	0.37
3.—Shifting Conveyor, Large Coal, per Ton	0	3.00

This payment includes starting and stopping Engine, and keeping same clear, &c.

4.—Standard Section of the Seam to be 2ft. 9ins. (TWO FEET NINE INCHES) in thickness, and, for each one inch below this thickness, to be paid extra at the rate of ½d. (ONE HALF-PENNY) per Ton.

5.—It is agreed that both parties shall each pay half the wages of the Dumper, and in the event of it being necessary to employ Two Dumpers, the Company will pay the second Dumper, and the men the first Dumper.

Any Deadwork item not mentioned in this List is governed by the Yard Seam List.

SIGNED on behalf of The Cambrian Collieries Ltd. :—

H. H. EVANS.
THOMAS JOHNS.
THOMAS REES.

SIGNED on behalf of The Workmen :—

W. H. MAINWARING.
NOAH REES.
DAVID WILLIAMS.
THOMAS WRIDE.

WITNESS to the above Signatures—THOMAS SPARKES.

DATED this 13th day of OCTOBER, 1927.

Part of price list for Cambrian Collieries, 1927.

the Mardy lodge could claim a victory in avoiding such humiliating terms; but even there the price for many was disqualification from unemployment benefit and poor relief, and above all the closure of the collieries for long periods.[20]

In attempting to salvage the situation,[21] the Federation tried to entice lapsed members back into the fold by wiping out their arrears and by issuing an account of its 'achievements' in pamphlet form.[22] The problem of rebuilding the Federation, for lodge committeemen like Oliver Powell of Tredegar, was immense:

> '. . . you never found so much hatred and bitterness amongst the workmen [than] when we returned after 1926. They would hold us responsible for the state they were in, middle-aged men who had saved up so much you know; [they] had no possible hope now of recouping what they had spent in the strike, and they directed their venom directly at the strikers (i.e. the young militants), most unpleasant. . . . But there you are, we were supposed to be left-wing militants, and we had to put up with all that.'[23]

In such an embittered situation, Oliver Powell and others like him in so many other towns and villages across the coalfield, were easily victimised with the collapse of good lodge organisation and the anxiety of the bulk of the men to get back to work. He was blacklisted by the Tredegar Iron and Coal Company for nearly twenty years, returning only on the eve of the nationalisation of the industry.[24]

Many of those who failed to be re-employed were forced into a nomadic existence. Terms of unconditional surrender had been exacted and the 'defeated army' was forced to seek work wherever it could find it. Police appeared at collieries armed with blacklists so as to turn back those who were to be victimised.[25] For those who had resisted the early breakaway at Cwmparc, the Ocean Company's local general manager exacted his own revenge, as one miner at the Dare Colliery recalled:

> *'How long were you off then?*
> I was out for twelve months after that (the lock-out).
>
> *Why didn't you get work back then?*
> Because we were 'strikers'. And this *one* here (the general manager) he had phoned right round the collieries, and they wouldn't accept us. . . .
>
> *There were a lot of people blacklisted, were there?*
> Yes, we had a form from the Labour Exchange then, we had to go round to start in Ogmore, Maesteg, Cymmer, Mardy, right round Ton, Bwllfa that way, right round, and you had to bring back every week before you'd get your dole. And signed by the manager.

How would you get around then, you walked?
Walked. No money, couldn't go on a bus. . . .

'How many of you were doing this then?
Oh a couple of hundred of us, sure to be, at the beginning. . . .[26]

For those who did get back, it was questionable whether they were better off than those who had been victimised, particularly in an atmosphere of repression, speed-up and mechanisation:

'. . . [we] had to go back under atrocious conditions. . . . And so the exploitation intensified from 1926. . . . Now in this period there was the introduction for the first time [in West Wales in any case] . . . of conveyor faces. And I can remember . . . developing a conveyor face, one of nine colliers in a team . . . going down that pit at half past six in the morning and catching a bus from the top of the colliery road at half past nine in the night. You had to work on in order to try to get this conveyor face going. . . . But this was the significant thing . . . nobody knew what each other were earning . . . [because] in the fear that next week, whatever he'd given extra to me, he would have *taken* back off you next week. . . .[27]

The degree of exploitation was felt all the more by the boys who started immediately after the lock-out. In some areas, fathers failed to get their places back while their sons were taken on until they were about eighteen when they became 'too heavy for a buttie to pay them'. There was no formal training so that a young collier was filling his curling box on his first day. If boys 'weren't good enough they were pushed from pillar to post. You would work with this man today and you would work with another tomorrow.'[28]

The intensification of production at the expense of what Cook called 'the safety of human life' became all too apparent within three months. On St David's Day 1927, fifty-two miners were killed in an explosion at Marine Colliery, Cwm, near Ebbw Vale. The event exposed the miners' conditions and their latent anger for all to see. Stanley Baldwin, the Prime Minister, visited the scene of the disaster, only to be jeered at and called 'murderer' by miners who seemed to have considered the visit a calculated insult. The Executive Council of the SWMF believed that in view of his behaviour during the lock-out, his presence was an act which 'justified the resentment of the miners who are now suffering as the result of the conduct of himself and his Government.'[29]

The unfortunate Evan Davies, the local miners' MP, who was rejected by the miners two years later, apologised for 'the work of a few

In Loving Memory

OF THE

MINERS WHO LOST THEIR LIVES

— IN —

WELSH COLLIERY DISASTERS

	Killed.		Killed.
1932—January 25, Llwynypia, Rhondda ...	11	1878—September 1, Abercarn	62
1931—Aug. 25, Caerau, Mountain Out-crop...	3	1877—March 8, Worcester Pit, Swansea...	18
1929—July 10, Milfraen, Blaenavon ...	9	1876—December 13, Abertillery	20
1929—Nov. 28, Wernbwll, nr. Penclawdd...	7	1875—December 5, Llan Pit, Pentyrch ...	12
1927—March 1, Cwm, Ebbw Vale	52	1875—December 4, New Tredegar... ...	22
1923—April 26th, Trimsaran	9	1874—July 24, Charles Pit, Llansamlet ...	19
1913—October 13, Senghenydd	436	1874—April 5, Abertillery	6
1905—July 5, Wattstown	119	1872—March 8, Wernfach	18
1905—March 10, Clydach Vale	31	1872—March 2, Victoria	19
1901—September 10, Llanbradach	12	1871—October 4, Gelli Pit, Aberdare ...	4
1901—May 24, Senghenydd	82	1871—February 24, Pentre	38
1899—August 18, Llest Colliery, Garw ...	19	1870—July 23, Llansamlet	19
1896—January 28, Tylorstown	57	1869—June 10, Ferndale	60
1894—June 25, Cilfynydd	276	1869—May 23, Llanerch	7
1892—August 26, Park Slip	110	1867—November 8, Ferndale	178
1892—Aug. 12, Great Western Colliery ...	58	1865—December 20, Upper Gethin ...	30
1890—March 8, Morfa...	87	1865—June 16, Tredegar	2
1890—February 6, Llanerch...	176	1863—December 24, Maesteg...	14
1890—January 20, Glyn Pit, Pontypool ...	5	1863—October 17, Margam	39
1888—May 14, Aber, Tynewydd	5	1862—February 19, Gethin, Merthyr ...	47
1887—February 18, Ynyshir	37	1860—December 1, Risca	146
1885—December 24, Mardy	81	1859—April 5, Neath Chain Colliery ...	26
1885—Naval Colliery	14	1858—October 13, Duffryn	20
1884—Nov. 8, Pochin Colliery, Tredegar ...	14	1856—July 13, Cymmer	114
1884—January 28, Penygraig...	11	1853—March 12, Risca Vale	10
1884—January 16, Cwmavon...	10	1852—May 10, Duffryn	64
1883—August 21, Gelli	4	1850—Dec. 14, New Duffryn Colliery ...	13
1883—February 1, Coedcae	5	1849—Aug. 11, Lletty Shenkin, Aberdare .	52
1883—February 11, Coedcae	6	1848—June 21, Victoria (Mon.)	11
1882—January 15, Risca	4	1846—January 14, Risca	35
1880—Dec. 10, Naval Steam Colliery ...	96	1845—August 2, Cwmbach	28
1880—July 15, Risca	119	1844—January 1, Dinas	12
1879—Sept. 22, Waunllwyd, Ebbw Vale ...	84	1837—June 17, Blaina (Mon.)	21
1879—January 13, Dinas	3	1837—May 10, Plas-yr-Argoed, Mold ...	21
1878—September 11, Abercarn	268		

"IN THE MIDST OF LIFE WE ARE IN DEATH."
Let's hope the Gallant Miners ha 't died in vain,
On God's own shore their friends might meet them once again.

C. P., TR.]

Religious memorial card, 1932. Two years later, Gresford exploded, claiming the
lives of 265 miners.

revolutionary Union, the United Mineworkers of Scotland.[41] With the lack of any concerted national action, the MMM's critique of leadership grew more intense. Nods to their mistaken sincerity were now left behind and the epithets, 'hypocritical', 'cynical', 'defeatist' and even 'Fascist' rolled out. The possibility of reform within the Union began to be discounted outright in some circles.[42]

Until this impasse was reached, however, there were continued attempts to spark off reform below, the main object of which was to change the structure of the SWMF so that it might correspond to the changes in the industry itself, most notably the gathering pace of amalgamation.[43]

The Government's Commission of Enquiry into Industrial Unrest, in 1917, had signalled this out as a cause of the deterioration of relationship between employers and employed in South Wales. In that year three combined concerns (Lord Rhondda's group; United National; T. Beynon & Company) produced 40 per cent of the coalfield's total output; with two large, uncombined firms (Powell Duffryn and Ocean Steam) producing almost one-fifth of the output between them. There had been some attempts to meet this organisational size before the war – the lodges in the Cambrian Combine in Mid-Rhondda, had been the principal organisers of the struggles of 1910–11, and, in 1912, the Ocean Combine Committee had been formed.[44] However, and despite the SWMF's official encouragement of joint committees,[45] these efforts remained local, indeed small-scale, as for instance the Tredegar Combine Lodges. And yet, the tendency was more and more to look for help to the Central Office. Harold Finch became a clerk in the Tredegar Valley District Miners' Office in 1917:

> At the time I entered the Miners' Offices at Blackwood there was an increasing tendency to consult the Central Office and seek the guidance of the Secretary, the Rt. Hon. Thomas Richards.[46]

The paradox was not easy to unravel. Only local effort, it was argued by the reformers, could make the Federation effective, but equally, only control of the Central organisation by a locally-based rank and file could ensure that District officials would be truly the men's servants; at the same time, these officials also supported an increase in the power of the existing Central by doubling financial contributions. Both camps then became caught up in the hopes for change (of whichever nature) set off by the War and its consequences. Hence the bitterness with which each side could view one another's efforts after 1926. In the meantime, this concentration on sweeping changes in the SWMF and MFGB's organisations had led attention away from the possibility of a more effective organisation from within. The need for an effective local reform had been clearly spelled out by two members of the SWMF in 1924 and 1925.

D. J. Williams,[47] in a pioneering work, showed the enormous rise in the power of the Combine Companies so that in 1920, four groups had control of three-fifths of the entire coalfield output. Williams indicated the covert control represented by informal alliances as well, as in the case of H. Seymour Berry who was a Director of twenty-four collieries with, between them, a production of 25 per cent of coalfield output.[48] Nevertheless, he saw no official recognition by the Federation of the changes this implied for trade union organisation, despite the intensification of disputes between men and management. His book was intended to sow seeds for the necessary changes:

In the main the Miners' Union still bears on its general structure the imprint of the pre-combination stage of Capitalism. Gradually, however, a consciousness is growing in the ranks of the miners that the present form of their Organisation is ill-adapted to face the new situation created by the growth of combines. In South Wales, where the combine movement has made such rapid strides, this is especially so, and already attempts have been made to bring the organisation of labour into line with that of capital.

With the growth of combines in the South Wales Coalfield, the miners in those districts where they exist have formed what are known as 'combine committees', representative of all the Miners' Lodges of the particular group of collieries controlled by a big company, these committees being found serviceable in securing co-ordination among the lodges when they happen to belong to different districts – one may be in Monmouthshire and another in the Rhondda, and so on. An interesting point has been raised as to the functions of such a combine committee. Should it possess the right, as acting collectively for the workmen, to interview the heads of the Company and discuss grievances? In other words, should it be 'recognised' by the colliery owners? Some time ago the Combine Committee of the Ebbw Vale Company's Collieries applied for an interview with the General Manager. This was declined, the General Manager, however, pointing out that he was fully prepared to receive representatives of individual lodges. The matter was subsequently taken up by the Monmouth Western Valley Miners' Council, who at their March meeting passed a resolution requesting the Executive Council of the SWMF to take steps with a view to the insertion of a clause in the new wage agreement, making it imperative upon the owners to recognise Combine Committees in the South Wales Coalfield (from *South Wales News*, 11 April 1924). . . .

. . . Almost every . . . capitalist combine in the coalfield has . . . been instrumental in bringing into existence a combine committee of the workmen.

It is early yet to estimate the precise significance of the committees in the affairs of the industry. In many cases they have been refused recognition by the coal-owners – a question which, sooner or later, the MFGB will have to take up. In almost every case they suffer from the inevitable immaturity of a new type of organisation. Up to the present, they have not been submitted to the acid test of a conflict with the power of the capitalist combines; nor have they put forward any positive proposals for dealing with them. In the main, the motive of their formation has been one of defence rather than aggression, and their efforts so far have been concentrated chiefly on the question of their recognition by the owners. In spite of all this, however, there can be no doubt that the idea of the combine committees will spread amongst the miners, and that, properly organised and directed, they contain vast potentialities as a step forward in the organisation of labour in the coal industry.

This was a lucid analysis of the shift of power within the industry; it contained, in addition, an acute prophecy of the future role of the Combine Committees, Even for D. J. Williams, though, in 1924 it was the long-term perspective that was the most absorbing:

. . . In so far as combines are the logical outcome of the development of economic forces, it is utopian to try to abolish them and reactionary to prevent their formation. The problem for organised labour is not to dissolve the Combines, but to wrest them from private control.[49]

The immediate problem was to maintain past standards in the face of concerted attempts to whittle them away. A case in point was the Anthracite area which was the last section to be developed and, in addition, was the one relatively prosperous area after the war. In 1913 there were 100 separate concerns; in 1923 Amalgamated Anthracite Collieries Limited was established, followed by United Anthracite Collieries in 1924. By 1928 the two principal concerns had themselves amalgamated, along with remaining smaller interests and, by then, controlled 80 per cent of production.[50]

Although the men had formed a Combine Committee within six months of the establishment of the Amalgamted Anthracite Combine in July 1923,[51] this did not stop the attacks on old-established customs, and in particular on the cherished Seniority Rule, which led in 1925 to a

bitter six-weeks' dispute and the dismantling of Ammanford No. 1 Pit
by management rather than allow the operation of that Rule. The men's
victory in maintaining that Rule elsewhere was tarnished by their
continued fears of further losses in wages and status.[52]

In what ways could a Combine Committee be more effective than the
apparatus of District negotiation and the skill of the miners' agent? In a
pamphlet published by the Mardy and Ogilvie lodges of the SWMF in
1925, Bryn Roberts tried to answer this in a defence of the
establishment of a Powell Duffryn Combine Committee on 4 October
1924. Again a Central Labour College student applied his learned
understanding of the monopolistic tendencies of Capitalism to a
discussion of the changes in labour relations that this entailed, changes
as drastic as that of the onset of mechanisation in coal-cutting:

> Unfortunately, the Miners' Organisation has not responded to the industrial
> changes so readily. While the 'purpose' of the Miners' Organisation is so
> definite and satisfactory, its structure can certainly be improved upon.
> 'Nothing endures for ever.' . . . True, discussions have taken place on the
> advisability of making the organisation conform to the new needs and
> changed conditions. This fact was manifested in the agitation [which
> appears to have been abortive] for 'centralisation'. In matters of
> organisation we are certainly most conservative. Very little attention seems
> to be given to moulding the structure of the Federation in keeping with
> coalfield development.
>
>   Sections of the Federation, however, have made gallant attempts to keep
> in step with 'Father Time'. The idea of 'Combines', which is an established
> idea, has been strenuously advocated as a 'second best' to 'centralisation'. In
> any case the 'combine' brought up to date, in the present circumstances, is
> certainly worthy of consideration. In any case its existence will mitigate the
> weaknesses of our present District Organisation.

This was, then, a way of by-passing the problems raised since before
the war without appearing to demand wholesale changes. It was a way,
in this instance, of uniting the Powell Duffryn pits in four separate
Districts (Aberdare, Garw, East Glamorgan and Rhymney). The
miners' agents would then present joint demands instead of dissipating
the workers' power by individual negotiation which could only result in
the difference of wages, between Companies, applying in pits under the
same company, as well. The pamphlet ends with a call for workers'
control and nationalisation (the two were still inseparable), but its real
punch was its indictment of the old structure:

Those in our ranks who now oppose the combine policy should consider the unquestionable defects of uncoordinated District Organisations. Each District acts as a Union within a Union. Each District adopts its 'District policy' without regard to the 'policy' of the adjoining district. Actually there is no pooling of resources or the least understanding between these bodies which have so much in common. Weak districts are not assisted by the more fortunate districts. The result of this is that progress is not uniform. One who has worked in one district and afterwards worked in some other can appreciate the great differences that exist within the South Wales Area. These differences must be minimised as much as possible. One of the most effective means of accomplishing this is by the formation of Combines . . . in given Areas.[53]

This plea could not, however, be fully met so long as the power for official action and negotiations was wielded by Central Office and District Officials. Even after the events of 1926, it was to be a long road to effective reorganisation.

At a Special Conference of the SWMF in May 1927, Tom Richards sounded a familiar note:

As General Secretary since the formation of the Federation and entering upon my 41st year as a miners' representative, I still have faith in the potency of the Federation as at present constituted. Any practical reform that after careful examination is found by the majority of the workmen to be desirable, will have my full support and every possible assistance to make it effective.[54]

Events were to overtake, indeed had already exposed, this grim determination to maintain the Union simulacrum for a society that had gone. The defeat of the miners in 1926 had been a total one – their demands on hours and wages had been ignored and the cherished District settlements of the owners were firmly entrenched. Certainly the owners had no cause for displeasure at the conclusion of the seven-month lock-out. At the Monmouthshire and South Wales Coalowners' Association meeting December 1926, Evan Williams who had led the owners at national level, was thanked for his services:

He, the Chairman [E. L. Hann], had a fairly long experience of Association affairs and of past Agreements entered into with the Workmen's representatives, but he was sure there was never an occasion for more satisfaction on the part of the coalowners than the present one.

In reply, Evan Williams underlined the opposition he felt that they had to face:

He felt that the industry had to make a stand for district settlements and that the owners could not negotiate with people whose endeavours were purely political.[55]

Since so many of the ills of the industry had been blamed, since 1919, on the 'political' drive for nationalisation by the MFGB, the defeat of the 'political' General Strike was sweet indeed. The owners lost no time in operating hard-line policies within their own companies; they could note, with special satisfaction, the birth of a rival union to the SWMF whose hold, since 1898, on the miners' loyalty was now directly challenged. Even Lord Davies of Llandinam, heir to the Ocean Coal Company and an advocate of arbitration whenever possible, held out no olive branches to the Federation itself. Thus, in June 1926 although he was advocating to his fellow owners that the men's wages should not be reduced if, in turn, they would work an eight-hour day, and even threatening to leave the Association because of its stubbornness, it was all in order to break the grip of the Federation over 'the more reasonable men'. He wrote summoning W. P. Thomas, his General Manager, to Llandinam: 'Don't you think the time has come when we should break away altogether from the Association? It appears to me that they do us no good whatever. I don't see that we can expect our men to break away from the Federation unless we take the first step of dissociating ourselves from the Association. The whole problem bristles with difficulties, but I cannot help feeling that the time has come when we must make a move. The essential point is whether if we did so there would be a response from our own workmen.'

In effect there would prove to be advantages in being 'non-associated' in certain collieries. Elsewhere an encouragement of the Industrial Union SWMIU and a reliance on non-unionism would suffice to tie the Federation down.[56]

South Wales, in common with other coalfields, had seen the phenomenon of men drifting back to work as the 1926 lock-out dragged on month after month. At the Raglan Colliery, Heol-y-cyw, near Bridgend, in June 1926 a miner called William Gregory left the Federation and persuaded others to go back to work with him. Gregory appears to have set up his own 'industrial union' whose lodge met in the colliery offices.[57] As a result of his subsequent career as the Secretary and driving force of the SWMIU the Raglan incident has been claimed as the beginning of the Industrial Union in South Wales.[58] There seems no substantial evidence, however, that Gregory's breakaway was distinguished from others in anything but his own determined personality.[59]

The crucial break with the SWMF centred around the new Taff-Merthyr Pit. The Taff-Merthyr Steam Coal Company set up by the Powell Duffryn and Ocean Groups,[60] had opened their new South Pit at Trelewis in January 1926,[61] and during the coal dispute of that year the company sought and obtained the permission of the SWMF to drive headings through the pit pillars to prepare the pit for production when the dispute was over. But, as James Griffiths, then President of the SWMF, was to complain in 1934: 'Permission having been granted advantage was taken of that by the colliery company to induce workmen to go to the pit, and they proceeded to develop a full coal-producing pit whilst the stoppage was still in progress.'[62]

Obviously no members of the Federation could produce coal whilst the strike lasted and so the most modern pit in the coalfield found 'new' men to match its new machines. A meeting of some of the men working at the new Colliery, whose intent was to break away from the SWMF, on Saturday night, 20 November, did not go unnoticed or unheralded by the *Western Mail* which declared: 'This is the first occasion in the coalfield for such drastic action to be taken and this example will probably soon be followed by many other colliery workers elsewhere.'[63] The meeting was a large one (there were already some 500 men at work in the colliery),[64] held in the Bontnewydd Hotel, Trelewis. It had been convened by W. A. Williams, the Secretary of the Nelson Conservative and Unionist Association, to consider the organisation needed by the Taff-Merthyr workmen in view of the potential development of the pit (it was thought 2,500 could be eventually employed there).[65] The meeting decided on the formation of a Taff-Merthyr Works Committee which would work harmoniously with the management, avoid politics and be entirely separate from the SWMF. W. A. Williams who was appointed Secretary of the new organisation underlined the distinctions between the SWMF and the new committee in a way that was to become familiar in later years. The new organisation's job was to provide sick benefit, funeral benefit, legal aid, and refer all disputes to arbitration, for 'the men object to the way in which their money has been wasted. We are not going to subsidise the Minority Movement, the Labour Party, nor the daily newspaper of any Party.'[66]

The movement did not stop there. A meeting the following week decided that a new name, the South Wales Miners' Industrial Union, should be adopted and their rules and constitution be registered.[67] The union was to include colliery workers of all grades at a membership fee of 2s. a month plus a voluntary 4d. a month for funeral benefits. The management recognised the new union immediately; the union rules confined themselves to clauses relating to compensation, allowances and benefits and, although the rules promised a weekly allowance to any member 'victimised, locked out, or on strike', it added that the EC would not call a strike until the disputed matter had been placed before an independent Court of Appeal. Nothing was more symbolic of the resentment felt against the SWMF than the final statement of intent: 'The union will be non-political. Any member raising a political issue at a lodge meeting shall be warned, and if he persists in his attitude the Committee shall have the power to expel him from the Union.'[68]

The new union was expansionist in tone from the start. Rule Number One stated: 'The Union shall be called the South Wales Miners' Industrial Union. The Union shall be composed of persons employed in and about the mines of South Wales.' To this end it had been decided that W. A. Williams should tour areas of the coalfield where new members might be recruited, beginning in the neighbouring Rhymney Valley.[69] By the end of the year there were reports of ballots organised by the SWMIU asking for a 'Yes' or 'No' to the question – 'Are you in favour of a Trade Union free from all party politics?'[70] At the Britannia Colliery, Pengam, where 251 men out of a total of 2,000 employed voted 'Yes', the SWMF miners' agent, Bryn Roberts, disclaimed the potential of the SWMIU but also spoke bitterly of the way in which a weakened SWMF was already being treated:

> The Colliery Officials are certainly assisting in the developing of this Union. It is their child. They allow notices in connection with the new organisation to be placed in lamproom and weigh-house windows and permit the organisers to visit all parts of the collieries to canvass members, while Federation representatives have been driven off the colliery premises, and our notices convening meetings have been torn down from the noticeboards at the Management's instructions. We have also been denied access to the collieries.[71]

The reasons for the initial success of the SWMIU were obvious to its supporters. A colliery free from the pernicious influence of the Federation had a wonderful opportunity to stay free from such interference because 'at the end of a 7 months' disastrous stoppage the Miners' Federation stands discredited and condemned by thousands of its most loyal members'.[72] W. A. Williams himself claimed to be an original SWMF member who, like others of the rank and file, was convinced that the Federation's political activities were against the functions for which it had been formed in 1898. He replied spiritedly to allegations that the movement owed more to the desire of the owners to break the SWMF stranglehold than it did to the sentiments of its members: 'I wish to state emphatically that it is untrue to say that this movement had its birth in the Unionist Association. It is also equally untrue to suggest that the men at the first meeting were not in a sober condition.'[73]

Undoubtedly the main factor behind the successful launching of the SWMIU was the opportunity presented to it to organise a lodge in a colliery where no SWMF lodge had ever been. Its later activities in Emlyn, Bedwas and Nine Mile Point Collieries all stemmed from a situation where labour had just been employed or even imported, but only in Taff-Merthyr was this the case from the very beginning. The SWMIU clung to its base there like a limpet. Further, in addition to the fact that the SWMF's main concern, at this time, was the momentous national issues, which tended to relax its vigilance at local level, there were special local factors at work. S. O. Davies, at this time miners' agent for the Dowlais District, replied, in 1930, to an enquiry about Taff-Merthyr in a letter both informative and pungent: 'The Colliery is a comparatively new one, and enforced membership of the "Non-Pol. Union" ... is a condition of employment. The workmen there are drawn from all over the Coalfield, many of whom are recruited from Tory drinking Clubs. The Colliery is in a virgin part of the Coalfield, outside the boundary of any of the Federation Districts. It is kept on a Day-to-day Contract – this is a most effective Victimisation weapon. It is no exaggeration to say that since the commencement of this Colliery, hundreds of men have been victimised because of their resisting the "Non.Pol. Union." The Dowlais District has now assumed responsibility for this Colliery, and we are concentrating upon the wiping out of this "Scab Union".'[74]

In 1926 there had been no such assumption of responsibility. The very hyphenated name of the colliery indicates its ambiguous position, located as it was in a small valley between the Dowlais and Taff and Cynon Districts of the SWMF. The colliery itself lay between the small villages of Bedlinog to the north-west and Trelewis to the south, with Treharris just beyond. From the bleak, isolated village of Bedlinog was to come much of the later militancy that characterised the trouble at

Taff-Merthyr. Even in 1926 the local Council of Action was concerned with the continued working at Taff-Merthyr and interviewed men and manager in an attempt to have it stopped.[75] Their minutes later in the year show their fear that the pit might be adopted by another district and, later still, the deep concern about the 'disorganisation' at Taff-Merthyr.[76] In practice, for a village depending on the pit for its livelihood, there was little that could be done at this stage. It was only in 1927 that the SWMF was able to turn its attention to the rival union that had sprung up but, by that time, its ability to curtail that union's growth was severely limited. The SWMF was not able to lick its wounds in a respite from gargantuan struggles with government; it was forced, immediately, to defend the very essence of a Trade Union, its right to exist where men desired it.

However, although the principle involved was early noted by Federation officials, the profundity of the threat was almost ignored. What was stressed was the temporary dislocation of the Federation, a position akin to the steep, but brief, fall in membership in 1922–3. Thus Oliver Harris, the General Treasurer of the SWMF, began his monthly column of 'Notes and Comments' in the January 1927 issue of *The Colliery Workers' Magazine* by admitting that no one regretted the passing of 1926 but denying that the MFGB's policy had failed. Now, he felt, the Federation had to be rebuilt in the face of attack by some owners desirous of revising price lists, abrogating established customs and victimising the men. In Harris' scenario the SWMF was a fallen 'giant' attacked by 'pigmies'; his prose skirts around open recognition of the facts in the coalfield as if he cannot quite bring himself to believe in the existence of a rival union:

> We understand that there are a few men, mostly frequenters of Tory drinking Clubs, who think this an opportune moment to try to entice the miners from their allegiance to the Federation, and they have, it is alleged, started a brand new union. It is rather difficult to understand what are the effects of this Union, other than to divide the workmen, because we are told that it will have nothing to do with politics, and co-operation with the Employers is to be its main guiding principle.[77]

At this stage even men whose careers were synonymous with moderation could see no available middle ground; for Harris, trade unions were necessarily 'antagonistic' to employers. The feeling was, of course, reciprocated by the owners in South Wales.

On 17 December 1926, Thomas Richards had circulated a letter to all Lodge Secretaries giving the Executive Council's thoughts on the new conditions:

> The unexampled duration of the struggle, unfortunately, exhausted the power of resistance of some of our members, while there were others who failed to realise that by leaving the ranks they were further imperilling the hope of securing reasonable wages and conditions of working for themselves and their fellow workmen in any settlement that may be arrived at.

So, in a mixture of sympathetic laxity and paternal sternness, all arrears in contributions owing to the Federation were written off; the first contribution due was for 6 December 1926, and the General Secretary warned that no man would receive any assistance or protection if, after four or more weeks in employment, he was not paid up.[78] This was, in the conditions that would now prevail, empty both as a gesture and as words. Ted Williams, the miners' agent in the Garw Valley, maintained this whistling in the dark the following month when he labelled the SWMIU a 'coffin club' which had been formed to prevent men who had themselves been 'blacklegs' in the strike from being themselves 'blacklegged' after it. He prematurely predicted its demise since the men now realised 'that it is more manly to fight for the living than to place their faith in a burial board'.[79]

Oliver Harris explored the same vein, in April, when he nonchalantly ignored the 'fizzling out' Industrial Union, in order to concentrate his fire on the poaching of colliery workers by other *bona-fide* unions; in May he was able to conclude that the SWMIU had shot their bolt:

> Full advantage was taken of the spirit of disgruntlement which always follows a prolonged struggle such as we passed through last year, but slowly the disgruntled ones are realising that it is no good to make matters worse by weakening the only organisation that has ever done anything for them.[80]

In the same month, in a May Day Speech at Aberdare Park, Tom Richards had been more forthright in his denunciation of the SWMIU as 'The Bosses and Boozers Crowd', a 'rag-tag and bob-tail Union' which could not be allowed to jeopardise standards of living in South Wales. The remedy was in the hands, he felt, of his audience:

> My mission here today is to declare that there is to be one organisation and only one organisation in South Wales. You have now been warned, and if you let this Union grow in your midst then it will be of your own doing.[81]

Slowly, though, the EC were making some attempts to meet the point that the organisation itself was not properly equipped to support its members in their desire to expunge the rival. In early 1927 they issued warnings to the Craftsmen's Union affiliated to the SWMF ('Beware of the fake unions that are favoured by the bosses, their sole aim is to divide you, and not to help you'), and then, in the case of the Werntarw Colliery, where deductions were made from the men's wages, in favour of the 'scab union', they promised full support for any action taken.[82] Shortly after this the EC made a number of important decisions. It decided to grant £100 to a deputation from the Garw District who were seeking central aid in rebuilding the Federation; it listened to a long report from S. O. Davies on the conditions at Taff-Merthyr Colliery and resolved that, as a temporary measure, the Taff and Cynon District should accept workmen employed at the colliery into membership; it extended its resolution of February[83] – 'That the Council supply speakers for the period of one month for the areas in which the Union develops' – into April, and it appointed a sub-committee to consider arrangements for 'Show Cards' with a view to intensive action being taken 'to complete the re-building of the Federation'.[84]

The inroads being made on their membership were being taken seriously, then, and a Delegate Conference was summoned to discuss the whole issue of Federation organisation. Lodges were recommended to appoint active members as Conference delegates so that full reports of all centrally-taken decisions could be given in their own areas. They decided to fix a definite date for the simultaneous holding of 'Show Cards' in the coalfield, whilst full membership returns would make clearer the areas that would need special attention.[85]

The Special Conference, held in May, had no set agenda. After listening to Enoch Morrell, the President, attack those trade unions that pretended to be able to serve their members without being political, and to Tom Richards' reaffirmation of faith in the SWMF, the 177 delegates (representative of some 91,389 members) made suggestions about propaganda work.[86] The EC shortly began to apply more strictly the rule about representation on the EC being related to the average membership of a District,[87] whilst a sub-committee on organisation was directed to draw up a series of leaflets for distribution (30,000 and 5,000 posters were prepared) as pro-Federation propaganda prior to the 'Show Cards' campaign.[88]

For all that, these campaigns, whether locally run or organised by the EC, could only scratch the non-union problem now, and until campaigns based on individual collieries succeeded rhetorical attacks the strength of the SWMIU, aided by the running sore of non-unionism, continued unabated. The membership of the SWMF at the beginning of 1927 was 136,250; by December it had fallen to 72,981; it fell further by December 1928 to 59,858, and only rose to 74,466 at the end of 1929.[89] The average membership, down to 1935, was about a half of those men in employment. At the Annual Conference in June 1928, a composite motion from three lodges was unanimously adopted. The words were:

That this Annual Conference instructs the Executive Council to conduct a campaign throughout the Coalfield against the non-Political Union which is being supported by the Owners. This Campaign should be a preliminary to the handing in of Notices for a Coalfield strike in an effort to destroy the last vestige of Non-Political Unionism, and also get the Non-Unionists to re-join the Federation.[90]

The words needed to be brave, for the coalfield was straining under the accumulated weight of years of social misery, the destruction of hope and a severe trade depression. Later years were to see a more severe incidence of unemployment but none reflects such bleak despair as 1928. The community had exerted its political, industrial and social institutions in an effort to stave off collapse; it had availed them nothing. By April 1928 there were some 70,000 unemployed in the South Wales coal industry; between January 1927 and April 1928, 56 collieries, employing 23,370 men, had closed; many more were due for closure, others were working short-time, local authority rates were rocketing.[91]

The Conciliation Board Agreement of December 1926, favourable in all respects to the Owners was not due to expire until 31 December 1929 but both sides could apply to an independent Chairman for revisions in the subsistence wage of 8s. $0\frac{3}{4}d$. a shift and the minimum percentage rate (of 28 per cent on the 1915 standard). Sir Francis Taylor, in 1927, refused applications to lower or to higher these rates of payment; at the end of 1928, he agreed to the owners' request for a reduction of the Subsistence Wage to 7s. $10\frac{1}{2}d$. a shift.[92] The SWMF were quite unable to halt this further reduction in their wages, which had declined from a total (for nine months, February to October) in 1920 of £49,519,760 to £16,871,505 in 1927.[93]

In 1927, the credit balance of the SWMF stood at £9,612; consequently they had to cut down the expenses that had enabled it to exert such a profound influence on the national labour movement before

1926. In October 1927, their excellently produced journal *The Colliery Workers' Magazine* ceased publication.[94] Then, in December 1927, the 11 SWMF-sponsored MPs agreed to forego £50 of the £650 p.a. paid to them by the Federation; during 1929 they came to an agreement with the EC to pool all monies received from the MFGB, to three of them, for postage and election expenses. Also in December 1926 the Council decided to recommend the cessation of support of the Central Labour College, which was costing the SWMF around £3,000 p.a., a sum too great even in the interests of producing yet another generation of leaders.[95]

In the late 1920s none of the several schemes for reorganisation that were presented to successive conferences proved acceptable. There were acute differences between those who wished an overall reform and those, mostly existing officials, who wanted a refurbishing of the Federation. Besides, the social and economic distress made any hint of more expensive services, from whichever side they came, unacceptable to the membership. In addition the Federation was in a chicken and egg situation in which inability to deal with non-unionism seemed dependent upon a centralisation of resources which could only come about when non-unionism was ended. Practical needs were foundering upon a divergence as much generational as political.

In 1931 A. J. Cook and Vernon Hartshorn died, and so did the man whose life had been the history of the SWMF, Thomas Richards:[96]

Never a man of advanced political views, he always advised moderation. The 'machine' was to him sacred. Any action which would damage the 'machine' had his stern opposition. The machine which he had done so much to create was the core of his being. The 'means' became more important than the 'end'. In his way, he was easily the biggest man produced in . . . 19th Century South Wales. It may not have been his fault that he failed to acquire a 20th Century outlook.[97]

In these hiatus years, after 1926, there was the prime necessity of maintaining the Federation. The period of adjustment was slow and painful, in short, because for a time the patient's will to survive seemed open to question.

In the wake of the 1926 defeat, with the change-over from essentially employed to unemployed mining communities and the decline of 'left unity' around the Minority Movement, political actions now became, of necessity, defensive. It was this defensive attitude within a confused situation of growing isolation, ostracism, diminishing size and influence, and its disastrous policy adopted between 1927 and 1932, which provide some of the clues to the role played by the Communist Party within the wider labour movement during the rest of the 1930s. For these were the years when, as we have seen, the SWMF had seemed to withdraw from the conflict position which it had adopted up to 1926. Into this vacuum, with only a modicum of effectiveness, came the Communist Party along with a variety of organisations, including the Left Wing Movement, the United Front, Workers' militias, anti-bailiff organisations, 'Friends of the Soviet Union', chalk squads, Councils of Action, the National Unemployed Workers' Committee Movement and the Minority Movement.

The first action which could be described as extra-parliamentary was the first Hunger March from South Wales in the autumn of 1927. The March was a protest against the grip of the Ministry of Health on the local Boards of Guardians in refusing (or limiting) relief notes to unemployed miners and their families, and against the new Unemployment Bill. Many Labour Guardians accepted the Ministry's rulings but the Bedwellty Union bankrupted itself so as to maintain poor relief in its area.[98] The initiative for this was apparently taken with a great flourish on 18 September at the 10,000 strong 'Red Sunday in Rhondda Valley' as the posters all over the valleys proclaimed. Organised by a Council of Action, the Rhondda District of the SWMF and the National Unemployed Workers Committee Movement (NUWCM), the demonstration on Penrhys mountain was addressed by A. J. Cook, Wal Hannington (secretary of the NUWCM) and the two Rhondda miners' agents, Lewis and Mainwaring. The posters also proclaimed:

CAMPAIGN AGAINST BALDWIN AND COALOWNERS.
WORKERS, AROUSE!

Join the Revolt Against the Coalowners' Government. NOW we want the 1914 spirit in the Workers' Fight. Organise Your Grumbles and fight Your Oppressors . . . Join Your Contingent in this Great March by falling in behind your Band and Banners. Special Attraction! The Mid Rhondda Section Young Comrades' League and Bands will render Working Class Music and Songs, and Lead Mass singing. Down with Baldwin! On for Workers' Government![99] [full poster reproduced overleaf].

The atmosphere was euphoric and the intent unmistakable: it was 1926, but the tide had ebbed. Cook had called for 'a great march to London' which would commence with the opening of Parliament on 8

RHONDDA MINERS' DISTRICT & COUNCIL OF ACTION

RED SUNDAY IN RHONDDA VALLEY

Campaign Against BALDWIN & COALOWNERS

MONSTRE RHONDDA

DEMONSTRATION

ON PENRHYS MOUNTAIN

On SUNDAY, SEPTEMBER 18th, at 3 o'clock.

The following Speakers will positively attend :

A. J. COOK

General Secretary, M.F.G.B.

WALL HANNINGTON

National Unemployed, London.

David Lewis,   **Arthur Horner,**   **W. H. Mainwaring**

Miners' District Secretary.   E.C. M.F.G.B.   Miners' Agent.

Chairman : T. THOMAS, Treherbert.

WORKERS, AROUSE! Line Up! Join in the Revolt Against
the Coalowners' Government. **NOW** we want the 1914 Spirit in the Workers'
Fight. Organise Your Grumbles and Fight Your Oppressors.

READ THIS TIME TABLE (Men and Women and Join Your Contingent in this Great March,
by falling in behind your Band and Banners.

RHONDDA FACH. Depart from Mardy 1.30 p.m., Ferndale Workmen's Hall 2 p.m., Queen's Square, Tylorstown, 2.30 p.m.,
Porth Square, Porth, 1.30, Workmen's Hall Ynyshir, 2 p.m.

RHONDDA FAWR. Depart from Blaenrhondda Station 1 p.m., Bute Square, Treherbert, 1.15 p.m., Stag Square, Treorky,
1.45 p.m., Ystrad Station 2.15, Butchers Arms, Penygraig, 1.30 p.m., Pandy Square, Tonypandy,
2 p.m., Partridge Road, Trealaw, 2.15 p.m.

SPECIAL ATTRACTION ! The Mid-Rhondda Section YOUNG COMRADES' LEAGUE and Bands will
render Working Class Music and Songs, and lead Mass singing.

Down with Baldwin! On for Workers' Government!

Thomas Bros. Printers

Rhondda demonstration at which A. J. Cook called for the first South Wales Hunger
March, 1927.

November. The intention was to interview Government ministers. Hannington explained its purpose:

> The march is not intended purely as an unemployed demonstration. It is also intended to draw attention to the serious crisis throughout the mining industry. . . . The unemployed miners are like rats in a trap. Pits are closed all around and there is no other industry for them to turn to. They are so poverty-stricken that they are unable to move into other districts for work.[100]

The plan was to get lodges to select marchers as their delegates, each of whom would carry a miner's lamp. It seemed the only way to take the message of their plight out of the valleys.[101] Whilst the tone of the posters was not again to be repeated, the Hunger March became a common enough form of expression in later years.

In the six weeks of preparation, however, the apparent broad base at the 18 September demonstration was somewhat whittled away. Neither the EC of the SWMF nor its Districts (except the Rhondda) was prepared to sponsor the March, partly because of the opposition of the TUC. Among the lone voices outside the Communist Party openly supporting the March were John Strachey (editor of *The Miner*, organ of the MFGB), A. J. Cook and S. O. Davies. Indeed Cook and his wife actually participated in a part of the trek.[102] The deputation to the Ministry of Health, however, was accompanied by six South Wales miners' MPs. But despite the TUC's opposition, the March met with support from every trades council in every town through which it passed, including Pontypridd, Newport, Bristol, Bath, Chippenham and Swindon.[103]

The two hundred and seventy marchers were drawn from the two Rhondda valleys, Caerau, Aberdare, Merthyr, Pontypridd, Tonyrefail, Ogmore, Gilfach Goch, Nantyglo and Blaina. Two miners actually died on the march. Arthur Howe of Trealaw was killed in a road accident. John Supple, aged fifty-eight, of Tonyrefail, died of pneumonia. He had been unemployed for over two years and left a widow and seven children. He wrote in his last letter to his wife:

> Don't worry about me. Think of me as a soldier in the Workers' Army. Remember that I have marched for you and others in want.[104]

The hostility generated against the March, particularly by the TUC, the press and the Government, was to be detected again on later demonstrations to London. On this occasion there was also alleged harassment *en route* by 'Fascists' and, anticipating provocation in London, the organisers took the unprecedented precaution of arranging an armed escort by one hundred members of the Labour League of Ex-Servicemen to meet them at Chiswick.[105] Para-military overtones were always in evidence. The marchers had from the outset been divided into detachments and companies and were expected to accept near military discipline. It was also frequently referred to as an 'army'.[106] Songs sung on the March included 'A Rebel Song' (by James Connolly), 'March Song of the Red Army' and 'The Red Army March'. Even in the pre-March build-up the Bulletins issued by the South Wales Organising Council appealed to ex-servicemen to 'use your military knowledge for the benefit of the March'.[107] Likewise, its extra-parliamentary nature was often in evidence. Wal Hannington, its 'chief officer', recalled shortly afterwards:

> . . . these men are lighting a lamp stronger and more powerful than that which they are carrying. They are lighting a lamp that reveals the tortuous path the *toilers* have had to follow, and which lights up the road of struggle for the battle with the forces of reaction and the conquest of power by the workers.[108]

Perhaps such rhetoric can only be seen in terms of attempting to raise morale. Certainly by 1928 and 1929 the hopes generated by the events of 1927 had turned to despair. Dozens of depressed mining communities crumbled. Many young girls went away into service and young single and married men tramped the country for work. One miner recalled how his friend tried to persuade him to leave for London:

> '. . .Let's go up to London, we'll have work up in London.' But he didn't have work. What he did catch was a cough like a sheep . . . with sleeping on the benches . . . up in London.[109]

The *Sunday Worker* was reporting in August 1928 that hundreds of young and old men from the South Wales coalfield were stranded and starving in London with nowhere to stay. By November 1928, the Pontypridd Board of Guardians was not paying relief to married or single able-bodied men. Relief of 10s. was paid to wives and 3s. for each child over three years, but only in vouchers.[110] In the absence of adequate relief, confusion reigned in some areas where political and non-political voluntary bodies vied with each other for the control of the very limited charitable resources. In Mardy, for example, the more political Distress Committee gradually lost out, as the reputation of

'Little Moscow' grew. The Quakers, the Labour Party and the Rhondda UDC became more acceptable bodies for outside benefactors to recognise.[111]

Within less than three years of the General Strike, South Wales miners were unbelievably being portrayed as 'scabs'. In January 1929, Arthur Horner, Tom Mann and A. J. Cook addressed a meeting of ex-miners in London so as to 'find a remedy for the intolerable situation'. The Government's transference scheme was regarded by the militants as a means of importing miners into workplaces so as to undercut wages and violate long-established customs. For example, it was believed that ex-miners were reputedly working in the High Wycombe furniture trade for 2*d*. or 3*d*. an hour. Most had been sent by Labour Exchanges but some had been tramping the country for work and would it was thought 'take anything to stave off actual starvation'.[112]

The SWMF then did not always have a direct significance for many militant miners in South Wales at this time simply because so many of them were unemployed, although all (if they had not been expelled for their political activities) kept up their SWMF membership. Erstwhile lodge militants redirected their energies into the National Unemployed Workers' Movement (NUWM) which became the archetypal extra-parliamentary movement in the South Wales valleys.[113]

By 1930, it was still difficult to organise the unemployed into a coherent movement and attempts at artificially stimulating campaigns such as that over the Workers' Charter in the autumn of 1930 met with little success.[114] In spite of this, small groups of NUWM members continued their agitation at local level representing the unemployed at the Labour Exchanges and the Court of Referees. They were also involved in extra-legal activities partly out of despair and partly because they felt their actions were morally and politically justified. The experience in mid-Rhondda were typical:

> I believe that unemployment . . . degrades and demoralises. I remember in the early thirties . . . trying to organise demonstrations to the Rhondda Council . . . [In an] Employment Exchange like Porth, where over 3000 were signing, you couldn't get a bloody hundred to walk. And in Pandy [Tonypandy] there would be 7000 signing . . . if you got two hundred on the bloody road you were doing well, you know. Oh no, it was demoralising . . . when you see men with a bloody fag and a pin stuck in the bottom of it and passing it around a bloody group, it's getting pretty desperate, isn't it.[115]

A similar situation existed in Abertillery in June 1931. NUWM membership had nevertheless increased to one hundred and fifty, a table and chair were placed outside the Labour Exchange every Friday for recruitment; branch meetings were held every Wednesday; and the NUWM scored successes at the Court of Referees. There were, however, still serious organisational problems:

> We have appealed by chalking the roads and printing notices for the unemployed to attend our branch meetings but so far we have not fully succeeded in getting them to turn up.[116]

Despair there was, but for the tiny minority of NUWM activists it was something of a fulfilment. Constant agitation on the dole was preferable to the 'starvation wages' for eight hours a day and more in the pit. One such activist was Edwin Greening of Aberaman, who later fought in the International Brigades:

> We were organising meetings and demonstrations all the time. We were continuously active. You see I had two things in the fire, my studies, . . . [and politics] and therefore unemployment meant nothing to me, right. I was getting 17/6 dole and then I was going out selling *Daily Workers* and getting another £1. I didn't smoke; I didn't drink, right and I didn't gamble, right; I was nicely dressed. Well, I studied in the day then I went out politicising in the evenings or in the weekends. . . .[117]

What changed the situation was the National Government's ten per cent Economy Cuts in unemployment benefit in September 1931. A groundswell of anger and protest made both the NUWM and the Communist Party look again at the possibilities of a broader strategy. NUWM activities now intensified and spread beyond its traditional strongholds of Merthyr, Rhondda and North Monmouthshire to most valleys in the coalfield.[118] The 'united front' tactic of forming councils of action was taken up. At Brynmawr, a 'united front' committee was formed in August 1931;[119] in September an 'all-in' conference was held in Bargoed and a Monmouthshire Council of Action was formed which included the Communist Party, the ILP, the Iron and Steel Trades Confederation, Dockers, the SWMF, Workers' Defence Corps, the National Union of Railwaymen and the NUWM.[120] Similar conferences against the cuts were also held in the same month at Ammanford and Tonypandy.[121] Much the most significant conference was held in Ystrad-Rhondda in October with one hundred and six representatives present including the NUWM, women's guilds, workmen's clubs, SWMF lodges and street committees.[122]

The NUWM event which accelerated activity considerably was the South Wales Hunger March to the TUC at Bristol in September 1931. On the theme 'Struggle or Starve', agitation for the March had begun with the Monmouthshire District Council of the NUWM, helped by the national chairman, Sid Elias, who went on a speaking tour of South Wales to rally support for the March.[123] Typical of the preparatory work was that undertaken by the Abertillery NUWM which distributed hundreds of leaflets, held pit-head meetings and made collections at shops, pubs and labour exchanges. With the £7 2s. 0d. they collected they were able to send eight marchers who were equipped with boots, socks, soap, towel and kit-bag. The local branch had still sufficient time to send a telegram to the Governor of Alabama protesting against a 'frame-up' of nine Negroes for rape.[124] Over one hundred men and twelve women set off on 5 September with nearly one-third coming from the Rhondda, and other contingents from Caerau, Merthyr, Monmouthshire, Cardiff and Llanelli. On reaching the Horsefair at Bristol on their way to the TUC Conference Hall, the March was broken up by mounted police using batons. The final indignity was yet to come: the TUC refused a hearing to a deputation of six marchers.[125]

Despite all the attempts at united action, the *political* campaigning on behalf of the unemployed by the NUWM was still narrowly based, made all the more so by their attacks on the 'Quakers' as at Treorchy where, according to the NUWM, they were trying to keep the unemployed busy by forming social clubs. The local branch of the NUWM sought to expose the meaning of their charity.[126] Meetings organised by a 'scab organisation' considered 'detrimental to the cause' were broken up at Tonyrefail.[127] (Presumably this referred to the development by the TUC of 'Unemployed associations' as a counter to the growth of the NUWM.) There was also hostility towards the work of the Educational Settlements and the National Council of Social Service which in particular provided numbers of wireless sets at miners' institutes and social clubs so as to give the miners 'recreation and new mental stimulus . . . to take an interest in subjects outside the daily routine of life'.[128]

A series of localised Unemployment Marches was mounted by the NUWM in 1932 including one to Bridgend in October, an all-Glamorgan March to the County Council in Cardiff in November and one at Abertillery again in November. Apart from this, there was a small March to London led by Idris Cox in 1930 and then a much larger one in 1932,[129] when three hundred and seventy-five marchers left on 14

October. In all a total of two thousand five hundred marchers set off from several parts of Britain.[130]

The intention was to present a petition to Parliament on 1 November demanding the abolition of the Means Test and the Anomalies Act, restoration of the 10 per cent unemployment benefit cuts and the cuts in the social services. The significance and impact of the 1932 National March was, however, not fully appreciated by the marchers at the time although they were made aware of some of the authorities' concern on their arrival in London. Metropolitan police files reveal excessively detailed preparations, including widespread cancellations of police leave, use of informers, extensive reports from those police stations located on the marchers' route and information on the criminal records of some of the Glamorganshire participants before the march arrived in London. There were elements of panic resembling that experienced by the authorities prior to the Chartist demonstration in London in 1848. The Assistant Commissioner for the Metropolitan Police even went so far as to attempt to frame Will Paynter, the Treasurer of the South Wales contingent. Described as a 'well-known Communist agitator', he had already been arrested at a Hyde Park rally (which had been broken up by mounted police) for 'wilfully obstructing police' and was fined £5. The Assistant Commissioner suggested that a van allegedly containing weapons such as sticks and iron bars should be linked with Paynter:

> Please get somebody good on to this at once and if possible connect P. with this van.[131]

Although by 1932 signs of a revival in spirit were clearly detectable with the marches and demonstrations, many activists amongst the South Wales miners (by now mainly unemployed) continued to feel relatively isolated and persecuted.

This is what invested the running debate over the dry details of reorganisation with such frenzy. The SWMF had never been an expression of the whole nature of coalfield society but the passionate political arguments within its ranks had been used to revolve around the nature of the organisation since all the political and industrial creeds supported by the miners derived their relative strengths from their base within the Federation. This is why the SWMF was emblematic of the possibilities for progressive social change; but since it was also, by virtue of its reflective nature, imbued with the paradoxes of its society, it re-acted, albeit massively, with bewildered ineffectiveness to economic calamity beyond its calculations. Some militants, disillusioned with failure to act consistently in line with professed politics, now attempted to by-pass it. Such action, developed in the context of Mond-Turnerism and spurred on by the inability of reformist politicians, nationally or locally, to affect events, ignored the reality of past coalfield militancy (that is, its molecular growth within the society). Without this the ideological manufacture of artificially required positions could have no hope of achieving any hegemonic control, and hence political or industrial success. The relative weakness of the SWMF, from 1927 to 1934, did not, on the other hand, signal its remoteness from its members for whom it remained the body most intimately connected with their daily experience, but rather its failure to mirror an altered society and, thereby, once more to formulate possibilities for social transformation. The bumbling prose of conference reports and of lodge records, with their creaking formality, so distinct in tone and interest from the colourful episodes of riot and demonstration in which the self-same people are presented to us via the press, should be interpreted as the language needed by men intent on creating an institutional pattern, for their actions and their thought, which might achieve a longevity, and a fruition, which would be denied to them if only expressed in 'spontaneous' revolt. This passionate involvement with the minutiae of administrative change, then, has to be understood as a conscious reaching, in lodge after lodge, for an organisation able to give a collective articulation to individual voices. The very remoteness of this mechanistic language from the accustomed speech of coalfield society has tended to obscure its role as a vehicle for social assertion. There is a disciplined self-consciousness in it that is quite removed from the threatening notes and language of such nineteenth-century coalfield phenomena as the 'Scotch Cattle'.[132] However, behind the formal and often mechanical presentation of themselves in the lodge and to the public, in imitation of the society beyond, there existed a clear, often sophisticated intent to pose as an alternative authority within that society.

NOTES

1. See SWMF Rules, partially revised in February 1920.
2. In fact he had stated his desire to resign one or other office (he had been MP for West Monmouth since 1904; the Constituency was redrawn after the war in

November 1919). His salary was increased to £750 in December 1919, and to £800 p.a. in July 1920. See Page Arnot, Vol. II, p. 181

3. SWMF Rules 1920, pp. 1 and 2.

4. For five months prior to the 1926 lock-out, the subscription fee was 1s per week, but this then reverted to 6d. a week (the pre-1914 fee) until the Second World War. See W. J. Saddler's *Contributions in Relation to Services* (1945), SWMF files.

5. Figures compiled from the SWMF Directory for 1926.

6. These were (1) Anthracite, (2) Aberdare, (3) Afan Valley, (4) Blaina, (5) Dowlais, (6) East Glamorgan, (7) Eastern Valleys, (8) Ebbw Vale, (9) Garw, (10) Maesteg, (11) Merthyr, (12) Monmouth Western Valleys, (13) Ogmore and Gilfach, (14) Pontypridd, (15) Rhondda No. 1. (16) Rhymney Valley, (17) Taff and Cynon, (18) Tredegar Valley, (19) Western. In 1920 Saundersfoot and Reynoldstown (in Pembrokeshire) had existed as a District in addition. See SWMF Rules, 1920, and SWMF Directory, 1926.

7. SWMF Rules, 1927.

8. SWMF Directory, 1926.

9. Bedwas and Mardy are, respectively, cases in point. See below chs. 5 and 9. The case of Gwilym Richards, a very able checkweigher who enjoyed the confidence of his men after the 1921 lock-out is, perhaps, the most clear-cut. Sir D. R. Llewellyn put Tower Colliery 'on a stop' until Richards removed himself voluntarily (the men refused to withdraw their support). See David Smith 'The Burning Mountain', *Cyffro* (summer 1972). Victimisation, of individuals and of whole committees, was widespread in the late 1920s.

10. Ness Edwards, *History of the SWMF*, Vol. I (1938), pp. 139–40.

11. *Colliery Workers' Magazine*, December 1926, p. 252.

12. See UCS, SWMF Circulars, 1915–26, 'Report of Conditions in the Various districts', 13 December 1926 (reproduced in Appendix III. A similar spate of victimisation occurred after the 1921 Lock-out.

13. See H. Francis, *Llafur loc. cit.* The contrast was in many ways remarkable and became all the more important in the revival of the Federation in the mid 1930s with victimised militants like Horner and Jack Jones of the Rhondda finding union positions in the Anthracite and Anthracite Agents, Jim Griffiths (1934–36) and Horner (1936–46) coming to the fore by becoming presidents of the SWMF. The significance of the Seniority Rule, the Sacred Cow of the proud Anthracite miner became legendary: 'The difference between the leader and the ordinary rank and filer in the Anthracite area is much less than in the steam coal. . . . In the Anthracite area, if you wanted to dismiss a man who was a bit of a 'trouble maker', they would have to take possibly a hundred men out before him (because of the Seniority Rule). . . . [Consequently] you see you had lambs roaring like lions in the Anthracite, and they had to be a lion to bloody well roar like a lion in the steam coalfield.' (D. D. Evans, interview, *op. cit.*, who was an Anthracite miner in the inter-war period, who later became general secretary of the South Wales Area of the NUM (1958–63). Some victimisation did however, occur in the Anthracite District (see Appendix III). There are no references at all in any South Wales coalowners' records to victimisation or blacklists which is odd given the amount of evidence from the miners' side.

14. See for instance SWMF minutes, 4 December 1926.

15. SWMF minutes, 7 January 1927; *SW* 2 January 1927.

Caenewydd miners (Gorseinon, near Swansea), about 1895
(*back row*) William Grenfell (Billy Sais), David Rhys Grenfell (later MP for Gower and Minister of Mines), David Rees (Dafydd Banc-yr-Eithin), Henry Howard, William Evans (Billy Boy) (*seated*) Henry Thomas (Rocking), William John Grenfell (W.J.), David Matthews (Coalbrook), Thomas Evans (Twm Arall – Billy Boy's father)

Photograph taken in 1906 by Willie Jones, a Pontypool miner. A pit pony hauls a tram coal, with a 'shaft and gun' linkage stopping the heavy load from crashing into the anima legs on slopes or when reversing; one miner holds a candle, the other has a primitive lamp and is smoking. He is at the Lamp Station, an area known to be gas-free where saf lamps could be relit.

Cwmfelinfach miners rat-catching, about 1913

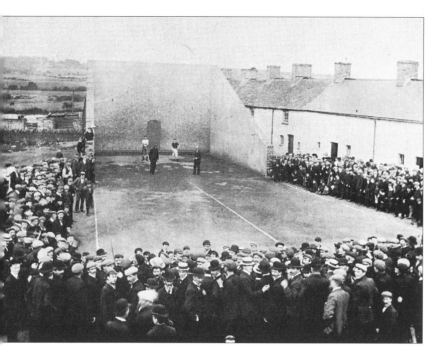

Hand-ball tournament at Nelson, Taff Bargoed valley, about 1914

Typical Tonypandy scene before the First World War

Six Bells, near Abertillery, about 1920. A typical South Wales mining valley community

West Riding Regiment guarding Market Square, Pontypridd, December 1910, at the time of the Tonypandy riots

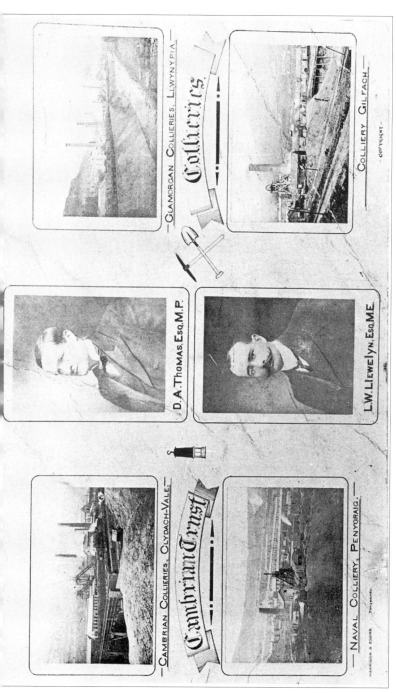

Postcard (about 1914) of the first Welsh Coal Trust

Nantyffyllon (Maesteg) boot-repairing depot in the 1926 lockout

A Pontypridd comic band, 1926 lockout

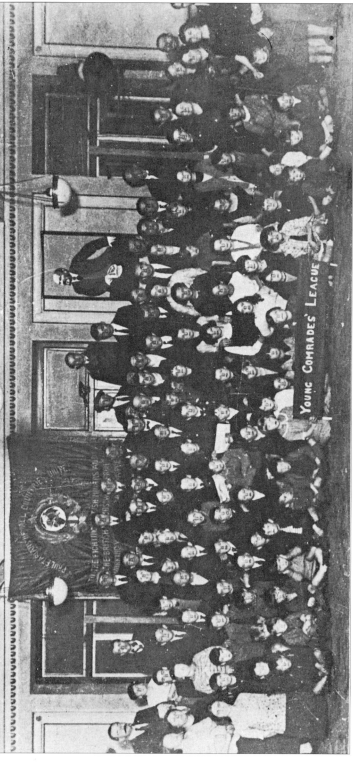

Mardy miners and their families with Soviet banner, December 1926

Mardy Council of Action 'anti-bailiff' defendants, 1932

Back row (left to right) George Thomas, Ben Williams ('Ben Coch'), Percy Moxam, John Thomas ('Social'), Daniel Childs, Ben Lewis, Martin Thomas, Tommy Rowe, Will Thomas, Sid Wharton, John Thomas ('Sioni bach y north'), Octavius ('Ockey') Hope, Ben Payne, Jim Evans, George Poole. *Front row* Will Rees ('Will Swank'), Sal Evans (and baby Betty), Betty Sweet, Ellen Tudor, Jesse Sweet, Pat O'Shea. *Kneeling* Joe Chambers

South Wales Hunger March to the Bristol TUC, 1931

Parc miners (Cwmparc, Rhondda) after their eight-day stay-down strike against the 'scab' union, October 1935. (The neighbouring Fernhill miners stayed down for twelve days on a wages issue in 1936)

Demonstration against imprisonment of local miners, Taff-Merthyr Colliery, 1936

Welcome home in Treharris for 'Taff-Merthyr' prisoners, 1936

Welsh volunteers in the International Brigades during the Spanish Civil War, before the Ebro offensive, 1938:
left to right (standing) Rowley Williams (Trelewis), Tom Howell Jones (Aberdare), Jack Roberts (Tonypandy), Arthur Williams (Penygraig), John Oliver, (Blackwood), Tom Evans (Kenfig Hill), Emrys Jones (Clydach Vale), Archie Cook (Ystrad-Rhondda), Goff Price (Bedwas), Sid James (Treherbert), Edwin Greening (Aberaman) *kneeling* Evan Lloyd (Bedlinog), Billy Griffiths (Tonypandy), Evan Jones (Llanelli), Morris Davies (Treharris)

County Councillor Lewis Jones welcomes Arthur Griffiths out of prison after serving a sentence following his part in the 1936 anti-Blackshirt demonstration in Tonypandy

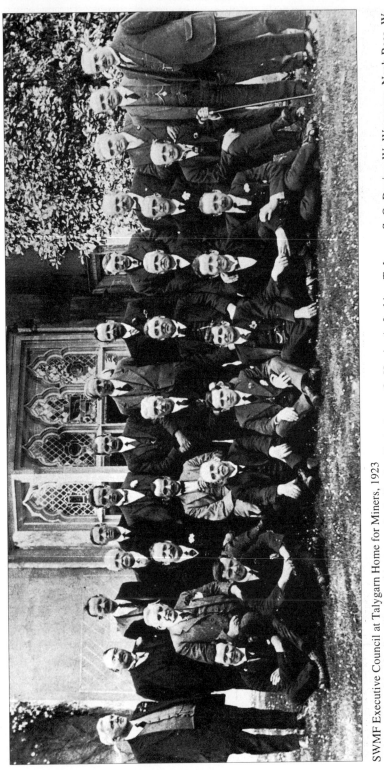

SWMF Executive Council at Talygarn Home for Miners, 1923
left to right (standing) J. James, D. J. Williams, D. L. Davies, T. Andrews, O. Harris, A. Jenkins, T. Lucas, S. O. Davies, W. Woosnam, Noah Rees, W. Lewis, T. Smith, H. Jenkins, W. J. Saddler *seated* Rt. Hon. T. Richards (General Secretary), V. Hartshorn MP (President), Major Linthune (Secretary of Home), E. Morel (Vice-President), D. Lewis, W. Hopkins, O. Powell, William Davies, *front row* T. Williams, S. Jones, E. Thomas, E. Williams, R. M. Rees, J. W. Grant, A. J. Cook

Ocean Combine Committee, 1935
(first person on left in each row and third in front row not known)
back row – standing (left to right) Goronwy Jones (Lady Windsor, Ynysybwl), Fred
Llewellyn (Ocean/Western, Nantymoel), George Thomas (Bute, Treherbert), Tom Johnson
(Abergorki, Treorchy), Chris Rimron (Albion, Cilfynydd), Phil Thomas (Nine Mile Point,
Cwmfelinfach), Harold Jones (Risca) *middle row (sitting)* Ike Jones (Deep Navigation,
Treharris), Alf Davies (Combine secretary, Garw Ocean, Blaengarw), Sidney Jones (miners'
agent, Rhymney valley)

SWMF Rank and File EC and Officials, 1936: *(back row)* Tal Mainwaring, W. H. Crews,
Jack Davies, James Evans, Dai Dan Evans, James Grant, Gomer Evans *(centre)* Obadiah
Evans, William Davies, Meth Jones, Mark Harcombe, Emlyn Thomas, D. R. Davies, Tom
Bateman, Ness Edwards, Tom Lucas, Will Paynter, Alf Davies, William Dunn, Sam
Garland, H. Aubrey, Idris Davies *(sitting)* John James, Oliver Harris (General Secretary),
W. J. Saddler (Vice-President), Arthur Horner (President), A. B. Meredith, Evan Evans
(kneeling) Albert Bennett, Sid Jones, Haydn Lewis

NUM (South Wales Area) Rank and File EC and Officials, 1972:
(*back row*) E. Cooper, G. Mann, E. John, A. Haywood, G. Pritchard, D. C. Davies, (*middle row*) D. Hayward, T. Walker, V. Court, I. Rosser, E. Jenkins, G. Rees, H. Matthews, E. Hughes, (*front row*) B. Jenkins, E. Williams (Vice-President), D. Francis (General Secretary), G. Williams (President), B. Morris, W. H. Thomas, J. Rogers

16. UCS, SWMF Circulars, 13 December 1926.
17. UCS, Ferndale lodge minutes, 13 December 1926.
18. UCS, Ferndale lodge minutes, 28 December 1926.
19. UCS, Cambrian lodge minutes, 2 January 1927; *SW* 30 January 1927.
20. *SW, ibid.*
21. UCS, SWMF Circulars, 17 December 1926.
22. SWMF, *An Outline of the Work Accomplished on behalf of the South Wales Colliery Workers* (Cardiff, 1927) pam.
23. Oliver Powell, interview, *op. cit.*
24. *Ibid.*
25. *SW*, 30 January 1927.
26. SWML interview with Will Thomas (Cwmparc, Rhondda), 19 December 1974.
27. SWML interview with Cyril Parry (Pontarddulais), 20 May 1974, who was working at Morlais Colliery in the Swansea Dry Steam or Western District at the time and who after a period of victimisation, returned to the same colliery after the war to become the lodge secretary for over twenty years until his retirement in 1971.
28. SWML interview with John Evans (Mardy), 13 June 1974.
29. SWMF minutes, 7 March 1927; *SW*, 6 March, 13 March 1927.
30. *SW*, 6 March 1927; Michael Foot, *op. cit.*, pp. 97–8.
31. *SW*, 17 July, 14 August 1927: *Report of Inquiry into the Cwm Disaster* (HMSO, 1927).
32. Cyril Parry, interview *op. cit.*
33. *Ibid.*
34. Interview with Will Lloyd, an Aberdare International Brigader, 9 July 1969.
35. See pp. 53–4 above.
36. See R. Martin, *Communism and the Trade Unions, 1924–1933: A Study of the National Minority Movement* (1969), *passim.*
37. Arthur Horner, *Incorrigible Rebel* (1960), p. 92.
38. *NMM, British Mineworkers' Union* (1927), *passim.*
39. See Horner, *op. cit.*, pp. 92–3, and Page Arnot, *The Miners in Crisis and War* (1961), Chapter X, *passim.*
40. *One Mineworkers' Union – Why?* NMM, pp. 8–9.
41. Page Arnot, *The Miners: Years of Struggle* (1953); L. J. Macfarlane, *The British Communist Party: Its Origins and Development until 1929* (1966).
42. See below, pp. 91–2.
43. *Commission of Enquiry into Industrial Unrest, No. 7 Division*, p. 6.
44. See David Egan, 'Abel Morgan, 1878–1972', *Llafur*, Vol. I, no. 2, 1973, p. 31.
45. See above, p. 25.
46. Harold Finch, *Memoirs of a Bedwellty MP* (1972), p. 25.
47. D. J. Williams had been a student at the Central Labour College and a miner. He became a lodge secretary in the Anthracite District, and Labour MP for Neath after 1945.
48. D. J. Williams, *Capitalist Combination in the Coal Industry* (London, 1924), p. 118.
49. *Ibid.*, pp. 172, 173, 174. In fact the owners refused to meet representatives of the Combines.
50. *The Second Industrial Survey of South Wales* (1937), pp. 54–5.
51. Williams, *op. cit.*, p. 173.
52. See Hywel Francis, *loc. cit.* A petition addressed to Lord Melchett of

Amalgamated Anthracite, in January 1929, by some of his workmen claimed a deterioration of relationship between worker and employer since 1924, and added:

> We are desired also, to emphasise the fear prevailing amongst the workmen, that the powerful 'Amalgamation' has been brought into existence, to lower the Standard of Life generally among the mining Communities within the area covered by the Amalgamation, by directly reducing the Rates of Wages of the Workmen, and in particular the Price Lists for Pieceworkers in the various Collieries now under the same centralised Management, a fear which has created a widespread indignation and a sullen anger that bodes ill for the future of the industry. SWMF files. Copy of the petition.

53. Bryn Roberts, Powell Duffryn Area Combine – *Why the Workers should support the Combine*. Copy in TUC Library.
54. *South Wales News*, 10 May 1927.
55. Monmouthshire and South Wales Coalowners' Association, Minute Books, 13 December 1926.
56. Lord Davies, Llandinam MSS. National Library of Wales, Box 3. *Letter* of 16 June 1926 to W. P. Thomas.
57. Montagu Slater, *Stay-Down Miner* (London, 1936), p. 23.
58. W. J. Anthony-Jones, 'Labour Relations in the South Wales Coal-mining Industry 1927–39' (Ph.D. Univ. of Wales, 1959); and Slater, *op. cit.*
59. In August the SWMF had scotched attempts by some men to sign on at Elliott's Collieries in New Tredegar; rashes of this sort continued to break out. In November a figure of 20,000 men were reported at work in the coalfield – *Western Mail*, 23 August and 5 November 1926. Gregory's action had not gone unnoticed, however. In Porth there was a Conference on the situation, as the Mardy Lodge was told: 'Lewis Lloyd gave a report of the Conference . . . re workmen at Heol-y-cyw and that they had decided that a Demonstration be formed up from both valleys to march to this place with the object of persuading the men to come out; after full discussion, owing to the distance to walk to this place that 12 volunteers be asked to attend there, and that 2/6d be given to each of them for expenses.' Mardy lodge minutes, 7 September 1926.
60. In 1922 the P.D. Company, with Ocean Coal and Wilsons Limited, had formed the Taff-Merthyr Steam Coal Company (each had half shares) to work an area of coal lying between existing collieries. D. J. Williams, *op. cit*, p. 98.
61. *Merthyr Express*, 9 January 1926.
62. *Western Mail*, 27 October 1934.
63. *Ibid.*; 22 November 1926.
64. *Idem.*
65. *South Wales News*, 22 November 1926.
66. *Merthyr Express*, 27 November 1926. However, the Chairman, Vice-Chairman and three Trustees were all Conservative Party members, it was alleged. The Treasurer had been an official of a Conservative Club and their Legal Adviser was the Conservative party Organiser for the Caerphilly Division, *Workers' Life*, 4 March 1927.
67. *Western Mail*, 6 December 1926.

68. SWMIU Rules, reported in *Merthyr Express*, 11 December 1926.
69. *Ibid.*, 11 December 1926; *Western Mail*, 6 December 1926.
70. *Western Mail*, 30 December 1926.
71. *Ibid*, 31 December 1926.
72. *Merthyr Express*, 4 December 1926.
73. *Ibid.*, 11 December 1926.
74. S. O. Davies Papers, letter book No. 14. Glamorgan Record Office.
75. Minute Book of the Bedlinog Council of Action, 7 and 10 May 1926. Loaned by Edgar Evans, delegate to the Council, which had been formed on 4 May 1926, for the purpose of coordinating strike activity in the locality. In 1928, now a Trade and Labour Council, it was still meeting.
76. *Ibid.*, 21 October and 22 November 1926.
77. *The Colliery Workers' Magazine*, January 1927.
78. The letter was reproduced in *The Colliery Workers' Magazine*, January 1927.
79. *Ibid.*, February 1927.
80. *Ibid.*, April and May 1927.
81. *South Wales News*, 3 May 1927.
82. SWMF EC minutes, 12 March 1927.
83. *Ibid.*, 5 February 1927.
84. *Ibid.*, 8 April 1927.
85. *Ibid.*, 27 April 1927.
86. *Ibid.*, 9 May 1927.
87. SWMF EC minutes, 17 May 1927 and 27 June 1927, when it was reported that the size of the EC would now be reduced to twenty-one.
88. *Ibid.*, 27 May 1927.
89. SWMF Annual Returns to Registrar-General. F.S. 12/137. 1160. T.
90. SWMF EC minutes, 25 and 26 June 1928.
91. *Western Mail*, 20 April 1928.
92. For details see Ness Edwards, *op. cit.*, pp. 141–3.
93. Figures quoted in *Workers' Life*, 30 December 1927.
94. *The Colliery Workers' Magazine*, October 1927. Even the Liberal *South Wales News* had to amalgamate with the *Tory Western Mail* in August 1928.
95. *Western Mail*, 29 December 1927; see Agreement and Correspondence in SWMF files.
96. See *Western Mail*, 14 March, 3 November and 9 November 1931.
97. Edwards, *op. cit.*, p. 152.
98. Michael Foot, *op. cit.*, pp. 108–10.
99. SWML poster collection, 'Campaign Against Baldwin . . . (1927)'.
100. *SW*, 25 September 1927.
101. W. Hannington, *The March of the Miners: How We Smashed the Opposition* (1927), pamphlet.
102. *SW*, 13 November 1927.
103. *SW*, 27 November 1927; Hannington, *op. cit.* Amongst the deputation of twelve marchers were Jack Jones (Blaenclydach) and Charlie Costello (Trecynon) both of whom ten years later volunteered to fight with the International Brigades. The Communist Arthur Eyles (Dowlais) was also amongst the deputation: he was one of the very few in the South Wales coalfield who joined Mosley's British Union of Fascists in the 1930s.

104. *SW*, 4 December 1927.
105. Interview with Tom Gale (Abertillery), 6 January 1976; *SW*, 20 November 1927.
106. Hannington, *op. cit.*
107. SWML, Hunger March (1927) collection, *London Marchers' Bulletin No. 2.*
108. Hannington, *op. cit.*
109. Glyn Williams interview, *op. cit.*
110. *SW*, 26 August, 25 November 1928.
111. *SW*, 18 January 1929; see also SWML, Mardy Distress Committee minutes, 1929, *passim.*
112. *SW*, 27 January 1929.
113. See, for example, Paynter, *My Generation, op. cit.*, pp. 82–108.
114. Marx Memorial Library (MML), Maud Brown and Wal Hannington MSS, *NUWM Monthly Report Bulletin*, No. 2, November 1930.
115. SWML, W. Paynter interview, *op. cit.*
116. *NUWM Monthly Bulletin*, No. 9 June 1931.
117. Edwin Greening, interview, *op. cit.*
118 cf. *NUWM Monthly Bulletins* No. 2, November 1930, and No. 11, September 1931.
119. *NUWM Bulletin*, No. 13, October 1931.
120. *NUWM Bulletin*, No. 12, September 1931.
121. *Daily Worker (DW)*, 16 September 1931.
122. *DW*, 13 October 1931.
123. *DW*, 15 August 1931.
124. *NUWM Bulletin*, No. 11, August 1931.
125. *DW*, 29 August 1931; Paynter, *My Generation, op. cit.*, pp. 85–7.
126. *NUWM Bulletin*, No. 7, April–May 1931.
127. *NUWM Bulletin*, No. 13, October 1931.
128. Quoted in G. A. Hutt, *The Condition of the Working Class in Britain* (London, 1933), p. 46.
129. Information provided in a letter 14 September 1970, from Idris Cox, CPGB District Secretary for South Wales in 1932; *DW* 29 September 1932.
130. Public Record Office (PRO), MEPOL 2/3065 *passim*, and MEPOL 2/3066 *passim.*
131. *Ibid.*
132. David Jones, 'The Scotch Cattle and their Black Domain', in *Before Rebecca* (1974).

CHAPTER FOUR

The 'Scab Union'

The existence of the SWMIU in the coalfield, down to 1938, was not a factor that impinged continually on the lives of the coalfield's population; its size and its location, small and scattered, militated against that. However, its removal came to be seen as the essential prerequisite of the re-establishment of Federation hegemony since, in its very existence, the SWMIU was a threat to the principles of unity on which the Federation had been built, and it was, in a time of sore relations between the men and the owners, a constant reminder of the willingness to organise unemployed miners to take the jobs of those in dispute.

It is difficult to write of the organisation of the Industrial Union in detail because none of its Minute Books is extant and it never published a balance sheet. No memoirs exist, nor the records of any individual Lodges. Its supporters are not vociferous in their recollections of it now. From the evidence that does survive, it is difficult not to avoid the conclusion that the major reason for this paucity of surviving evidence is the added light it would throw on the collusion of the Industrial Union and the coalowners themselves. This, certainly, was the Federation's contention from the start. When A. J. Cook spoke at Llanharan in May 1927, he did not hesitate to link the owners, the union and the newspaper that reached all parts of the coalfield, the *Western Mail*:

> The Non-Political Union was born in the colliery office, supplied with Tory beer, and fed in the Tory clubs, and when the employers withdraw their support from it, it will die. The *Western Mail* is its mouthpiece. You have never found the *Western Mail* advocating lower hours or increased wages, nor increased compensation for injured workmen. We have in South Wales the dirtiest and the most vile press in the country which has done all it could to utilise its columns, to try to support the Non-Political Union and smash the Miners' Federation.[1]

The free publicity it received explains perhaps the grievance of the

Press in being barred from admission to the SWMIU's first Annual Conference at the Grand Hotel in Cardiff, in September 1927, since the 'union owes its phenomenal growth to press publicity more than anything else.'[2] There were 121 delegates representing the 121 branches claimed but no membership figures were available. The union delegates emphasised their desire for peaceful co-operation with the SWMF.[3] But how phenomenal had their growth been and how peaceful was its expansion in reality?

In early 1927 the SWMIU continued to grow. Twenty-one branches were formed in January, principally in the Rhymney Valley, and a membership figure of 30,000 claimed.[4] None the less, the hub of its activity remained the Taff-Merthyr Pit. There, the local branch of the SWMIU appointed a new Secretary, Gordon Harris of Nelson, to replace W. A. Williams who had been elevated to the position of Organising Secretary. At the same meeting it was announced that 10,000 application forms for membership had been distributed in South Wales, along with 5,000 Rule Books – numbers considerably less than the blown-up estimate of 30,000. They had issued a pamphlet elucidating their belief in the separation of political and industrial matters and denying any connection with the owners. They turned the jibe that the union was a 'Coffin Club' into a boast that they would bury the SWMF – 'True it [that is, payment of £10 to a member's wife on his death] sounds very much like a coffin club but it will be the Miners' Federation's Coffin, don't forget.' The pamphlet ended with a confident slogan – 'Join the Miners' Industrial Union – the Union for Peace and Happiness. Ignore the Miners' Federation – the Union of froth and shabbiness.'[5]

The SWMIU was registered as a trade union in June 1927 with a Chairman, a Vice-Chairman, an Organising Secretary and an Executive Committee of eighteen. The positions of President and General Secretary went unfilled; these posts were to be held 'during the will and pleasure of the majority'. The Executive Committee came from Monmouthshire (5) and East Glamorgan (12), with a solitary representative of the Anthracite area. The Rules were eloquent about the rights of membership and the manner in which full balance sheets would be prepared so that the use made of the members' money could be seen. Rule 15 concluded:

> None of the Funds of the Union are to be used for Political purposes, propaganda, or for defraying any Election expenses whatsoever.

The weekly contributions were 6d a week, and the funds were to go to secure the best wage rates possible, and 'to regulate the relations between Employer and Employees in order to secure the best working arrangements for the Industry'. Before a strike could be called, and after exhausting all possible arbitration, there would have to be a three-fifths majority of the membership in favour.[6]

There had been, in such sentiments as these, enough power to have the Union registered formally, with a sizeable support for its views. It spread sporadically, often where there had been trouble during the lock-out. This had happened in the Rhondda in October 1926 when there had been demonstrations for several days against men working in the pit at Cwmparc,[7] and where, by January 1927, it was reported that some 200 men had joined the SWMIU despite active Federation propaganda.[8] As early as February 1927, the Industrial Union tried to co-ordinate their activities by holding a Delegate Conference at the New Inn Hotel in Pontypridd, a geographically central location. Over fifty delegates attended, representative of twenty-seven lodges, but, of course, there were no exact membership figures.[9] William Gregory was among those elected to the Executive Council, but most of the delegates were from the Eastern part of the coalfield. W. Gooding from Nine Mile Point Colliery, near Risca, made the key-note speech in which he proclaimed the unwillingness with which the Industrial Union would fight the Federation, which they had rejected because of the Bolshevik policies it had adopted since 1921, policies which would have made the older leaders cry. W. J. Batterbee, a solicitor from Bargoed, and their Legal Adviser, indicated the new kind of industrial relations being sought. Pithead Committees would attempt to settle all disputes; in the case of failure, the General Secretary and the Executive Council would intervene, and as a last resort an Arbitrator would be consulted. If a majority desired a strike, then this would be done, 'But . . . such words as striking, victimisation and fighting are words that the new union must dispense with forever.'

William Gooding was made Chairman and W. A. Williams the Organising Secretary, both for six months, at annual salaries of £275. Full confirmation was deferred, presumably to allow them to show their worth. Gregory's minor role, at this time, underlines his obscurity in the movement and gives further point to Gooding's paean of praise for Taff-Merthyr:

It was due to Taff-Merthyr Colliery that this new organisation was initiated.

Although many sections in the coalfield were desirous of a change in the administration of their affairs, it was the Taff-Merthyr men who first launched the scheme. Whatever may happen in the future, one can always look back upon Taff-Merthyr as its founders.[10]

The following months saw no slackening in the SWMIU activity. In March, 61 branches were claimed,[11] in April 81 branches,[12] and 35,000 members. And, in the course of May, from 103 to 150 branches.[13] W. A. Williams addressed meetings all over the coalfield as branches sprung up as far apart as Senghenydd and Port Talbot, and Abertillery and Kenfig Hill. There was, of course, a considerable difference in opening up a branch, and claiming a proper membership, and then actually sustaining one; the number of branches claimed, if accurate, might have much to do with the annual salaries of £10 promised to Lodge Secretaries.[14] Then, in April 1927, the union moved their headquarters from Bargoed to Cardiff and appointed four full-time organisers: J. Bevan (Taff-Merthyr), William Gregory (Raglan), G. Reynolds (Treorchy), and W. H. Nuttycombe (Ogmore Vale).[15] The union had funds enough to run two cars,[16] and salaries, it was claimed, in excess of Federation ones, and this despite its very recent origin.[17]

The membership claimed was always an exaggeration. Oliver Harris, for example analysed their returns to the Registrar of Friendly Societies, for 1928. They had claimed in January 1928 a membership of 6,435, rising to 7,635 by December. At 6d. a week in contributions, their income should have been £9,925 10s. 0d. but their returned income was £3,356 13s. 5d., and this was verified by an accountant. Therefore, he concluded, the full average financial membership in 1928 was 2,486.[18] In effect, after the undoubted fluctuations of 1927, the membership of the SWMIU settled down to a figure that ranged between two and six thousand, depending at any particular time on how many pits it controlled, for its success lay almost entirely in its ability to maintain itself, or infiltrate itself into any one particular colliery rather than to any general support. Thus, in January 1936 it could claim a membership figure of 5,991; this declined to 443 by December of that year. The former figure refers to the membership in the Nine Mile Point, Dare and Bedwas collieries which were all lost to the Federation between the autumn of 1935 and the winter of 1936, leaving a rump in the Taff-Merthyr colliery which was boosted by recruits from elsewhere to 589 by December 1937.[19]

Initially, their breakthrough, partial or sustained, benefited from the hard-line taken up by the owners towards the Federation. Churchill, then Chancellor of the Exchequer, had said in September 1926, after meeting with the MFGB and failing to get them to consider a National settlement:

> They were obviously determined to break up the Federation and their arguments against any form of National Agreement were clearly disingenuous.[20]

Victory in December, allied to the success of Spencer's breakaway in the East Midlands coalfield, did nothing to temper the drive towards the destruction of the MFGB whose very power in 1919, when the coal industry had been so effectively arraigned by the Sankey Commission, now drove the owners on to end any threats of nationalisation for another twenty years. Thus, the essential holding of 'Show Cards' on colliery premises, if the SWMF was to rebuild membership, was now actively disrupted by the owners, despite the custom being allowed at any individual colliery in the past, as, according to the Conciliation Board Agreement, every custom allowed before 1915 could continue. The Owners' Association printed two Show Card Reply forms – 'A', to be sent in when any information was received about the holding of a 'Show Card', and giving the intentions of the Company, and, 'B', a reply after the action was taken indicating the extent of disruption, naming the occupation of the card examiners and asking the numbers involved.[21] During May 1927, Evan Williams reminded Association members of their policy decision to refuse 'Show Cards' on colliery premises and to institute legal proceedings if this were done anyway. Circulars reminding individual Companies of this were prepared and sent out so that none might default, for:

> Whatever the consequence, it is the duty of all the Members to protect men who are not desirous of being members of a Trade Union, and it is not to be a condition of employment that the men shall be a member of any Union.[22]

This attitude prevailed throughout 1927 and 1928 wherever the Federation tried to act as they had in the past. There were bitter altercations at the Britannia Colliery, Pengam, with the SWMIU and the SWMF both holding 'Show Cards',[23] and complaints at the Monmouthshire Standing Committee, by such notables as Alderman Arthur Jenkins, concerning police refusal to allow him on to the premises of Blaenserchan Colliery, despite past custom. The Chief Constable of Monmouthshire, Victor Bosanquet, succinctly described the police's attitude, then and later, when he justified this by the fact that there were two unions at the colliery, that the police had to protect men irrespective of their union, that miners had complained of Federation interference and that he had 'read reports that members of the Markham Lodge of the MIU, and miners at other places had been "elbowed out" when applying for lamps and that in other places miners had been turned back because they were not members of the Miners' Federation'. He had ordered this to be stopped.[24]

Many of the suggestions made by the organisation sub-committee of the Federation were, therefore, necessarily concerned with bolstering attempts to hold 'Show Cards' in the face of such pressure, by sending out speakers and paying for them, producing leaflets and issuing circulars advocating methods.[25] If a local district, or group of lodges, proved too active, then the Companies came down hard. The Tredegar Combine Lodges produced pamphlets and handbills on non-unionism and the payment of the political levy by the signing of contracting-in forms,[26] and then, the following year, organised as by custom, simultaneous 'Show Cards' at all the Tredegar Companies' Collieries. The result was an injunction against them and the dismissal of all the Committee men (forty-seven of them) at the Oakdale and Markham Collieries, on the ground of interference with the men. The Federation's legal advice was that an injunction did not prohibit the holding of 'Show Cards' but it did prevent any interference with the workmen.[27] This, of course, was to make an effective 'Show Cards' an impossibility since it gave the legal right but not the practical possibility of it. In this the owners had the support of the 1927 Trade Disputes Act.

Direct collusion between the owner and the SWMIU is, with certain exceptions, not easy to find since both sides were vehement in their denial of any such link. More likely than any direct connections would be an arrangement with 'sympathetic' bodies, such as George Spencer's stronger Nottinghamshire Non-Political Union and Havelock Wilson's Seamen's Union. Wilson, who had opposed the General Strike and whose union was expelled from the TUC in 1928, visited South Wales in the course of 1927, and ardently supported the foundation of a National Non-Political Miners' Union.[28] The EC of the SWMF were concerned about his actions, which extended to circularising colliery companies to urge them to buy copies of the *Non-Political Miners' Journal* to issue to workmen.[29] They referred the matter to the Disputes Committee of the TUC which found that the MIU had been formed during the course of a trade dispute with the encouragement and assistance of the employers' and that the NUS had aided it, promoted it, 'and reaffirmed its intention to give substantial financial assistance'. In fact, Wilson's EC had voted £10,000 to the Non-Political Miners' Union (by 13 to 12) and had it confirmed in Conference.[30] Notwithstanding this, or the attempt to make Frank Hodges the President of the new organisation,[31] a 'National' Union was cutting across if only in its nomenclature the very point that the owners had so fervently supported since 1921. (District agreements and the power to manage individual concerns without being embroiled in wider disputes with wider support for the men, either on a District or on a National basis.) Within the coalfield, therefore, the SWMIU's real strength came from the accretion of individual pits, or parts of pits, rather than in its paper growth down to 1929.

This was managed by a mixture of propaganda and availability. The propaganda consisted of claims that the men employed at the SWMIU-controlled collieries enjoyed better wages than their Federation counterparts,[32] that death benefits were an insurance for relatives, and that the contribution (at 3d. a week in 1932) was low because arbitration ensured that compensation was settled out of court, whilst there was no need for a strike fund.[33] Direct appeals to colliers as a group were comparatively rare, unless there was reason to think that a breakthrough was possible, as in the case of the Ocean Colliery, Treharris, where proximity to Taff-Merthyr emboldened the SWMIU so far as to rent 'the front room of a house in the main street leading from the colliery' where two agents spent four hours on Friday, 11 November 1932. Again the argument was that 'co-operation' was the key to justice, whereas poverty and ruin had come from 'the old system':

> Surely no sane-thinking man can deny that it is through any other cause but STRIKES, STRIKES, STRIKES. . . . Abolish strikes from our industry, and introduce in its place co-operation with a system which will bind both employer and employee to the true findings of a Court of Arbitration in all your disputes and Agreements, which will ultimately mean – increased wages, less disputes, and a better understanding between employer and employee. This system can only be found in one Miners' Union, and that is – The South Wales Miners' Industrial Union.[34]

Tom Andrews, the Secretary of the Taff and Cynon District, wrote to Oliver Harris enclosing the leaflets and explaining that he had advised his District Meeting to ignore 'these pests' rather than advertise their activities. He gives a rare insight into their procedure in an 'unfriendly' area:

We put a watch upon the house. No one entered or even took the trouble to cross to read the invitation to do so. In the enclosed circular they say otherwise. That is a lie. I watched the house myself during the busiest time of the day at the Colliery. No one attempted to read or look. . . .

There have been statements made by these Agents to the workmen of Treharris and other places to the effect that the Company will contribute the whole of the Collective Life Insurance for the first year if they succeed in getting 200 names upon their books from this colliery. They issued a small leaflet, typed to that effect, but I have been unable to get hold of a copy. They were discreet in the distribution of that leaflet and did not distribute in the same way as the one enclosed. The local management say they know nothing of any of the doings of this Union and have no part in it . . .' but '. . . you will quite realise that in this place, Taff-Merthyr – are some men who lend themselves to the very lowest type of procedure. They get on to the local committee and cling there, the drink and the pay entices them. . . . We have only verbal statements respecting the attitude of the local companies to this project. These people on the crossroads and in the clubs say they have the consent of the management concerned.[35]

They were more adept at recruiting labour, *en masse*, as during a colliery dispute or, in small numbers, where a particular colliery wished to call men in from outside their own district rather than employ locally unemployed men who had given offence by their previous actions. In this matter the Ocean Coal Company proved the front runner, especially after the dispute in the Garw Valley and at Nine Mile Point Colliery, over non-unionism, in 1929.[36] During 1930 the Ocean Colliery in Garw was idle for 105 days, and then, again, in 1931, down to 7 November was idle for 119 days, with 15 days for a strike. The lodge sent a memorandum in to the Central Office complaining that throughout this period the 'Non-Pols' worked every shift, having been brought in from outside, given travel vouchers and lodgings and guaranteed work. They cited a case where seven men were brought, on Sunday, 25 October, from Pontypool to fill coal on a Sunday night, in pursuit of management desire since 1927, and flatly against the men's customs.[37] A statement was signed by four of these men, from Pontycymmer, expressing ignorance of the use to which they were put, and explaining how the guarantee of 'regular work whether colliery worked full or not' lured them.[38]

The Executive Council took the matter up with Ocean Coal Company's Head Office. It was pointed out that men being offered jobs in other parts of the coalfield caused bitterness amongst the local unemployed whilst those who refused put their benefit at risk. Even men at work found their places 'badly scamped' and had to spend time ripping instead of filling coal because the company was using 'strangers' to work these places when they were supposedly idle and giving them preferential treatment in other ways.[39] The Company insisted that the local managers, those in charge, denied the complaints anyway and refused to meet with any Combine Committee drawn from its separate pits.[40] In this manner, no tangible results would be achieved with an unrepentant management, for 'While the company emphatically deny working in collusion with the 'Non-Pols', the practice of working in collusion with them continues'.[41] At this stage all that could be done was to call a conference of all lodges under the Ocean Coal Company to discuss further steps.[42]

Fortunately, the truth of these allegations of collusion can be fleshed out, to an extent, by the use of documents that came, at various times, into the Federation's hands. Between August and October 1931, correspondence between the SWMIU's General Secretary and a 'Harry Blount, Esq're' of Pontllanfraith, give chapter and verse, in an episode of which traces remain to us. On 10 August (in reply to the 'lost letter' of the 8th), Gregory writes:

> I can get you work in the Garw Colliery under the Ocean Colliery Company as a collier. The representative came to see me today (Monday) and informed me that there are several good places now opening. Although there is no work there at the moment, our members work regular, even when the colliery is on stop. He suggests that you go to Blaengarw and see for yourself . . . will pay your expenses down there.[43]

However, the Ocean Collieries did not reopen as quickly as Gregory had anticipated so Blount received assurances, a cheque for £2 'as a loan from the organisation', and then a further £2 'to help you over'.[44]

Blount was evidently 'placed' elsewhere and, himself, began to arrange for the employment of colliers at Nine Mile Point but, with his 'rise' in the union, he became too concerned with the rights of the men so that he is reprimanded for being 'bombastic' – 'very much against our wishes and principle' – and given 'a word of advice':

> Do not shout so much when you are in the Public House on a Saturday evening. It was given to us that you were heard to have said last Saturday night that before you had finished with the Officials of the Point, you would straighten them up a bit. . . . Now please be careful where you step, and keep quiet, for your own good.[45]

Clearly, the SWMIU had no wish to offend a management that sustained them in key instances and was able to manufacture employment for them in others. After they had suffered a setback in their hold on the Ocean Company's Dare Colliery, in 1935,[46] Gregory wrote to a T. Roberts, his organiser in the Rhondda, suggesting a canvass of all the men at the Dare to find out their 'sympathies' now that 'they have had some time in which to think the matter over'. He suggested a visit and chat with all so that close contact might lead to 'our re-establishment at the Colliery' and the men might 'feel we are taking a genuine interest in themselves'. The punch came at the end:

> I am today writing Mr. John Griffiths (the General Manager) to see whether there is a possibility to assist us by keeping the Collieries on slack time, as I believe this would assist us immensely.[47]

It was, then, undoubtedly this kind of contact that allowed the SWMIU to exist. The union did try to maintain links with a wider ideology, as in its substitution of May Day by an Empire Day in collieries under its control,[48] its meetings with, and complaints to, the Imperial Policy group in Parliament, headed by Kenneth de Courcey (full support was promised), and the eventual election of George Spencer as its President in April 1936.[49] Two hands, clasped in friendship, over colliery winding gear, with a miners' belt encircling the picture, and the watchword 'Co-operation', was its official insignia. Gregory, himself, seems to have been a formidable figure, with decided views. An interview he granted, in 1935, though it fought shy of revealing any official statistics concerning the SWMIU was clear about his professed aims:

> Our main principle is that we do not believe in strikes. . . . The main plank of our programme is co-operation with the employers. . . . The recent troubles [i.e. of 1934 and 1935] are not a fight to worsen conditions or to lower wages but a fight against Communism which is taking a firm grip of the Miners' Federation in South Wales. It is a fight . . . for the freedom, protection and liberty which we are entitled to as subjects of the great British Empire, under the British flag. . . . Our men are beaten up going to and from their work. And this we intend stopping.
>
> We believe that tyranny can be overcome with the assistance of the Government. There is sufficient legislation for the protection of our members in the Trade Disputes Act of 1927, which we are demanding the Government put into force.[50]

By this stage Gregory was the linchpin, because the short internal history of the SWMIU had been, and would afterwards be, characterised by anything other than 'co-operation'. At the outset, W. A. Williams' heir-apparency to the General Secretaryship had been contested by two rivals who wished to put the matter to a ballot vote,[51] and then in late July 1928 Williams was dismissed as Organising Secretary by the Executive, with Gregory, now General Secretary, explaining the position to the Taff-Merthyr men. Williams, himself, attended this meeting but declared himself mystified as to the cause of his dismissal. Several Lodges approached him, it was reported, to form another union, and he declared he was 'at the service of any body of workmen who felt there was room for a new union'. No amoeba-split occurred, though Williams added that 'he was loathe to say anything which would prove detrimental to the work of the Union, but it was an open secret that numerous Lodges had ceased to exist'.[52] The shake-up continued when, in August, Morgan Lewis of the Britannia Lodge, Pengam, the Vice-President and Trustee of the SWMIU resigned both offices 'owing to internal troubles'.[53]

The union continued with Gooding as President until his death in 1934, when James Jenkins, of Pontypool, was appointed to succeed him *pro tem*.[54] Now the SWMIU were engaged in a crucial struggle to maintain Taff-Merthyr.[55] Within a twenty-six-day period, they received cheques amounting to £875 from George Spencer. The letters from Spencer to Jenkins made the reasons for this considerable financial support quite clear:

> By now I hope there is a great victory in sight. If this can be achieved it will discourage any similar effect elsewhere.

Two weeks later he wrote:

> I do hope the Colliery Company stands firm over this dispute. One good stand of a successful character would change the psychology of South Wales.

That Spencer was acting as a clearing-house for money supplied to him is underlined by these documents, as is the lack of openness about the SWMIU's finances:

> I personally would prefer to make them [i.e. the cheques] out to the Union but G [i.e. Gregory] says it is very inconvenient, and that the amounts would have to be shown as grants; . . . personally, if they are to be made out to persons, it would be better if there were two; . . . I may inform you that Mr

Iestyn Williams [the Secretary of the Coalowners' Association] places great confidence in you, and looks to you to see that business is conducted according to strict business principles, I need say no more about it.[56]

For whatever reasons, and perhaps the SWMF's ability to gain a foothold in Taff-Merthyr was one, the SWMIU was not able to shrug off its internal dissensions. In early 1935, Gregory turned sharply on his own ranks in a memorandum which, significantly enough, was addressed to the agent of the Taff-Merthyr Colliery. Gregory was dissatisfied with the conduct of James Jenkins whose interests, he claimed, kept him tied up in Pontypool (i.e. a shop and two sons at work in Tirpentwys); the pro-tem President was 'entirely lacking of all initiative and fighting spirit. His methods are vacillating and his suggestions hesitant.' Therefore, 'As the position of President is still unfilled [permanently] I am prepared to take the position, *if such is in accordance with your wishes* [my italics], provided a President who will fight back is appointed.'

The General Secretary proceeded to lay down the law about the nomination of a third Trustee and a Vice-President, attacking the suggestions made by his colleagues (one nominee had a family which was '100 per cent Communist', another was disabled), and to ask that a new Executive Council 'be appointed' to break up the 'clickism'. 1935 was a year of retrenchment for the SWMIU and Gregory recommended the reduction of Branch officials' salaries where their contributions did not cover maintenance and 'the Salaries allotted to them by the secret circle'. This latter body is not revealed though a sum of £26 p.a. is mentioned in a document originally attached to the memorandum but subsequently lost.[57]

So, although George Spencer was made President at the Annual Meeting in Cardiff, in 1936, the one figure who had remained, through thick and thin, was Gregory. Not, however, without storing up resentment against his sticking power. During 1936, James Jenkins and W. C. Williams, the former Secretary of the SWMIU Bedwas Lodge who had been dismissed in March, began to hold a series of meetings designed to reveal chicanery within the Industrial Union. Naturally, the SWMF were only too pleased to help in arranging meetings to further the rift they were hoping for in Bedwas. There, and in Bedlinog, accusations against the MIU were fleshed out by these former officials, whilst in Dowlais a meeting called by Williams and Jenkins was disrupted when a bus load of SWMIU men arrived. A free fight ensued.

Thirty-six SWMIU men were charged with incitement to disorder.[58]

The accusations mounted by these ex-MIU officials (four altogether) were published in leaflet form, and included excerpts from the memorandum sent to the colliery agent, W. E. Jayne; the circular published by W. C. Williams promised all:

> Corruption, victimisation, double-dealing, collusion. These are the themes of a story of filth in the South Wales Coalfield which will be unfolded to you within the forthcoming week. Coalowners, public men, Members of Parliament, Peers and others will figure prominently in these disclosures. Within the plot to deprive British workmen of their right to belong to a legitimate Trade Union, the Company Union has its place.
>
> Behind the fabric of British society, with the connivance of legal institutions a plot has been hatched which would make a fitting theme for an Edgar Wallace thriller. In the perpetration of this plot to destroy the liberties of the Welsh miners, thousands of pounds have been supplied, both by English and Welsh coalowners.

Revelations of strike-breaking at Bedwas and Nine Mile Point would follow financial disclosure and 'all these things shall be unfolded to you so that the names of these people shall stink in the nostrils of every decent-minded miner in the South Wales Coalfield'.[59]

The ability of the SWMIU men, at high and low levels, to withstand hostility often stemmed from the cohesion of family groups. William Gregory's brother Eli, was a Trustee of the Union, Mansel Gregory was an Official living in Cardiff, Tom Gregory was William's son, and a Chairman of the Junior Imperial League, Haydn Gregory worked in Bedwas, Harold Adams, Eli's son-in-law, worked in Bedwas. All these, along with George Gregory, were involved in the fray at Dowlais.[60]

Whatever the full truth about the SWMIU's involvement with groups like the 'Cliveden Set', and with the police themselves,[61] the real value of the MIU, throughout, lay in whether or not it could organise a pliable work force for a particular owner. This was the consistency behind all of its activities, and made its interventionist role the cause of violent disputes throughout its existence. And it was here that the SWMF had to take on, and defeat, the SWMIU if its own basic rebuilding was to come to anything.[62] However, between 1927 and 1930, the interconnection of the owners' hostility, the existence of the Industrial Union (and D. B. Jones' smaller Craftsmen's Union) and the almost overwhelming pressures of non-unionism were brought home to the SWMF, particularly in the Garw and Sirhowy Valleys, in such a way that their own weakness was underlined even further.

As part of the SWMF's general drive against non-unionism in early 1927, there had been a brisk campaign of meetings and 'Show Cards' in the Maesteg area. In late May fourteen days' notice was given in order to coerce the defectors into joining but, on their expiry on 4 July, there remained 6 non-unionists, 21 in arrears and 100 members of D. B. Jones' South Wales and Monmouthshire Colliery Enginemen, Boilermen and Craftsmen's Association. Consequently a strike at all the Maesteg Collieries (except for Oakwood where work had only just restarted) now began.[63] About 8,000 men had come out on an issue which quickly resolved itself into the refusal of fifty craftsmen to join the Federation.[64] Finally, on 7 July, the craftsmen did agree to join and the strike was ended. At which point a backlash, that was to become increasingly familiar, hit the Federation – the agent for Messrs. North, the colliery owners, locked the men out on the grounds that work was unavailable. This was a clear indication that the owners were intent on punishing like actions by the SWMF. Nothing could have been more calculated to enrage the 'Lord of Maesteg',[65] its MP, Vernon Hartshorn.

Hartshorn had emerged from the First World War with an enhanced reputation as a responsible 'labour leader' and convinced that the responsibility evinced by official labour during the war would bring its own reward. His dislike for the militancy of the SWMF from 1919 to 1921 led to his resignation from the Vice-Presidency in 1920. Hartshorn was no firebrand, although a convinced Parliamentary Socialist, so with his background of conciliation in mind, one can gauge the vehemence of the words he addressed to the mass meeting at Maesteg:

> As far as I am concerned – and I say it with great deliberation – from this moment forward here is a rebel, a rebel of the deepest dye. Let any of the Coalowners talk to me any more about good relationships, co-operation or good will, and they will hear what I have got to say about them.[66]

What troubled Hartshorn, as a practical man, as much as anything else was the vindictiveness of the owners' action, for nothing could result from it but further strife. D. B. Jones of the Craftsmen claimed that a brass band and 6,000 demonstrators terrified his members into affiliation, not the weight of argument, whilst the editorial column of the *Western Mail* warned that those who struck could not expect collieries to reopen at will,[67] but the lock-out at Maesteg reasserted in Hartshorn's mind the legitimacy of the struggle against the owners. As he argued convincingly in the pages of the *Western Mail* only by extending the struggle begun at Maesteg to the entire coalfield could industrial peace be brought to South Wales. A permanent weakening of the MFGB was not permissible:

> The responsibility of coalowners or others who may seek to foster disruptive influences will be a very grave one indeed. No matter how long it may take, nor what losses may be involved to the coal industry or the community, the work of re-establishing the undisputed supremacy of the Miners' Federation as the sole representative and champion of the Mineworkers shall be done, and done right thoroughly.[68]

For the first time a prominent miners' leader spelled out in precise terms the impossibility of *ever* accepting another miners' union. Not until the late 1930s when Arthur Horner, using a different phraseology, also underlined the momentous implications of such an acceptance were the inchoate, instinctual feelings of the rank-and-file given such clarification. Both Horner and Hartshorn, despite their political differences, were convinced, by their own experiences, that the trade unions were the fundamental bedrock of their political creeds.

The abnormality of the struggle, thought Hartshorn, had caused the abnormal dimensions of the disruption, providing men and leaders with a huge task and one in which failure was impossible 'because failure would mean the disappearance of liberty from the coalfield, and when that issue is made clear neither the workmen nor the leaders will surrender. The power of the wage earners to protect their interests, and the liberty of the wage earner which has no secure foundation except on that power has to be re-established at all costs.'

There were two adverse influences to be isolated – the lethargy that led to non-unionism and 'mongrel organisations' planted in the coalfield by others – 'These spoon-fed organisations, subsidised by quarters hostile to an independent and virile Trade Union and Labour Movement find it not very difficult during the period of reaction following a long struggle, to mislead some workmen'. Hartshorn, flushed with the success at Maesteg, was convinced that they would be uprooted as 'hope and determination' replaced 'inertia', but he was prophetically aware that the struggle would be more 'costly, intensive and prolonged' than ever before. And he knew why.

> This is due entirely to the Coalowners and to the press, both Liberal and Tory, who on this occasion have openly thrown in their power on the side of the influences which are working for the permanent crippling of the SWMF.

> These are the new factors. . . . For the first time during my official con:.ection with the Miners the Coalowners have given encouragement and support to two disruptive sections. The two I refer to are the Craftsmen's Union and the Non-Political Union. These are the two pets of the Coalowners, and through their instrumentality the Coalowners hope to smash the Federation. But by the time we have done with those two new pets, even their fathers the Coalowners will not recognise them.[69]

The *Western Mail* having provided Hartshorn with a platform to preach the guilt of the coalowners, the newspaper reiterated its view, and the claim of the SWMIU, 'that these organisations are not fostered or planted by the coalowners but are the voluntary unions of men who have grown disgusted with the policy of the Federation and who have risen in revolt against the methods which have involved them and the Federation in financial ruin'.[70]

In the meantime, outside the realm of accusation and counter-accusation, eight thousand men remained idle in Maesteg. The SWMIU which had not been, at Maesteg, the principal object of the SWMF's campaign now issued their propaganda in the area.[71] Eventually, on 13 July, work recommenced at the pits with 100 per cent Federation membership assured, though the *Western Mail* now having a running battle with the 'formerly sane leader' Hartshorn bestowed on him its most opprobrious epithet by likening him to Lenin.[72] The exchange closed with a classic confrontation of views so different, that the tenacity with which opposing sides held them goes far to explain the continued reputation as a storm centre that South Wales was to hold in the 1930s.

Hartshorn declared that if the coalowners continued 'their fool's policy of allowing the coal industry to drift to ruin, while at the same time they encourage and support movements to destroy the Miners' Federation, I will fight them with the gloves off and the knuckle dusters on'; while the paper that all, in South Wales, regarded as the spokesman of the owners retaliated: 'We know that it is the declared policy of the Miners' Federation to make private ownership impossible by making the mines unremunerative.'[73] On that irreconcilable basis the lines were drawn.

The victory had been costly both in terms of individual hardship and drainage of both local and central funds. In Garw 2,500 out of the 7,500 miners previously employed were now idle as the pits closed. Hundreds of these men had exhausted all the benefits to which they were entitled over a period of unemployment extending in some cases to two years.[74] A grant of £5,000 was made by the SWMF for distribution to the workmen made idle because of the non-union dispute; the paucity of funds made a larger grant impossible.[75] Obviously no massive anti-Industrial Union drive could be made all over the coalfield, when non-unionism itself proved so tenacious a plant.

The conflicts of 1928 followed a spasmodic rhythm, with the Federation making few inroads into its problem,[76] but 1929 gave notice early on of its more violent and protracted intentions, with the SWMIU making a successful onslaught on what had seemed an entrenched position. Again, the SWMF found itself up against the willingness of the Ocean Coal Company to jettison them in favour of their more accommodating rival, and their legal right, helped by the police, to guard the right to do so.

The Nine Mile Point Colliery, in the lower Sirhowy Valley, Monmouthshire, consisted of three pits – the Rock Vein, the East and the West. The colliery had belonged, in the past, to Burnyeat, Brown & Company, had been acquired by the United National Group in 1927, and in 1928 had been sold to the Ocean Coal Company.[77] Industrial relations had not been good at the colliery for a while and 'during the long period of ownership . . . by Messrs Burnyeat, Brown & Company, disputes and stoppages were all too frequent . . . [so that] it was largely because of these spasmodic outbreaks that the colliery was sold to the Ocean Coal Company for something like a round million'.[78] The latter, with every intention of surviving in the harsh days that had fallen on the coal industry, decided on an abrogation of local customs in order to make the pits more remunerative.[79] The miners' agent, in the locality, estimated that this would have meant a 4s. 6d. a day reduction in the colliers' wages, and an increase in the hours, spent at work, of most grades.[80] The owners had given a month's notice of their intentions and, when the terms were not accepted, the pits closed on 3 November 1928.[81] Fourteen weeks of unemployment were now in store for the colliers of Nine Mile Point.

The Ocean Coal Company was by now experienced in dealing with the Industrial Union so it was not surprising that when the Rock Vein pit reopened on Monday, 28 January, the nineteen men who turned up to work did so under an agreement reached between the Company and the SWMIU. The SWMF had held a meeting at the Workmen's Hall, Cwmfelinfach (the village of the colliery), on Sunday to dissuade men from taking the fifty places of employment available at the colliery. The *Western Mail* warned (erroneously) that men refusing work would 'lose their benefits under the Unemployment Insurance Acts'.[82]

The SWMIU had negotiated a minimum wage for the men working the Rock Vein seam and boasted of this fact though, as Tom Richards pointed out, a minimum wage was assured to every collier by statute. The real issue was over the price-list for the seam since this determined how much more the colliers (who were, of course, pieceworkers) could earn.[83] The Federation was particularly grieved over the Ocean Company's policy of attempting to reduce wages outside the Conciliation Board Agreement, as well as refusing to submit their terms to the Conciliation Board. Richards complained, 'A repetition too often of what is happening in this case will destroy the faith of the workmen in the system of collective agreements, and hasten the return to guerilla warfare days.'[84] The Federation, for the present, were only fighting when the battle was carried to them.

For all that they were assured of support from the men in the locality. The agent of the Ocean Coal Company, Lewis Lewis, had informed the local Labour Exchange that work was available at the colliery for 600 men in the Rock Vein pit and for 700 men in both the East and the West Pits. The Company had been approached by the local branch of the SWMIU to reopen the colliery so, said the Company, in view of the Federation's three month refusal to come to an agreement, they opened negotiations with the Industrial Union though no one seeking work had to join that union prior to his employment.[85] Over the week-end of 1 February to Monday, 4 February, it was reported that some 200 men, mostly from outside districts, were travelling to work at the pits. The SWMF men, anxious for their former jobs, sent their representatives, George Davies (the miners' agent) and William Lewis (the chairman of the Nine Mile Point Lodge) to interview Lewis Lewis. They drew a blank for now they were told that they did not represent anyone in the Company's eyes, that men should first apply for work, on an individual basis. The colliery agent undercut what Tom Richards had called 'the generally admitted first function of a Trade Union in dealing with the terms and conditions of employment of its members',[86] when he insisted that: 'The Management was offering terms to persons as individuals at present, but, of course, if those individuals, after obtaining work formed themselves into a union, then the Company would discuss terms with the union's representative.'[87]

The SWMF called a special meeting of the Executive Council to consider the whole position. They declared themselves convinced that 'the Company's attitude violates every practice and custom in the coalfield in settling terms and conditions between employers and workmen'.[88]

The support guaranteed, the men kept up their spirits. On the Tuesday only a dozen men were at work. A body of men from the Rhymney Valley who had arrived for work, cried off after the local miners had protested to them. Those who ignored the protest were jeered and pushed, at the end of the shift, by a crowd of over a thousand. Each workman's home was in need of police protection.[89]

On the Wednesday three local men and about six from the Rhymney Valley went to the colliery. When they emerged from the pit a '500 strong crowd' were waiting for them with chants and stones. The police whose number had been increased (to forty), and who were under the personal supervision of the Chief Constable of Monmouthshire and a Superintendent Spendlove, initiated a baton charge to clear a way for the three workers. When the police charged there were considerable numbers of women and children in the crowd – 'Some who tried to resist the charge of the police were felled to the ground, several with blood streaming from gashes on the head.' The three workers were then allowed home whilst the Rhymney Valley men were taken to the train, and escorted home on arrival at Pontllanfraith by the police.[90]

The expense involved in guarding such a small number of Industrial Union men was obviously not commensurate with the results achieved, nor had there been any sign of weakening in the Federation ranks. This last, however, could not be guaranteed if the dispute was prolonged, so a joint meeting was arranged by W. P. Thomas (the General Manager of the Ocean Coal Company) and Tom Richards.[91] At the pit head the police were increased from forty to sixty. On the night of 13 February the conditions agreed upon by the Company and the Federation were submitted to the men. Pre-stoppage conditions would be in force until 1 March when there was to be a joint report, on the terms offered, by two representatives from each side and their award as independent arbitrators was to be retrospective and binding. For the Federation preference was to be given to the workmen previously engaged in re-employment but there was to be no interference with those already at work. The terms were hardly glorious and though the Federation had achieved some concessions these were slight compared with the recognised existence of the SWMIU in the colliery.[92]

Company unionism had become an issue that, in communities

almost totally dependent on the coal industry for their livelihoods, had far wider than merely industrial implications. An interesting debate now took place over the right of the community to break the law in pursuit of what it deemed just objectives.

The Monmouthshire Standing Joint Committee's Labour members attacked the conduct of the police at Nine Mile Point in baton-charging and in their subsequent search of people's houses. Aneurin Bevan, who had won a seat for Tredegar on the County Council in March 1927,[93] made one of the remarkable speeches for which he was later to attain fame. He said that 'affairs had reached a point in this district in which the police were rapidly losing any control of the civilian population at all. The point that would be reached would be that these miners who, a few years ago, were being praised as capable of the utmost heroism, would show a bigger heroism against the brutal action of the police. An utter contempt for the law was being created. . . . The men went to work there largely in consequence of the criminal lying of the South Wales press. If anybody was to be charged it should have been the Editor of the *Western Mail*. They broadcast a deliberate lie that there was work to be obtained for two thousand people, and the same lie was put on cinema screens at Tredegar, and people started to go to Nine Mile Point, and some actually started before they discovered the real reason why the collieries were idle.' Bevan was convinced that 500 to 1,000 men would not be scattered by fifty or sixty police, except voluntarily, for 'we should eat them up in a conflict of physical force. What drives them away was that there still remains, *unfortunately*, a degree of law-abiding conduct amounting to a broken spirit among the miners of the district.'[94]

The Chief Constable confined himself to remarking that the charge was short and sharp. However, the *Western Mail* launched a slashing attack on the Standing Joint Committee's vilification of the police since that body's prejudice 'demonstrates the utter unfitness of Socialist-controlled bodies to be entrusted with the administration of the force necessary to the maintenance of public order'.

A similar divergence of views was taken on the meaning of the strike. Either work was available for 2,000 men who, in a misguided folly, refused it at the time only to have to accept it later on terms they could have had before, or to accept work from the beginning would have meant the end of the men's union as a negotiating body. Bevan emphasised the dilemma of the men along with their reasons for refusing this work when he wrote:

Mr Lewis was trying to terrorise the miners of Nine Mile Point into accepting his conditions of employment by the threat to fill their places with other men, but if the worker and the employer do not recognise each other's status, then work, 'in the practical sense of the term is "not available"', and 'lastly, work is not made "available" to me if, on taking it, I have to violate every principle of good conduct, offend the moral code, and break down those standards which protect the lives of me and my kind.'

Therefore, not in the industrial, nor in the legal, nor in the moral meaning of the term was work available for two thousand men at Nine Mile Point.[95]

Bevan, like Hartshorn before him, was insisting on giving a dispute, ostensibly about a price-list, a much wider importance. No matter, though, how powerful their rhetoric, Federation officials were to remain relatively powerless in the face of concerted attacks to alter established conditions. At Nine Mile Point the SWMIU continued in existence with the SWMF until 1935. Rebuilding had to come first if any limited bargaining power still left to them, could be utilised. Whenever they stepped up their action, in this respect, the owners reacted as if a first-line of defence was being broached, with most costly results so far as the Federation were concerned.

When the General Election of May 1929 had been concluded, the SWMF once more moved on to the offensive, especially as the SWMIU was issuing manifestoes appealing 'to the womenfolk to see that their husbands and sons join the Industrial Union' in order to ensure that the better trade conditions should not be spoiled.[96] Efforts made at Taff-Merthyr bore no fruit at this stage,[97] so they proceeded with a cautious determination elsewhere, especially where earlier ground seemed to have been lost and where employment was increasing.

Thus, the Garw District had, as early as March, received the Executive Council's support in the form of money and speakers to organise men at the Meiros Colliery; in April a deputation from the District led by its chairman, Charles Forester, had requested a grant to carry on their campaign of 'Show Cards' and meetings; so well was the business going that in June financial assistance was promised to the Garw men if they were refused work after a termination of the non-unionist question.[98] By August 700 men at Raglan Colliery, William Gregory's old colliery, had rejoined the Federation although, as Ted Williams, the agent, reported the MIU still had friends in the management, trying to continue to deduct MIU dues from the pay.[99]

The campaign in this District had gathered enough steam for the men employed in most of the local collieries to hand in fourteen days' notice

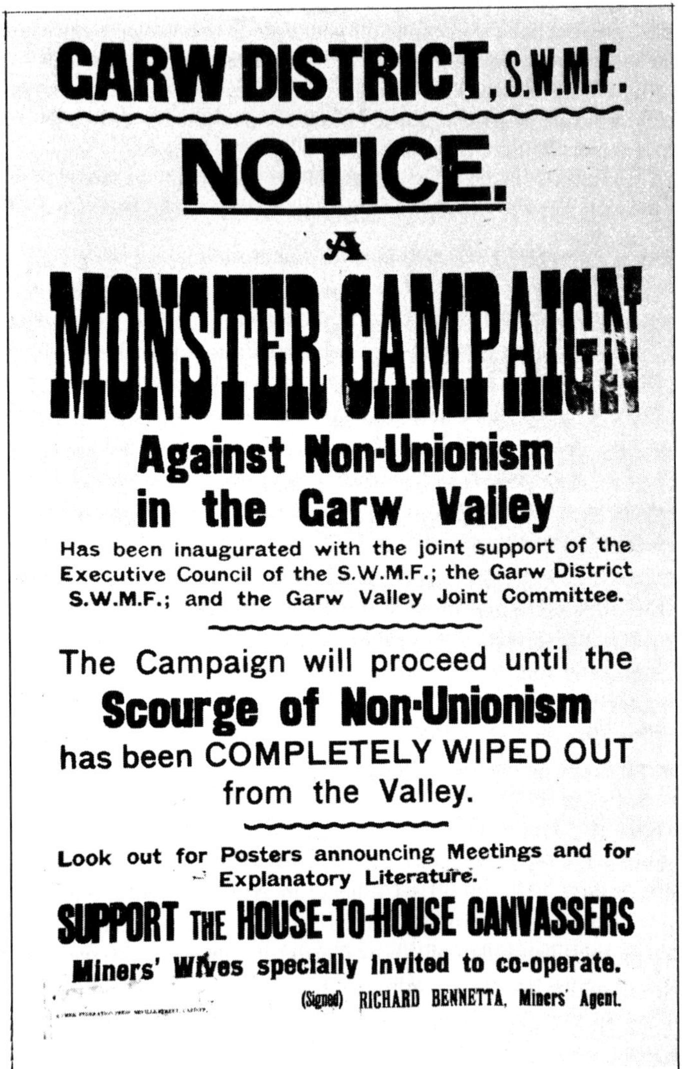

GARW DISTRICT, S.W.M.F.

NOTICE.

A

MONSTER CAMPAIGN

Against Non-Unionism
in the Garw Valley

Has been inaugurated with the joint support of the Executive Council of the S.W.M.F.; the Garw District S.W.M.F.; and the Garw Valley Joint Committee.

The Campaign will proceed until the
Scourge of Non-Unionism
has been COMPLETELY WIPED OUT
from the Valley.

Look out for Posters announcing Meetings and for Explanatory Literature.

SUPPORT THE HOUSE-TO-HOUSE CANVASSERS

Miners' Wives specially invited to co-operate.

(Signed) RICHARD BENNETTA, Miners' Agent.

Garw Valley non-unionist campaign, 1929 (poster).

from 7 October to secure a 100 per cent membership in the valley. For the second time in 1929, though in differing circumstances, the SWMF was to find itself embroiled in a direct clash with the owners who now regarded any non-unionist campaign as a direct attack on their legal right to employ whatever labour they wished irrespective of the union to which the men belonged.

Almost immediately the SWMIU issued a statement to the effect that the pits were open for work irrespective of union membership; the counter-blast from Tom Richards at the Workmen's Hall, Blaengarw, said that the Federation would soon 'be back where it was in 1926'.[100] The campaign affecting three pits and 2,500 men covered the Ogmore Valley, Maesteg and the Garw Valley itself, where Ted Williams had appealed to churches, chapels and clubs to support the Federation.[101] At Pontycymmer, 2,000 miners and their wives had supported the strike by a show of hands. The Industrial Union men had been reduced to twenty-seven, so it was a confident Ted Williams who was reported as saying that 'he firmly believed the strike would be settled in 24 hours. He had the chapels, churches, clubs and every institution in the Garw Valley behind him in this struggle, which would be carried on until they had a clean sheet.'[102]

At a meeting of the South Wales Joint Conciliation Board the owners had told the SWMF that the dispute was 'outside the purview of the Board'.[103] However, as the struggle carried on, the Coal Owners' Association granted 'a special indemnity of one shilling per ton to the Colliery Companies involved, in addition to the fixed rate of 1s. 8d. a ton', making the fight central from their viewpoint as well.[104]

By Tuesday, 22 October, the non-unionist dispute was over in Ogmore Vale though there was no restart at work. In the Garw Valley, some twenty-one men, now protected by a large force of police, remained outside the Federation, working in the Ocean Colliery, Blaengarw, and the Ffaldau Colliery, Pontycymmer. The men were members of the Craftsmen's Union. On that Tuesday afternoon, four of them, escorted by six policemen and two officers in front, and a 'strong escort' behind, left the pit to face a shouting demonstration of about 2,000 people. The reporter from Cardiff was duly impressed by the resulting pandemonium: 'First it was a dull roar, then a howl, which was followed by savage hissing. The women seemed possessed by frenzy as they beat a barbaric tattoo with their feet on the corrugated roofs of the garden sheds and poured imprecations on the heads of the workers.' The men who had worked were taken home safely, though as four of them approached their homes at The Avenue, Pontycymmer, women at the back of the houses signalled their approach by 'the loud beating of tin cans, kettles and frying-pans, a great deal of booing and jeering'.

Women seem to have taken a prominent part in the demonstrations in this valley, undoubtedly because, with unemployment benefits unavailable and poor law relief exhausted, they felt a special grievance against the small number who had driven 2,500 men to hand in their notices. Here, anyway, the SWMIU propaganda had fallen on stony female hearts.[105]

The following day a large body of imported police escorted the men home in an imposed silence. These scenes were repeated throughout the week as three 'blacklegs' kept working.[106] The SWMF paid the strikers 10s. that week, with smaller grants to wives and daughters, and, the following week made the decision to pay out money to the strikers at the equivalent to unemployment benefit rate. This was a new departure in Federation policy on non-union strikes. The outraged *Western Mail* consoled itself with the reflection that this switch 'raises the interesting question how the Federation is to deal with any financial problem which may be created by a prolongation of the Garw strike or by an extension of the strike policy to other areas'.[107]

The same thought cannot have been far from the minds of the SWMF leaders for at their meeting on 2 November, Enoch Morrell reported that several collieries now had a 100 per cent leadership. Work should restart on Monday.[108] Although Morrell had congratulated the men, the officials, and their wives on the patience they had exhibited, the mass meeting of the men on Sunday night, 3 November, to call off the three weeks' strike was rather stormy. Many were discontented that the strike was called off whilst some men remained in the Craftsmen's Union and they heckled their leaders, Charles Gunter, the local chairman, as well as Ted Williams. Gunter put a bold face on it by pointing out that 583 men had rejoined the Federation since the strike began. Non-unionism was cleared in the valley whilst the numbers of the Non-Political Union or the Craftsmen's Union had been reduced to negligible proportions. Ted Williams was more to the point, however:

> The Executive considered that as the Garw Valley had made its full contribution to the coalfield problem they should not prolong the strike any further. As far as non-unionism was concerned, they had stamped it out in the Garw Valley, a fortnight ago, and they had since been directing their efforts to eliminate craft unionism from the valley.

The Garw men had received Federation 'dole' for the first time in the organisation's history because the issues affected the coalfield as a whole. The only way of prolonging the struggle would have been to withdraw the safety men, thereby flooding the pits, or to use 'more extreme methods'. The former would have resulted in the pits being manned by the armed forces, the latter, physical pressure, was self-defeating. Once more the awareness of the men that they were engaged in absolutely basic self-defence can be seen in Williams' otherwise rather inflated statement, that 'they had gained one of the greatest victories in Trade Union history'. Others characterised it as 'industrial cannibalism' which had failed.[109]

Rearguard actions of this sort could not be extended across the coalfield if each one was to prove any financial cost. The skirmishing between the rivals over the following three years was often vigorous, but inconsequential. The SWMF remained too feeble to root out the SWMIU, not fully able to wipe away non-unionism even where an individual lodge proved militant in its desire to do so,[110] and hampered all the way by adverse legal decisions.[111] Continued failure to make an impact at Taff-Merthyr and a protracted strike at Bedwas[112] meant that their weapons of action in 1930 were blunt indeed.[113] They were reliant, almost entirely, on the ability of individual Lodges to maintain control. A common, because not outstanding, example could be that of the Windber Colliery Lodge, Cwmdare, whose activities in organising men were not spectacular, nor, in the short term, rewarding but which show the dogged persistence necessary.

In early January 1928 the Committee discussed whether 'it was now desirable to reorganise the workmen back again into the union'. The decision to rebuild led them on over the next few years to innumerable 'Show Cards', reduction in entrance fees, propaganda meetings. Then, in the course of 1930, the 'Show Cards' scrutineers reported a reduction in the number of non-unionists from 54 to 27 (almost half of whom were boys) and recommended that letters be written to their wives or parents to persuade them to join. Not so dramatic an event as a march or a riot but, equally, the utilisation of social pressure within a community. By June 1931 the success of the previous year had evaporated; in 1932 'a short committee meeting was held to consider the best way and means to increase the membership of the Lodge Federation. It was decided to ask every member to gather every name of those in arrears and also non-unionists and to question them of their intention with regard to their Trade Union' -- the tone was that of an outraged parent; the cycle continued in 1933, 1934 and 1935.[114]

So, despite whatever efforts were made the numbers of those employed in the coalfield who were in the Federation remained, constantly, low. There were some 75,480 in the SWMF at the end of 1930; this dipped to 62,089 in December 1931 and was still only 63,337 at the beginning of 1934.[115] This is the chief explanation for the vacillation with which the EC conducted negotiations over wages and hours in 1930, and with which they finally led the coalfield into the only coalfield-wide stoppage of the 1930s, that of January 1931. This weakness had for four years been the cause of increasing disaffection amongst its Left-wing militants as well. The coalfield strike proved to be the zenith of that discontent.

NOTES

1. *Western Mail*, 7 May 1928.
2. *Merthyr Express*, 1 October 1927.
3. *South Wales News*, 27 September 1927.
4. *Merthyr Express*, 8 January 1927.
5. *Ibid.*, 15 January 1927.
6. Members Rule Book of SWMIU (SWMF files).
7. *Rhondda Leader*, 23 October 1926 – Captain Lionel Lindsay, the Chief Constable, had organised a baton charge to disperse the demonstrators; several people were knocked unconscious.
8. *Ibid.*, 8 January 1927.
9. *Ibid.*, 12 February 1927; *Merthyr Express*, 12 February 1927.
10. *Merthyr Express*, 26 February 1927. Further light on its origins may be its extensive publicisation in the *Merthyr Express* – owned by the Seymour Berry Combine which was the head of 'the most powerful capitalist combination in the South Wales coalfield ... the Berry-Llewellyn-Rhondda group. This is not a combine in the ordinary sense of being a registered company, but it is more powerful and its influence is more far-reaching than any of the formally organised combines in the coalfield. The interests of this group extend like red threads through the mesh of capitalism in South Wales, and, as in a tangled skein, it is impossible to say where they begin and where they end. They extend from coal to steel, patent fuel companies, transport shipping, engineering, banking, finance, etc. Mr H. Seymour Berry is a director of 24 South Wales colliery companies with an annual output of about 13 million tons (or a quarter of the total coal output of South Wales).' D. J. Williams, *op. cit.*, p. 99.
11. *Ibid.*, 12 March 1927.
12. *Ibid.*, 2 April 1927.
13. *Ibid.*, 9 April 1927; 7 and 21 May 1927. The variations and exaggerations render these figures meaningless except as propaganda.

14. *Ibid.*, 26 February 1927.
15. *South Wales News*, 7 April 1927.
16. *Merthyr Express*, 9 April 1927.
17. See the attack on the financial sources (i.e. the owners) of the SWMIU by A. J. Cook and S.O. Davies, at Trelewis; *Merthyr Express*, 23 April 1927. Presumably this referred to Lodge Secretaries because Tom Richards' salary, on his death, was £700 p.a.: SWMF EC Minutes, 22 November 1931.
18. Circular No. 95, SWMF Circulars.
19. Registry of Friendly Societies. SWMIU and Benefit Society file, 1936–7. There are no membership returns available at the PRO, whilst this file is the only one on the SWMIU possessed by the Registry of Friendly Societies. The others were, it seems, destroyed when the SWMIU merged with the SWMF in June 1939. The only source of income given in this file is that of members' contributions (£1,245 in 1936) but an attached Auditor's Report mentions £141 15s. 10d., as a portion of income received from other organisations, under the heading *Sundry Grants*, the remainder of which (not specified) being paid to the General Secretary, personally, for use for the benefit of the Union.
20. Quoted in Patrick Renshaw *The General Strike* (1975), p. 232.
21. Show Card Reply Forms (4 volumes of them) in papers of Monmouthshire and South Wales Coalowners' Association.
22. Minutes of the Monmouthshire and South Wales Coalowners' Association, 3 May 1927. This was, of course, precisely the case where the SWMIU ruled the roost.
23. *Merthyr Express*, 9 April and 21 May 1927.
24. *South Wales News*, 23 June 1927.
25. SWMF EC Minutes, 8 and 27 April, 27 May and 8 August 1927.
26. Pamphlet and handbill announcing 'Show Cards' (6 and 7 December 1927) in Papers of Coalowners' Association.
27. SWMF EC Minutes, 20 September 1928. Aneurin Bevan was the Chairman of the Combine and he emphasised that there had been no interference.
28. *Western Mail*, 8 July 1927.
29. SWMF EC Minutes, 8 November 1928.
30. SWMF Circulars. No. 7 (n.d.) *Workers' Life*, 15 July 1927.
31. *Western Mail*, 8 July 1927. Hodges, who had been nominated by 'branches' in Kenfig Hill and Mountain Ash ('We remember the past services he wholeheartedly and ungrudgingly rendered to us and the contemptible manner in which he has been treated'), refused the post but did warmly recommend the new union – 'There is no doubt that the men are demanding new leaders and evidence is in abundance that they will require new leaders. There is a growing feeling among the men that their present leaders do not and cannot help them. . . . When I have thoroughly surveyed the position and weighed up the possibilities I shall give an answer, and that answer will be entirely dictated by my judgement as to whether, by my accepting this proffered position, I can co-operate with the miners to improve both their lot and that of their industry. . . . The mere fact of the controversy that would arise from my acceptance of the position would not in the slightest degree deter me from helping the miners to the maximum of my ability.' (See *Merthyr Express*, 18 June and *South Wales News*, 20 June 1927). And Sir Samuel Instone (who owned Bedwas Colliery) wrote:

If Mr Hodges accepts it will in my opinion be a milestone in the affairs of the coal industry . . . [he] enjoys the confidence of owners and men alike. . . .' (*Letter* to the *Morning Post*, 21 June 1927).

32. SWMF EC Minutes, 19 November and 3 December 1932.
33. SMWIU leaflet addressed to workmen of the Abercynon Collieries (date is 1932). SWMF files.
34. SWMIU leaflet addressed to workmen of the Ocean Colliery, Treharris (date is 1932).
35. Letter from T. Andrews to Oliver Harris, 11 November 1932. SWMF files.
36. See below pp. 129–36.
37. Memorandum of the Garw Ocean Lodge, by Alf. Davies, SWMF files.
38. Statement in SWMF files.
39. *Letters* from Oliver Harris to W. P. Thomas of the Ocean Coal Company Limited, 7 and 20 November 1931; 1 January 1932.
40. *Letters* from W. P. Thomas to Oliver Harris, 11 and 23 November 1931; 22 January and 11 March 1932.
41. *Letter* to Oliver Harris from R. Benetta (miners' agent of Garw District), 10 December 1931.
42. *Letters* from Alf Davies (Secretary of the Ocean Combine Committee) to Oliver Harris, 23 November 1931, 19 March 1932. At the Conference held on 12 March 1932 ten out of fourteen pits were represented.
43. There are photostats of letters, supplied, it seems, by a 'friendly' source. See a letter from William Gregory to H. Blount of Pontllanfraith, in which the latter is asked to copy out an appended note disclaiming a letter (of 8 August 1931 – now lost) in which travelling vouchers and the agent of the Ocean Colliery Company, Nantymoel, is mentioned. This letter had, apparently, been shown to Mr Davies, the Agent in question.
44. *Letters* from William Gregory to H. Blount, 10 August, 14 August, 20 August and 18 September 1931. SWMF files.
45. *Letters* from Gregory to Blount, 30 October and 14 December 1931.
46. See below pp. 290–2.
47. *Letter* from Gregory to T. Roberts, 3 February 1936.
48. *Western Mail*, 30 April 1929.
49. *Ibid.*, 23 October 1935 and 7 April 1936.
50. *Stay Down Miner* (1936), Montagu Slater, pp. 29–30. Slater, admittedly not a friendly reporter, described the SWMIU's offices at 177 St Mary Street, Cardiff, as 'cramped' with a couple of junior clerks and a typist, whilst Gregory was a 'short, grizzled man' with a 'rough accent, overlaid, with the sort of refinement that comes of association with conservative manufacturers'.
51. *Merthyr Express*, 1 October 1927.
52. *Ibid.*, 28 July, 1928. No ballot was held so far as we can ascertain. Presumably Gregory's superior organisational talent had emerged. The gossip columnist from Nelson wrote: 'I knew nothing whatever of the reasons which actuated the Union to "drop the pilot", but I do think that to dispense with the services of such a live wire as Mr Williams . . . is not exactly helpful to the future of the union . . . a non-political organisation which has undergone many changes since its birth at the latter end of 1926.'

53. *Western Mail*, 15 August 1928. Gooding had moved from chairman to president in the course of the year.
54. *Ibid.*, 10 April 1934.
55. See below pp. 211–43.
56. *Letters* from George Spencer to James Jenkins, 5 and 19 November 1934, SWMF files. Spencer had long nursed a grievance against the 'psychology of South Wales'. See Alan R. Griffin, *The Nottinghamshire Miners* (1962).
57. Copy of a document, entitled *Points for Consideration* signed by Gregory and sent to W. E. Payne. SWMF files. There is no date, but, from the context, it must be early 1935, probably February.
58. *Western Mail*, 7 and 28 April 1936. *Merthyr Express*, 2 and 30 May 1936. Six of the accused were near relatives of William Gregory. Two panels of magistrates failed to agree on the case and it was eventually dismissed.
59. This was read, from the leaflet (one of eleven produced) by the SWMIU's defence counsel at the hearing. *Merthyr Express*, 20 June 1936. Only eight of these leaflets have come to light. For a discussion of whether the SWMIU was a company union or a non-political union, see *Bulletin* of the Society for the Study of Labour History, No. 35, Autumn 1977 pp. 30–1; No. 36, Spring 1978 pp. 22–32 No. 37, Autumn 1978 p. 13. We are of the view that, irrespective of whether it had the support of one or fifty companies it remained a company union and for that reason it deserved to be called a 'scab' union. See also A. R. and C. P. Griffin, 'The Non-Political Trade Union Movement' in *Essays in Labour History*, Vol. 3 (1977).
60. *Merthyr Express*, 30 May 1936.
61. Interview with W. H. Crews (6 June 1969). And see *Western Mail*, 20 June 1936, where, at the Glamorgan Joint Standing Committee, it was alleged that Captain Lionel Lindsay had met with Gregory at the house of a 'titled lady' near Newport. Presumably this was a reference to Lady Rhondda.
62. There were some easy successes. An SWMIU meeting at Mardy was completely disrupted, and in Treorchy A. J. Cook held a mass meeting simultaneously with an SWMIU meeting in the Parc and Dare Hotel; Spencer, though, announced to speak, did not appear. *Rhondda Leader*, 2 and 23 April 1927. At the Aberbaiden Colliery, Kenfig Hill, terrorisation of those who had been involved in 'blacklegging' was reported, and social ostracism, which caused a local Federationist to write that the local unemployed were being ousted and that 'it only goes to show that the "strength" of this new union is expressed in the support they expect from their employers for the excellent service they rendered in helping to defeat their own comrades, for the personnel of the new union in this district is as well known by myself as anyone.' *South Wales News*, 1 and 7 April 1927.
63. *South Wales News*, 4 July 1927.
64. *Western Mail*, 5 July 1927.
65. This was A. J. Cook's phrase in reply to Hartshorn's jibe of 'The Emperor of the Rhondda'. *South Wales News*, 13 November 1921.
66. *Western Mail*, 7 July 1927.
67. *Loc. cit.*, 8 July 1927.
68. Hartshorn had, for years, been given a platform for his views in the *South Wales News*; now the *Western Mail* afforded him the same chance. Although both papers disagreed with him, this is a firm indicator of the cogency of his arguments

and their belief that his was one of the more 'responsible' voices in the coalfield, on the men's side anyway.

69. *Western Mail*, 12 July 1927.
70. *Idem*.
71. *Ibid.*, 13 July 1927. Precisely the development feared most, as by this time a week's wages had been lost.
72. *Ibid.*, 14 July 1927.
73. *Ibid.*, 16 July 1927.
74. *South Wales News*, 19 July 1927.
75. SWMF EC Minutes, 19 July 1927. The owners broke with their past traditions in being willing to pay North's Navigation Company's costs in an appeal brought by the workmen against an award of damages made to North's over a 'breach of contract' incurred in the dispute. Coalowners' Association minutes, 1 November 1927. All of which lends further point to Hartshorn's declaration to a meeting in Maesteg that: 'I do not think that this is really North's policy but that of the Coalowners' Association and I say that whether I live one year or ten years the remainder of my life will be devoted to their overthrow.' *Western Mail*, 7 July 1927.
76. See above pp. 84–5.
77. W. J. Anthony-Jones, *op. cit.*, pp. 63–4.
78. *Merthyr Express*, 16 February 1929. But Anthony-Jones, *loc. cit.*, believes that the colliery 'prior to the 1926 General Strike . . . had enjoyed a long period of industrial harmony'.
79. Anthony-Jones, *op. cit.*, p. 64. The owners estimated there was a loss of 3s. 5d. a ton on coal produced; they proposed an abandonment of payment for 'through coal' and a reversion to the pre-1916 practice of paying only for 'large'.
80. *Western Mail*, 6 February 1929.
81. *Ibid.*, 29 January 1929.
82. *Western Mail*, 6 February 1929. This newspaper continued to claim this despite vociferous denials by the SWMF. Aneurin Bevan wrote to them (*Western Mail*, 19 February 1929) that, 'The Umpire, set up by the Ministry of Labour, had ruled that a genuine offer of work had not been made to the Nine Mile Point workmen. Work was therefore "Not available", in the Employment Exchange sense of the term.' Nevertheless 600 men did eventually exhaust their benefit and the EC had to grant them £1,000 to relieve their distress.
83. *Western Mail*, 6 February 1929.
84. *Ibid.*, 31 January 1929.
85. *Ibid.*, 1 February 1929. This, however, seems a meaningless distinction since acceptance of employment automatically meant membership of the Industrial Union, as at Taff-Merthyr.
86. *Ibid.*, 21 January 1929.
87. *Ibid.*, 4 February 1929. Lewis Lewis was in this way allowing individual acceptance of 'SWMIU' negotiated terms before that individual worker was in the Union.
88. SWMF EC Minutes, 5 February 1929.
89. *Western Mail*, 6 February 1929. The 'foreigners' who decided against work on arrival were breakfasted in the Workmen's Hall and entertained by the local brass band.

90. *Ibid.*, 7 February 1929. Where there are conflicting accounts of numbers involved in demonstrations we have adopted the lower figure or indicated that it is not definite. As a result of this 'riot' questions were asked in the House, by both sides.
91. *Ibid.*, 9 February 1929.
92. *Ibid.*, 14 February 1929 and Anthony-Jones, *op. cit.*, p. 64. The Arbitrators reported in favour of the 'yardage' system of payment, not 'tonnage' as desired by the Federation; the hewers had to take the company's price-list; hauliers received an extra allowance for extra hours.
93. *Western Mail*, 12 March 1927; The announcement ran – 'Mr Aneurin Bevan arrives! Socialist critic of Socialists.'
94. *Ibid.*, 14 February 1929. In 1933 Bevan crossed swords with the official Labour Party in South Wales in his suggested scheme for the enrolment of British youth in a movement that would combine discussion, cycling, hiking and physical training. The body would have been in opposition to 'Fascism which is . . . growing in South Wales'. Working-class groups would train, take an oath of allegiance, and not be affiliated to the ILP, LP, CP or any existing political body. See *Western Mail*, 20, 22 and 28 May 1933. In fact some 'militia' groups did form (see below, pp. 192–8).
95. *Letter* from Bevan, *Western Mail*, 19 February 1929. In the same issue, the SWMIU president, complained that the 'coalowners instead of fighting side by side with the non-political workers, seemed to have backed the Miners' Federation'. *Letter* from William Gooding. This, in view of the facts, can only have been meant as a disavowal of any formal connection with the owners.
96. *Western Mail*, 18 June and 18 September 1929.
97. See below pp. 212–13.
98. SWMF EC Minutes. 14 March, 13 April and 3 June 1929.
99. *Ibid.*, 1 August 1929. The return to the Federation was only a prelude to a two-and-a-half month strike in 1930 over a reversion to the pre-1926 price list. A yardage system had been substituted when the SWMIU had moved in. *Western Mail*, 18 July 1930.
100. *Western Mail*, 19 October 1929. Vernon Hartshorn was serving on the *Simon Commission on India*.
101. *Ibid.*, 21 October 1929: At the Wyndham Colliery, Ogmore Vale, the non-unionists had already been reduced to four, when the notices took effect on 19 October.
102. *Idem.*
103. *Ibid.*, 23 October 1929.
104. Anthony-Jones, *op. cit.*, p. 59.
105. *Western Mail*, 23 October 1929. It was claimed that the resolve of the MIU men was stiffened by the personal grievances held against the Federation by them.
106. Ted Williams, the agent, objected strongly to this show of force, particularly to the numbers of 'foreign' policemen present. This objection probably had more to do with their extra numbers than with any preference for local policemen. 123 summonses were issued in the aftermath. *Daily Worker*, 17 January 1930.
107. *Western Mail*, 30 October 1929.
108. SWMF EC Minutes, 2 November 1929.
109. *Western Mail*, 4 November 1929. Williams thought that work could be restarted

within a week or two. At Maesteg the fourteen days' strike notice had been withdrawn after a 'clean sheet' had been obtained.

110. In March 1932 a campaign at the International Colliery, Blaengarw, ended with twelve of the 600 employed outside the Federation and notices handed in. The SWMF had to consider whether to finance the stoppage and decided 'that the matter was bristling with difficulties and with a possibility that if some stoppages were financed and others were not a situation would be created that would tend to discourage lodges from pursuing their normal activities to increase the membership. With our limited resources it would be impossible to give financial assistance to all the lodges that may desire to take strike action.' SWMF EC Minutes, 23 April 1932, and *Western Mail*, 22 March 1932.

111. For example, at Newport County Court, in Bedwas Navigation Company v. Bowen and others (the twenty-four defendants were members of the Bedwas Lodge), £5 damages were awarded against the men for their attempt to hold a 'Show Cards' at the colliery in June 1929, on the grounds that the 1926 Conciliation Board Agreement, and Section 3 of the Trade Disputes Act of 1906, permitted the holding of 'Show Cards' but that the 1927 Trade Disputes Act forbade intimidation. Then in April 1931, the Federation lost a test case against the Bedwas Colliery Company in the Chancery Division when members of the lodge were found guilty of conspiring to commit illegal acts at a 'Show Cards' in February 1930. Mr Justice Bennett allowed that they were entitled to hold a 'Show Cards' but that pickets were not entitled to insist on workmen answering their questions or that they produce their cards; nor were men to be prevented from working by not allowing safety lamps to be issued. Federation costs were £20,000. *Western Mail*, 13 January 1930 and 2 April 1931.

112. See below pp. 213, 315.

113. They were prepared to finance District action against non-unionism short of a stoppage. Thus £350 was granted the Garw District. SWMF EC Minutes, 13 May 1932.

114. Windber Colliery Committee Book Minutes: 24 January 1928, 6 June and 4 July 1929; 11 and 26 March 1930; 20 April 1932. Books in possession of the family of the late E. W. Davies (Secretary), Llwydcoed, Aberdare.

115. SWMF Annual Returns to the Registrar-General. *Loc. cit.*

CHAPTER FIVE

The Fate of 'Little Moscow'

The push for a revision of the rules of the SWMF was seen, in 1927 and 1928, as the means of reorganising the Federation as a first step towards revitalising the MFGB. The CP and the MMM had had influence in framing policy in South Wales, in 1926, and its membership grew in the aftermath of the General Strike.[1] The period was one of confusion as the great national struggle was reduced to local fights to maintain past standards, with, at the same time, the CP attempting to maintain a wider impetus so as to salvage something out of the wreckage. MMM conferences were held, in South Wales and elsewhere, in an attempt to derive lessons from the events of 1926.[2] This was linked to the demands made for a centralised National Union, alone capable of ending the imposed District Agreements. The leading spokesman of this policy was Arthur Horner, who had himself recognised that the struggle 'will be transformed into a series of local Lodge fights . . . in defence of local customs'.[3] Within a year of the General Strike, Horner was still trying to argue for both policies:

> A one hundred per cent organisation is not an alternative for One Miners'
> Union, nor One Miners' Union an alternative to 100% organisation. They
> are complementary parts of one problem – one is essential to the other.[4]

It is a theme he pursued after the MFGB's Southport conference at which Herbert Smith had likened the CP's agitation to that of Spencer Unionism. Horner saw this as a trap that should be avoided:

> We must not run away or tolerate for a single moment the idea that our
> people should leave the Union, or even remain inactive within it. . . . On,
> therefore, for 100% membership, One Mineworkers' Union, and rank and
> file control of the organisation.[5]

Horner's view that the MFGB (and the SWMF) could be won for militant policies was, at this time, accepted. He himself was still an MFGB EC member for South Wales. Attacks on the incumbents of official positions had, necessarily, to follow and it was this that led to more bitter denunciations from the CP and, finally, to an abandonment of Horner's strategy. The seeds were already there in 1927, for the CP had to face again the paradox of its role as a revolutionary party operating within reformist structures.

Thus, parallel to a call for a rebuilding of the existing Federation, was an attempt to resurrect pit groups in the wake of the 1926 defeat. There had been sixteen pit papers in the coalfield prior to May 1926; three had ceased production entirely by early 1927, but ten were coming out again in the summer. It was stressed, strongly, by full-time Party organisers that pit and factory group organisation was the only form possible for a revolutionary working-class party.[6] Efforts to operate as an alternative to the Labour Party, however briefly successful, were doomed from the start even when, as in the Rhondda and in Maesteg, the official Labour parties passed into the hands of CP members. The result was the disaffiliation of the Rhondda Borough Labour Party, and its consequent re-establishment in 'official' Labour Party hands. Horner had attended Labour Party conferences as an accredited delegate in the past; now the Executive's decision from the Centre was seen to have teeth in its local organisations. Similarly, the TUC refused to allow Trades Councils to affiliate to the MMM, and the MFGB chose to regard it as an alternative authority to itself, and therefore to be censured.[7] So the tandem of building up the Federation and of demanding wholesale changes was stressed, with opponents being seen as barriers to progress.[8]

The tightrope on which leaders like Horner were operating was a perilous one, and his policy was more convincing in practice, in the later 1930s, than it ever was in theory. The paradoxical dilemma emerged in full at the Ninth Annual Congress of the CP in Horner's speech, still supported by the Central Committee, in which he lambasts a reformist leadership only to demand their replacement, in a worsening situation, by others who may do their jobs even better, albeit in a revolutionary spirit:

> We must never forget that the first barricade in the capitalist defences is the reformist leadership; that leadership can only be replaced to the extent that we can prove to the masses that our policy is capable of finding a solution to their every-day problems and that our members can be trusted to operate that policy so as to make it effective, and finally lead the way to the Dictatorship of the working-class. . . . We are faced . . . with the certainty that our future fights will be mainly of a defensive character. In a state of

intensifying decline a resistance to further reductions is as revolutionary as a fight to increase wages. . . . We must be careful not to get into the habit of thinking that once a man becomes a Trade Union official he becomes a renegade and a traitor. We must not, we will not, fall into the trap which the Right Wing is laying for us. We shall try and discover good Left Wing officials in the localities who can be separated from the reactionary influences of the Right-wing. And when Party members are elected to official positions we must see that the job is done in all ways better than it was before.[9]

Radicalisation of the coalfield, in the meantime, had to be pursued and this led, in turn, to widening rifts even amongst old allies,[10] whilst the growing despair of 1928 elicited plans for an immediate take-over of the organisations that had grown too feeble. Horner, as the chairman of the District Party, and Idris Cox, as its organiser in South Wales, sent a joint letter to all Party members in South Wales spelling this out. The letter began by enumerating the economic and industrial difficulties with which the coalfield was burdened. It poured scorn on any appeal to the owners to help salvage the industry[11] since the latter were only concerned with breaking local customs and with encouraging the Non-Political Union whose success had its roots in a dissatisfaction with the present leadership of the Federation and their recalcitrance in extirpating the menace. The result was that workers were being threatened with dismissal unless they paid the SWMIU. The circular went on to draw conclusions, issue warnings and give its own advice:

Under such circumstances it must be admitted that this [i.e. joining the SWMIU] is a great temptation to workers who might be deprived of their means of livelihood. In fact, there might be a tendency to argue that it would be a good 'tactic' to pay to the Scab Union and still maintain connections with the SWMF until the opportune time arrives to attack the Scab Union.[12] Or it might be argued that it is just as well to join the Scab Union leadership and the leadership of the SWMF. We want to say quite emphatically that both these arguments must be strenuously opposed by our Party members.

   To join the Scab Union would be to give it an incentive to go forward with the same policy in other areas as well. To confuse the leadership of the SWMF with the SWMF itself is to fail to recognise the potentialities of the SWMF when provided with a militant leadership. Now is the time to fight the Scab Union. If the present leadership refuse to fight, we must provide a new leadership for the SWMF.

   It must be realised that a fight against the Scab Union must also resolve itself into a fight against its supporters the Coalowners. There can be no formal separation of opponents in such a struggle. We realise that the EC of the SWMF is unwilling to face the task. Such a struggle would destroy the friendly co-operation with the coal-owners.

This was, virtually, to suggest collusion, and even more harshly, they proceed to deny any 'real' difference between the official Federation policy and that of the SWMIU:

> There is no 'mid-way' in the present struggle in the coalfield. There is no room for friendly co-operation with the coalowners. There is no 'Centrist' position between the policy advocated by the CP and MM and that practised by the Scab Union. Faced with these two alternatives, the EC of the SWMF prefer to tolerate the Scab Union rather than accept a policy of struggle against the coalowners.
>
> Our party members are capable of conducting this struggle, even against the will of the EC of the SWMF. In the process the present leadership can and must be changed. A change of leadership will pave the way to One Mineworkers' Union, which can be used as an organ of struggle on behalf of the British Miners.[13]

The Rules Conferences of that year were, therefore, important arenas for the projection of such policies, since the 'existing machinery' was 'utterly incapable of safeguarding the workers' interests'.[14] This was a local, one-industry equivalent of what was happening on a wider front as the CPGB increased its denunciation of the 'reformist' ILP and any future Labour Government, in their move to replace social democratic parties as the mass organisation of the working-class. In Scotland the dissension within Fife, where CP members had been voted in, led to the MFGB's support of the 'old officials' irrespective of those elections, and the insistence by the MFGB that only Labour Party candidates receive official support in elections.[15] This battening-down on the opportunity for CP dissension, within the wider trade union and labour movement, inevitably drove the militants into the cold. Short of a mass revolt in their direction, they were limited to crying 'Foul' and to attacking those who had 'fouled' as the consorters with capitalism, men of paralysed wills.[16] The climax of this came at the Llandudno Conference of the MFGB when the elected Lanarkshire delegates were refused their credentials, and amidst speeches from the gallery, Herbert Smith jumped on Horner in an unseemly scuffle.[17] The alteration of the rules of representation of the MFGB EC meant that the South Wales representatives were now reduced to two, Tom Richards and S. O. Davies, with Horner as the sacrificed third member.[18] This Conference had laid down strict rulings about the rights of MFGB members (employed and unemployed) in elections, coupling this with an onslaught on CP and MMM tactics in Scotland especially. Horner issued a manifesto criticising the resolutions arrived at, and eighteen officials signed it, including Cook and S. O. Davies. This open defiance was now to be stamped out.[19] It was the high-water mark of the old alliance of 'lefts'; low tide now settled in very quickly.

At first, the criticisms in South Wales were launched, as before, against the 'reformist' leadership, though now there were more personal remarks made against them. Tom Richards had been sitting in on the Mond-Turner talks as MFGB representative, and had been scathing in his denunciation of Communist disruption; he was easily 'the biggest man' in the SWMF and, therefore, a prime target. Why not re-christen the SWMF 'Richards Bros.', it was asked, since it is only an old-established family concern in which the General Secretary received £700 p.a., his step-brother, the Assistant Secretary, took £350 p.a., and on the staff were Tom Richards' son and daughter, along with the son of his step-brother, whilst a son-in-law was employed at Talygarn Convalescent Home.[20] Meanwhile, A. J. Cook was writing to Horner to complain of the General Council's plans to further their co-operative talks with the employers, and himself taking side-swipes at Tom Richards:[21]

Wacth [sic Watch?] Tom – expenses paid double and inquir [sic] – Welfare Fund (District Expenses South Wales £3,500) Gibson [Finlay Gibson, Coalowners' Secretary] and Richards with their families make a good thing out of it. At Welfare Committee demanded explanation that is budget for 1928 while they spent in expenses (District Headquarters in 1927) £4,342 (Mason £1,000 and £621.6 legal expenses.) These blighters [indecipherable word above] only in movement for money. . . . Get South Wales going. Love to all from one in a lone struggle here but trusting to you to carry on.

In fact, what Horner did was to write articles suggesting financial peculation by Federation officials in South Wales (the payment of excessive expenses for attendance at MFGB EC meetings, and, more seriously, a suggestion that the £30,000 received from the MFGB for disbursement in the cause of miners' relief, since January 1927, had not been so used).[22] Idris Cox had made speeches to the same effect so that the SWMF EC decided to issue their statement of accounts, indicating what had been spent, and to take legal opinion, which advised them that the articles and speeches were slanderous and actionable.[23] Horner remained unrepentant. He saw this appeal to a 'capitalist court' as 'the final stage in the treacherous journey of this Privy-Councilled and self-appointed body . . . all except two of its members, including the officials, are there by virtue of their rank as agents in the districts and not as the result of being elected to sit on that body', and declared:

> My position is clear. I withdraw nothing of what I have said concerning dual payments, extra train fares, spurious cab allowances, and reservation of federation funds, industrially and politically, at the expense of Russian and other relief moneys. These charges I am ready and anxious to sustain before any working-class tribunal.[24]

He was not given this chance before any tribunal, for the matter was dropped in 1929, by mutual agreement.[25] By this time the CPGB had swung decisively into its 'Class Against Class' or 'Third Phase' period. A. J. Cook, himself, was taken to task for repudiating the Llandudno manifesto he had signed and in joining with official MFGB strictures on Communist interference; his call for a Labour Government was written off as 'pathological' in its folly.[26] Ultimately, and obviously reluctantly, Horner wrote an open letter bewailing Cook's 'capitulation' to the 'Trade Union and Labour bureaucracy', and pointed to the 'inevitable treachery of a Labour Government'. Cook wrote a heartfelt reply which looked for any way of lessening the suffering of the coalfield.[27] With this break ('Arthur Cook and I were like brothers and when we quarrelled we quarrelled like brothers and our quarrels were very bitter'),[28] South Wales' leading militant had relinquished his last ally within the MFGB, the man he had described, a few short months before as 'the only man amongst the National Officials who stands for a policy ("organisational changes . . . centralisation of our forces") which can rebuild the Miners' Federation'.[29] Cook had indeed suggested that new unions were a mistake and that the reorganising and centralisation of the existing ones was the only possible course, a view with which Horner did not disagree.[30] Only the manner of the implementation of the policy was in dispute in 1929.

Already, in late 1928, the MMM had formed, in South Wales and elsewhere, a 'Save the Union' Committee which had, in turn, called a conference representative of 10,432 organised workers (but only ten miners' lodges), addressed by Horner and Nat Watkins, of the MMM. A further three were called at different venues with speeches against 'Mondism' in industry and for one mineworkers' union in each case. The manifesto they issued came closer to home with its statement that 'non-unionism and Scab Unionism' were 'caused by the betrayals of the official leaders'.[31] Horner produced a pamphlet, *The Bureaucracy in the*

Miners' Federation, which sought to pin the failure of trade unions to capitalise on the revolutionary potential of the working class on to a leadership that was too concerned with its own preservation. It was this, he argued, that led to the suppression of 'all those elements' who persist in fighting:

> They are clinging to office because they are clinging to life, for to them official position is synonymous with livelihood. . . . I have been very doubtful in the past of the wisdom of allowing the fight between the 'right' and the 'left' to become personal, and under very great provocation from the leaders, I have tried to confine the argument . . . as to questions of machinery and policy [but this he now saw] as cowardice, emanating from a disinclination to let down one's 'colleagues', even though their defence involved evading the paramount struggle of the masses.

The criticism had to be made (and he details, once more, the 'double' payments made to MP's from the MFGB and the State, the expenses claimed, in addition to salaries, by District and sub-District officials, the continued payment of 'cab allowance' though London now had buses and Tubes, and the use of 'relief moneys' for normal union business) because of the power wielded by 'the bureaucracy' in selecting delegates to Labour Party and TUC conferences, and in forming policies irrespective of their membership's wishes. South Wales is used as his prime example:

> In the South Wales District the Executive Committee . . . is made up, with two exceptions, of Agents in the full-time employment of the South Wales Miners' Federation, not a single one of whom occupies a seat . . . in virtue of having been elected. They are not subject to any real control, and invariably act without consultation with the members they claim to represent. This Committee exercises enormous powers. It enters into agreements with the South Wales Coalowners and generally determines the policy of the organisation in between Conferences. . . .
>
> The Annual Conferences of 'lodge' delegates are utilised by the Executive as safety-valves for the discontented rank and file, who are permitted to blow off steam to their heart's content. The issues dealt with in special conferences, on the other hand, are usually so compromised by the steps already taken by the Executive as to render it impossible to strike out on an independent line.
>
> Thus we have a state of affairs in which a self-appointed Executive Committee controls the destiny of nearly 200,000 men. . . .
>
> If and when the workers protest against the decisions of such bodies, they are invariably told that they have elected the leadership, and must permit it

to lead, until by ceaseless repetition of a lie they are persuaded into accepting it as a truth.[32]

Horner may have been clear in his own mind about the distinction to be drawn between an organisation and its present leadership but his own loss of power within that organisation (he no longer sat on the EC of either the MFGB or the SWMF, and his own lodge was, to all intents and purposes, an unemployed one)[33] was not an encouraging example. This was especially so in the climate of left sectarianism in 1929 when Horner was exposed to criticism from within his Party as some now advocated that the logic of his exposition was to abandon the old TU structures altogether, just as Horner had been willing, and still was, to jettison their political wing, the Labour Party.[34]

The mining issue figures prominently at the Annual Conference of the CP in early 1929, with Horner successfully warning against forming new unions, unless this was inevitable as a result of the bureaucracy's refusal to budge, and insisting that the MFGB could still be won over, and that no CP member had been expelled because of his party membership. The rest of the year saw the ground moving under his feet; at first Cook was rejected as an ally, and then the 'Save the Union' Committees were re-designed as Miners' Committees of Action not necessarily dependent, anymore, on the established Union structure.[35] Horner was beaten into third place, by a Liberal, in Rhondda East in the General Election,[36] whilst the return of a Labour Government only intensified the campaign against 'reformers'. Horner had now to argue that it did not matter how the workers were won over to CP policies, only so long as they were; there were no absolute principles on the formation of new unions or not. This was to shift the position he had taken before. At a National Minority Movement Conference, he said:

> We have made very serious mistakes in the past year . . . not the result of desire or determination to do wrong things, but the outcome of blind subconscious hanging on to old methods when objective conditions have changed. After the General Strike we realised things could never be the same but we failed to realise the complete transformation in the role of the bureaucracy; that old avenues had been poisoned by treachery.

The alternative was to turn Committees of Action into Councils of Action, to operate amongst non-union labour as well. In a wider perspective, the Party was shifting attention away from the primacy of the miners' struggle into a demand that all the workers be politicised in the deepening crisis of capitalism.[37] To this end a revolutionary leadership of the CP was called for in place of the old discredited one, and new organisations that could contact the masses.[38] Within South Wales, the consequences were in opposition to everything that Horner had believed in. Soon he was to be isolated even from the Party Committee in South Wales itself, as old ways of struggle were declared outmoded. The Garw disturbances against non-unionism were described as 'wasted valuable enthusiasm' which should have gone into the formation of Committees of Action to press for a minimum shift payment.[39] Worse was to follow, as the SWMF's campaign of 1929 for 100 per cent unionism, with its success in the Garw Valley, was designated 'a reactionary game' since, in certain pits in the Maesteg Valley, 'the management have privately told the men that they *must* be members of the SWMF or lose their job'. This meant that the SWMF was being transformed 'into a Company Union'. Certainly the wheel appeared to have spun full circle now. Openly, the suggestion of the CP in late 1929 was that the previous struggles for reorganisation had to be seen, now, as a delusion, for the SWMF 100 per cent campaign

has to be understood, not as a move towards struggle with the coalowners, but rather as a move (i) to sidetrack the rising spirit of the miners into the 'safe' channel of a fight against the boss; (ii) to consolidate their own somewhat weakened position, morally and financially, by posing as 'militants'; (iii) thereby to counter the new policy of the CP, and to make it easier for themselves to crush the miners' revolt against the latest proposals of the Labour Government.

The 100 per cent slogan, which used to be a militant slogan at an earlier stage, has now become a reactionary slogan.

The Party, in South Wales has not, as was frankly recognised at the enlarged DCP on 2 November, realised clearly and quickly enough what has been happening.[40]

What had already happened was the 'disgrace' of the 'right' leadership of such as Campbell and Horner, with Pollitt as one of those excused by the Party's oracle, who now demanded 'energetic and enthusiastic fighters for the international line . . . closest to the masses, however crude and inexperienced'.[41] It was a foregone conclusion that the 11th Congress of the CPGB would call on the miners to imitate the action of the United Mineworkers of Scotland, as their blow against the 'social fascism' of the Labour Party. This was to leave the old militants in South Wales completely high and dry, so they opposed, vainly but vigorously, this revolutionary shadow-boxing.

Horner warned that the CP might become 'a leadership without an army to lead' and that so long as the 'reformist unions' had 'a grip on the majority of workers' they ought to stay there and 'not run away and form new unions whenever we are insulted'. In all of this, Horner insisted that the question of 'independent leadership' was not tied to the issue of 'old and new unions' for the only thing that mattered was being able 'to get at the masses to be led'. Enoch Collins, of Llanelli, reiterated this and reminded the delegates that 'Arthur Horner, who had real mass contacts, was more valuable than "gramophones" who remained at H.Q.' D. L. Davies, who had been Horner's co-checkweigher at Mardy, talked of the 'black fascism' he had witnessed grow in the coalfield as the result of repression, faster than any 'radicalisation' talked of in resolutions. The Central Committee had been advocating more pit groups; within two months the most radical lodge in the coalfield, Mardy itself, would have been expelled from the SWMF; this was said to have 'exposed' the Federation. Dai Lloyd Davies' words were not heeded:

> It was not so easy to get 'roots in the factory or Pit' as it was to talk about it. It was not so easy as in London, where the next-door man didn't know you. But in the mining villages, once you were a militant you were known by everyone in the village and in the district.[42]

The case of the Mardy Lodge was, in retrospect, to prove instructive just as the history of *the village* exhibits, in microcosm, many of the integuments of South Welsh society from the late nineteenth century to the 1930s.

As late as the 1870s, Mardy, at the very top end of the Rhondda Fach, separated from the Rhondda Fawr and the Aberdare valley, on either side, by precipitous mountain slopes and almost enclosed in a bowl, was a reminder of that sylvan Rhondda whose trees, streams and hills were, after thirty years, in the grip of the coal-getters. In 1847 the Marquis of Bute, with the characteristic caution of the self-improving aristocrat, declined purchase of Lot 20 of the Miskin estate, viz. the land and mineral rights of the 999 acre Maerdy farm (the name, Maerdy, or Mardy, as it was spelled, derived from the farm house). It was left to Mordecai Jones of Brecon to purchase those rights, in 1873, for £122,000 and, in partnership with Wheatley Cobb, also of Brecon, to sink Mardy No. 1 pit in 1875 and Mardy No. 2 in 1876. They hit good coal-bearing seams and sent their first coal to Cardiff in 1877. Matters moved apace; in 1878 the enterprise was leased out to Locket & Company who sank No. 3 pit in 1893, incorporated themselves as Locket's Merthyr Steam Coal Company in 1894, and sank the last shaft in 1914.

The obvious economic prosperity of this venture was reflected in the transformation of the settlement. By the late 1870s the workmen had begun to hold religious services for Calvinistic Methodists and Congregationalists, in the old farmhouse; the latter left to build their own chapel when the Welsh Baptists moved in, but it is not clear whether this was because of pressure of numbers or due to the schismatic tendencies which seem to have been as endemic to nineteenth-century nonconformity as they are to twentieth-century socialism. Aside from make-shift huts, the chapels were the first buildings to go up – the Congregationalists with Siloan in 1881, joined shortly after by Zion for the Baptists and Bethania for the Calvinistic Methodists. The chapels were the organising foci of such settlements. They allowed worshippers, by dint of their collective, and democratic, procedures to find individual expression, whilst their religious precepts gave a communal strength to individual frailty. Thus mere aggregations of men became, with the help of such institutions, communities, held together by more than economic pressure but only allowed to cement their unity by their relative prosperity. By 1909 there were approaching 7,000, housed in 880 dwellings, many of which had been built on owner occupier schemes: the usual settlement pattern of a main street, Mardy Road, with terraces rising in parallel lines above and below it, had been established. The village created its own social capital. The Mardy Coffee Tavern with its attached Reading Room and Library were supplied, in 1881, by a philanthropic director of the company; by 1905 this had been transformed into the Workmen's Institute, the largest and most central building in the community. It comprised a large hall, with a balcony, that could hold 1,200 people, a billiard room and gymnasium, and two reading rooms, one especially for ladies. This was, down to the 1920s, very much a Welsh society, although as early as 1886 the Church of England had opened a rival establishment, whilst in 1906 there were two English chapels (Baptist and Wesleyan) to add to the Welsh ones. In 1899 the railway line for passenger services reached Mardy whose growing population caused the school, erected in 1880, to be enlarged five times in twenty-six years. The basic services offered by the pioneering shopkeepers of the early 1890s were now extended by jewellers, watchmakers, newsagents and booksellers, chemists, banks, a commercial hotel, a doctor, the Mardy Electric Light Company, fish and chip shops and a veritable tribe of Italian ice-cream vendors, confectioners and café owners (Pessione, Zerbino, Bacigalupo, Carpanini, Belli, Angelo Fecci and Peter Gambarini), all of whom followed in the wake of the early-established, and thereafter epony-mous, Bracchi Brothers. However, so desperate was the craving for sugared balm that a sole Welsh-owned sweet shop, that of Nellie Elias, managed to survive all this Latin competition; by 1920 a grateful denture maker had set up business.

The cultural appurtances of Edwardian South Wales were not lacking. In 1909 the Siloah Choral Union consisted of 40 sopranos, 38 contraltos, 29 tenors and 34 basses; prominent soloists and organists were imported for special performances in the Institute, whilst the large Ebenezer chapel, opened in 1911, was as much a cultural centre as a place of worship. The role and significance of these chapel choirs, and that of their gargantuan male-voice counterparts, has yet to be assessed for Welsh history – clearly they are another example of the collective organisatión of talent so necessary for the dignity and self-respect of the raw townships and literally, in this case, symbolic of harmony. However, their prime characteristic, on which appraisal of them in an eisteddfod or a *gymanfu ganu* rested, was their technical rendering of a piece for which intricate practice was required in order to compete (a hallmark of the brass bands and of the rugby teams too). There was no aesthetic subversion in such virtuosity for in style and in content these choirs expressed a solidarity of confirmation, not of destruction. The ballad tradition of the Durham coalfield, with its rural and Irish heritage, played a minor part in South Wales. It was, then, the culture of social accommodation in a society that, for the most part, had managed a political consensus. Mardy before 1914 had not broken this shell. On 18 June 1899, when the railway station was opened, the school-children and the underground door-boys were treated to refreshments by the wife of the colliery director who had given the Reading Room (and chose and supplied the improving books he was glad the men read); the colliers presented the four company directors with gold and silver mounted walking sticks and, in turn, were given £100 to be shared between the chapels and churches, the school and the Reading Room. As if to underline the connection between such mutual regard and the agencies of social discipline required by new industrial societies, the children of the Boys' School gave a concert to mark the opening of the Institute, in 1905, at which the following verse was sung:

When babies go to school all dressed so neat and tidy,
To learn their lessons as a rule from Monday until Friday,
They toddle in, they toddle out, their little hearts are yearning,
To do their best, to pass the test of HMI of learning.[43]

Although much of coalfield society can be designated 'militant'
against its own past traditions after 1918, it was Mardy that came to
stand for South Wales along with the 'red villages' of Durham and
Scotland, and that attracted as its nickname, 'Little Moscow'. In
the early days of the 1926 lock-out the *South Wales Daily News* ran a
report under the heading 'Little Moscow' subtitling it – 'Lawless
Mardy – "Red" Reign of Terror'. The reporter wrote that strangers
(presumably himself) were called 'spies' in the streets, that the children
wore red sashes at funerals and that even a Communist soccer team
existed. Worse than this, H. E. Maltby, the general manager of the
collieries, had been defeated for the Rhondda Council by the
Communist checkweigher, D. L. Davies:

> It is extremely difficult for a person who has not come into contact with the
> young Communists of Mardy to form any conception of their extra-
> ordinary mentality. The power they have acquired in the town has gone
> to their heads like wine, and as they have had no experience in any
> town except Mardy, they are unable to realise the weight of public opinion
> against Communism in the country generally, and believe that soon other
> towns will be controlled by Communists.[44]

By the 1930s this had become the legend to which all commentators
on the Rhondda paid homage of one sort or another. Lewis Jones,
leader of the NUWM in South Wales, entitled his novel about the
Rhondda *Cwmardy* (1937) as a tribute to those tendencies he saw as
replete with future hope of revolutionary change. A year later, H. W. J.
Edwards in a chapter called 'Red Rhondda' in his volume *The Good
Patch* wrote in a different vein:

> The industrialised life of Rhondda . . . produced the almost inevitable
> rebellions knows as strikes, which flared up in Tonypandy's little war, which
> so unjustly gave Tonypandy the name of Tonypandemonium . . . Rhondda
> [became] a byword for Red Politics. Mardy became known as little Moscow,
> and London philanthropists returned thence with the feeling they had risked
> their lives.

What explains this fearsome reputation? There is, of course, a simple
answer. On May Day 1919, Arthur Lewis Horner was elected as a

checkweigher for Mardy Colliery although he was, at the time, still in
Cardiff gaol for having refused to be conscripted in the war. When he
was released, shortly after his election, and after a hunger strike, Horner
clearly enunciated the position that had led him earlier to support the
establishment of Soldiers' and Workers' Councils in the wake of the
Russian Revolution, and to fight in the Irish Citizen Army. He told his
first lodge meeting that 'he repudiated the rumours of his not being
willing to fight, and stated he was willing to shoulder a rifle to fight for
the working classes, but not for the enemy of the workers, the
capitalists'.[45]

Horner was then twenty-five years old, with almost ten years of
commitment to socialist politics behind him. He had been born the son
of a railwayman in Merthyr in 1894 and had progressed, via evangelical
religion, and a brief stay in a Birmingham Baptist College, to work as a
miner in the Rhondda. He had sat at the feet of Noah Ablett and
became chairman of the South Wales Socialist Society, itself a rag-bag
of syndicalist, industrial unionist and socialist tendencies. Along with
the Society, Horner went into the CPGB in late 1920, and, by 1923, he
was ensconced on its Central Committee. His years in Mardy, 1919 to
1934, are synonymous with the years of Little Moscow so, QED, the
phenomenon is explained.

There is, however, a more complex answer as well. Mardy enjoyed,
as did all the coalfield, an ambivalent existence. The fabric of
accommodation could be perforated. In 1885, two days before
Christmas, eighty-one men died in an explosion in the new Mardy pits;
it was not an isolated happening in the volatile steam-coal pits of
Rhondda. Between 1887 and 1905, another 294 men and boys were to
be blown up in Rhondda mines. Maerdy had its necessary pubs: and by
1914 a County Police Station with a sergeant and three constables.
That, too, was to be enlarged by 1926 and opened by the local Labour
MP and former miners' agent Colonel Dai Watts-Morgan who had
himself raised a battalion to serve in France. Its existence ('big enough
to house an army') underlined the words of Dai Lloyd Davies, a
Mardy man, a Welsh-speaker and formerly a lay-preacher, who
defined the politics of control:

> The ruling classes govern with the necessary measure of force, not too
> much, not too little, but the necessary measure. . . . If a fine will do they will
> impose a fine, if imprisonment is needed it is imprisonment. And if the
> necessary measure means hanging, well they will hang you.[46]

Dai Lloyd Davies acted as Horner's co-checkweigher; he, too, joined the CP. But unlike Horner, he was rooted in Mardy society and in the tradition that is militant before 1920. As a new and booming part of the Rhondda coal-rush, Mardy had been able to attract outstanding men to serve its colliers as checkweighers – T. I. Mardy-Jones (Ruskin College student, FRES, and later to be MP for Pontypridd), Ted Williams (Horner's immediate predecessor, then agent for the Garw, MP for Ogmore, and after 1945, Governor-General of Australia), whilst in 1910 the English-speaking Noah Ablett was appointed to a colliery whose lodge minutes were kept, until 1914, in Welsh as well as in English. Under Ablett's guidance Plebs League classes, dispensing the Marxist history and economics of the Central Labour College, were held in Mardy during the First World War. Horner attended these classes before taking his enforced Irish holiday.[47]

The war forced social antagonisms into a clearer focus; it disrupted communal ties in places like Mardy. In 1917, the shop of Alf Evans, a grocer, a Lib.-Lab. Councillor, the secretary of the Welsh Baptist chapel, and a JP, was ransacked. He had claimed that he did not have certain goods in stock but:

> . . . somebody had spotted he had a haul in on a Friday . . . [and] . . . on the Saturday night when they came out of the pubs – they must have been talking in the pubs and clubs – and a crowd congregated outside the shop. Well, by the time that all the pubs came out there was thousands of people there. . . . And somebody threw a brick through the window . . . and they raided the shop. . . . They were carrying everything out through the windows when the police came and they read the Riot Act from the top of a tram . . . the Union boys had to persuade the crowd, with the police, and then they agreed that if everybody would turn up on a Sunday morning, everybody would get a share of what was in the shop. So everybody dispersed and on the Sunday morning they had the police there, and the Federation there, and the queue was right down Mardy Road . . . and they cleared the shop out.[48]

Although it would be impossible to analyse Mardy without emphasising that it was a part of Rhondda society (with a population of 169,000, the peak figure, by 1924), there remains its distinctiveness. In part this stems from the comparative lateness and swiftness of its growth; mostly it is a function of its geographical isolation. It was only in 1912 that the first Rhondda tram reached Mardy, and not until 1920 that a bus from Tylorstown, down the valley, could take passengers over Penrhys mountain into the other Rhondda. Ribbon urban development made for intense, narrowly local communities which lacked a central focus: conversely, where there was a widening of the valley bottom, and thus a concentration of population with the provision of more shops, and perhaps a music hall and one or two cinemas, then the inhabitants of villages less well endowed would, periodically, mount an 'invasion'. There were dances in the Mardy Institute to a four-piece band every Thursday and Saturday night, in the 1920s, for a 3d. entrance fee, but for a real 'night out' boys and girls would travel to Judges' Hall in Trealaw, in mid-Rhondda, learn a new dance (tango or fox-trot, perhaps) and take it back to Mardy like some purloined terpsichorean bauble; there was a cinema committee for the Institute with a projectionist from the early 1920s, and amateur drama as well, but the fruits of a secular post-war world could be tasted more quickly in Porth's Coliseum or Tonypandy's Empire Theatre; shopping expeditions down the valley or, on foot, over the mountain to Aberdare, were not uncommon. But, for most of the time, the Institute and Hall represented a central focus of social life in Mardy – it was dance-hall, cinema, meeting-place, theatre, reading room, library and sports arena; it was, above all, the forum for discussion of pit work and of politics. It housed, in microcosm, the diverse interests of the village.[49]

Similarly, Mardy was, in miniature, a reflection of Rhondda's cosmopolitanism. Thus its work-force was mobile and variegated – some from nearby Blaenllechau, Ferndale or Tylorstown, others entrained from Cardiff, some Maltese, 'Cardis' from West Wales and enough Italians underground to have one district christened 'Italy Fach'. The increasing pace of post-war militancy had strong echoes in Mardy where there was an early attempt to have Horner ejected as checkweigher and from where, in the lock-out of 1921, men marched down the valley to Wattstown to withdraw safety men. The customary gaol sentences (three months each for Horner and D. L. Davies) were doled out.[50]

There were, none the less, still countervailing forces within the society. There had been since 1906 a Conservative Club (in 1928 they organised an Empire Day tea party for over 500 children; Horner who led other children in a counter-demonstration said they had been 'secured by tyranny, intimidation, bribery and corruption that was as corrupt as the Empire itself');[51] there was a League of Young Britons, a Women's Unionist Association and sundry non-political groups from the Amateur Dramatic Society to the Salvation Army, from the Boy Scouts to the Carolina Coons. It was indeed a pluralist society in which the

Committee of this 'red' Institute could consider, in March 1920, whether to request a police constable to keep children in order when meetings and lectures were on, and that ordered, in August 1925, for the Reading Room, not only *Lansbury's Weekly* but also *The Statist* and *The Cheltenham and Gloucester Chronicle*. No group was denied free access to the Institute's facilities 'for political, religious or other purposes', provided they did not require them for the 'procurement of private profits' but rather for 'the furtherance of their cause or movement'. The English Baptists had no difficulty in securing the Lesser Hall in 1919, nor the Spiritualists either, though their request, granted as it was, in February 1926 for the loan of an urn and boiler, does give a new gloss to speculation on links between religion and the labour movement.[52]

Activists within the CP never exerted a 'total' control over life in Mardy. Indeed, they did not attempt to do so although the committees of both the lodge and the institute were so dominated. Beyond this they were not in a physical majority, whilst support was bunched into three streets, and scattered elsewhere.[53] The existence of 'Little Moscow' was, rather, an attempt, often deliberately, to create a counter-community within an existing one but based on its past traditions, frequently imitative of existing social formations, never excluding them whilst constantly offering what was thought of as a better alternative because more political, more proletarian, more conscious of its purpose. It was for these militants a question of directing the energy that raised funds and managed to rebuild the Institute, after it had burned down in 1922, within two years; Mr H. E. Maltby, the colliery manager, was in no doubt as to the ultimate direction of those energies for, in June 1926, he resigned as a trustee. The company thus signalled its withdrawal of support from an institution they had once seen as serving a useful purpose.

There were overt signs of this counter-community though its emblematic presence often smacked of a recolouring of old designs: there were the Young Pioneers and the 'Redlets' for the children removed from the Scouts and the Wolf Cubs, competitions for boxers for Russia, and to raise a soccer team to visit the Soviet Union, 'Lenin weeks' in the coalfield and secular funerals that replaced one form of pomp with another – red ribbons in place of black ties, with wreaths in the shape of the hammer and sickle not the cross, and rendition of the 'Red Flag' or the 'Internationale' instead of Welsh hymnology;[54] Comrade Bessie Baker, from Monmouthshire, and Comrade Wharton,

from Mardy, both aged thirteen, went on a Children's Delegation to the
Soviet Union – the lodge requested their reports on 'Workers' Russia'.
More purposefully, all the offshoots organised by the CP, in the 1920s,
excited within Mardy – the NUWM, an ICWPA society, and the
MMM in which Horner was a leading light. Prominent political figures
were constant visitors to mass meetings. The causes of women's right to
contraception, anti-Fascism in Italy and the Indian workers' movement
were just some of the many wider issues supported. Horner and Dai
Lloyd Davies both visited the Soviet Union, more than once, in the
1920s and Mardy received unofficial Soviet delegates too.[55] All of this
was a manifestation of the belief of those who had joined the CP from
South Wales that a national, and indeed an international, organisation
with a clear political purpose was alone capable of organising the
inchoate militancy that, from time to time, had grouped itself around
such bodies as the Unofficial Reform Movement. Beneath the symbols
of an alternative society lay this reality in which the Mardy CP and its
SWMF lodge were firmly rooted. It is not the existence of a mythical,
monolithic 'Little Moscow' that is important so much as the attempt
made to formulate, and act out, an alternative world-view that could
organise existing tendencies to reject a received culture by giving them
power. And just as the sinking of the pits was the basis for the creation
of that society, with all its ambiguities, so the pit lodge was the rock on
which all attempts to seize control for the society itself had to rest.

Mardy was not only brimming with the self-confidence of its own
creation and the conscious optimism of over a decade of 'socialist'
education; it was, too, economically buoyant. Between 1919 and 1925,
its pits employed between 2,000 and 2,500 men; their numbers added
weight to Horner's views. In turn, he proved a capable negotiator –
standard rates were higher in Mardy than in neighbouring Ferndale
despite company attempts to reduce them.[56] The minute books of the
lodge, down to 1926, reveal that prosperity which instilled confidence,
all over the coalfield, to break the cocoon of dependency. The books are
stuffed with the detail of day-to-day business on customs and price-lists
and ballots and minor disputes, but the tone of their resolutions fixes
these clearly within a wider perspective. The men arbitrate over such
issues as purloined tools or misappropriated places; they deliver moral
judgements as when, in June 1924, a collier worked through his shift
though his boy had been injured. They resolved:

... that we disapprove of Hamlet Cooksley's action of not taking the boy out, and in future any member will be held responsible for taking his boy home, or partner, after he meets with an accident, failing to do so that we cease work until that member is stopped from working at the colliery,[57]

The implicit solidarity of intent that is to be found in this willingness to discipline themselves had its corollary in a determination to dictate to management. The lock-out of 1921 had been combated with vigorous measures by lodges in the Rhondda Fach – the Mardy Lodge went even further by refusing to release any coal trucks from the railway sidings until they were given twenty trucks for distribution amongst needy members;[58] all threatened prosecutions for pilfering had to be withdrawn. When Horner and Dai Lloyd Davies returned after their brief prison spell the management proved incapable of removing either of them; nor could it restart the pits until they had agreed to appoint men on a seniority basis. At the same time their intransigence was not able to prevent reductions in price-lists when, after months of distress, the collieries restarted in 1922. The tension that was to arise later between A. J. Cook and Horner, and between the Mardy Lodge and Cook's successor as miners' agent, W. H. Mainwaring, surfaces as early as 1922 in Cook's frustration at their stubborn will and the lodge's public chastisement of Cook for having spoken to the press. From this date the lodge is unswervingly to the left of all official union, TUC and Labour Party policies, though it still tries to operate within their structures. The crisis that erupted in 1926 proved the zenith of this policy with Horner, seconded to assist the CP at national level from late 1925, as its reporter on almost every important conference of the day.

During the General Strike itself, the lodge became, literally, the executive power of the village. The committee called the grocers before them and issued a declaration on food policy which amounted to rationing certain items, forbidding any bulk-buying by those in a financial position to do so, allowing supplies only to long-established customers, and maintaining fixed price levels. The *Western Mail* and the *South Wales News* were banned from the Institute since they were printed by blackleg labour, and newsagents were asked not to distribute them. The lodge controlled all transport in the area and decided on priorities – thus a charabanc was given to take a party of mourners to a funeral but refused to the Methodist churches who wished to attend a 'gymanfu ganu'. A strike committee with wider representation than the miners' lodge was formed from delegates of railwaymen, the unemployed, women's guilds, the CP and ILP. This committee supervised the feeding of school children, the provision of entertainment, the organisation of publicity and of picketing. Any breach of the regulations was dealt with swiftly. This masterful control of Mardy showed no sign of weakness when the strike was brought to an end – it was basis of survival during the seven months' lock-out that followed.[59]

The defeat of the MFGB was a particular one for Mardy. The pits never reopened on the old basis, the village was drained of vitality and of population, left only with spasms of feverish activity. By 1929 the lodge was a rump of what it had once been. Horner was re-elected checkweigher, in early 1927, for No. 3 pit by a large majority, but the management now refused all past customs in the pits, slashed price-lists and insisted on employing whoever they wanted. There were sporadic negotiations over particular seams, and intermittent working, but, in general, the lodge was resolute in its rejection of imposed terms. Mardy moved into the years of mass, long-term unemployment. Symbolically, by August 1927 the local branch of the NUWM had merged with the lodge. Such unconstitutional action continued with their support of the MMM despite its official proscription after 1928. The splits in the labour movement in the late 1920s were faithfully reflected in the lodge's uncompromising support of CP policy.

Fleeting control of the Rhondda Borough Labour Party's delegate conferences, or those of the Rhondda No. 1 District, were hollow victories in the light of the disaffiliation and expulsions that followed. At local level the lodge, for eighteen months, refused all suggestions that they accept work on terms that involved an absolute suspension of all past rates, no guarantee of re-employment of old Mardy workmen (and hence no redress against victimisation), and with no negotiations possible over any subsequent difficulties encountered in working a particular seam. In this stance, with its attendant sacrifices, they were supported officially by the SWMF. The attempt to form a branch of the SWMIU was successfully resisted but they were not able to prevent some men from working on company's terms.[60] In 1927 there were 377 employed members of the Mardy Lodge and 1,366 unemployed, for 1928 and 1929 the figures were, respectively, 8 and 774, and 25 and 325.[61] The continual hints that the pits would reopen if the control of the old lodge was dispelled, led a number of the men in work (after a meeting in Ebenezer vestry) to write to the EC of the SWMF to request permission to form a new lodge. They were, at first, advised to join the old lodge which promised to make special provision for their representation. By the end of 1929 these men still refused to join what they designated as an unemployed and unrepresentative lodge.

Certainly the EC of the SWMF might, with good reason at a time of rampant non-unionism, wish to have Mardy workmen organised; undoubtedly, though, the hard line they took from September 1929 was dictated by their insistence that the Lodge should conform to the 'political and industrial policy of the MFGB, TUC and Labour Party' which was broken by their support of Horner against the official Federation and Labour Party candidature of Watts-Morgan in the 1929 general election. The lodge were informed that they had to 'desist from the political associations and activities . . . contrary to the policy of the SWMF'. In reply the Lodge insisted on proceeding with its own 'past policy' in order 'to go forward to fight the struggle of the workers'. There was no breakaway 'Red' Union in South Wales, but the bitter dissension of 1930, within the Federation ranks, was to provide a clear definition of the political isolation at which the society of 'Little Moscow' had arrived. The old acceptance of the ambivalence in coalfield society, the attack on policies rather than personalities, the burrowing from within, had given place to a direct onslaught on existing officials, to an aggressive refusal to adopt the stance required of a minority position, and, finally, to punishment by those they described as 'Fascist Federation officials'. This was the rhetorical defiance of a splinter society that had outstripped its parent body; unemployed and expelled, it had to look now to international chimeras, to listen to Lewis Jones lecture them on 'a general survey of the revolutionary position of the world's workers'.[62]

The Executive Council applied the writings of the MMM directly to its principal home in the coalfield and warned that disaffiliation would follow further unsatisfactory replies; at the same time they convened a meeting of the employed and unemployed, in Mardy, through the Rhondda District to discuss the whole situation. The lodge, on the other hand, insisted on calling and holding its own meeting, although finally the lodge attended the one convened by the EC as well, at which, with S. O. Davies in the chair, they were asked to reconsider their attitude over affiliation to the Labour Party.[63] After this meeting the EC responded firmly. W. H. Mainwaring, the agent for the Rhondda, moved:

That in view of the declared policy and aims of the CP and their activities in various parts of the coalfield in seeking to set up official Committees with the intention of leading the workmen and dealing with disputes, together with their campaign of slander and open charges of betrayal on the part of the SWMF, this Council shall consider what steps are necessary to counter all of these activities.

After a long discussion it was resolved that the lodge be given until 11 January 1930, to reply. When they did so, it was only to reiterate their refusal to withdraw from the disaffiliated Rhondda Labour Party. They were then informed that this refusal 'to support or act in conformity with the policy and rules of the MFGB, to whom the SWMF is affiliated' would mean 'that the Mardy Lodge shall no longer be recognised and that the Officials of that Lodge shall not be entitled to receive contributions on behalf of the SWMF'; a new lodge would be established.[64] It was discovered that the lodge had the right of appeal to a Special Conference so this was requested, though still defiantly, as an eight-point resolution was forwarded (drafted by Horner) which insisted that the 'Class against Class' struggle would be pursued. Other points were equally uncompromising:

II. To resist all attempts to form a Scab Company Union Lodge under the auspices of the SWMF which attempts are being prepared to assist the local Colliery Company, to safeguard the Fascist Federation officials and to be subordinate to the Capitalist Labour Government.
III. To render greater assistance to the newly formed Pit Committee of Action for the achievement of more unity in the struggle in defence of the workers employed by Locket's Merthyr.
IV. To carry out a widespread campaign at the Pits and in the Lodges of South Wales in order to expose the Pro-Coalowner splitting tactics of the Executive Council.[65]

Although the Special Conference was allowed, this news reached Mardy after Horner had left for Russia (he was the Secretary of the International Miners' Propaganda Committee) so that D. L. Davies attended as the Mardy delegate, authorised by the lodge only to abide by its previous decisions. The resulting conference began in an uproar, discussion was curtailed and the motion for expulsion simply put, with 150 for and 9 against.[66]

In effect the Mardy Lodge had 'broken away' from the SWMF. Horner, for all his brinksmanship at the time, appears to have recognised the significance of the point when he wrote later:

If I had had the telegram telling me of the decision [to allow an appeal to Special Conference] I would have postponed my trip [to Russia]. The Conference was held. I knew that S. O. Davies, as Vice-President, would be in the chair instead of the President, Enoch Morrell. S. O. Davies had come to our house in Mardy after I had left. He had planned to make a statement which would give us a chance to withdraw with dignity. Unfortunately the Mardy representative did not know this. They refused to give way with the result that the suspension remained. And Mardy Lodge remained expelled.[67]

The expelled lodge continued to function, but the employed were now all in the official lodge; more left the village. Beyond this, the unity of the SWMF had been broached. All of this was to lead Arthur Horner into 'Hornerism' when he returned from Moscow, in December 1930. In his absence the Mardy expulsion was given an altogether different significance by those who were wrecking the format under which the MMM had been successful as a 'ginger group'.

The expulsion was explained, solely, in terms of the desire of the colliery owners to reopen the pits at lower rates than before 1926 (something the old lodge had refused categorically), and in the desire of the 'Social fascist' SWMF (now a 'Mondist Union') to accommodate them. The reorganisation of the SWMF, then, could only proceed by rejecting its past traditions and proceeding to the formation of independent pit cells.[68] A Mardy Solidarity Committee was organised in the coalfield, with the nearby lodges of Tylorstown and Ferndale at its head. They were now, in their turn, warned to desist.[69] This was interpreted as a blow-by-blow campaign against all 'militant Lodges' with the concomitant that fighting back within the Federation was doomed. The victory of militants in winning elections was no longer adequate, indeed it was now seen as symptomatic of 'trade union legalism' in its refusal to approach 'the miners independently at the pit' and in its 'opposition to all forms of activity outside the lodge'.

Undoubtedly this was an accurate designation of the attraction of lodge activity in the coalfield, though it was, equally, a woeful failure to understand the power of lodges in the communities and the difficulty of 'independent' organisation at the pit. Notwithstanding this, the CPGB, in its aberrant 'Third Phase' which effectively cut it off from its industrial bases and destroyed its own MMM (the last National Conference was in August 1929), proceeded to advise the South Wales miners to imitate the United Mineworkers of Scotland and establish 'independent Pit Committees of Action' of organised and 'unorganised' (i.e. non-union) miners. In the meantime, the lodges were advised to 'withhold dues'; within ten days, this was altered as being 'premature', as being out of step with the 'real situation' in South Wales, i.e. the absence of any mass campaign.[70] At this stage confusion reigned supreme in the mess that an ill-calculated campaign had caused. However, unwilling as yet to see the 'new line' as folly, it was decided that the only cause for the weakening of the militant Left in the coalfield, was the pessimism and apathy induced by the 'old line' which relied, too heavily, on 'one or a few leaders'. In a blistering reference to Horner, the grave was dug deeper:

> This must be rejected, especially if the comrade in question is one who is still not clear and firmly convinced of the new line. A comrade who is not politically fit for Party leadership [the purge had come at the 11th Party Congress in 1929] is likewise not fitted to lead one of the Party's most important mass campaigns [Mardy], which is a concrete application of the new line.

In effect a generation of experience of the actual struggle in South Wales for a 'fighting' Federation was rejected, and those who had led it were told they had not appreciated the importance of the Mardy issue for:

> Around this struggle we can rally the miners and lay the basis for a big mass movement. . . . Reorganisation is connected with all the tasks of the Party. We must proceed at once, and not stop until the entire district is reorganised on a factory and pit cell basis.[71]

Even the proponents of the 'new line' split into factions, until again the synthesis, from on high, was revealed – it was a 'right' mistake to press for a conference on the Mardy expulsion and a 'left' mistake to drop the fight for its reinstatement and refuse dues. An immediate 'economic campaign' had to be launched as the basis of widening the struggle. Beyond this, the enthusiastic circular of the South Wales DPC calling for strikes on any and every issue, with adequate preparation, was condemned by the Political Bureau, who sent one of their leading members down 'to raise the political level'. This included the attack on 'Social Fascist May Day Celebrations' and their substitution by 'Red Day' (1 August).[72] The blood-letting had only just begun, as the DPC admitted all its mistakes, removed seven old members and added eight new ones, with new organisers for South Wales and Cardiff. The past 'right opportunism' and present 'left sectarianism' were both exorcised, with the 'returned Lenin School students' as a 'shock group' to 'carry out the Party line and to establish the Communist Party as the leader of the working class in South Wales'. At the District Congress where these pronunciamentos were made, the Mardy local was absent.[73]

So severe had been the body blows delivered that they were absent too at the Rhondda Fach 'Red Day' celebrations; the Mardy Solidarity Committee was said not 'to exist'. Amidst cries for a 'Red Union', CP and MM members in other lodges were barred from holding office, and in some cases expelled from the Federation for 'interfering with the proper working and conduct of the lodge'.[74] The clearest expression of Federation grievance and justification occurred in a case where Jack Jones of the Tillery Lodge (Monmouthshire Western Valley District) had been expelled by the District because 'at street corner meetings, and in leaflets that were distributed among the workmen and the general public, [he] had made made attacks of a most scurrilous character on the miners' agent, the SWMF, and the MFGB, and urged the setting up of a revolutionary organisation under the auspices of the CP and Minority Movement'. The lodge had queried their right to do this, disclaiming any responsibility for what had been said, but pointing out other SWMF members who supported the Liberal and Tory parties instead of the Labour Party – 'they thought that a member of the CP was as much entitled to remain a member of the Federation as any Liberal or Tory'. In a reply, which the lodge accepted, the EC laid down its ground rules:

> We pointed out that the Federation was primarily an industrial organisation. It is true we were affiliated to the Labour Party and desired all our members to be loyal to that Party, but we could not make that a test of membership of the Federation. As long as they carried out the industrial policy of the Federation, and refrained from attacking the organisation, they were entitled to remain members.
>
> In the case involved in this dispute, however, the member had scurrilously attacked not only the Officials, but the Federation itself, and had called for its destruction with the view of creating a revolutionary organisation on its ruins. In any case, it was our view that if the member felt aggrieved the Rules provided for an appeal to the EC, and if necessary, to conference. It was the duty of the Lodge to carry out the decisions of the District, and the EC and to allow the member to take whatever steps he desired in accordance with the Rules of the Organisation.[75]

Soon, the MMM in South Wales, was 'very weak indeed',[76] and at Mardy (D. L. Davies had now left) the lodge was no longer any force at all, however valiantly remaining members maintained their contacts and lectures.[77] The consequence was the virtual impotence of the CP in the coalfield, with the majority of the local branches having 'heavy membership arrears' for May, June and July and failing to fulfil 'elementary obligations'. The only answer to this seemed the parroting of a demand for the unification of unionists or non-unionists against 'the united front of the SWMF and the South Wales Coalowners', with a swipe at the 100 per cent membership drive in the Rhondda that autumn as a 'cover-up for treachery'.[78]

The reports from the coalfield must have struck Horner, still in Russia, as bleak indeed. He attempted to rally the depleted ranks by insisting, in a special article (first major one he had contributed in 1930) that he was not the victim of any political persecution, rather that he saw the mistakes he himself had made in trusting 'pseudo-lefts' like Cook, S. O. Davies and Ted Williams, and that apathy should have no such excuses:

> The defeats inflicted on us during this period have created a measure of pessimism and passivity in our ranks, especially in Mardy . . . [but the] new leadership of the Communist Party acted quite correctly in the course taken against the foremost members of the old leadership.

Horner urged support for the Workers' Charter Campaign of the MMM and its basis of struggle, the industrial and economic fight in the pits.[79] When he returned in early December (assuring his old lodge that he was 'home . . . without being imprisoned for 5, 7, 10 or 15 years in Russia'),[80] Horner threw himself into the crisis that was brewing, over wages and hours, in South Wales. The Mardy Lodge now sent a delegate to the Unity Conference called by the MMM and he could report that 'during the past two or three weeks in Mardy there has been increased activity, and everything goes to show that Mardy will again take its place in the forefront in the fight against capitalism'.[81]

In fact the strike of January 1931 would, for Horner anyway, finally reveal the folly of working outside the SWMF, lead to his almost breaking with the CP, and bring to an end a highly-coloured period of 'left' activity within the coalfield which, in the words of one historian, resulted in 'suicide during a fit of insanity'.[82] The basic problem of reorganisation of the SWMF, the hopelessness of which had led to such extremes of despair, would remain for another three years the focus of all hope for change.

NOTES

1. L. J. MacFarlane, *op. cit.*, p. 177. He estimates there were 1,500 in the CP in 1926, and 2,300 by October 1927. Thereafter numbers fell away.

2. *Workers' Life*, 1 and 8 April 1927.

3. *The Mineworker*, 4 December 1926.

4. *Workers' Life*, 27 May 1927.

5. *Ibid.*, 26 August 1927.

6. *Ibid.*, 17 June 1927. There were pit papers like the *Cwmaman Flare*, *The New Star* (Wattstown), *The Cambrian X-ray*, *The Red Observer* (Tylorstown), *The Gilfach Rebel*, *The Llanbradach Liberator*, *The Taff-Merthyr Star*. 29 July, 21 October 1927. For others see the note 'Pit Papers' by David Egan and Hywel Francis, *Llafur*, Vol. I, No. 4, 1975.

7. *Ibid.*, 18 and 25 March 1927. The Rhondda BLP had voted in March 1926, at a delegate conference, to allow full rights for the CP. The LP Executive acted a year later. *Rhondda Leader*, 26 March 1927.

8. *Workers' Life*, 15 and 22 July 1927, where Hartshorn is praised for the non-union struggle in Garw and attacked for setting up a 'scab' Labour party against the one that had been pro-CP.

9. *Ibid.*, 7 October 1927.

10. In late 1927, Hannington of the NUWCM came down to South Wales to organise a march of unemployed miners (see above pp. 99–102). Cook supported this, despite strictures from the MFGB and TUC. Then he in turn was supported for condemning a Strachey–Shinwell plan to nationalise the mines without workers' control and with compensation for the Royalty owners; and, at the same time, attacked for implicitly accepting compensation for the colliery owners. *Workers' Life*, 28 October, 11 and 18 November, 2 December 1927, 27 January 1928.

11. This was a reference to a suggested approach by the SWMF EC and owners to the Railway Companies to secure lower railway charges. It was alleged that this would involve lower wages for railwaymen. *Workers' Life*, 13 January and 2 March 1928.

12. This is precisely the policy that was later adopted by Horner.

13. *Workers' Life*, 17 February 1928.

14. Horner, *ibid.*, 16 March 1928.

15. *Workers' Life*, 20 April 1928. MacFarlane, *op. cit.*

16. *Ibid.*, 13 April and 11 May 1928. SWMF leaders met in the House of Commons with leading coalowners; Horner asked why Hartshorn should think only a Labour Government could do anything for the miners, that this was tantamount to a justification of non-unionism.

17. *Ibid.*, 20 July 1928. *Western Mail*, 19 July 1928. Horner, *op. cit.*, pp. 98–9.

18. Horner, *op. cit.*, p. 100. He had beaten Enoch Morrell into third place in the previous year.

19. *Workers' Life*, 21 September 1928. The MFGB EC enquired of the Districts whether any of the signatories were authorised to sign.

20. *Ibid.*, 20 July 1928.

21. Letter from A. J. Cook to Horner, 26 June 1928. Horner MSS. The letter is written in pencil on MFGB notepaper. It was obviously done in haste since the spelling and punctuation are rudimentary, the hand difficult to decipher and the internal logic not always clear. Nevertheless, as one of the only three surviving pieces of private correspondence between the two men, it is of considerable value.

22. *Sunday Worker*, 23 September 1928; *Workers' Life*, 28 September 1928.

23. SWMF EC Minutes, 15 and 20 October, 10 November 1928. They issued a manifesto declaring that the CP wished to substitute revolutionary destructive action for the SWMF, and engaged in 'an orgy of falsehoods'; a balance sheet was appended which gave receipts [in tot] as £318,433 1s. 2d. and outlay as £336,129 12s. 4d. (for relief) and £11,672 4s. 3d. in legal costs in defence of prosecuted members (647 had been defended, and 431 released or bound-over). *Western Mail*, 12 November 1928.

24. *Letter* from Horner, in *Western Mail*, 14 November 1928.

25. These accusations ceased; there was, too, opposition from the lodges to any intended prosecution. No official reasons were given. *Workers' Life*, 7 December 1928, 1 April 1929.

26. *Ibid.*, 19 October, 26 October, 15, 22, and 29 March 1928.

27. Letters in *Workers' Life*, 1 and 26 April 1928.

28. Horner, *op. cit.*, pp. 106–107. None the less, Horner and Cook restored their personal relations.

29. *Workers' Life*, 5 October 1928.

30. *Ibid.*, 26 April 1929; Horner, *loc. cit.*

31. *Ibid.*, 9 and 23 November 1928.

32. Arthur Horner, *The Bureaucracy in the Miners' Federation* (Miners' Minority Movement, November 1928), pp. 5–6, 15–17, 9. Circular No. 81 of the SWMF refuted this 'campaign of abuse', and added, 'The full heinousness of this campaign can only be realised when it is known that Mr Arthur Horner who initiated it, was a Member of the Council during the distribution of this fund, and must be fully conscious that he is responsible for writing and stating a deliberate falsehood, that his expenses as an EC member, or the salaries of the officials, were paid from Relief funds.'

33. The No. 1 Rhondda District had had its representation cut, on the EC, with a fall in financial membership, so Horner, though still on the MFGB EC, could not attend meetings in Cardiff. The District pressed that he be allowed to do so until 'such a time . . . as the District is in a position to elect him in the ordinary manner as one of its representatives'. Monthly reports of No. 1. Rhondda District, 30 January 1928.

34. Horner declared that non-political trade unionism was an offshoot of the disillusion with paying a political levy to 'a capitalist party, not to be distinguished from the Conservative or Liberal Party'. *Workers' Life*, 18 January 1929.

35. *Workers' Life*, 25 January, 22 February and 8 March 1929.

36. *Western Mail*, 1 June 1929.

37. *Workers' Life*, 30 August, 4 October 1929. The Miners' Page that *Workers' Life* had carried since the 1926 lock-out was now discontinued.

38. Article by R. P. Dutt, *ibid.*, 8 November 1929.

39. *Ibid.*, 8 November 1929. It was said that Cook 'will do things that would make Spencer and Hodges blush'.

40. Article by Andrew Rothstein, *ibid.*, 15 November 1929.

41. Article by R. P. Dutt, *loc. cit.* Lewis Jones of Clydach Vale wrote to ask why any distinction had to be made between 'good' and 'bad' rights when the task was to purge *all* reformist tendencies within the CP.

42. *Ibid.*, 6 and 20 December 1929.

43. Details of the growth can be found in various years of *Kelly's Directory of Monmouthshire and South Wales*; see also E. D. Lewis, *The Rhondda Valleys* (1959) pp. 253–4; *Notes on the History of Maerdy* (unpublished MS.) complied by Bill Picton; SWML interview with Arthur Morgan (Mardy). It is not easy, or advisable, to distinguish Mardy as such from Ferndale which also housed Mardy workmen or, even more, the hillside community of Blaenllechan (or 'Blaen' as it was then, and is still, known). The Rhondda MOH Reports reveal a low rate of house-building and doubtless a disguised population size in the years of expansion down to 1914 so that official estimates could be revised upwards.

44. *South Wales News*, 25 May 1926. However, 'Little Moscow' could also be a state of mind – its exact geographical location depending on the complainant's proximity to a 'radical' spot. Thus, J. Vyrnwy Morgan in 1925: '. . . what we call Little Moscow in Wales . . . is the Aberavon parliamentary division, with Cwmavon, which the writer has known from boyhood, as the storm-centre. In no other part of industrial Wales has Communistic-Socialism found a more fertile field for its revolutionary propaganda, or where the Bolshevik-Lenin banner has been flaunted with more provocative agressiveness. . . . We cannot understand what satisfaction Mr Ramsay MacDonald can derive from the fact that he represents in Parliament this Little Moscow in Wales.' J. Vyrnwy Morgan, *The Welsh Mind in Evolution* (1925) p. 230, p. 232.

45. Minute Book of the No. 3. Pit, Mardy, 14 May 1919.

46. E. D. Lewis, *op. cit.*, SWML interview with Frank Williams (Ferndale).

47. Minute Book of No. 3 pit, 6 June, 11 July 1910; 7 December 1917; 21 January 1918; 11 March 1919; 1 May 1919.

48. SWML interview with Bill Picton.

49. SWML interviews with Octavius Morgan, Velinda Evans, Fred Morris.

50. *South Wales News*, 25 May 1921.

51. *Ibid.*, 25 May 1928.

52. Minute Book of the Mardy Workmen's Institute, 24 September 1919; 31 March 1920; 9 June, 20 August, 5 November 1925; 4 February 1926, 16 June 1926, and *passim* for a flavour akin to that of a novel.

53. Thus the slide of the 'King's person' was removed when pictures were shown (in 1925) but children who refused to stand for God Save the King in school were caned. Institute Minutes, 11 September 1925. SWML interview with Mary Evans.

54. *Workers' Life*, 20 May 1927, 6 and 20 January, 13 July 1928. *Rhondda Leader*, 11 August 1928.

55. Mardy Lodge Minutes, *passim*; Horner, *op. cit.*, p. 65, p. 111.

56. SWML interview with Reg Fine.

57. Mardy Lodge Minutes, 6 June 1924.

58. *Ibid.*, 6 April 1921.

59. *Ibid.*, 1, 5, 8, 13, 16, 18, 23, 27, 29 May 1926.

60. *Workers' Life*, 2 November 1928. David Lewis and Mainwaring 'resigned' because of disruption but their resignations were refused by the Rhondda District Committee. And see Mardy Lodge Minutes, 1927, 1928 and 1929, *passim*.

61. See *Rhondda No. 1. District Annual Reports*. By contrast the average financial membership of the lodge in 1919 was 1,933; in 1920, 2,020; 1923, 1,666; 1924, 2,421. The constitution of a new lodge in 1930 did not reverse the downward trend – in 1930 there were 102 full members, none unemployed and, in 1931, 62 and 16 respectively.

62. SWMF EC Minutes, 29 April and 10 September 1929. Mardy Lodge Minutes, 24 and 26 September 1929; 5 October 1930.

63. SWMF EC Minutes, 12 and 26 October 1929. Mardy Lodge Minutes, 16 and 30 October, 17 November, and 24 December 1929.

64. SWMF EC Minutes, 24 January 1930.

65. Mardy Lodge Minutes, 29 January 1930.

66. SWMF EC Minutes, 10 and 20 February 1930; Mardy Lodge Minutes, 19 and 28 February 1930.

67. Horner, *op. cit.*, p. 109.

68. *Daily Worker*, 1 and 3 February 1930. Article by Idris Cox and report to a DPC meeting. It was claimed that 'pit cells' could begin in eighteen separate pits.

69. Will Paynter had been expelled from the Cymmer Lodge for supporting a CP candidate in a local election. *Ibid.*, 24 February, 25 February, 4 and 8 March.

70. *Ibid.*, 12, 14, 20, 22, 24 March 1930. Mardy delegates had been repulsed by the police in their attempt to attend a Rhondda No. 1 District meeting. Thirteen defendants were fined.

71. Article 'The Coming Fight in South Wales and the Party's Task' by J. W. Mills. *Ibid.*, 5 and 7 April 1930. All 'pessimistic comrades' must 'be removed'.

72. *Ibid.*, 9, 10, 11 April 1930.

73. *Ibid.*, 7, 9, 20 May; 18 June 1930.

74. *Ibid.*, 6 May, 27 June. The Naval Lodge barred CP members from office; George Maslin was expelled from the Tylorstown Lodge. SWMF EC Minutes, 10 July 1930.

75. SWMF EC Minutes, 13 September 1930.

76. *Communist Review*, August 1932. Quoted in Woodhouse, *op. cit.*, p. 397.

77. Mardy Lodge Minutes, 2 March, 19 August, 5 October 1930.

78. *Daily Worker*, 9, 17, 18 September 1930. As late as March 1935, there were still, surprisingly, only five fully paid-up members of the CP in Mardy, all of whom were unemployed.

79. *Ibid.*, 25 September 1930.

80. Mardy Lodge Minutes, 7 December 1930.

81. *Daily Worker*, 13 December 1930.

82. Woodhouse, *op. cit.*, p. 398.

CHAPTER SIX

Starting Out in the Thirties

The election of the Labour Government in 1929 gave new hope to the beleaguered mining areas looking for some National Agreement on Wages and Hours. In South Wales the Agreement (due to expire at the end of 1929) was extended for a year, both sides having the right to apply for an alteration in the light of the expected legislation. This came, in July 1930, in the shape of a Coal Mines Act which established a reduction in working hours from 8 to $7\frac{1}{2}$ (though allowing a 'spread over' whereby on some days men could work 8 with consequent reductions, or 'stop-days', later) and set up a National Industrial Board with powers of recommendation. This Board was never properly recognised by the owners who did not see it as 'independent'. Nevertheless, they did implement its proposal in November 1930 that existing wages and conditions be kept, with a 'spread-over' of five days of 8 hours, and a Saturday of 7 hours operating in the first week, with five days of 8 hours in the second. Reluctantly the SWMF conference, with a protest, accepted this; the meetings in individual districts were uniformly critical and 'made more bitter by a recognition of the weakness of the organisation'.[1]

Patently, there was no desire on the part of the SWMF to begin industrial action whose outcome they could not predict with any certainty; there always lurked the possibility, now, of a complete fragmentation of the already battered Federation. So, although the MFGB did not consent to the 'spread-over' arrangement, the EC continued to negotiate, mostly pressing the Owners on the matter of hours of work. Finally, with a blank rejection of the National Industrial Board, the owners posted up terms, unilaterally, that demanded the retention of the present terms until 31 January 1931, or, if hours were reduced to $7\frac{1}{2}$ a shift, then day-wage men were to lose one-sixteenth of their wages. This was an either/or dictation of the kind that gave the SWMF, even in its parlous state, no alternative, so the Conference called to discuss the Industrial Board's suggestions, but suddenly

confronted by the owners' ultimatum, decided to let the existing
agreement lapse. The only coalfield-wide strike of the 1930s began on
1 January 1931.[2]

At this point the total membership of the SWMF was 75,480 but the
work-force was in excess of 140,000. The rationalisation that had
proceeded apace in the late 1920s had cut a swathe through the smaller
concerns with the result that 138 pits, employing 18,300 men, had
closed permanently, in the eighteen months since January 1929.[3] The
SWMF EC were anxious for a settlement and the Government pressed
the owners to make concessions over what Noah Ablett called 'trivial
issues'. The strike itself was fairly solid except in patches where
SWMIU members, or Craftsmen, continued at work, notably at Taff-
Merthyr, Emlyn Colliery and Parc and Dare collieries.

The significance of the strike was that the Federation felt it could
afford to sink no further in its loss of wages. They calculated that the
owners' terms would mean 50,000 men being in receipt of between
31s. 3d. to 37s. 6d. for a full week's work, that this would therefore
mean more poor relief and consequently still higher rates:

> We further call the attention of the business people to the fact that if the
> wages of the South Wales Miners had been regulated on a cost-of-living
> basis the workmen would have received during the last $3\frac{1}{2}$ years nearly £11
> million pounds in additional wages, and the business community would have
> benefited thereby.[4]

It was unimaginable that any independent arbitration could leave
them worse off, so the talks with William Graham at the Board of Trade
were pursued assiduously, and, with a sense of relief, a provisional
agreement was reached after two weeks that was to last three years. The
terms were the maintenance of the November 1930 rates of pay and a
$7\frac{1}{2}$-hour day, but the minimum percentage and subsistence wage were
to be considered immediately by a new Independent Chairman whose
award would be operative from 31 March. On this basis the strike was
ended by a Delegate Conference, voting 169 to 72. The EC declared
themselves satisfied for, in difficult circumstances, the 'intentions of the
Owners had been thwarted, and the Organisation was maintained
unbroken even in parts that were known to be fragile'.[5]

Even this limited satisfaction was to be of short duration. F. P. M.
Schiller, KC, reported as independent Chairman of the Conciliation
Board, on 6 March 1931. He reduced the minimum percentage payable
on the 1915 standard base rate from 28 to 20 and he brought the

subsistence wage down from 7s. 10½d. a shift. For daywage men this meant a reduction of anything from 8½d. a shift, with all grades not attaining that level, for some reason or other, receiving a subsistence wage of 7s. 6d. if married with children, 7s. 3d. if a married man, and 7s. if single. The award was unfeeling in its assessment of social needs and provocative in its payment of three rates for the same job. The 'impossible' had occurred, the living conditions of miners were to be depressed yet again.[6]

There was immediate disquiet in the coalfield, with strike action in some pits and stormy meetings elsewhere, though most of these lasted only a day or so, as officials urged the end of any isolated actions. Nevertheless, the delegate conference called to hear the EC's recommendations to the Lodges ended in uproar, as anger and criticism burst out. The EC had declared:

> The heartless cynicism of the award is indicated by the suggestion that 3d. a day is enough for a workman's wife to subsist upon and that 6d. a day is sufficient to provide all comforts necessary for a wife and children in a working-class home.

The delegates were not content with strong words. When they reassembled on 21 March, resolutions for a further strike and for the EC's resignation were put. On a card vote of 787 to 747 (a 2,000 majority out of 76,700 cast) the conference narrowly accepted a recommendation to appeal to Government for an amendment to the Minimum Wage Act of 1912 so that present rates be at least equal, in real terms, to those of 1914.[7] They added:

> While the EC fully share the general resentment towards the Award, they are definitely of the opinion that a South Wales stoppage would be calamitous to the workmen of the Coalfield, and consequently, they urge the Lodges to adopt the recommendation of the Council.[8]

Whatever gloss was put on it this was an unmitigated defeat, only confirmed by the summer when the MFGB, despite the opposition of South Wales and Yorkshire, accepted the Government's decision not to bring in a 7-hour day by legislation but rather to accept a 7½-hour day, with a guaranteed maintenance of wage rates for a year. For South Wales this was, of course, only to guarantee disaster. Without MFGB or Government support, the EC felt helpless to do anything else; with great reluctance the lodges, by 2-1, acquiesced.[9]

The failure of this stratagem of the EC entailed also a further loss of prestige. To rub salt in their wounds, the Taff-Merthyr men who had worked through the strike received bonus payments of £1 per man. The MMM had advocated a continuation of strike action throughout, accusing the leaders of betrayal, calling the terms given 'slavery', and demanding an independent fight without the Federation's backing.[10] An analysis of the actual militancy upon which they could call, however, only confirms the dejection of the Federation leadership.

At the start, Horner headed the MMM attempts to form strike committees of 'organised and unorganised' labour (as at Mardy) and spoke at a Conference of some 55 delegates. The South Wales Central Strike Committee declared, on the return to work, 'While our basic organisation is the pit we can only successfully carry this through by consistent work within the Lodges'. This, consistent with Horner's basic convictions, was to pay lip-service to the Party line on pit committees. In Mardy itself the old lodge, though protesting against the new lodge's vote in favour of acceptance of terms, could only advise those men, in work, who supported them to go back. Eventually they even referred to themselves as a 'Group' and constituted themselves as such, within the MMM.[11]

The crucial test of the efficacy of the projected line would come with the acceptance, or otherwise, of the new terms offered. The Central Strike Committee were told this, in no uncertain terms, by a Political Bureau unhappy with their handling of the situation:

> To the extent that our activities in the coalfield are intensified it will be possible in South Wales on 1 March for the Miners to break the shackles imposed by the SWMF Officials and to come out under the leadership of the MM in alliance with the miners in Scotland, Durham and Northumberland whose temporary agreements also expire on 1 March, and also to bring the Lancashire miners into the struggle. . . .

But, despite some strengthening of the Party's role, its independent stance 'was almost completely submerged during the strike, and there were no independent party pronouncements bringing out clearly . . . fundamental aims . . . in relation to the immediate strike issue'. Horner, it seems, had returned unreconstructed in the essentials of his industrial philosophy for the 'widespread conviction that the Federation's decisions are decisive and the lack of conviction of the possibilities of independently carrying the fight forward after the Federation betrayed the strike, was most clearly revealed in the character of the discussion in the extended District Party Committee meeting on 17 January'.[12]

The proposals that were being put were to continue the strike unofficially: Horner recalled: 'I opposed this action. I said, "You can begin a strike and build it up but you cannot carry it on in pieces after the initial strike has disintegrated. The only result of carrying on the strike unofficially in these circumstances will be to isolate the militants from the rest of the miners in the coalfield and [then] it will be perfectly easy for the Owners to victimise the militants."'[13]

This appraisal was written off as pessimism, as 'lagging behind the masses', as a failure to see that 'in this period there is *no* other leadership than that of the CP and MM'. Horner resigned as Chairman of the Strike Committee in South Wales and was removed from his post as Secretary of the MMM whose conference called for a strike on 1 March. Horner was credited with sabotaging the success of the strike by failing to give a clear lead 'for the continuation of the struggle' and by his 'active opposition' to the 'policy of independent leadership'; whilst after the strike ended, it was maintained that 'Comrade Horner has persistently refused to recognise these mistakes'.[14]

When the Award was given, there were sporadic strikes at nine collieries (five in the Rhondda) but only at the Glamorgan Colliery, Llwynypia, where the men struck from 9 to the 19 March, was there any concerted support for the CP's call.[15] Horner had written to the Party's Central Committee on 21 January to the effect that there had not been 'the elementary machinery for carrying on a dispute, in the event of the reformists calling it off, whilst the tactics employed to continue the struggle on Monday morning were infantile'.[16] The point, for Horner, was not that the ending of the strike was justifiable but that there existed no possibility of maintaining the struggle, 'in the present circumstances', however strong the desire to do so on the part of the militants confusing anger with the resolution necessary to maintain an extended stoppage.

The MMM ceased to exist, for all practical purposes, in the coalfield from now on,[17] though its role as leader of 'rank and file pit strike committees' was still broadcast. Horner's retraction was demanded in view of the potential growth of militancy revealed, and this despite the fact that the Llwynypia strike alone could be cited in evidence.[18] The distinction being made was between acceptance of the trade union 'bureaucracy's' views and a complete rejection of any but 'revolutionary leadership'. The latter only made sense if the economic and social dislocation was such that the call to revolution would not prove isolationist. Horner believed that an emphasis on the unemployed

or the unorganised was mistaken and that a radicalisation of the
organised workers was a first essential. He was pilloried ceaselessly and
unmercifully for almost six months in the party press. His views were
labelled 'Hornerism', with an emphasis on the opportunism that saw his
paying lip-service to party discipline even whilst disobeying in practice.
In fact, he refused to submit to a confession of error and came near to
leaving the party until prevailed upon to put his views before the
Comintern against the CPGB's Central Committee. After this, he did
accept that there had been 'a correct analysis of my mistakes' though
this was now presented as a mere tactical difference. Horner had
decided to stay within the CPGB, and in so doing swallowed some
medicine, but his lone stance against the vagaries of the 'Third Phase'
assured him of his own continued independent judgement.[19] By the end
of 1931 that policy was in ruins anyway and the European parties
would soon be moving, step by step, from a 'united front from below' to
a 'United Front' and eventually to the 'Popular Fronts' of the late
1930s. Within South Wales this would mean, from 1932 on, that the
militant 'Left' would again, under Horner's leadership, engage in
building a rank-and-file movement whose intention would be to replace
an existing leadership within a reorganised SWMF rather than to
destroy the latter. Policies would again be attacked rather than
personalities.

This traumatic episode over, the pieces were picked up again. Horner
contested Rhondda East in the October election of 1931, polling over
10,000 votes, and then, in early 1932 he was given fifteen months' hard
labour for having prevented, with others, a bailiff from taking away a
man's furniture for allegedly not paying his rates.[20] This action
prevented the removal of furniture from the house of Bill Price in North
Terrace, Mardy, on 10 November 1931. The Mardy Council of Action
(virtually an anti-bailiff committee) was thus in existence before the
change in Communist Party line and was sufficiently broad to include a
member of the Salvation Army who participated in the fateful events of
10 November 1931. Whenever the threat of an eviction or seizure of
furniture arose, Ben Payne, who acted as a kind of town-crier on such
occasions, would rouse all those who were members of the organisation.
This, it appears, is what happened at North Terrace.[21] In the words of
Trevor Davies, a leading member of the Salvation Army:

Well, we were having this meeting in the Hall and someone came in and said
that the bailiffs (or the bums as we called them) . . . were going up to North

Terrace to take possession of this man's house. Well he was the son-in-law of the undermanager Lewis that was in the collieries at the time you see, and he was a fireman when we was working, that is one of the bosses, like see. So Arthur Horner got up and started shouting . . . agitating them to try to get the men . . . [to] march up to North Terrace. As *usual* I was in the front again, because I was used to being in the front with the Salvation Army Band.

How many of you were there?

About fifty or sixty, quite a crowd. And Arthur Horner and Dai Lloyd [Davies] and Charlie Goch [Jones] and myself, we went into the house. . . .[22]

Horner was told by the bailiff that the furniture was to be taken away because of non-payment of rates, an allegation which Mrs Price vigorously denied (it later transpired that she was correct.) Horner made an agreement by telephone with the Treasurer of the Council that when Bill Price arrived home from work he would consult with the Treasurer. He then informed the bailiff that he could not take the furniture away. In the meantime the crowds had grown and 'things looked ugly'. Horner 'gave orders that no one was to touch the furniture van. I told Charlie Jones my main supporter that if they tried to take the furniture away, all he had to do was to put a man at each of the wheels of the van and when they tried to move it, stick a knife in the tyres. We didn't have to carry out our threat and there was no rough stuff at all.' By the time the police under Inspector W. E. Rees arrived from the surrounding districts the bailiff's empty van was already leaving.[23]

None the less, thirty-two men and three women were summoned to appear before Porth Magistrates' Court by the end of January 1932, charged with unlawful assembly and incitement to riot. Only thirty-four proceeded to the Glamorgan Assizes at Cardiff on 18 February: it had been decided to drop charges against the member of the Salvation Army who was one of the leaders of the action and he was dismissed with a caution and five shillings costs.[24] Those who remained were deemed by the *Western Mail* and the Glamorgan Constabulary to be 'Bolshevists' or their sympathisers. A certain amount of hysteria was whipped up during the trial by the *Western Mail* which had, according to a general belief, originally given the label 'Little Moscow' to Mardy in 1926.[25] References were made to the defendants at the 'Little Moscow trial' as 'agitators', 'desperadoes', 'conspirators' and 'inveterate enemies of society . . . organising anarchy'. When Horner was given fifteen months' gaol, the *Western Mail* complained that it was a light sentence and would have preferred 'that this pestiferous fellow should be permanently segregated from his kind'.[26]

In all, twenty-nine were found guilty of unlawful assembly but none of incitement to riot: they were sentenced to a total of seven years' hard labour. The bulk of the evidence (provided by the Glamorgan Constabulary) was of a political character which provoked the *Manchester Guardian* to demand an enquiry because politics was allegedly used to sway the judgement. The Chief Constable, Lionel Lindsay, stated that it was important to provide the political background of the defendants because 'definite proof was difficult to obtain'.[27]

There was little evidence directly referring to the events of 10 November 1931. Much of it related to detailed biographical information of the defendants, particularly Horner who was described as assuming the role of 'dictator at Mardy'. It was implied that he was a paid Russian agent and that during his absence Mardy was normal. The decline in the value of houses, from £350 to £50 and the incidence of mass unemployment were all attributed to Horner and his friends, some of whom were described as his bodyguards and lieutenants.[28] One of these was Frank Owen who was later killed serving with the International Brigades whilst seven others had fought in the Great War (one of whom had lost a leg).[29]

The views expressed by the Glamorgan Constabulary and the *Western Mail* were not shared by the people of the Rhondda nor the Labour Movement in general. A Mardy Defence Committee was set up with representation from lodges, Women's Guilds, NUWM, TUC unemployed branches and Co-op Guilds. George Hall, MP, and D. R. Grenfell, MP, asked the Home Secretary if the sentences could be reviewed, whilst David Watts-Morgan, MP, despite ill-health (he died within a year), was involved in getting three months' remission for Horner and five others.[30]

There can be no doubt that all the defendants had failed to get re-employment after 1926 (or were wives of the unemployed) and had been deeply involved in politics, the SWMF and the NUWM. Their activity could not be explained by youthful exuberance (their average age was thirty-seven years). They were very much part of that trapped generation with family and mortgage ties which prevented any uprooting to Slough, Coventry or elsewhere. Frustrated, and left with little legitimate political or trade union action at their disposal, they were prepared to use extra-legal activities to defend what little they had left.

The circumstances and nature of the trial inevitably encouraged a feeling within the Labour Movement that a deliberate conspiratorial attempt had been mounted to crush what 'resistance' remained in Mardy. Already suffering from mass unemployment and already expelled from the SWMF, it seemed that with the elimination of thirty-four of its most ardent activists, 'Little Moscow' had finally fallen. What it did succeed in doing was to end Mardy's isolation from the coalfield. It also drew together, at least temporarily, those who had bitterly attacked each other in the preceding four years. Attacks on Horner and Hornerism ceased overnight in the *Daily Worker* and S. O. Davies, prominent in the Mardy Lodge expulsion, campaigned for Horner's release. It did in some ways clear the ground for the united front and anti-fascist perspectives later in the 1930s.[31]

When he was released in the summer of that year, he was to find a situation before him that was much more amenable to his views and abilities, both in terms of his own party's development and as regards the Federation itself.

The latter, through all these tribulations, had been tinkering with reform proposals until the cold-water shock of the 1931 award, coupled with the election of Oliver Harris as General Secretary in February 1932, finally pushed them into decisive action. In 1929 the schemes drawn up by the Organisation Committee were variations on the previous pattern, with suggestions for more centralised control of agents but a continued insistence on a balance between the Central and Districts in terms of representation on the EC.[32] It was only in late 1931 that a more ruthless pruning came to be seen as necessary as they addressed themselves, again, to the difficulties of non-unionism. The Organisation Committee produced a comprehensive report that summed up the strategy to be pursued in the 1930s. There was the usual insistence on Lodge efficiency, production of leaflets, payment of speakers and the like, but there was also the suggestion that the coalfield should be divided 'into suitable areas' which would consist of one or more districts, and that Conferences of the Lodge Delegates should be held. Further, they suggested the eight areas into which the coalfield could be divided – an effective halving of the district structure. These eight areas, with minor adjustments affecting a lodge or groups of lodges, was the exact prototype of the scheme of centralisation adopted in 1934. Significantly, they also gave their view 'that in dealing with non-unionism among the employed persons in this coalfield it is necessary to arrange to organise all unemployed colliery workers and to link them up in some form with the SWMF'. The echo was that of Horner, in his quarrel with the CPGB: 'I contended that the source of power must be the organised workers because they alone had some organised strength. I said the organised working-class *in work* must be the basis of organisation. I said we must concentrate on strengthening the trade unions and then building an alliance between the employed workers and the unemployed.'[33]

During 1932 the Organisation Committee, having refused to finance every non-union stoppage initiated, were able to report on their 'experience of recent successful district Conferences on organisation'. Their proposals, at this stage, were limited to urging more and better communication between the various levels within the Federation, whilst the continued pressures for reorganisation were still framed in terms of an amalgamation of existing resources only.[34] So when in August 1932 the EC again presented the lodges with a scheme (of eleven suggested Districts), its only new features were the Central's obligation to meet all existing District debts, and proposals for new Central appointments of a Compensation Secretary and an Organisation Secretary with special responsibilities for unemployment. District expenses would thus be lessened, so the Central would receive a higher share of the monthly contribution (i.e. 5*d*. to the lodge, 4*d*. to the District and 1*s* 3*d*. to Central). The unwillingness to relinquish control was shown by the proposal for a 'Joint Committee' (one delegate per lodge) where collieries had a common ownership, which would always be presided over by the SWMF President and only be called by the Executive Council to deal with matters the EC deemed fit. Rather tetchily the committee declared that this was 'its last word on the question of a new division of the districts'.[35] Once more the idea was to retain an outmoded structure by suckling the weak.

The scheme was put before a Delegate Conference in November and pressed most strongly by the Executive Council. After a long disputed session, on a card vote, the scheme was rejected (48,750 to 40,700) and the Conference proceeded to establish its own sub-committee (to consist of delegate and Executive members) to draft another one, on the principle of Centralisation. Enoch Morrell told the Conference that he hoped when this was done that there would not be 'schemes submitted to be ruthlessly turned down one after the other'.[36] Undoubtedly, the EC were stung, as they had been in the past by Delegate Conferences, but this time there would be no residue of pride in their own autonomy, on the part of the Districts, to underwrite the compromise for in 'parts the organisation was dying of a pernicious economic anaemia'. However, in late 1932 the 'work of destroying the trade union feudalism of the South Wales Miners' Federation had commenced'.[37]

It had, in short, become unavoidable, though the individual jealousies of the separate Districts had taken a long while to whittle away since 1925 when D. J. Williams had written:

> No one will hold today that [our Districts] are efficient fighting or even administrative units. In no sense are they productive or economic units. They are in fact, arbitrary geographic divisions; inevitable, at one time, it is true but now nothing more than anachronisms. The collieries within them belong to different owners, often to different combines; they offer no unifying force to bring the workers together and in a conflict with the owners ... would stand no chance. Certainly a new orientation is needed in trade union structure in South Wales.[38]

Since 1926 the financial position of the Districts, even of large and powerful ones, had become parlous, since they were so dependent on the prosperity and number of their lodges. The officials of Rhondda No. 1 District complained, annually after 1925, that the Lodges were using more than their five-sixths quota towards local expenses, and in 1931, told the Lodges that 'the arrears have again accumulated'.[39] For December 1931, 35 per cent of the insured population engaged in mining in Wales and Monmouthshire were unemployed (76,917 men) and by December 1932 the number had increased to 42.6 per cent (93,254).[40] There was no sense, in this worsening crisis, in amalgamating Districts solely to relieve them of some financial costs, as the Executive had proposed, and the Districts had desired,[41] for the lodges were receiving no benefit from a three-tier system any more. W. J. Saddler, then General Secretary, was entitled to write, in 1945, that before 1934 'the old district form of organisation had become exhausted and obsolete. They were unable to give service to our men because of the bad state of organisation, and were, in fact, unable to pay the salaries of the officials in those districts'.[42] The very viability of the SWMF was at stake in the early 1930s, with its purposes questioned by the SWMIU, the MMM and even other trade unions who felt, as the AEU did, that they could protect engineering workers in collieries more effectively than the Miners' Federation.[43] It was a prerequisite of

Federation survival that it alter form as drastically as the coalfield of which it had been such an important part.[44]

By March 1933 a draft scheme for centralisation had been prepared and explained to Conference; the lodges were advised of the Central's desire to retain 1s. 8d. out of the monthly contribution, with 4d. going to the lodges, and the whole matter brought up at Conference in June.[45] There, by a majority of 2-1 (1,042 to 592 on a card vote) the scheme, with an amendment only allowing the Central 1s. 7d., was accepted.[46] At last the old organisation had been superseded by a plan that left almost nothing untouched.

Eight new numbered Areas replaced the existing Districts and themselves were only designed as councils for reporting purposes, and in order to link together those lodges outside any large combine.[47] The Combine Committees now came into their own, for although 'in the past . . . organised very incompletely in a few groups of collieries', under the new rules they were to 'be organised generally' and 'in a few cases cover an area extending from Monmouthshire to Mid-Glamorgan'.[48]

Of most importance was the creation of a rank-and-file Executive on which only the President, Vice-President and General Secretary would sit as ex-officio members. Agents could only sit, in rotation and at invitation, in an advisory capacity. Executive members were elected by ballot for two-year periods, and were eligible for re-election. Each Area was entitled to one EC representative for every 6,000 members, and an additional one for every 6,000 above that. The agents (and the number of them) were to be decided by the EC and the lodges, as were their salaries. The Area Councils were to meet every two months to receive reports from the Agents and the EC lodge delegates would elect the chairman in each Area from their own ranks. The 'Joint Committees' (or Combine Committees) were to meet 'at least once every two months' with 'special meetings . . . if any lodge or lodges affiliated to it so desire'; and this formalisation (indeed insistence upon) Combine Committees would be no rubber-stamping of the Central, for each one would appoint its own Secretary, President and Treasurer, with its finances coming from the lodges affiliated.[49]

Thus the direct links between the lodges and the Central, the members and the officials, were strengthened by this abolition of the Districts. Power now flowed the way of the non-official sectors of the Federation. It was not completely what The Miners' Next Step had advocated, since the General Secretary, for instance, remained a full-time appointment, but no paid official could dominate policy-making, as in the past, without securing the support of the Council directly in touch with, and to an extent recallable by, rank and file members. Even full-time lodge secretaries were debarred from election. Almost immediately arrangements were made for a ballot vote so that the new EC might have some experience before the scheme came officially into operation on 1 January 1934. The ballot was to be on the transferable vote scheme, with employed and unemployed financial members being allowed to vote. In the first instance there were three EC members of Area No. 1, and one each for the others, with the exception of Area No. 2, who, at that stage, did not warrant one.[50] The new EC was a reflection of the respect accorded to experienced men by the members and of the prosperity of the Anthracite District which had, in November 1932, elected Jim Griffiths as Vice-President in place of S. O. Davies, who became the first organiser (two other new appointments were Evan Williams, Maesteg, to the Compensation Department and William Dunn, Blaina, to the Finance Department).[51] The EC reviewed the staff formerly employed by the Districts and reallocated the agents and secretaries involved. They decided against the retention of any advisory Agents in the way that the old Districts had retained MPs. Rates of expenses and travel allowances were fixed for Area and Central meetings, and the location of Area offices agreed.[52] By the end of the year they had decided that one agent from each Area would periodically sit on the EC for specified times.[53]

In addition, the question of the relationship of the unemployed members to the organisation was considered vital. For a number of years they had organised their own unemployment rather haphazardly, reducing the contribution to 1d. a week, and allowing continuation of membership. By the late 1920s they had taken action to ensure that the unemployed could only take decisions on matters not affecting 'working conditions', still hoping for an improvement in conditions. When these did not materialise, they again tightened the procedure by a stricter application of the rules in favour of employed members. Thus, in 1931, a Circular declared:

Hitherto we have given the unemployed members the same rights as are enjoyed by the employed financial members whose contributions provide the means for keeping the organisation in existence. It is regrettable that this privilege has been abused in too many instances by the unemployed in interfering in matters that concern only the employed members, and in some cases by furthering policies other than those for which the Federation stands, thereby creating friction in the Lodges which has been injurious to the organisation.

What happened now was that lodges of collieries definitely abandoned were dissolved, and where wholly idle, but not abandoned, the lodges could deal with unemployment, and questions of re-employment, but could not vote at either District or Conference meetings. Similar restrictions applied to partial closures, with the unemployed only allowed a limited representation on the committee.[54]

There was some tension at this period, of course, within the Federation ranks, so this move can be seen, in part, as a political manoeuvre, just as the SWMF did not favour the activities of NUWCM or its hunger marches. The TUC had plans to create unemployed associations based on Trades Councils. These met with a mixed reception from the SWMF, since they wished to maintain their links with unemployed members but, at the same time, did not wish unemployed demands (such as the possibility of 'sharing work') to gain ground. Oliver Harris admitted to a TUC representative 'that the unemployed lodges were getting a menace to the employed members. In many districts the votes of the unemployed members would carry decisions on policy, and the coalowners were refusing to discuss proposals which had been carried in this manner, and claimed that they could only meet representatives of their own employees. In addition, the South Wales Miners' Federation has been reorganised. . . . From October . . . no full-time officials will be eligible[for the EC]. In this way, unemployed lodges will be able to influence the return of some members of the Executive.'[55]

In fact, the SWMF clung to its old policy of organising its own unemployed and they took a definitive stand on the issue, in accordance with their new constitution, in April 1934, with the issue of their 'Regulations Respecting Unemployed Members', which clarified the one they had issued, to some protest, in January:

> In view of the prolonged state of unemployment in the coalfield, and, unfortunately, a prospect of its definite continuation, the regulation of the position of the unemployed colliery workers . . . should be dealt with on lines different from those contemplated when the old rules of the Federation . . . were adopted [and] intended only to apply to cases of individual members, or small bodies of men, being unemployed for short periods . . . not designed to deal with a situation where tens of thousands are idle, a large number . . . for long periods.

The irregularity of these circumstances was now regularised by emphasising still the primacy of the employed members' rights and restricting the unemployed, whether as individual members of a lodge, or as an unemployed lodge (where a colliery was partially open or not definitely abandoned), to matters affecting unemployment or re-employment only, but also allowing unemployed lodges of not less than 50 members to send a delegate to Area Council Meetings and Annual Conference. Further, they now set up in some areas 'Branches of Unemployed Mineworkers', with the right of a delegate if they had a membership of at least 100.[56] This effectively gave the unemployed a voice within the SWMF, and so provided a most valuable outlet for their frustrations, whilst restricting their powers of decision. Naturally this elicited considerable protest, over a number of years, from the unemployed themselves who felt shuttled off from the Federation proper, but it placed the control of administration firmly in the hands of the employed.[57]

The SWMF could approach 1934 with more confidence than it had enjoyed for some time, with its component parts streamlined and more responsive, its members having weathered the worst crisis in its history. Further grounds for hope lay in the unity that was again being forged from below as the CPGB and its allies reversed their earlier pronouncements. There was still dissension, of course, but disruption was ruled out in the push to change the trade unions from being 'organs of collaboration to organs of class struggle'. Even before the end of 1932 South Walian militants were writing to the *Daily Worker* criticising the CP's isolation from non-party militants. The swing away from 'Red Unions' was almost complete and the CP Central Committee reconfirmed their emphasis on 'revolutionary mass work in the reformist Trade Unions'.[58]

The old Mardy Lodge itself began, in August 1932, to press for readmission into the Federation as, with Horner still in gaol, the colliery company was rumoured to be reopening the pits. The EC refused a deputation on the question, since the men were unemployed and because, as one member pointed out, it was 'in accordance with the policy of the CP that their members should seek to re-enter the trade unions'.[59] Horner, on his release in early December 1932, had been elected checkweigher by the men in work. Promptly the pit closed again, though the ballot itself ('I regarded this a great tribute') had been declared void because Horner was not a member of the SWMF. The old lodge could only press for re-entry of 'expelled militants' and the 'recruitment of those not at present members of the Federation'.[60]

Although Horner contested Rhondda East in the by-election of March 1933, caused by the death of Watts-Morgan, and came near to toppling the Labour candidate and Rhondda miners' agent, W. H. Mainwaring, [61] the main arena for militancy in the coalfield was still seen, even in the election itself, as the reconstruction of the Federation whose weakness and 'bankruptcy' were attributed to 'the leadership of those who co-operate with colliery managers against workmen'. This was a hit against Mainwaring, as agent, for allegedly recommending the Mardy men to go back to work in 1927 on management's conditions. The moral now drawn, however, was not that the Federation was hopeless but that 'it can and will become an effective instrument in the workers' struggle against the coalowners by the removal of those autocrats who have captured power and used this power against the militants'.[62]

With the success of fascism in Europe the demand for 'a united front' grew, whilst the SWMF's decision to centralise in late November 1932, provided the hope of a more effective militant voice being heard via the lodges. It was resolved to build up a 'rank-and-file movement' on the pattern of the old Unofficial Reform Committee and to set up a paper. Sympathisers in the lodges were circulated and conferences held with an agenda on 'The United Front in Action' and 'Rank-and-File Movements in South Wales'. Progress was not spectacular, in a numerical sense, but the stated line of approach was one of immense significance, for the future, for it was now adumbrated that:

> The old idea that unity is only possible with workers who are close to the CP is a dangerously wrong one. The United Front must be one of the mass of workers on questions of immediate concern to them, in which Communists must prove themselves in words and deeds the best fighters for the demands on which the United Front is based. . . . There are scores of Lodge Officials and Labour Party officials who are bitterly opposed to the CP, who have attacked the CP in local and Parliamentary election, public meetings and lodge meetings, but who are deeply concerned about the situation in the coalfield and anxious that something should be done. All these elements must be won and can be won to support the rank and file movement.[63]

At a Militant Miners' Conference in Pontypridd, Horner outlined their programme which consisted of the usual demands for increased wages, a 7-hour day, against victimisation and the abrogation of local customs, and it enshrined, as its foremost plank, the push for 100 per cent membership of the Federation. The movement re-elected its Provisional Committee and decided on further Conferences. The stress was on the potential in the issues before the workers with the Party's own ideas being soft-pedalled. Or, as Idris Cox put it, 'What we want is not unity in organisation but unity by action.'[64]

Its most effective weapon was the paper launched on 22 June as a fortnightly, edited by Horner and entitled *South Wales Miner*, the 'official organ of the rank-and-file movement of the South Wales miners'. Its policy, it stated, was 'to advocate militant Trade Union policy throughout the South Wales coalfield' and to this end it denounced 'co-operation with capitalists'. All miners were urged to join the Federation to 'build once again the fighting strength of the lodges in the coalfield'. Throughout 1933 the paper covered the issues where disputes seemed likely and it pressed for an end to 'the district complex', for an acceptance of Combine Committees as an end to 'the inglorious isolation of the lodges', and help to advertise local rank-and-file conferences.[65] Immediate success was slight but it was sowing well for future reaping.

The breakthrough in the Left's isolation came in November 1933 when Horner, who had been invited to stand by some lodges, topped the poll in the first ballot for miners' agent in the Gwendraeth. The most prosperous area in the coalfield had already elected Jim Griffiths as Vice-President. Now the growing power of its left-wing, fed by an unlikely confidence in their own economic strength, would ensure that Horner's voice in the SWMF would be listened to again, backed by the employed. He was elected, an English-speaking outsider in this most Welsh part of all the coalfield, after a bitter contest, on the third ballot with the technicality of his not being a member of the Federation evaded because of the Anthracite District's precedent of having previously allowed non-members to stand and by virtue of the EC being unwilling to contest the point. He began at once, though not officially until 1 January 1934, so that the reorganisation scheme would not upset his position. By the end of the year he was sitting, after an absence of six years, on the EC.[66]

The old Mardy Lodge had given its blessing to his departure and was, itself, under the SWMF's new unemployed regulations merged with the new lodge *en bloc*, in February 1934.[67] In all senses, then, the prodigals had returned, though not to a fatted calf and not repentant either. Horner, for example, insisted on defying an SWMF censure against his support for Wal Hannington, the CP candidate, at the Merthyr by-election in May and June 1934, arguing that he had the right to espouse his own political principles whatever job he held.[68] It would take some time before old wounds were healed; but indicative of the new spirit was the SWMF's refusal to do more than rap Horner over the knuckles by distinguishing between freedom of opinion and loyalty to Federation policy, and the willingness of Horner and Mark Harcombe to address the same meeting in the Rhondda in a non-union campaign.[69] For the rest, disagreement was phrased now in terms of tactics, with the most important area of strife being that of wages which had been 'frozen', by mutual agreement between the MFGB and the Government, through 1932 and 1933.[70]

But all this occurred against a dramatically changing international scene in which the most serious event was the emergence of Nazi Germany. Activists in the coalfield, whether consciously or unconsciously, from now onwards began to view their localised preoccupations in internationalist terms: it was one 'united front' anti-fascist struggle. Their political strategies seemed to change overnight and yet they were in an uncanny way part of the now well-established extra-legal, extra-parliamentary pattern. But these events in Europe did accelerate the trend. The para-military proposals which emerged in South Wales in the Spring of 1933 to counter fascism in Britain centred around Aneurin Bevan, MP for Ebbw Vale, who was to invoke the memory of the Monmouthshire Chartists' March on Newport in 1839 to bolster his argument.

Bevan need not have reached as far back as that to justify his scheme within the traditions of the coalfield. There had been elements of para-military 'political' organisation in the valleys since at least the mid-1920s. Quite apart from the obvious militaristic overtones of the Hunger Marches between 1927 and 1932 and the well-organised 'anti-bailiff' Mardy Council of Action, there were several other examples. A Defence Corps had been set up by Amman Valley miners at the height of the Anthracite strike and riots of 1925 and S. O. Davies, the Vice-President of the SWMF at the time, had called for a 'United Army'.[71] A 'Council of War' was called by the Afan Valley miners in September 1926 as a means of combating the increase in the police forces during the lock-out.[72] In October 1932, miners in the Aberdare Valley formed a 'Defence Corps'[73] and in October 1931, seventy ex-service men in Porth formed a 'Defence Force' to head demonstrations because of the police hostility towards open-air meetings.[74]

The initiative to establish these 'united front' para-military bodies in 1933 seems to have come from Aneurin Bevan, supported by his socialist followers within his own parliamentary division, and his close friend John Strachey. Strachey had been associated with Bevan and Oswald Mosley in their criticism of the Macdonald Labour Government, and had, unlike Bevan, stayed with Mosley when his New Party was launched. With Mosley's rapid drift towards fascism and Hitler's rise to power, Strachey realigned himself with Bevan.[75] They had spent Easter together at Strachey's Bishop Stortford farm and must have discussed the possibilities of a new movement. Such ideas could not bear fruit in South Wales without the total support of the Communists whose organising skills and experience of illegality were necessary. This was appreciated by Strachey and Bevan. Strachey thus wrote on 18 April to their most important leader, Arthur Horner, who had only been released from prison the previous Christmas. The letter was understandably vague, presumably because of the dubious legality of the subject involved:

Thank you for your letter which I was indeed glad to get. Aneurin Bevan, who has been with us over Easter, is writing to you also. I shall be deeply interested to hear what you think of his proposals. My own view is that they may just possibly be the germ of the one thing that can possibly save us. Aneurin and I are passionately anxious that the CP should work with and not against them. I trust that you and Aneurin will talk the whole thing over soon. Will there be any chance of you coming to London after that? If so I will make a point of coming [*word illegible*] to London having a talk – at any time or place that you find convenient.

My own feeling is that until you have had a chance of discussion with Aneurin and, if possible, we have met, it would be better not to go into further details with King Street. As you know Aneurin has already had a full talk with Harry, and I don't see that until you and Aneurin, at any rate, have got some preliminary work done in Wales, and are in a position to see how things are going, then there is much more to say. What do you think?[76]

Bevan simply wrote briefly but in urgent tones on 30 April:

I will come over to Mardy to see you on Wednesday afternoon at 3 o'clock. If you cannot see me on Wednesday at 3 o'clock, please let me know where you can see me. If Cardiff or Newport, I will see you because I am particularly anxious to have a discussion with you about this matter.[77]

As we have seen, Horner had fought a bitter Parliamentary by-election in Rhondda East against the Labour candidate W. H.

Mainwaring, who had been the miners' agent responsible for carrying out the expulsion of the Mardy Lodge.[78]

When Bevan visited Horner after the election, he explained that, although being in different parties, he would have spoken on Horner's behalf, had he stood as a miners' candidate. This qualified support for Horner along with their earlier differences over the prolongation of the 1926 lock-out and Bevan's refusal to be associated with the Miners' Minority Movement, may explain the apparently cool reception the Communists later gave to Bevan's proposals.[79]

In the meantime, the Communists buoyed by their near miss at Rhondda East and their gaining of four district council seats in April (at Nantyffyllon, Caerau, Cilfynydd and Ferndale) responded optimistically to the Communist International's call for working class unity. By the end of April, the South Wales District of the CPGB and the South Wales Divisional Council of the ILP had agreed on a detailed plan of united front action which included eleven area May Day demonstrations, the main themes for which were to be solidarity with the German workers, action against war and the 'capitalist attack on the workers'. The joint appeal issued by the two organisations linked up the international struggle against fascism with the localised struggles of the Bedwas strikers and demands for free school meals and free fuel for the unemployed. Emphasis was also significantly placed on appealing to unorganised workers and the need for uniting the employed with the unemployed.[80]

Bevan seemed to have pressed on quietly and independently with his proposals. Closed meetings of his supporters (admitted by invitation card only) were held in his constituency in the week preceding a Cardiff Conference convened to discuss the growth of fascism in Europe. Bevan basically relied on his 'Query Club' which he had successfully developed in the 1920s as a secret socialist society in Tredegar to conquer all the centres of power in the town. It was the 'Query Club' which was to form the organisational backbone to what became known as the 'Tredegar Workers' Freedom Group'.[81]

Oliver Jones, who had presided over the meeting at Tredegar and who prided himself all his life on having spoken as a boy to one of the last surviving Monmouthshire Chartists, did release some tantalising background details of the proposed organisation to the *Western Mail*, even though the meetings and the proposals were cloaked in secrecy. He maintained that the demand for a disciplined socialist youth movement had come from all over South Wales and that

Bevan was merely giving articulation to this spontaneous response. It was felt that the cinema, dance-hall and other similar kinds of recreation were obstructions to the Labour movement. The new organisation would include study circles, propaganda meetings, educational meetings, physical culture classes, hiking, cycling and swimming. It was left to Bevan himself to reveal his proposals to the Labour movement in Cardiff on 20 May.[82]

It was the South Wales and Monmouthshire Division of Trades Councils who had called the conference of working-class organisations at the Cory Hall to protest against the growth of European fascism and to discuss various proposals to counter a similar development in Britain. The conference accepted the proposition made by James Griffiths, the SWMF agent (and later MP for Llanelli), which simply called for demonstrations against Nazi atrocities, the printing of *Vorwarts* for German workers and the establishing of a relief fund. He was followed by Aneurin Bevan who asserted that capitalism had no hope of recovery. In order to survive, British capitalism had already declared war on democracy and gave as his evidence of this the reorganisation of the Metropolitan Police Force. But civil war in Britain, he claimed, could be averted by the working class being 'well organised, disciplined and courageously led'.[83]

Bevan nevertheless must have been only too well aware of the paradoxical situation in which he was about to find himself: a British Member of Parliament ready to launch an extra-parliamentary para-military organisation. He seemed confused, spoke at great length and for once was unable to rebut a remark at the rear of the Hall: 'What is this, Mr Chairman, Tennyson's "Babbling Brook"?'[84] He ended, however, appropriately enough by invoking the past to justify the practical proposals he was about to make. The *Western Mail* reported that he quoted a Pontypool boy's letter on Chartism.[85] This must have been the letter from the nineteen-year-old George Shell who was one of the twenty-two killed during the Chartist Rising at Newport in 1839:

> Pontypool, Sunday Night, November 4th 1839
> Dear parents, – I hope this will find you well, as I am myself at present. I shall this night be engaged in a struggle for freedom, and should it please God to spare my life, I shall see you soon; but if not, grieve not for me. I shall fall in a noble cause. My tools are at Mr Cecil's and likewise my clothes.
>
> Yours truly,
> George Shell.[86]

He finally suggested that anyone interested 'in the development of a new form of united organisation should stay behind and have a chat over things'. This tactic was ruled out of order by the chairman, Alan Robson, of the Cardiff Trades and Labour Council, who maintained that everything should be discussed openly by the conference already convened. After some disagreements, Bevan and his supporters, amongst whom were several Communists, left the conference and eventually proceeded to Charles Street Labour Hall where they took possession of a room. It was here that Bevan first made public his proposals. Every district would organise a Workers' Freedom Group which would not exclude the ILP, the Communist Party or any other bodies outside the Labour Party. They would be specifically aimed at youth, they would provide for organised training and would have a first aid detachment. Among the objects of the group would be the 'cleansing of working class bodies' and the organising of resistance to war. Every member was also expected to take an oath of allegiance.[87]

Even in the more exclusive meeting in Charles Street, Bevan met with some criticism, particularly from Labour Party members, who were concerned about the democratic control of the groups and were afraid that Bevan wished to become a 'British Hitler'. His answer was that the groups would not be democratic, but he was not concerned about self-aggrandisement. With more than an echo of von Clausewitz's *The Art of War* which had apparently made an impact on Horner while in prison the previous year,[88] Bevan answered his critics:

> It will be a dictatorship of conditions and not of persons. . . . A general must direct his army by relationship to the conditions in which he finds himself.[89]

With the organisation remaining in the hands of a committee of fourteen, the adherents to the new cause returned to the valleys. In the following week, Bevan was at pains to explain that he was not forming a new party, that there was no intention to organise a movement on a militaristic basis and that it was not a Communist organisation.[90]

James Griffiths again attacked Bevan's proposals by alleging that any attempt to set up bodies outside the trade unions and Labour Party would aggravate the very problem the conference had been called upon to discuss. Another miners' agent, W. H. May of Pontypridd, expressed the mood of the major trend within the British Labour movement in the 1930s:

Force has never been any remedy. In this country we have got the most democratic Government in the world and the people can put into power any members they like, so that they get the Government they deserve. Speaking for my district I do not think our men will show any enthusiasm for this scheme.[91]

None the less, the movement was launched but against a background of hostility from the Labour Party and ridicule from the *Western Mail* whose fictitious column written by the 'Junior Member for Treorchy' dubbed Bevan, 'The Cymric Hitler'.[92]

Groups were set up in other parts of the coalfield, mainly in the Rhondda but they quickly fell under the control of Communists and consequently Bevan dropped them 'like hot cakes'.[93] Elsewhere, as in Nantyglo, Bevan's emissary, Archie Lush was met with hostility by the local Communist Party: they already had their own youth movement based upon cycling, parades and leafleting. His proposals were thus rejected.[94]

Effective groups, however, were launched in Bevan's own constituency, particularly in Tredegar itself and in such outlying villages as Abertysswg and Pontlottyn. There was at one time a combined total of some seventy members most of whom were probably unemployed miners (although there is no precise evidence of this). The centre of activity was a room over a coffee tavern in Tredegar's Commercial Street where members gathered wearing specially commissioned badges with a design which resembled a coffin and a flash. Route marches across the mountains (which might well have been crossed by Chartists nearly a century earlier for this same purpose), would be organised but weapons were never apparently used. Activity petered out within a matter of months so that the organisation became known jocularly even to its members as the 'coffin club'.[95]

Although sharing the central idea that the freedom groups were first and foremost anti-fascist, the Communists in South Wales viewed them in a slightly different way from Bevan's socialist supporters. They believed that Bevan was correct in outlining what seemed to be deliberate and increased police and state persecution of working-class demonstrations and the need for greater democratic control over Members of Parliament and local government. The Communists however, did not seem to be prepared to follow his initiative. Workers' Defence Forces had existed previously in South Wales and elsewhere and were to continue into the mid-1930s particularly in countering fascist demonstrations in Manchester and London. Some were deliberately organised and others were more spontaneous, as at Tonypandy in 1936.[96]

Even though the Tredegar Workers' Freedom Group disappeared almost as quickly as it had been launched, there was one revealing sequel nearly a decade later. In one of the war-time debates in which Bevan achieved notoriety, he was cut short by Brendan Bracken, the Minister of Information, who suddenly gave vivid and copious details of the Tredegar Group as if to challenge Bevan's loyalty to constitutionalism and parliamentary democracy. The detail must have surprised Bevan, but also sheds some light on the gravity with which the authorities must have viewed his group.[97]

The real significance of the Workers' Freedom Groups was not their success, for they achieved few or none of their avowed aims, but the revelation of an underlying, combative, even para-military element and form of organisation in the coalfield. Three of the members, Bob Jones and Bob Cox of Tredegar and Jim Brewer of Abertysswg (who had been brought up to take pride in his great-grandfather being a Chartist) continued their anti-fascist activities by later joining the International Brigades. Bevan himself was also one of the foremost parliamentary supporters of the Brigades and had once said to Brewer that he would have liked to have gone to Spain with him.[98]

It was important also as being one of the first anxious responses in Britain to the growth of fascism in Europe. That this response took this particular para-military form in the South Wales coalfield was not without its historical and contemporary relevance. As we shall see later, the received Chartist tradition of 1839 was, whether consciously or unconsciously, always in evidence.

Bevan's Freedom Groups can be seen as nothing more than a brief and rather romantic episode. They did not succeed because they were outside the established institutions of the Labour movement and did not grapple with the central problem of mass residual unemployment and the rebuilding of the SWMF. The question for Bevan and Horner alike, in representing two militant trends within South Wales, was how to remove themselves from the periphery to the centre of politics.

Inevitably it was the wage negotiations which were the constant backdrop to 1934 with the EC asking for a revision of the Schiller Award (with a 35 per cent minimum above the 1915 standard), a $6\frac{1}{2}$-hour shift on Saturdays and twelve days' holiday a year. These were not as much as the provisions set out at an earlier militants' Conference but, despite an intervention by Horner demanding a campaign around a Charter and the immediate handing-in of notices, this carried the day. Jim Griffiths agreed with all of Horner's attack on the coalowners but insisted that the economic circumstances of the industry were not conducive to strike action, and, of course, the unstated fear was that the Federation was still not strong enough. It was Horner's first speech at a Delegate Conference in years; he recalled that the attitudes he found there 'made me realise how much less militant was the coalfield' than in 1928.[99]

Jim Griffiths, who had become President when Enoch Morrell retired, in April 1934 (with Arthur Jenkins as Vice-President), was intent on negotiations rather than confrontation. The stumbling-block was the refusal of the owners to accept arbitration by an independent tribunal. The Federation were not prepared to see another Schiller or anyone 'who knew little about the industry'. They prepared public statements pointing out that the labour of 66 men out of 1,000 in a colliery went towards paying royalty owners and insisting they wanted a machinery established that might avoid conflict over wages, but that the owners' restrictions on the choice of arbitrators made it impossible to ensure that the latter were competent.[100] Finally, the Federation put their case to the National Industrial Board where they pointed out that a third of all South Wales' colliery workers were unemployed, that in ten years, 2,379 men had been killed and 330,731 injured in South Wales, that poverty was rife in an area whose colliery work-force had declined from 260,502 in 1920 to 129,719 in 1933, and that the Schiller Award was 'an insult'. The Board, after six weeks, pronounced that, in view of a slight trade upswing that made 1934 a better commercial year than 1928, the percentage awarded by Sir Francis Taylor should be restored and the Schiller differentials abolished. However, even this partial justification of their case, was irrelevant, for the owners had categorically refused to recognise the Board, to give evidence before it, or recognise its findings.[101]

The proceedings had been protracted, the results discouraging. The EC decided to recommend a month's notice to terminate the agreement that had been in abeyance since 31 January, and a Delegate Conference agreed.[102] Before this ran out the owners finally agreed to allow the Ministry of Labour to set up an Independent Tribunal which would report by 31 October 1934, with an award which, if it was an increase, would be retrospective to 1 October and, if a decrease, would not operate until 1 October 1935. This was accepted by a Delegate

Conference on a card vote of 67,000 to 14,000 so that there was an overwhelming majority in favour of the arbitration. The militant call for strike action had the proviso attached that South Wales should not fight alone, but rather approach the MFGB, a suggestion so bereft of reality that it is rather an indication of their unwillingness to push the matter to the limit.[103]

The standing ovation accorded Jim Griffiths, at this Conference, is a firm indication of the support his moderate policies were receiving, especially since they were coupled to a firm resolve to make the new organisation as efficient as possible in conditions of 'general impoverishment'. In March, the SWMF had launched a news-sheet again, *The Miners' Monthly*, to further contact between members and levels of the Federation. The President had written that, 'the task of the Federation has been one of fighting against fearful odds, and it is a tribute to the Federation that it has weathered the storm, and that, both in membership and spirit, it is recovering and is showing a determination that lost ground must be recovered and that new ground must be won'.[104]

The old ground had to be recovered in terms of membership. Early in 1934 yet another non-unionist campaign had been launched, with the MPs roped in, and the entrance fee reduced, for the sake of uniformity, to 5s. for a three-month period. The Organisation Committee began to collate information to determine where the most forthright work should be concentrated (Areas 4, 5 and 6 were designated), and requested Lodge Committees to exchange information so that non-unionists living in each other's localities could be chased up, with a 'Show Cards' as the end product. The Annual Conference resolved that even stronger action be instituted and that:

> . . . the EC be instructed to organise an intensive campaign to secure 100 per cent membership of the Organisation. The machinery of the Combine Committees should be utilised to the full for this purpose, and Show Cards should be held regularly every eight weeks on the same day throughout the coalfield. In the event of a failure to secure the necessary 100 per cent membership, 14 days' notice should be tendered simultaneously throughout all the areas, particularly those covered by the Combines.[105]

Old ground had been, mostly, maintained with successful non-union stoppages,[106] but as William Gregory stated, with some semblance of truth in the light of Nine Mile Point, Bedwas and the Dare Collieries, 'all previous attempts to "exterminate" the non-political union had resulted in some increases in the membership of that organisation'.[107]

He was speaking at a time when the first big Federation breakthrough against the SWMIU was being achieved. The Emlyn Colliery, opened in 1904 with its No. 1 slant; then, in 1924, the No. 2 slant had been started and began to raise coal in early 1926. During the lock-out a non-political branch, despite several attempts to stop it, had been formed. It had survived other attacks in 1931 but, from March 1934, began to receive the attention of the new Organisation Department, under S. O. Davies, with backing from neighbouring lodges. It was estimated that 80 per cent of the men were paying SWMIU contributions under duress.[108] The colliery, near Penygroes, Ammanford, came under Horner's purview as agent and he directed attention towards addressing mass meetings of the men on top of the slant despite being 'warned off' by the company.[109] Instead of a complete turnabout, in the situation, the SWMF used its propaganda for subtle purposes:

> We first of all carried out a campaign to get as many men as we could to join the Federation. Many of the men decided to be members of both Unions and the Company had no idea that they had rejoined the Federation.[110]

By the end of April the Industrial Union Lodge was disbanded, with its former chairman elected chairman of the new Federation Lodge and a new checkweighman, the Communist Evan J. Evans, elected. A trial of strength, the backlash of eight years, over the issue of minimum wage payments (there had been no payment for small coal at No. 2 slant) and the lodge's right to decide questions of seniority, now erupted with 900 men out for nine weeks. The men, despite having to pay some damages for their action, won their demands and achieved a new price-list.[111] This was a real victory, the first of its kind since the 1926 lock-out, and it did demonstrate 'the possibility of bringing about the final elimination of the South Wales Miners' Industrial Union'.

It was, by no means, an 'Open Sesame', for the chances of victory in the grimmer conditions prevailing in the eastern part of the coalfield were harder to forge and to grasp. None the less, it was to prove the only effective way of re-establishing Federation control even if, as elsewhere, at the cost of considerable sacrifice, financial and otherwise. By 1934 the Federation had explored every alternative avenue to all-out attack, and had had the necessity of using industrial action underlined for it. In December 1933 they had asked a Cardiff barrister about taking out an injunction to prevent a colliery company from terminating its contracts with workmen because they wished to be SWMF members. The opinion delivered was deafeningly eloquent about the non-existence of legal means to combat legal rights:

> ... no action will lie against the Colliery Company for dismissing workmen because they wish to become members of the SWMF, because ... the Colliery Company on their initiative and of their own free will, are in law perfectly free to engage whomsoever they like and whensoever they like and are free upon giving due notice to their present workmen, that in the future they will only appoint coloured men or men of a particular Nation and persons who are so dismissed upon proper notice being given have no remedy against the Company, because the Company have done nothing unlawful.[112]

A London barrister, Upjohn, confirmed this for Jim Griffiths in early 1934[113] and Stafford Cripps ended all debate on the matter when he said in 1936 on being asked for his general advice on the problem of non-unionism:

> The matter is one which can ... only be dealt with through the usual channels through which industrial disputes of this type are dealt with and not by legal proceedings.[114]

On the matter of 'usual channels' the SWMF naturally, needed no elucidation. Their problem had been to assess their ability to use those channels. There was, in 1934, the beginning of an upsurge of confidence within the coalfield again. It is difficult to pin it down for it is hardly assignable to a new prosperity in trade, slight as it was, or in wages, whilst the unemployed in mining did not diminish at all. Perhaps it lies in the recognition that no salvation lay in waiting for a Labour Government or the intervention of the MFGB, both fairly moribund in the early 1930s, and, therefore, that any grand national advances, political or industrial, were not to be looked for. The fight was very much in the localities. It would be arduous and gradual in its progress, but it was the necessary foundation. There is an indefinable tone of resurgence in the pronunciations of leaders of all shades, in the press, and from the platform. The reorganisation of 1934 had provided a focus for this recovery, as S. O. Davies, no longer lamenting the 'disgraceful condition' of the organisation, saw when he exposed the new scaffolding of the Federation and pointed to the building for which it had been designed:

There is now concrete evidence to show that our people are once again realising that there is no hope of protection or improvement outside the Federation. The great change recently effected in the structure of our Organisation and the response made to the change, show a revival of the old spirit that made history among the workers of the country. These changes have brought the members, employed and unemployed, in to Central Control. They are now the Executive Power of the Organisation, its work and its policy. The autonomy and mobility of the lodge have been maintained and enormously strengthened. It has now not only direct contact with the Central Authority, but is linked with other lodges at collieries owned by the same Company.

Further, lodges within and outside the big Combines are brought together at our Area Councils. There the officials of the Area and the Executive Council representatives give an account of their stewardship; conditions at collieries, Combine and non-Combine, are discussed, and a common policy, where practical, is evolved.

Your New Organisation recognises the need of a more effective co-ordination of our work throughout the Coalfield. It intends to obviate the duplication of costly and unrelated efforts as in the old days. It proposes to substitute for the old, isolated and independent action in one place, action directed from the Central, in order that its results may become the common property of the whole Coalfield, and thereby derive from it a common advantage.[115]

The SWMIU's existence at some pits meant a 'common disadvantage' for all others; since the bastion of the Industrial Union was, in 1934, as it had been all along, Taff-Merthyr, it was here that the SWMF, with its wage-claim gone to arbitration, decided to concentrate its energies so that the 'common advantage' could be gained by the Federation asserting, once more, its domination of every aspect of coalfield life. It was, as had been the case since 1926 (and some had argued, even before), a case of the Federation putting its own house in order first, in controlling, first, all colliery workers. The remaining years of the 1930s, contain this story and demonstrate the consequences of a revitalised SWMF in the politics and society of South Wales.

NOTES

1. Ness Edwards, *op. cit.*, p. 145. He goes into the wage negotiations in some detail. *Western Mail*, 1 October, 5, 19, 27 November, 1 December 1930.
2. Edwards, *op. cit.*, pp. 146–7. *Western Mail*, 23 and 31 December 1930.
3. *Western Mail*, 10 December 1930; 1 January 1931. The figures were supplied by Shinwell as Minister of Mines.
4. *Ibid.*, 2 and 8 January 1931. The SWMF issued an appeal to the rest of the community in South Wales. The Editor of the *Western Mail* described this 'plea for pity' as either an 'unpardonable miscalculation or sheer recklessness', and warned that fifteen-sixteenths of a wage was better than none at all.
5. *Ibid.*, 8, 9, 10, 16, 19 January 1931; Edwards, *op. cit.*, p. 149.
6. *Ibid.*, 7 March 1931.
7. *Ibid.*, 9, 10, 11, 17, 23 March 1931.
8. SWMF EC Minutes, 21 March 1931.
9. *Western Mail*, 4, 6, 11 July 1931.
10. *Ibid.*, 19 and 24 January 1931.
11. *Daily Worker*, 5, 8, 23 January 1931. Mardy Lodge Minutes, 18 January, 1 February 1931.
12. *Daily Worker*, 28, 29 January 1931.
13. Horner, *op. cit.*, p. 110.
14. *Daily Worker*, 10, 12, 23, 28 February 1931.
15. *Western Mail*, 9, 10, 11, 19, 20 March 1931.
16. *Daily Worker*, 7 March 1931.
17. Woodhouse, *op. cit.*, pp. 397–8.
18. *Daily Worker*, 17 March, 10 April 1931.
19. *Daily Worker*, March, April, May 1931; 8 October, 6 November 1931. Horner, *op. cit.*, pp. 111–12; Pelling, *The British Communist Party*, pp. 58–61. Will Paynter, then a checkweigher at Cymmer, wrote in support of Horner to the *Daily Worker* and later 'the experience left me a little sour for a time'. Paynter, *My Generation* (1972) p. 48. The whole episode is rather complex. Perhaps, for the history of the CPGB, two facts stand out, (1) that Horner was too important a figure to lose despite remarks to the contrary and (2) that Horner was strong enough to stand out against the Party but committed to it as the best hope of revolution to the extent that he could, having won the vital point, concede the game on a technicality.
20. *Western Mail*, 28, 29 October 1931; 25 February 1932. Horner, *op. cit.*, pp. 113–19.
21. SWML interviews with Trevor Davies (Mardy), 3 July 1973 and Mrs. V. Evans (Mardy), 11 June 1973.
22. *Ibid.*, Trevor Davies interview.
23. Horner, *op. cit.*, pp. 113–15.
24. Trevor Davies, interview, *op. cit.*
25. See p. 157 above.
26. *Western Mail*, 23 February, 25 February, 27 February 1932.
27. *Ibid.*

28. *WM*, 25 February 1932.
29. *DW*, 4 March 1932.
30. UCS, Mardy Defence Committee MSS.; 29 June, 11 August 1932.
31. W. Picton interview, *op. cit.*, *DW*, 3 March 1932.
32. Circular No. 61, SWMF files.
33. SWMF EC Minutes, 14 November 1931. Horner, *op. cit.*, pp. 110–11. The eight suggested areas were:

      1. Pontypridd and Rhondda
      2. Rhymney, East Glamorgan and Tredegar
      3. Ogmore and Garw
      4. Aberdare, Taff and Cynon, Merthyr and Dowlais
      5. Monmouthshire Western Valleys, Ebbw Vale and Blaina
      6. Eastern Valleys
      7. Maesteg and Afan Valley
      8. Anthracite and Western

34. SWMF EC Minutes, 23 April, 13 May, 2 July 1932.
35. Circular No. 157, 25 August 1932.
36. SWMF EC Minutes, 21, 22, 23 November 1932. *Western Mail*, 22 November 1932.
37. Edwards, *op. cit.*, p. 153.
38. *The Colliery Workers' Magazine*, January 1925.
39. Annual Report and Statement of Accounts, Rhondda No. 1 District, 1925, 1927, 1928, 1929, 1930, 1931.
40. *Western Mail*, 3 December 1932. The SWMF, quoting official figures, had issued a Christmas appeal for parcels of clothes, boots, bedclothes for 'sad cases': 'Women and girls with threadbare skirts and scanty or no underclothing; stockings darned until very little of the original stockings remain, bedclothes worn out, and no means to buy new ones; men without underclothes, and lack of boots common to all.'
41. See, for example, East Glamorgan District Minutes, 12 October 1932, when Morrell and S. O. Davies attended and had their proposals accepted.
42. W. J. Saddler, *Contributions in Relation to Services* (1945). SWMF files.
43. *Letters* between Ebby Edwards (MFGB President), Oliver Harris, officials of the Garw District (where AEU poaching was alleged), the General Secretary of the AEU and E. W. Davies (District Secretary of the AEU), December 1931–January 1932. SWMF files.
44. Jack Jones recognised this, in his novel *Rhondda Roundabout* (1934), a semi-documentary fiction, Shoni, his lodge delegate, is talking about the less drastic scheme of 1932:

> 'Yes, son, . . . our Federation is a very important body . . . you could no more think of South Wales and Monmouthshire without our Federation than you could think of the sea without ships. . . . Why, most of the South Wales MP's are our Federation chaps. . . . We've got nineteen districts like the Rhondda in four counties. Nineteen though it's true that more than half of 'em are gone to the dogs since the war. Nobody working in 'em, pits all closed down, like in the Dowlais District. And the others not much better, yet they all got their

Miners' Agents, offices, secretaries, clerks and the rest of it same as when things were going well, though they send in little or nothing to the Central Office which has got to foot the bill for all the outstanding compensation cases as got to be fought. So we're going to reduce the nineteen districts to eight by tacking a couple of bad 'uns onto a good 'un, or knocking three into one. – Anyway, the nineteen got to be reduced to eight in order to keep things going. And a good idea, I think, though I'm mandated by my Lodge to vote against it' (p. 234).

45. SWMF EC Minutes, 6 March, 12 and 13 June 1933.
46. *Western Mail*, 13, 14 June 1933.
47. These were:

Area No. 1 – Anthracite and Western Districts
No. 2 – Afan Valley District and British Rhondda Lodge
No. 3 – Garw, Ogmore and Gilfach, and Maesteg Districts
No. 4 – Rhondda No. 1 and Pontypridd Districts (excl. Abercynon Lodge)
No. 5 – Aberdare (excl. British Rhondda Lodge), Taff and Cynon, Merthyr and Dowlais District, and Abercynon Lodge
No. 6 – Rhymney Valley and East Glamorgan Districts
No. 7 – Tredegar Valley and Ebbw Vale Districts
No. 8 – Monmouthshire Western Valleys, Blaina and Eastern Valleys Districts

48. Circular No. 166, 17 May 1933. SWMF files.
49. SWMF Rules, 1933.
50. SWMF EC Minutes, 25 August and 25 September 1933. The ballot was on 13 and 14 September. The elected members were:

No. 1 – W. J. Jones; Evan J. Evans; Gomer Evans.
No. 3 – Alf Davies
No. 4 – Mark Harcombe
No. 5 – Idris Davies
No. 6 – W. H. Crews
No. 7 – Sam Garland
No. 8 – Obadiah Evans

51. Edwards, *op. cit.*, pp. 154–5.
52. Area No. 1 was to have 4 agents.
No. 2 was to have 1 Agent and 1 Secretary
No. 3 was to have 2 Agents and 1 Secretary
No. 4 was to have 2 Agents and 1 Secretary
No. 5 was to have 2 Agents and 1 Secretary
No. 6 was to have 3 Agents and 1 Secretary
No. 7 was to have 2 Agents and 1 Secretary
No. 8 was to have 1 Agent and 1 Secretary

Area Offices were to be, respectively, Swansea, Port Talbot, Bridgend, Porth, Aberdare, Bargoed, Pontllanfraith, Crumlin. SWMF EC Minutes, 16, 23, 28 November 1933.

53. SWMF EC Minutes, 7, 30 December 1933. These were initially:
   Area No. 1 – John James (4 months)
      No. 2 – John Thomas (4 months)
      No. 3 – Thomas Lucas (3 months)
      No. 4 – W. H. May (6 months)
      No. 5 – Noah Ablett (6 months)
      No. 6 – Ness Edwards (3 months)
      No. 7 – Sydney Jones (6 months)
      No. 8 – W. J. Saddler (6 months)
   Craftsmen's Representative – J. W. Grant (6 months).
54. SWMF Circulars of 20 June 1927, 1 February 1928, 9 March 1929, 9 July 1931.
55. *Memorandum of Interview* (Organisation of the Unemployed) between Oliver Harris and E. P. Harries. 31 July 1933, TUC 135.6.
56. Regulations Respecting Unemployed Members, April 1934.
57. See *Letters* to and from Oliver Harris, by various lodge secretaries, 18, 25 February, 3 March, 31 July, 24 December 1934.
58. *Daily Worker*, 11, 21 October, 2, 9, 10 November 1932.
59. Mardy Lodge Minutes, 12 August 1932. SWMF EC Minutes, 12 September 1932. Jack Jones wrote a scene in which Comrade Trevor Short (or Arthur Horner) addresses a mass meeting of Rhondda Communists and scores points off Comrade Tellem (Pollitt) in a telescoped and rather fantasised version of events:

> 'Now as to our work in the trade unions, of which the Comintern doesn't appear to be well informed, for if it was Comrade Tellem wouldn't have been instructed to come into the Rhondda to talk about the decline of Communist influence in the trade unions. Why, the fact of the matter is that the Communists of the Rhondda have been *too* influential. You all know the history of the Mardy Lodge of the Miners' Federation, which is the only trade union that the Rhondda knows. In Mardy we captured every office in the Lodge, we controlled the Workmen's Hall – and damned near controlled the town. Humph, no wonder it got to be known as "Little Moscow". Our Lodge at Mardy was the shining light and proud boast of the National Minority Movement. Then you know what happened. Alarmed at the growth of our influence in the Rhondda and throughout the coalfield, the Federation Executive decided to expel, or as they put it, "disaffiliate", the Mardy Lodge, which they did, and then secured the election of tame-cat officials to run what is now known as the "*official* Mardy Lodge", thereby placing us, an unofficial lodge, outside the trade-union movement. Yes, we worked ourselves "beyond the pale". . . . Many other Lodges that were rapidly coming our way were frightened by the threat of disaffiliation and beat a hasty retreat. Now, Moscow was informed of all this, and we were told by the All-Russian Central Council of Trade Unions that on no account were we to cut ourselves adrift from the trade unions of this country by attempting to form Communist trade unions. When expelled owing to your great influence we were as good as told, get back into the unions as individual members and work, not only to capture the machinery of trade unionism, but, in your second attempt, see that you win the membership as well. Keep close to the workers; remain part of the National Minority Movement *within* the trade unions.'

Rhondda Roundabout (1934), p. 46.

60. *Western Mail*, 23 December 1932, Horner, *op. cit.*, p. 147; Mardy Lodge Minutes, 27 and 29 December 1932, where the reasons for closure are given as inadequate safety precautions and capitalism, not communism, is blamed for the ruination of the village.

61. *Western Mail*, 29 March 1933. Mainwaring polled 14,127 to Horner's 11,288.

62. *Horner Election Special* (March 1933), and Leaflet entitled *Labour Last Minute Lies and Slander!* (March 1933). The lodge had agreed in September 1927 to suspend rates for one year provided the seniority rule and all working conditions and customs were safeguarded; the management refused and wished to employ whichever men they chose.

63. *Daily Worker* 9 February, 2, 9, 12, 30 May 1933. There were some 84 organisations involved in South Wales, including 13 lodges and 15 TU branches, but the rest were limited to the 'fringe' of women's groups, CP locals, ILP and NUWM branches.

64. *Ibid.*, 5, 7, 16 June 1933.

65. *South Wales Miner*, No. 1, 22 June 1933; No. 2, 6 July 1933; No. 3, 20 July 1933; No. 7, 28 September 1933. The paper ran for forty-two numbers, until 10 July 1935. It was always in financial difficulty, and made constant appeals. At a time when the SWMF itself had no paper, its impact seems to have been of some weight. Horner, who typed out all the articles and counted the words because they could only afford so much printing, certainly thought so:

> ... when the paper arrived, I used to parcel it up, take it to the stations to be sent to the lodges all over the coalfields. We had a circulation of about three thousand (cost 1*d.*), but it was read by nearly all the active trade unionists in the area, and I think it had a lot to do with my victory when I came to stand for the Presidency.

Horner, *op. cit.*, p. 133.

66. *Western Mail*, 25 November 1933; *South Wales Miner*, No. 10, 9 November, and No. 12, 7 November 1933. Horner, *op. cit.*, pp. 129–30. SWMF EC Minutes, 16 December 1933.

67. *South Wales Miner*, No. 11, 23 November 1933. Sam Davies, Secretary of the Old Lodge, wrote to refute Horner's running for agent for personal gain though he was on unemployment benefit: 'We challenge all comers to show another person who has sacrificed as much as Arthur Horner for the principles he believes in. We deny that he has ever before tried for any position which would involve leaving Mardy, though he has had many offers to do so if he would give up his principles. He is now contesting for the position of Miners' Agent only by the consent of the Mardy workmen who think it is a crime he should be shut out of Federation activity in the period of grave crisis for the miners.' Mardy Lodge Minutes, 20 February 1934. Their typewriter was 'given to the local branch of the NUWM'.

68. *Western Mail*, 4 June 1934; SWMF EC Minutes, 1 August 1934; *South Wales Miner*, No. 23, 21 June 1934. The post of organiser was not taken up again now that S. O. Davies was an MP.

69. SWMF EC Minutes, 18 August 1934. *South Wales Miner*, No. 22, 22 May 1934.

70. Edwards, *op. cit.*, pp. 153–4.

71. *SW*, 16 August 1925.

72. *SW*, 17 October 1926.

73. *SW*, 9 October 1927.

74. *SW*, 21 October 1931. Similar bodies were being set-up throughout Europe inspired by the ICWPA and the CI. See George Lansbury, *The ICWPA at Work* (London, 1926) pam.

75. For a full account of this period, see M. Foot, *op. cit.*, pp. 97–169. Similar anti-fascist militias were being formed throughout Europe, and in Spain itself they were the bodies which organised the 1934 rising which reached a peak in the Asturian coalfield.

76. UCS A. L. Horner collection, Strachey to Horner, 18 April 1933.

77. UCS A. L Horner collection, Bevan to Horner, 30 April 1933.

78. *WM*, 28 March 1933.

79. Idris Cox, interview, *op. cit.*, 9 June 1973. No evidence has survived to signify Horner's actual response to the proposals.

80. *DW*, 2 May 1933; SWML, J. S. Williams (Dowlais) collection, B/ii. *Joint Appeal for United Action of the Workers*, issued by the CPGB and ILP of South Wales, n.d.

81. *WM*, 20 May 1933; see also M. Foot, *op. cit.*, pp. 52–4, 65–7, 85.

82. *Ibid.*, Oliver Jones, *The Early Days of Sirhowy and Tredegar* (Tredegar, 1969), p. 8.

83. *WM*, 22 May 1933.

84. Oliver Powell, interview, *op. cit.*

85. *WM*, 22 May 1933.

86. *Merlin*, 23 November 1839. Quoted in David Williams, *John Frost*, (London, 1969 edition), pp. 230–1. David Williams casts some doubt on its authenticity but points out that it was accepted as evidence at the trial of the Chartist leaders for a premeditated attack on Newport.

87. *WM*, 22 May 1933. The Group's manifesto was first published in full in M. Foot, *op. cit.*, p. 172. Foot believed that the idea derived some of its inspiration from the Schutzbund in Vienna, the workers' para-military organisation which was drilling to fight off fascism.

88. Horner, *op. cit.*, p. 125.

89. *WM*, 22 May 1933.

90. *WM*, 23 May 1933.

91. *Ibid.*

92. *WM*, 25 May 1933.

93. Oliver Powell, interview, *op. cit.*

94. Phil Abrahams, interview, SWML.

95. SWML interviews with Sir Archie Lush (Gilwern), 11 May 1973, and Oliver Powell, *op. cit.* Also interview with Jim Brewer, an Abertysswg volunteer in the International Brigades, 30 October 1969.

96. Idris Cox interview *op. cit.*, (9 June 1973).

97. Oliver Powell interview, *op. cit.* Powell attended the debate, listening from the visitors' gallery amazed that the authorities could have been as well-informed of their activities.

98. Jim Brewer, interview, *op. cit.*

99. *Western Mail*, 12 January 1934 and 22 January 1934; Horner *op. cit.*, p. 132. The teasing effects of Welsh rugby can be seen in the fact that the delegates who wanted to extend the debate were overruled by the 'scores of delegates who

wanted to go to the International Rugby Match between England and Wales and who shouted Vote, Vote, Vote'. *South Wales Miner*, No. 16, 10 February 1934.

100. *Western Mail*, 8 and 19 May 1934.

101. *Ibid.*, 4 July, 2 August 1934.

102. *Ibid.*, 14 and 27 August 1934.

103. *Ibid.*, 28 and 29 September, 1 October 1934. *Daily Worker*, 1 October 1934. *South Wales Miner*, No. 30, 9 October 1934.

104. *The Miners' Monthly*, April 1934.

105. SWMF EC Minutes 22, 30 January, 15 February, 13, 14 and 28 April, 24 May 1934.

106. There had been one of a week's duration in the Garw Valley, in February, the first since 1929, to get nineteen men at the Ffaldau Colliery into the Federation. *Western Mail*, 5, 6, 12 February 1934.

107. *Ibid.*, 10 April 1934.

108. *Miners' Monthly*, March 1934.

109. *Letter* from E. G. Cox, Secretary of the Emlyn Lodge, to C. J. Prosser (Hon. Sec.) of the Gwendraeth Valley SWMF Group, November 1935; 'Who was instrumental in bringing this change [the removal of the 'Scabs' and 'D. B. Jones' lot] at Emlyn? Mr Horner has the biggest slice to his credit.'

110. Horner, *op. cit.*, p. 133.

111. *South Wales Miner*, No. 25. 17 July 1934. *Western Mail*, 20, 21, 22, 23, 24, 25 August; 6 September 1934. *Letter* from Cox to Prosser, *loc. cit.*

112. Opinion of Joshua Davies. December 1933. SWMF files.

113. James Griffiths, *Pages from Memory* (1972), p. 36.

114. *Letter* from Oliver Harris to Ebby Edwards, 16 December 1936, quoting Cripps' opinion which was, that provided there was insufficient evidence of a conspiracy to injure the SWMF, there was no remedy in law, for if '. . . the sums are deducted on the signed instructions of the workmen and paid to a third party [i.e. the Union] by the employei s, the provisions of the Truck Act are not offended against. In this case the deductions are not illegal on this ground.'

115. *Miners' Monthly*, April 1934.

CHAPTER SEVEN

Taff-Merthyr: The Crucible

The full impact of the development of company unionism in the
coalfield can only be seen when the perspective is narrowed
geographically. It existed, as has been shown, at the behest, if not the
direct request, of the owners, and notably the Ocean Coal Company, to
serve the purpose of maintaining a work-force that would make none of
the traditional demands of the Federation. A pit, in its control of the
economic destinies of a number of men, was difficult to win back,
especially when elementary rights of organisation were denied, but the
social counterpart to the pit, one or more villages, was not so easily
dominated. Here there were countervailing tendencies that resisted the
implications of economic dictation even if the 'take-over' had to be
suffered. The village of Bedlinog, in the narrow Taff-Bargoed valley,
with no real outlet at its top end, and the Taff-Merthyr pit, like a cork in
a bottle, at the other end, were perfect examples of both tendencies, a
microcosmic example of the reality behind the struggle in the coalfield
after 1926. Would the cork be able to hold the pressure building up in
the bottle, and if so, at what cost?

   The village of Bedlinog grew as a direct result of the late opening of
two pits, Bedlinog and Nantwen, both sunk in the late 1870s by the
Dowlais Iron and Steel Coal Company, and followed by people,
railway, houses, shops and chapels in the usual simultaneous social
explosion of late nineteenth-century coalfield society. If the village had
any distinct characteristic, apart from its topographical lunacy (the
main street and its tributaries ascend, from the village square, a 1-in-3
hill), it might be the relatively high proportion of North and mid-
Walians (with others, Welsh and Irish, travelling to work from Merthyr
and Rhymney) whose isolation allowed for a strong Welsh-speaking
tradition in its history. The pits came under the old Dowlais District
of the SWMF (the agent, John Davies, being succeeded by the
youthful S. O. Davies in 1919), and when both, within months of each
other, closed in 1924 the economic crutch of the place was kicked away

just as the social fabric of the village – its religious life, a considerable degree of adult education, active political involvement, the start of an institute – had come to an early fruition.[1]

In the stormy years of the early 1920s, Bedlinog reacted with a fierceness that was later to become synonymous with its name, as when, in June 1923, eighteen of its inhabitants (seven of them women) were arraigned for unlawful assembly. They had 'terrorised' D. B. Jones, in a crowd of around 1,000, and some of the members of his Craftsmen's Union during a non-union campaign against Jones' breakaway group. There had been an earlier demonstration in Dowlais where 'Mr S. O. Davies appealed to the passion of the mass'.[2] There was then, early on, a clear idea of the primacy of natural justice in Bedlinog, and men prepared to remind them of it as A. J. Cook had done, when, chastising the miners of the Taff and Cynon District in nearby Trelewis, in March 1926, for failure to pay their dues he had added:

> There were enough men and women in that meeting to make it impossible for non-unionists to live in that locality.[3]

Of course, the sea-change in village life occurred with the opening of the new Taff-Merthyr pit and its organisation by the newly-formed SWMIU by the winter of 1926.[4] This was the most bitter pill of all, for it offered a species of economic salvation at the cost of social humiliation.[5] In the conditions prevailing in the immediate aftermath of 1926 there was little that could be done to affect the Taff-Merthyr pit itself which provided employment when the Merthyr and Dowlais areas were becoming deserts. The SWMF had to tread a delicate line between establishing their control at the expense of an unwanted closure.

Old Federation members tried to maintain contacts with those in work but, unemployed themselves, their efforts were hamstrung in forming a Federation lodge and in attracting membership. There were complaints about the lack of official activity in the area which, it was argued, combined a sizeable number of men who could be won over. The position worsened as the complement of men employed grew.[6] S. O. Davies and other speakers held meetings, leaflets were distributed but without much effect. The local Trades and Labour Council did not meet, formally, after April 1928; the whole problem remained to fester.[7] By 1929 there were 1,500 men employed in the colliery, and further attempts were made to have a Lodge formed, both by S. O. Davies for the Dowlais District, and Enoch Morell and Tom Andrews for the Taff and Cynon District. Meetings were sparsely attended although some

1,100 men intimated that they no longer wished their subscriptions to the MIU to be deducted at source. The Company's reaction was swift and compelling. They gave their employees the choice of instant dismissal or the signing of individual authorised declarations in favour of deductions for the SWMIU. Despite the fact that some men paid a reduced subscription rate of 1d. a week to the SWMF, and thereby retained a dual membership, the weakness of the SWMF was firmly pointed up.[8]

In February 1930, the SWMIU entered into an arrangement with the Taff-Merthyr Company for an industrial insurance scheme for the men employed;[9] the EC now attempted to co-ordinate their earlier sporadic forays, under the leadership of S. O Davies, who reported to the EC on his actions. They resolved again to test the feelings of the workmen concerning their compulsory membership of the SWMIU.[10] The initial response to a series of meeting and a canvass of the men, in March, seemed so favourable that a confident S. O. Davies could write:

> I am enclosing the latest effusion of the 'Non-Political Union'. It is obvious they are anxiously concerned about the future of their 'Union' at Taff-Merthyr.
>
> My information last evening was that numbers of the men are very anxious if not panicky in this matter, and that the officials of both the 'Non-Pols' and the Company are extremely active in all forms of intimidation, etc.[11]

A ballot was organised to see if the SWMF was to be favoured and, as a result of it, Tom Richards handed into W. E. Jayne, JP, ME (the General Manager of the Taff Merthyr Steam Coal Company Limited), some 876 personal applications for the company to cease deductions for the MIU, adding that no pressure should be put on the men to make them agree to these deductions.[12] The company denied any such pressure had been used and that all the authorisations were voluntary, whereupon Tom Richards wrote to the press insisting that:

> With the information in possession of the Council, great astonishment was expressed that such untrue statements should be made, especially in writing. Even at the ballot taken this week of the workmen, colliery officials endeavoured to do all that was possible to prevent the workmen taking the ballot, and they were assisted by a police officer, presumably in the employ of the Company, about which further enquiries will have to be made.[13]

The SWMIU alleged that 400 of the men had re-signed their authorisation forms and that many of the SWMF ones were signed by men canvassing for the Federation. Whatever the exact accuracy of these figures, it was undeniable that the threat of the loss of jobs was difficult to combat – the SWMIU might boast of the 'best wages' and 'best conditions' in the coalfield, but it was the company's active help that was their real weapon. The weekend after the SWMF ballot, they posted the following notice at various points on the pit-head:

> A number of notices have been received purporting to be signed by the workmen employed at this colliery, withdrawing authority to deduct from their wages contributions to the Miners' Industrial Union. A number of letters have also been received from workmen stating that their signatures to these notices have been obtained under pressure and against their wishes. Under the circumstances the Company does not feel justified in acting upon these notices without confirmation, and, therefore, invites any person who wishes to cancel the authority originally given to the Company to call at the office for the purpose of confirming his signature.[14]

This was a straightforward means of isolating the workmen, individually, in order to break any collective resistance. The SWMF in the face of complete non-recognition by the owners, were reduced to exhortation and promises. They issued a circular leaflet to all workmen in the colliery assuring them that they would be supported in their recent vote, that there would be no entrance fee charged and that a 'holiday with full pay' would be guaranteed if this was the price that had to be paid to end 'the reign of terror'. At last, the SWMF had recognised the key importance of Taff-Merthyr:

> These people realise that the end of the 'Non-Pols' at Taff-Merthyr Colliery means their finish in the coalfield.
> The SWMF is determined to concentrate all its forces with a view to your being granted (a) the right to choose your Trade Union (b) the same contract of service, which is a 14 days notice, as the other miners in this coalfield.
> The vicious day-to-day contract must end.
> If you are determined to end this terrorism, it shall be done. . . .[15]

S. O. Davies, now at full steam in the area, reiterated the offer of full wages for the men in the event of a strike, but the earlier enthusiasm of the unemployed militants at Bedlinog had no counterpart at a time of denunciation of the SWMF itself,[16] so the early intensity of the campaign fizzled out,[17] as the agent himself explained to a correspondent from an Afan Valley lodge to which an expelled Taff-Merthyr man had gone in search of employment:

The Dowlais District has now assumed responsibility for this Colliery and we are concentrating upon the wiping out of this 'Scab Union'. Recently we succeeded in obtaining the signatures of between 75 per cent and 80 per cent of the men to a document prohibiting the employers from making any deductions towards the 'Non-Pols'. These were handed in to the Company by Mr Tom Richards. But within two weeks most of this work was undone. The workmen were seen individually, and by means of trickery and threats of victimisation many of them were compelled to withdraw their signatures.

We are now concentrating on an attempt to stop this colliery. The Executive Council are prepared to back that policy to the hilt, with full financial support.

Unfortunately, our strongest men there are weeded out by victimisation, and very many of the rest have been unemployed for three to five years.

Nevertheless, we are very hopeful that when the Raglan struggle ends, we shall be able to straighten out matters of this Colliery.[18]

The Raglan struggle, the inevitable fight after the displacement of the SWMIU in 1929, had ended by mid-July with the men accepting the present, post-1926, price list but the owners agreeing to accept Conciliation Board Agreements, in future,[19] but in Taff-Merthyr, where the MIU Lodge was functioning even to the extent of holding elections, matters were much more intractable.[20] It was, therefore a much more despondent S. O. Davies who wrote on 28 July 1930:

The SWMF has decided to concentrate on Taff-Merthyr for a further period of eight weeks, but in the event of no appreciable progress being made re: membership of the Federation during that time, the SWMF will have no alternative I fear, but to abandon that Colliery to the tender mercies of the 'Non-Pols'. For the eight weeks the Federation are financing from 8 to 10 Collectors, with a view of ascertaining definitely whether there is a real disposition to join the SWMF.[21]

The salesmen of the Federation had little tangible success. During the coalfield strike of January 1931, Taff-Merthyr, with a work-force of 1,600 men produced 2,000 tons daily, whilst the Federation men at the nearby Deep Navigation pits, in Treharris, stayed idle.[22] This was an acute psychological blow, as it was in the Rhondda and elsewhere where police guarded the smaller numbers at work.[23] However, wages not non-unionism was the real issue in 1931, as the comparative lack of incidents over non-unionism indicates. At Taff-Merthyr, at least initially, the wages of the men did not go down when the Schiller Award went against the SWMF.[24] The following years saw no further activity on this front as instead the Federation wrestled with the dispute at

Bedwas and their own reorganisation. When these had been settled in 1934, the latter favourably but the former not, the question of a new wages agreement again brought Taff-Merthyr to the fore, for it was vital, in the event of another stoppage, to insure against back-stabbing. In the event of a strike the Rhymney Valley would have been flanked by the two company union pits, Taff-Merthyr and Bedwas, so once more the SWMF considered the thorn in their flesh, especially as it would affect their new Area 6.

Ness Edwards was the agent; W. H. Crews (the EC member for the area), Noah Ablett, the Merthyr agent, and he made up a small organisation committee which, with the help of Glyn Jones (the Secretary of Penallta) began to tour the Taff Valley, throwing out feelers. They discovered that only the unemployed would talk to them freely and that the men employed were very much 'selected', especially if they came from Bedlinog itself. They produced a leaflet, 'A Call for Action', sketching the role the Federation would like to see adopted by men working in the two collieries. They found that the call met with an 'unexpectedly cordial' reception from Taff-Merthyr men, and decided to visit Bedlinog 'to see what were the chances of establishing a base for an attack upon the problem'.[25]

This cordiality had been preserved, in no small measure, and particularly in Bedlinog, by a small group of activists in and around the CP, led by local ironmonger, Edgar Evans, whose meetings at a brick hut on Bedlinog Square (the 'Kremlin') initiated many young, unemployed miners into the YCL and the CP. There was no Labour Party as such in Bedlinog; even the Chamber of Commerce had, for a time, a CP majority.[26] It was to these men that the EC of the SWMF armed with their new, more flexible organisation and equipped, by their Unemployment Regulations, to formulate plans that could unite the unemployed to the Federation, now addressed itself.[27]

Ness Edwards was given the job of informing the coalfield of the story that now unfolded:

> We found that a collecting station for the Dowlais Lodge . . . existed at Bedlinog for the unemployed, but that there were no direct organisational contacts. The long valley from Nelson right up to Dowlais was a wilderness from an organisation point of view. We canvassed the idea of forming an Unemployed Lodge in Bedlinog, and eventually W. H. Crews and myself made a report to the EC which gave permission to establish the Lodge, subject to the agreement of the Dowlais Lodge. This was obtained, and on Friday, 21 September, we called a meeting of the Unemployed and set up the

Taff Merthyr Lodge (Unemployed). The meeting appointed a Committee and Officers, and these were given the task of distributing the Non-Pol's Balance sheet, which we had ready in leaflet form, with a critical commentary. This had already been done at Bedwas. These leaflets were distributed that day. The base had been formed and the attack commenced. The battle for Freedom had commenced.[28]

On that same Friday the EC had received the Organisation Committee's full report on Taff-Merthyr and endorsed their authorisation to their representative in the area to take whatever steps were necessary; an intensive campaign officially under Ness Edwards and W. H. Crews (the EC member for Area No. 6) was now mounted.[29] Unofficially, Arthur Horner had been given six months' leave from his duties as an agent in the Anthracite area and was active in the area, knitting together in himself the CP and the SWMF and, thus, ensuring the full co-operation of the local militants with the Federation's line.[30]

The Unemployed Committee, and the leaders drafted in, distributed different leaflets each day, mingled with the shifts as they came off, and began speaking to the men at the pit with the aid of a loudspeaker (from Edgar Evans' ironmongery). The arguments used revolved around past oppression and the present inability of the company to sugar that pill any more by paying good wages:

This ruthless Colliery Company, accompanied by their poodles, by their control through the stomachs of our wives and children, has succeeded in smashing every form of working class organisation that existed here. First to suffer was the Taff-Merthyr lodge which was 100 per cent organised in 1926, then the Labour Party, and afterwards the Trade and Labour Council, all inside the space of 2½ years. For eight years the same gang through different agents has tried to pinch the Bedlinog Workmen's Hall and Institute Fund so as to still further control your social lives but due to the persistence of several loyal comrades, this attempt has so far been frustrated. But conditions at Taff have changed considerably since these events took place. Selected colliers cannot get such good places to earn good money, that is now ancient history. 'Cross Measures' is no more, 'North East' is going 'West', and the 'Six Feet' has taken their places, which with the 'driving' that's being adopted there, will soon land you into your final 'six feet'. . . . Are you going to wait until the colliery is worked out. The time to fight is now. The place to fight is inside the ranks of the SWMF.[31]

The police at the colliery multiplied from one Colliery Sergeant to

150; the Industrial Union brought in a barricaded lorry, with two loudspeakers, which blared their answer – distorted gramophone music. When the police banned both sets of loudspeakers, mountainside meetings were held (Taff-Merthyr had no houses within a mile of it, either up or down the steep-sided valley), and it was at a meeting held on Friday, 5 October, addressed by George Hall the MP for Aberdare, that an already sharp campaign reached its first climax.

At the meeting, after a number of leaders had spoken, the afternoon shift was asked to vote one way or the other. The Federation's official account still rings with euphoria:

> Five in favour of the Company Union; the rest in favour of the Federation. Federation Cards were issued and gladly received. The day shift meeting held with the same result. The train men clamoured for cards. That night over a hundred paid contributions at Bedlinog. The afternoon shift was met coming from work that night. The same result again repeated. Success followed success. Liberty was in the air. Enthusiastic meetings were held in all the surrounding villages that night. The valley that had been held in the grip of silent terror was at last on the verge of Freedom.[32]

Although euphoria may have justified the use of majuscules, in reality only the first round was over. For the Industrial Union, William Gregory derided the reports of disaffection at the colliery as delusion induced by the presence of unemployed men, whilst D. B. Jones, the General Secretary of the South Wales and Monmouthshire Colliery Enginemen, Boilermen and Craftsmen's Association, was convinced the Federation's campaign would cripple themselves as they slowly died 'from a cancerous growth known as Horneritis'.[33]

None the less, the EC decided that the work would go on, aided by more EC members and MPs, whilst a similar campaign would be begun at Bedwas.[34] Through the following week, at the pit, in the villages, at the railway stations, literature was passed to the men and information disseminated.

On Tuesday, 9 October, the company made it clear that they would back the Industrial Union when at least twelve men were dismissed for having joined the Federation. C. B. Tellyn, the Chairman of the Taff-Merthyr SWMIU Branch, gave as his reason (though, officially, it was the company that fired the men): 'We are only adopting the same methods as the Federation. Our members won't work with Federation men.'[35]

As a result the Federation propagandists switched to slogans of solidarity – 'All out or all in' and 'One man victimised, all men out' – claimed that 1,100 out of the 1,650 employed at Taff-Merthyr had accepted Federation cards, threatened a stoppage and guaranteed the victimised men the equivalent of 'unemployment pay'.[36]

Throughout the week dismissals continued; nor were the campaigners free from injury. Outside the Navigation Colliery at Bedwas, a gang of Industrial Union miners, armed with short iron bars, attacked and smashed up a motor car (with loudspeaker) which contained, among others, Edgar Lewis, a Carmarthenshire County Councillor, and Jack Davies, the new Secretary of the Bedwas Federation Lodge.[37] On the same night a car stopped outside Edgar Evans' shop in Bedlinog High Street and flagons were thrown through the shop window, causing considerable damage.[38]

Neither side was to succumb to intimidation. The Federation's drive reached a new high point on Friday, 12 October, when a day-long effort was mounted, backed by such speakers as James Griffiths, Arthur Jenkins, Oliver Harris, Ted Williams, MP, W. H. Mainwaring, MP, Ness Edwards and W. H. Crews, and a large force of police. The effort was directed towards taking Federation contributions openly, near the pit:

At 3.30 a.m. the Unemployed Committee men carted a temporary structure to the side of the road. By the light of torches it was erected before the night shift started to leave the pit. As the night shift left the Colliery streams of men queued up to join the Federation amidst scenes of tremendous enthusiasm. 'Cwm Rhondda' and the 'Red Flag' were sung repeatedly. The night shift was solid for Freedom. The day shift repeated this success. At 9 o'clock that night we were there to receive the afternoon shift. About 50 or 60 of the Scab Union touts had arrived before us. Beer had inflamed their debased minds. They were there to repeat the 'thuggery' of Bedwas. Some of them had flagons in their pockets. Flagons which they used to smash the windows of our men at Bedlinog, were now to be brought on our heads.

But a noise came from the Colliery. Shout upon shout floated up to us. Two sons had been instantly dismissed for joining the Federation. Their father, a Colliery official, was dismissed as well. The Manager was busy writing out notices. 250 men were to be dismissed for having joined the Federation. The men had taken matters into their own hands. 'All work or none.' Above the din arose a tremendous cheer. The night shift had decided to strike. They trooped back to the pit head bath and from it came the huge roar of the night shift singing the 'Red Flag'.

The Scab Union touts disappeared like melting snow. With bared heads we joined the singing that came from the pit head bath.

As dawn broke on Saturday morning, the day shift was met. Unanimously they voted to strike for the right to join the Miners' Federation.[39]

The information issued by David Hughes, the manager of the colliery, did not move with such technicolor brio. After establishing that those who joined the Federation would not be admitted to the colliery again, he declared that, on the Friday, eighty-four men who had joined the SWMF had returned home, but 240 had gone down the pit as usual, whilst only 217 men in the total complement, had joined the Federation.[40]

The management refused to meet a Federation deputation. The SWMF EC decided to give 'financial support, on Unemployment Benefit basis', to all the men on strike at Taff-Merthyr.[41] In the meantime Oliver Harris wrote identical letters to Lord Davies, Plas Dinam, as Chairman of the Ocean Colliery Company, and to E. L. Hann, the Chairman of the P.D. Company, indicating that 90 per cent of the men at their colliery wished to join the Federation but that Jayne (the colliery agent and General Manager) and Hughes (the local manager) would not discuss the matter. He ended with a pertinent reference to the arbitration procedure adopted over the wages negotiations:

> Recent events in this coalfield indicate that there is a possibility of creating a more peaceful atmosphere, and more cordial relations, between the workmen and the Coalowners, than has prevailed for many years, but so long as some Coalowners including Taff Merthyr deny to some of the men the elementary right to join the Organisation which is responsible for the wage arrangements in this Coalfield, peace will be impossible.

Hann denied the truth of the Federation's statements; Lord Davies replied, at length, later.[42] One answer came at Treharris Workmen's Hall, on Sunday afternoon (the 14th) to which Taff-Merthyr workmen were taken, free, by buses; a second overflow meeting was held in the Co-op Hall, and another, in the open air. ('Outside the Public Hall, remarkable scenes were witnessed. The audience sang Welsh hymns and choruses with great fervour, and were entertained with vocal and instrumental solos.')

Inside, under the chairmanship of Ness Edwards, the entertainment was of a more serious kind. The chairman added 'Independence Day' to his eighteenth-century repertoire of 'Liberty' and 'Freedom', and told the men that 1,200 men had joined the Federation. A lodge was appointed, with officers and a committee of sixteen, and the meeting resolved:

> That the Federation be authorised to continue negotiations for recognition of the Federation and the reinstatement of the victimised men. Also that mass picketing be arranged outside the colliery, the stoppage to continue until all the objects of the Federation are achieved.[43]

Gregory, for the SWMIU, took the Federation to task for counting unemployed men as new members when, he alleged, they had been handed their threepenny first contribution by outside Communist agitators. Loyalty was still felt by the men to the Industrial Union. These words rang empty on the Sunday night when only thirteen men in addition to officials and safety men went to work on a shift that normally employed 400. Oliver Harris, warming to the occasion, likened the Federation to the biblical father who had welcomed his prodigal son home, and added, patriotically, that the Federation would 'use all its resources to see to it that men shall be able to exercise the British right of joining a Trade Union'.[44]

The Federation had no desire to dissipate its energies elsewhere at this time, so they clamped down on eruptions in other parts, and quietened down their campaign at Bedwas.[45] There was no complete stoppage on Monday, despite picketing, though figures differed widely (from 250 at work, out of a total of 550, to under 100). Two new factors were against a speedy resolution of the dispute – forty new men had been signed on; bus drivers at Merthyr, Bedlinog, Quakers Yard and Nelson had decided against running the usual workmen's services to the colliery because of the threats they had received.[46]

When the colliery company openly issued an invitation to any men to work at the colliery, provided they broke with the Federation, the latter had no choice, after their EC meeting on Tuesday the 16th, but to issue a call to arms:

> In view of the attitude of the colliery company in trying to force the men to remain members of, and contribute to, the Miners' Industrial Union, and the refusal to recognise the Miners' Federation, of which 90 per cent of the men are members, the Council decided that it had no alternative but to warn the Secretaries of lodges throughout the coalfield that possibly it would be necessary to call a coalfield conference to consider the situation and decide upon some action with the view of enforcing the principle that men should be entitled to join the union of their choice.

The Ocean and PD Combine Committees were to meet, whilst the NUR, ASLEF, the Railways Clerks' Association and the Transport Workers' Union would be asked for their co-operation in not carrying men to the colliery. The unemployed were told that 'they are entitled to refuse to accept employment at the Taff-Merthyr Colliery without in any way jeopardising their unemployment benefit'.

On the other hand the SWMIU declared itself prepared 'to fight for the principle that men will have the right to join the Non-Political Union if they desire and not become pawns of the Miners' Federation'. Bedwas, Dare and Taff-Merthyr collieries were now 'free from trouble and strife'; the boast was rather inappropriate. Relentless picketing continued, along with hostile receptions for the men at work when they returned home to Bedlinog, Trelewis and Nelson (order was maintained by the police). The numbers of men at work still increased, despite this pressure. The Industrial Union men at Treharris faced the usual jeers but in the three villages above a new tactic was used:

> Crowds assembled . . . the streets being lined on both sides. Women formed a large percentage of the crowds, and, as the workmen passed along the streets silence was observed. The crowds doffed their hats and caps, remaining bare-headed until the men passed out of sight.[47]

This was the form of 'respect' normally accorded to a funeral procession.

From the Rhymney Valley, a special train (quickly christened the 'ghost train'), was now transporting workers to the pit where the afternoon shift had never been stopped.[48] Indeed the company warned that whatever the outcome of the dispute there would be 400 fewer men employed in future. The company had stipulated that the men to whom pay was due should collect it at the time stated, but the local strike committees ignored this in favour of mass mountainside demonstrations on the Friday (19 October) to watch the men who had arrived in two long processions; one up the valley from Bedlinog and Dowlais, the other from Trelewis, Nelson and Treharris, collect their pay. The men were escorted by the police in batches of twenty to the pay office whilst their companions sang the 'Red Flag and Welsh Hymns'.

Once more there were silent demonstrations, in the villages, against the 'scabs'; this time women carried wreaths to make their point clear. Now the deep rift in these isolated formerly tightly knit communities had widened considerably. If impoverishment had removed the smack of enrichment from the social life of other Welsh valleys, here hatred and distrust gave a new gloss to poverty as the village communities wrecked their own social institutions in a determination to allow no prevarication.

At Bedlinog there were intimations that church services attended by Industrial Union members would be boycotted; at Nelson, all committee members and players of Nelson Welfare AFC were forced to resign 'in the interests of the club, and of the safety of the people concerned in view of the feeling prevailing in the district'. An open-air Federation meeting, of some 500 people, cheered the news loudly. The Taff-Merthyr Workmen's Silver Band and the Trelewis and District Male Voice Party were similarly disrupted.[49]

The *Western Mail*, thanks to its 'special representative', now mined a new seam of Welsh social life for its readers by informing them that a novel species of industrial warfare had come to the Bedlinog Valley:

> It is something that is making the valley a place of fear and terror; preparing dynamite and playing with a spark. . . . It is not new in the history of the world; it is the vendetta of Corsica and the terrorism that has swept parts of Europe in more recent times and swallowed democracy in its malefic progress.[50]

Almost at the same time, the SWMF's resident terrorist, Ness Edwards, had used similar hyperbole in his description of life in the valley *before* the strike:

> For eight years [i.e. 1926–34] liberty has been unknown and democracy has had no existence. All forms of social life in both villages have been under the domination of the Company Union and Colliery Management. In Trelewis, up until a month ago, only one person could be found who would exhibit a bill in his window announcing a Labour meeting. Only few people dared attend a meeting to hear the local Member of Parliament [Morgan Jones, Caerphilly]. A silent terror had laid hold of the lives of the people and made them follow paths approved of by the Colliery Management. The Company Union was the instrument of this terror; the workers in this valley were in bondage.[51]

Disruption of these 'forms of social life' was inevitable once an attempt to switch allegiance to the Federation was made. Previously, those who had been open members of the SWMIU and silent members of the SWMF had had no choice but to co-operate if they were to remain in work. Social anonymity was not possible in the villages.

The instruments of the Taff-Merthyr Workmen's Silver Band were removed, at a midnight hour, from the Band's HQ, the Bontnewydd Hotel, Trelewis, and taken to the colliery by the Band Chairman and C. B. Tellyn of the Industrial Union. The officers of the Trelewis Bowling Club, along with their President, D. Hughes, the manager of the colliery, also resigned.[52]

In a more generalised way a 'social boycott' of almost all those connected with the Industrial Union now took place. In Bedlinog shopkeepers, milkmen and bakers who had dealings with the SWMIU were boycotted; the secretary of a local singing festival had to resign because he had a relative in the pit; whole cinema audiences walked out if blacklegs were found there, until the management co-operated by refusing entrance to blacklegs or their relatives; school children were kept away from those classes where teachers refused to discriminate against Industrial Union children, and in Nelson a hairdresser's trade plummeted because of his son's membership of the SWMIU. Men drank at different pubs. Although over a hundred police were billeted in the area, the windows of 'scabs' were broken, doors were blacked with tar at night, and pigs let loose on to the mountains. Nothing for the opponents of the strike was more 'despicable', 'un-British', 'illicit' and 'cowardly' than this treatment meted out to men who were, for one side, 'blacklegs' and, for the other, men exercising, bravely, their 'liberty of choice'. The SWMF in no way openly supported these social tactics though there would have been little point in, or desire to, disclaim them – in the Bedlinog Valley it *was* a question of who would control the workmen's lives, and phrases extolling 'the tolerance of the British way of life' cut no ice in communities where the only tolerance afforded to others would be from a position of solidarity. For the people of the valley those who broke the solidarity demanded had put *themselves* outside the code of natural law, beyond the pale of society, of the only society that mattered anyway. Talk of legality was as meaningless as it had been to the landless Irish in the nineteenth century, or to the 'primitive rebels' of the Mediterranean. In some ways the *Western Mail*'s reporter was not so far wrong after all.[53]

In the midst of this furore, the SWMIU began to defend itself, in some detail, aided by letters to the Welsh press from George A. Spencer, the Notts Miners' Leader, and President of the Non-Political Trade Union Movement. Spencer alleged, blissfully unaware of his self-contradiction, that the SWMF was 'still ruled by the most extreme Communist section of its members, who are bitter because they have failed to force a general strike' (i.e. over the 1934 wage negotiations) and, since the MIU was the cause of the failure, this body was now being attacked, though futilely, since it had 'the whole resources of the Non-Political Trade Union movement behind it, and because there is loyal co-operation between the colliery companies, where agreements exist, and the thousands of workmen'.[54]

William Gregory, in two long articles, extolled the wage structure of Taff-Merthyr (slightly higher than rates elsewhere), and explained the lack of expenditure on compensation cases by the fact that they had been settled out of court. The main burden of his attack lay in a denunciation of 'tyranny, coercion and intimidation' which were the by-products of 'socialism'. For Gregory the fight for the Industrial Union was a fight against the SWMF's 'threat to British freedom'. With remarkable mental dexterity the secretary of a union which operated very much in the dark, raised the curtain on yet another example, albeit of local significance, of the 'plot theory of history'. What, he asked, was the real reason for the campaign that began months ago at Emlyn collieries?

> To those interested we say in all sincerity that Communism alone, under the direction of Arthur Horner and Evan Evans, with others of the same ilk, is responsible for the campaign waged against the SWMIU.

The proof was that Horner, with the 'ruin of Mardy behind him', was now dominating the 'destinies of the western coalfield' and controlling even the highest officials of the SWMF; indeed 'with the smashing of the SWMIU Horner would have a clear field. It would not be a very big risk to prophesy the complete subjugation of the SWMF to Communism within a short while.'[55]

When, in 1936, by a series of accidents Horner became President of the SWMF, Gregory's cup was full. After Horner's election, since the 'Red Menace' did not stalk the coalfield, references to the 'Communist domination' of the SWMF perceptibly decreased; yet, in 1934, the SWMF found it extremey difficult to make its point to the coalowners, even when the point was made by such 'respectable' officials as Oliver Harris and Sir William Jenkins, MP for Neath and chairman of the Glamorgan Standing Joint Committee. Harris wrote again to Lord Davies contending that since the Federation had just signed a three-year coalfield agreement, they had given good faith of their peaceful intentions, but that the whole coalfield would be embroiled in the dispute, if the Taff-Merthyr case remained unresolved. Lord Davies, not a notorious fire-eater by any means, replied, at length, in a manner that evaded the reality of life in the Bedlinog Valley as calmly as the existence of Plas Dinam denied the substance of rows of miners' cottages

> We [i.e. the Ocean Coal Company's Directors] feel that the dispute at Taff-Merthyr is primarily a dispute between the Federation and the Industrial Union, and is therefore one in which we are not directly concerned. If we acceded to the request of your colleagues it would be tantamount to taking sides, or at any rate it would be interpreted as such by the partner to the dispute. However, we have, as you know, an agreement of long standing with the Industrial Union which we cannot terminate without their concurrence. Further, we deny that the men employed at this pit have voluntarily joined the Federation, and we have evidence to show that a campaign of terrorism and intimidation has been going on incessantly during the last few weeks. I am sure you will agree that in these circumstances it is impossible to secure any free expression of opinion on the part of the Taff-Merthyr men. This is a most deplorable state of affairs, and I am sure that if you were in our place you would be the last to agree to any new arrangement which had been brought about by these methods . . . and we have no right, as employers, to dictate to the men at this Colliery, or indeed any other Colliery, what Union they shall belong to.

Since such 'dictation' was, palpably, the case at Taff-Merthyr and Dare collieries, Lord Davies' reply caused even the phlegmatic Sir William Jenkins to comment pungently:

> It is perfectly clear that the employers at Taff-Merthyr are taking a definite side, and they say that only men belonging to the Non-Political Union can work at that Colliery. If that is not taking sides I do not underatand the English language.[56]

Since all the attempts to negotiate with management had failed because of these semantic difficulties, the SWMF proceeded with orthodox industrial pressure. The weekend 19–21 October, culminated in a mass demonstration at Treharris Football Field, preceded by a mass walk from Trelewis (a mile away) headed by the Taff-Merthyr Band (until midnight still in possession of their instruments). The meeting was addressed by S. O. Davies, Horner, William Betty, Ness Edwards and Crews, and unanimously resolved that the struggle for the right to join the SWMF would continue. The declaration of support made by the PD and Ocean Combine Committees was welcomed (a delegate conference representing the 35,000 men there employed had met, in Cardiff, on Saturday), as was the Rhymney Valley men's 'refusal to travel in the "ghost train"'.[57]

Throughout the third week of the strike over 200 men kept working at the colliery. The management, who had already abolished the afternoon shift, now made it known that one of the two pits would be dismantled, thus ending another 500 jobs. All the attempts of the SWMF to organise a secret ballot failed; a train was to run from Pontypool, Crumlin and Pontllanfraith; the weekend saw yet another 3,000 strong demonstration at the pit and vigorous speeches from Federation leaders, or, as the *Western Mail* put it, 'After all this oratory the crowd sang the Red Flag and bared their heads to the symbol of tyranny.'[58]

Failing to break through to complete success, the Federation now convened a delegate conference to discuss Taff-Merthyr.[59] For the Industrial Union, the law was involved – a writ was issued against Gelligaer Council claiming an injunction to restrain them from refusing to carry workmen and officials employed at the colliery in their buses; charges of intimidation were to be heard at Bargoed and Pontlottyn.[60] Whilst these events were moving apace, the coalfield learned that the Bridgeman Tribunal had, at long last, awarded the miners a wage increase, albeit a small one. The arbitrators, headed by Viscount Bridgeman who had been the Secretary for Mines 1920–2, had awarded a $2\frac{1}{2}$ per cent increase on the base rates and a flat subsistence rate of 7s. 8d. a day for all adult workers. The new percentage rate was $12\frac{1}{2}$ per cent less than that requested by the SWMF, and $5\frac{1}{2}$ per cent less than that 'awarded' by the National Industrial Board, but it was of some importance that the Schiller Award with its absurd distinction and anomalies had gone. This was the first time wages in the coalfield had gone up (albeit to a continuingly low figure) since 1924. James Griffiths, quite rightly, saw the award as a fillip for the miners:

I hope that the award will strengthen the faith of the members in the Federation, and will bring back those men who are outside the Federation, so that when 1935 comes and a further review takes place the Federation will be able to speak for a united body of workmen.
Finally, the award will do much to re-establish the workmen's faith in the Federation, which was so shattered by the award of 1931.[61]

The Conference convened for Wednesday, 7 November, was preceded by the now accustomed mass rally at Treharris and other villages on Sunday; the SWMF thought 1,400 men formerly employed at Taff-Merthyr were now on strike.[62] Delegates representing 85,000 miners followed the Executive's recommendation to tender fourteen days' notice after a consultation with the lodges. There was no avenue left open to the Federation at this stage – the local management would not meet Federation officials, nor would the directors of the parent companies, nor would the Conciliation Board intervene. Since a secret ballot was also refused (and this was seen as the 'vital principle at stake of importance to the coalfield and to the whole Trade Union Movement – i.e. the right of the workmen at any coalfield to decide which organisation shall represent them in dealing with wages and conditions of employment') the dispute had to be widened if the SWMF initiative was not to fail.[63]

At the same time more men were signing on at the colliery, the Bedwas trouble of 1933 had ended badly for the Federation, despite a threatened coalfield strike, and, with many miners still outside the SWMF there was reluctance to run down funds on what could be a long struggle. There seemed to be no diminution of enthusiasm for the cause in the Bedlinog area where mass meetings had been developed to a fine art. Motor coaches brought the strikers to a point a mile outside the Palace Theatre, Treharris, a procession was formed, each man carrying a lighted torch, and the men on Sunday, 11 November, marched in to be cheered by a large crowd. Distinguished speakers were inevitably followed by renderings of 'Cwm Rhondda' and the 'Red Flag'.[64]

Unknown to the weekend demonstrators, Oliver Harris had received a letter from E. L. Hann, the PD Company's chairman, finally agreeing to meet the three top Federation officials.[65] This news was broken to the reassembled delegate conference on Monday and, as a result, a large majority agreed to postpone the tendering of notices. For the Federation there could be only one interpretation of this turn of events – the company had, albeit tacitly, afforded them recognition.[66]

The owners of Taff-Merthyr were certainly looking for some accommodation now. Lord Davies, in particular, was more frank about the situation, in private, than he had been in public. On 7 November 1934 he had drawn up an important memorandum[67] on the Taff-Merthyr dispute which, perhaps, influenced his fellow directors. He began by asserting the right of employers to employ whomsoever they chose and of employees to join whichever union they chose. However, he proceeded to discuss the actual situation and purpose of their policy so that its bankruptcy in 1934, as opposed to 1926, might be revealed:

Briefly [present policy] may be described as *divide et impera*. As an expedient this may serve for a time, but in the long run I believe it will fail because it is based on fundamentally wrong principles

1. Because by insisting upon all our employees belonging to one Union, and dismissing all who may join the Federation, we violate the principle of freedom of choice – but we rightly condemn Federation intimidation.

2. By granting privileges to one Union which we deny to others we, in effect, offer inducements to our employees to join a particular Union.

3. By deducting contributions from wages and handing the proceeds to the Industrial Union we place the individual miner at the mercy of officials of the Union and our managers. For fear of losing his job the man is compelled to pay his subscription to a Union of whose policy he may entirely disapprove.

4. By being a non-associated Colliery we reap all the advantages without any of the responsibilities. But we risk, by our isolation, embroiling the whole coalfield in a stoppage.

If it was not for the depression, then there is every likelihood that the present dispute would have produced a complete stoppage in South Wales.

This was a remarkably clear-sighted, and revealing, document. Lord Davies was quite aware that the new Tribunal that had been established, in the wake of the Bridgeman award, strengthened the miners' hand on the Conciliation Board:

Owing to the conditions which followed the coal strike in 1926, it may have been feasible to do many things which will not be possible or practicable in future. . . . No one suggests that we should let down the Industrial Union. On the contrary, my object is to insist upon its representation on the Conciliation Board. If it really represents the views of our men at Taff-Merthyr they will stick to it. If, on the other hand, it is merely a spoon-fed organisation, depending entirely upon the support of the Company, it is bound to bust up sooner or later.

With masterly acumen, Lord Davis acknowledged the satisfaction of repelling 'vile intimidation and coercion' and the immediate economic advantages of stopping one shift in a manner that laid blame at the Federation's door, but insisted that there might be greater advantage in not pressing on with an outmoded policy:

For the moment, no doubt, we shall win. We shall dispense with the services of a number of redundant men when we revert to one shift, and we shall get as many men as are required for the Colliery. But are we quite so sure that this will not become a Pyrrhic victory? And I don't believe it will end there. Taff-Merthyr will become the battle-cry of every Federationist in South Wales, and the Federation is not down and out yet, and are we quite so sure that by helping to down the Federation we are not playing the game of the

Communists and extremists, which will render the existing machinery –
Conciliation Board etc. – perfectly useless and produce an anarchical state
of affairs throughout the coalfield. We should then be compelled to look
forward to another period of fighting and skirmishing. Having imposed
upon our men at Taff-Merthyr a new régime of coercion – however much we
may try and delude ourselves that it is not – the Federation, pushed by their
wild men, will also resort to their old tactics and will continue to harass us
more than ever at every point.

The days of 'delusion' were over for one important owner whose
views had undergone some change since the owners had pressed home
the advantage wrung in 1926. For Lord Davies the answer to industrial
strife, not one jot diminished in its potential disruptiveness despite the
wearing down of the SWMF, lay in association with the other collieries
and a willingness to submit all demands to the Board and to the
Tribunal for ultimate settlement. Apparently he convinced the others, at
least to the extent of not outlawing the Federation from Taff-Merthyr
completely. It was a policy of ambivalence he knew well how to pursue,
whether in industrial matters or in his much-vaunted search for
international peace via arbitrators like the League of Nations. His
actions would make his words ring hollow.[68]

Meetings with Hann, and his fellow director, Sir Stevenson Kent,
went slowly but on the basis that no more 'strangers' would be
employed, and that once strike notices were withdrawn there would be
a settlement of difficulties, the Federation were reluctant to discontinue
them.[69] They therefore persuaded both a mass meeting of the Taff-
Merthyr workmen and the reassembled delegate conference to
withdraw notices so that the negotiations might be fruitful.[70]

At the end of the sixth week of the strike,[71] the men attended a
mass meeting in Trelewis, under the chairman of the Taff-Merthyr
Federation Lodge, Staffron Bolwell. The negotiated settlement, after a
four-hour discussion, was accepted with thirty dissentients. It called for
an end to all propaganda and picketing at the colliery, the re-
engagement of workmen employed on 30 September 1934 at the
colliery, before any 'strangers', grievances to be dealt with, jointly, by
Jim Griffiths and E. L. Hann, and the SWMIU insurance scheme to
continue for a period. The Federation's true verbal victory (for the
situation was only to be a guaranteed limbo) lay in the clauses:

Until the ballot of the men is taken neither the officials of the Miners'
Industrial Union nor the officials of the Miners' Federation will be

recognised at the pit. . . . The owners being assured that the colliery is working satisfactorily and that complete cessation of propaganda by both the Miners' Industrial Union and the Miners' Federation has been established, and after a reasonable lapse of time . . . a secret ballot of the men then employed at the colliery shall be undertaken under the auspices of an independent person. . . . The men shall be asked to decide whether they prefer to join the Miners' Industrial Union or the Miners' Federation.[72]

From the very beginning there had been an underlying tension within the Federation's ranks between those who saw militancy as spreading in concentric circles from the original incident and those who saw the circles becoming fainter as they receded from the centre. In particular local militants who wished to drag the net wide felt frustrated at the Federation's compromise. On the same evening that the negotiation settlement was accepted, a protest meeting, convened by leaders of the unemployed, was held in Treharris. A thousand men, women and children listened to speeches by Edgar Evans, Sid Elias (the NUWM leader from London) and Jack Davies (the chairman of the Cambrian Combine Lodges, a CP member). They argued that, with the battle almost won, coalfield notices should not have been withdrawn, and that now the rank and file's original demands were being betrayed by their leaders. Once more the Federation had 'sold' the strikers. Interestingly enough Elias apologised for the absence of Arthur Horner who had been announced as one of the speakers: 'Mr Horner [he said] was a member of the Federation Executive and they did not intend to offer him up on the altar of sacrifice.'[73]

This seems a little disingenuous in view of the fact that Horner had not hesitated to clash with the EC in the past, and had that very year been censured by them, whilst the settlements he himself later reached, against the arguments of local activists, bear a remarkable similarity to that negotiated in 1934. So, although he appears to have disputed the 'principle of the ballot', there is little doubt that he was not personally convinced that more could have been achieved at this juncture without losing the support of the Taff-Merthyr employed:

Unfortunately events moved too rapidly . . . with the consequence that a strike was provoked before enough had been done to win over the large majority of the workmen at the pits.[74]

The feeling of those who had borne the burden, in Bedlinog and elsewhere, for so long without any aid of consequence was none the less highly charged with indignation that their 'glorious fight' had 'been again marred by the reactionary, knee-trembling leaders'.[75] Their demand was for the complete, unconditional withdrawal of all 'blackleg' labour and recognition of the SWMF, but 'in view of every member of the Executive and the Agents who were conducting the Taff-Merthyr campaign . . . prolongation of the stoppage would lead to a debacle'.[76]

The protest meeting had, of course, been composed of those not employed in the colliery. Understandably they felt by-passed by the agreement reached, angry at the Federation's removal of the unemployed to the sidelines. When the coalfield conference had come and gone, W. H. Shore of the Garw Unemployed Lodge had written in protest of the EC's refusal to allow the attendance of the unemployed:

> The Unemployed should at least have been allowed to attend even if they did not vote. It is only by the solidarity and efforts of the Taff-Merthyr Unemployed that a lodge has once more been formed in that area.
>
> If the unemployed are expected to remain scab proof and loyal to the organisation they must be allowed to know what is going on especially when they are required to do the spade work in reforming Lodges which have gone out of existence due to the lack of interest or faint-heartedness of the employed men.

This was an acute comment and one that the Federation would respond to more generously in the course of the next year. Harris replied, brusquely, that only employed men could vote and that the Unemployed Regulations of the SWMF were against the participation of the unemployed in such matters.[77]

A large number of men had sacrificed their employment in the pit. Tension remained near to breaking-point through December 1934 with court cases still being heard on charges of intimidation.[78] By the middle of December, less than a month after the settlement had been reached, the secretary of the Treharris Joint Lodges was complaining that the company was not keeping to its bargain over the re-engagement of old workmen and he pleaded for a definite EC statement because 'we do not want it said that the Federation is impotent in a matter of this kind'. The General Secretary could only point to the reduction in the full complement of men employed, and that, once this was overcome, the company would have less excuse to take advantage of the proviso, in re-employing senior men, that this be 'subject to the ability of the man'.[79]

As 1934 closed, over 600 men involved in the recent strike were still idle, and the Taff-Merthyr Lodge requested that the SWMF EC attend to answer their questions and worries.[80]

The policy of the Executive was, clearly, to consolidate the partial victory they had achieved in November but this seemed cold comfort to men who had sacrificed their jobs in the fight.[81] In this situation the views of those who thought the strike had ended too soon gathered eager listeners. From December the militant rank-and-file journal *South Wales Miner* had warned that the Agreement was 'no absolute guarantee'. The journal returned to the point in its next issue with the dire warning that 'whenever the ballot is held, the owners can at any time guarantee a majority for the Company Union because they have the full right to decide who is to be reinstated'. Therefore, it was argued, that the Lodges should demand as priority points that the Federation be recognised immediately and that all strikers be immediately reinstated on the basis of seniority.[82]

This was the doctrine of attack preached by the local activists and the one that Ness Edwards had to face when he attended two stormy Lodge meetings at Taff-Merthyr in January. The clash that had been long brewing between the outside organiser and the men who had maintained the struggle, albeit fitfully, from 1926 now turned into an open quarrel. Although Edwards was prepared to explain the official Federation policy he was no longer prepared to brook what he regarded as obstructionist CP tactics – 'He strongly resented the interference of a certain political party (the Communists) in the dispute, and so long as he was the Agent for the District he would not allow any political party to dictate to him. Bedlinog was the only place in the district where party strife was introduced into an industrial dispute.'[83] – with the result that, at the second meeting he refused to discuss matters with the Committee, at all, until Edgar Evans, a Communist member of Gelligaer UDC, and his supporters, withdrew.[84]

Disgruntlement was running high for all that. The militants' journal claimed that 950 former Taff-Merthyr colliers were still out, and that of the 1,000 employed at the colliery only 250 had been strikers, whilst the latter were directed to the worst 'places' and the non-Federation men to the best. This time the demand was for a Coalfield Conference.[85] Although Federation Officials could parry demands of this sort, they were unable to ignore the mounting evidence of failure to implement the Agreement. The Secretary of the Treharris Joint Lodges, a highly respected SWMF leader, noticed the quickening of Industrial Union activity, in his area, both in Treharris where a man named Pilt was visiting men at present working and those about to return 'telling them that their work is secure if they will join the local Lodge of that organisation', and in Trelewis where 'quite a number of those active with the affairs of that Union are engaged daily and nightly in an endeavour to create an impression that a quicker return to work is possible if they will signify a readiness to join their branch. They assure those at work, that in the event of management being made aware of *their* intentions their work is 'safe'. You can imagine the effect of this kind of tactic. . .'.[86]

In order to maintain their grip on a steadily worsening situation, the EC decided to call a Special Conference.[87] The SWMIU had been steadily working against the spirit of the agreement since the official end of the dispute. Early in January the Industrial Union set up a branch in Bedlinog itself and on the last day of January had organised a secret ballot, at the colliery, under the supervision of Messrs. Gilling and Goodfellow (Cardiff Solicitors). The result, hardly in doubt in view of the personnel employed at the colliery, was 5-to-1 in favour of the SWMIU.[88]

It was immediately condemned by the SWMF as held without their knowledge, without a reasonable lapse of time and as a violation of the agreement signed by the Directors of the Company. Those who organised the ballot stated that it had been held because of the wishes of the men employed who had tired of being the pawns of the Federation and of the Company. This disavowal of the Company was common practice on the side of the SWMIU, hardly convincing in view of the knowledge the Company must have had of the running of the ballot on its premises.[89] For the Federation the position was becoming as grave as ever.

There could be little hope of a permanent settlement so long as Gregory remained actively supported in his plans by the Coalowners. None the less, the SWMF continued to place its faith in good-will and negotiations, in which they were encouraged, before their Conference of 9 February, by a request from the Secretary for Mines, Mr W. L. Cook, to meet, in London, for talks with him and Company representatives.[90]

The delegate conference was, therefore, adjourned until the London meeting had produced some result. Gregory, who now claimed 604 of the 715 men employed at Taff-Merthyr were loyal to the MIU, was indignant that the Minister should negotiate with the SWMF in these circumstances.[91] Eventually at the Annual Conference of the SWMF, Griffiths asked, again, for the EC to be allowed to continue their laborious negotiations, despite the vehement demand for another strike voiced by the Taff-Merthyr Committee. The President allowed that the

Agreement was not observed, and that, at least 168 men were employed in place of a similar number who were, despite their prior claims, still unemployed; but what, he asked, was the best policy to be pursued in the interests of these men?

At the end of April a special delegate conference confirmed that the EC be empowered to meet with Ernest Brown and that the non-Union struggle be confined to the mines owned by Powell Duffryn Associated Collieries and the Ocean Colliery Company. Although strike demands were again rejected the SWMF stiffened its resolve by deciding that, in the event of a collapse of negotiations, 14 days' notice were to be tendered by the men employed at those mines, that they be supported by a weekly levy of all the miners in the coalfield and that the MFGB and TUC be asked for moral and financial support because of 'the vital principle involved in this dispute'.[92]

In early May the Federation Leaders were in a position to summon yet another Conference for 13 May after first circulating the Lodges as to the details of the new proposals. The new ingredient was the active intervention of the Secretary for Mines who would refer, to a single arbitrator, all cases of men claiming the right to be re-engaged in accordance with the Agreement of November 1934 and all such cases in future disputes. The men were to have a nominated individual to represent them in arguments over the price list. On their side the Colliery Company expressed their willingness to allow men to join the Union of their choice, that membership of any Union would not be a condition of employment, nor would Union contributions be deducted from the pay. Since these protracted talks and redrawing of the lines of agreement had stemmed from the furore surrounding the holding of a ballot in January, it was now specifically stated that the agreements would operate until employment reached a normal level in the future. In the meantime there would be no more propaganda meetings or 'interference' with the workers in or near the colliery.[93]

Although the terms were accepted (963 votes against 641; or 46,150 against 32,050), 60 delegates from Taff-Merthyr complained bitterly that the Company had ended the second shift at the colliery out of spite (there were 800 to 900 unemployed and only 300 at work, of the SWMF men). Unemployed men had marched twenty miles from Bedlinog, Trelewis and Treharris late Sunday night, slept on boards at the Workmen's Hall at Caerphilly, in order to attend the Monday Conference. Their admission to the hall for twenty minutes was of no avail against the insistence by Jim Griffiths and Oliver Harris, that non-acceptance of the terms would mean a complete closure of the colliery.[94]

Oliver Harris's point that workmen could now explicitly join the Union of their own choice when they wanted so that there was nothing in the way of an SWMF colliery taking shape immediately,[95] was an admirably lucid piece of theorising. It hardly tallied with the realities being faced by those in work who saw little advance in the November position when SWMIU men were being allowed to circulate a petition against the arbitration just agreed. The militants' paper, whilst deploring the acceptance of the EC's recommendations, felt worried that 'many good fighters in Taff-Merthyr and elsewhere are talking of breaking away from the Federation and even organising militant lodges and combines into an alternative Union.' This was familiar territory and its denizens were warned that such a step would be fatal.[96]

When arbitration did begin in the summer of 1935 matters hardly improved since he ruled that 'length of service' (the basis of re-employment) did not mean the number of years worked in the pit but rather the time a man had been employed in a particular grade. This meant, in turn, that a man might work for 10 years, change his grade and thereby be junior to a man who had only been employed for 18 months. Men did not often remember the exact date of a change in grade which itself was a frequent occurrence in a highly mechanised pit. Nor did the Company's books always record a change. Consequently, almost all the cases submitted by the Federation were disputed. When W. L. Cook gave his ruling in July 1935, in favour of 113 men, still idle, who should have been re-employed, the Company still had no obligation to take them back except at their own pace. Only in October 1935 were all the named men engaged again, but 12 men not mentioned in the Award had been taken on in September, and no-one who had started since September 1934 was dismissed.[97]

In no sense can the SWMF be credited with an overwhelming success in Taff-Merthyr in 1934 and 1935. On the other hand, it was arguable that the SWMF had shown a resolve missing from its policies since 1926. This, in itself, would mark out the struggle at Taff-Merthyr as a turning-point in its affairs. Within 12 months of that campaign being fought despair would become elation as the Federation regained the initiative in the direction of coalfield society.

NOTES

1. There are two excellent local histories *cum* personal reminiscence *The Right Place, the Right Time* (1972) and *Ups and Downs* (1975) by Walter Haydn Davies. Alun Morgan has conducted a community study of Bedlinog, based on tape-recordings, *Bedlinog Study – Pre-war Society in a Colliery village* in *SSRC Coalfield History Project – Final Report* (unpublished, 1974).
2. Copy of Depositions taken in Merthyr Tydfil, 30 June 1923. S. O. Davies MSS.
3. *Merthyr Express*, 20 March 1926.
4. See above, p. 91.
5. The humilation could be personal as well. Noah Ablett was suspended from the SWMF EC for a while because, during the lock-out, he had arranged a settlement at Hill's Plymouth Collieries, Merthyr. He accepted total responsibility although, in fact, the SWMF's General Secretary gave it his official imprimatur. Before Ablett died (of cancer in 1934) he gave a document to Horner – a sheet of Tom Richards' private notepaper.

> Saturday, 13 November 1926.
>
> The possibility of the dismantling and abandonment of the Plymouth Collieries having become imminent, we are informed that they can be acquired and carried on by another company if a general 8 hours working day is conceded by the workmen.
>
> Under the circumstances the workmen are asked to record their vote upon the following proposal.
>
> The Proposal:
>
> That if a general district arrangement for the South Wales coalfield is not of such a character as to make the proposal necessary, the workmen are prepared to authorise their representatives to make an equivalent concession to meet the position.
>
> Signed Thomas Richards
> Noah Ablett
> W. M. Llewellyn
> Isaac Edwards.

This was produced in Ness Edwards' *History of the SWMF* (vol. II) which was unpublished; there is an uncorrected proof copy in Nuffield College Library, dated 1936. Ablett, in fact, resigned from the National Executive of the MFGB (replaced by Horner). He said:

> This is the ugliest situation I have ever faced. I have sacrificed my reputation and my position as a member of the National Executive, which represent all my ambitions in life, for the sake of Hill's Plymouth and the town of Merthyr.

Merthyr Express, 27 November 1926.

6. Though a SWMF contingent of 307 out of 700 working was claimed in early 1927. *Workers' Life*, 4 February 1927 and 22 April 1927; 10 February 1928.
7. Minutes of the Bedlinog Trades and Labour Council. 10 and 24 January 1927; 30 April 1928.

238 THE FED

8. *Western Mail*, 26 June 1929. Anthony-Jones, *op. cit.*, pp. 61–2. Interview with Will Howells, miner, Bedlinog, 1969.

9. *Merthyr Express*, 8 February 1930. It was a Co-operative Group Life Insurance Plan.

10. SWMF EC Minutes, 10 February 1930.

11. Letter from S. O. Davies to Oliver Harris, 2 April 1930. S. O. Davies Papers. Letter Book 12, Glamorgan Record Office.

12. Document in SWMF files, from Richards to Jayne. The men had also declared in favour of joining the Dowlais District. *Merthyr Express*, 19 April 1930.

13. *Western Mail*, 14 April 1930. The 'intimidation' can be seen in a letter from Frank Rogers, of Trelewis, to S. O. Davies, about his son's dismissal from the pit for travelling the 'haulage at prohibited hours' (this would mean no dole so the boy refused to accept the reason for his dismissal). A note from the son, Cyril, was added: 'The statement by my late employer is wrong. I had my timekeeper which was wireless time, also there were six others with me and they were not given notice to terminate their contract the reason is obvious, I am a member of the SWMF and the other members of the SWMIU, and I maintain I am not guilty of any contravention of the rules of the mine.' Letter Book 12, 27 May 1930.

14. *Western Mail*, 14 April 1930; *Merthyr Express*, 19 April 1930. The owners won a case in Chancery giving them an injunction against any further 'obstruction and intimidation'. Anthony-Jones, *op. cit.*, p. 62.

15. *Western Mail*, 28 April 1930.

16. See above pp. 149–54.

17. *Merthyr Express*, 10 May 1930. It was sharply suggested that his interest in Taff-Merthyr was 'personal': 'The fact of the matter is that the district for which Mr Davies is the agent has been so sadly reduced in its membership through the closing down of Dowlais collieries that it has almost been wiped out. Finding himself in such an anomalous position Mr Davies is naturally keen on getting Trelewis into his district so that he may be the direct representative of the workmen employed there on the Federation.'

18. S. O. Davies papers. Letter Book No. 14, 29 May 1930.

19. *Western Mail*, 29 April, 18, 23 and 24 July 1930. There had been, still, forty non-union men employed prior to the strike.

20. *Western Mail*, 7 July 1930, reported that Charles Tellyn was returned unopposed as Lodge Chairman, and that James Bevan, the incumbent secretary, defeated 'Mr W. A. Williams, the founder of the Union, by 511 votes to 316'.

21. S. O. Davies papers. Letter Book No. 14. The letter was offering a job as a collector, to the dismissed workman, Cyril Rogers. The collectors earned 10s. a week each and a commission of 6s. 8d. in the £.

22. *Merthyr Express*, 10 January 1931.

23. Some 500 men were alleged to be working in Treorchy and police, transported from Barry, lined the roads. At Hirwaun where some Industrial Union and Craftsmen's Union men worked, women and children who had congregated to protest against these Tower Colliery men were dispersed. Six SWMIU members worked in the Ocean Colliery, Blaengarw. *Western Mail*, 3, 7, January; 24 February 1931.

24. *Merthyr Express*, 24 January 1931.

25. Edwards, Vol. II, *op. cit.*, Ch. XIII; *The Miners' Monthly*, October 1934.

26. Interviews with Edgar Evans and Len Brooks in 1969 and 1970. The latter had

been in the YCL, a 'rioter' and a 'stay-in-striker'. Edgar Evans (b. 1900) joined the CP in 1926 and was Branch Secretary at Bedlinog, 1926–43, as well as being on the Welsh Committee of the CP, 1933–57. He won a seat on Gelligaer Council in 1934, though as a result of his 9-month imprisonment for 'incitement to riot' in 1936, he was deprived of his Civil Liberties for ten years ('as a bonus' was his ironic comment); he regained his seat in 1947.

27. Edgar Evans thinks that the Taff-Merthyr campaign was inaugurated as the result of a letter from him to Idris Cox, the CP organiser in South Wales, in which he mentioned the Ocean Combine's non-union attacks. Cox then suggested that Taff-Merthyr be included so Alf Davies, the Ocean Combine Committee's Secretary, agreed and, as a result, Ness Edwards met Evans.

Horner, though, wrote: 'The Taff-Merthyr pit . . . remained in the hands of the Industrial Union from 1926 to 1934 when the Executive of the South Wales Miners decided to attempt to secure recognition for the Federation' (*op. cit.*, p. 135), which is in accord with Ness Edwards' version and that of James Griffiths, 'When I became President in 1934 . . . I had decided upon the bold plan of attacking the rival union at the Taff-Merthyr Colliery' (Griffiths, *op. cit.*, p. 35). It is probably impossible to trace the steps now; it would seem that all three organisations involved (the CP at District and branch levels, the Ocean Combine Committee and the SWMF EC) were, simultaneously, moving towards action at the colliery – a sort of ground-swell in the 'united front' that was to operate in the coalfield from 1934 on.

28. *Miners' Monthly*, October 1934. The collecting station for the Dowlais Lodge was a remnant of S. O. Davies' earlier efforts; Noah Ablett, the agent for the new Area 5, agreed to the setting up of an Unemployed Lodge at Bedlinog.

29. SWMF EC Minutes, 21 September and 13 October 1934. Edwards and Crews were placed 'in charge of the Taff-Merthyr and Bedwas campaigns'.

30. Interview with Edgar Evans who said that Albert Thomas, the agent from Bargoed, had surprisingly told the EC that 'Horner was the only man who could make a mark in Bedlinog, or impress the essential people there'. See also a letter from a 'Taff-Merthyr Workman' in *Merthyr Express*, 6 October 1934, where the writer refers to Horner, 'The Federation's CP enemy', as leading the attack for the previous two weeks and asks:

> Is it likely that the Taff-Merthyr men will run the risk of the place being turned into another Mardy through political influences? Hundreds of men have to travel from Dowlais to Bedlinog to work at this colliery owing to the collieries where they usually worked being closed through activities of this kind.

31. *Federationist* No. 2, 5 October 1934. Issued by the Taff-Merthyr Lodge. SWMF. No other numbers survive.

32. *The Miners' Monthly*, October 1934.

33. *Western Mail*, 8 and 9 October 1934. A pernicious opposite of 'Hornerism', no doubt.

34. SWMF EC Minutes, 6 October 1934. The Bedwas campaign was regarded as a 'holding operation' with Taff-Merthyr the principal target. Several prominent miners' leaders took part, Will Betty (a Glamorgan County Councillor), E. J. Evans (Area No. 1. EC member), Alf Davies (Ocean Combine Secretary), Dick Bennetta (miners' agent), Edgar Lewis (Carmarthenshire County Councillor), Jack

Davies (Llwynypia), Nun Nicholas (Marxist teacher), W. H. Mainwaring, MP, Ted Williams, MP, George Hall, MP, J. W. Grant (Craftsmen's representative), Dick Beamish (Abercrave), William Paynter (then unemployed), almost all the lodge officials in the vicinity and the mining members of the Standing Joint Committees of Glamorgan and Monmouthshire. See Edwards, Vol. II, *op. cit.* Interview with Edgar Evans who put many of them up – Horner slept in the same bed as Edgar Lewis, Cross Hands, who was Horner's defeated, and disgruntled, rival for the job of agent in the Anthracite.

35. *Western Mail*, 9 October 1934. Tellyn claimed twenty dismissals.
36. *The Miners' Monthly*, October 1934.
37. *Western Mail*, 10 October 1934.
38. *Merthyr Express*, 13 October 1934. The culprits escaped.
39. *The Miners' Monthly*, October 1934. In fact the men on the night-shift were 'advised to go back and keep the men working. The Friday night temper of a night shift was not too reliable.' Edwards, Vol. II, *op. cit.*, p. 189.
40. *Merthyr Express*, 20 October 1934.
41. SWMF EC Minutes, 13 October 1934.
42. Letters from Oliver Harris, 13 October 1934. SWMF files.
43. *Merthyr Express*, 20 October 1934.
44. *Western Mail*, 15 October 1934.
45. There was a brief non-union stoppage (14–16 October) at Fernhill Colliery, Treherbert, which was exceptional for the removal of safety men for the first time since 1921. The non-unionists were roped in. A campaign was begun in Ogmore Vale against men in arrears in late October. *Western Mail*, 15, 17, 29 October 1934. The SWMF EC resolved to continue the Bedwas campaign but to avoid a precipitate stoppage. EC Minutes, 28 October 1934.
46. *Western Mail*, 16 October 1934.
47. *Ibid.*, 17, 18, 19 October 1934.
48. The importing of blacklegs from the coalfield's bottomless pool of unemployed labour was, of course, the greatest danger in all the Federation's struggle. Ness Edwards (Vol. II), *op. cit.*, p. 190: 'During the week "blackleg" recruiters were busy in all the pubs at which they could find toleration. In the derelict northern end of the Rhymney Valley, the poor despairing unemployed miner would see glimpses of rolls of pound notes, "which we can get with your Union at Taff". In the Merthyr area the same tactic – "subs" of 25s. and free transport. A guarantee of employment and the pick of the work. The chance of a lifetime as against the black bitter despair of the derelict area. Steal another man's job, become a tool of the company, rat on your fellow workers; forget your tradition, remember your own kids want boots and clothes; get drunk and become a blackleg. The policeman will save you from the deserts which you know rightly belong to you. Such was the individual drama.'
49. *Ibid.*, 20 October 1934.
50. *Ibid.*, 26 October 1934.
51. *Miners' Monthly*, October 1934.
52. *Merthyr Express*, 27 October, and *Western Mail*, 8 November 1934.
53. *Western Mail*, 26 October 1934. Interviews with Bedlinog inhabitants. Blacklegs were despised as bought pawns, constantly referred to as 'twp', and, even when they showed courage in the face of mass demonstration still dismissed as 'bastards

all the same'. A constant allegation was that in return for 'easy places' at the coal-face the 'scabs' would allow pit officials to have sexual relations with their wives and daughters. Unfortunately the bedroom door is closed to the social historian but the extent of these allegations, at the very least, indicates the intensity of feeling aroused. For a comparative comment on 'blacklegging' see David Smith 'The Struggle Against Company Unionism in the South Wales Coalfield', pp. 367–9. *Welsh History Review*, Vol. 6, No. 3.

54. Letter from George Spencer in *Western Mail*, 20 October 1934.
55. Articles by Gregory in *Western Mail*, 22 and 23 October 1934.
56. Letters from Oliver Harris to Lord Davies, 22 October 1934; from Lord Davies to Sir William Jenkins, 29 October 1934, and Jenkins to Lord Davies, 31 October 1934. SWMF files.
57. There was no diminution of 'unorthodox' pressure, however. On Friday, 19 October, Charles Tellyn, SWMIU chairman, was assaulted by 'a hostile crowd' and received facial injuries in Trelewis High Street. *Western Mail*, 22 October and *Merthyr Express*, 27 October 1934.
58. *Western Mail*, 24, 27, 29 October 1934; *Merthyr Express*, 27 October 1934.
59. SWMF EC Minutes, 28 October 1934.
60. *Western Mail*, 31 October, 3 November 1934. Nine men were sent for trial at Swansea on charges of intimidation and unlawful assembly. They included the three miners' agents, Bennetta, Betty and the Rev. J. Buckley Jones, Minister of Moriah Chapel, Bedlinog, an ardent supporter of the strikers. They were accused of threatening, along with 500–600 other people, Daniel Jones, an Industrial Union Committee man. They were discharged on 23 November after promising not to use intimidation for 'political purposes' again.
61. *Western Mail*, 17 October and 5 November 1934. The arbitrators had also agreed that the ascertainment system, in force since 1921, does not give any complete picture of the profits and losses in the coalfield under the conditions which now prevail' i.e. the subsidiary companies (and coal by-products) with which the collieries were profitably linked. See J. Griffiths, *Pages from Memory* (1972), p. 40.
62. *Merthyr Express*, 10 November 1934.
63. *Western Mail*, 8 November 1934.
64. *Merthyr Express*, 17 November 1934.
65. *Letter* from Hann to Harris, 10 November 1934.
66. *Western Mail*, 13, 16 and 17 November 1934.
67. Lord Davies. Llandinam MS., Box 15. *Memorandum on Taff-Merthyr Dispute 7 November 1934*. The document is of very special interest as it is the only candid, unofficial memorandum by a coalowner that survives. The Hanns, in particular, later destroyed all their material so that only the 'non-controversial' official Association papers were stored in the National Library of Wales (information from L. J. Williams, Esq.).
68. *Loc. cit.*, *Memorandum of an Interview with Sir Connop Guthrie at Claridge's* on 24 January 1934, when Lord Davies was informed that Sir Connop thought there would be a strong 'confiscatory' Socialist government in power within six years and that investment abroad was to be favoured. American dollars were suggested, Lord Davies preferred Canadian investments. Furthermore, it was thought war between Russia and Japan was likely in the spring with Britain possibly drawn in on Japan's side. Sir Connop added 'that all the armament firms are doing extraordinarily well.

Lord Davies wishes Mr Edwards to ascertain which particular industries would benefit in the event of a war in the Far East. It may be possible to buy shares in aviation and other Companies for a rise within the next few months . . . Lord Davies would contemplate investments on these lines not only for Cambrian and General but for himself personally.'

69. SWMF EC Minutes, 16 November 1934.
70. *Western Mail*, 19 November 1934. It was felt, by the EC that a deadlock had been reached with 'blackleg' members holding steady and likely to increase with a detrimental effect on the morale of the strikers. Edwards, *op. cit.*, Vol. II, p. 195.
71. There continued to be window-smashing incidents and some violent clashes between opposing sides in the area.
72. *Western Mail*, 19 November 1934. *Agreement between the SWMF and the Taff-Merthyr Steam Coal Company Limited*, in SWMF files.
73. *Merthyr Express*, 8 December 1934; *Western Mail*, 3 December 1934.
74. Horner, *op. cit.*, p. 135.
75. *South Wales Miner*, No. 34, 3 December 1934, and No. 35, 17 December 1934.
76. Edwards (Vol. II), *op. cit.*, pp. 197–8.
77. Letter from Shore, 8 November 1934 and Reply from Harris, 12 November 1934.
78. *Merthyr Express*, 24 November and 1 December 1934. Oliver Harris complained that the Chairman of the Bench trying the cases was the brother of the man who had brought the charges, i.e. the Chief Constable, and that this man had had to make public apology (and pay damages) to the SWMF some years before for slandering Federation officials. *Miners' Monthly*, November 1934. The Chief Constable's own report to the Glamorgan Standing Joint Committee described the origins of the dispute as a refusal of SWMIU members to join the SWMF, whereas the strike itself, of course, erupted because of the company's refusal to employ SWMF members. *Western Mail*, 11 December 1934.
79. Letter from T. Andrews to Oliver Harris, 18 December 1934; a reply dated 27 December 1934. SWMF files.
80. *Western Mail*, 31 December 1934.
81. E. J. Parsons, of Bedlinog, may stand as an example (extreme perhaps) for many. He wrote to the EC to complain that he was still out of work after the dispute and receiving only a 10s. a week disablement pension and 16s. strike pay, whereas his wages at the colliery had, with his pension, been £3 11s. 7d. He had lost part of one foot, was sixty-six years old and had 'hesitated to come out at once with the others, though loyal in spirit with them, because of my condition and the special job given me to do at the colliery, feeling that if I did I should never get back'. Persuaded that the Federation would stand by him, and 'in the truth of the slogan "every man back to his place", "All in or All out"', he had struck. His reply was that there were always hard cases and all possible would be done to secure justice for those loyal to the Federation. Letter from Parsons to Harris, 21 December 1934 (reply attached). SWMF files.
82. *South Wales Miner*, Nos. 34 and 35. 3 and 17 December 1934.
83. *Western Mail*, 4 January 1935; *Merthyr Express*, 12 January 1935.
84. *Western Mail*, 18 January 1935; *Merthyr Express*, 19 January 1935.
85. *South Wales Miner*, No. 36, 9 January 1935.
86. Letter from Tom Andrews to Harris, 14 January 1935. SWMF files.

87. This was after the SWMF EC had received two delegations from the Taff-Merthyr Lodge Committee. EC Minutes, 22 January and 2 February 1935.

88. *Merthyr Express*, 12 January and 2 February 1935; *Western Mail*, 1 February 1935. The actual figures were:

For the SWMIU	542
For the SWMF	112
	430 majority

89. *Western Mail*, 4 and 5 February 1935.

90. *Ibid.*, 8 February 1934; SWMF EC Minutes, 22 January 1935.

91. *Ibid.*, 11 and 20 February.

92. SWMF EC Minutes, 11, 12 and 13 April 1935. *Western Mail*, 29 April 1935. The EC was not cheered by the news that Sir Wingate Saul, KC, umpire at the Industrial Court, had reversed the decision of the Bargoed Court of Referees (after an appeal by the chief insurance inspector of the Ministry of Labour) and had denied the Taff-Merthyr strikers any unemployment benefit. This decision confirmed the legal advice given to the SWMF, i.e. that the conditions of employment offered the workmen were not illegal under the Truck Acts of 1831 and 1887 (i.e. membership of the SWMIU); that the dispute lay between employers and employees and that, therefore, the claimants were disqualified under the provisions of Sec. 8 (1) of the Unemployment Insurance Act, 1920. Taff-Merthyr (on which £13,709 4s. 3d. was spent in strike pay in 1934 and £1,333 19s. 6d. in 1935, with £4,287 17s. 6d. in litigation costs. SWMF Balance Sheets 1934 and 1935) was becoming an expensive liability. See *Western Mail*, 12 December 1934; 1 March 1935.

93. *Western Mail*, 8 May 1935.

94. *Ibid.*, 14 May 1935.

95. *Miners' Monthly*, May 1935.

96. Edwards (Vol. II), *op. cit.*, Ch. XIV: *South Wales Miner*, No. 40, 22 May 1935. Edwards wrote, in 1936, 'On Wednesday, 22 May 1935, both W. H. Crews . . . and myself visited the roadway opposite Taff-Merthyr Colliery at 11 a.m. Outside the clerk's office on the colliery premises, Bevan, the Secretary of the Taff-Merthyr Lodge of the Industrial Union, was standing talking to Milsom, the colliery cashier. We saw the cashier hand to Bevan a ledger-like book.' *Loc. cit.*

97. Edwards (Vol. II), *op. cit.*, p. 204.

CHAPTER EIGHT

Marching Out and Staying Down

The SWMF emerged from 1934 in better shape than for many years —
there had been a small increase in wages aided, in purchasing power, by
the trough of deflation (1932–4); there had been some restoration of
prestige *vis-à-vis* the SWMIU; the split between its various political
factions had, to some extent, been healed; and, at last, it had restruc-
tured its own organisation which was now run by an executive elected
by direct ballot vote. The most immediate impact could be seen in its
membership figures which now rose by 13,612 in the course of the year
(to 76,949) and did not decrease again until 1941 when membership
went down slightly. There were, in addition, some 24,000 unemployed
members and the number of these did not drop dramatically until the
outbreak of war (to 11,037 in 1940). The increase in membership was
achieved despite a fall in the average number employed in collieries in
Wales during the year of some 6,000 (140,396 in 1933; 134,286 in
1934). It was this latter fact that had come to temper all upsurges of
optimism by the mid-1930s. The Federation had shown themselves
aware, finally, of the need to define the role of their own unemployed
with care, but almost equally pressing was the necessity to defend the
position of the unemployed within communities where, in any one street
or any one family, there was no real separation, socially, of the two
categories. The numbers wholly unemployed from the collieries
fluctuated between 1932 and 1934 but never dropped below 50,000,
and for most months, could be much higher. Even more appalling was
the inescapable fact that many men were becoming habituated to the
state of unemployment by virtue of the length of time they had been out
of work. Over 20 per cent in 1934 had been out for over four years,
whilst 75 per cent had been unemployed for over a year. Their well-
being could no longer be seen as a matter for temporary adjustment.
When, in 1934, the Government resolved to clean up the anomalies in
the rates of unemployment benefit and to separate the unemployed, for
administrative purposes, into different categories, the Federation

showed itself to be aware of the implications for South Wales and to be capable of organising the only 'direct action' that succeeded, in the 1930s, against Government decision.[1] They were the tip of the iceberg.

The last two Hunger Marches from South Wales to London (in 1934 and 1936) were the two most significant examples in South Wales of the United Front in practice (unlike the previous Marches which fundamentally were confined to the CP, the NUWM and their supporters). But they also represented something much more than a mere political strategy: the breadth of active support which propelled them forward was an instinctive United Front which embraced non-political organisations. The depth of concern felt about the permanence of mass unemployment in the coalfield, lack of governmental action and the destructive social effect of the Means Test regulations were now being harnessed for the first time. The social structure of valley society was such that a working-class consciousness was often indistinguishable from a community consciousness, so overwhelmingly proletarian were the communities. Just as in the seven-month lock-out of 1926, valley society felt besieged, with whole communities threatened with extinction. It was the recapturing of the unique community consciousness of 1926 and all its related socio-political activities which made the last two Hunger Marches and all the extra-parliamentary 'explosions' of the 1930s so powerfully dynamic. The *Local Unemployment Index* reveals that unemployment was uniformly high throughout the steam coalfield for most of the 1930s. Although there were obvious local and regional differences, it cannot be concluded that high rates necessarily led to either militancy or inaction. The equation was never as simple as that. Rhondda's plight was as desperate as Bargoed or Merthyr but their degree of activism was never the same. Rhondda had more in common politically with parts of the Anthracite coalfield which suffered considerably less unemployment: their respective historical and contemporary circumstances drew them closer together in the early 1930s, particularly through a new rank and file movement launched in May 1933.[2]

The official organ of the movement, the *South Wales Miner*, edited by Horner, was launched on 22 June 1933 and during its short life (it folded through lack of finance on 10 July 1935), it did succeed in bringing Communists and non-Communists together on a militant platform at a time when the new executive council was being launched (two of its supporters were elected on to it) and when the combine committees were re-emerging as a force in the vacuum left by the

SOUTH WALES MINER

ONE PENNY   FORTNIGHTLY

No. 38.   *The Official Organ of the Rank-and-File Movement of the South Wales Miners.*   March 25th, 1935.

JOINT ACTION WITH THE UNEMPLOYED

The campaign against the Slave Act continues with great vigour in South Wales, and all parts of the country. Three thousand Scottish marchers are on the road to Glasgow, tramping nearly two hundred miles to place their demands before the Scottish Unemployment Board. In every town and village they are greeted by thousands of unemployed and EMPLOYED workers, and on March 25th, Scottish workers employed in industry will join with the marchers in Glasgow, together with Scottish miners in several pits who have declared for a one-day strike on that date.

SOUTH WALES LAGS BEHIND.

South Wales started the fight against this Slave Act, and gave a lead to the whole country. The Cambrian miners gave the lead in building the United Front and organising the biggest mass demonstration ever seen in the Rhondda. The South Wales Conference on January 26th brought together for the first time the workers in the different industries and the different trade unions. It gave the inspiration in every part of South Wales for building United Front Committees to lead the fight against the Slave Act and to bring down the National Government.

But South Wales is now lagging behind other parts of the country. While the meetings and demonstrations in South Wales end in pious resolutions, the Scottish workers are MARCHING against the Slave Act. While the campaign in South Wales is limited to speeches, the Scottish workers are organising JOINT ACTION with the unemployed.

NATIONAL GOVERNMENT GOES AHEAD.

The National Government has not been slow to grasp this opportunity of a breathing space to go forward with its war preparations, expressed both in the extra £10,000,000 for armaments in the coming Budget and in the militarist propaganda which is the essence of the Jubilee celebrations. The unemployed "cuts" are suspended, but the Slave Act regulations REMAIN and can be reimposed at any moment the National Government thinks fit. It would "spoil" the Jubilee celebrations to do it now, but the preparations are well in hand to reimpose the "cuts" when the Jubilee celebrations are over.

Are we to wait for the National Government to choose its own time for the next attack? Are we to allow the Government to go on with its war preparations and Jubilee celebrations, when this is just the BEST time for us to organise JOINT ACTION to withdraw the Slave Act and to bring down the National Government? To remain satisfied with fine speeches and pious resolutions is to play into the hands of this National Government. The only way forward is to organise JOINT ACTION of the unemployed and EMPLOYED in demonstrations to the local Unemployment Boards and Public Assistance Committees, and united strike action in the pits and factories.

LEADERS AGAINST ACTION.

The attitude of the so-called South Wales Council of Action makes it clear that this body will NEVER organise joint action against the Slave Act. The only action it takes is AGAINST the joint action of the workers. The first time it met after the historic January Conference, was for the purpose of PREVENTING the joint action of the Cambrian miners with the unemployed by holding forth the prospect of joint action in South Wales. The second time it met was for the purpose of declaring AGAINST action on a South Wales scale by holding forth the prospect of national action. Now, it proposes to become a "consultative" body acting under the direction of the National Labour Council.

This policy leads to the BREAKING UP of the United Front. How can the National Labour Council, which refuses even to discuss the United Front, lead the movement for UNITY in South Wales? The scope of the movement in South Wales goes far beyond the narrow limits of the vision of the national Labour Party and Trade Union leaders who impose "black circulars" to split the Trade Union movement, and who co-operate with the capitalists but not with militant workers.

DEMAND CONFERENCE.

The South Wales miners can change this situation. Every big meeting and demonstration is in favour of a one-day strike. But it is necessary for INDIVIDUAL miners' lodges to demand a Coalfield Conference to take an official decision. Twenty individual lodges have the right to demand the E.C. to call a Conference. SEND IN NOW.

Organise Joint Action of All Workers!
Support the Scottish Marchers.
Prepare for one-day strike in S. Wales.

Yours fraternally, *Editorial Board.*

The Rank and File newspaper, 1935.

elimination of the Districts.[3] It was probably a decisive factor in getting
two victimised Rhondda militants back into the Federation via the
Anthracite coalfield, by campaigning on their behalf: Horner was
elected miners' agent in the Gwendraeth Valley in November 1933[4] and
Jack Jones, of Clydach Vale and later an International Brigader, was
elected checkweigher at Cross Hands (also in the Gwendraeth) in
August 1934.[5]

Militant initiatives within the SWMF now came more and more from
the Anthracite coalfield in the west, particularly from the Amalgamated
Anthracite Combine Committee (AACC). Significantly, one of their
agents, James Griffiths, was elected President of the SWMF in 1934,
and in the same year the only South Wales Miners' Industrial Union
foothold in the Anthracite, at Emlyn No. 2 Colliery (Penygroes), was
swept away after a vigorous campaign. Both events, in their own way,
proved to be sources of inspiration to the SWMF.[6]

Stoppages over non-union, semi-political (the South Wales Miners'
Industrial Union in the Steam coalfield) and political issues (non-
intervention in Spain) were called for by the AACC (and on occasions
actually carried out). Often they invited the rest of the coalfield to follow
their example, as in July 1933, over their call for a one day anniversary
protest strike against the loss of the 7-hour day.[7]

At one stage, the Executive Council of the SWMF felt its power was
being challenged by the AACC and attempted to reprimand it, but to no
avail. On the contrary, the SWMF acknowledged the AACC's
resources by borrowing some of its leading members for the campaign
against the South Wales Miners' Industrial Union at Taff-Merthyr
Colliery in 1934.[8] The Anthracite miners were in the fortunate position
of working in a relatively prosperous industry – production reached an
all-time peak in 1934. It was largely because of the 1925 'victory', when
the whole of the Anthracite District struck in support of Ammanford
No. 1 miners who were defending a breach of the seniority rule which
protected militants, that so few lodge officials were victimised after the
1926 lock-out. The Anthracite miners also suffered less in the seven-
month lock-out because, being a semi-rural coalfield, many could live
off the countryside whilst others were still part-time farmers. Many
miners also owned their own houses and would 'eat them' before being
starved back to work (although house ownership was not uniformly
high). Superimposed on this comparative industrial and trade union
security was the development of independent working-class education
throughout the area. It was claimed that as a result of NCLC classes

under D. D. Evans (Ystradgynlais), Jack Griffiths (Cwmllynfell), James Griffiths (Ammanford), Nun Nicholas (Trebanos), D. R. Owen (Garnant) and D. J. Williams (Gwaun-cae-Gurwen), the Anthracite miners had a Marxist lodge leadership second only to the Rhondda.[9]

Despite this 'apartness' of the Anthracite coalfield and the longstanding variations between and within valleys, there was one kind of uniformity which distinguished the whole of the South Wales coalfield from other depressed industrial areas. The whole region continued and increased its loyalty to the Labour Party in the difficult General Elections of 1931 and 1935. Whilst unemployment was a leveller it cannot be assumed that variation in it necessarily led to a particular degree of politicisation. This was more a function of the nature of political, trade union and 'independent' educational opportunities and traditions in a given locality, alongside the vital immediate relationship with capital.[10] One indicator of this difference was the struggle for and by the unemployed centring on the Hunger Marches.

The 1934 March had been preceded by growing local agitation. The NUWM, revitalised by a Welsh Council organised by Lewis Jones, had decided to organise an all-Monmouthshire Hunger March on 30 August 1933 when 500 of the unemployed were to converge on the County Council Offices in Newport. There were 40,000 unemployed persons in the county in May 1933, of whom 37,000 were on transitional benefit and subject to Means Test regulations. Some areas of the county were almost totally derelict. Blaina (80 per cent), Abertillery (85 per cent), Risca and Pontypool (both 30 per cent) were amongst the worst hit. But conditions of the employed and part-time workers appeared no better with, for instance, children of the employed in Abertillery receiving food in feeding centres set up for the children of the unemployed. In 1933, the Monmouthshire County Health Department reported that 80 per cent of the children were physically incapacitated in one degree or another and only 10 per cent were in normal health. In the previous year a medical practitioner in Pengam reported that children had contracted rickets in their mothers' womb. The NUWM claimed that the only areas in the county which provided regular school feeding (for example 3,000 Abertillery children received two meals a day) were those which had been subjected to their militant pressure.[11]

The 1933 March demands included the restarting of work on the Newport–Chepstow road at trade union rates; that Public Assistance Committees ignore Means Test regulations and grant full benefits to all

THE

Rhondda

Price One Penny

No. 1.   September, 1935

The Official Organ of
—— the Rhondda ——
Borough Labour Party.

Clarion

TWO BOB A DAY MORE !

The Miners' Campaign for a Living Wage

THE CLAIM FOR A NATIONAL AGREEMENT

By JIM GRIFFITHS, President S.W.M.F.

ONE of my earliest recollections is that of being taken in my father's care to a miners' "Mabon's Day" meeting. Mabon himself was the speaker, and the burden of his speech was expressed in the slogan:—

" Wyth awr i weithio,
Wyth awr yn rhydd,
Wyth awr i gysgu,
Ac wyth awll y dydd."

A generation has passed by since then—and it is a terrible commentary upon our industrial system—that the last line of the slogan is one we might still repeat! "Eight shillings per day"—said the old slogan. Last year the average earnings per person employed for the year in the mines of Britain was £115 11s. 5d.—44/6 per week—7/5 per day, divided by six days in the week. Less than 1/- an hour. And that is the average for all persons employed below the status of under-manager. There are tens of thousands of miners who are lucky if they have 30/- a week to take home.

MORE WORK—LESS PAY.

To-day the miner works harder than he has ever done. He produces more coal per shift than he has ever done, and he receives less wages than he ever did. Look at these figures.

In 1920 for an average daily output of 14.84 cwts. the miner received £4 5s. 9d. per week.

In 1934 for an average daily output of 22.94 cwts. he gets £2 4s. 6d. per week.

In 1934 the miner works half-an-hour longer per day than he did in 1920; he produces 8¾cwts. more coal per day than he did in 1920; and he gets 6/8 per day less than he did in 1920.

*WHAT THE MINER GETS—
AND WHAT HE PAYS.*

That is what the miner gets for his work. What does he pay in Blood and Tears ?

In 1934—1,078 persons were killed in and about the mines, and 132,859 persons were injured.

In 1934—the number of accidents occurring in the coal mining industry was six times the number occurring in Factories and Workshops.

The miner works harder. He runs the greatest risks, and he is the lowest paid.

He is the "Cinderella" of Industrial Britain.

AND NOW THE MINER SAYS "STOP !"

For fifteen years the miner has suffered either the stark tragedy of poverty on the road—or abject poverty at work.

Amalgamations are closing the pits, and throwing him on the scrap heap.

The machine in the pit is reducing him to slavery.

And the Miners' Federation of Great Britain says "Stop !"

The miner must no longer be the "Cinderella." We must organise ourselves into a strong force once again. We must rouse the Nation's Conscience. We must compel the owners, we must force the Government to take action.

We are asking for 2/- more per day, and we intend to get it.

The M.F.G.B. is conducting a Nation-wide Campaign to bring the miners' cause to the forefront. In October a Special Conference is to be called to decide what action shall be taken to enforce our modest demand—TWO BOB A DAY, AND A NATIONAL AGREEMENT.

During the coming months every nerve must be strained in order to develop to the full our industrial and political strength. Let every man take his place within our organisations. The Federation, as the basis of all our power, must again be made strong. Every miner should rally to this call—if they desire to make victory certain.

LABOUR ON THE COUNCIL.

By IORWERTH THOMAS, D.C.

The advent of the Labour Party to the position it now holds upon the Rhondda Council is an accomplishment that registers one phase of the general advance made by the working classes towards self-government. To attain a majority of Labour members has meant years of hard work and involved much sacrifice. Years ago it was customary for working classes to take all their troubles to the family butcher, grocer, or local tradesman. Spiritually and temporally the working man placed all his faith in somebody else. He would go cap in hand to somebody else in the village to appeal and invite Mr. Somebody to represent him on the Council. If we examine the composition of the Council during these days, we would discover that it was a collection of tradesmen, colliery managers, and solicitors, etc. As the result of propaganda in the pioneering days, working men and women were persuaded to have faith in themselves and put out their trust in others.

Gradually the idea of independent working class representation took root. Eventually working men from the coal face and women from the home were returned to the Council, until finally we gained power. The purpose of the activities that will appear in this paper each month will be to show how working men and women organised under the banner of the Labour Party have utilized the machinery of government in the Rhondda for the benefit of the workers of the Rhondda. We shall educate you about the problems of local government. We want you to understand the work of the Labour Party, its plan and policy.

etc. We want to convince you that working men can govern. As an example of Labour's record, let us quote the efforts made to assist the unemployed. Let it be clearly understood here that the Labour Party realises that unemployment can only be eliminated by the abolition of Capitalism. But we cannot wait and pray until this capitalist system collapses. We must do something now for the suffering people of the Rhondda. The Rhondda Labour Council has done excellent work for the unemployed in the provision of work schemes. Since 1928 we have spent on Rhondda work schemes about £490,000. This has provided employment for 70,000 man weeks, approximately 3,400 man working for a period of thirteen weeks each. We have in hand for the coming winter additional work schemes for unemployed. The Labour Party has submitted proposals for relief work amounting to £315,000, which would provide work for 49,000 man weeks or work for 4,000 for a period of thirteen weeks each. We anticipate that during this winter we shall put into effect work for which we shall have gained from the Commissioners over £100,000. Included in this will be provision for three new swimming baths. In conclusion we take pride in the fact that our Council is to the fore in its endeavour to do something tangible for the unemployed and not merely shout about it. Every month we shall outline in this paper Labour's policy on the Council.

**Our next issue will be published
on September 26th.**

Survival of the Fittest

In northern climes, the polar bear
Protects himself with fat and hair,
Where snow is deep and ice is stark,
And half the year is cold and dark,
He still survives a clime like that
By growing far, by growing fat.
These traits, O. bear, which thou transmittest,
Prove the Survival of the Fittest.

To polar regions, waste and wan,
Comes the encroaching race of man,
A puny, feeble, little bubber,
He has no fur, he has no blubber,
The scornful bear sat down at ease
To see the stranger starve and freeze—
But, lo! the stranger slew the bear,
And ate his fat and wore his hair;
These deeds, O! man, which thou committest,
Prove the Survival of the Fittest.

In modern times the millionaire
Protects himself as did the bear;
Where poverty and hunger are
He counts his bullion by the car;
Where thousands perish still he thrives;
The wealth, O! Crœsus, thou transmittest,
Prove the Survival of the Fittest.

But, lo! some people, odd and funny,
Some without a cent of money—
The simple, common human race,
Choose to improve their dwelling place:
They had no use for millionaires,
They calmly said the world was theirs;
They were so wise, so strong, so many,
The millionaires?—there wasn't any.
These deeds, O! man, which thou committest,
Prove the Survival of the Fittest.

Mrs. Charlotte Stetson.

Local Labour Party newspaper, 1935.

claimants and take no account of other income by the employed or his relatives; that two substantial meals be provided for school children every day; that two cwts of coal be given to all unemployed; and that the seven hour day for miners be reintroduced.[12]

Although the United Front strategy was attempted, little organisational contact was established outside the NUWM, mainly because the March was an implied criticism of the Labour majority on the County Council. The Labour Party members in South Wales as elsewhere had decided to try to administer the Means Test 'humanely', which to a degree they had succeeded in doing. Nevertheless, Marchers' Councils in several parts of the county did collect 17,000 signatures for its petition and the Urban District Councils of Abertillery and Caerleon passed resolutions of support. The march was also discussed in chapels and churches. A Risca church took a collection and placed the church at the disposal of the marchers. The potential of the chapels was emphasised in a published account of the march in which reference was made to two Blaenau-Gwent deacons who had been expelled from their chapel for not supporting the 1839 Chartist march on Newport. The memory of the Chartists was constantly being evoked and every participant was reminded:

> If their Chartist forbears had marched in the Hungry Forties of the last century, their descendants would march in the Destitute Thirties of our era.[13]

The march organisers asserted that the 'smug' administrators of the county had been opposed to the Chartists, their demands had been impossible, their leaders had been irresponsible; so it was with the march and the demands of 30 August 1933. But whilst the Chartists could contemplate overthrowing the social system, their descendants could do no more than make a 'public parade of their destitution and the horror of their child-life'.[14]

Despite the lack of a broad organisational front, the march inspired considerable enthusiasm. Whole towns and villages with their bands turned out in their support. Between Crumlin and Cwmcarn alone, 50,000 people are said to have been on the streets showing their solidarity. The demonstration at Newport involved 20,000 people. The County Council conceded only two minor demands: that a deputation be received and that the marchers be provided with free transport home.[15]

With the organising of marchers' councils and committees in most of the valleys of the steam coalfield, the march of February 1934 proved to be the largest, most representative and best organised to leave South Wales (apart from the final one in 1936.) The main protest was against the new Unemployment Insurance Bill, the so-called 'Slave Bill' which would replace the local Public Assistance Committee with an Unemployment Assistance Board with nationally determined relief rates which could not be influenced by localised pressure. There was the additional concern that the unemployed who had exhausted their statutory benefits were to be hived off and treated differently. A wider fear was that the unemployed could be turned into an army of conscript labour to work without wages in the so-called 'fascist' type labour camps, industrial training centres and public works schemes.[16]

The march was organised by the NUWM and various United Front organisations, and consisted of seventeen regional contingents from all parts of Britain, culminating with a Congress in London on 24 February and again on 4 March. The marchers were to be elected from a wide range of bodies including trade union branches, Ex-Servicemen's Clubs, unemployed branches, Co-operative Guilds and mass meetings.[17] Preparations and instructions on the usual military style lines (quartermasters, cooking squads, fatigue squads and section leaders) were sometimes detailed almost to the point of absurdity but all for a precise purpose. That they were accepted without criticism reflected the seriousness and discipline of the marchers:

> Marchers found soiling seats of lavatories etc. will be expelled from the march. There is ample lavatory accommodation and each marcher should pull the chain after him. . . . No gambling will be allowed for fags or anything else because the losers become disgruntled when they have no smokes. . . . No cobbling, haircutting or shaving must be done anywhere but in these places [allocated].[18]

The Treherbert Marchers' Council must have been typical in its preparations. Meetings and rallies were held in schools and in the local Labour Hall. Street collections were made, marchers elected and messages of support obtained from the Treherbert Loco NUR branch, the local Workers' Club and some Labour councillors.[19]

The unity drive was not without its difficulties in at least one area. At Merthyr, Arthur Eyles, a member of the British Union of Fascists who had recently defected from the Communist Party and had been on the previous march, attempted to disrupt the first meeting of the Borough's Marchers' Council, while its chairman resigned over the allocation of street collections. There were also organisational problems between the

ILP (which was still relatively strong in the area) and the NUWM which was taking the lead in the preparations.[20] But with the representatives from the Communist Party, the ILP (and its Guild of Youth), the NUWM, the General and Municipal Workers' Union, women's groups and two chapels, it was assured of wide support within the Borough.[21]

The continuing concern shown by the police and the Government again manifested itself. Hostile attitudes expressed at the outset of the march by the Home Secretary prompted the founding of the National Council of Civil Liberties because of a fear that the police incidents of 1932 might have been repeated.[22] Informers, as in previous marches, were again used by the Metropolitan Police,[23] although it is now apparent that certain leading members of the NUWM were throughout aware of the identity of the informer in their midst. They chose not to take any action even though (or possibly because) the person involved was a central figure in the NUWM hierarchy. In the event, there were no reports of serious clashes with the police.[24]

What was more telling, at the time, were the summonses taken out against Tom Mann, then treasurer of the NUWM, and Harry Pollitt, for 'seditious' speeches they allegedly delivered in Trealaw and Ferndale. They were compelled to answer the summonses on the day of the Marchers' Congress in London and were therefore effectively prevented from addressing it. Pollitt addressed the Court with the words:

> It is well-known in South Wales that when Communists walk into the Court, justice flies out of the window.[25]

When they finally came to trial in Swansea in July, it was found that the police constable whose evidence had been accepted by the Pontypridd Stipendiary Court could not take down short-hand when subjected to a test by D. N. Pritt, Tom Mann's Defence Counsel. The Judge stopped the trial and acquitted both defendants. Pollitt, who had intended defending himself and had spent weeks preparing a political speech, never had the opportunity of delivering it. The whole episode further embittered relationships between the local police and the unemployed. At the outset of the trial, Lionel Lindsay, the Chief Constable of Glamorgan, had tried to stop all supporters of the defendants and a 'Workers' Jury' from entering the Court. The Court was ringed by police and the Judge was given a motor-cycle escort. The Clerk of the Court informed the police that they had no authority to stop any members of the public attending the trial and the Judge apologised for the interference.[26]

But what was most revealing was the campaign in support of Mann and Pollitt. Twenty SWMF lodges, two BISAKTA (steel union) branches and one National Union of Railwaymen branch contributed to their defence fund.[27] This indirectly reflected a growing coalescing of the 'unemployed struggle' with that of those in employment. Hitherto, the two had been quite distinctly separate. None the less the co-operation was still narrowly based.

Other changes occurred in 1934 which accelerated this process. For the first time since 1927 numerous SWMF lodges (twelve in all) sponsored a hunger march.[28] Similarly, a miners' sponsored MP (Aneurin Bevan) also for the first time since 1927, supported a march.[29] All this was not happening in isolation. With the coming of the rank-and-file executive council on 1 January 1934, it was possible for an unemployed miner to get elected on to the controlling body of the SWMF. This ultimately happened with the election of Paynter in 1936. Whilst the SWMF officially remained guarded about unemployed members, unemployed lodges and the NUWM, with the rising tide of militancy and unrest in the coalfield it became increasingly apparent that the unemployed could and would play an important 'solidarity' role in the actions which were being organised. The partially successful strike at Taff-Merthyr in October 1934 against the South Wales Miners' Industrial Union relied for the first time on the systematic harnessing of the unemployed by the SWMF in picketing, boycotting, in social ostracism and vendettas throughout a wide geographical area.[30] The revived community consciousness of such villages as Bedlinog, Trelewis, Rhymney and Fochriw during the Taff-Merthyr strike united those employed and unemployed who supported the SWMF, but drove a permanent wedge between the 'blacklegs' and the communities of which they were once part.[31]

When Horner remarked in January 1935 that it was not an 'unemployed question but a working-class question' he was expressing a sentiment which had been gathering momentum for twelve months. What made it all the more evident was the growing concern during the autumn of 1934 that the scales of benefit in Part Two of the Unemployment Insurance Act (coming into operation in February 1935), would result in further cuts for most of the unemployed. The continuation of the Means Test regulations under the 1934 Act unified the whole South Wales mining community, and was fully expressed in the greatest volcano of socio-political protest ever experienced in the region. What really secured this enormous united protest was the destructive effect of the Means Test. In a region still priding itself in its community ethos but now suffering long-term mass unemployment, the breaking up of families by the regulations and worsening benefits, would ultimately lead to the collapse of the whole community.

The Governments of the 1920s had clung to the idea that widespread unemployment was a temporary phenomenon. By 1929, the insurance scheme basis for payment looked increasingly hopeless for those on 'transitional benefit' (or 'dole'); the old Boards of Guardians were abolished and relief was to be administered by Public Assistance Committees formed by local authorities. The National Government that won the 1931 election cut benefit by 10 per cent, limited the number of weeks in which a man was entitled to draw 'standard benefits' and placed the administration of transitional payments into the hands of the Public Assistance Committees who were asked to enforce a 'means test'. Unemployment continued to rise to a peak in 1933, with the old regions of heavy industry worse hit. The Labour opposition in Parliament did not number fifty MPs and these could do little more than draw the country's attention to the plight of their constituents. The one opportunity that existed, however limited it was, for cushioning the misery of the unemployed, lay in the PACs which, in areas dominated by Labour Councils, as in South Wales, were able to interpret the Means Test as generously as possible. The result was that scales of benefits and the nature of Means Test investigation varied widely.

In 1933 this ramshackle structure received the attention of an arch-administrator determined to establish a sound financial and logical base for the 'dole'. Neville Chamberlain's Unemployment Act of 1934 had two parts and two aims. The first part was intended to deal with those able to draw benefit for 26 weeks on their paid insurance; the second, and controversial, Part II of the Act was intended to remove financial control of Treasury funds, paid out as transitional benefits, from local bodies so that payments could be standardised and administered through the local offices of a new Unemployment Assistance Board. Overall, the Government expected they would have to pay out more money as a result and not less.

Their first miscalculation was that the new relief scales would be higher than those replaced; in many cases this was simply not so. Secondly, in matters demanding great care and discretion, they tried to operate a rigid set of rules that were, all too often, mechanically interpreted by the new officials appointed. The household means test was calculated on the assumption that family members would contribute equal amounts to the household budget. Again, this was not always the case. The assumption, translated into practice, embarrassed fathers made dependent on the meagre income of a son or daughter. It seemed as if the Government was insisting that the money that remained in the coalfield, after the end of prosperous days, should now be shared out rather than provide additional funds. The unemployed were to receive full attention, at last, but only in exchange for accepting some responsibility for their own plight, whilst their chances of complaint were diminished by the replacement of local, elected bodies by a nationally directed bureaucracy.[32]

When the Bill was being read, in the summer of 1934, Aneurin Bevan had said, in the House:

> The Bill is a studied attack on democracy. It perpetuates the means test, imposes concentration camps on the poor, deprives the poor of the right of representation and puts up barriers to progress.

The Bill had become law in mid-December; by the end of the month its implications, as Bevan had warned, were becoming known. Local MPs in South Wales began to call meetings, the NUWM issued tables comparing the old scales with the new. Local Councillors warned people of its effects. It was pointed out that Barry, the only place in Glamorgan without a Labour majority, had, under the old PAC given maximum benefits to far fewer; they had knocked off 'the assistance' thrice as many as had Committees faced with similar cases elsewhere.[33] George Hall, MP for Aberdare, who was very active in disseminating information about the Act, pointed out that neither MPs nor local councillors could challenge the Board, since it had been placed outside political influence. Since the election of their local Councillors had been almost the only control, however inadequate, within the grasp of the people themselves, the bureaucratisation of relief was a harsh threat indeed. Mark Harcombe estimated that Glamorgan's unemployed stood to lose at least £1 million p.a. under the Board, whilst Iorrie Thomas who moved a Council resolution condemning the new Regulations that was carried unanimously, thought that Rhondda would lose about £200,000 within twelve months.[34]

The sole institution that could co-ordinate the groundswell of protest that was arising was the SWMF since within its own ranks it contained the different parts of the coalfield, varying political persuasions, supplied most of the local councillors themselves and was, still, the primary union. They were not slow to seize the nettle. On 5 January, two days before the Act came into force, George Hall led a group of MPs in a discussion with the EC on the Regulations. It was decided to summon a Conference 'of all parties interested in South Wales' to meet in Cardiff on Saturday, 26 January.[35]

Even before this 'all-in-Conference' assembled, protest against the Act had been transmuted into action, with small demonstrations outside the UAB's offices in Rhondda, in Abertillery, Pontypool and Abersychan, as well as a continued round of meetings explaining its provisions. The pattern of the astonishing demonstrations that were now to erupt, however, was established on Sunday, 20 January, in the Rhondda where, in pale wintry sunshine, from all over the two valleys, 50,000 people marched into De Winton field, Tonypandy, to hear the speakers on five platforms – the two MPs (Will John and W. H. Mainwaring), Mark Harcombe and Arthur Horner. This was not so much a new unity as the residual testimony of that thriving community (in all its aspects) that had flourished so briefly, and spectacularly, before 1914:

> People who have lived in the valley all their lives were emphatic that they had never witnessed such a scene of protest and indignation against regulations condemned as unjust and inhuman. It was not a movement initiated by any particular Party, but a united front of Lodge Officials, Communists, Ministers of Religion and business and professional men, with Members of Parliament, Magistrates and Councillors rubbing shoulders with all sections of the populace.[36]

The meeting had resolved on further conferences, and even strike action. Meetings in halls and cinemas proceeded, as on 22 January in Porth where W. H. Mainwaring talked to 450 delegates, 288 of whom represented the churches of Rhondda. Unemployed associations and local lodges continued to organise local protests on whose platforms sat representatives of all parties and organisations. They became, in effect, *ad hoc* United Front Committees. On the march of 20 January, the Rhondda Federated Chamber of Trade and the mid-Rhondda Evangelical Council rubbed shoulders with CP leaders who were, indeed, the most ardent advocates of united action and who accused the Rhondda Borough Labour Party of being dilatory in response to their call. There was, from the start, a split between those who advocated demonstrations in protest and those who insisted that the PACs should make good the differential in the scales, so that some marches were directed not only against the UAB offices but against the former administrators of benefit as well, whose total control ended on 1 March.[37] During the meetings and marches themselves, and in particular villages, the United Front was, nevertheless, a reality.

In the Aberdare Valley, at Trecynon and Cwmaman, there were meetings, organised by the local Federation Lodges where CP and Labour Party spokesmen sat on the same platforms and advocated strike action; Aberdare's English Methodist Church and Soar Congregational Chapel passed resolutions, after services, against Part II of the Act; the Rotary Club was warned by George Hall that the money paid to the local unemployed would reduce from £6,500 a week (or £34,000 p.a.) by £1,500 under the new regulations. This universality of protest was indicative of the understanding that any worsening in the position of the unemployed would have reciprocal effects on the rest of the community. Horner referred to 'the question which is called an unemployed question', and added, 'I say it is not an unemployed question but a working-class question [in which] it was up to the workers to show to their leaders that the whole of the workers, employed as well as unemployed, were solid behind them . . . and that they did not intend to take this dictatorship lying down.'[38]

The 'All-In' Conference convened by the SWMF met on 26 January, with some 1,600 delegates representing various unions, Co-op Societies and Labour Party organisations. With Jim Griffiths presiding it passed a resolution condemning the Act and it appointed a Joint Council of Action with instructions to interview the Minister.[39] The meeting was a massive success, as Griffiths recalled:

I have taken part in many Conferences in our capital City, but the Conference to protest against the Means Test in 1935 stands out in my memory. It was more akin to a religious gathering than a Conference. The singing was even more expressive of our feeling than the speeches.[40]

The unity was not entirely complete for although Horner, as an EC member, addressed the conference and hoped that this first-ever joint trade union action in South Wales would occur thereafter, for similar objects, his call for the union's EC to consider a one-day general strike was rejected, whilst no CP or NUWM members were allowed into the hall. The attitude of the latter was summed up by their principal spokesman in South Wales, Lewis Jones, who, before the conference, had said: 'In spite of the fact that the organising committee desires to exclude representatives of militant organisations the numbers of delegates mandated for action against the new Act ensures that a terrific fight will be made to make the conference the stepping stone to an even greater mass mobilisation of workers.'[41]

On the Sunday after the conference there were, again, mass demonstrations. To Aberdare Park 30,000 (out of a total population of 48,000) marched; in Ynysangharad Park, Pontypridd, 20,000 assembled. The weather was cold and frosty; the demand was for an extension of the 'United Front' and a one-day general strike.[42]

In the week that followed the volume of protest increased,[43] as all over South Wales, the machinery of organisation for another monster march, on Sunday, 3 February, was put into motion. The secretary of the Rhondda Borough Labour Party, Tom Duggan, acting for the Rhondda Joint Central Committee, called ward meetings attended by trade union branches and lodges. The meeting held in the Gaiety Cinema, Treherbert, was described as 'unparalleled in the town's history for enthusiasm and unanimity'. Local Committees of Action were formed from LP, CP, and ILP members, from Co-op Society delegates, from Churches and Chapels and from unemployed Clubs. Local papers carried times and places for the different groups to assemble for the projected march. Brass bands gave their services free. Advertisements detailing the march's procedure were shown in the cinemas, free. The British Legion and ambulance services offered to help.[44]

On that Sunday, all over South Wales, at least 300,000 people marched. In the Rhondda all traffic was stopped as they came, twelve abreast, some 60,000 to 70,000 people, into De Winton Field, Tonypandy; at Blackwood, Nye Bevan addressed several thousand people and called for an end to all Means Tests, pointing out that the children of working-class families had always supported their parents in need, and vice versa, but that there was an enormous difference between a voluntary act and a legal compulsion. Pontypool saw its biggest meeting ever, with over 20,000 listening to Ernest Bevin. There were meetings in Neath, at Briton Ferry, in Merthyr, and even in Barry.[45] In the Aberdare Valley an unprecedented 50,000 people marched to Mountain Ash in a procession two-and-a-half miles long through a bleak wind and fine, persistent rain. The local reporter caught an essential feature of all these disciplined and orderly demonstrations, their deliberate exposure of an indignation as restrained and respectable as it was deeply felt:

Keen as the resentment is throughout the whole valley, indignant as almost every section of the community is against the new Part II regulations, the procession had the atmosphere of a Gymanfu Ganu or a Sunday School rally.

There were smiles, jokes and laughter on every side. Men, women and children wore their 'best' clothes. Colliers, their faces pallid and limned with lines that came from underground toil, care and anxiety, wore good-looking overcoats and suits, young fellows, many of them unemployed, wore smartly-cut clothes, shining shoes and even yellow gloves, looking the mirror of fashion; young women walked in attractive hats, smart coats and dainty high-heeled shoes. There was little outward indication of poverty and want such as the majority of the families of the unemployed are experiencing now.

A true-blue Tory supporter of the 'National Government would undoubtedly have pointed an accusing finger . . . and said, 'Bah! where is your poverty and hardship?'

But it was Sunday afternoon and all this arose from the peculiar psychology of the Welsh miner and his family in regard to the sartorial requirements of the Sabbath. That 'well-dressed' atmosphere of the procession did nothing to obscure the issue that a man and his wife cannot live on 8s. 3d. a week each after paying the rent; that to expect a young man over 21 to exist (apart from live!) on 10s. or 8s. a week is colossal vanity on the part of our country's Government. The miracle of it all was that such good-looking clothes could ever have been obtained by many of the marchers.

There was no mistaking the procession as a vividly unified protest against the regulations, for in the march, in addition to miners, employed and unemployed, were teachers, tradesmen, UDC employees, printers, shop assistants, Salvation Army officers, British Legionnaires, Co-op employees, many women's organisations, representatives of Churches and Sunday Schools, indeed no section of the community one felt was disassociated from the march.

. . . It was for all its pathos a magnificent gesture of protest; a cry from humanity for humanity. The Government cannot refuse to listen to the cry of the people. . . .

When one remembers that thousands of these people, including women and children, had walked to Mountain Ash from Hirwaun, Llwydcoed, Cwmdare, Trecynon and had to walk back again – many of them tramping 16 miles all told in the wind and rain one is impressed by the determination of the people in making this great protest. The Government *must* listen.[46]

The previous Friday, the Minister had received a deputation from the South Wales Joint Council which returned with no answer to their facts and arguments.[47] In the meantime, the Cambrian Combine, in mid-

Rhondda, was pressing for a strike. On the following Monday (4
February), an NUWM-led deputation of 1,000 women and 2,000 men
went to the Merthyr UAB office at Iscoed House and destroyed the
records. Prominent in the attack were three leading Communists: J. S.
Williams of Dowlais (later an International Brigader), Mrs Ceridwen
Brown of Aberdare (whose son was to serve in Spain), and Griff Jones,
an unemployed miner, active in the NUWM (another later to serve with
the International Brigades). Jones recalled scenes in the town which
might be considered reminiscent of 1831. Once again, Merthyr had
become the focus of a national crisis sharpened by a spasm of violence:

> But now the Act took effect, and they were knocking them off, I remember I
> was knocked from fifteen shillings . . . [to] five shillings I received that week.
> And everybody was the same you know. . . . We had a meeting for a further
> demonstration and this was to be a women's demonstration to Merthyr,
> Iscoed House. . . . I remember us starting off from Pengarnddu with banners
> and all the rest of it, there was about thirty started from Pengarnddu. We
> stopped at Dowlais, there was people there with banners. By the time we
> reached South Street they were coming in from Pant, Caeracae, and all the
> rest of it. Then down on the new road . . . they were coming from all
> directions, well down through the town, you could see it was a huge
> demonstration. Then when we reached Pontmorlais, they came up from
> below, from Twyn, Penyard and Swansea Road. . . . Well the place was
> packed. . . . But I remember when they were all crowded there the actual
> gate of Iscoed House gave in and they started moving in. . . . Well when we
> got in the garden somebody threw a stone, through the window you know,
> that started it off . . . some clerks upstairs had been making faces at us . . .
> and there were stones flying from all directions . . . well they smashed all the
> windows, all the windows were in. And the police came there but they were
> helpless. They [the demonstrators] went inside, through the windows, they
> pulled the stairs away, ripped everything, all the fittings, phone and
> everything and tried to burn the papers there. Well the papers were all flung
> in a heap. And at that time they had some speakers there, John Dennithorne,
> the Quaker now, and John he got up to speak on the window sill. They called
> him down, they called him 'Old Bug Whiskers' and all the rest of it. 'Get
> down from there.' John appealed to them of course, not to carry on, against
> violence and all the rest of it, that we would make a special appeal, we would
> march up to London to see the Government and all the rest of it. But they
> wouldn't have it see. 'Get down.' And there was a fellow with us, he was with
> the Party at that time, George Nicholas, a Greek. George got up to speak.
> No good. A few others got up to speak, they wouldn't have it, the only ones
> who could speak were Jack Williams and Crid Brown from Aberdare. They
> spoke.[48]

Then, quite suddenly, on the day following the Merthyr disturbance,

Oliver Stanley, the Minister of Labour, without previously consulting his Cabinet colleagues, announced in the Commons that the UAB scales would be suspended and that an applicant for relief would be entitled to receive benefit on either the old PAC or the new UAB scales, whichever gave him most. All losses incurred (and in over half the cases the old scales had been higher) were to be restored; this 'standstill order' was regularised on 13 February.[49] It was a great victory, the only time in the 1930s when direct action caused a government to change its course and capitulate to demands from outside Parliament.[50]

The jubilation felt in the coalfield was matched by an equal resolve to remove the Act entirely, for the Government were revising the code of regulations to bring them in on 16 November 1936, for men on transitional payments and on 1 April 1937, for men on relief. Two week-ends after the 'Standstill Order', South Wales was, albeit in diminished numbers, still marching; there were celebration meetings at various places, and, a crowd of 20,000 in the Rhondda itself.[51]

None the less this very success took some steam out of the movement whilst the 'United Front' itself began to break up as old pressures reasserted themselves. It was, partly, a question of future tactics and partly of future control. The local 'Committees of Action' had been superseded, from the middle of January, by 'Representative Committees' which more accurately reflected the preponderant strength of organisations affiliated to the official Labour Movement.[52] Where, as at Merthyr, the Trade Council and Labour Party refused to co-operate with the NUWM, there was mutual recrimination, with S. O. Davies describing the women who marched on the local UAB offices as a 'rabble' and their leaders as 'yellow', and in turn being howled down by ILP and CP supporters at the celebratory meeting in Penydarren Park.[53] The Pontypridd Council were told by Councillor Llew Jenkins (CP) that further obedience to the law would send hundreds into the 'British United Fascist Party' and the council itself into 'fascism'. Those who looked to build a united *political* movement on the basis of the demonstrations were to be disappointed. At dwindling meetings Labour MPs and councillors were met by chants of 'We want the United Front' and demands for NUWM or CP speakers.[54] The Cambrian Combine decided on a one-day strike on Monday, 25 February, and persuaded the mid-Rhondda Chamber of Trade to close their shops for a day but this was opposed by the Rhondda Joint Central Committee and by the SWMF EC who requested the lodges 'not to take any sporadic, unauthorised action which will not assist the unemployed and may endanger the unity that has been secured in South Wales . . . in this campaign'.[55] In fact, the Chamber of Trade reversed its decision and general meetings of all the mid-Rhondda collieries did the same.[56]

The South Wales Council of Action was itself proposing to become a consultative body under the aegis of the National Labour Council; there was no desire to propagate militant demands for further marches on the UAB offices, whilst the 'black circular' from the TUC was a clear direction not to allow Communists to act as delegates for trades councils:

> This policy leads to the breaking up of the United Front. How can the National Labour Council which refuses even to discuss the United Front, lead the movement for Unity in South Wales? The scope of the movement in South Wales goes far beyond the narrow limits of the vision of the National Labour Party and Trade Union leaders who impose 'black circulars' to split the Trade Union Movement, and who co-operate with the capitalists but not with militant workers.[57]

The invitation to Citrine to be an official speaker at the Council of Action's Conference was seen as an insult 'to Welsh miners'. Attempts from within the United Front Committees to expel CP members generally failed, whereupon Labour members would leave. By the summer of 1935 all the organisations affiliated to the Rhondda Borough Labour Party and Trades Council had agreed to leave United Front movements.[58] Attempts to turn informal co-operation into formal unity failed yet again.

Yet the protests and demonstrations continued, particularly where the incidence of long-term unemployment was severe. There was confusion over the retrospective payment of the old scales. The NUWM was also not prepared to let slip the advantage it now had with mass mobilisation of communities behind the banners of the Councils of Action. The subdued sullen discontent caused by the 1931 cuts, years of unemployment, living on the edge of starvation, deteriorating health and the break-up of families, had come to the surface in January 1935. The new regulations, whilst obviously making the situation worse for many, merely provided the occasion for protest. The long-standing grievances remained, and the unemployed were not to be denied. In the northern reaches of Monmouthshire's Ebbw Fach Valley (comprising Abertillery, Brynmawr, Nantyglo and Blaina), protests had been particularly widespread. The local SWMF sponsored Labour MP, George Daggar, had urged the unemployed to take 'any measures necessary' against the Government.[59] On 25 February, Nantyglo school children refused to go to school and shopkeepers closed their premises.[60] In the same village, Communists gained fifty new members, fifty others joined its Working Women's Clubs and a further seventy joined the Communist Social Club. There was a Communist County Councillor and District Councillor (elected in February 1935) in the valley.[61] Unrest had been accentuated by the new regulations, but hostility towards an established authority was deep and widespread. The chanting and singing by the demonstrators throughout the period of crisis reflected this:

'Who's afraid of the big bad wolf?'[62]
'One, Two, Three, Four, Down with the Unemployment Bill.'[63]
'One, Two, Three, Four, Five, Six, Seven – Struggle or Starve.'[64]
'We are the working class, down with the ruling class.'[65]
'We'll make Queen Mary do the washing for the boys
When the red revolution comes,
We'll put the Prince of Wales on the Means Test. . . .'[66]

After a demonstration in Abertillery on 15 March, twelve of the leaders were charged with intimidating officers of the Unemployment Assistance Board, unlawful assembly and disturbing the peace. The intention had been to occupy the offices but, although the leaders had come prepared with packages of sandwiches, they were met by a force of police inside the building. As only eight of the leaders knew of the plan it was suspected that one had informed the police. The defendants claimed that the anti-Royalist songs sung on the demonstration were not likely to disturb the peace of Abertillery and the case was dismissed. Three of the defendants, the brothers Clarence and Harold Lloyd, along with Bert Vranch, were Communists who later went to Spain. A fourth defendant, Len Hill, was secretary of the Abertillery Trades and Labour Council.[67]

Before the case came to trial at Monmouth in April, a much more serious incident occurred. The Relieving Officer and the Guardians' Committee at Blaina refused to meet a deputation led by the Communist County Councillor Phil Abrahams. The deputation's demands included payment of rent and coal allowance where applicable, payment of maximum scales, civility to those attending the Relieving Office and the right of representation for all organisations. When Councillor Abrahams was also refused the right to inform the Committee of cases of hardship in his Ward it was decided to organise a mass demonstration involving the whole of the Valley.

It was after this demonstration and the subsequent disturbance had occurred that the twelve were summonsed so as to create, according to the Communist Party, an atmosphere of disorder in the area. The local police would thus have been justified in banning the march to the Blaina Public Assistance Committee. The police informed the NUWM and the March Committee that they would take 'whatever steps may be necessary to prevent [them] from interfering with the lawful duties of the PAC'. (In the meantime, the Abertillery Public Assistance Committee after representations had been made by a deputation, granted similar demands on 20 March.) On the morning of the demonstration (21 March) the police apparently granted permission and then withdrew it later in the day although by that time many contingents were already assembling.[68]

Demonstrators from Blaina, Nantyglo, Abertillery and Brynmawr were to meet outside the Blaina Public Assistance Committee offices at 6 pm. The Nantyglo and Brynmawr contingents arrived first and were told by the police that as the Committee was not meeting, the march should disperse, because it was causing an obstruction. The scene was described by a local newspaper reporter:

> While the leaders spoke together there were some tense moments. Women, girls and young children looked on the scene from the surrounding coaltips. Then a child would cry and be hushed by its mother with the words: 'It's alright, your daddy isn't going to be hurt.' . . . The red banners too had to be lowered when a horse shied. The horse was quietened and with the red banners out of his sight, he plodded on with his cart behind him.[69]

These two contingents withdrew in an orderly fashion partly because the other contingents had not arrived but mainly because the police drew their batons. A short scuffle did occur and a few of the unemployed were injured when contingents from behind forced the demonstrators forward. The Abertillery contingent had been halted by the police but individuals made their way in small groups towards the Blaina contingent. When they finally arrived near the Blaina Inn, where seventy police had been billeted, Superintendent Baker ordered them to return. The police were now confronted on two sides. Apparently before the leader of the Blaina contingent could tell his demonstrators of the order, Superintendent Baker ordered the police to draw their batons on the contingent.[70] According to one of the Abertillery demonstrators:

Well, you weren't in a pub for nothing. But they smelled of booze: I can't say they were drinking but they smelled of it. Rank some of 'em was. And in my opinion they were so intoxicated that they didn't know what they were doing. They had to, because they were beating down their own people. . . . They came out, and Baker was there, and he faced us, and he just looked at us, and he said 'Into the buggers boys, into 'em.' And they came into us. Now, he'd had another body of police up by the Blaina Hospital. Now they came behind the Brynmawr and Nantyglo contingent and they backed them in there. But it was a running fight, and the next thing I remember I woke up in Nantyglo hospital.[71]

The Nantyglo and Brynmawr marchers charged the police who were now batoning the Blaina and Abertillery contingents as well as, it later transpired, innocent bystanders. The police were also showered with stones from the mountains and tips on the roadside. The whole affair lasted only a matter of minutes but about a dozen police and over a hundred demonstrators were injured.[72]

Phil Abrahams advised the demonstrators to keep together in crowds up until midnight to prevent police attacks. The Communists believed the police to be 'demoralised by their defeat'. Later in the evening thirty to forty police failed to disperse a crowd at Garn Cross. According to the Communists, the police were looking for the leaders of the demonstration that evening. Doors of houses were left open so as to give them free access. When the leaders signed on at the Labour Exchange a 'guard' was formed for them to prevent their arrest.[73] Some of the leaders fled, in the style of the 1831 Merthyr rioters who were harboured in Brecon. Clarence Lloyd left hospital without permission and joined his brother, who with others walked across the mountains to Abergavenny where they were kept in hiding on two farms. They later returned to face the charges against them.[74]

In the aftermath of the riot, the feeling in the district was one of anger against the police and a continued buoyancy on the part of the unemployed reflected in the large street demonstrations. A campaign of protest throughout the coalfield was also launched. The local MP, George Daggar, demanded that the Home Secretary set up an inquiry into the behaviour of the police as there was a widespread feeling that they had panicked.[75]

But within two weeks of the disturbances taking place, eighteen people were charged that they 'unlawfully and riotously did assemble to disturb the public peace and then to make great riot and disturbance to the terror and alarm of His Majesty's subjects'.[76] After the preliminary hearing at the local magistrates' court in May the case proceeded to the Assizes at Monmouth. Among the eighteen were five of those dismissed over the Abertillery demonstration. The most prominent defendants were Communist County Councillor Phil Abrahams and Communist District Councillor Jack Jones; Len Hill, secretary of the Trades and Labour Council and a strong supporter of the United Front; the Lloyd brothers, Frank Landon and George Brown. All were leading local Communists (except Hill) and members of the NUWM.[77]

The prosecution relied heavily on evidence provided by the police who had taken part in the 'riot'. Apart from the police, the Assistant Relieving Officer was the only other prosecution witness to be used. Abrahams was cross-examined about his political beliefs and his views on the pamphlet *For Soviet Britain*. The defence counsel, D. N. Pritt, KC, alleged that the police had committed perjury. One of the defendants, G. Penry of Nantyglo, was accused of having a hammer which was never found and brought forward as evidence. Penry was found not guilty. Pritt further alleged that if there was so much stone-throwing why was it that none of the windows of a bus behind which the police were sheltering were broken. But the most serious allegation made by Pritt was that the 'police enjoyed flogging the men'. In cross-examination several policemen stated that they believed it was their duty to 'hit people while they were running away'.[78]

The defence case relied on the testimony of three American students who were Rhodes Scholars at Oxford University. They had participated in the march and had taken notes on the day. Two of them had previously given evidence at the magistrates' court hearing. They had then alleged that the police had given no warning of their charge, had hit out indiscriminately and that one police sergeant hit a woman in the face. At the trial, one of the students described the scene:

> I was in the demonstration going up to Salem Corner. The crowd was very gay. I was surprised that the people of that derelict valley could be happy and gay. The first thing I knew was the attack of the police. They charged into the crowd and scattered them. The police continued in pursuit, striking as they went. I was just lucky I was not hit.

When asked if he thought the mention of a Chartist by one of the speakers in the demonstration was an invitation to violence, he replied:

> I have heard an American Minister make a reference from the pulpit to the American Revolution, but it does not follow the congregation are going to leave the church and attack anybody.

But a doubt was cast over their evidence when the prosecution implied that the University October Club to which they belonged was a Communist organisation.[79]

Before the sentences were announced, the judge apparently consulted with the Home Secretary who, according to Pritt, advised terms which would not outrage the coalfield too much as there was already a petition circulating on behalf of the defendants. There was also a fear that, since the charge was for 'great riot', the defendants could have received life sentences.[80] In the event, the four most prominent leaders, County Councillor Phil Abrahams and George Brown of Nantyglo and Frank Landon and Bill Madden of Blaina received nine months each. Six others received sentences of four to six months.[81]

The trial seemed to mark the end of the campaign which had started seven months earlier with the introduction of Part Two of the Unemployment Act. Four of the most articulate and active spokesmen for the unemployed in North Monmouthshire were removed from the scene by heavy prison sentences and Phil Abrahams, on release, was unable to resume as councillor because he had been stripped of his civil rights for ten years.[82] A campaign for their release was mounted, involving demonstrations, a workers' commission of enquiry, a conference and a deputation to the Home Secretary. The main objection was that the prosecutions threatened the right to demonstrate and to hold public meetings.[83]

The churches and chapels which had been active in the big demonstrations earlier in the year now showed themselves to be as concerned about 'moral' deterioration as they had been with physical. They identified their enemy not as the Labour Party, with many of whose members they had close ties, but with 'atheistical' Communism which was singled out by those Christian activists injecting new vigour into Social Christianity in the coalfield.[84] A deputation of representatives of the Churches in Wales met the Prime Minister, Ramsay MacDonald, in April 1935, and warned of the dangers to the State and to society of an army 'of parasitic young men who have never known the discipline of work ... it has no conception either of responsibility or loyalty'. The Rev. Alban Davies, an Independent minister from Ton Pentre who had been in Rhondda for some ten years, testified that:

... South Wales [might] soon become a skimmed community with a lack of vitality such as to make it a veritable hotbed of Communism. During the last

few weeks Communism has been spreading through the Rhondda Valley
with the force of an epidemic . . . during the last few weeks a day to day
Communism is becoming a real active force in the life of the valley . . . it
does not spring from any definite knowledge of the philosophy of
Communism but . . . is caused purely . . . by the . . . adversity prevailing
amongst the people.[85]

He was certainly right, at least, in his definition of vitality. The
Communist Party was to play a catalytic and increasingly decisive role
in this growing unity of employed with unemployed, in the general
resurgence of extra-parliamentary, extra-legal militancy, which
climaxed first in 1935–6 and finally in the 'Spain' campaigns of 1936–9.
By the end of 1934, after seven years which in reality were spent in the
political wilderness, the Communist Party could report that it was
growing considerably in membership and influence. Its District
Congress Discussion Bulletin, although complaining of the unequal
development of the Party during the year, also revealed its growth on
many fronts and the leading role its members had played in all the
campaigns. There was, for example, the nine-week strike at the Emlyn
Colliery against the 'company' union, and similar actions at Treorchy
and Taff-Merthyr. There had been unemployed demonstrations in East
Glamorgan, anti-war and anti-fascist committees in West Wales,
Rhondda and Aberdare. Communist and 'militant workers' representatives' were now on councils in the Rhondda, Monmouthshire,
Caerau, Aberdare and Risca. The Miners' Rank and File Movement
and the Young Communist League were gaining wider support, whilst
the *Daily Worker* from time to time carried special Welsh pages which
signified a growth of readership in the area. The paper also had, in
George Thomas of Treherbert, its own South Wales correspondent.
The emphasis was now on the co-ordination of local struggles, and
hence the effect of National Government policy on South Wales
resulted in the improvement of the Party's organisation and the United
Front. An indication of its increasing influence was its poll of over
40,000 votes in the local elections of March 1934. In twelve localities
where Labour and Communist candidates contested, both in 1933 and
1934, the average Communist vote increased from 839 to 1,300 and the
Labour vote from 1,015 to 1,498. (The Communist Party claimed that
the Labour totals must have included many Tory and Liberal votes). In
most areas, where over a thousand votes were recorded for the
Communist Party, there were invariably less than twelve Communist
Party members.[86] Even in Merthyr, where the Communist Party had

never been strong, it mustered 3,409 votes in the by-election of June 1934, less than one hundred votes behind the ILP whose seat it had been for thirty-four years.[87]

Within less than a year, this support began to be translated into increased membership, often attributable to the example and sacrifice of charismatic members in particular localities. In some cases the Communist Party was built around one or two dynamic individuals who, after years of plodding away in oblivion, were at the centre of the resurgence. Edgar Evans, the Communist ironmonger of Bedlinog, became a District Councillor and effectively led the struggle at Taff-Merthyr and was imprisoned for his activities. Mavis Llewellyn, a school teacher and a Communist Councillor, championed many local causes particularly relating to unemployment and health. Phil Abrahams, an unemployed Nantyglo miner, was another Communist councillor who was imprisoned for his activities.[88] J. S. Williams of Dowlais was a leader of the unemployed in his locality and in common with all the other colourful and energetic figures, marked out because of his affiliation: he was known locally as 'Jack Williams the Communist'. It was the Communists who were now invariably to be found wherever there was a local flashpoint. By April 1935, the Party was claiming that its membership had trebled over the previous six months.[89]

The Labour Party was beginning to see it as a serious threat to its monopoly position[90] and by the mid-1930s the Communist Party felt confident enough to launch its own proposals for the reconstruction of South Wales, in the pamphlet, *The People can save South Wales*.[91] By 1935, the Rhondda Communist Party had seven councillors (there were nine others elsewhere in the coalfield) and was producing its own fortnightly newspaper, *The Vanguard*, with a circulation of 8,000 at its height.[92] There were as many as 352 Communists now in the SWMF, mostly in responsible positions (three years previously, almost all had been expelled from official positions), whilst in the Neath area alone, there were twelve pit cells and a mining group of forty-eight members. There were also activists in transport, steel and amongst seamen. Whilst still small compared with the Labour Party, the Communist Party was now extending its influence for the first time into areas such as the Dulais Valley.[93]

Considerable as this influence was, it was frequently exaggerated and misinterpreted by the *Western Mail* with its references to red plots, red-hands, secret societies and well-paid propagandists as the major source of all the industrial unrest in 1935.[94] A local minister of religion added to this atmosphere when he claimed during a local election contest in the Rhondda in March 1935 that if the Communists came to power they would abolish Sunday-school trips to Barry.[95]

But this increased growth and influence, whilst associated with individuals and their role in various campaigns, can best be explained by the strategy it used. It had long abandoned its isolated, aggressively sectarian policies and was now prepared to concede the 'vanguard' position to broader bodies such as the SWMF, the South Wales Council of Action and at a local level, to Combine Committees and even lodges.[96]

Its major problem seemed to be to harness and direct the rising tide. Its tactics not only anticipated the consolidation of the United Front at the Seventh World Congress of the Communist International in August 1935, but more remarkably the Popular Front of 1936. Parts of South Wales in 1935 had more in common with France and Spain in 1936 than the rest of Britain. Whilst local United Front type committees 'against Fascism and war' had received some backing in South Wales before 1935 (and this was crucial in understanding what happened in the mid-1930s), what distinguished it from elsewhere in Britain was the breadth and depth of support it received, which was not always necessarily political or institutional. In some ways it was the re-emergence of a political consciousness on a wide geographical basis for the first time since 1926; a broad socio-political alliance once again became commonplace. Such was the interest in the uniqueness of the South Wales situation that J. R. Campbell was sent down to compile a special report for the Central Committee of the CPGB.[97] But the upsurge in 1935 was not sudden and spontaneous. The activities of the Communist Party and the NUWM from 1933 onwards, and particularly in 1934, helped in altering the mood in the coalfield. In 1936, Horner reflected that the 'most marked feature of the previous year was the change from a general defensive position . . . to a partial counter-offensive'.[98] This had already partly happened in 1934 in South Wales and without it the confident offensive of January 1935 and after would never have materialised to the same extent.

In 1936 the amended code of Regulations was due to come into action and again people were galvanised into mass action. On 20 July 1936, a crowd of over 60,000 turned out in the Rhondda, addressed by two county councillors, Lewis Jones and Mark Harcombe, as well as the local MPs. There were mass meetings in other areas and, again, the South Wales Joint Unemployment Council denounced the Regulations and proposed another 'All-In' Conference.[99] On Sunday, 27 July, the demonstrations were as big as they had ever been, with 100,000 marching in Rhondda, 50,000 in Aberdare and large crowds in Merthyr, Pontypool, Cardiff, Ogmore and Ebbw Vale. The Spanish Civil War had broken out on the week-end of 18-19 July; Spain and France were invoked at these meetings and Aneurin Bevan declared that if 'those who by accident or fortune or by peculiar circumstances had reached the leadership of the movement did not take the initiative of leading the struggle against the Regulations, then the people of South Wales would lead a rank and file movement throughout the country and do so'.[100]

There was a serious attempt to create a Popular Front in British politics, at this time, which had a definite basis behind it in South Wales, particularly on the issue of unemployment. But there was also now a new international dimension.

The last and most representative hunger march to leave South Wales was seen from the outset by its chief organiser to have international significance. At one of the many rallies in South Wales against the new Means Test regulations, Lewis Jones appealed, in the same way as Cook had done in 1927, to the 60,000 gathered at Tonypandy on 26 July, less than ten days after Franco's rising in Spain:

> Can we from this vast demonstration call for five hundred men and women who will march on London and take the fight of the Labour MPs, both inside and outside the House, against the cuts. . . . Let us see that the struggles in France and Spain be an example which we in this country shall follow. We have shown our power today, now we must decide what to do with it. . . . Let us strengthen the unity shown here today which makes Rhondda the vanguard of the democratic forces of this country.[101]

When the 504 marchers left South Wales in October, they represented in many ways, a broader Popular Front than existed in either Spain or France. The organising body, the South Wales and Monmouthshire Joint Council Against Unemployment, boasted support from trade unions in every industry, political parties in every constituency, religious organisations of every denomination, trading associations and civic bodies. It also included nominees from the Trade Union Unemployed Association and many from non-mining areas.[102] It was confidently claimed that the Joint Council co-ordinated area councils of action which in turn were made up of united front committees embracing representatives from the whole Labour Movement.[103]

But probably the most significant indicator of the breadth of community support, apart from the official backing of the SWMF and the Labour Party (both for the first time), was the role of the religious and civic bodies. The Rhondda Urban District Council officially supported the march and donated £30.[104] The vicar of Treherbert gave a religious send-off to the seventeen local marchers. The crowds and the marchers recited 'The Lord's Prayer' and the vicar then told them that the Church in Wales supported their fight and asked them to be well-behaved. At Cardiff, the Rev. W. Jones told the marchers that if Jesus Christ were on earth he would have been on the march.[105] At Merthyr, the Borough gave the local marchers a civic send-off[106] and in Blaenavon there was a religious service. The Salvation Army launched the Cwmbran contingent with prayer and music ending with 'God be with you till we meet again'.[107]

The NUWM which had organised the earlier marches had travelled a long way since its narrow base of 1931 and 1932. The march of 1936 reflected the mood of unity of the time and the NUWM deliberately kept a low profile allowing emphasis to be put on the wide range of support. As a result, there was no harassment on the part of the Home Office or the Metropolitan Police, although informers continued to be used extensively. It was still nevertheless very much an extra-parliamentary action, relying heavily on revolutionary enthusiasm and strict military organisation and discipline (which lent itself well to the Spanish situation later). Although it could be argued that they were not strictly extra-parliamentary (in that demonstrations were constitutionally acceptable ever since 1689) they were certainly being viewed and treated as such in Government circles. Of the march leadership, elected at Cardiff by the marchers, four were to serve in the International Brigades (Tim Harrington, D. R. Llewellyn, Will Paynter and J. S. Williams), and two were 'rejected' volunteers (Arthur Griffiths and Lewis Jones).[108] When everything is considered, it is not surprising that the marchers sent a telegram to the TUC demanding that the British Government lift its arms embargo on Republican Spain.[109]

The mood was hopeful as Idris Cox, who had become a CP representative on the South Wales Joint Council Against Unemployment, wrote in a mixture of confidence and frustration:

United action has brought new life to the Labour Movement in South Wales. There is hardly a town or village in which there is not a united front committee of Labour Party, Trade Unions, CP and Co-operative movement representatives. The local Committees are combined into councils of action which direct activities over an area roughly correspondent to a Parliamentary constituency; and these in turn are directed by the South Wales and Monmouthshire Joint Council Against Unemployment, also representing all shades of opinion in the working-class movement.

The Labour movement in South Wales is ten times stronger by means of this situation. There is a spirit of enthusiasm in all its activities. A spirit which is completely absent in all the big official conferences dominated by those who'll stop at nothing to prevent working-class unity.[110]

The implicit weakness of this situation was made explicit in the course of 1937 as Popular Front overtures were rejected and the position of men like Bevan became one of isolation. There were moves to alter the composition of the Joint Council so that, as at the first 'All-In' Conference, only trade union delegates, if of other parties than the Labour Party, might be members and indeed, though without calling a formal meeting, the Labour Party did so pronounce. This was in line, of course, with their formal expulsion of the Socialist League itself, which was an effective scuppering of any attempt to widen out the 'United Front' movement.[111] The SWMF opposed the plans to turn the Joint Council into a Regional Council of Labour, and hoped that the latter would allow trade unionists the same rights of representation as the former had. When this was refused the SWMF considered holding their own 'All-In' Conference, but, again, in the interest of not disrupting any unity whatsoever over issues like unemployment, the Spanish Civil War and trade union work itself, the Federation reluctantly agreed to allow the newly formed Regional Council to take the lead in any subsequent appeals against Unemployment Regulations. From the autumn of 1937 the demand was for abolition of the Means Test and a 10 per cent increase in all allowances.[112]

There were, once more, organised demonstrations before the second appointed day on which the last part of the Regulations were to be implemented. They did not, however, abolish the Act nor cause such a storm of protest as hitherto. The one held in Rhondda in early November had banners proclaiming 'Down with the Means Test', but also ones demanding an increase in the existing scales, more money for pensioners, better pensions for widows and so on. The protest, then, had been made diffuse, with the massive indignation of early 1935 now channelled into organisations with a more effective watching brief or erupting in smaller-scale demonstrations to specific area offices.[113] Besides, the protest of 1935 had been successful in that the scales projected in 1934 were never implemented. More importantly the Boards learned to be more flexible and humane in their approach to individual needs. The first Annual Report of the UAB said:

> Any action must be gradual and must be carried out in full association with local opinion, so as to give effect to the considerable differences in the locality.[114]

The miseries of long-term unemployment had not been banished but any worsening in alleviation of it had been met head on. The success of the 1935 demonstrations revitalised political activity in the coalfield, made a 'united front from below' an actuality, and demonstrated the continued determination of entire depressed communities not to succumb any further to atrophy of the will. The significance of these monster demonstrations lies in their difference from the gay, hopeful jazz bands of the summer of 1926, from the grim, determined mass meetings of the lock-out, when what had seemed the ultimate protest weapon, the General Strike, had failed, and, too, from the hunger marches of 1927 and 1934 in which people trooped from the devastated valleys and then trooped back again; these were not the complaints of particular groups against an officious bureaucrat or a colliery manager, it was as if, on those Sundays, the whole of the coalfield had moved out of doors in a proud, defiant act of communal exposure distinguishing their continuing humanity from the blighted, ghost-towns around them. Gwyn Thomas who himself participated in these demonstrations (along with a guest contingent from the Oxford University Labour Club) later wrote:

> The thirties gave South Wales their political peak. Coal, already a ruptured industry, had stepped down from first place as a battle-cry. The world's brow was hot, and we were out to fan it with banners. We suggested a possible definition of Wales as a non-stop protest with mutating consonants. Navels distended by resting banner-poles became one of the region's major stigmata. During the demonstrations against the Means Test and other bits of crass social legislation that put Britain in deep-freeze during the Baldwin period, we marched almost as a way of life. . . . In 1935 some climax of disgust brought the entire valley population on to the streets. As one watched the huge streams of protesters pouring up and down the two gulches on their way to Tonypandy, one could have sworn that the very blood of the place was on the boil.[115]

The people, of course, were the very blood of places like the Rhondda; there was no explanation of the existence of the coalfield without them. Unemployment after the heady days of full prosperity, was a type of social leukaemia, whilst migration was an open wound. 1935 can be seen as a turning-point in the coalfield's inter-war history in which societies who had suffered agonies that were, in no sense, self-inflicted still claimed the worth of their self-made communities. As the year wore on, there was to be another echo of this resurgent determination.

At their Annual Conference in 1935 the Federation claimed a justifiable credit for having been the moving force behind the calling of the 'All-In' Conference in January. Jim Griffiths was quick, however, to underline the daily grind of the assistance given by Federation officials and agents, from the centre and in the localities, to individuals. This was tied in to the constant theme of the necessity of maintaining the organisation's strength, a task that could only be completely achieved from the ground up, in the face of hostility from the company officials themselves:

The power of the Federation depends on the strength of the Lodges at the Collieries; the personal service and protection which the individual member can receive depends very largely on the state of the Organisation at the Colliery at which he is employed, and he should realise that never in our industrial history was it more necessary that he, whether employed or unemployed, should be joined up with his fellows for their mutual protection. Anything the Executive Council can do to assist in this great work will readily be done, but they cannot do much without the co-operation of the men themselves.[116]

The pace at which colliery amalgamations, with their attendant rationalisation, was proceeding was a growing threat to the ability of an individual lodge to stand up for itself. It was here, at the base of all the organisational problems, that the Combine Committees came into their own from the mid-1930s. Early in 1935 Welsh Associated Collieries Company merged with the Powell Duffryn Company, thereby, with a capital of £17 million and control of seventy-five pits, becoming the largest coal combine in Britain. The potential output of 20 million tons was about one-third of the total coalfield output; and by 1937 was 40 per cent. The fear was that this would mean 'fewer pits, more machines, and less men'.[117] Indeed, by 1935 the reorganised

Federation had to recognise the full import of the trend of amalgamation within the industry on employment. Even though the
average percentage of unemployed in the industry rose to a peak in
1932, and dropped slightly thereafter, there was no real cutting into the
numbers of those wholly unemployed, whilst the fluctuation in those
'temporarily stopped' that had reflected, hitherto, alteration in trade
conditions flattened out with increasing amalgamations. This, however,
was also not completely satisfactory, for the explanation of it only
serves to emphasise the reserves of surplus labour in the coalfield:

> First, the natural effect of prolonged depression is to liquidate the more
> costly and purely short term methods of meeting a sudden failure in demand,
> such as short time working, and second, more unified control in the industry,
> the most notable example of which is the recent extension of the Powell
> Duffryn Co., leading to the permanent closing of certain pits and the
> concentration of production in others. Other things being equal this means
> higher efficiency in the industry, but that higher efficiency is dependent
> upon a smaller number of workers being in full employment, rather than
> a larger number of whom many work intermittently.[118]

With this stabilisation of the work-force, albeit reduced, after 1934 it
was of paramount importance that the Federation eradicate non-
unionism within the separate combines if those combines where wages
or conditions did not meet requirements were to be in turn combated.
These combines – the Anthracite, the Ocean, the Cory, the Tredegar
and the Powell Duffryn – varied in size and potential power; but where
their officials were determined their attitude proved militant. This was
particularly true of the Ocean Combine and its secretary, Alf Davies,
and the Cory Combine, where Archie James had succeeded George
Thomas, in 1931; here, in the steam-coal area, the issue of non-
unionism was rife. The combines were limited in their powers,
ostensibly coming together (one delegate from each lodge) solely for
purposes of information. The EC was still wary of creating any duality
of power within the coalfield, particularly where a powerful combine
like that of the economically sound Anthracite area might replace the
old District organisation and thereby challenge central directives. The
Combine Committee for the Cory group met once a month but an
active Secretary would co-ordinate its day-to-day activities. In this way
pressure could be applied at weak points without the Central having to
rely either on an individual lodge or having to bring into play the rest of
the coalfield. The only time difficulty would arise might be when the

enthusiasm or determination of the Combines came up against a more wary EC.[119]

During the summer of 1935 the Cory and Ocean Combines decided to mount a 'Show Cards' campaign in July and August. The EC were in support of this, but not for any consequent tendering of notices. None the less, the Combines pressed the point, with Archie James writing to the effect that every effort would be made to avoid giving notices on 16 September, yet adding:

... while we fully appreciate the EC's refusal in not granting permission, consequent upon the success of other efforts, we believe that the only real steps necessary to ensure certain success is that we have your official permission to tender notices. Because we are determined to obtain a 100 per cent on this occasion.

The EC agreed on condition that they receive a further request first.[120] On Monday, 30 September, after an intensive campaign, the 14,000 miners employed in the collieries owned by Cory Brothers Limited, and the Ocean Coal Company Limited, came out, with the support of the EC, who declared themselves confident that the men outside the union (2 per cent of those involved) would join within a few days.[121] The non-unionists involved here were not members of the MIU or of any other union; this was strictly a push towards an 'all-in' policy where the SWMF held the whiphand. The direction taken by the stoppage, however, underlines once more how it had become impossible for the SWMF to continue to reorganise without becoming entangled in yet another inter-union dispute.

From the outset feelings ran high. At Risca two men returning from work at the United National Colliery, Cross Keys, were harassed by angry men and women; there, and at Blaengarw, police had to intervene. Although the stoppage was widespread it was difficult to assess its full proportions since many pits were on short-time working. At the Glenavon Collieries, 2,000 miners called the strike off after one day since their object had been achieved. In Rhondda only safety men were at work, except in the Dare Colliery, Cwmparc, where the MIU maintained its hold; at Parc Colliery some fourteen men continued at work. The position was unchanged over a few days, but in the Garw the SWMF proved successful. The EC reported that only thirty-three men at Cory and Ocean pits were still outside the Federation. At Cross Keys and at Blaengarw the five men working were greeted by hostile crowds;

eighty-six police protected the solitary Cross Keys man. At Nine Mile
Point police protected a number who had begun work.[122] Presumably
as a tit-for-tat, the Special Purposes Committee of the Coal Owners'
Association authorised the Cory and Ocean Combines to keep their
collieries idle for up to six days after the dispute had ended.[123]

As the week continued the Blaengarw non-unionists gave in and the
number at work in the Parc Colliery was reduced from fourteen to eight.
Although there was no official campaign against the MIU men in the
Dare pit, police were protecting some homes and 100 of them were
needed to escort two men from their homes in Ton Pentre to the Parc
pit. A man who started in Blaengarw had his door tarred, and thereafter
a police guard and escort.

On the weekend the stoppage at the Cory Collieries was ended with
only two men outside the fold; the struggle at the Ocean Collieries, with
twenty-four men outside, was to continue. This, too, was called off on
Thursday, 10 October. However, the Ocean Company's favourable
attitude towards the MIU was fast becoming an inescapable issue. Thus
at the Deep Navigation pit, Treharris, very near to Taff-Merthyr,
although non-unionism had been eradicated, the men refused to return
until the company stopped dealing with the MIU. In the Rhondda
matters were near to breaking-point as twenty men, protected by 130
police drafted in from Pontypridd and Aberdare, continued work in the
Parc Colliery.[124] When the storm finally broke, though, it was in
Monmouthshire at the Nine Mile Point Colliery where, during the
second week-end after the strike had started, the struggle took on a
dramatic form. For Jim Griffiths, what happened was 'the answer to the
problem of what to do to get rid of the Spencer Union – the "non-pols",
for it was when the Federation men came out that they went down the
mine: if we stayed down, they would stay out'.[125]

At Nine Mile Point Colliery, both the SWMF and the SWMIU had
been recognised since the dispute in 1929.[126] In April 1935 there had
been 1,600 men employed at the colliery but then three Districts had
closed, cutting the work force to 800. The Federation men had struck
against non-unionists during the October strike, with a little success; on
the return to work, though, they found that others had been drafted in to
work in the east pit, where the bulk of the SWMIU men were, at the
expense of Federation men. Only mild demonstrations had greeted
blackleg buses during the strike. Nor were the scenes in any way
different on the afternoon of Saturday, 12 October, when the non-
unionists were brought to the surface earlier than the other men in order

to avoid any clashes. Their coach was escorted from the area by another coach, full of police.

Shortly after this the news reached the surface that the men on the day shift in the West Pit had decided on a hunger strike to last until the Industrial Union men were removed. There were about seventy-eight men underground. Apart from Jack Marsden and John Prosser (the chairman and secretary of the Federation Lodge) no one on the surface, not even the men's wives had been aware of the plan, whose immediate origin lay in the men's fear that after Saturday they would lose their places completely to MIU men. One said, 'Many of us knew that Saturday was going to be our last shift in the mine. On Monday the Management was going to bring in more "scabs" to do our work. We decided to fight and that is why we stayed down the mine.' Apparently, most of the men were also ignorant of the decision, at least as to its timing. 'The whole thing happened on Saturday afternoon when it was decided that we should remain down. We had reached the pit bottom and there it was done.'[127] The actual organisation underground was done by a militant miner, Billy Mitchell, who talked to others during a food-break.[128]

At first there was some confusion as to whether it was to be a hunger strike or just a 'stay-in'. This was itself dependent on the attitude of the company, which, at first, refused to allow supplies to be sent down so that the men ate nothing between 10 a.m. Saturday and early Sunday. However, the company yielded to pressure 'and thereafter each day would witness a procession of wives and mothers to the pit-head bringing sandwiches and Welsh cakes and flasks of tea to sustain their husbands and sons'.[129]

The awareness of these men that a dispute of any sort with the Ocean Company would, in all probability, lead to the importing of SWMIU-organised labour (as had occurred in 1929) was the catalytic element that produced this do-or-die effort in the colliery. The village of Cwmfelinfach was relatively isolated, and certainly dominated by its pit. Life revolved around the Institute, and to a lesser extent, the Pioneer Hotel. The old company, Burnyeat Brown, had brought much of the labour force with them from their pits in the Rhondda so the men were, from the start, well organised. The setback of 1929 was a particular blow since the men had been fierce in their defence of existing customs hitherto, even to the extent of attempting to force the manager to revoke company orders.[130] The lodge had been the dominant force in the society, able during the lock-out of 1928 to organise 'soup kitchens' and food supplies in all the villages where Nine Mile Point men worked.[131] Now, in 1935, they were not prepared to countenance any further loss of their power. Hence it was that some lodge representatives (including Marsden and Mitchell) floated the idea of a 'stay-down' to local SWMF officials, like Harold Finch, and the agent, Sydney Jones. These counselled caution and an approach to the EC. Jim Griffiths recalled:

> This confronted me, and the Executive Council, with a dilemma. It was a breach of the Coal Mines Act to stay down the mine beyond the permitted hours. If we called upon our men to stay down we would be in breach of an Act of Parliament designed to protect our safety. To this some of the enthusiasts had an answer. 'You close your eyes – we will do it on our own.'

Certainly, there was no prior 'official' knowledge of it. Harold Finch told them to think hard about any action but they '. . . replied to the effect that with every day which was passing, Industrial Union men were getting control at the pit and the position was desperate. However, they said they would consider the position. The next I heard, a few days later, was the sensational news that the "stay-down" had actually begun.' There had been, then, vague discussion but little encouragement from any officials.[132]

The idea of occupying the pits stemmed from the action of a thousand miners in Hungary who, in 1934, threatened mass suicide in the pit unless they were granted an increase in wages.[133] Newspaper reports of this action had been read and discussed in the lodges, and on the combine committees. Indeed, the spread of such strikes as if by a kind of industrial osmosis can only be understood, as distinct from concerted action for which no evidence exists, as a trigger mechanism releasing notions that had been mulled over in many pits and areas. Even before this, occupation of the pits had occurred to some as a means of exerting their control over the work-place. Thus, in Bedwas Navigation Colliery, in 1929, after a 'Show Cards' had ousted all non-unionists, one SWMIU member was still employed. When he descended the pit, the Federation men refused to leave the pit bottom until he was sent home.[134] The first genuine 'stay-down' in South Wales had happened at Waunlwyd slant of the Brynhenllys Colliery, in the Swansea Valley, at Cwmtwrch in October 1934 when twenty-two men refused to come up, after their shift, for $6\frac{1}{2}$ hours, until the management revoked an earlier decision over the payment of a minimum wage for abnormal places. One of the men who had used this 'new weapon' said 'Don't think this was a novel stunt. We wanted to make an effective protest and we succeeded. We will fight in every way for what we want [if] we have a just case.'[135]

The intense non-union struggle of September and October 1935, allied to the inspiring demonstrations against Part II of the 1934 Unemployment Act, had created an atmosphere in which such action might be attempted on a wider front. Conventional methods, in both parliamentary and industrial spheres, had proved unable to cut the knots that bound them. United Front committees had served to link militants, inside and outside the CP, within the SWMF. Meetings of local party cells, as this one described by Lewis Jones in his novel *We Live*, were typical:

> When he spoke it was in a whisper, as though he were afraid of what he was saying.
>
> 'Comrades, we've been bullied and battered for staying up the pit. What about staying down for a change?'
>
> The brief sentence was followed by a momentary pause, then a gasp of surprise as the audacity of the idea made itself felt. When the Party meeting broke up, the decision was made and worked out the same night in a secret emergency committee of the Federation.[136]

At Nine Mile Point, the Federation Committee had swung into action immediately by sending men through the village to ask shopkeepers, hoteliers and proprietors of clubs to express their sympathy with the men by closing early and providing food supplies. These requests were granted, whilst at the pit-head on the Saturday evening a large crowd was led in community singing by a brass band. The men below were not alone in their struggle for most of the crowd kept a vigil throughout the night and swelled in numbers during the day. That Sunday, prayers for the strikers were said in some of the Chapels. Three men had ascended the pit early Sunday morning because of illness in their families, and in the case of Samuel White, aged fifty-six, from near-exhaustion. The men received their first supply of food (tea, coffee and sandwiches) that afternoon. White explained that the men were grouped, in a body, in the colliery stables. Conditions were not comfortable although in general the men were 'like crickets and if they are not taken ill they will remain there. They are Britons. They are happy and pass the time singing and going after the rats.'

The Federation, represented by Oliver Harris and Sydney Jones (the miners' agent), had met with Levi Phillips (the General Manager of the United National Group of the Ocean Coal Company), though to little avail since the latter refused to consider the question of non-unionism at the colliery until the men came up. A statement issued by Phillips was, in itself, a summary of the men's grievances:

> The method of coercion which is being adopted [i.e. to effect dismissal of men in *another* pit], either on their own initiative or by the advice of unreasoning leadership, is calculated with the intention of creating a tyrannical force to compel workmen to be members of a Union which they individually have . . . refused to join [and] it was not a matter of surprise [i.e. when the original non-union strike was proposed] that other workmen who have been idle for years should seek to obtain employment in collieries which obviously had to remain open for work.[137]

The delegate conference called by the EC which met on Monday was faced with a situation that was escalating by the hour. Sixty men on the morning shift in the Rock Vein pit announced, as soon as they had gone underground, that, with the exception of the boys, they were 'staying-in'. A similar move by forty men on the afternoon shift in the East Pit was thwarted by the management's refusal to let them go down. More than this, however, the action of the original strikers sparked off a massive wave of pit occupations across the coalfield. In the uncertain, frustrating period that had followed the non-union campaign, the move at Nine Mile Point appeared startling in its simple effectiveness. The response of their fellow workmen became an emotional catharsis for entire communities.

At nearby Risca during the non-union stoppage, several arrests, including that of a local councillor, had been made. Three hundred miners in Risca stayed down on Monday morning in sympathy with the Nine Mile Point men.[138] At Blaenavon a mass meeting reaffirmed an earlier decision to stop until the Nine Mile Point men surfaced, so 1,540 men from Big Pit and Garn Drift Colliery were out. A further 800 men struck at the Wylie Pit.

At the Delegate Conference, James Griffiths took the line that the Federation's authority was being directly challenged by the Ocean Colliery Company's unprecedented departure from neutrality in a non-union dispute. He requested an 'open mandate' from the lodges to take whatever action was necessary and stated that men were visiting derelict villages to tempt the unemployed into working as blacklegs by offers of bribes amounting to £5. The conference was adjourned.

When it met again on Wednesday afternoon, there had been stay-in strikes at Nantymoel, Blaengarw, Treherbert, Ton Pentre, Treharris and Cwmparc, though the total of 1,690 down in these collieries diminished during the day to 940. There were, according to the Federation, 335 men down in the Nine Mile Point pits and at Risca. At Tredegar, a number of collieries (5,600 men) decided to come out in sympathy; in the Garw Valley the same decision was taken; in the Sirhowy Valley 4,000 men were out; elsewhere the resolutions were in favour of waiting for the conference's decision.

The tight clandestine organisations, bred in the mining communities and nurtured by the years of experience from 1926 onwards, lent themselves to this situation. Many of the militants who had been squeezed out after the lock-out had now found their way back to the pits where they now organised in a careful, guarded way. This tradition was of the essence in October 1935. At Nantymoel, a local school-teacher, Mavis Llewellyn recalled:

> ... Fred [her uncle] had been to a combine meeting on this Saturday evening. He came home, didn't say anything. My father was working nights in the pit, so he went to work on the Sunday night. Monday morning he would normally be home before I would get up. Father would come in, light the fire and call when it was time to get up. My mother came and said, 'Mav, your father's not come home from work.' 'Oh he's working on.' 'That's unusual, because if he's working on he sends a message.' Well, I didn't pay much attention, I went on getting the breakfast. Mother kept on going back and fore to the front door, she was uneasy because he hadn't come home from work. And presently she said, 'Hey, have a look, the boys are coming home!' The pit was at the top here and the youngsters were coming down the road. So she said, 'What's happened?' 'Oh, they're staying down.' 'Staying down?' 'Yes, and they've sent us up, we're too young. So we've given them our food and our water.' Well, it was the first we knew. Fred had come home, he had confided in my father, and – what I always felt was so interesting – in the old days, if there was a dispute, and they'd have a pithead meeting, one man had to take the cork out of his bottle or his can, and empty his water, and once they started emptying their water, that meant 'We're not going down.' That was it, it was settled, once you started. But that time instead of saying 'Empty your water', he said 'Take care of your water'. That was Dad's job then at the bottom of the pit to tell the men when they got down, 'Go easy with your water.' And when they sent out the old men and those who were ill, they all left their water down with them. Well, that was such a complete change and it was a new way of fighting the bosses.[139]

One of the significant features of the stay-in strike was the depth of community consciousness it tapped. Nantymoel was typical of the solidarity above ground:

I heard the town crier, there was to be a mass meeting in the Workmen's Hall. Well, the school was close, and as soon as twelve o'clock came, I was down at the Workmen's Hall, and the Hall was absolutely heaving, mainly with women. 'How are we going to get food down to them?' We were supporting the strike, of course, but 'How are you going to get food down to them?' Well, the instructions were, 'Go home, and if you've got a man down the pit, find a shoe box, fill it up with food, tie it up and put his name on it, and we'll see that it goes down the pit.' Until eventually we begin to organise a soup kitchen on top of the pit, now instead of a soup kitchen for children. Anyway, the women were the people working in the Hall, making cocoa and what have you, and oh, stacks . . . and there are some very funny stories about that because it was new to everybody. And one old lady, the son is still alive, they had had an argument on the Saturday, he was betting, she didn't approve of him betting and gambling on horses. But she was so concerned that she'd had this quarrel with him, that in his shoe box she had put the Echo, and a shilling for a bet. And we were trying to tell her – 'You can't. . . .' 'Oh never mind, let him know, all is forgiven.'[140]

The hordes of national reporters who had flocked to Cwmfelinfach were not disappointed for news. Cardiff City police and men from the Newport Borough force had been on duty at the pit head, mostly concerned with escorting the non-Federation men to their train, throughout Monday. On Tuesday the train carrying eighty men to the colliery was damaged when a rock (weighing about 1 cwt) was dropped from a bridge in Wylie Village and tore a huge hole in the roof of the empty guard's van; the engine was also damaged. Any such 'ghost trains' were now liable to prolonged attack by stone-throwing miners. The 250 policemen who were on duty by Tuesday had little trouble, however, in escorting the blacklegs through a crowd a thousand strong to their train after the shift, although the railway line and each compartment had to be guarded.[141]

Another statement by the Ocean Coal Company maintained an intransigent stance as well as accusing the Federation Executive of being unable to exert any authority over its membership:

Time and time again the Miners' Federation has failed completely to control its constituent members in the individual collieries and carry out its side of the agreement which exists between the Federation and the Coal Owners, and the failure has always been due to the influence of the left wing or extremist element. The Federation has in the past pronounced against Communism but has not effectively excluded it.

For the Ocean Coal Company, set in its belief that ruin was thus being foisted on the coal industry, the existence of the Industrial Union seemed, as it had done in 1926, an escape from continual strife. The only difference they acknowledged between this dispute and any other was that there existed in the coalfield 'a comparatively strong Union in opposition to the Miners' Federation and this Union took advantage of the opportunity of finding collieries where there was employment offered for men who were genuinely seeking work *and who were members of their organisation*, and these men having secured work their employment has been continued'.[142]

If the Ocean Coal Company was concerned with peaceful industrial relations then it would long ago have abandoned its support of that 'strong union' in opposition; if, on the other hand, its concern was to keep the SWMF's finances in a parlous situation, then the Industrial Union remained a valuable pawn in any attempt to excise any Federation control.

In the meantime the Secretary for Mines (Captain Crookshank) had once more intervened in order to bring the two sides together. The Company now agreed to meet James Griffiths, despite continuation of the strike. Although they insisted on closing the three pits at the colliery, they also agreed to meet Federation officials, after a short period, to discuss resumption of work. No mention was made of the SWMIU so on this basis the EC and the Delegate Conference recommended a return to work.

At the various pits 'on stop' the decision received a mixed reception. Most of those who had stayed down in sympathy came up; at Nine Mile Point the feeling was that the agreement was 'not sufficiently protective of the interests of the Federation members in view of the sacrifices made by so many men in remaining down the pit for so long'.[143]

The leadership had underestimated the intensity of feeling now running throughout the affected areas. Crowds marched through surrounding villages until the dawn. Solidarity with the strikers had spread to local branches of the NUR and ASLEF who had refused to carry blackleg labour to Nine Mile Point, whilst at Merthyr the local unemployed lodges had persuaded men to refuse offers of work at the colliery.[144] The Delegate Conference had had a three-hour stormy meeting before the EC had been supported and at meetings held by the lodges in the early hours of the morning of Tuesday, 17 October, extremist proposals were voiced again. Men at North and South

Celynen Collieries who accepted the EC's decision were prevented from working by a crowd of 2,000 men and women who marched up the Sirhowy Valley. There was more confusion than certainty in the coalfield as conflicting opinions were put.

There had been other news that Wednesday as well, the effect of which resulted by Friday in the temporary victory of the more militant proposals. At Taff-Merthyr, Federation members who had decided on a stay-in strike to force a resolution of the situation at the colliery engaged in a fierce hand-to-hand struggle with SWMIU men and colliery officials. They were thrown into coal trucks and taken up in the cage; some were severely hurt. Another forty men were cut off by cordons of officials and thus unable to move from an exposed position.

As a direct result of this the men still at work were greeted, at the end of their shift, by an exceedingly hostile crowd which broke through the police cordon and engaged in a running fight on the mountainside with the 'scabs' and the police. Stones were used freely; when two trains appeared on the line that ran below the road, the shout was 'Here comes the scab train' and showers of stones greeted their arrival. In Trelewis there were fights in the streets and windows were smashed.[145]

The other turn in events was a stay-in strike at the other SWMIU stronghold – Dare Colliery, Cwmparc. The net result was that on Friday there were still 'stay-in' strikes at Nine Mile Point, Parc and Dare Collieries, at Garw Colliery, Blaengarw and at Fernhill, Treherbert, whilst the 'sympathy strikers' were again on the increase, there being 25,000 men involved on Thursday.

Elsewhere men were obeying the EC's decision to return to work and at Risca 170 miners came up after three days underground. The general mood, however, was one of determination to expunge the MIU. After meetings on Thursday, there were 40,000 men concerned in the strike and another 'stay-down', this time at Wyndham No. 1 Pit, Ogmore. At some pits in the Rhondda the owners would not allow work in case the men refused to ascend.[146]

The greater part of this activity was in support of the Nine Mile Point men to whom the EC had to address itself if the rash of strikes was to be ended. The local lodge officials met with representatives of the EC for three-and-a-half hours before agreeing to vacate the pit if the men underground agreed. The crucial point they had secured was a written guarantee, not verbal promises, from the owners that there would be no victimisation and that only the SWMF would negotiate over the reopening of the Colliery.[147]

James Griffiths and Arthur Jenkins arranged to go down the West Pit where the trouble had started and where seventy men had been down for 176 hours, almost seven-and-a-half days:

The . . . days below had left their mark; the elderly looked weary – the young had grown beards. I was greeted by the 'patriarch' who had opened and closed each day with prayer, and in between had transformed the stay-down strikers into a choir. The leader escorted me to the platform – an upturned tub – and called for order. They listened to me intently as I announced the terms of the settlement, and plied me with questions. Then the leader announced that a vote would be taken for or against the acceptance of 'our President's recommendation'. It was one of the proudest moments of my life when every lamp was raised. We sang 'Bread of Heaven'. This was the bread they could not deny us.[148]

However, at the Parc and Dare Pits the men underground sent up a note declaring that they were 'prepared to stick down until they achieve their demands, providing the dispute does not last longer than the Great War'. The fight against the SWMIU was at the forefront in Cwmparc, again, just as it had been before the unexpected action of the Nine Mile Point men. Oliver Harris had written to Lord Davies to complain of the conditions at the Dare Colliery and his letter had been discussed by the Board of the Ocean Coal Company. As at Nine Mile Point, their decision was to declare innocence. Lord Davies replied:

. . . I was requested to advise you that the present position at the Dare Colliery has arisen as the result of a unanimous request from the Company's employees at this pit. [This referred to the agreement reached in August 1934 with the MIU after a temporary closure.] It was wrong, therefore, to suggest, as you do in your letter, that the conditions of employment have been imposed by the Company upon its employees. On the contrary, these conditions are part and parcel of an agreement which was suggested by the workmen themselves, and to which we consequently agreed.[149]

The SWMF were, of course, aware that the reply would be dusty. Earlier in the year it had told its members:

Unfortunately, the Federation organisation at that colliery has been unsatisfactory for the last few years, and the men, therefore, became easy victims of this oppressive policy of the company. The council is taking steps to deal with the situation, and we have every reason to believe that we shall be able to secure the freedom of the Dare workmen.[150]

One of the steps not pursued by the EC was Lord Davies's suggestion that any workman who objected to paying his subscription to the MIU should report, in person, to the colliery manager with no fear of reprisals. All previous attempts to oust the MIU men at the Parc and Dare Collieries had failed over a period of eight years.

Both unions had been in existence in the Upper Rhondda since 1927, following a return to work of some men during the lock-out. The riots that had taken place then had resulted in the imprisonment of the local checkweigher and lodge chairman, Iorwerth Thomas (later MP for Rhondda West 1945–67), along with some others. He was released after two months and reinstated as checkweigher by a ballot vote of the men.[151] None the less, the Federation's control in the Dare Pit remained slight as the management employed those whom they chose to employ. Attempts to oust Thomas by ballot also having failed, they then refused to make deductions at the colliery office for his wage. This led to a court case in February 1931 in which Thomas, and two other checkweighers claimed £1 from John Nicholls and others as a proportion of the wages due to them from men employed at the Dare Colliery. The checkweighers had been appointed in 1921, and reinstated in 1926, but the defendants had joined the MIU in 1926 and thereby objected to the payment. Judgement was given for the plaintiffs.[152] The activities of 'General' Reynolds (the local SWMIU organising agent) continued in 1932 with the publication of propaganda leaflets; when men were laid off they were not being re-engaged on any basis of seniority, and again there were concerted attempts to displace the elected checkweigher.[153]

The SWMF EC appointed Jim Griffiths (the Vice-President) and Richard Bennetta (Garw miners' agent) to assist W. H. Mainwaring in an investigation into the situation. The report they delivered was a black one: on stop-days SWMIU members were given any work available, they were the first taken back, the checkweigher was obstructed in his duties. They suggested that the Central finance the campaign conducted by the Lodge and that attempts be made to pressure the directors. Nothing could be more eloquent of the plight of the SWMF in maintaining their position within the old Districts, than the fact that during the discussion that followed 'it was revealed that the local lodge committee was composed entirely of unemployed workmen, and it was suggested that efforts should be made, to get men who are at work to become members of the committee'.

An interview with W. P. Thomas, the General Manager, merely elicited the reply that there was no preferential treatment for the Industrial Union,[154] so that in early 1933 the local campaign proceeded. For the most part of January 1933 there were meetings in the locality in order to expunge what Bennetta, rejecting the notion that the SWMIU was a 'rival union', referred to as 'a disease upon the Miners' Federation'. Iorwerth Thomas railed against the Ocean Coal Company's financial assistance and the special privileges accorded to the MIU.[155] At best only a *status quo* was maintained, for by the end of the year the complaints were the same, with the Secretary of the Ocean Combine Committee reporting the difficulties of the Federation Officials in the Parc and Dare pits over organising the men. Oliver Harris confirmed that despite the management's denial of any restriction 'emissaries of the Industrial Union had been going around intimidating the workmen'.[156]

So, despite the fact that wages and conditions at the Dare Colliery had been, since 1926, those negotiated under the Conciliation Board Agreement, there was an effective ban on Federation 'interference' in the pit, originating in the refusal of local officials to countenance the break-away proposed in 1926. Finally, in the summer of 1934, the SWMF felt able, after a number of meetings held in the pits, to organise a secret ballot – the result was 7 to 1 in favour of the Federation. The following day all the men at the Dare pits were given notice of fourteen days and the miners' agent, now W. H. May, was told 'that they were closing down the Dare Pit, the Garw Ocean, and one other pit, through lack of orders'.[157] Following this, after an SWMIU meeting, the pit was reopened under an agreement whereby all the men at work agreed to contribute to that Union.[158]

The management explanation of this turnabout was that the SWMIU, who claimed a 90 per cent membership at the Dare Colliery, urged them to keep the pit open on a day-to-day contract basis. They entered into an agreement with the MIU because the men appeared to desire it, but 'we have never taken any steps to induce our men to join the Miners' Federation or the Industrial Union'.[159]

The local SWMF officials now complained that they had been told there was no possibility of the pit ever opening again, whereas the opposite information had been conveyed to the Industrial Union. In support of this allegation of collusion, the Ocean Combine Committee declared:

Events . . . now proved that this was correct. As a result . . . the union officials [i.e. the SWMIU] immediately got in touch with the management of the colliery, and in a few days notices were posted up in the locality to the effect that work would be resumed, conditionally upon the men signing a new contract book embodying the terms arranged between the management and the MIU. Public notices had been posted up notifying men in certain districts to attend at the office with a view of signing the new contract book, and that the management had resorted to the practice of inviting men individually to attend the offices for that purpose.[160]

Iorwerth Thomas added bitterly – 'Any man who refused to allow the company to deduct from his wages moneys in support of this union was rejected.'

Despite strike threats, pleas to the Executive and mass meetings there was little that could be done to reverse the situation. Once again a particular Ocean pit had been winkled out of the Federation fold, presumably, on this occasion, because of the possibility of a coalfield stoppage over the wages issue on 1 October. The Ocean Combine Committee promised to stop all Ocean pits if need be but the crucial appeal had, first, to reach into the Dare Colliery.[161] In the meantime they could only rail against a company which, with Lord Davies at its head, was a fervent supporter of the Free Church Council and the Peace movement:

> They shout out for religious liberty, for peace among nations, and equality for all, but they move heaven and earth to prevent this spirit entering their pits.[162]

Through 1935, with the MIU representing men in the Parc pits too, this deep hostility continued, with all 'open' attempts to re-establish the Federation being repelled.[163] So the 'stay-in' at Parc No. 2 on 15 October 1935 could be seen as angry frustration; not so, however, a 'stay-in' the following day at the Dare Colliery where the men were all supposedly stalwarts of the MIU. There were now 200 men on strike underground.[164] Local Federation officials had indeed acted, though not in the way suggested by Lord Davies:

> What the managment didn't know was that the men in the Dare pit had been in conference with the Federation and we had advised them to stay in the Scab Union while we were consolidating our forces. They were members of both Unions. We had built up a membership of 30 to 40 per cent in that pit and that was why we were able to strike such a devastating blow. So now we had a complete strike in Parc No. 2 and the Dare pit. The management stopped work in Parc No. 1 pit fearing that there, too, we might have infiltrated into their Industrial Union.[165]

The immediate spark of these 'stay-ins' lay in the determination of the

Parc No. 2 men who had taken 'extra rations' down after the restart when the non-union dispute was over; a haulier was then delegated to go through the connecting door to the Dare Colliery in order to pass the message to 'stay-in' there. Once again the organisation was local, a rank-and-file response to the ideas and discussions that had filtered down via the EC and the Ocean Combine Committee.[166] The men were determined to 'stay down' until their particular grievance was ended; this was not to be a mere protest but the culmination of a long period of secret infiltration and planning.[167]

So, despite the end of the first phase of the 'stay-down' strikes another serious dispute had arisen in the Rhondda where the EC's call for a return to work was openly disregarded. Men at the nearby Fernhill Colliery stayed down in sympathy. Although, at times, it appeared as if the bitterness might come to violence here, too, the Ocean Coal Company's capitulation at Nine Mile Point made it possible for them to resist in Cwmparc.[168]

When the Delegate Conference met, in Cardiff, on Monday, 21 October, an agreement had already been drawn up with the officials of the Dare Colliery which made explicit provision for the men to withdraw their agreement to the deductions made in favour of the MIU from 25 October and that work would begin again, thereafter, when the officials met with the representatives of the majority of the men (the SWMF had claimed that 648 of the 750 men in the Dare Colliery had joined them during the strike). Nor was this all. There was to be no victimisation, nor further employment of the 'blackleg' labour used in the non-union strike (the two Ton Pentre men were signalled out) and no deductions for the MIU at all, even for any minority support they might still possess. At the Parc No. 2 pit all MIU members had now signed up with the Federation.

Not surprisingly a mass meeting of the Parc and Dare workmen on the surface accepted these terms, and this was followed by the acceptance of the men underground. On Wednesday, these men, after almost 200 hours underground, came up at last. The men from the Dare Pit were met by the miners' agent W. H. May, Iorwerth Thomas and a throng of people who saw the occasion as symbolic of the attainment of daylight in more ways than one. As if to underline the complexity of the nature of protest in these communities, the people, led by the Dare Colliery Male Voice Choir, many of whose members had 'stayed in', sang various hymns and then 'came the "Doxology", and as the first bar of the hymn, "Praise God from Whom all Blessings Flow" sounded, every head was bared and the crowd, some thousands strong, stood silently in an attitude of reverence.'[169]

Not even the *Western Mail* could attribute this particular event to Communist influence, though the drama of late 1935 did induce a clutch of articles headed 'Red Hand behind Coal Strikes' whose evidence was limited to 'militant' quotes from CP literature. Will Paynter wrote, in reply:

> The South Wales Miners need no agitators – Welsh or non-Welsh – to convince them of the necessity of sweeping Company Unionism from the coalfield. They are determined to do it and they will succeed.[170]

Although local CP militants advocated much of the strike action, the leadership and certainly the rank-and-file support were wider based, as Paynter argues. The only disagreement between the EC and the militants (inside and outside the Party) was over the extension of the action. However, this particular form of militancy had paid handsome dividends and there was little dissension over the return to work; for unity, with a limited victory won, was seen as more valuable now than any temporary heightening of industrial action at the expense of the organisation itself. In his second novel, *We Live*, Lewis Jones has his hero, Len, a 'stay-down' striker, reluctantly agree to follow the CP line (that is, support of the EC) in an argument that encapsulates the determination, and the discipline, of the 'United Front' in 1935:

> 'We have nothing to expect from the company, from the authorities, from anyone. No, nothing can serve us but our own strength, determination and unity. . . .' His voice broke a little and became sad as he continued, 'That is why I believe the Executive is right and we ought to ask our men to come up the pit. Look . . . everywhere our men are split. Some are fighting underground like ours, others are on the surface, and working . . . we must on this issue fight together or lose the fight.'[171]

In the sense that the initiative had now passed, irredeemably, from the SWMIU, the 'stay-in' strikes do mark a turning-point. They were, by no means, the end of company unionism, however, for its hold in the two remaining pits of Taff-Merthyr and Bedwas was one that a 'stay-in' by itself would not be able to dislodge. This had been seen in Taff-Merthyr in October, and was again shown in November. The Federation's success, had apparently, wrung concessions even here since the Company, for the first time, agreed to curtail the distribution of Industrial Union pamphlets, as under the 1934 Agreement they were bound to, and to terminate their practice of allowing SWMIU men up the pit early on union business. Within twenty-four hours this promise had been broken and, then, two weeks later six Federation men who had 'stayed-down' on a Saturday were dismissed (four of the thirty strikers in October had not been restarted for 'geological reasons') with the result that ten SWMF members staged another 'stay-in'.

This incident, itself set off by the abortive strike on the preceding Saturday, was the result of growing frustration as their demands for an end to the 1934 Agreement and the sole recognition of the SWMF indicate. The men barricaded themselves in the No. 9 District but were forcibly ejected by being blasted, alternately, with stone dust, compressed air and water. The men had been down from 6.30 a.m. to 10.40 p.m., led by Morgan Jones, secretary of the local Federation lodge, who said that the earlier strike, on the Saturday, had not been authorised and was, he believed, 'a trap' set by the company.[172]

Although these men were reinstated following negotiations and an 'apology' to the management, they were not restarted until 16 December, and when they did they

> noticed that a number of colliery officials and the Industrial Union committee men were assembled outside the pit-head baths. About 100 men already had descended the shaft. About 40 men were together, who took a decision not to work with the 10 'stay-in strikers'. It was freely alleged that colliery officials were advising the men to attend the meeting and 'Stop the Federation blighters'. The Company thereupon stopped the pit for the day and sent down the pit to get those up who had descended. The Company made the first MIU strike 100 per cent.[173]

This flurry of ineffectual, and disconcerting, activity in Taff-Merthyr led the Executive to examine, yet again, their own procedural techniques. Edwards and Crews appealed for a full-time appointment to be made 'over' the colliery, and Alf Davies was delegated. Of more significance was the realisation that in Bedwas 1,000 men were paying 4*d*. a week to the SWMIU and that a full onslaught there might so cripple their finances as to make existence at Taff-Merthyr alone an impossibility. Bedwas was, therefore, marked out for the next move by the EC.[174] The latter were intent on asserting their full control over any such move; indeed some had seen the spontaneous outbreaks of late 1935 as akin to anarchy; and so they insisted that any action on the non-union issue could only be taken after the organisation committee had both vetted and approved the proposal.[175] The ability of the new combine committees to organise action, allied to the new-found militancy of some lodges, it was felt, had to be supervised by the Central so as not to impair any concerted action. Oliver Harris spoke for them when he voiced his disquiet over unofficial stoppages in early 1936:

> All of us are reluctant to give up our right to withhold our labour when we feel there is justification for so doing, but I want our members to seriously ask themselves, apart altogether from the breach of contract which they have entered into, [if] the unconstitutional stoppages that have taken place in this coalfield, often over comparatively small matters, are justified? I am sure that when they think the matter over calmly they must admit that generally the game has not been worth the cost.[176]

Certainly, whatever the leap forward of 1935, it was not the only, nor necessarily the best, manner to proceed thereafter. There were some forces within the coalfield which were difficult to overcome, since local authority oversight of them did not include any ultimate control – that lay with the Home Office. In this respect, the police force had a free hand, and perhaps for this reason the relationship of the community to the custodians of law and order had been worsening for a number of years, for too often the police had been the visible enemy. On the very week-end that the December strike at Taff-Merthyr was settled, 300 summonses were issued to people allegedly involved in the 'riots' at the colliery in October 1935.

There had been the now customary protests at the Glamorgan Standing Joint Committee over the Chief Constable's report in which he had defended the calling in of 300 policemen from outside forces (fifty men from both Swansea and Bristol, and 100 from both Birmingham and Liverpool) during the strikes of the autumn. This was, he claimed, because of the requests for protection he had received from the GWR and the SWMIU, as well as Home Office insistence. Captain Lindsay told the committee that it 'was gratifying to observe the influence the increased police strength had on the unruly elements. The position immediately began to settle down, and on 24 October, fifty of the Liverpool contingent stationed at Bridgend and fifty Birmingham police stationed at Porth returned home.' As Sir William Jenkins caustically commented: 'Anybody reading that report would consider that the strike had ended through the efforts of the Chief Constable or through the police.' The Chief Constable's statement was excluded from the minutes.[177]

The actions taken by the police in prosecution could not be so lightly excised. The trial of those accused led to the conviction of fifty-two men and three women, with twenty-one bound over, and the sentences ranged from fifteen months' hard labour to three months' imprisonment. Mr Justice Humphreys described Bedlinog as a 'disgrace to the valleys' and seemed as intent on meting out punishment for what had happened in 1934 as with the actual case in hand. He incurred the wrath of the coalfield by his injudicious remarks. Edgar Evans, he thought, should have had no part in it since 'he was a shopkeeper and not a collier', whilst, as a local councillor, he should have been 'on the side of peace'. To Margaret Jenkins, 'that wild woman' as he called her, he said: 'You were the person who committed the first act of violence by pulling a man from his bicycle. Because you are the mother of seven children and have a respectable husband, you will be bound over. I am going to keep this matter hanging over your head for three years.'[178]

What normally hung over the heads of demonstrators was the Damoclean baton of the police force, or, as in a march to the Bridgend PAC in October 1933, a droning aeroplane, symbol in the decade of totalitarianism, of disembodied technology. This 'control' over their actions was deeply resented by those who had to march out of the valleys to come near to a personal confrontation with those who made the decisions. As Aneurin Bevan wrote: 'Silent pain evokes no response.'[179]

After the sentences of 1936 there were huge demonstrations organised in the area around Treharris at which S. O. Davies, Horner, Alf Davies and others spoke; at the trial in Swansea the representatives of the Anthracite Area protested. The feeling aroused was as much directed against the police as against the severity of the sentences. Horner refuted the notion of impartial justice:

> To put it bluntly no one has the right to be violent or to riot unless he was dressed as a policeman, and the arch-thug is the Chief Constable of Glamorgan, who does not hold his job by the voice of the people or by the wishes of the Standing Joint Committee, but by the desire of the capitalists.[180]

The EC issued a stern statement to the same effect, though couched in colder prose, when they referred to the resolutions received in indignation 'at the grossly unjustifiable sentences', and added that the EC 'fully shares this indignation and emphatically protests against the obvious bias of the Judge who tried the defendants and his improper remarks about the workmen of this area. We call upon the Standing

SWM TILLERY SEARCHLIGHT
COMMUNIST PIT GROUP

No. 11.   MAY 15th. 1936.   Price 1d.

DAMAGING EXPOSURE OF SCAB UNION.

Seven of the thirty-three Taff-Merthyr prisoners were released last week
and were given a great welcome. Prisoners they were and twenty-six are
still prisoners but according to disclosures shown by one time officials
of the so-called Non-Political Union they should not have been prisoners.
                     Everyone knew it was in trying to ensure freedom to be
members of the S.W.M.F, in preference to the scab-union that gave the
police the pretext on which to charge the Taff members. Also that the
Owners at the collieries were forcing the workmen to be members of the
scab-union or be penalised in different ways.   This so-called
union it now transpires is none other than an organisation thrown up by
the Owners.   W.C. Williams of Twill Rd, Bodwas, has issued several
leaflets in which he takes damning accusations against William Gregory
the Non-Pols Secretary and acting President, and also against George A.
Spensor of Nottingham. He also asks W. Gregory to answer many questions
etc. W.C. Williams points out that in a letter from George Spenser to
Gregory that Spenser gives a list of six cheques totalling £875 which
he sent to Gregory in one period of less than a month. Another letter
where Spenser thinks that these amounts should be shown as contributions
of members to make the position of the scab-union look strong which would
discourage any action members of a genuine union wish to take.
Here is a quotation from the entry, George A. Spenser to Gregory "If at any
time thou are in doubt write me, I do hope the colliery company stands
firm over this dispute. One good stand of a successful character would
change the psychology of South Wales".   Thanks to the stand the
Federation members made the scab-union was knocked very badly, despite
the imprisonment of thirty-three.   (Cont.Page 4.)

"THEY BUILT A WALL AROUND THE JAIL
TO KEEP THE FOLKS AWAY."
Popular song

"THE HOME SECRETARY KNOWS NO REASON FOR REMISSION OF SENTENCES"
HOME OFFICE

A pit paper protests against Taff-Merthyr sentences in 1936

Joint Committee of Glamorgan to institute an inquiry into the conduct of the police . . . and the brutal batoning of innocent men, women and children.'[181]

The man who had been behind so many of these police actions, since he succeded his father in the job, in 1891 (via a post as Inspector of Gendarmerie in Egypt) did finally retire in 1936, at the age of seventy-five. Sir Rhys Williams of the Standing Joint Committee lamented that there was 'no son to carry on the family tradition'. A hollow laugh must have echoed in the coalfield, for as Alderman D. D. Davies, Chairman of the Glamorgan County Council, said, 'Sir Rhys does not speak on behalf of the work-people of Glamorgan.'[182]

They had, of course, spoken for themselves in a spectacular fashion in late 1935. There is no simple explanation of the outbreak which was, essentially, a compound of frustration and desperate anger. It was if the biting *social* militancy that had gathered around an industrial boil in Taff-Merthyr in 1934 had been diffused through the bloodstream. The actions of the men, whose form was without real precedent in South Wales, had taken their own leadership by surprise. Ness Edwards, writing in the immediate aftermath of these events, said:

> The rank-and-file, in desperation, had taken its head. All the petty victimisation and repression, the low wages, the breakneck speed of mechanised mining, the open encouragement of the Scab Union, all these things had created a psychology ready for such dramatic incidents as 'Stay-in-Strikers.[183]

In all the pits of South Wales since 1926 the men had had little redress against victimisation, petty or otherwise; their wages, despite the Bridgeman award, remained abysmally low; they had proved powerless to eradicate the SWMIU or to prevent its open encouragement; their own non-union problem remained of considerable dimensions. Increasing mechanisation and abrogation of old customs to ensure economies further alienated the miner from his pride in his work as a coal-cutter, a craftsman, to become what he regarded as an automaton with a machine (more coal cut less safely for less money and more profit); he was alienated too from the financial undertakings, the banks and shipping companies, that had replaced the entrepreneur, the coal magnate, the local (or at least Welsh) owner.[184]

The 'stay-in' strikes were the only form of direct action left to a reduced and battered working-force; occupation of their work-place did have elements in it of a turning of the tables by the slave of the mine.

The joke that went the rounds was that the latest offer at Nine Mile Point was 30s. a week and 'live in'. Colliers lived in communities that literally dug away their own foundations; it was a work that had no end-product, only an endless round of destruction of the earth and an exporting of its riches whilst they themselves grew more impoverished. The contrast was sharper in that the crazy underground world in which they laboured produced a comradeship that had institutional echoes above ground in a world, apparently rational, but in fact falling about their ears. This was a society almost tailor-made for rejection of any imposed outside hegemony, whether economic, physical or social.[185]

For the men themselves there was now the euphoria induced by the victory at large and a particular camaraderie amongst the 'stay-in strikers' themselves. They fashioned walking-sticks during their underground stay, as souvenirs, a horse-shoe was made into rings. The eyesight of many was permanently impaired. Within months they were holding celebration dinners and concert parties, paid for by their workmates.[186] So, although, as Jim Griffiths warned of the 'new weapon', 'We must not use it lightly lest it become farcical',[187] it was quite clear by 1936 that the people of the coalfield had themselves given a firm indication that, wherever possible, they were prepared to make even more effort to wrest back whatever control they could over their own lives, and that in this the SWMF was seen as the principal channel of protest and of hope.

It was this growing refusal to submit to the pressures and miseries inflicted upon them in any passive manner that Jim Griffiths was putting a gloss on in his final presidential address when he came to review the momentous events of 1935 which, he said, 'revealed a new spirit of revolt amongst our people, which, if wisely led and directed, can lead to a permanent improvement in the conditions in the coalfield':

> God knows that those conditions can do with improving. . . . For years a feeling of despair has lain over South Wales. We have stood almost silently by and watched our industrial and social life decaying. It has been like a vigil at the death-bed of a community, with the watchers paralysed by the feeling that nothing could be done to ward off the dreaded end.
>
> At long last I believe we are freeing ourselves from the paralysis of our social will.
>
> There is growing up everywhere in South Wales a determination to fight for our economic existence, and a realisation that this calls for a supreme effort. I will do all I can to foster this spirit. This South Wales of ours, with its cultural heritage, is far too good to die. It is worth fighting to preserve, and in that struggle the Federation can and will take its rightful place.[188]

NOTES

1. Statistics (official ones are quoted) taken from the SWMF Annual Report 1934–5. The unemployment figures relate to the coalfield itself. SWMF Annual Returns to the Registrar-General.
2. *DW,* 13, 30 May 1933. See also below, pp. 245–8.
3. A complete file of the *South Wales Miner* (*SWM*) exists in the British Museum Newspaper Library at Colindale.
4. *SWM,* 7 December 1933.
5. *SWM,* 7 August 1934. Horner was fortunate in that the the all-Welsh rule for Anthracite agents was dropped before the election, apparently for the convenience of another candidate. Jones had the advantage of being Welsh-speaking. Such a qualification was a considerable advantage in a coalfield which was in every respect Welsh. Lodge committee meetings and even general meetings in such collieries as Cwmllynfell were conducted in Welsh as late as 1959, and those miners who had their origins in Merthyr and did not speak Welsh were considered 'English'. Interview with Will (Post) Rees (Cwmllynfell), 4 August 1971.
6. *Miners' Monthly* (official organ of the SWMF), March 1934.
7. *SWM,* 22 June 1933, see also UCS, Amalgamated Anthracite Combine Committee minutes, 1935–8 *passim.*
8. D. D. Evans interview, *op. cit.* The growth of the AACC encouraged a semi-syndicalist outlook amongst Communist and other miners who saw it as an all-important trade union and political forum. This was certainly so of D. D. Evans and Dick Beamish. Among those borrowed were Dick Beamish (Abercrave), Haydn Lewis (Ammanford), Joe 'Brickman' Jones (Cwmllynfell), Will Betty (Glyn-Neath), Sidney Jones (Cross Hands), Nun Nicholas (Trebanos) and Evan (Ianto) Evans (Ammanford). See also above, pp. 239–40, n 34.
9. For a fuller account of the Anthracite miners in this period, see Hywel Francis, 'The Anthracite Strike and Disturbances of 1925', *op. cit.* For Anthracite production figures betweeen 1894 and 1944 see D. Ivor Evans, MC, FGS, *South Wales Institute of Engineers Presidential Address,* (Cardiff, 1946), pam.
10. *WM,* 27 October 1931, 16 November 1935; British Museum State Papers Room, BS 23/24, Local Unemployment Index (HMSO), 1931–9, *passim.* See also Appendix IV.
11. Monmouthshire Marchers' Council, NUWM, *Monmouthshire Hunger March* of August 1933, (Abertillery, nd) pam. *passim.*
12. *Ibid.,* p. 2.
13. *Ibid.,* pp. 6–7. This extraordinary revival of interest in Chartism can in part be explained by the importance attached to that movement in the syllabuses of the Plebs' League and the NCLC, see for example, UCS, D. J. Williams collection (A) Educational Activities. An interesting parallel is found with the Ystradgynlais miners of the Swansea Valley who, on being told about 'Scotch Cattle', by an ex-Labour college student, proceeded to imitate them during their picketing activities in the 1926 lock-out, see above, Ch. 2, pp. 62–3. But the importance of oral tradition and the 'received memory' cannot be over-emphasised, see for example, Ch. 12, p. 477.

14. Monmouthshire Marchers' Council, NUWM, *op. cit.*

15. *Ibid.*, pp. 9–10.

16. Wal Hannington, *Ten Lean Years*, (London, 1940), pp. 120–1; National Congress and March Council, *Manifesto of National Hunger March and Congress*, (London, 1934), pam. *passim*.

17. PRO, MEPOL 2/3071, file on National Hunger March 1934.

18. SWML, J. S. Williams, *op. cit.*, D(ii)3(a), 'Instructions to Section Leaders' (n.d.).

19. UCS, George Thomas (Treherbert) collection (D) Hunger Marches MSS.

20. SWML, J. S. Williams, *op. cit.*, D(ii) 1934 Hunger March MSS. *passim*.

21. SWML, J. S. Williams, *op. cit.*, D(ii)1(a) Report of Conference to elect Merthyr Borough Marchers' Council, 15 January 1934; E(i)3(a) Appeal for Merthyr Conference on 15 January 1934.

22. W. Hannington, *op. cit.*, p. 110.

23. MEPOL 2/3071, *op. cit.*, *passim*.

24. Information obtained in conservations with R. Page Arnot, July 1973. The police use of informers is discussed by Ralph Hayburn, 'The Police and the Hunger Marchers', *International Review of Social History*, Vol. XVII, 1972.

25. Idris Cox MSS, *op. cit.*, pp. 58–61; W. Hannington, *Unemployed Struggles 1919–1936* (Wakefield, 1975 edition), p. 284.

26. Idris Cox MSS., *op. cit.*

27. J. S. Williams, *op. cit.*, K/V Pollitt-Mann Defence Committee.

28. *DW*, 10 February 1934.

29. National Congress and March Council, *op. cit.*, p. 8.

30. See David Smith, 'The Struggle Against Company Unionism in the Wales Coalfield, 1926–39', *op. cit.*, pp. 369–70. Interview with Griff Jones, a Merthyr volunteer in the International Brigades, 18 October 1969.

31. SWML Interviews with Dick Beamish, 7 November 1972, and Edgar Evans, *op. cit.*, and 9 July 1975. This identification of a community consciousness in political terms could be challenged on sociological grounds, but the resurgence of the mid-1930s cannot be explained or quantified in a satisfactory manner in any other way.

32. See Bentley Gilbert, *British Social Policy, 1914–39* (1970), pp. 162–92.

33. *Aberdare Leader*, 12 January 1935 where W. J. Edwards presented the evidence and gave examples, e.g. a father earns £2 10s. His son is unemployed. The new UAB would allow the father 5s. personal allowance and 5s. for stoppages. Clear earnings would be £2. The Board's family scale was 24s. for the parents and 10s. for the son; a total of £1 14s. Since this was less than the father's earnings, the son would receive nothing. Under the old scales the unemployed son would receive 17s. a week; family income (minus 5s. stoppages) would be £3 2s. or £1 0s. 8d. a head; as opposed to 11s. 4d. a head under the new regulations.

34. *Rhondda Leader*, 12 January 1935; *Rhondda Fach Gazette*, 2 February 1935.

35. SWMF EC Minutes, 5 January 1935. George Hall and George Daggar, MP, were co-opted on to the Organisation Committee, as was E. Alan Robson of the Cardiff Trades and Labour Council.

36. *Rhondda Leader*, 26 January 1935; *Rhondda Fach Gazette*, 26 January 1935. *Western Mail*, 21 January 1935.

37. *Western Mail*, 23 January 1935, 24 January 1935.

38. *Aberdare Leader*, 26 January 1935; *Daily Worker*, 28 January 1935. Even the

youthful Welsh Nationalist Party tried to get in on the act; but since its President, Saunders Lewis, decided that the SWMF was too closely linked to 'English' unions and rejected Government help in favour of 'Welsh self-help' it is not clear what their practical proposals were. At Aberdare, Lewis said that South Wales' Utopian ideals would lead to evil consequences and moral rottenness:

> The Welsh Nationalist Party . . . offered the simple life instead of the Pentecostal Utopianism that was the curse of the country. Freedom [is] not a bounty but a responsibility, and the Welsh Nationalist Party stands for liberty, responsibility and prosperity.'

Aberdare Leader, loc. cit.; *Western Mail*, 21 January 1935.
39. *Western Mail*, 28 January 1935.
40. Griffiths, *op. cit.*, p. 43.
41. *Daily Worker*, 24 and 28 January 1935.
42. *Western Mail*, 28 January 1935; *Aberdare Leader*, 2 February 1935; *Daily Worker*, 29 January 1935.
43. In the House of Commons, W. H. Mainwaring, after promising the Minister a 'safe custody' if he would travel down to South Wales, said:

> The Minister, perhaps, can make some attempt to imagine the depth of the feeling [in Rhondda] when I tell him that . . . there is a total population of less than 140,000, and a week ago yesterday, 100,000 people demonstrated there. There was nobody in that district who was not demonstrating except those who were in hospital. Every man and woman in that area and practically every child of over sixteen demonstrated spontaneously. It was not a whipped up or organised demonstration. It was simply a rising of mass indignation against the system. I only wish to God that the same thing prevailed in London and the surrounding boroughs. If that spirit prevailed, the people would mass round this ancient institution and shake this Government to its foundations.'

See *Rhondda Leader*, 2 February 1935.
44. *Rhondda Leader, loc. cit.*; *Aberdare Leader*, 9 February 1935.
45. *Rhondda Leader*, 9 February 1935; *Western Mail*, 4 February 1935.
46. *Aberdare Leader*, 9 February 1935.
47. *Western Mail*, 1 February 1935; J. Griffiths, *op. cit.*, p. 43.
48. SWML Interview with Griff Jones, 23 November 1972, G. A. Williams, *The Merthyr Rising* (1978).
49. See Gilbert, *op. cit.*, p. 185.
50. There had been demonstrations, though not so large, elsewhere, notably in Lancashire and Yorkshire where, in Sheffield, there was a three-hour fight between police and 20,000 demonstrators. See Allen Hutt, *The Post-War History of the British Working-class* (1937).
51. *Western Mail*, 25 February 1935.
52. *South Wales Miner*, 6 February 1935.
53. *Daily Worker*, 9 February 1935; *Western Mail*, 21 February 1935.
54. *Rhondda Leader*, 2 March 1935.
55. *Western Mail*, 21 February 1935; SWMF EC Minutes, 21 February 1935.
56. *Ibid.*, 25 February 1935. *Daily Worker*, 25 February 1935.
57. *South Wales Miner*, 25 March 1935. The Pontypridd Trades and Labour Council

had agreed (by 38 votes to 22) to join the Pontypridd United Front Committee, in February. All these mergers 'from below' were to be ruled out. See the Minutes of the Pontypridd Trades and Labour Council, 18 February 1935 (in Pontypridd Public Library).

58. *South Wales Miner*, 22 May and 19 June 1935; *Rhondda Leader*, 16 March 1935; *Western Mail*, 26 March 1935.

59. *South Wales Guardian*, 1 February 1935.

60. *DW*, 26 February 1935.

61. *DW*, 4, 26 February 1935.

62. This was always sung when the local Deputy Chief Constable, Supt. Baker was in the vicinity. Interview with C. Lloyd, (Cwmtillery), 14 November 1969.

63. *SWG*, 29 March 1935.

64. *Ibid.*

65. *Ibid.*

66. E. B. McLeod, 'The Social and Economic Conditions leading to the Blaina and Abertillery Riots' (n.d.), p. 47, n 3 (copy in South Wales Miners' Library).

67. SWML Interview with Clarence Lloyd (Cwmtillery), 17 May 1974; *WM*, 8 April 1935.

68. UCS, Phil Abrahams (Nantyglo) collection, *The True Story of the Police Attack Upon the Blaina Demonstration on March 21st 1935* (cyclostyled leaflet published by the South Wales District of the CPGB, 2 April 1935).

69. *SWG*, 22 March 1935.

70. P. Abrahams, *op. cit.*, n 68.

71. C. Lloyd interview, *op. cit.*

72. P. Abrahams, *op. cit.*, n 68.

73. *Ibid.*

74. C. Lloyd, *op. cit.*

75. *DW*, 23, 29 March 1935.

76. *DW*, 4 April 1935.

77. *DW*, 9 May 1935; *WM*, 8, 10 April 1935.

78. *DW*, 12, 13, 16 July 1935.

79. *DW*, 17, 18 July 1935.

80. P. Abrahams interview, *op. cit.*

81. *DW*, 20 July 1935.

82. P. Abrahams interview. *op. cit.*

83. *DW*, 27 August, 24 September 1935.

84. See Letters to *Western Mail*, 6 and 8 April 1935, from the Rev. R. J. Barker of the Central Hall Methodist Church, Tonypandy, and T. George Thomas, then a Ward Chairman of the Rhondda LP (and later, of course, an MP for Cardiff and Secretary of State for Wales). And C. E. Gwyther, *Methodism and Syndicalism in the Rhondda Valley, 1906–26* (University of Sheffield Ph.D. 1967).

85. Premier's Papers 1/182. PRO. And see T. Alban Davies, 'Impressions of Life in the Rhondda Valley' in *Rhondda Past and Future* (1975), pp. 16–17.

86. *DW*, 6 April 1934.

87. *WM*, 6 June 1934.

88. See above, Ch. 3 *passim*, and pp. 260–7; and below, pp. 283–4.

89. *DW*, 22 April 1935, quoted by H. Pelling, *op. cit.*, p. 84.

90. James Griffiths, *Pages from Memory* (London 1969), p. 199.

91. Idris Cox, *The People can Save South Wales* (London 1936) pam. This was a 'best seller' and was reissued in a slightly amended form by the South Wales District, *A Programme of Life Health and Work for South Wales* (Cardiff, 1937), pam.

92. *Rhondda Leader*, 5 October 1935; W. J. Griffith, interview, *op. cit.*

93. *Party Life*, June 1935, *DW*, 3 April 1935.

94. *WM*, 28 February, 26 March, 9 October, 21 October, 22 October 1935.

95. *DW*, 3 April 1935.

96. For a discussion of this strategy, see Will Paynter, 'The United Front in South Wales', *Labour Monthly*, April 1935.

97. Edgar Evans, interview, *op. cit.*, 9 July 1975. It was only in South Wales that the Communist Party's United Front strategy received significant mass support (H. Pelling, *op. cit.*, p. 84), although demonstrations did occur in Glasgow, Maryport, Sheffield and elsewhere (C. L. Mowat, *Britain between the Wars 1918–1940* (London 1966) p. 472. By 1937 the Communist Party was claiming that direct or tacit agreements with the Labour Party had been made in local government elections. Its eight county council candidates averaged 944 votes, contrasting with the total failure to adopt any candidates in London. Idris Cox, 'South Wales Shows the Way', *Discussion*, No. 14, April 1937.

98. A. L. Horner, 'Problems of Trade Unionism in 1936', *Labour Monthly*, May 1936.

99. *Rhondda Leader*, 18 and 25 July, 1 August 1936; SWMF EC Minutes 11 July 1936; *Western Mail*, 13 and 15 July 1936.

100. *Western Mail*, 27 July 1936. *Daily Worker*, 27 July 1936.

101. *DW*, 27 July 1936.

102. South Wales and Monmouthshire Joint Council, *The Plea of the Workless* (Cardiff, 1936), pam. p. 8.

103. *DW*, 25 October 1936.

104. *Rhondda Leader*, 12 September 1936.

105. *Rhondda Leader*, 31 October 1936.

106. UCS, Claude Stanfield (Troedyrhiw) collection, *Diary of 1936 Hunger March* by W. E. Rowlands, Troedyrhiw.

107. UCS, Eddie Jones (Cwmbran), collection, *Report and Diary of March to London* (1936).

108. Claude Stanfield, *op. cit.*

109. *Ibid.*

110. *Daily Worker*, 25 October 1936.

111. *Ibid.*, 22 January 1937; 28 January 1937.

112. SWMF EC Minutes, 22 February 1937; 13 April, 11 May, 1 June, 7 June, 28 June, 4 August, 2 November, 18 and 20 November. The Council was established in August 1937. See *Daily Worker*, 13 August 1937.

113. *Rhondda Leader*, 6 November 1937, 4 December 1937. Lewis Jones was bound over for twelve months for allegedly threatening to use force if a local UAB office did not increase its rates.

114. Quoted in Gilbert, *op. cit.*, p. 188. He comments:

> The new attitude towards the unemployed was one of accommodation. . . . Officials were now willing to make enquiries about adequate bedding and

cooking facilities and to make substantial lump sum payments above regular maintenance for exceptional needs. Relieving officer discretion, the absence of which had been so much a part of the previous trouble, was now used to the fullest. The practice of substantial exceptional payments for unusual family situations – and nearly every family situation was exceptional – which had become common for obvious reasons during the political turmoil of the standstill, continued even though theoretically these were at an end with the introduction of the new regulations.' Pp. 188–9.

115. Gwyn Thomas, *A Welsh Eye* (1964), p. 18, p. 24.
116. First Annual Report of the EC, 1934–5.
117. *The Miners' Monthly*, April and May 1935.
118. *Second Industrial Survey of South Wales* (1937), Vol. I, pp. 63–8.
119. SWML, interviews with Archie James (Secretary of the Cory Combine, 1931–8) and Will Paynter, *op. cit.* No minutes of any large Combines, apart from that of the Anthracite, have been found.
120. *Western Mail*, 22 July 1935; Letters to Archie James (Cory Combine Secretary) and Alf Davies (Ocean Combine Secretary) from Oliver Harris, July 1935; and letter from James to Harris, 26 August, and reply, 13 September 1935.
121. *Western Mail*, 30 September 1935.
122. *Ibid.*, 1, 2 and 3 October 1935.
123. Anthony-Jones, *op. cit.*, pp. 64–5.
124. *Western Mail*, 4, 5, 8 and 7 October 1935; *Daily Worker*, 2, 3, and 10 October 1935.
125. Griffiths, *op. cit.*, pp. 36–7.
126. See above, pp. 129–33.
127. *South Wales Argus*, 12 and 14 October 1935; *Western Mail*, 14 October 1935; *Daily Worker*, 14 and 19 October 1935.
128. Interviews with John Moon (last chairman of the Lodge) and Len Evans (a 'stay-in' striker) on 20 November 1971.
129. Griffiths, *op. cit.*, p. 37; *South Wales Argus*, 14 October 1935.
130. This happened in February 1922 when the manager who had, on the orders of the United National Company, laid off sixty-five men was dragged from his office by 800 others and marched to the Institute where, after a long harangue, he was made to sign a document to the effect that 'all previous customs at this colliery' were to prevail in future. The men issued a manifesto attacking the management for trying to end their customs during an economic crisis. Fifteen men were arraigned; three had six months, four had three months, two were bound over, and six found not guilty of charges of riotous assembly, assault and intimidation. Harold Finch, *Memoirs of a Bedwellty MP* (1972), pp. 78–9.
131. Nine Mile Point Lodge Minutes, 9 and 10 December 1928.
132. Griffiths, *op. cit.*, p. 37; Finch, *op. cit.*, p. 81.
133. *Merthyr Express*, 19 October 1935; see also Horner, *op. cit.*, p. 133, and Griffiths, *op. cit.*, p. 37, where the 'stay-down' miners are described as Rumanian.
134. *Workers' Life*, 1 August 1929.
135. *South Wales Evening Post*, 27 October 1934. There is a cryptic note in *The Call*, 27 March 1919, entitled 'South Wales Straws' by 'W.M.' (presumably W. H. Mainwaring) which says:

> Strikes are booming. Two teachers' strikes, one in Pembroke, the other in

Rhondda . . . and a stay-in strike at one of the Rhondda valley pits. This last is surely a move in the right direction. We have been unable to find any further reference to this strike which was, it seems, part of the unofficial rash that followed in the wake of the men's discontent with the MFGB's acceptance of the Sankey Report. See *South Wales News*, 24, 25, 26, 27, 28, 29 March 1919. In late 1923, the men employed by the Cambrian Combine in mid-Rhondda were in dispute with management over the dismissal of some men and the withdrawal of customary rights, including the application of a seniority rule that the men determined to enforce. They decided to adopt 'a policy known locally as the "stay-in strike", namely refusal to work overtime and refusal on the part of each miner to do any work outside his own particular grade. This policy was calculated to have a serious effect on output.' *Western Mail*, 3 December 1923; *South Wales Daily News*, 17 December 1923. This is clearly an echo of 1920 and of *The Miners' Next Step* whereas the great strikes of the mid-1930s are quite distinctive as 'stay-downs', though also known at the time as 'stay-ins'.

136. Lewis Jones, *We Live* (1939), p. 256. Lewis Jones (1897–1939) was educated at the Central Labour College, joined the CP in 1923 and was victimised in 1929 when a Cambrian lodge checkweigher. He became the foremost leader of the unemployed in South Wales. See David Smith, *Leaders and Led, loc. cit.*, pp. 55–6.

137. *Western Mail*, 14 October 1935.

138. *Ibid.*, 15 October 1935; Horner, *op. cit.*, p. 134.

139. Mavis Llewellyn interview, *op. cit.*

140. *Ibid.*

141. *WM*, 15 and 16 October 1935; *South Wales Argus*, 16 October 1935. A 'blackleg' train from Merthyr to the colliery did not run when the driver refused the forty-minute journey because of this incident. However, not all police duty was unpleasant. 'The police at the pit head had the unusual experience during the night of listening to the singing of the strikers in the depths of the pit. The solo passages were sung by a miner with a fine tenor voice, and the rest of the men joined in the choruses. "Cwm Rhondda" was sung over and over again, and "Hold the Fort" was another favourite.'

142. *Ibid.*, 16 October 1935 (authors' italics).

143. *Ibid.*, 17 October 1935; *South Wales Argus*, 17 October 1935.

144. Minute book of the Dowlais Unemployed Lodge, 30 September 1935. S. O. Davies papers, Glamorgan County Record Office.

145. *Merthyr Express*, 19 October 1935; *Western Mail*, 17 October 1935; Horner, *op. cit.*, p. 135. A police sergeant was knocked out by a stone; Trelewis Post Office was smashed when the postmaster attempted to interfere with an attack on a blackleg.

146. *Western Mail*, 22 October 1935.

147. *South Wales Argus*, 19 October 1935. A crowd of 200–300 had greeted the EC men when they arrived at 7 a.m. for their meeting.

148. Griffiths, *op. cit.*, p. 38. The numbers underground decreased as men ascended for family or health reasons; youths under twenty-one had been sent up a couple of days before. The men had been refused chewing-gum, tobacco and newspapers after the first few days, and then received food only.

149. Letter from Lord Davies to Oliver Harris, 11 October 1935; reprinted in SWMF EC minutes, 12 October 1935.
150. SWMF Annual Report 1934–5.
151. *Rhondda Leader*, 23 October 1927; *Workers' Life*, 15 April 1927.
152. *Western Mail*, 4 February and 4 April 1931. The decision had been that they were checkweighers within the meaning of the Coal Mines Regulation Act of 1887.
153. Letter from the Rhondda No. 1 District to the SWMF EC Minutes, 3 December 1932.
154. SWMF EC Minutes, 3, 10 and 24 December 1932.
155. *Rhondda Leader*, 7 and 21 January 1933. An indication of the difficulties facing the SWMF is perhaps the apology in the local paper to the MIU 'for the inconvenience and annoyance caused' by publication of the *report* of Thomas's remarks.
156. SWMF EC Minutes, 6 November 1933.
157. A leaflet entitled 'A Brief History of the Trouble at the [Ocean Company] Dare Pit', by W. H. May (miners' agent). No date, but the internal evidence suggests August 1934.
158. *Western Mail*, 14 August 1934; *Rhondda Leader*, 18 August 1934.
159. Letter from John Griffiths, the General Manager, in *Western Mail*, 15 August 1934.
160. *Rhondda Leader*, 18 August 1934.
161. *Ibid.*, 25 August 1934; *Western Mail*, 20 and 27 August 1934.
162. Leaflet by W. H. May, *loc. cit.*
163. Iorrie Thomas was physically ejected from the premises of the Dare Colliery and arraigned for trespass. Iorwerth Thomas MSS.
164. *Rhondda Leader*, 19 October 1935.
165. Horner, *op. cit.*, pp. 137–8.
166. Interview with Will Whitehead (then a local militant), later South Wales Area President, 9 August 1972. He relates how messages were sent below by wrapping them in lead weights put into pop bottles from lodge committee men to those 'leading' underground.
167. Interview with Mrs Anne Thomas (wife of Iorwerth Thomas) who points out that men wishing to leave the 'non-pols' were encouraged to remain. One man was deputed to become an active committee member; so well did he play his role that his wife left him. (Interview with W. Whitehead.)
168. *Western Mail*, October 1935; Rhondda Leader, 26 October 1935. When the management threatened to cut off food supplies to the men they were warned that 'the women of the village' would 'attack the pithead'. Horner, *loc. cit.*
169. *Western Mail*, 21 and 24 October 1935; *Rhondda Leader*, 26 October 1935.
170. *Western Mail*, 21 and 22 October 1935.
171. *We Live* (1939), p. 301.
172. *Western Mail*, 26 and 27 November 1935; Edwards, Vol. II, *op. cit.*, pp. 204 and 212; interview with Edgar Evans, 1 April 1969, who recalls that the proposal to 'stay-down' was made by Rhys 'Trotsky' Davies at a lodge committee meeting; when the men came up their mufflers were covered by an inch thick layer of dust.
173. Edwards, *loc. cit.*, p. 216. He also pointed out that on 14 December the MIU gave a banquet in Cardiff attended by colliery owners and officials. See also, *Western Mail*, 17 December 1935.

174. Edwards, *loc. cit.*, p. 212.

175. SWMF EC Minutes, 10 December 1935.

176. *Miners' Monthly*, February 1936. He had made a similar point in June 1935 (*Miners' Monthly*) when he wrote that 'strikes or lock-outs are very poor weapons for settlement of disputes'. On that occasion the *South Wales Miner* had replied in a tone that was muted by 1936: 'Oliver seems to think that strikes or lock-outs are due to "unreasonableness" on the part of the men or owners. The conflict between wages and profits, we would assure our naïve general secretary is as old as capitalism itself and will be solved only when profit is eliminated as the motive for production. Wages versus profits, propertyless versus private ownership, represents a conflict no arbitrator can placate.'

177. *Western Mail*, 10 December 1935.

178. *Ibid.*, 28 March 1936.

179. *Ibid.*, 9 October 1933; Aneurin Bevan *In Place of Fear* (1952), p. 5.

180. *Ibid.*, 30 March, 1 April 1936.

181. SWMF EC Minutes, 31 March 1936.

182. *Western Mail*, 28 July and 8 December 1936.

183. Edwards, *loc. cit.*, p. 211.

184. For a working miner's feelings about this see B. L. Coombes, *These Poor Hands* (1939) and *Those Clouded Hills* (1944); there are comments on these developments, from different angles, in Lewis Jones' *Cwmardy* (1937) and Richard Llewellyn's *How Green was My Valley* (1939). And for an attempt to penetrate the smokescreen of their unstated assumptions consult David Smith, 'Underground Man: the Work of B. L. Coombes, "miner writer"', *Anglo-Welsh Review* (Winter 1974) and 'Myth and Meaning in the Literature of the South Wales Coalfield: the 1930s', *Anglo-Welsh Review* (Spring 1976).

185. For an extended discussion see David Smith, *Leaders and Led, loc. cit.*

186. *Rhondda Leader*, 26 October 1935; Horner, *op. cit.*, p. 138; invitation card issued by the Blaengarw Ocean Lodge. SWMF files. Nine Mile Point Lodge Minutes, 4 May and 15 June 1937 – a cold spread, a concert, and a drink were provided out of the remnants of the 'stay-in strike fund'.

187. *Miners' Monthly*, December 1935.

188. *Miners' Monthly*, April 1936. Arguably there was a symbolic portent in December 1935 when a fourteen-man Welsh Rugby team scored a one-point, last-minute victory over the All Blacks at Cardiff Arms Park.

CHAPTER NINE

The Ishmaelites of South Wales

On a wider front, 1935 had some significance in that it saw the MFGB attempt to break down district isolation once more in their campaign for a national 2s. a day increase.[1] In early 1936 the miners accepted the owners' offer of a slight increase that benefited the lower-paid men rather more, and brought the average day-wage over 8s. a shift for the first time, in South Wales, since 1930.[2] There was, as yet, no hope that the MFGB would be able to exert any decisive influence over wages despite the slight improvement in trade conditions, but 1935 had been full of positive signs of future change. Arthur Horner told a meeting in Bedlinog that not 'since 1925 has there been such a spirit prevailing. The historical role of the miners of this country is to lead the workers of this country. The miners have always led the workers and now we reclaim that right.'[3]

In South Wales itself the political domination of the SWMF had, by 1936, become the subject of some discussion and not merely amongst their traditional opponents. Wherever the Parliamentary seats of South Wales had come to be regarded as 'mining seats' the Federation were staunch in the defence of their candidates, rapping the knuckles of those SWMF lodges and officials – for example those who supported the CP in Rhondda East – on the grounds that 'the action of these people' was 'calculated to destroy the unity and solidarity of the Federation in industrial as well as political matters' because they were 'disloyal to the decision of the Federation'.[4] The identification of local government with Labour politics, invariably linked to or backed by the SWMF, extended throughout the coalfield and on into Parliamentary representation, so that in the 1935 Election out of thirteen Labour-held seats in the coalfield itself, ten were represented by men who had been prominent in the SWMF. This was the result, not just of the physical majority of miners and their families, but also of the spread of Federation activity. It had come to be seen as synonomous with *all* institutions in the community:

The Miners' Federation Lodges were pillars of the communities because the Miners' Institutes and Welfare Halls provided places for the social and cultural activity, and their domination of the local Labour Parties decisively influenced local politics. It is not surprising, therefore, that this kind of background produces a loyalty to the Union so strong and primary that the Union is regarded as a substitute for a political organisation.[5]

Paradoxically, as the Depression had strengthened its grip on the coalfield so the SWMF came to increase its domination of Parliamentary politics. George Hall had won Aberdare in 1922, as a miners' candidate, against the volatile C. B. Stanton; Merthyr itself had gone to R. C. Wallhead, the ILP successor to that ILP Scot, Keir Hardie. However, when the ILP left the Labour Party in August 1932, their hold on the seat weakened. Within a year Wallhead had resigned the ILP and rejoined the Labour Party, causing bitterness in the local branch. When he died almost a year later, the ILP claimed Merthyr as their own constituency – Campbell Stephen was nominated by them, as was Wal Hannington for the CP, before the local Trades and Labour Council had made a move. The delay was the fruit of dissension – 'It is an open secret that there is keen rivalry behind the scenes between the miners and their co-operators. The latter are disposed to go outside South Wales in search of a candidate. They hold that the miners have already more seats in Parliament than their actual strength in the country entitles them to. Merthyr . . . is not a miners' seat.'[6]

Nevertheless, S. O. Davies who had recently won a seat on the local council (though his new job as organiser for the SWMF would sever his direct links with Dowlais) was nominated by a narrow majority and proceeded, of course, to win the seat and hold it continuously until his death in 1972. The ILP candidate was beaten into third place behind the Liberal over whom S. O. Davies had an 8,629 majority. Although subsequent jibes at the number of seats held by the miners can, in part, be seen as stemming from a polemical purpose of divisive intent, there was a genuine resentment amongst other trades who had legitimate claims.[7] The trend continued in 1935 when Pontypool was won by the SWMF Vice-President, Arthur Jenkins, despite the appeal of Tinplatemen who had previously been represented by Tom Griffiths, and then, in 1936, on the death of Dr J. H. Williams who had held Llanelli for Labour since 1922, the SWMF again put forward a 'favourite son', their locally-born president, Jim Griffiths. Once more there was disgruntlement at a miners' candidate, although the redistribution of the constituency did mean that, with the Amman and Gwendraeth Valleys attached to the town, over half the population was of mining stock. Jim Griffiths defeated the other nominees but took pains to point out that his elder brother and two sisters had both worked in the Tinplate Mills. Oliver Harris was adamant that the SWMF were only interested in claiming the right to nominate a candidate and would then accept the local Labour Party decision – both Arthur Jenkins and Jim Griffiths were accepted by these bodies before they came under the Federation's political scheme for MPs.[8] This was the high-water mark of the miners' political control of Parliamentary representaticn in the coalfield.[9]

The by-election in Llanelli was the most portentous of all those fought in the inter-war years. The press mounted an almost hysterical campaign against Jim Griffiths' victory not because they resented another mining MP so much as they feared what his departure as SWMF President would entail. The CP, locally and from a wider area, supported Griffiths fervently and put up no alternative candidate. In all this was detected a Communist plot since, if Jim Griffiths were 'elected . . . the heir presumptive to the Presidency of the SWMF [would be] none other than the chief Communist agitator of the South Wales coalfield'.[10] No plot, of course, could have induced Jim Griffiths to stand for Parliament; the truth was, however, that Horner would now be placed in a most favourable situation to become the first Communist to win one of the leading SWMF offices. In turn, the reasons for this were not Machiavellian but rather a coincidence of fortunate timing and Horner's own personality. The full-blooded United Front policy that the CP had sustained in the coalfield was akin to Horner's firmest political and industrial beliefs, so there was no danger of his being cut off from any political base within the CP, whilst, at the same time, he could make the widest possible appeal to the 'left' Labour Party. He was backed by the most prosperous area of the Federation (the Anthracite) which had put Jim Griffiths into both his previous offices so that any 'electoral' weight within the SWMF was also his. Horner's past reputation, from 1920 on, was unmatched and his stock remained high in his old stamping-ground in the steam-coalfield; his abilities as a negotiator and as an orator had been revealed again, since he had become agent in the Anthracite in late 1933, at Emlyn and at Taff-Merthyr collieries, whilst his experience at national level surpassed that of any other SWMF official still active. Finally, he was very popular because so likeable as an individual. The biggest single industrial triumph of the CP 'united front' policy was, in retrospect, a foregone conclusion.

The only major stumbling-block was the willingness of both Griffiths and Jenkins to remain in office, if requested to do so by the Annual Conference. The EC themselves recommended that the offices could not adequately be filled by MPs and that if the Annual Conference accepted this view that the elections should take place at a subsequent conference. The conference did so decide, meeting again, after the lodges had been mandated, within a month.[11] 235 delegates represented 110,000 members; there were five candidates for president and Horner won at the first ballot with 155 votes over the 43 of his nearest rival, W. J. Saddler of Newbridge, who was subsequently elected vice-president over Alf Davies.[12] The position of president was not, of course, a fulltime one, but power within the SWMF flowed not merely from an office but also from the strength of an individual incumbent; Oliver Harris, moderate and a sound administrator, was not the strong personality Tom Richards had been, and since his election, in 1934, Jim Griffiths had made a considerable impact upon Federation affairs. Horner was to continue the tradition of making the presidency the decisive office within the SWMF.[13]

He came to the office fully tempered by the vicissitudes of a rather stormy career, sure of his members' needs, a leader solidly rooted in 'the led':

> By the time I was elected to the Presidency, I had pretty well formulated my philosophy as a trade union leader. It had grown out of my experience in the struggle . . . and my period of meditation . . . in Cardiff jail. The function of a Trade Union is to sell a commodity. The function of the employer is to buy that commodity.
>
> . . . you have to seek to place the buyer in the position where he cannot buy from anybody except you. This of course is the basis for the drive for 100 per cent Trade Unionism. . . .
>
> It was my conviction that this was the fundamental basis of Trade Union struggle which caused me to put such emphasis in the struggle against the breakaway organisations in South Wales. . . .
>
> The Owners realised that 100 per cent organisation was *our* strength, and that was why they poured out money and gave every support to the attempt to keep the breakaway Unions going. The next stage after securing 100 per cent organisation of the Miners was to work for a national leadership and national negotiations. . . .
>
> This was my philosophy, and these were my basic objectives as I took up any new post. But I also outlined our immediate tasks in the first message

... sent out to the members after [the] election. .... We stressed the importance of every unemployed miner as well as those in work joining the Union and the need to establish 'the broadest united front embracing all the sufferers from capitalist depression'.

We set as our goal the carrying on of the fight against Company Unionism until the last semblance of 'this devilish coalowners' instrument has been swept away. ....

... The most difficult situation was at Bedwas ... where the Company Union was still ... in control.[14]

The campaign planned since 1935 against the Bedwas Colliery had been put into operation even before his election. The attack was on two fronts — first, informal approaches to the Company and, simultaneously, attempts at local organisation.[15] Bedwas was the last colliery controlled by the SWMIU that had ever been fully in Federation hands; its recapture was thus a matter of some importance for the prestige of the SWMF. More than this, it would symbolise the end of a long period of rot because Bedwas, at one time a very strong lodge, was a particular and heightened example, of the industrial and social decline within the coalfield since the mid-1920s. The story of the struggle against company unionism, in Bedwas, is, as it was in Taff-Merthyr, inseparable from the development and organisation of the pit, the village and the lodge.

The two pits at Bedwas had been sunk in 1911 and 1913, high enough to escape the water of the Rhymney River, but, at the edge of the rising strata of coal. This made the gradient very steep and hence caused difficult conditions. By 1918 Bedwas had attracted workers from the Upper Monmouthsire Valleys where trade union traditions were long-established. The villages of Trethomas and Bedwas grew around the colliery, more than doubling in population between 1881 and 1911. There had been two small local pits working in the 1880s but with the sinking of the new pits by the Navigation Steam Coal Company Limited the social character of the District was completely changed. A predominantly rural area, with its two annual fairs and attendant services, and a predominantly farming community emerges as a miniature cameo of the coalfield's chameleon society. In 1912 an Urban District Council of 12 members was formed (there were now chapels for English and Welsh Baptists, Congregationalists and Wesleyans), and by 1914 there was a workmen's institute and library, three banks, a public elementary school (founded in 1903), a cinema called with the aptness attached to novelty *The Cinema*, and the inevitable Bracchi Brothers. By 1921 the colliery company was reconstituted as a subsidiary of S. Instone Limited, Shipping Agents (based in Newport), as the Bedwas Navigation Colliery Company (1921) Limited. Instone proved a benevolent employer, contributing generously to the Workmen's Hall, and establishing a modern by-product plant connected with the colliery. All seemed set fair for the future.[16]

However, another portent of the future lay in the fact that the plant, owned by another company but also under Instone's control, made non-unionism a condition of employment. At the same time the general depression in coal prices after 1920, coupled with Bedwas' geological difficulties, led the company into a financial crisis. Instone loaned money to the colliery company from the parent concern (£300,000 at 6 per cent interest), and Barclays Bank contributed £1,000,000. The interest payments on this overdraft led, in 1928, to the appointment of H. Stuart Martin, representative of the Bank, as an 'adviser', or consulting engineer, to the management. The price-lists and the old customs that had been in operation under the old company were regarded as the biggest obstacles in the path of financial solvency but the management found themselves confronting a well-organised and very determined lodge committee.[17] The latter was headed by its Secretary, W. J. (Billy) Milsom, a fearless, uncompromising character who had been responsible for many of the good customs and conditions in the past, and was now to prove an obdurate opponent for both management and the SWMF officials.[18] At the same time, there was an active Minority Movement headed by W. J. (Billy) Nind and Garfield Williams who produced a pit paper, *The Bedwas Rebel*, which attacked the old Lodge Committee whenever they detected signs of conciliation. Generally, though, the men supported Milsom to the extent, on one occasion, of sacking the majority (ten) of a Committee who supported a Communist Party denunciation of Milsom's negotiations with the Company.[19] Certainly this was an active and confident lodge capable of demanding that the management notify them before signing on men, of insisting on the provision of pit-top lavatories, of threatening strike action if officials were not civil to the men, and of maintaining near 100 per cent membership down to the late 1920s. Milsom in his frock-coat, winged-collar and spats, as their full-time secretary, was a living embodiment of Bedwas' Lodge's independence and pride when he met the Instone Brothers in London. He was the representative of a Lodge which, when asked to accept a 10 per cent reduction in price-list, refused point-blank, accused management of gross inefficiency and persuaded the company to meet a deputation every other Wednesday to receive the men's complaints about lack of materials for the job and their suggestions as to how to work the colliery more efficiently.[20] By 1927 Bedwas was out of step with the rest of the steam-coalfield in that it was still insisting on maintaining old customs and price-lists whilst collieries closed all around them; their rebelliousness was part of a developed 'pit-consciousness' that could, they felt, stand on its own, as two men involved with the colliery recalled.[21]

> Bedwas was a unique colliery . . . it was owned by the Instones' and they were not the old bear of coalowners that we had in South Wales. . . . Now Bedwas was a colliery that was isolated from the coalfield, it was not a part of the coalfield. The owners themselves made it that, they gave conditions to the men that were different from what obtained in the rest of the coalfield. Bedwas men became a law unto themselves, they behaved vastly different from the rest of the men in the Rhymney Valley, and in the steam-coalfield generally. . . . It was like an oasis in a desert.
>   . . . you wouldn't hear anybody talking about the Fed. down there, it was our Lodge, it was us you know . . . we were the union, not some amorphous bloody body.

Despite their attitude of defiance, in 1928 the lodge had to accept a threepence a ton reduction in the price list; a single shift system on the basis of seniority of service was introduced with the employed paying 2d. in the £ to unemployed members. Contrary to this agreement, management then introduced double-shifts in certain pit districts and then, in late 1928, demanded a system of payment by yardage instead of tonnage. The men were not willing to accept this since it meant wage cuts of between 20 and 30 per cent; with no terms offered, the colliery closed. The Board of Guardians relieved married men with families of four or more children, but dole was refused on the grounds that the colliery was 'open' for work.[22]

After almost two months of being out, the men returned with slightly better terms (though still on a yardage basis), and having lost the company's agreement to adopt the lodge's 'seniority list'. For the next few months the lodge was busy re-establishing Federation membership amongst the 2,500 men at work. By June 2,258 were in the Federation again, but Milsom had to be granted a month's holiday to recover from a 'breakdown' whilst the Company was applying for injunctions against the holding of 'Show Cards' and the prevention of non-unionists from working. An arrangement was reached whereby, in return for a production of 14,000 tons a week, the management promised 'to deal with all non-unionists so that "Show Cards" would not be necessary', adding another oddity to the Bedwas Colliery. However, the management could not withdraw their summonses, so that 'Show Cards', despite the injunctions issued, continued to be the means of organisation. By March 1930, the lodge was again, after 'Show Cards' had been held by different men, 100 per cent for the Federation.[23]

Clearly management was only making limited progress in 'disciplining' the lodge who continued to oppose successfully any attempts to sign on men who had not been previously employed at the colliery.[24] In desperation the management served notice on the men, in November, applying for a complete alteration in existing working arrangements and when this was refused, 2,700 men were locked-out from 18 November 1930. They stayed out through the coalfield strike of January 1931 and, despite some intermittent negotiations from December 1930, did not return until 6 July 1931, when the company agreed that the men should return to the working places they had occupied before the stoppage. Within three days the 500 men who had been re-employed struck once more, until 20 July, alleging the company were not, in fact, operating the seniority rule. A further agreement was drawn up and the men returned again at the request of the EC who promised to invoke Conciliation Board procedure in any dispute that might arise.[25]

The management, represented in the pit by Messrs Cornick and Colley as manager and agent, and at board level by Mr Stuart Martin had, it seems, decided on a policy of direct confrontation, for throughout 1932 the EC was deluged with complaints and requests from Bedwas. The local lodge officials and the new District agent (the young Ness Edwards had replaced the venerable Hubert Jenkins, who became an advisory agent, in 1932) could not obtain interviews with the management to consider disputes; the company failed to carry out their agreement to re-employ first of all those employed before November 1930; and they would not refer disputes to the Disputes Committee of the Joint Conciliation Board. Worse than this, though of the same pattern, was the inevitable employment of 'strangers' in preference to local unemployed men. A deputation attended the EC:

It was stated that the workmen were getting very restive, and were anxious to tender notices in order to enforce a settlement. The complaint of the men chiefly was that the company were engaging strangers in preference to the old workmen who were out of employment, in contravention to the arrangement [and] the company prevented the lodge secretary to attend on the colliery premises to deal with any disputes.

The EC, having no wish to let another colliery slide away, duly gave permission for fourteen days' notice but, recognising their own weakness, strove to come to a settlement by having the mines department to intervene. At last interviews were obtained and outstanding grievances settled in November. And yet, on Christmas Eve, the men were again complaining that the management had broached the agreement.[26]

Since the resumption of work in 1931 conditions at the colliery had steadily worsened. The conveyor system, introduced in the 1920s, had been troublesome in that the gradient of the coal was so steep that 'it was more like a bloody chute than a conveyor', so that men at the top end of the face were filling coal that was falling off the conveyor, and the men, at the bottom, were busy putting it back on rather than filling their own. Milsom introduced a 'pool system' so that all the men would receive a wage on the basis of the total amount of coal cut. From the late 1920s the management began to undermine this sort of control – first, they brought men in to work week-ends (not a practice the lodge approved), and instead of paying them separately paid them out of the 'pool system' (i.e. they benefited from the work left uncompleted by men on the previous shift); then, they introduced mechanical picks, and later coal cutters, taking $2d.$, and then $4d.$, a ton cut off the men's wages, i.e. making the men pay for the use of machinery that benefited management. Finally, in 1931 they began to put the work out to contract to a man who, in turn, sub-contracted – 'a company within a company', a procedure from the Nottinghamshire coalfield:

> . . . that started the ball rolling, because men objected to that. If there was to be contract, well, the men had to be the contractors, and not sub-contractors working for someone else . . . that was a thing absolutely unheard of until they brought it in. So, if a chap had a job to do, and he took it on contract, or paid by the yard, or by the ton, or whatever it was . . . then he'd make the contract with the boss, a verbal contract, and they were honoured too . . . if you made a contract with the under-manager to do a job at a certain price, you got paid, and there was no argument for it. Well now, when you were putting out these contracts, instead of the men on the job making the tender . . . this other fellow was always making a tender that was accepted. And

then the whole pit work was run on sub-contract work. That caused a lot of trouble.[27]

This was the constant backdrop to work in the pit in 1932 as the management employed boys on the screens instead of men, used chargehands to cut coal and do repairing work, instituted week-end working and brought in 'contractors'. They even requested some men to work the coal on May Day. The lodge's protests and occasional demonstrations availed as little as the EC's intervention until the final threats to strike in late 1932 appeared to have brought some redress.[28] Palpably, this was a forlorn hope, for management were set on full 'rationalisation' rather than a literal interpretation of the 1931 Resumption of Work Agreement. The lodge, all set in late 1932 to hand in 1,007 notices, had become disgruntled with the EC's failure to force the company to honour the agreement. They had finally persuaded the EC to consider legal action when the company tried its patience for the last time:

Following upon reports of the workmen of strangers being set on at the Colliery and had taken the place of Workmen who had been given notice by the Company to terminate their Contracts, it was *resolved* to call a General Meeting to decide on action after discussing all complaints, on Sunday 19 February.[29]

The company had brought in some men to work on a conveyor in place of the old workmen (55 per cent of whom were still unemployed). Now, without the authority of the EC, the men struck. Over 1,000 men came out, but the 'strangers', already sixty in number, continued work.[30] The lodge committee, in the absence of Milsom who had been ill, had been reconstituted, with the approval of a General Meeting, at exactly the same time as the 'strangers' had been employed. In addition to ten members 'who are working at the colliery' there were to be eight unemployed members having full status on the committee, able 'to consider all committee matters'. Ness Edwards was of the opinion that this new committee, with an unemployed ballast not really acceptable to the SWMF, fell into a trap and took precipitate action.[31]

Management refused any meetings at all prior to a general return to work. Affairs deteriorated rapidly. The East Glamorgan District, through the EC, gave £1,000 to the Bedwas men; within a week there were 200 new men at work in the Colliery, recruited from Merthyr and the Upper Rhymney Valley.[32]

On Monday, 6 March, the SWMF summoned a special delegate

conference to consider the position.[33] There were now almost 500 men at work who had not been previously employed at Bedwas. The EC, under pressure from the delegates, and after a brief adjournment, recommended that the lodges tender fourteen days' notice to enforce a settlement.[34] Particular resentment was felt in that the original Resumption of Work Agreement had been negotiated by the Ministry of Mines and the SWMF considered the Government should intervene. In the meantime the NUR and the Railway Clerks' Association were asked to black trains carrying men to the colliery.

The blacklegs were also organised. On 26 February the company had formally recognised the SWMIU, and the latter now swung into the attack. The Bedwas men were accused of having broken the coalfield agreement to tender fourteen days' notice before a strike, and hence they had no cause to complain if the colliery remained open. The company reiterated this and added the standard plea of the coalowners that, for the safety of the colliery, 'the discretion of the management in the employment of workmen cannot be interfered with'.

The police forces at Bedwas were increased as the next step in this formalised ritual, but, apart from minor demonstrations against blacklegs in Caerphilly and Abertridwr, all remained quiet. Certainly the Bedwas men were content, at this stage, to allow the SWMF to continue their propaganda drive, backed up by the threat of a coalfield strike.[35] On 13 March the adjourned conference met and, acting on instructions from the lodges, decided to tender notices, 'throughout the coalfield on Monday next, 20 March'.[36] Matters were not as clear-cut as they seemed. There had been 236 delegates present, representing 89,000 men. It was the lodges, however, who had voted, and there had been no ballot of the rank and file. Ordinarily this would not have mattered so much, but with so few employed, the coalfield's mood was resentful and sympathetic, rather than militant.[37] The SWMF EC was pinning its hopes on the coalowners being so desirous of avoiding a costly dispute that they would pressure the Bedwas Navigation Colliery Company into negotiations. They had some hopes of this in statements such as Sir Alfred Cope's (Amalgamted Anthracite) to the effect that 'because some colliery could not manage its affairs properly, his colliery was in jeopardy and the men were in jeopardy'. Theodore Instone, however, the Vice-Chairman of the Bedwas Company, advised Cope to acquire the facts from the South Wales Coalowners' Association. The latter body indicated to the SWMF that a conciliation board meeting would be to no point.[38]

In the Caerphilly and Rhymney Valley areas, trains and buses were vetted by the miners' leaders, as well as the usual picketing of the colliery; at Cardiff, however, an emergency meeting of the EC was not over sanguine. James Griffiths reported that with 500 men working, the position was extremely difficult, and the General Secretary, Oliver Harris, stressed the importance of persuading the men at work to refrain so that the coalfield could avoid a strike. Harris was unhappy:

> The result of a couple of years of economic pressure . . . had deprived men of the spirit to fight and they could not resist the temptation of accepting work offered them.

Towards the end of the week allotted before the handing in of notices, the EC began to move away from the strikers. On Saturday the 18th, after a day long debate in which the EC split into a minority who thought vacillation was the worse policy and a majority who considered a strike would be calamitous, notices were postponed until a further conference, and the campaign at Bedwas was to proceed.[39]

The divergence of opinion was even more marked in the locality. On the Friday a police escort for workmen had been stoned, but this was a mere prelude to the trouble that took place even as the EC were arriving at their decision. The police, reinforced after Friday's incident, were escorting a workman home when the crowd that had gathered to demonstrate began to tussle with them. As a result two women were arrested and taken half a mile away to Trethomas police station. W. J. Milsom, the Lodge Secretary, had entered the station to arrange bail when the demonstrators who had followed the police, possibly assuming he had been arrested, charged the station with sticks and stones until police dispersed them with drawn batons.[40]

Undoubtedly the riot stiffened the resolve of the local men who argued strongly that the EC should continue the struggle. By the middle of the week, however, the EC was convinced of the futility of the struggle and, after negotiations, resolved that they should instruct the Bedwas men to return to work. A furious lodge committee insisted that EC members tell the men of the decision themselves and, for this purpose, a mass meeting was held which lasted four hours, became boisterous and reached no decision. Here, indeed, was a dilemma to tax the leadership – at Bedwas the mood was fierce and unrelenting, elsewhere it was shaky; the longer the men stayed out, the more firmly did the Industrial Union dig itself in. Despite the efforts of the Bedwas Lodge to have a Conference called, after addressing meetings throughout the coalfield, the EC reaffirmed their decision.[41] In face of this, though still reluctantly, a further mass meeting at Bedwas agreed to return to work, by a majority of nineteen.[42] In retrospect the whole affair seems messy, predictable and unfortunate; Bedwas men were signing on at the Unemployment Exchange once more and the Industrial Union was established at another colliery. Oliver Harris wrote to the secretary of the SWMF Lodge at Abercrave, near Swansea, explaining why no strike had been called. He emphasised that not a third of the Federation members in the coalfield had signed the notices to terminate contracts so that it would have been to invite disaster to carry on, and then he turned to the specific situation at Bedwas:

> The Bedwas Colliery was rapidly filling up with blacklegs. The EC members did all they could by meeting these men in groups, and at their homes, to dissuade them from going to the colliery, but notwithstanding all their efforts there was a steady increase in the number of blacklegs. When the strike was called off there were nearly 700 working and if the strike was continued the colliery would have been full of blacklegs and there would have been no places left for any of the old Bedwas workmen.
>
> The Non-Pols were also active and if we did not call off the strike when we did we should have had another Taff-Merthyr and Emlyn situation at Bedwas.
>
> Unpalatable though it was I am sure your members will agree that under these circumstances the EC did the right thing.[43]

The unpalatable fact was that if a dispute arose in an individual colliery the men, even backed by their Executive, were, in the midst of mass unemployment, powerless to stop a determined company from importing labour. A saga all too familiar now played itself out – by the end of April only about 250 of the original Bedwas workmen had been reinstated, whereas more men from outside areas had been signed on whilst 'the representatives of the Industrial Union were given every facility at the colliery to recruit members, and a number of men had been dismissed for their refusal to join this union'. The Federation were now in the position of having, from scratch, to organise the men now employed into the SWMF but the SWMIU were allowed to inaugurate a full campaign to enrol the workmen, backed up by the management. Shortly all new men had to sign a card that stated:

> I, as a member of the South Wales Industrial Union, hereby authorise you [i.e. the company] to deduct 4d. a week from my wages in respect of the wages of our Miners' Examiner.

Failure to sign meant the loss of work.[44] The Bedwas men were out in the cold, and there, despite a brief flurry of SWMF activity in 1934 during the Taff-Merthyr campaign, they remained until 1936. The company had proposed to the Coalowners' Association that the MIU be recognised, instead of the Federation, in all future coalfield-wide agreements. Not even the Association would take this step, so, to avoid being constrained by any new agreement that might be reached in 1934, they withdrew from the Conciliation Board procedure.[45] Some 1,300 of those employed by mid-1933 were blackleg labour, recruited by the MIU, working with reduced wages and altered conditions:

To maintain this . . . a complete espionage system was started in the pit. Each conveyor, each heading had its spy.

Away from the pit, where the workmen lived, each village had its spy.

The comings and goings of men known to have had negotiations with the Federation were faithfully reported.

Employment could only be obtained by nomination of notorious strike-breakers and stewards and officials of Conservative Clubs. The nominations were entered in a book for further scrutiny and report by the spies. Complete slavery had been imposed where freedom previously reigned.[46]

None the less, there were gaps in the fortification erected – many of the old Bedwas men had drifted back under the pressure of unemployment and the need of management to employ men more skilled than those drawn in by the MIU, and, secondly, there was the dissension within the MIU caused by Federation successes in 1934 and 1935.[47] This had a direct effect in Bedwas where W. C. Williams, the local MIU agent, who had been replaced by one Harry West, began to issue leaflets giving 'inside' information against his former associates. The most telling part of this propaganda was that it associated colliery owners (viz. Instone and the Ocean Coal Company) with financial contributions made to the MIU in its disputes, challenging Gregory to account for various 'refunds' and the salaries paid out, and to deny having reached arrangements with the Bedwas Colliery Company to sack all men over fifty-five, since their 'insurance premiums were too heavy'. Williams and his son, the son of James Jenkins (the ex-MIU President), Edgar Miles (ex-chairman of the Bedwas MIU branch) and others had all been sacked from Bedwas, for allegedly opposing Gregory. They had demanded to see an MIU balance sheet for the time since Bedwas had been given to the MIU. W. C. Williams claimed that he had been appointed by Cowley, the colliery agent, and Gregory, just as his successor had been appointed at Stuart Martin's house. In 1936, the financial backing of the owners and the political support of the Conservative Imperial Policy Group in the Commons and the Lords, were seen in 'European' terms:

> The views of this group find expression in a weekly journal called *The Patriot*. In this anti-Jewish, pro-Nazi, and pro-Fascist paper, the strike breaking and blackleg organising work of the Non-Pols finds favourable comment and support. Here is an account of a dinner held in the Philharmonic Hotel, Cardiff, in December last, organised by Gregory to meet the Tories. It is taken from *The Patriot* of January 1936:
>
> 'With me were MPs, men of great authority in Empire work, Colliery officials, Union Leaders, G. A. Spencer, Barristers, etc. These MPs and another group of gentlemen representing a very important public body . . . guaranteed their unstinted support in our cause.'
>
> Will the workmen of Taff-Merthyr and Bedwas realise that the gang that has been imposed upon them as the Non-Pols are merely the counterpart of Mussolini and Hitler? The Jew-baiter, the gangster, the blackleg organiser, the public meeting thugs, all come out of the same bag. . . .
>
> Does Lord Davies want to subsidise the destruction of the League of Nations?
>
> Does Sir Samuel Instone want to subsidise the persecution of his race?[48]

Arthur Horner, with others, had visited Bedwas in March 1936 to review the situation. Now, in May, as president he declared:

> The fight against fascism is the fight for trade unionism . . . 100% conscious militant Trade Unionism is the most important safeguard against fascism. . . . Scab Unionism is fascism in embryo.[49]

Bedwas' symbolic role was put into the broader perspective that dictated the political colour of the coalfield down to the war; it became of a piece with the SWMF's fervent support of the Spanish Republic and opposition to Nazism. Its primary importance, for all that, lay in its defiance of the right of the SWMF to organise coalfield labour. The Bedwas campaign was the best planned and directed of all the forays against company unionism. From the first, it was the EC that took control by appointing three of its members, D. R. Davies (Ebbw Vale), Jack Davies (Llwynypia) and Dai Dan Evans (Swansea Valley) to assist W. H. Crews and Ness Edwards in the ground work. These men arranged meetings at the end of each shift and lived in the locality for weeks, adapting their tactics to the circumstances at the pit. D. D. Evans recalled these events in a graphic manner:

We were getting up in the morning at about five o'clock, and going to the pit to meet the men . . . there were two entrances to the Bedwas Colliery, the Trethomas end and the Bedwas end . . . most of the men who were coming in by bus were going to the Trethomas end, but they were coming in by train to the Bedwas end, you see . . . and the Bedwas end was much more ripe for action than the Trethomas end . . . they had to wait for the train to come . . . until the whole of the men would be there for the train . . . and you would have possibly three hundred, four hundred men on the train . . . together at the same time and you had a chance to make a sustained statement to them, [but] if you were at the Trethomas end, you only had time to make a speech . . . as long as the bus filled, and away they went . . . the buses were continually fetching them . . . so you didn't have time to make a sustained statement. . . . At the Bedwas end you could have possibly a quarter of an hour, and when you started speaking you would have 50 per cent of your audience at the time, and they would be drifting in, drifting in, drifting in until the whole of the audience was there, you see.

We were able to call public meetings but the people you would get at the public meetings would be the men that were idle there . . . we would hold meetings in Caerphilly, we would hold meetings in Llanbradach . . . all the way up the Rhymney Valley, and all the way up the Merthyr Valley. But the people that would come there would be in the main the people that were unemployed. . . .

To conduct a campaign amongst the old Bedwas men was easy, you see, but they were not part of it, they were idle, the people you were campaigning to come back into the Union now were 50 per cent scabs, who had been recruited from a ten mile radius . . . to the Bedwas Colliery. So that now you didn't have the same situation that you had in Taff-Merthyr . . . Bedlinog men were employed there but Bedlinog was a stable community . . . and a large number . . . were Federation men . . . driven to the scab union . . . because of sheer poverty. . . . Whereas, in Bedwas . . . you had the hard core of the scab union . . . that had drifted in there [wherever others] came out to fight.[50]

So at Bedwas the MIU men, in the main, had to be persuaded to leave their union. Ness Edwards, in a leaflet that poured scorn on the MIU's lack of safety regulations or care for compensation for injury, warned of strife and more strife until company unionism in the coalfield ended and asked the men to 'get back into the general movement' as a matter of pride:

Can you resist taking your part in this human endeavour to build up a condition of freedom and decency in this coalfield upon which we all depend?

Premature disruption was avoided like the plague, until by mid-July the Federation believed that over 800 of the men employed were with them. There had been 'peace' in Bedwas for three years, a state of affairs planned for by the management, and doubtless enjoyed by them. The real struggle would, once more, lie between the SWMF and the owners themselves as the latter made plain when, confronted by Federation encroachment, it chose to make an uncompromising stand, in a letter addressed to all its employees. This stood four-square behind the existing agreement with the MIU which body, it claimed, was representative of all the workmen; none other would be recognised. The sting came in the tail:

> Consequently, the Company will not accept any notice or any forms or cards presented . . . by the Miners' Federation, and any workman wishing to alter the terms of his existing agreement will be requested to present a written notice himself personally to the Company or present it through the representatives operating for him under this agreement with the Company. Any such form must of necessity be regarded as an intimation by a workman of his desire to terminate his employment at the Colliery.[51]

Since individual workman could be marked out, the tactics were to be the same as those operated in the Emlyn and Dare Collieries – men, operating underground in committees of three, contacted those who wished to leave the MIU and signed them for the 'Fed' at a reduced rate of 2d. a week. A 'shadow' leadership thus formed underground, able to hold back any spontaneous combustion amonst the men.[52]

The shoals of propaganda issued by the SWMF was most skilful in its emphasis on the importance of the issues at stake, knitting together local miseries and grievances with their wider implications. An account of them reveals the analysis of a trade union firmly convinced of its own political and industrial role.[53]

Leaflet No. 1 offers the services of the Federation to the isolated workmen of Bedwas, asks the men to listen to the propaganda 'in mass' and then to join all together. There is the same striking reference to 'manhood' as at Taff-Merthyr in 1934: 'We are sure that *Every Self-Respecting* man amongst you must *Feel The Humiliating Position* you are in by being tied to an organisation so *Foreign To All The Best Traditions* of the British workmen, and of the South Wales miners in particular.'

Leaflet No. 2 recalls the Federation's past services, but in No. 3 the SWMF make their main appeal.

South Wales Miners' Federation.

Re BEDWAS COLLIERY.

THIS or THAT

A LEAFLET WITH YOUR DOCKET.	A DOCKET WITH PROPER WAGES.
RUMOURS.	THE TRUTH.
CHAOS, SPYING, INTIMIDATION.	NORMAL DECENT RELATIONS.
DISTRUST AND SUSPICION.	TRUST AND SOLIDARITY.
COMPANY IMPOSED UNION.	UNION OF YOUR OWN CHOICE.
POT-HOUSE PRICE LISTS.	KNOWN AND NEGOTIATED LISTS.
SPECIAL TREATMENT FOR SPIES.	EQUAL TREATMENT FOR ALL.
COMPANY BELIEVES THAT 100% ARE BEHIND THEIR AGREEMENT.	FEDERATION KNOWS THAT MAJORITY HAVE NEVER SEEN THE AGREEMENT.
"I CANNOT DO ANYTHING."	AN ORGANISATION TO PROTECT YOU.
SHADES OF THE BARRACKS.	A COALFIELD CONFERENCE.

Show your choice by signing your Revocation Card.

Vote for the help of 100,000 workmen to assist you in smashing this Slavery.

BE READY FOR THE CONFERENCE DECISION.

THE BEDWAS PIT COMMITTEE (Pro Tem).

A Bedwas leaflet, 1936.

This leaflet demands the right of choice and asks the men to follow the Fed's lead. It sets out, in eight points, the EC's *Charter for Bedwas*, as follows:

1. The right to belong to the Miners' Federation.
2. The cancellation of the Pit Agreement which compels you to be members of a company union.
3. To establish freedom for normal trade union activities.
4. To give the workmen full control over their trade union contributions.
5. To give the workmen the right to appoint their own representatives without interference from the colliery company.
6. To abolish intimidation of the workmen by the colliery management.
7. To establish the Federation Lodge to give the workmen adequate protection regarding compensation, wages, price lists and employment.
8. To abolish the twenty-four hour contract and replace it with a normal fourteen days' contract.

These demands were to be the basis of subsequent negotiations. The Federation, in its next leaflet, showed its belief in the wider implications of the fight; opposition to fascism and the corporate state were tied to the Bedwas dispute. In this leaflet the company was likened to the Nazi state, the 'blackleg barracks' (sheds that could house 600 men had been erected on the pit-top) to concentration camps and the persecution of Welshmen to that of Jews. Underneath, two juxtaposed tables comparing conditions 'In Germany Now', and 'In Bedwas Now', the Executive issued a double warning:

> *The Patriot*, the political organ of a die-hard group of Tories, regards both 'Fascism' and the 'Non-Pols' with equal favour. It regards 'World Jewry' and the Miners' Federation with equal hatred.
>
> Do the owners of the Bedwas Colliery realise that they are nourishing a viper that will bite the hand that feeds it? [Instone was a Jew].
>
> Do you workmen of Bedwas realise that you are being compelled to support the industrial counterpart of Hitler and Mussolini?'[54]

Requests for the men to sign their revocation-cards (postage paid) so that the Federation could be assured of a majority were pressed home as the men were urged to throw off intimidation.

This is Britain – Not a Mad House (Leaflet No. 20).[55]

The SWMIU was attacked both for its role as a company tool, and for its failure to safeguard the interests of its membership (Leaflet Nos. 28 and 29 provided details of medical cases ignored, and of paltry expenditure on pit examinations). Although most of the leaflets were signed by the EC, some of them came out under the name of the Bedwas Pit Committee (*pro tem*):

> At the Meeting at the Caerphilly Workmen's Hall on Sunday you were shown the 'Bible' of the Company Union gang. What did you think of it?
> Detailed accounts of your activities outside of the Pit were contained in it. Even present 'spies' of the Company Union were reported by the older 'hands'. Some of you even were reported for dismissal by your present allies (Leaflet No. 38).

It was with confidence that this committee could declare in late July, 'The day is fast approaching when we will come to you with our policy' (Leaflet No. 42). And so the company's letter to its workforce escalated the campaign further since the Federation was given no choice but to retreat, whilst it had every indication that its campaign from May to July had been most successful.

Both the Bedwas Pit Committee and the Executive Council issued leaflets denouncing the veiled threats of victimisation contained in the company's circular to the men. Interestingly, they stressed their desire to avoid a harsh confrontation:

> We want no dislocation. We are capable of carrying out 'Agreements' but we must make those Agreements ourselves. We are still ready to peaceably make the transfer from Slavery into Freedom. If the Company forces a fight we shall fight back, in our way and in our time (No. 38 from the Pit Committee).

Whilst the Executive Council had decided to call a conference for 12 August to recommend to delegates the need for action in support of Bedwas, they continued to stress that they preferred to work within the terms of the Conciliation Board Agreement (Leaflet No. 48). Bearing in mind the abortive strike action in 1933, the EC was patently anxious to maintain synchronisation between local and coalfield-wide action. On the one side they assured the Bedwas men 'You Will Not Fight Alone', adding:

> Your fight for freedom must be timed to begin when the forces of the Coalfield have been prepared to take simultaneous action.
> We must keep in step with the Coalfield. . . . With discretion and courage resolve to play the part of men' (Leaflet No. 45).

And, at the same time, they had to be certain that the men in Bedwas were prepared – 'As an indication that you want to play the part of men, sign the Revocation Cards.'

Let the men of the Coalfield know that Bedwas is ready (No. 48).

This became the crucial area of attack in the two weeks leading up to the Conference. 'Revocation cards' were posted to those at work in the colliery asking them to revoke their written consent to allow deductions from their wages for the SWMIU, its group life insurance scheme and other funds (the men were asked to put their signature, address, lamp number, occupation and the date as well as having it witnessed). Business-reply envelopes and a letter from the Pit Committee accompanied the cards:

> We are anxious that our majority shall be overwhelming. We want to tell the Conference of the SWMF ... that practically all our men at Bedwas Colliery have signed. If we want the coalfield to help us we must show our readiness to do our part. We must not let the coalfield down.[56]

The EC, with about 1,000 of the 1,600 men now employed, having signed cards prepared to recommend the coalfield to give notices,[57] and it was decided, by the 250 delegates, to issue notices on 24 August (to expire on 5 September) if any of the men who had signed the cards were dismissed when the Federation presented them to the company. The cards themselves would be given in at the most favourable opportunity. In the meantime the EC wished to continue its attempts at negotiation, although, so long as the Bedwas Company remained outside the Coalowners' Association, it was not easy to bring them to the table.[58]

Failing this, the campaign had to continue as before – a mixture of local attacks on particular grievances to show the SWMIU as an incompetent manager of their members' affairs,[59] an insistence that Bedwas be ready for action by 24 August (Leaflet No. 52), and wider appeals to justice as in the Pit Committee's direct challenge to the company, headed 'An Open Letter to the Bedwas Colliery Company'. This was published in the press, and the effect was to provoke Sir Samuel Instone to reply himself. Over the week 16–23 August, the protagonists in the case all threw their argument into the public arena for debate.

The Open Letter demanded, as in previous propaganda, the 'elementary' right to belong to a trade union but distinguished itself by personifying the issues in individual, and indeed, in biblical terms:

> We have all been employed for periods of over twelve months by you. Some of us have been at Bedwas for over three years. You have made no complaint as to the quality or quantity of our work. Our behaviour has been

unquestioned. *Are you afraid to trust us to do the right and proper thing in the relations between Employers and Workmen?*

We are desirous of maintaining employment. We have homes and wives and children to maintain. We know the dread effect of unemployment. Our homes are as sacred to us as yours are to you. . . .

For the rest of this Coalfield there exists the Conciliation Board Agreement. For the Owners there is the Coalowners' Association. For the Miners there is the Miners' Federation. *You compel us to be the Ishmaelites of South Wales.* From all the advantages of collective agreements you shut us out. We are treated as if we were not as other men. . . .

We have asked for the right to join our own Trade Union. You have imposed a sham upon us and called it a Union.

You have no Moral Right to Do This.

We are still prepared to peacefully alter these things. We want no strife. We do not want to see this Coalfield again thrown into a state of possible anarchy. The course of events will be your responsibility. The sacrifice of 120,000 workers and their families will be laid at your door. The economic dislocation of the industry will be the result of your actions.

We ask, in all sincerity, *Is Peace Impossible*? (Leaflet No. 53)

The Industrial Union's stereotyped reaction equating 'Communism' with the Federation was no answer to this fervent but reasoned plea.[60] Instone's pamphlet, issued on 21 August, 'The Bedwas Colliery – the Truth', was a much more cogent attempt to put the Company's point of view. What emerged from his long statement can be seen as the root-cause of the strife since 1926, that is, the conviction that the SWMF was operating beyond the confines of normal trade union activity and, as such, had to be stopped in the name of freedom and 'business-sense'. However, no matter how much the SWMF was disliked throughout the coalfield, at Bedwas, as elsewhere, company unionism could only be established under special circumstances – with the active encouragement of the company concerned. In his recount of the events at Bedwas, Instone underlined this active role, asserting that the SWMF's domination of the colliery between 1921 and 1933 had led to so many strikes that the pit was 'idle' for two years:

There was hardly a day that the manager and his officials were free from having to meet deputations on questions, many of which were simply irritations concocted by the extremists who were running the Miners' Federation Lodge at that Colliery.

It became intolerable for the management to carry on, and maintain that control which would ensure the safety of the mine, and the safety of the men employed in it, much less endeavour to make the colliery a paying proposition to those who had invested their money in it and to secure prosperity of workmen therein.

In February of 1933, the position had reached such a stage that the right of management to employ what men they liked or to select men best fitted for the work that had to be performed was directly challenged, and a precipitate strike occurred without any notice or warning of any description. The mine was in danger, and the business of the company was brought to a standstill with consequent loss and misery to the entire neighbourhood.

Instone claimed that at this juncture the company were approached by a 'sound body of unemployed men' who were seeking 'regular employment' and who had no desire to work with Federation members, and, bearing in mind their past experience, the company agreed to employ only those who joined the SWMIU. The latest campaign, in his view, was marked by intimidation and false claims. The signed revocation cards were merely the products of a desire to be free from molestation by the Federation, whilst, if they were genuinely intended, they could not be accepted from the Federation's hands.

Instone's view of the Federation was that it was a minority-controlled organisation which enjoyed little effective support in the coalfield, whilst the SWMIU enjoyed widespread, but mostly scattered support. Where it was established, as at Bedwas, relationships were amicable, and voluntarily arrived at for:

> It is and always has been a principle of the employers in the coal trade that they would not interfere with their workmen or influence them in any way to belong to any particular union . . . The only reason why Bedwas is in the Miners' Industrial Union is because the workmen demanded it, and the company as any other company would, being satisfied that the intention was towards the betterment of the men's conditions and towards the advantage of the concern itself, had no option but to agree.

The wider freedoms demanded by the Federation, therefore, were dismissed as a smokescreen for a reversion to the old 'harmful' practices and domination of the now-unemployed Federation membership. The existence of this core of former employees was to prove a stumbling-block in subsequent events; at the time of the pamphlet, however, the company was obviously intent on digging in all along the line, refusing to make any concessions at all.[61] A full statement was prepared, in reply to Instone's pamphlet, by the EC. The strike situation had arisen in 1933 because the company had refused to fulfil the terms of the arbitrators' award, and following the stoppage, with the help of the Industrial Union, they staffed the colliery with men from other valleys. A key argument employed by the SWMF, here and elsewhere, was that, by 1936, the men employed were, in fact, old Federation members:

> A large number of the men recruited during that stoppage [i.e. 1933] proved to be quite unsuitable and gradually they have been replaced by other men, old federationists so anxious to get work that they even agreed to pay to the Industrial Union as the price of a job.

Revolt had broken out because of the company's attack on wages and conditions and their arbitrary policy of dismissals. The Federation had restrained the men so that there might be a peaceful settlement but there had been no reciprocal gesture by the owners with the result that 'this is the only question which is likely to disturb the peace of the coalfield'.[62]

A deputation from the EC, along with 3 MPs, met on 24 August, with officials from the Mines Department, to try to end the impasse caused by the Bedwas company's withdrawal from all the usual negotiating machinery in the coalfield,[63] and on 26 August the Secretary for the Mines Department met with Instone separately. The Government met the intransigence hitherto reserved for the Federation – all their suggestions were rejected as Sir Samuel, declaring that the MIU was the only 'sane solution', said he would stand or fall in 'a fight for freedom from tyranny', for if 'the SWMF succeeded in smashing the Miners' Industrial Non-Political Union now then every colliery in the South Wales coalfield should realise what to expect in their turn'.[64] None of this was very convincing to Captain Crookshank who believed that Instone was wrong not to meet the Federation or to consider the Conciliation Board or to take seriously any evidence of Federation support:

> Sir Samuel Instone thinks . . . that the Federation is playing a game of bluff, but to count on this is taking too great a risk since the stoppage might be the final blow to the South Wales coalfield.[65]

Instone's vehemence was rooted in a refusal to concede control of the colliery's working conditions, won since 1933; profit was, he openly admitted, the principle. The real obstacle he had to overcome, though, was neither the 'terrorism' of the SWMF nor the moral pressure of the Mines Department and his fellow-coalowners anxious to avoid a stoppage, but rather the only 'truth about Bedwas' that mattered, the intolerable nature of the employment in the colliery. It was this that the Bedwas Pit Committee returned to in their lengthy reply to his own pamphlet, for his 'facts' concealed more than they revealed.

Again they insisted that the Arbitration Award of 1931, negotiated by two representatives from each side, had stipulated that ex-Bedwas men would be the first to be re-employed; no mention had been made of management's right to employ whomsoever they chose. The Award was, in its defence of the old conditions and workmen, in the way and openly flouted before the strike of 1933:

> If Sir Samuel wants further proof let him consult the report made to himself and his co-directors in March 1933, which mentioned *interalia* that the destruction of the Arbitration Award would put 'thousands upon thousands of pounds into the pocket of the company for the lifetime of this colliery'.
>
> This stoppage of February 1933, was deliberately provoked to destroy the effect of conciliation and arbitration.
>
> Immediately the stoppage commenced, the recruiting of blacklegs was embarked upon. Three days after the stoppage commenced it was reported to Sir Samuel that some 300 outside men had been employed, and the policy was being pursued. Hardly a dozen of the normal Bedwas men had re-commenced, and this held good for the five weeks and three days of the stoppage. . . . When the stoppage concluded, on guarantee that the Bedwas men would be re-employed, not 100 men were given work from the villages of Bedwas and Trethomas. The old workmen were shut out. The districts surrounding the Colliery were victimised. Trains and buses brought in some 1,500 men whilst the local men were kept idle.

Throughout this record of grievances, what rankled most was the destruction, deliberate as they saw it, of the relatively new, but united, community around Bedwas. It was this redirection of the pattern of men's lives in the aftermath of 1926 that hurt their sense of pride/control as much as the heavier brutality of the economic depression:

> Sir Samuel, who had naturally helped in creating a community spirit among his workmen in the area, as manifest in the magnificent Workmen's Hall, now sought to wipe it out. Behind this apparently senseless expression of hostility a motive made itself quite plain. . . . Behind the backs of even the flotsam and jetsam that had been used to 'man' the pit, an agreement was concluded with the Industrial Union cancelling all Price Lists, Standard Rates and Conditions and making the deduction of contributions for Company Union a condition of employment. Not a single man now at Bedwas knows the terms of that agreement.

Oakdale Miners' Institute Library, 1945

rc and Dare Workmen's Hall at Treorchy, built between 1907 and 1913, is one of the nest examples of miners' institutes in South Wales. Following the closure of local llieries, it has become a public hall under the local authority (Rhondda Borough Council)

Gwaun-Cae-Gurwen Silver Band (Band y Waun) in 1902, a famous band with a lo
association with the miners' struggles, particularly in 1925 and 1926

Tredegar Workmen's Institute Billiard Team, 1934–5: *(back row)* R. C. Thomas, W.
White, A. James, H. A. Davies, L. Edwards, A. Tillings *(front row)* D. Arthur, F. Foxhall,
Phillips, H. James, C. Hill, T. J. Morgan

ew Jones (Llew North or Llew Wern) using drill, bow and stand in Ynyscedwyn Colliery
stradgynlais), about 1940

ven Sisters Colliery (Dulais Valley), 1942. As seen in *The Silent Village,* an anti-nazi film
ide with the co-operation of the SWMF. The colliery has been completely demolished,
velled off and grassed

Looking south down the Rhondda Fawr, the greatest coal-producing valley in the world.
photograph, taken about 1945, shows Fernhill Colliery and the community of Blaenrhon
(left centre)

Demonstration at Cardiff in 1952 against withdrawal of Section 62 of the unemployment
insurance regulations

A rescue team near Bridgend, about 1920

MAR/APR, 1961
VOLUME 9. No. 2

THE MINER

Contents

THE MAGAZINE OF
THE SOUTH WALES AREA
OF THE NATIONAL UNION
OF MINEWORKERS

Area journal with picture of Six Bells miners after explosion at their colliery in 196

Gala. The Markham and District Colliery Band is one of the striking features of the
Wales Gala – invariably leading the parade

1959 Gala: *left to right*
Glyn Williams, W. H.
Crews, D. D. Evans, Ness
Edwards, MP, Ben Morris,
Tom Mantle, Joe Hughes,
Will Whitehead, L. R.
James, Aneurin Bevan, MP,
Tommy McGee, Abe
Moffatt, Wendell Jones,
Jack Jones, W. R. Jenkins,
Dai Francis

The Cwmbach Male Voice Choir, founded during the 1921 lockout and frequent winners in the Miners' Eisteddfod, at a Movement for Colonial Freedom Concert with Paul Robeson, in the Royal Festival Hall, 1960

South Wales lobby against
pit closures, 1963:
Monmouthshire miners
with retired NUM General
Secretary, Arthur Horner

Last day of Abercrave Colliery (Swansea Valley), 17 March 1967: *left to right* Joe Walsh (collier), Sid Charlton (development ripper), Emlyn Adams (collier), Arthur Shaw (cutterman), Jack Davey (ripper), Emlyn James (deputy), Rhydian Griffiths (cost clerk), Haydn Williams (borer)

Cardiff miners' pickets outside a power station at a date during 1972 strike.

Wales Miners' lobby of NUM NEC during Deep Dyffryn anti-closure campaign, April 1979

Ray Davies and Tom Morgan look through the roof-control chocks in the M22 fa[...]
Markham Colliery. The coal-cutter and conveyor are working a seven-foot seam i[...]
meadow vein, illuminated by a new electric lighting system (picture taken in 1977)

The men's reply then goes into details about victimisation, about the extra wages given to 'spies', about 'thuggery', and the other incidents that occurred. What is most interesting, however, is their denunciation of the failure of the Industrial Union to represent the men, even on its own terms – not even the appointed committees are aware of the price lists imposed, supposedly negotiated, by management. This was a denunciation of the MIU from the inside. More could be won over, so they grappled with the accusation that the men at present employed would be replaced by the old Federation men in the event of an SWMF victory, but 'on this point we have ample guarantees, both in the pledges of the Federation President and the Federation Constitution. The present Pro-Tem Federation Committee on which we sit, consists of only one old Bedwas workman, the rest of us being residents of other districts. . . . As to the control of our own affairs, we are satisfied that it will remain in our own hands. We have had full lodge status already in the Federation campaign. The old Bedwas Lodge has agreed, and the Federation constitution imposes, that the Bedwas Employed Lodge shall be completely separate from the Bedwas Unemployed Lodge.'[66]

The Federation's concession of this point, and, eventually, Instone's acceptance of it was to prove the key factor in the final stages. In the meantime, threats and counter-threats continued, with the company not denying that men could join the Federation, provided they remained members of the Industrial Union, Gregory telling the press that men were lined up for jobs at Taff-Merthyr and Bedwas in the event of a general stoppage, and the Federation calling for a secret ballot at Bedwas to establish, publicly, their strength.[67] Horner insisted that Bedwas had to be settled to establish the right of 'free combination' and that it, with Taff-Merthyr, represented the sole threat to peace; for 'in recent days there has been evidence of a general readiness on the part of the South Wales coalowners to regard the SWMF as a decisive influence in the affairs of the coalfield. This has been shown by the establishment of more effective machinery for the settlement of normal disputes.'[68] Of course, the Bedwas Company had withdrawn from that machinery to escape its obligations; and in the same vein they now rejected the Federation's offer of a ballot, made through the Secretary for Mines.[69] On 5 September, a Saturday, the coalfield was due to stop working.

At Bedwas the barrage of leaflets had continued even to the eve of the termination of contracts, emphasis being placed on the rights of those in employment to continue at Bedwas and the Federation Lodge to be composed 'only of men now employed at the Bedwas Colliery'.[70] However, a new factor emerged when on Thursday, 3 September, about eighty men stayed down in the North Pit of the colliery, at McCarthy's working. The men behind this action were the local 'officials' intent on preventing importation of blackleg labour in the event of a wider strike; they made their own demands, which reflected the Federation's, with a prominent call for 'removal of barracks from pit tops'. At the same time the team sent in by the Federation were, without doubt, aware of the action to be taken, and in this, as most other things at Bedwas, showed themselves to be well in control.[71] Elsewhere in the coalfield the strikes that had followed in the wake of the Nine Mile Point dispute appeared to be in the offing – at the Parc Pit, in Cwmparc, thirty-eight men stayed down on Thursday night to prevent the reintroduction of 'blackleg' labour; at the Bute Colliery, Treherbert, 180 men 'stayed in' out of sympathy with the Bedwas and Fernhill troubles. By Friday, the Glamorgan Colliery, Llwynpia, was also involved (sixty-five men underground) and a total of 6,000 men were idle in the Upper Rhondda.[72]

The Mines Department had at last managed to meet Instone again, this time securing his agreement to have talks with the SWMF provided the notices were withdrawn.[73] This was agreed to on condition that there would be no dismissal of the 'stay-down' strikers or attempts to engage new workmen during the negotiations. At the same time further 'propaganda meetings' were called off. At Bedwas, after a mass meeting, work was resumed on the Sunday night, and in the Rhondda the other strikes (now in five pits) ended too.[74]

In London, on Wednesday, 9 September, the EC met, with the endorsement of Saturday's Delegate Conference,[75] with the representatives of the Bedwas Company under the neutral chairmanship of J. Forster (a barrister in London and the south-east circuit). This initial meeting was ended almost straightaway by the news that a fresh stay-in strike had erupted at Bedwas, though the Joint Committee were to meet again on the Saturday if the strike was ended. Horner had it called off the same day[76] and the following day reported, in person, to the men at Bedwas.[77]

When the joint meeting was resumed, it was against this background of unease (Gregory issued statements declaring the Industrial Union's refusal to agree to a ballot under circumstances of 'terror' and said 'Russia has come to Bedwas'), but the EC were intent on establishing their firm but limited aims. Horner had declared that the question of the

SWMIU, as a union, was neither here nor there, for what was to be decided, by the company, 'is whether there shall be a ballot to establish the wishes of the men in a manner which can leave no doubt in the minds of anyone as to their desires', and then, whether they would continue to support the SWMIU no matter what the result.[78]

In fact, on Sunday, 13 September, at a mass meeting addressed by Horner, Saddler and Ness Edwards, the men were told that the company had agreed to give their reply on the question of a ballot in seven days. The men resolved, unanimously, to assist their representatives in their attempt to settle the policy with the Company in a peaceful manner; the Pit Committee issued leaflets calling for restraint in the face of any provocation (No. 64).

Although this was, indeed, the eventual outcome it was so on terms that met with some severe opposition. Neither side was quite so intent on a struggle as it had appeared. For the SWMF, though they had no other choice ultimately, a coalfield stoppage would have quickly depleted their funds and without the certainty of eventual success this was to gamble away the position that had been slowly regained. What they learned at the Joint Meeting of 12 September, however, was that the Bedwas Company was not in a healthy financial position either. In Horner's words, the Company 'was carrying more than a million pounds of debt. If there was a strike for a week or so at the colliery, the Company would be smashed. It would be the easiest thing in the world to close the Bedwas Colliery for good. But we had no desire to destroy the men's employment at the cost of wiping out the company union, and so we set out to get the best possible agreement.'[79] The point was that this gave the SWMF their victory but, unless it were to prove a pyrrhic one, at the cost of restricting their effective demands. The extent to which the Federation were prepared to meet the Company can be seen in the final terms negotiated, but, nowhere so clearly as in a fragmented transcript account of the early negotiations over the question of the ballot, that has, fortunately, survived.[80]

The EC representatives (Horner, Saddler and Harris) proposed that a ballot be held to enquire into the state of opinion; that if the Federation were accepted then Horner would act as agent for the colliery.[81] In their turn the company's representatives (Samuel and Theodore Instone and Stuart Martin) were concerned to establish the SWMF's attitudes in the event of a ballot and its outcome, whatever it might be. Much of the subsequent discussion concerned the difference between a ballot of enquiry and a decisive ballot since, in the event of the latter, the

Federation wanted assurances about its own 'propaganda machine' being on an equal footing with that of the Industrial Union. In the course of their reply the SWMF made plain what they were *not* demanding. Instone was concerned about the position of old Bedwas employees in the Federation Lodge:

> *Mr Horner:* . . . That matter is settled by the fact that the persons referred to are not now in the employ of the company, and the lodge will be composed of the employees of the company . . . we are not going to put forward any claims for the reinstatement of what are known as the ex-Bedwas workmen.

This was a reference to those who had not been re-employed after the 1933 stoppage; Instone pursued this by asking whether the Seniority of Resumption of Work Agreement then drawn up would also be shelved. Horner and Harris said this was the case, and, more than that would be forgotten too:

> *Mr Horner:* I want to make it quite clear that we are not claiming the restoration of the old conditions.
> *Sir Samuel Instone:* Nor customs?
> *Mr Horner:* Nor customs.
> *Sir S. Instone:* You want the birth of a new colliery?
> *Mr Horner:* Yes.

Although the Federation would press for the reinstatement of the 'thirty-odd men' who had been dismissed in the present dispute, the rest would only return as 'an act of grace' (the Chairman's phrase) on the company's part whilst Stuart Martin promised 'to deal with them all, with the exception of a few. There are a few you know.'

The Instones were obviously startled to find so much granted to them. They were intent on hearing Horner promise again and again, that the sole object was to re-establish the Federation.

> *Mr Theodore Instone:* . . . Does that mean that the present conditions as to working price lists and everything else will be maintained as they are?
> *Mr Horner:* Yes. That is definitely understood. For the chairman's information I think it ought to be understood that there are things such as the definite pre-1933 condition, which have gone. There was a definite Resumption of Work Agreement. So far as those two matters are concerned they are dropped by us. That is understood. . . . All the lot.

On the wider issues of Federation demand for total control of collieries in South Wales and whether they would accept an MIU victory, Horner skilfully skated over the points – in neither case did the

Bedwas Company have any reason to follow these chimeras for they had received the substance of their wishes. Not surprisingly, they agreed, a week later, to a decisive ballot vote provided a truce was maintained over propaganda activities.[82] The SWMF negotiators had, during the week, been backed up by the EC over the three major issues: a decisive ballot within a few weeks; membership of the Bedwas Lodge to be confined to men in work; and that there would be no restoration of the 1933 Agreements, conditions and practices.[83] At Bedwas the victory, in principle, for a ballot was welcomed. The Pit Committee called for support on the basis that a Federation Victory 'will entitle us to all the privileges and safeguards contained in the Conciliation Board Agreement' (No. 65) – such as fourteen days' guarantee of employment and full protection on customs and conditions. Already the latter had been resigned; soon the former was to disappear as well.

It was now decided to hold a ballot for elections to a 'public' Federation Lodge; out of 1,452 men employed at the pit, 1,022 had asked to have their contributions to the MIU revoked by signing and returning cards issued to ascertain the SWMF's strength after the breakthrough. The SWMF had asked for 2d. a week (not the usual 6d.) until the men did not have to continue membership of the SWMIU (4d. a week).[84] Although negotiations were proceeding between the SWMF and the company, Sir Samuel Instone continued to feel aggrieved. He gave vent to his exasperation at the AGM of Instone & Company at which he told his shareholders that he had only met with the Federation representatives to avoid a national calamity and under pressure from a 'very high place'. He claimed that the agreement which was in the offing was being placed in jeopardy by the SWMF's continued harassment of his work-force, and recollecting he was talking to those whose interest was in the minerals, not the men nor even the topography, of South Wales, he concluded:

> It is not like being in London, where you can go wherever you like. You must visualise these colliery villages and understand how easily one man can get to another, and how difficult it is for one man to get away from another.[85]

Despite this last-minute attack the SWMF and the company were able to agree to have a secret ballot, to be held on 28 and 29 October and this, in turn, was presented to a mass meeting at Bedwas which accepted the terms negotiated.[86] The full terms, by which both sides agreed to be bound as the result of the ballot, were not made fully public until a week later. Already there was some unease at the terms, particularly since on 25 September the Industrial Union had produced a leaflet which contained extracts from the earlier negotiations at which Horner had agreed that the old Bedwas men and customs would not be reinstated. The SWMF's position of strength would be frittered away if there was any delay, especially since there was evidence that 'new men' were being signed on at the colliery whilst others, dismissed during this campaign, had not been reinstated.[87]

In the weeks leading up to the ballot, both sides once more issued 'propaganda' leaflets. The SWMF concentrated on exposing the dubious financial arrangements of the SWMIU, eagerly pointing out that its expenditure on motor cars and vacuum cleaners was high whereas on fighting compensation claims, wage negotiations and pit examinations it was absolutely minimal. For all that, the Industrial Union's strong point was that the minimum wage rates at Bedwas for colliers and repairers were slightly higher than the coalfield's general rate, and it was this, allied to the terms of the agreement, that made their strongest case.

The agreement was a body blow to those who had naïvely assumed that the Company was completely on the run. True, it agreed to accept the SWMF if the ballot was in their favour, and to accept a committee of men employed at the colliery, but it also had written in a form of disputes procedure that was unique in the coalfield. Unique, that is to say, in Federation-run pits and, *ipso facto*, tantamount to reflecting Industrial Union practice.

The men had to agree to take any dispute that arose first, to the manager, then, failing mutual satisfaction, to the pit committee; after this, the colliery agent and the miners' agent (in this case Horner would act) were to be consulted, with the Consulting Engineer as a further guide. The hard part to stomach, though, was the insistence that, in the end, a prickly dispute would be referred to an arbitrator whose decision would be binding. The agreement read:

> The parties signatory hereto and the workmen undertake that no restriction of effort or strike action of any kind shall take place, nor shall any stoppage of the colliery be brought about by them under any circumstances whatsoever, provided that any and every dispute which may arise is dealt with in a manner provided in the foregoing and that the ultimate decision is applied by the company.

What the Federation had done was to accept the management's rule in the pit (with some safeguards) in return for the vital recognition of the

SWMF. Thus, the Federation agreed that it would regard the dismissal of any workman who broke the agreement as self-protection by the company, and not victimisation; it accepted the day-to-day contracts for another twelve months; it agreed to hold no 'Show Cards' on colliery premises, nor to engage in campaigns without the management's consent; and, of course, the rejection of the old Bedwas employees and customs was made explicit, with all the present terms, conditions, customs and procedures to continue to apply.[88] Since the agreement was to last until 30 September 1941, the SWMF had theoretically resigned away their right to strike for five years. It is hardly surprising that few who had struggled for victory could claim this as a famous one. Nevertheless, provided the ballot went in their favour, the SWMF had won the most essential battle of all, and with it the war, for the end of the SWMIU at Bedwas would remove that Union's strongest financial prop, to open up the way for the final assault. Arthur Horner had to defend the settlement, tenaciously, at the time; he admitted later, that it had not been an entirely convincing deal:

> We had to make some concessions. In particular, we had to agree that the men's committee at the pit which would operate negotiating and conciliation machinery set up under the agreement would be composed of representatives of the men employed in the colliery.
>   This was demanded by the Industrial Union men because they did not want to be controlled by the old Federation Committee. It was also laid down that I, as President, and Saddler, as Vice-President, should carry out the job of miners' agent at the pit. To the credit of the members of the old Bedwas Lodge they agreed.[89]

It was Horner's ability to secure this local support that ensured the acceptance of the agreement, despite vehement attacks both within the SWMF, and from outside it. The SWMIU now began their part of the leaflet war by pouring scorn on the Federation's broken promises – primarily, the failure to have the Conciliation Board Agreement implemented at Bedwas, and the retention of the day-to-day contract (Leaflet No. 1, SWMIU). It was, after all, plain that the main planks of the MIU Agreement at Bedwas, i.e. price lists, customs, holidays, and the rest, had been retained (only the 'personnel' would be altered), so the question became – 'Why change?' It was now the Industrial Union's turn to assure the men that if they won the ballot, no one would be dismissed for his past Federation activities. Their battle-cry was one, they claimed, that the SWMF had tried, in the agreement, to copy – but why take the copy?

> A vote for the Federation is a vote for the 'dole'
> So vote for the Union, make Security your goal (Leaflet No. 2).[90]

The ballot itself took place under the supervision of the Clerk to Monmouth County Council, and with policemen as polling-booth stewards. The propaganda machines this time worked in a low key, though even the injured were carried to vote. Some 1,624 men were entitled to vote (W. H. Crews had earlier checked these figures for the Federation), and 1,487 did so (a 91 per cent poll). The result, announced on 29 October, fully vindicated the SWMF's claims with 1,177 cast for the SWMF and 309 for the Industrial Union. When the result was known SWMF sentiments were to assure the men that their interests would now be safeguarded, and at the same time, that they would fulfil the agreement completely. These two promises did not seem to some to be entirely consistent.[91]

Nevertheless, at the Delegate Conference called to receive the President's report, the discussion ended in almost unanimous acquiescence. The key argument employed, here, was that since the Bedwas Company was no longer a party to the Conciliation Board Agreement, a different one had had to be drawn up.[92] There matters rested for a while, and it was with some degree of petulance, that Oliver Harris repeated this decision to Lodge Secretaries who wrote, on behalf of their members, to condemn the agreement, and its acceptance by the EC before consultation with the Coalfield. One added, 'Personally, I realise the difficulties that you were faced with, but no word of mine could convince them that you did the right thing.'[93]

Despite the fact that the former militants, at Bedwas, remained loyal,[94] there was, without doubt, a need to quiet the unrest felt in the rest of the coalfield ('I was attacked by some of my left-wing colleagues because I made those concessions,' Horner recollected),[95] a feeling of disquiet increased by the praise lavished on the agreement by the local press, and on the SWMF President, by Sir Samuel Instone, who told the annual meeting of the British Benzole and Coal Distillation Company that 'in the shape of Mr Horner . . . an entirely new phase has come over the mentality of the men'. This was a new experience for Arthur Horner, one under which he seemed to wriggle uncomfortably (he had replied that the SWMF would hold its end up if the Company did the same)[96] – and it was only his forthright defence in the December issue of the

Miners' Monthly that finally ended these doubts, and, incidentally, encapsulated the philosophy of trade unionism that Horner espoused.

The article, called 'The Truth behind the Bedwas Settlement', reviewed the history of the Bedwas Lodge from the 1933 dispute when 'one of the strongest lodges of the SWMF was driven off the colliery it had controlled for many years'. Horner accepted that there had been no strike because the coalfield was not ready, and that the Bedwas Lodge had to become an unemployed one. In a touching reference to W. J. Milsom (who died in 1935) he said, 'Their leader died – in the main because of the humiliation arising from seeing his men beaten and sacrificed, whilst blacklegs worked in the pits.' Horner reviewed the stirring events of 1934 and 1935, not forgetting to emphasise the subsequent financial weakness of the Federation, leading to the end of the SWMIU deductions (on a compulsory basis anyway) at Taff-Merthyr, leaving Bedwas as the financial bastion of the MIU – 'Taff-Merthyr was of secondary importance from the angle of time'. His account of the EC's attitude to the campaign in Bedwas is of a piece with the entire policy of the SWMF under his tutelage:

> At times they called for stay-in strikes, coalfield action, etc. in their anxiety not to lose the ground gained, or exultation arising from unexpected success. Always the EC said 'Go back. Keep on doing the job. Win a majority, and then the coalfield will join in.' This team of EC members carried out this policy loyally, very often against all their inclinations to go over the top.

And so on, down through the handing in of coalfield notices (90 per cent this time, as opposed to 40 per cent in 1933) to the negotiations with Instone and the discovery that the colliery was in a parlous financial state. Horner's real task, though, was to convince his membership that the Federation had not weakened at this crucial stage.

First, he dealt with the question of their discarding the Conciliation Board Agreement:

> The answer: Because the Company had given concessions to the Industrial Union to maintain its prestige with the men, such as 8s. 2d. a day subsistence wage instead of 8s. 1d. for the coalfield, and we could not take less than the men had through the Industrial Union.

Perhaps this ignored the old arguments over former price-lists and customs, but it laid a correct emphasis on the fact that such a matter might have had a prejudicial effect on the Fed's chances of victory at the ballot.

The wage-rate system (there were no percentages on the basic rates —
they were merged together) was, he claimed, the same in substance only
simpler in form as the rest of the coalfield's; that the twenty-four-hour
contract was for a limited period only and a man could appeal against
dismissal; that bonus turns were safeguarded. These were minor
matters, open to interpretation, the biggest issue was that of Clause 13
that set out the machinery for dealing with disputes. Horner bluntly
admitted to the differences, making expediency his only excuse:

> . . . The Committee must be composed of men employed at the colliery. This
> guarantee was not first given to the company. It was given to the men
> employed in Bedwas Colliery, so as to reassure them against being con-
> trolled by the more experienced Old Bedwas Lodge committee members.
> It was not a condition we liked, but after consultation with the Old Bedwas
> Committee and the Bedwas workmen, we mutually agreed that it was not a
> provision we would close Bedwas Colliery to prevent — without this,
> negotiations would not have reached settlement.

Certainly, he was right to recognise the self-sacrifice of the old
Bedwas Committee as being instrumental in achieving that end. For the
rest, the President had no trouble in defending the Bedwas scheme of
Independent Arbitration against the Coalfield's Finality Committee (a
'halfway house to Arbitration for the settlement of ordinary disputes'),
and insisted that there was no conceivable reason why a settlement
could not be found for every local dispute that might arise, especially
since the Company had bound itself to accept independent judgement.

As for general coalfield disputes, again, Horner could see no worry:

> It is said there cannot be a strike at Bedwas for the life of the agreement. If
> there is a coalfield fight Bedwas can do as every other colliery; each
> individual member can terminate his contract and secure release from the
> agreement, as is done every time notices are given contrary to agreement in
> the coalfield.

All in all, this was a most persuasive (if, at times, Jesuitical) display. It
did, however, skate over thin ice, in its assertion that, at Bedwas, 'there
is nothing to strike about' any longer, since the axiom of union
negotiations is the ability to move quickly, and unfettered, to deal with
any situation, however unprecedented, that may arise. Opposed to this
theoretical freedom was the complex series of events that had led to the
Bedwas settlement — and the feature that had to be kept in focus, in
Horner's opinion, was the success of the Federation in reinstating itself.
Everything had to, and could if need be, stem from that. Strikes were

only a means to an end, and a poor means if they weakened both the union and the enemy. Bedwas had the appearance of an anomaly but the reality had altered, whilst the Agreement had 'not endangered coalfield solidarity' but paved the way, in a period of relative weakness, for the final elimination of scab unionism from the South Wales Coalfield.

> Let the 'rights' sneer who failed with men and money to win Bedwas; let the 'lefts' who secured isolation for themselves and security for scab unionism jeer. The fact is that scientifically applied class struggle has given us Bedwas without undue loss of expenditure of man-power.[97]

It certainly meant that the remaining struggles against the twin foes of company and non-unionism were altered into the guise of mopping-up operations; perhaps the most fitting tribute to Horner's eloquence in defending the Agreement, and his success in reuniting the coalfield, were the requests made for further copies of his speech in leaflet form.[98] The tight rein that the EC had kept over the Bedwas dispute was evident in its attitude elsewhere. The sense of purpose was maintained.

Nowhere was this more true than in Bedwas itself where the men who had given up their employment, for reasons more particular than any general economic crisis, continued resolute in accepting their own victimisation, but still appealing for others. W. J. Nind, ex-lodge chairman of the Bedwas Lodge and then Secretary of the Bedwas (Unemployed Lodge) of the SWMF wrote to Oliver Harris in 1939 to complain of the Company's failure to re-instate local labour:

> During the three months ending 30 September 1939, 43 men engaged by Bedwas Colliery Company from Exchanges of the Caerphilly area. 35 of these were *nominated* by the Company, 13 were from Caerphilly area and 22 from such districts as Aberdare, Merthyr, etc.
>
> Since that time a list of 80 men from the local exchanges have been submitted. Up to now 2 have been employed.
>
> We feel the time has come when some *action* should be taken to force the company to carry out their promise to employ local labour. When we say local labour, we do not mean the members of the old Committee, because we are still where we were in 1936, but we feel the other members should be employed.[99]

The lasting victory of the SWMF surely lay in its capacity to elicit such a response from those who had most reason to feel aggrieved; it was an understanding that rose above individual consideration. Billy Nind never worked in Bedwas Colliery again but the satisfaction he had, as a member of a community, and the proponent of the SWMF cause, found expression in a poem that uses the imagery of the American 1930s, knowing as Brecht did that the meaning of the connection drawn was not so far-fetched:

> *'Bedwas Workmen's Farewell to M.I.U.'*
>
> Poor *Old Greg* your time has come,
> For barefaced cheek you take the bun.
>
> From far and near you spread the cry,
> That Bedwas men you'd satisfy.
>
> But they were waiting for the day,
> When they could openly have their say.
>
> That day has come and you must go,
> Where trouble you will cause no more.
>
> No longer will you meet the boss,
> We've settled that matter with a cross.
>
> We could have settled quick with dusters,
> But Bedwas men are no mean rustlers.
>
> We took the tip of Arthur Horner,
> To send you where it's very much warmer.
>
> In Taff and Notts you're *'On the spot'*
> Try Chicago it's not so hot.
>
> Al Capone will know you well,
> For all you guys have a peculiar smell.
>
> Tell Capone you have done your best
> But Bedwas men have sent you west.
>
> > *So Long Old Pal*
> >
> > > W. J. Nind
> > > *Shortfellow*[100]

NOTES

1. See Page Arnot, *The Miners in Crisis and War* (1961), pp. 156–60.
2. *Western Mail*, 7 January, 4 February 1936; 2nd Annual Report of the SWMF EC. The minimum percentage on the standard rate went up from $22\frac{1}{2}$ to 25 per cent.
3. *Daily Worker*, 13 January 1936.
4. 2nd Annual Report of the SWMF EC, 1935–6.
5. Will Paynter, *My Generation* (1972), pp. 110–11.
6. *Merthyr Express*, 6 and 27 May 1933; 12 and 19 May 1934.
7. *Ibid.*, 19 May, 9 June 1934.
8. *Llanelly Star*, 8, 22 and 29 February; 7, 14 and 28 March 1936.
9. The 'backlash' can be seen in the case of the by-election at Pontypridd in 1938. This was a seat held successively since 1922 (when it was captured from the National Liberals) by T. I. Mardy-Jones (who resigned in 1931) and D. L. Davies (who died in 1937), both miners' officials. The Divisional Labour Party voted in Arthur Pearson (a chainworker in the local works and the chairman of the UDC) on the fourth ballot after W. H. May (the miners' agent) had led the field of five in each vote but the last when Pearson picked up all the other votes. This caused some anger amongst the local miners' lodges who felt that May had been deliberately excluded because he was the miners' nominee. Finally, with Horner campaigning for Pearson, the cracks were papered over. See *Western Mail*, 26 November 1937; 17, 18, 19, and 22 January; 4 and 14 February 1938. None the less when Morgan Jones, MP for Caerphilly, died in April 1939, the SWMF nominated Ness Edwards the local agent as its candidate despite protests that this would give them thirteen out of a total of eighteen Labour seats. Edwards was duly elected. *Western Mail*, 24 and 28 April, 6 July 1939.
10. *Western Mail*, 25 March 1936.
11. SWMF EC Minutes, 31 March 1936; the *Western Mail* alleged that, with some absentees, the vote was 8 to 6. 16 and 20 April 1936.
12. *Western Mail*, 25 May 1936.
13. By a happy omen Mardy No. 1 pit, closed since 1932, was to reopen in 1936. *Western Mail*, 24 June 1936.
14. Horner, *op. cit.*, pp. 148–50.
15. SWMF EC Minutes, 28 April, 2 and 12 May 1936.
16. *Kelly's Directory of Monmouthshire and South Wales*, 1884, 1895, 1914, 1920.
17. *Miners' Monthly*, July 1936. This was a special number devoted to Bedwas and Taff-Merthyr.
18. Interviews with Leo Price, 21 November 1971, and D. D. Evans, August 1973.
19. *The Workers' Weekly*, 28 September 1923, where it is alleged whisky and bottles of Bass provided by the manager softened the committee's line on non-unionism; Bedwas Lodge Minutes, 4 and 11 December 1927.
20. Bedwas Lodge Minutes, 12 July 1925, 1 September 1925, 29 February 1926, 23 and 30 October 1926, 30 July 1927.
21. Interviews with Leo Price and D. D. Evans, *loc. cit.*
22. Bedwas Lodge Minutes, 7, 8 and 20 January; 8 and 10 April; 22 July; 18 and 25 November 1928. *Workers' Weekly*, 14 December 1928.

23. *Workers' Weekly*, 11 January 1929; Bedwas Lodge Minutes, 7 and 29 January; 16 and 21 June; 20 August 1929. 12 January 1930. 9 March 1930.

24. *Ibid.*, 13 April, 20 July 1930.

25. *Merthyr Express*, 20 June, 11 and 25 July 1931; see also Anthony-Jones *op. cit.*, pp. 66–7. Milsom's negotiations with the company were attacked bitterly by W. J. Nind and other militants.

26. SWMF EC Minutes, 12 and 26 August, 1 and 26 September, 5 and 19 November, 24 December 1932.

27. Interviews with Leo Price, 21 November 1971 and 17 May 1974.

28. Bedwas Lodge Minutes, 3 and 24 April, 1 May, 28 August, 25 September and 23 October 1932.

29. *Ibid.*, 12 February 1933. The Bedwas Lodge Minutes do not start again until December 1936, i.e. after the SWMIU had been ousted.

30. *Merthyr Express*, 25 February 1933.

31. Edwards, Vol. II, *op. cit.*, p. 169; D. D. Evans agreed with this. See interview *loc. cit.* Bedwas Lodge Minutes, 12 February 1933.

32. SWMF EC Minutes, 21, 25 and 28 February; 3 March 1933.

33. *Western Mail*, 3 and 4 March 1933. Ness Edwards was worried about the numbers and origins of those recruited: 'We strongly resent the action of the Ministry of Labour in issuing unemployment books to men to work at the Bedwas Colliery who were never employed in the mining industry before and who were debarred by the Mining Industry Recruitment Act.'

34. SWMF EC Minutes, 6 March 1933.

35. *Western Mail*, 8, 9, 10 and 11 March 1933.

36. SWMF EC Minutes, 13 March 1933.

37. *Western Mail*, 14 March 1933. Thus, it was alleged, at the Bute Merthyr Colliery there had been no meeting of the men, but the Lodge Committee was for the strike; at Blaengarw where 600 were employed, 28 men had split – 19 for and 9 against; at the Albion Colliery, Cilfynydd, 50 out of a possible 750 attended, of whom 30 were for the strike. The Tredegar Combine Lodges had a membership of 1,000 and an attendance of 150.

38. SWMF EC Minutes, 15 March 1933; *Western Mail*, 14 March 1933. The Special Purposes Committee of the coalowners supported the Bedwas Company's stand, but not their request for money. Anthony-Jones, *op. cit.*, p. 67.

39. *Western Mail*, 15, 16 and 20 March 1933; SWMF EC Minutes, 15 and 18 March 1933.

40. Pieced together from *Merthyr Express*, 25 March 1933, and *Western Mail*, 20 March 1933. Half a dozen police and twenty others were injured. 100 summonses were heard at Caerphilly Court on charges ranging from intimidation, stone throwing and indecent language to plain obstruction. Most cases were fined but twenty-four people were sent to Monmouthshire Assizes where four men and seven women were jailed for periods of three to four months each. See *Merthyr Express*, 8 April 1933; *Western Mail*, 17 June 1933.

41. SWMF EC Minutes, 23 and 25 March 1933; *Western Mail*, 25 March 1933.

42. *Western Mail*, 27 March 1933.

43. SWMF letter files. Letter from Harris to Jim Evans, 11 April 1933.

44. SWMF EC Minutes, 22 April, 8 and 27 May, 15 August 1933; SWMIU

Authorisation Card in possession of the authors; *South Wales Miner*, 22 June 1933.

45. Anthony-Jones, *op cit.*, p. 67.

46. *The Miners' Monthly*, July 1936.

47. See above, Chs 7 and 8, *passim*.

48. W. C. Williams published eleven leaflets (of which eight are in the SWMF files) in April 1936. The quote comes from No. 10.

49. *Daily Worker*, 25 May 1936.

50. SWML Interview with D. D. Evans, 7 August 1973.

51. *Western Mail*, 1, 8 and 24 July 1936; SWMF EC Minutes, 19 May and 30 June 1936. Ness Edwards, 'An Open Letter to the Bedwas Workmen', 3 June 1936.

52. *Miners' Monthly*, July 1936; interview with Leo Price, who had been asked to work for the Fed. in the pit, 21 November 1971. Some Dowlais men, at work in the pit, had been cajoled after three secret meetings not to start a 'stay-down' over a minimum wage dispute.

53. What follows is based on a collection of leaflets put out at the time. Although the numbered series is incomplete, it is the fullest evidence of its sort that is extant. Most were collected and kept by Leo Price and are now in the SWMF files.

54. Horner relates that some men approached him with the notion of smashing Jewish shops because Sir Samuel Instone was a Jew:

> I said . . . 'Nobody is going to touch a Jew because you don't like . . . Instone', and later I raised the matter at a conference of the South Wales coalfield and said, if anybody started anti-Jewish activity on this issue I would resign the Presidency of the South Wales Miners in protest.

Horner, *op. cit.*, p. 152. There had been anti-Semitic riots in Tredegar in 1911. See Geoffrey Alderman, 'The Anti-Jewish Riots of August 1911 in South Wales', *WHR*, Vol. 6, December 1972.

55. There is a gap between Leaflet No. 4 and No. 20; and further gaps occur in the series.

56. *Western Mail*, 29 July and 10 August 1936.

57. SWMF EC Minutes, 11 August 1936.

58. *Western Mail*, 13 August 1936.

59. There had been an alteration in the MIU constitution whereby the Comfort Fund had been put into the hands of the Cardiff Officials, and the men had to be idle for six consecutive weeks before they could claim any money. Leaflets demanded that West (the Agent at Bedwas) stand up against this 'overlordship' of a 'local' fund. Other complaints concerned the nature of the Price Lists under which the men worked (Leaflet Nos. 48 and 69).

60. *Western Mail*, 20 August 1936.

61. 'The Bedwas Colliery – the Truth' by Sir Samuel Instone, SWMF files. There is a copy of the full text in the *Western Mail*, 22 August 1936.

62. *Western Mail*, 24 August 1936. William Gregory's invited reply referred to agitators and terrorism, denied allegations about spying and Company Union 'gangs' and added that the Bedwas men did not request help from the Federation but 'it was merely the case that the Federation took advantage of the

disgruntlement of dismissed officials of the Union to bring the union into disgrace with its members. In this they have completely failed.'

63. The Assistant Secretary of the Coalowners' Association, Iestyn Williams, had written to Oliver Harris denying any responsibility for Bedwas since that Company was no longer 'associated'. See Letter from Iestyn Williams to Oliver Harris, 21 August 1936.

64. *Western Mail*, 27 and 28 August 1936.

65. Note by Secretary of Mines (Captain Crookshank) for Premier, 27 August 1936. Prem. 1/201, PRO.

66. Proofs of Pamphlet by Bedwas Pit Committee (Pro Tem). SWMF files.

67. *Western Mail*, 29, 31 August 1936. By midnight Sunday, 30 August, a stay-in strike, involving sixty-four men, had been under way for sixty-five hours at the Fernhill Colliery, Treherbert. The dispute, totally unofficial, concerned the grievances of twelve men who had not received a minimum wage payment for filling small coal. When the strike ended, on 9 September, a 'world record' of 292 hours underground had been achieved.

68. *Ibid.*, 2 September 1936.

69. Letter from R. N. Quirk (Sec. to Crookshank) to E. B. Speed (Premier's Sec.), 27 August 1936; Letter from Crookshank to P.M., 3 September 1936; Letter from Crookshank to Runciman, 4 September 1936. Prem. 1/201, PRO. These reveal several approaches, all in vain, to Instone to agree to a meeting with the Federation to consider a secret ballot; they considered exerting pressure through Barclay's Bank; they felt that a strike would be 'practically complete throughout the coalfield' and would probably use the 'stay-in' method.

70. Leo Price MSS., Leaflet No. 63.

71. *Ibid.*, an original pencilled document, on the back of an envelope, stating demands. See also *Western Mail*, 4 September 1936; interviews with Will Paynter, W. H. Crews and D. D. Evans, *loc. cit.*

72. *Western Mail*, 3, 4 and 5 September 1936.

73. Letter from Quirk to Speed, 5 September 1936; Crookshank to Runciman, 7 September 1936. Prem. 1/201, PRO.

74. SWMF EC Minutes, 5 September 1936; *Western Mail*, 5 and 7 September 1936.

75. EC Minutes, 8 September 1936.

76. *Western Mail*, 10 September 1936. There is some uncertainty as to the motives behind this short strike though Leo Price (see interview) suggested it was to hasten on the negotiations. Whatever the reason it is indicative of the men's conviction that it was a victory weapon. There may have been a further reason in the rumours circulating about the intentions of the SWMIU since the Federation had in its possession a 'spy' report of the meeting held by the SWMIU Committee in Cardiff, on Sunday, 6 September. The Report (a single typewritten sheet) gives the names of the committee members and William Gregory's report on his negotiations with the company about their willingness to meet the Federation: 'Gregory regarded it as a hole in the hedge for the SWMF to escape the consequences of a stoppage. He regarded the position as very satisfactory and things would be normal after Wednesday.' They also resolved to hold their own 'stay-down' strike on Tuesday or Wednesday (i.e. the date of the Joint meeting in London) – seventy men could be got to do this so that Gregory could tell the Secretary for Mines that Bedwas men were behind him – 'and they would only

come up on condition that all Federation men were sacked'. The anonymous spy concluded: 'I had the impression that the Company were acquainted with the whole plan and were raising no opposition. I could not prove it but that is my impression.' SWMF files.

77. *Western Mail*, 11 September 1936.
78. *Ibid.*, 12 September 1936.
79. Horner, *op. cit.*, p. 151.
80. Photostat copy of transcript in SWMF files. Original was in possession of the late W. H. Crews.
81. This was in order to by-pass the currents of antagonism stirred up locally and to ensure any dispute of priority.
82. *Western Mail*, 21 September 1936.
83. SWMF EC Minutes, 17 September 1936.
84. *Western Mail*, 28 and 29 September 1936. Gregory claimed that the signatories had been intimidated by 'unemployed' men and that the figures were not accurate.
85. *Ibid.*, 1 October 1936. There were now 1,086 reported in the Fed.
86. SWMF EC Minutes, 6 October 1936.
87. Letter from Ness Edwards to Horner (enclosing the SWMIU leaflet), 26 September 1936. SWMF letter files.
88. *Western Mail*, 14 October 1936.
89. Horner, *op. cit.*, pp. 151–2.
90. Leo Price MSS. contains two SWMIU leaflets.
91. *Western Mail*, 29 and 30 October 1936.
92. *Ibid.*, 2 November 1936; *Miners' Monthly*, November 1936,
93. Letter from the Secretary of Maindy and Eastern Lodge, 12 November 1936; Letter from Bargoed Steam Lodge, 23 November 1936. SWMF letter files.
94. Letter from Harris to W. J. Davies, the Workmen's Hall, Bedwas, 9 December 1936, expressing on behalf of the EC, 'our appreciation of the splendid and loyal services rendered by the Unemployed Committee of the old Bedwas Lodge. Furthermore, it was decided to make a grant of £55 to the eleven members who, we are informed, have been actively engaged in this long campaign.'
95. Horner, *op. cit.*, p. 152.
96. *Western Mail*, 18 and 20 December 1936.
97. *Miners' Monthly*, December 1936; *Western Mail*, 23 December 1936.
98. Letter from James Morris, Secretary of the Cambrian Lodge, 3 January 1937. The article proved too expensive to publish as a pamphlet.
99. Letter from W. J. Nind to Harris, 20 November 1939. SWMF letter files.
100. The poem and the information (now in the SWMF files) was supplied by S. Nind (W. J. Nind's son).

CHAPTER TEN

From Tonypandy to Madrid

Now I'm fairly certain of this that most of the people living in other countries who had struggled . . . on behalf of their workers . . . and if they were incarcerated in any way there would be one voice that would protest against their incarceration. They could be in whatever dungeon . . . despite the fact that their voice was unheard, the voice of the South Wales Miners' Federation would be one that would be protesting. . . . So when the Spanish Civil War came . . . it was automatic (D. D. Evans, 5 December 1972).

An internationalist commitment rooted in pacifism and radical nonconformity had existed in Wales since the end of the eighteenth century. The response within the South Wales coalfield to the Spanish Civil War, however, belonged to a more recent proletarian tradition. The diverse support given to the Spanish anti-fascist cause was not spontaneous but the culmination of a process in which a particular class consciousness was created.

The coalfield provided the largest regional-occupational grouping within the British Battalion of the International Brigades. This was not simply the result of a revolutionary internationalist outlook reaching back to the Great War when the miners' bargaining power, the growth of Marxism and a heterogeneous population coincided to form a distinctive proletariat.

The response can only be understood by examining the nature of the miners' resistance from 1926 onwards. As we have seen, with the SWMF's power eroded and the change from employed to unemployed communities, the principal features of resistance included extra-parliamentary actions which relied on an intense community consciousness indistinguishable from a class consciousness. An alternative culture emerged, out of step with the norms of British society and its Labour movement, in which the political prisoner, Hunger Marcher and International Brigader became folk heroes. Spain represented the climax of this unorthodox political tradition.

ex↑↑↑↑

By 1936, the SWMF in supporting the Popular Front and in identifying its problems in anti-fascist terms, had more in common with Spain than Britain. The growing influence of the Communist Party over extra-parliamentary activities and the SWMF reached a peak in 1936 which explains the strength and direction of the response to Spain.[1]

By the mid-1930s the Executive Council of the SWMF was the most powerful single political forum in South Wales. By 1939, it represented 135,000 miners, sponsored thirteen Members of Parliament, its members participated substantially in the control of most local authorities in the coalfield, and it was internally and politically united. The SWMF was therefore in a unique position to initiate and control most of the activities in Wales in support of the Spanish Republic.[2]

As we have already seen, there was a well-established internationalist outlook within the SWMF.[3] Lodges, combine committees and the Executive Council of the Federation itself consistently passed resolutions against the imprisonment of relatively obscure Socialists and Communists in fascist and neo-fascist countries. The Cambrian lodge was typical when it sent a protest to the Greek Legation demanding the immediate release of Nikos Zachariades, the Greek Communist.[4] There had also been a long-standing interest in Spanish working class affairs, particularly within individual combine committees and lodges. The action of the Cambrian Lodge was symptomatic of a growing sympathy for the harsh struggles of the Spanish miners. A letter sent to the Spanish ambassador stated, 'The two thousand miners organised in the Cambrian Lodge, SWMF, at their mass meeting on Sunday, February 24, 1935, demanded that you take immediate steps to secure the unconditional release of Gonzales Pena and all other heroic miners and socialists now held in the prisons of Spain under danger of execution.'[5] This moral support was transformed into more tangible terms by the volunteering of three working members of the Cambrian Lodge to join the International Brigades.[6]

Neither was the organ of the rank-and-file movement of the South Wales miners, the *South Wales Miner*, oblivious to the plight of the Spanish miners, although its time and energy were almost wholly taken up with the domestic matter of winning the SWMF over to more militant industrial policies. The Spanish Prime Minister intended importing Welsh coal in 1935 in order to defeat the Asturian miners' strike. The *South Wales Miner* called on its supporters in the following vein to show their solidarity:

Not an ounce of coal to scab on our Asturian comrades: This must be our fighting slogan. Resolutions should be sent immediately to the EC demanding an immediate investigation of what companies are filling these orders, and preparing coalfield action to stop it.

Comrades: it is urgent; not a moment to lose if we would help in a practical way our courageous Spanish comrades.[7]

But such enthusiasm fluctuated from area to area within the South Wales coalfield, although all localities carried out some activities on behalf of the Spanish Republic. The South Pit Lodge, Glyncorrwg, in the Afan Valley, was typical of a considerable number of miners' lodges which rarely if ever, discussed international political events. Yet this lodge, so quiescent since being the focal point of such turbulence in 1926, nevertheless was so concerned by events in Spain that it formed a Spanish Aid Committee and carried out regular pit-head collections.[8] The 'Spain' activities of these formerly passive lodges could not be compared with the work carried out by the traditionally militant lodges.

The greatest interest in international affairs and in particular the Spanish situation came from the traditionally militant centres which formed a central triangle within the coalfield, especially its so-called 'red villages'.[9] Substantial interest was also clearly shown by many lodges in the Anthracite coalfield.[10] The Ferndale Lodge was not untypical of the lodges in these areas in protesting against the shooting of Spanish miners during their abortive rising in 1934.[11] Furthermore, it was the lodges and Executive Council members from this central triangle in the coalfield and the Anthracite lodge to which the Abercrave Spaniards belonged which encouraged the SWMF to send financial aid of £100 to the miners' families involved in the 1934 rising.[12]

The SWMF at every level appeared to be ever vigilant with regard to the growth of fascism in Europe whether it was in Germany, Austria, Spain or within its own mining communities. Its Executive Council needed little prompting from lodges and often would take initiatives itself.[13] But such seemingly spontaneous reactions were never orchestrated from above. As early as April 1934 an area annual conference protested against fascist terror in Europe and, anticipating its later commitment to Spain, pledged itself 'to use every means at its disposal to combat the spread of Fascism at home and abroad'. With this end in view, it called for a nationwide campaign 'to rouse the workers to the dangers of Fascism and to organise the entire forces of the working class to resist it'.[14]

The response of the SWMF to the Spanish War was predetermined, but its commitment intensified to such a degree in the course of the bitter struggle that Spain was to mean something more considerable than mere food parcels and lame conference resolutions. In every facet of the organisation it assumed great significance even when there were many pressing domestic problems. Support manifested itself in three different ways: through individual members who volunteered for the International Brigades; within mining communities where lodges were to the fore in organising various collections and often in setting up Spanish Aid Committees; and at all levels of the SWMF which used organisational, moral and political pressure on behalf of the Spanish Republic. All were interrelated, were often inseparable and reacted upon each other and had one common denominator, the influence of the Communist Party. It was this diversity and its comprehensive nature which made its reaction so distinctive.

Miners' lodges were amongst the first to show signs of giving military help. On 13 August, the Cambrian Combine Committee accepted a suggestion from Harry Dobson of Blaenclydach Lodge (he was later to die on the Ebro Front) that the EC of the SWMF should send a delegate to Spain to show their solidarity with the Republic. (This anticipated the blessing given to Paynter later.) This was one month before the formation of the International Brigades.[15] Later the Cambrian Lodge (in December 1936) and the Merthyr and District Unemployed Lodge (in February 1937) asked the EC of the SWMF to organise volunteers.[16]

Although the Spanish War began with the military insurrection of July 1936 against the Popular Front Government, and British volunteers on the side of the Republic had started to enlist at a very early stage, no Welsh miners volunteered for the International Brigades until the beginning of December 1936. The first volunteers took part in the dramatic defence of Madrid and in the Battle of Jarama. Their delay in arrival can be partly explained by the bulk of coalfield activists being involved in the Hunger March of 1936 and such other domestic struggles as anti-Blackshirt demonstrations and stay-down strikes. Indeed, the majority of these International Brigaders had a background of deep political, trade union and educational commitment. As one volunteer, D. R. Llewellyn, remarked, 'We paid our union dues before the rent.'

They were largely from that central coalfield triangle bounded by the Rhondda, Abercare and Merthyr Valleys, where class conflict had been most intense since the beginning of the century and where the Communist Party and mass unemployment had been prevalent in more recent times. The more immediate their struggle, whether it was the Taff-Merthyr dispute in the Bedlinog-Trelewis area (seven volunteers) or the anti-Fascist demonstrations in mid-Rhondda (fifteen volunteers) the greater was the response. Over 25 per cent were union officials, like Tom Howell Jones of Tower Lodge, and their average age was thirty with 18 per cent being married. They saw the European anti-fascist movement in microcosmic form in the South Wales coalfield. As Will Lloyd, an Aberdare volunteer explained, 'The Powell Duffryn Coal Company is fascism.' Such a recognition of the 'common enemy' was also seen in an anti-company union handbill which compared the situation in 'scab'-infested Bedwas with Nazi Germany. Although they were not all Party members by any means, they were overwhelmingly communist in outlook.

The 174 Welsh volunteers dominated as they were, politically and numerically, by the 122 from the mining valleys of South Wales (and to a lesser extent the thirty-four from the adjoining coal ports) were probably one of the most homogeneous groups within the International Brigades. Indeed, the contingent from the South Wales coalfield was the largest ethnic grouping of its kind within the British Battalion whose total strength has been estimated at 2,500 volunteers.

The extent of their political commitment can be seen by the number of volunteers who had taken part in all the working-class protest movements within the coalfield between 1926 and 1936. Jack Jones, Frank Owen, Will Paynter, Fred White and J. S. Williams had been prominent on several hunger marches while Sid James (Tydraw), Morris Davies (Treharris) and Leo Price (Bedwas) had led stay-down strikes against the company union. Over 20 per cent of the contingent had been summonsed or imprisoned for their political activities. Harry Dobson, imprisoned for his part in the 1936 anti-fascist demonstration in Tonypandy, volunteered the day he was released. He was killed, along with thirty-two other Welshmen. It became as much a test of integrity to join the International Brigades in the late 1930s as it was to go to gaol in the early 1930s.[17]

One South Wales miner who would have gone to Spain 'to take his bullet' was Lewis Jones, the Rhondda Communist Councillor, novelist and leader of the unemployed. Urged not to go because of his value as a propagandist, he died, according to folk memory, from exhaustion and a broken heart after addressing over thirty street meetings on Spain, the week Barcelona fell to Franco in January 1939. His two novels, *Cwmardy* and *We Live*, drew on the trade union and political experiences of his generation of South Wales miners.[18] *We Live*, published posthumously in 1939, reaches its climax when the hero of the two novels, Len, volunteers for the International Brigades. In the last chapter, entitled 'A Letter from Spain' news arrives of his death at the front, coinciding as it did with the late arrival of his last letter to his wife. The book ends with this air of pathos, if not pessimism and fatalism. He might well have been dwelling on the fate of his close friend, Jack Jones, who was in Spain and about whom there had been no news for many months, following his capture and incarceration in San Pedro Concentration Camp.[19] It had been Lewis Jones's intention to write a third novel, or possibly a play, which would have been based ironically on the successful return of the Welsh International Brigaders who would, he believed, have provided some momentum for a social revolution in Britain. He died believing that Jack Jones, later a miners' agent and upon whom Len was largely based, was dead. *We Live* vividly illustrates in human and political terms the effect on individual families and the internal and external turmoil of the Communist Party in the South Wales valleys over the Spanish question. In this sense, of all the Welsh writers, it was he who came nearest to describing what 'Spanish Aid' really meant.[20]

Apart from the question of the volunteering of miners which involved the enormous problem of personal political commitment, the most obvious indicator of the strength of genuine feeling for the Spanish Republican cause was seen within the mining communities themselves. The willingness of lodges to initiate collections was only equalled by the spontaneous response from Federation members and their families who had often suffered hardship and poverty for over a decade. Will Paynter, who was at the time an EC member of the SWMF recalled:

> . . . going into the streets of Trealaw and Tonypandy, in Trehafod and Porth, with a trolley, knocking on the door of people, most of whom were unemployed and destitute, pleading for a tin of milk or a pound of sugar, and there wasn't a home, facing the impoverishment that they were facing, that wouldn't make a contribution, during that period, to help the fight of the Spanish people.[21]

The miners of the Gelliceidrim Colliery in the Amman Valley even decided to cease their contributions to their local workmen's hall and diverted them to what they considered to be 'a more worthy cause – the relief of Spanish workers'.[22]

On the initiative of the Maindy and Eastern Lodge, all local organisations in the Ton Pentre area of the Rhondda participated in a collection in February 1938 which resulted in what the *Rhondda Leader* considered to be a revelation and called 'a total of 2,799 sacrifices to the cause'. The collection said as much about the diet of an impoverished community as it did about its expression of international solidarity.[23] In the Anthracite coalfield undoubtedly the best example of 'Spanish Aid' was in the tiny village of Onllwyn in the Dulais Valley north of Neath.[24]

Events in Spain were made all the more immediate by the existence of the small community at Abercrave less than three miles away in the neighbouring valley. Some of the Spaniards worked at Onllwyn No. 1 Colliery and were active politically within the Communist Party, and on the Spanish Aid Committee. The Spaniards, all of whom described themselves as 'Marxists', had been stirred by the Asturian Rising of 1934 and had collected sums of money. One of the collectors was Frank Zamora, later to be killed in Spain. They were amongst the first to respond in 1936 and on one occasion the whole adult population of the community (totalling thirty) volunteered for military service with the Republican Government.[25]

The Onllwyn Committee was set up on the initiative of local Communist miners who convened a meeting which was addressed by representatives from the Neath Spanish Aid Committee. The committee elected at the meeting was representative of the whole community and the adjoining villages of Coelbren and Banwen. The local headmaster became the chairman and among the organisations represented were the miners' lodge, the CPGB, the Labour Party, miners' welfare associations, religious denominations, the local NCLC class and even a knitting class. Two of its members, Jim Strangward and Frank Zamora, joined the International Brigades, and both were killed in action. So widespread was the support that only the colliery manager failed to contribute to the committee's food and financial collections.[26] At one concert in October 1937, held in Onllwyn Chapel, at which the artistes and local choir had performed without fees, it was announced that the village had collected three tons of foodstuffs and £23.[27]

Whilst such activities as house-to-house collections, concerts, football matches and dances raised modest sums,[28] what really distinguished the village was the work of the miners' lodge. It decided, with the consent of its members, to purchase milk tokens for Spanish Aid from the local Co-operative Society out of the profits from its 'powder fund'. This fund comprised the proceeds from the sale of explosives to the miners, the profits from which were normally distributed to the members every quarter. At the end of one quarter, £60 was spent on the tokens and it has been estimated that over £150 was raised in this way. This appears to have been the only scheme of its kind operating in the coalfield. One member of the committee later claimed that Arthur Horner had stated that the village of Onllwyn had raised more money per head of population for Spanish Aid than any other town or village. Similar committees, which imitated in some ways the Councils of Action of 1926 and 1935, were eventually set up throughout 1937 in most parts of the coalfield with the Communist Party or the miners' lodge (or both together) usually taking the initiative.[29]

The official policy of the SWMF, determined by its governing body, the Executive Council, and its Annual Conference, early on in the war, was largely to campaign against the British Government's support of non-intervention and to agitate against the Labour Party's inactivity on the Spanish question. This early period was also characterised by the passing of resolutions giving strong moral support to the Spanish Republic.[30]

Such a limited policy was shortlived. When the War became more protracted and when it was realised that it would be difficult to change the policies of the British and French Governments, more energy was concentrated on giving material support to the Spanish Republic. Precedents for financial support for Spanish miners had already been set in 1935.[31] This was continued in August 1936 with the contribution of £200 to the TUC Relief Fund for distressed Spanish workers and their families.[32]

A real alteration in policy came when substantial and long-term committed help was promised on 16 March 1937 by the Executive Council. It was decided that a grant of six pounds per week be made to the International Brigades Dependants' Aid Fund and that the lodges be asked to contribute a weekly sum.[33] At a coalfield conference on 3 April 1937 the lodge delegates decided to increase the grant to twelve pounds per week.[34] This change in attitude from giving financial support on seemingly compassionate grounds to one of contributing considerable aid towards something of a political and military crusade in the form of the International Brigades must have been accentuated by substantial pressure from the lodges.[35] Such pressure was so intense that when the Merthyr Unemployed Miners' Lodge suggested that the SWMF should call for volunteers to the International Brigades from among its own unemployed members, the General Secretary, Oliver Harris, only turned the suggestion down on 'practical grounds', because volunteering had been made illegal with the reinforcement of the Foreign Enlistment Act, 1870.[36] The Cambrian Lodge had also asked the Executive Council to appeal to each lodge for volunteers.[37]

By 3 May 1938 the SWMF Executive Council had further committed itself financially by suggesting to the MFGB that it should contribute £50,000 for relief work in the Spanish Republic and that the SWMF would be prepared to contribute its quota.[38] The MFGB asked for £12,500 to which the SWMF immediately agreed. This grant from the SWMF central funds was the equivalent of a half-crown levy on all members. It was to be partly reimbursed by a voluntary shilling contribution by members.[39] Eventually the money raised was directed towards three causes; these being the Basque Children's Fund, the International Brigades Dependants' Aid Fund and the Spanish Medical and Milk Fund.[40] There had never been such a levy as this in the history of the British coalfields. Where a levy had been called to raise money to support fellow miners in an industrial dispute it rarely amounted to more than a fraction of a member's union contribution. But this sum to aid Spanish workers was ten times that of a normal sized levy called the previous year.[41]

Response to the collection of the shilling voluntary levy varied somewhat from one lodge to another depending upon their individual histories but more importantly on the intensity of the economic depression in particular localities. The Anthracite district, a generally militant and comparatively prosperous part of the coalfield, produced the best response. The Emlyn Lodge, Penygroes, flushed with its victory in driving out the SWMIU, succeeded in levying the full half-crown from all its seven hundred and seventeen members.[42]

The Swansea Dry Steam area, traditionally less radical than the rest of the coalfield, and also hit more harshly in the prevailing economic situation than the adjoining Anthracite area, found greater difficulty in paying the levy. Edgar Williams, the secretary of Garn Goch Number One Lodge, whilst showing sympathy, expressed the difficulties facing the lodges in the area:

Since February this year, the above lodge has been working on half-time and some weeks has not worked a single shift. At a general meeting held last week to consider the above question, I was asked to write you pointing this fact out, at the same time it was felt that in as much as the men had only been working half-time that under these circumstances the levy should be reduced to half. May I say here, that under normal working conditions my members would not hesitate to meet this levy, realising the magnificent struggle that is being made by the workers of Spain to retain democracy, but intermittent working and the consequent effects have hit our men rather hard. I would be obliged if you would forward me your guidance on this levy and thanking you for your past assistance.[43]

Only one lodge expressed any resentment at being asked to pay the levy although this was only in the form of a protest against the process by which the decision was taken. The Lady Windsor Lodge, Ynysybwl, at its general meeting, decided that it would have preferred authorisation from the lodges. But its secretary, John E. Morgan,[44] qualified the criticism in his letter:

This is not done owing to any hostility among those present to the levy, in fact some of those present expressed a willingness to contribute very much more, but they feel that the method taken by the council is rather autocratic.[45]

Furthermore, only one member of the SWMF seemed to have expressed any criticism of paying the voluntary levy and this largely arose out of the over-zealous activities of the Nantymoel Ocean Lodge Committee in its method of collection.[46]

Collecting by lodges in certain areas, however, presented considerable difficulties. Local lodge officials were hindered by police interference, but this occurred only in those localities where relations between miners and police had been traditionally bad, and where police had made it a practice to acquaint themselves with local political activities, especially in the Rhondda. Police prevented collections near colliery premises by the Cambrian (Blaenclydach), National (Wattstown) and Lewis Merthyr (Porth) lodges, all of which were in the Rhondda.[47] The Assistant Chief Constable of Glamorgan gave humanitarian rather than political reasons for his refusal of collection permits:

... in view of the unemployment and depression which exist in the County area, such permits are now limited to efforts by authorised organisations for local charitable objects only.[48]

The Spanish question served only to accentuate an already aggravated situation in the Rhondda where harassment and provocation of 'militants' was a long-standing police preoccupation. The memory of police action in mid-Rhondda against strikers in 1910–11 was still vivid. Even more vivid was the memory of police involvement in a 'rates eviction' in Mardy in 1931 which resulted in six heavy gaol sentences based on circumstantial evidence provided by local police.[49] More significantly, hostility towards the police was so intense because of what many local miners considered to be the indiscriminate arrests of thirty-six demonstrators against fascists who were being protected by the local police at Tonypandy on 11 June 1936.[50] Throughout the 1930s activists, in particular those from the Rhondda, had felt that they were being persecuted by the local police and were being fined heavily and bound over to keep the peace for minor offences.[51]

Despite the economic depression and difficulties involving the police, the equivalent of nearly 45 per cent of the membership contributed to the voluntary Spanish levy which was a considerable achievement for an impoverished coalfield.[52] Between 1935 and 1940 the SWMF contributed £16,020 10s. 3d. to four separate funds.[53] This represented about half a crown per member. These funds were the International Brigades Dependants' Aid Fund, the Spanish Medical and Milk Fund, the Basque Children's Fund and the Spanish Miners' Fund. It is likely that the SWMF contributed more financially to the Spanish Republican cause than any other British trade union, certainly more than any other regional union.[54] Yet, as late as 19 October 1938 the President, Arthur Horner, was complaining that not enough effort was being made to collect the shilling levy.[55]

In May 1939 the SWMF decided to commute the payment of the £12 per week to the International Brigades Dependants' Aid Fund by making a grant of £500 to the International Brigades Memorial Fund. Fred Copeman, secretary of the Memorial Fund, in a letter of thanks to the general secretary, stated:

> . . . I take this opportunity of thanking you and your Federation and the members of your Union for the very fine gesture they have made in donating this sum. I am sure that if all unions will respond in such an excellent manner as your own, we will very quickly reach the £20,000 which our Committee has decided is necessary to make the basis of our Trust Fund. . . . I am sure that the members of the British Battalion and their dependants will have no

South Wales Miners' Federation.

AID FOR THE SPANISH PEOPLE

AN APPEAL.

The dreadful sufferings of the Spanish people, the ruthless slaughter of men, women and children, and the destruction of their homes by the rebel Franco and his FASCIST accomplices, ITALY and GERMANY, call for the active sympathy of ALL Workers.

The Fight of the SPANISH WORKERS against Fascism IS YOUR FIGHT.

The success of Fascism in Spain would endanger the liberties of the Workers in all Countries.

Fascism means the horrors of the Concentration Camps, Imprisonment and Death.

Help the Spanish People in their heroic struggle.

A Collection will be taken at your Colliery on FRIDAY NEXT, JULY 16th, to help to relieve distress caused by the Civil War.

THE SPANISH PEOPLE ARE GIVING THEIR LIVES, WE ASK YOU TO GIVE A GENEROUS CONTRIBUTION. THE EXECUTIVE COUNCIL.

CYMRIC FEDERATION PRESS, CARDIFF.

SWMF poster appeal for Spanish Republic, 1938.

reason to forget the SWMF and the Spanish people will forever remember the generosity which your Federation has shown in the cause of freedom and humanity.[56]

Material support by the SWMF was expressed in several other ways. Official sanction was given to Will Paynter, an Executive Council member, to join the British Battalion as a political commissar.[57] This sanction, probably the only one given to a volunteer by a British trade union, proved to be useful to Paynter in impressing anarchists in Barcelona who had hitherto refused to release cargo for the International Brigades.[58] The President, Arthur Horner, was also given permission by the SWMF to visit Spain as an observer.[59] Horner so timed his visit that he returned on the eve of the 1937 TUC Conference and was partly responsible for winning the TUC over to a policy of complete support for the Spanish Republic and against non-intervention, by using his first-hand information in his speech on behalf of the MFGB.[60]

In collaboration with the Cardiff Trades and Labour Council, the Executive Council of the SWMF set up the South Wales Council for Spanish Aid which inspired the formation of many local committees. It also helped to finance and organise several Basque children's homes in South Wales, notably at Brechfa in Carmarthenshire and Caerleon in Monmouthshire.[61] The SWMF made itself responsible for paying for the treatment of wounded Welsh International Brigade members on their return[62] and made available to them the Talygarn Miners' Rest Home which the Miners' Welfare Commission owned at the time.[63]

This financial support was merely an expression of the political and ideological unity and especially the consistency of the SWMF throughout the period of the Spanish Civil War, although its policy did change slightly according to the prevailing national and international circumstances with, for instance, more emphasis being placed on the International Brigades and their dependants in the early spring of 1937 because of the recent formation of the British Battalion.[64]

The SWMF saw the Civil War as a straightforward international fascist assault on a constitutionally elected 'popular front' government which had won power democratically on a programme of fairly radical social change. The Communists on the SWMF EC, in particular Paynter, who was usually the organisation's spokesman on Spain, believed that limited and realistic demands in support of the Spanish Republic, with only moral and organisational pressure being used, would be the best ways of securing maximum results. In this sense, the SWMF supported the policy of the CPGB and the CI.[65]

The ILP's position of supporting the POUM and its contention that first priority should be given to the pursuing of a successful social revolution in Spain rather than saving a 'bourgeois' republic from fascism, was unacceptable to the leadership of the SWMF. It was also unacceptable to the rank and file of the Federation.[66] There was no support for what has been described as a 'social revolution of unprecedented scope' taking place in the months following the Franco insurrection, involving the spontaneous seizure of lands by peasants and factories by workers.[67] Horner, on returning from Spain in August 1937, spoke in favour of crushing the POUM after the 'Barcelona rising' of May 1937 and claimed that the anarchists were obstructing the war.[68]

This political position held by the SWMF leadership and its rank and file could be explained by the general lack of information on the situation in Spain. Few national newspapers enthusiastically supported the Spanish Republic and those that did, such as the *Daily Worker* and the *News Chronicle*, tended to play down the revolutionary tendencies in Republican territory.[69] The main reason for this relatively uncritical support for the Spanish Republic was, however, due to a long 'domestic' conditioning of the political outlook of Welsh miners and their union. To a very significant extent, the nature of the economic and political conflict in the South Wales coalfield, largely created by the defeat of the 1926 strike and the economic depression, had tempered the political ideology of militant miners to such a degree that they could no longer realistically contemplate a millennium or even a social revolution within the immediate future. A defensive militancy had permeated the coalfield. This rearguard action of staving off the political and economic encroachments entailed in the Means Test, company unionism, the incursions of the British Union of Fascists into the valleys and perpetual heavy unemployment, led to an anti-fascist rather than a revolutionary ethos. Whether the conflict involved 'creeping' state fascism or 'naked' Mosley-type fascism, the political activity of the SWMF was inevitably defensive, rather than an offensive towards social revolution.[70]

Above all, to the Communists and Labour Party members in the SWMF, it did not seem possible to carry out a successful social revolution in Spain, during a period of growing fascism, declining social democracy and general trade union weakness due to heavy unemployment throughout most of Europe.[71]

The resolution passed at the Special Conference of the SWMF in June 1937 typified both its limited demands and its political standpoint:

> This Conference, representing over 120,000 miners of South Wales, welcomes the declaration of a new policy towards Spain by the IFTU [International Federation of Trades Unions] and the Labour and Socialist International. This policy, requiring pressure upon the Government members of the League of Nations to assist the Spanish Government to (1) recover its political and territorial independence; (2) obtain commercial liberty, including the right to purchase means of defence, shall have the support of this Conference to the utmost of its power.[72]

Such a standpoint, determined not so much by events in Spain as by a political outlook created by the long-standing and prevailing conditions in the coalfield, was consequently consistent throughout the duration of the Spanish Civil War. This consistency was not disturbed even by such a cataclysmic event as the 'Barcelona rising' of May 1937, which, on the contrary, seemed to harden the SWMF position.[73] The consistency of policy was emphasised by Horner at the 1938 SWMF Annual Conference. His speech also sheds light on the unusual political, financial and military commitment of the SWMF to the Spanish Republic:

> Our policy as a federation has always been clear. We are for the defence of Republican Spain and we accept the contingent upon this in terms of men and resources. We still have faith in the undying courage and inventiveness of the Spanish people to win victory, subject to the world working-class securing for the Spanish Government the right to buy arms to defend its people. . . .[74]

These political aims were shared at every level of the SWMF but the means of realising them were questioned by certain lodges and combine committees.[75] In reality, the Executive Council limited its activities to pressurising the MFGB, the TUC, the National Council of Labour and the British Government; wholeheartedly supporting, especially by financial means, the Spanish Republic, the International Brigades and the National Joint Committee for Spanish Relief; and agitating in the coalfield through meetings, demonstrations and film shows for financial and material aid. The intensity of activity in the coalfield is seen in the report of 2 November 1937, submitted by the EC sub-committee on Spain. It drew up the following plan of action which it conceived as an initiative which other sympathetic bodies and individuals in South Wales should follow:

1. That mass meetings be organised throughout the coalfield on Sunday, November 14, 1937, to protest against the threatened extinction of the Asturian miners.
2. That circular letters be sent to the areas, EC members, Agents and Lodge secretaries, advising them to jointly assist in holding the meetings.
3. That 100,000 special leaflets dealing with the Spanish situation be sent to the lodges for distribution.[76]

In all its activities, the SWMF achieved a limited success in the sense that it won working-class organisations over to its views. In the process of decision making within the whole framework of the MFGB, initiative for action on the Spanish question was frequently, if not always, taken by the SWMF EC and full-time officials.[77] Furthermore, Welsh miners' delegates invariably moved or seconded Spain resolutions at the MFGB, the TUC and the Miners' International Congress.[78] The SWMF leaders, in particular Horner and Paynter, were also responsible for spearheading the MFGB towards compelling the TUC to demand arms for Republican Spain.[79] In this way, the SWMF played a major role in the decision making of the MFGB.

With the constant support of the two important areas of Durham and South Wales, the MFGB was consistent and steadfast in its demands on behalf of Republican Spain.[80] From the very beginning, it opposed the Labour Party policy of supporting non-intervention early in the Civil War.[81] It even went to the extent of calling a special national delegate conference for 28 April 1938. The conference arose out of the worsening position in Spain and the refusal of the TUC to take decisive action on the question of the British Government guaranteeing financial credits for Germany and Italy.[82]

The peak of SWMF influence over other working-class bodies with regard to Spain came later. At the 1938 TUC, Will Paynter, representing the MFGB, seconded a successful resolution on arms for Republican Spain and unmistakably imprinted on the British trade union movement the unique 'trade union' orientated outlook of the South Wales miners towards the Spanish War.[83]

The conquest of Spain can well mean the commencement of further attacks upon other European democracies, and therefore I am pleading with this Congress that we should regard this matter, not merely as one of solidarity, but as an issue of self-preservation for trade unions in this country. I feel that the outcome of the war in Spain will not only determine the circumstances of our political existence, but will ultimately determine the industrial efficiency and the industrial existence of our trade union movement.[84]

But such pleading only influenced working-class organisations and failed to change markedly British Government policy or the fortunes of Republican Spain. Within six months of the 1938 TUC the British Government had recognised General Franco[85] and by 28 March 1939 the Spanish Republic had fallen to his armies.[86]

Some miners' lodges and combine committees differed with these tactical means of supporting the Spanish Republic. It was felt that the SWMF EC should use its most powerful weapon, a token strike, to show political solidarity and as a means of attacking non-intervention. This difference of views was accentuated both by the failure of the SWMF to achieve any substantial change in the policy of the British Government concerning non-intervention, and by Federation members fighting with the International Brigades.[87]

The first sign of opposition came from the Cefn Coed Lodge, in the Dulais Valley, in November 1937 when it asked the Executive Council to place before a special conference on unemployment and wages due for 20 November, a proposal for a day's stoppage as a protest against the Government policy on Spain.[88] But the Executive Council only agreed to place a much more moderate resolution before the conference. Other than urging an intensification of the collection of milk and food, all the resolution really called for was:

> ... the TUC to consider decisive action to secure a reversal of a [Government] policy which has brought the name of Britain into contempt among the democracies of the world.

The resolution was accepted by the conference partly because it was moved by the ex-International Brigader, Will Paynter.[89] But frustration with the failure of the SWMF to achieve a decisive change in the national and international situation again showed itself in April 1938. Once more, the opposition came from the Dulais Valley but this time the plans were better organised. The Dulais Valley Joint Lodges Committee[90] sent a delegation to the Executive Council to gain support for a token strike, with the view of placing a resolution before the 1938 SWMF Annual Conference. In the meantime, this rank-and-file movement had already enlisted the support of lodges in the Abercrave and Glyn-Neath areas.[91] But the Joint Lodges Committee was only allowed to place an amendment to a very mild resolution concerning an embargo on coal for Germany and Italy and the urging of the TUC to call a special conference on Spain. The amendment, moved by Onllwyn delegate and seconded by the Seven Sisters delegate, called for an immediate strike by South Wales miners 'to enforce the release of arms to the Spanish Government, to prevent the supply of any material to the fascist powers who were supporting the fascist rebels, and also to bring about the downfall of the present pro-fascist British Government'. The resolution was carried overwhelmingly, largely helped by Will Paynter moving it.[92]

Support for a token strike was also voiced at a meeting of the AACC which was specially convened to discuss Spain. A forthright appeal was made by D. J. Williams,[93] the chairman:

> The South Wales coalfield should give a lead to the British Trade Union Movement to take action on behalf of Spain. Situation in Spain is at the eleventh hour. . . . If we cannot get the top to lead we must lead from the bottom.[94]

Although there was strong support for strike action at this meeting, there was opposition not only from the usual quarters, but also from the President of the SWMF, Arthur Horner, who was still an agent in the Anthracite coalfield. He stated that strike proposals did not have the support of the Communist Party. He urged instead full support for an MFGB National Conference on 23 April on Spain and the possibility of levying a day's wages from all members. As a result of the strong differences of opinion, a vote was not taken on the strike proposal but the committee decided to send representatives to the National Conference on Spain and to send its suggestions for a pay levy to the SWMF EC.[95]

Discussions of strike action were revived much later, in October 1938 by the Cambrian Lodge Committee which asked the EC to call for a day's stoppage against the blockade of Spain.[96] The issue was not raised at any subsequent EC meetings.[97] Yet, as late as January 1939, the Fernhill lodge of Treherbert (Rhondda) once again raised the question of a token strike.[98]

Such militant proposals as strike action for essentially political reasons could not hope to succeed without the support of the Communist Party which played such an influential part in moulding the political policy of the SWMF. The Communist Party, at a time when it was working for a United Front, seemed convinced that success could only be achieved by orthodox, united action through the MFGB, the TUC and the National Council of Labour, rather than by localised industrial action which was believed would only atomise and not unify action in support of Republican Spain.[99]

Although attention paid to Spain should have naturally diminished with the withdrawal of the International Brigades from September 1938 onwards, and the defeat of the Spanish Republic in March 1939, the SWMF persisted for a considerable time in following Spanish events very closely. It sent £5 to every Welsh International Brigader held at the San Pedro de Cardenas Concentration Camp in Spain, and an extra £2 each for the Christmas of 1938.[100] The Federation was also concerned with the release of these prisoners, at least five of whom were Welsh miners.[101] The last Welsh prisoner, Tom Jones of Rhos, North Wales, was released in March 1940, helped by the work of the SWMF, but more especially by the persistence in the House of Commons of Will John, miners' MP for Rhondda West.[102]

Furthermore, five Spanish refugees who had been arrested in May 1939 as aliens in Cardiff were accommodated at the Ship Hotel, Penarth, on SWMF expenses.[103] Later, other refugees were helped in getting employment by the SWMF promising to maintain them if they became unemployed.[104] As late as 12 November 1940, four refugees who had landed in Cardiff in a 'terrible condition' were provided with clothes.[105] Arthur Horner was also sent by the MFGB to France in February 1939, to help set up a Miners' International Federation home for Spanish miners' orphans. Horner was later selected to attend the opening of this 'Spanish' house at Commune de Borderes near Farbes on 20 September 1939.[106]

Of all the international crises of the late 1930s it was Spain, with the failure of a democratically elected government to survive a military uprising and a foreign invasion, which finally shed the last vestiges of post-war pacifism in Wales, especially within the Labour Party. None the less, whilst there was sympathy for the Spanish Popular Front Government, and even James Griffiths respected the motives of Stafford Cripps in proposing a British Popular Front,[107] the immediate result of the defeat in Spain was recrimination in South Wales. Bevan along with a few miners, including Dick Beamish were expelled for their support of Popular Front agreements with the Liberals and the CPGB.[108] Less than a month after the fall of the Republic internal dissension in the Labour movement in South Wales was the dominant feature, with the SWMF once again almost totally isolated in its defence of Bevan. On a speaking tour of the Rhondda in April 1939 the expelled Bevan outlined his strategy and the lessons to be learnt from the

Spanish situation. It was a cry of despair and pessimism that he uttered at Tylorstown Welfare Hall:

> But I say again our Popular Front is better than the Unpopular Front we have with Chamberlain. . . . I would remind you that the most class conscious, the most advanced, the most democratic section of the working class supports us – and that is the South Wales Miners' Federation. . . . No one will deny for one moment we did not as a Labour Movement supply the government with unity. We have walked behind them in very docile fashion. We did all we could to make our people to respond. But there is something infinitely more than that. Co-operation was followed (in the first year of the Spanish War) by support of non-intervention. The blood of our Spanish comrades is on our hands. The working class of this country could have beaten Franco. The real enemy we had was Neville Chamberlain. . . . Our Labour Movement at that time hadn't got the guts to break away.[109]

This scathing and withering attack, impregnated as it was by an overwhelming sense of chronic despair, was a critique of the British Labour movement as a whole which was still failing, in Bevan's judgement, to equal the internationalist vision of the organisation in which he had been nurtured and which he described as 'the most advanced . . . section of the working class'.[110]

The history of the SWMF in the 1930s falls into three distinct parts: decline, revival and consolidation. The first period up to 1933 was composed of a decline in membership and of a bitter splenetic conflict between the Communist and Labour Parties. The mid-1930s was a period of revival helped by a more democratic union structure, greater tolerance by Communists and Socialists, a full-scale attack on the Means Test, company and non-unionism and an increase in membership. It was only on the basis of this revival that the SWMF was able, in its period of consolidation towards the end of the 1930s, to extend its anti-fascist activities into international politics and play a major role on the side of Republican Spain. It is only in this domestic context, as well as in consideration of its long militant and internationalist record, that the SWMF's relation with Spain can be adequately understood.

R. Page Arnot's description of the MFGB as something of a political party in its relations with the Spanish Republican cause is even more apt when considering the SWMF.[111] Such a departure from the normal function of a trade union had a profound and lasting impact on the policy and the members of the SWMF. The enduring syndicalist expression 'lodge politics' was never more appropriate for the coalfield than during the Spanish War. The SWMF's consistent internationally orientated and anti-fascist policy after the late 1930s can be traced directly to the period of the Spanish Civil War when policy precedents were set in giving enormous and diverse aid to Republican Spain. The SWMF was as one International Brigade volunteer later recalled, 'the link here with things international'.[112]

The survival of a form of fascism or francoism until the Spanish general election of 1977 meant that the internationalism of the South Wales miners continued to focus on Spain. The plight of the illegal Spanish trade unions had always been a major preoccupation. In the new situation following Franco's death, a delegation of Asturian miners attached to the socialist trade union centre (UGT) left Spain illegally and attended the Annual Conference of the South Wales miners in May 1976. This was followed by the Area EC giving a donation of £500 to help establish a legal miners' union in the Asturias. The South Wales miners were the first British trade union (apart from the TUC itself) to send a legal delegation into Spain. On the delegation, in March 1978, was Lance Rogers who had served with the International Brigades.[113]

At the unveiling in January 1976 of the plaque to commemorate the Welshmen killed serving with the International Brigades, Will Paynter articulated an internationalist outlook which had been endemic in the day-to-day activities of the South Wales miners ever since the outbreak of the Spanish War, but it was a perspective rooted as much in history as in contemporary reality:

> ... I'm hoping that we will take advantage of this situation this morning, when we pay tribute and salute the memory of those Welshmen who died in Spain, to rededicate ourselves in our determination to give all the assistance we can in the days ahead in order to ensure that the struggle of the Spanish people will be a successful struggle.[114]

Those slogans on the international lodge banners carried in the 1970s were, as that Cambrian miner who went to Spain had believed in 1938, 'clothed in flesh and blood'.[115]

NOTES

1. For a comprehensive account, see Hywel Francis, 'The South Wales Miners and the Spanish Civil War: A Study in Internationalism' (University of Wales, Ph.D., 1977). A forthcoming book by Hywel Francis, *From Tonypandy to Madrid*, will deal in detail with the background of the Welsh International Brigaders and their service in Spain.

2. D. B. Smith, 'The Rebuilding of the South Wales Miners' Federation, 1927–39', *op. cit.*, pp. 410–11.

3. See above Ch. 1, pp. 10–13; Ch. 2, pp. 52–4.

4. UCS, Cambrian lodge minutes, 15 December 1936.

5. UCS, Cambrian lodge minutes, 24 February 1935.

6. These were W. J. Griffiths, B. Jones and J. Roberts all of whom at various times served on the Cambrian lodge committee.

7. *SWM*, 9 January 1935.

8. UCS, South Pit lodge minutes, 9 April, 6 November 1937; 18 May 1938.

9. UCS, for instance Cambrian, Ferndale, Mardy lodge minutes, 1936–9 *passim*.

10. UCS, AACC minutes, 1936–9 *passim*.

11. SWMF EC minutes, 31 December 1934.

12. SWMF EC minutes, 1935 *passim*.

13. SWMF EC minutes, 15 February 1934; 27 May 1935; 8 December 1936.

14. SWMF Annual Conference minutes, 13–14 April 1935.

15. UCS, Cambrian Combine Committee minutes, 13 August 1936.

16. UCS, Cambrian Lodge Committee minutes, 29 December 1936; letter from Merthyr and District Unemployed Lodge to SWMF EC, 13 February 1937.

17. See Hywel Francis, 'Welsh Miners and the Spanish Civil War' in *Journal of Contemporary History*, Vol. 5, No. 3, 1970, pp. 177–91. *Idem*. 'Rhondda and the Spanish Civil War', in *Rhondda Past and Future* (1975), pp. 66–83. For more general information see Bill Rust, *Britons in Spain* (1939) and Hugh Thomas, *The Spanish Civil War* (1961).

18. Lewis Jones, *Cwmardy* (1937) *idem*, *We Live* (1939). Both have now been reprinted (1978) with a new Introduction by David Smith.

19. *Ibid.*, pp. 325–34; W. J. Griffiths, interview, *op. cit.*

20. Interview with Mavis Llewellyn (Nantymoel), 23 September 1969.

21. 'Will Paynter on Spain', *Llafur*, Vol. 2, No. 1, Spring 1976.

22. *South Wales Voice*, 21 May 1938.

23. *Rhondda Leader*, 18 February 1939.

24. See Gwyn Evans, Onllwyn: 'A Sociological Study of a South Wales Mining Community' (MA University of Wales, 1961) *passim*.

25. *DW*, 4 January 1935, 12 October 1936; SWML interview with David Francis (Onllwyn), 21 June 1976.

26. D. Francis interview, *op. cit.*, SWML, Onllwyn Spanish Aid Committee minutes *passim*.

27. *South Wales Voice*, 6 November 1937.

28. £7 was sent both to the International Brigades (Dependants' Aid Fund and the Relief Committee for Victims of Fascism) on 22 and 23 December 1937 respectively.

29. D. Francis interview, *op. cit.*, information from David Francis, 6 June 1977.

30. The following resolution was typical: 'That this Council representing 120,000 mineworkers expresses its deepest sympathy with the Spanish people in their heroic defence of the constitutional Government elected by the Spanish people themselves, and we urge the National Council of Labour to organise a campaign in this country with the view of giving every assistance possible to help the Spanish people to resist the attacks made upon them by rebels who are supported by the Fascist Governments of Germany and Italy', SWMF EC minutes, 28 November 1936.

31. See above, p. 352.

32. *Miners' Monthly*, August 1936.

33. SWMF EC minutes, 16 March 1937.

34. SWMF EC minutes, 3 April 1937.

35. By 16 March when the permanent financial commitment was made, several lodge officers were already fighting with the International Brigades. These included Sam Morris, chairman of Saron Lodge, Ammanford; Morris Davies, chairman of Treharris lodge and Frank Owen, member of Mardy Lodge committee. Many others followed later, notably T. H. Jones, Chairman of Tower Lodge, Aberdare, and H. Dobson, member of the Blaenclydach Lodge committee, both of whom were killed in the Ebro offensive.

36. UCS, SWMF collection, Merthyr Unemployed Miners Lodge committee to Oliver Harris, general secretary SWMF, 13 February 1937; reply from Harris, 15 February 1937.

37. UCS Cambrian Lodge minutes, 29 December 1936.

38. SWMF EC minutes, 31 May 1938.

39. SWMF EC minutes, 31 May 1938.

40. UCS, SWMF collection, O. Harris to Empire Lodge committee (Cwmgwrach), 24 February 1938.

41. R. P. Arnot, *The Miners in Crisis and War*, *op. cit.*, p. 267.

42. UCS, SWMF collection, E. G. Cox, secretary Emlyn Lodge committee to O. Harris, 14 November 1938.

43. UCS, SWMF collection, Edgar Williams, secretary Garngoch Number One Lodge committee, to O. Harris, 10 September 1938.

44. Morgan's son, Morien, had been serving with the International Brigades but, having been captured, was at the time languishing in San Pedro de Cardenas Concentration Camp.

45. UCS, SWMF collection, John E. Morgan, secretary Lady Windsor Lodge committee to Oliver Harris, 16 July 1938.

46. UCS, SWMF collection, Thomas Jenkins to Oliver Harris, 1 July 1939.

47. UCS, SWMF collection, Cambrian Lodge to Oliver Harris, n.d.; Lewis Merthyr Lodge to Oliver Harris, 25 October 1937.

48. UCS, SWMF collection, Chief Constable of Glamorgan to Evan Samuel, Lewis Merthyr Lodge secretary, n.d.

49. See above, Ch. 6, pp. 180–3.

50. Hywel Francis, 'The South Wales Miners and the Spanish Civil War', *op. cit.*, pp. 205–10.

51. *Ibid.*, pp. 94–6.

52. SWMF EC minutes, *Annual Accounts*, 1937–40.

53. SWMF EC minutes, *Annual Accounts*, 1935–40.
54. According to the Honorary Secretary of the International Brigades Dependants' Aid Fund, the South Wales miners in contributing over £1,000 gave more than any other British trade union for the year 1937, *Miners' Monthly*, April 1938.
55. SWMF EC minutes, 19 October 1938.
56. *Miners' Monthly*, May 1939.
57. W. Paynter, *My Generation, op. cit.*, pp. 63–9.
58. W. Paynter interview, *op. cit.*
59. SWMF EC minutes, 13 July 1937.
60. *DW*, 8 September 1937.
61. Interview with John Harris, secretary South Wales Council for Spanish Aid, 27 October 1969.
62. Interview with Pat Murphy, Cardiff volunteer in the International Brigades, 12 May 1969.
63. Interview with John Oliver, Blackwood volunteer in the International Brigades, 27 September 1970.
64. SWMF EC minutes, 1937, *passim.*
65. W. Paynter, *My Generation, op. cit.*
66. There is no reference in the correspondence or minutes of the lodges or in the EC of the SWMF indicating any support for a revolutionary approach to the War.
67. N. Chomsky, *American Power and the New Mandarins* (London, 1969), pp. 62–129.
68. *DW*, 28 August 1937.
69. H. Thomas, *op. cit.*, p. 292; W. Rust, *The Story of the Daily Worker* (London, 1949), pp. 39–49.
70. See above, Ch. 3 and Ch. 6 *passim.*
71. W. Paynter, *My Generation, op. cit.*, The most succinct accounts of the SWMF's approach were contained in a poster appeal to its members in July 1937 in which it emphasised the need for a common struggle against fascism, and a four-page pamphlet it published probably early in 1938 and entitled *Britain is in Danger!* (Cardiff, n.d.). As the title implied, the SWMF placed less emphasis on Spain and the nature of fascism and more on the need for international unity against it. It also called for the removal of the 'Chamberlain government' without which Britain could not be saved (poster reproduced on p. 361).
72. SWMF Special Conference minutes, 26 June 1937.
73. Interview with W. Paynter, 19 April 1969, *op. cit.*
74. *Miners' Monthly*, April 1938.
75. See below pp. 366–7.
76. SWMF EC minutes, 2 November 1937.
77. For example, the MFGB EC on 24 March 1937 sent on a resolution originating from the SWMF to the TUC General Council calling for a Special Congress of the TUC on Spain, R. P. Arnot, *op. cit.*, p. 255.
78. Horner seconded resolutions at the Miners' International Congress, 3 August 1936, and at the TUC on 7 September 1937. He also moved a resolution at the Special MFGB Conference on Spain on 8 September 1938. R. P. Arnot, *op. cit.*, pp. 244–75.
79. Horner at the 1937 and Paynter at the 1938 TUC spoke on resolutions demanding arms for Republican Spain, *ibid.*

80. *Ibid.*
81. *Ibid.*, pp. 251–2.
82. *Ibid.*, pp. 261–2.
83. Paynter 'drew such an eloquent picture of the atrocities in Spain that the resolution was carried without opposition from the platform or from the body of the hall' (*Manchester Guardian*, 9 September 1938); and he was allowed to continue speaking long after his allotted time had elapsed (W. Paynter, interview, *op. cit.*). Unquestionably, his prestige as an International Brigader counted for much, for the General Council had unaccountably failed to oppose a resolution whose carrying now entailed a reversal of its policy. This was all the more remarkable in that it followed a bitter attack in an earlier private session on the international situation. Arthur Deakin, General Secretary of the Transport and General Workers' Union and a member of the General Council, in replying to a speech by Dai Dan Evans, tried to undermine the South Wales miners' prominent role in the Spanish campaign by alleging that their integrity was in question. He claimed that miners from South Wales 'blacklegged' on Bristol dockers during the 1926 General Strike. His allegations were immediately answered by Horner, *TUC Annual Report*, Private Session on the International Situation, 8 September 1938.
84. SWML, transcript of speech by Will Paynter at TUC, 8 September 1938.
85. *WM*, 28 February 1939.
86. *WM*, 29 March 1939.
87. *WM*, 6 April 1938.
88. Interview with Tom Williams (Onllwyn), 19 January 1970, a member of Dulais Valley Joint Lodges Committee. He was the stepbrother of J. S. Williams of Dowlais who was at the time serving with the International Brigades.
89. *Miners' Monthly*, April 1938.
90. The Joint Committee included the Onllwyn lodge which had been so important in setting up a Spanish Aid Committee in the village. Among members of the Onllwyn lodge were H. J. Strangward who was about to go to Spain where he was to be killed in the Ebro offensive and several Spaniards from the Abercrave community whose enthusiasm for the Republic was well known, see above, pp. 356–7.
91. SWML, Tom Williams to David Francis, n.d.
92. *Miners' Monthly*, April 1938.
93. D. J. Williams was the author of *Capitalist Combination in the Coal Industry* (London, 1924), a student at the Central Labour College and Ruskin College, checkweigher in the Fife coalfield in 1926, Secretary of the Gwaun-cae-Gurwen joint lodges committee in the 1930s and miners' sponsored MP for Neath, 1946–64.
94. UCS, AACC minutes, 19 April 1938.
95. *Ibid.*
96. UCS, Cambrian Lodge minutes, 30 October 1938.
97. SWMF EC minutes, 1938–9 *passim*.
98. UCS, Ferndale Lodge minutes, 26 January 1939.
99. D. D. Evans interview, *op. cit.*
100. Interview with Morien Morgan, an Ynysybwl volunteer in the International Brigades, 15 October 1969.
101. SWMF EC minutes, 29 November 1939.

102. SWMF EC minutes, 2 April 1940.

103. SWMF EC minutes, 2 May 1939.

104. SWMF EC minutes, 15 June 1940.

105. SWMF EC minutes, 12 November 1940.

106. R. P. Arnot, *op, cit.*, pp. 273–4.

107. J. Griffiths, *op. cit.*, pp. 59–67.

108. M. Foot, *op. cit.*, pp. 271–300; Beamish, *op. cit.*

109. *NLW*, W. H. Mainwaring Papers, Verbatim Account of Speech by Aneurin Bevan, April 1939.

110. *Ibid.* Among the Welsh organisations to support the Popular Front were Mountain Ash Trades and Labour Council (*Aberdare Leader*, 11 February 1939).

111. R. Page Arnot, *op. cit.*, p. 271.

112. Jim Brewer (Abertysswg) to Hywel Francis, 30 September 1970.

113. National Union of Mineworkers (South Wales Area), *Annual Report, 1976–7.*

114. 'Will Paynter on Spain', *op. cit.*, p. 76.

115. W. J. Griffiths, 'Spain' (unpublished MSS.), p. 1.

CHAPTER ELEVEN

Ends and Beginnings

When Horner addressed his first Annual Conference, as President, in April 1937 he gave the protracted events of the summer and autumn of 1936 in Bedwas pride of place, claiming it as an 'outstanding victory':

> For four years this was a problem which haunted almost every Coalfield Conference. It will no longer haunt the Federation as in the past. Whilst we have not achieved everything we would like to have at Bedwas, and many difficulties still exist, we have at least established ourselves at a colliery where we had been outcasts for four years.[1]

The organised membership of the SWMF in 1936 was greater than at any time since 1926, though still not fully 100 per cent,[2] a situation that was seen as the product of an accelerating morale since 1933. The Bedwas settlement was the clearest indication of the EC's resolve to win disputes at limited cost to its financial and organisational capital; the back-log of resentment that built up in any one pit over time should, they felt, be defused by means of the existing machinery. 'Sporadic stoppages,' as Saddler the vice-president explained, 'weakened the organisation, and imposed sacrifices on our members which were not justified by the results.'[3] In other words, the 'Popular Front' that had won out within the SWMF was now arguing that since militancy could be effectively channelled, by institutional means, there was no further excuse for unofficial outbreaks.[4] The EC had earlier appointed its officials and four EC members to consider the whole question of unofficial stoppages, and especially 'stay-ins' which tended to deprive elected officials of 'leadership' over the men.[5] This had worried some, even when the issue was as fundamental as it had been in 1935. Now in the post-Bedwas situation it appeared to be a weapon that might disrupt hard-won unity. Iorwerth Thomas believed that its ability to allow a minority to dictate to others, without consultation with lodge officials even, undermined what had been achieved:

Whilst the power and authority of the organisation have been gradually moving towards centralisation we are confronted with the possibility of an industrial throw-back to where we were 40 years ago.

Undoubtedly the psychological consequences of a 'stay-in' were profound, with a whole village focusing on the action taken, perhaps to the exclusion of the actual issue in contention:

> There emerges but one opinion: the men down the pit must be supported. Hero worship and a general idealisation of the strikers as martyrs develop. Mothers, sisters, fathers, sweethearts, brothers, bask in reflected glory. Down below, as the days go by, dignity, pride, egotism, become increasingly manifest. A form of industrial eroticism arises . . . In such a situation local leaders of the Federation, men with long records of steadfast loyalty to the miners, invite disaster to themselves if they assert their honest convictions. . . . Arthur Horner . . . sounded the correct note at the last conference when he warned the coalfield against the perils of sporadic action. Discipline is essential; the alternative is industrial anarchy.[6]

In fact, from the late 1930s there was no serious possibility of any widespread discontent taking on an anarchic form (albeit in industrial guise) in the coalfield. The desire for a united 'Labour Movement', with the CP affiliated to the Labour Party, so ardently supported by the SWMF, and so firmly rooted in its own union structure, prevented this. Thus, both the Bedwas agreement and the new Wages Agreement of 1937, had the wholehearted support of both political groups on the EC.[7] The latter was an important stage in the industry's history. The economic 'boomlet', stimulated by rearmament, allowed an ending of the subsistence wage by discarding the old standard rates of 1915 in favour of higher ones, and by increasing the minimum percentage payable on them from 25 to 30 per cent. This meant that no man's wages would have to be brought up to 8s. 1d. a shift since the lowest would now receive 8s. 5¼d. Wage increases varied between 2s. 2d. and 10s. a week. More than this, however, the complicated grading of jobs in the coalfield, with pay differentials, was reduced from the thirteen underground and six surfacemen grades, to four main ones that now ensured one rate for the job throughout the coalfield. This was a vital, if underestimated, advance in tying the men together economically, and it was accepted, for a four year period, by a large majority.[8] Horner reflected that Sir Evan Williams, who had headed the coalowners' side in the negotiations, had been amenable 'because he knew that we were

SOUTH WALES MINERS' FEDERATION
NEW WAGES AGREEMENT

CLASSIFICATION OF WORKMEN OVER 21 YEARS OF AGE:

Grade "A" - 6/6 Minimum Standard Rate   Grade "C" - 7/2 Minimum Standard Rate

Grade "B" 6/10   "   Grade "D" - 7/6   "

Plus 30%

Class of Workman in Grade "A"

UNDERGROUND.

Coalcutters's Assistants; Cogcutters; Colliers Helpers; Dumpers; Fitters Labourers; Flitters (ordinary) Gob and Waste Labourers, including the necessary walling; Jig Hitchers; Labourers; Lamplighters; Lamplockers; Subsidiary Haulage Enginemen, up to and including 100 H.P.; Oilers; Ostlers; Subsidiary Pumpmen; Shacklers and Spragmen; Slummers; Trammers over 18 years of age; Watermen, watering roads.

SURFACE.

Ashmen; Assistant Banksmen; Blacksmiths Strikers; Brakesmen; Carpenters' Labourers; Coal Throwers; Engine Cleaners; Fitters Labourers; Flue Cleaners; Granarymen, small; Hauling Enginemen, small; Hauliers and Shacklers; Labourers; Lampmen; Masons Labourers; Mortarmen; Ostlers; Platelayers, ordinary; Small Pumpmen; Quarrymen; Rubbish Tippers; Sawyers' Assistants; Screenmen; Screen Enginemen; Stone-dust Mill-hand; Timber Fillers and Unloaders.

Class of Workman in Grade "B"

UNDERGROUND.

Coal Cutters' Assistants posting (i.e., Anchor and Stampermen); Fitters, semi-skilled; Hitchers, ordinary; Hauliers (over 18 years of age); Main Haulage Enginemen; Subsidiary Haulage Enginemen, over 100 H.P.; Pipemen; Pumpsmen, main; Repairers Assistants; Rippers' Assistants (men actually assisting in ripping); Riders and Rope-changers, over 18 years of age; Roadmen; Sheavemen; Signalmen and Wiremen; Timbermen's Assistants; Wallers who do strip packing and build pack walls.

SURFACE.

Air Compressor-men; Boilermakers, semi-skilled; Carpenters, semi-skilled; Crane Enginemen; Electric Generating Enginemen, up to and including 3,000 K.W. rated capacity, actually running and in charge; Electric and Acetylene Burners; Fanmen; Fitters, semi-skilled; Granary Chargemen; Lampmen in charge of each Shift; Locomotive Shunters; Platelayers, Leading; Pumpsmen, Large; Quarrymen; Smiths, semi-skilled; Stokers; Stone-dust Mill-hand in charge; Switchboard Men in Power Stations up to 3,000 K.W. rated capacity actually running and in charge; Other Switchboard Men; Tip Enginemen; Tram Repairers; Wagon Repairers, semi-skilled; Wiremen (Electric light wiremen.)

Class of Workman in Grade "C"

UNDERGROUND.

Borers; Bottom cutters; Electricians, skilled; Fitters, skilled; Flitters, leading; Hitchers, leading on coal winding shift; Main Haulage Enginemen, men bringing coal to pit bottom or surface with 200 H.P. haulage or over (including Slant Enginemen); Masons; Pitmen; Punchmen and Automatic Pickworkers; Second-class Repairers and Timbermen; Rippers; Roadmen (men who can and do lay "T" head partings, check rails, &c., i.e., men in charge); Ropesplicers; Steel Prop Drawers; Timber Drawers.

SURFACE.

Banksmen; Boilermakers, skilled; Carpenters, skilled; Electric Generating Enginemen, over 3,000 K.W. rated capacity, actually running and in charge; Electricians, skilled; Electric and Acetylene Welders, skilled; Farriers; Fitters, skilled; Haulage Enginemen, large (over 200 H.P.); Locomotive Drivers; Masons; Ropesmiths and Splicers; Sawyers; Smiths, skilled; Smiths, sharpening Tools; Shoeing Smiths; Stokers, in charge of boilers other than their own; Switchboard Men in power stations over 3,000 K.W. rated capacity actually running and in charge; Wagon Repairers, fully skilled and competent all-round wagon repairers who can and do perform all-round wagon repairing work.

Class of Workman in Grade "D"

UNDERGROUND.

Conveyor chargemen; Coal cuttermen; Electricians, fully skilled and competent all-round electricians who can and do effect all kinds of skilled repairs to motors, and who are capable of, are called upon to and do dismantle and erect electrical plant; Fitters fully-skilled and competent all-round fitters who can and do perform all-round fitting work underground or on surface; Hard heading men; Masons, fully-skilled and competent; Pitmen, leading; Timbermen, first class; Steel Arch and Girder erectors; Colliers on minimum or daywage, 7/3.

SURFACE.

Boilermakers, fully-skilled and competent all-round boilermakers who can and do perform all round boiler-making work; Carpenters, fully-skilled and competent all-round carpenters who can and do perform all-round carpentering work underground and on the surface; Electricians, fully-skilled and competent all-round electricians who can and do effect all kinds of repairs to motors, and who are capable, are called upon to and do dismantle and erect electrical plant; Electric and Acetylene Welders, fully-skilled and competent all-round welders who can and do perform all-round welding work; Fitters, fully-skilled and competent all-round fitters who can and do all-round fitting work underground and on surface; Masons, fully-skilled and competent; Patternmakers; Smiths, general, fully-skilled and competent all-round smiths who can and do perform all-round smithing work; Shoeing smiths, who can and do actually make and fit shoes; Winding enginemen.

Boys Underground.		
Years of Age.		Standard Rate.
14 to 15	.. ..	2/6
15 to 16	.. ..	3/-
16 to 17	.. ..	3/6
17 to 18	.. ..	4/-
18 to 19	.. ..	4/6
19 to 20	.. ..	5/-
20 to 21	.. ..	5/6
	Plus 30%	

Boys Surface.		
Years of Age.		Standard Rate.
14 to 15	.. ..	2/4
15 to 16	.. ..	2/8
16 to 17	.. ..	3/-
17 to 18	.. ..	3/4
18 to 19	.. ..	3/9
19 to 20	.. ..	4/3
20 to 21	.. ..	4/9
	Plus 30%	

April 5th 1937.

OLIVER HARRIS, General Secretary.

CYMRIC FEDERATION PRESS, NEVILLE STREET, CARDIFF.

SWMF poster on 1937 Wages Agreement.

strong enough to make our demands'.[9] So the calmer waters into which the SWMF had sailed implied no slackening in its determination to win total control of the labour-force in the collieries. With a grim finality the Federation turned once more to consider Taff-Merthyr.

The Federation had maintained their activity there during the Bedwas campaign, using the same tactic, though at a lower level of intensity, of building up support within the pit first. However, the leaflets they issued assuring the men that the Company would not 'victimise' them if they joined the Federation were repudiated by the Company itself, although the Federation insisted that such a verbal guarantee had been made.[10] E. L. Hann, a director of the Company, pressed the Federation to hold a ballot as under the 1934 Agreement, but the failure of the Company to re-employ those who had been imprisoned over the disturbances in 1935, allied to constant allegations that the colliery officials claimed that any full recognition of the Federation would lead to a further reduction in the labour force, all convinced the Federation that 'normality' (the pre-condition of a ballot) had not been established.[11]

The SWMIU assured its members that the SWMF's 'Red tide of Communism' would be held back so that the men at Taff-Merthyr could be assured of their jobs. This was a tactic that the Federation had had to face in Bedwas, and now, as then, they insisted that they were no longer demanding the dismissal of men who had been employed during the period of strife. The vehemence of this particular leaflet war[12] was tempered by the 1934 Agreement's strictures on the use of colliery premises or open places nearby for mass meetings. The neighbouring villages had not recovered from the savagery with which their social cohesion had been disrupted (it lingered on, in many ways, for decades), nor was the Colliery itself back to full working. There were only 700 men employed on two shifts – one for repairers and one for colliers since the third shift, for colliers, had not been restarted after 1934. In December 1936, three of those imprisoned for riot were still in gaol. Normality, then, was an elastic term.

It was a puncturing of ingrained hostility *within* the pit, that the Federation had to achieve if they were to win it over; hence their disclaiming of any intention of rejecting the present work-force. The Federation were anxious for 'normality': 'It is our earnest desire . . . that you [i.e. the workmen employed] . . . with ourselves may be able to restore to the district an atmosphere of friendship and goodwill, resulting in incalculable value to the religious, social and industrial life

Taff Merthyr Lodge, S.W.M.F.

INDUSTRIAL UNION RECORD.

Extracts from Balance Sheets of M.I.U.

IS THIS WHERE THE FOURPENCES GO?

1934	One Motor Car	-	-	£325
1935	One Motor Car	-	-	£468
1936	The Price of a Hearse?			
1934	Legal Charges - Compensation			Nil
1935	Legal Charges - Compensation			£4 7 0
1934	Pit Examinations	-	-	£12 0 0
1935	Pit Examinations	-	-	£5 10 0
1934	Vacuum Cleaner	-	-	£20 0 0
1935	Vacuum Cleaner, Balance			£8 0 0

More spent on a Vacuum Cleaner than on Pit Examinations.

200 times more spent on Motor Cars than on Compensation Cases.

What was spent on Negotiations for Wages Increases? NOTHING!

What was spent on Conferences for Members? NOTHING!

To-morrow we will give the record of the SOUTH WALES MINERS' FEDERATION - the only Organisation that is fighting for the South Wales Miners.

JOIN THE FEDERATION!

Cymric Federation Press, Neville Street, Cardiff.

A Taff-Merthyr leaflet, 1936.

of the whole.' Conversely, the SWMIU reply addressed itself directly to the indignities suffered by those who had 'blacklegged': 'We invite you to tell these people . . . that least of all will you join an organisation which has subjected you and your dependants to every form of insult and injury within their power, and has ground your face in the mud in an attempt to impose their will upon you.'[13]

But perhaps the most convincing indication of the efficacy of such reminders (and they did bear fruit) is a letter in the local press, signed 'A Faithful Scab', which attacked the 'militants' of Taff-Merthyr in a familiar fashion, yet whose real eloquence lies in its depiction of a rival 'scab' community around Taff-Merthyr, one that had grown as tenacious as the one which had supported the Federation:

> . . . We have been hounded out of the churches; we should not associate with any of our friends; we could not enter a public house; in fact we were driven into a community of our own. This is what the local Communists call 'victory'. For two years we were called all the despicable names that a Communist tongue could utter. We were jeered at in the streets. But in spite of this humiliation we remained united to a man.[14]

This 'rival community' had help in maintaining their unity from the Company, which pursued its own interpretation of the 1934 Agreement on re-employment:

> They are transferring men from the old Bedlinog Pits who have been in employment for the last year or so whereas the loyal Taff-Merthyr men who are still unemployed are not being reinstated with the exception of a small number who started a short while ago. Again, members are reporting on the activities of certain Non-Pols who are very active and are making statements such as, Don't pay the Federation and we will get you work. This meeting [a mass one called by the Taff-Merthyr Federation Lodge] is of the opinion that the Company is still as determined as ever to prevent a Lodge being established there and urges the EC to carry out its pledges to do everything in its power to establish a Lodge of the SWMF at Taff-Merthyr.[15]

The impatience of the local men, strengthened as it was by the final ending of the Industrial Union in Nottinghamshire (though not on terms approved of by the SWMF),[16] had its roots in their conviction that the campaign was having effect. Even Gregory, after the end of Spencerism elsewhere conditioned his insistence that the SWMIU 'had not gone out of existence' by the phrase 'if it does' – if it did then there was to be a resurrection as a South Wales Conservative Workmen's Association.[17]

So, despite continued allegations about the employment of 'new men' in 1937,[18] the men engaged in organising in the district became convinced that the SWMF could win a ballot. The EC, by no means so optimistic, finally succumbed to these pressures to hold a decisive ballot as soon as it could be arranged. A series of meetings with the Company produced the agreed date of 7 October for the ballot, with the EC agreeing, after expressing their unwillingness, that 'no propaganda' should be conducted.[19]

The acceptance of this provision, in a situation of continuing tension and the employment of new workmen (who brought the total employed to 900 men) proved fatal to the Federation's hope. The result was the only such victory ever enjoyed by the MIU — 453 voted for them, and 448 for the SWMF. Gregory declared that it was a result to be expected when men were freed from intimidation.[20]

This was a grievous blow to the Federation. Horner himself had opposed taking the ballot on the grounds that the 'scum of the coalfield' had been gathered together in Taff-Merthyr and would not be easy to skim off;[21] certainly the existence of such a counter-community is indicated by the voting figures and by the social misery that continued to haunt the local villages.[22] When Horner came to explain the subsequent settlement to the Taff-Merthyr men he emphasised that it had been local pressure that had induced the Federation to go ahead with the ballot:

> We sent people here to try and bring about a situation where we could conduct the ballot with some degree of certainty . . . the Taff-Merthyr Committee and others told us, in no uncertain terms, to take the ballot. . . . I had a letter from one of your members stating that it would be a mistake to take the ballot, but our EC members here and the officials of the Lodge had told the EC that if we took the ballot we were bound to win; but we did not win the ballot.[23]

So far had the situation altered, however, that neither the owners nor the Industrial Union had any desire to use their slender majority to prolong matters. At the same time, the SWMF's defeat put the SWMIU back into a position of strength in the talks that now took place over amalgamation. The Industrial Union, in South Wales, had not been wound up at the same time as its Nottingham equivalent because the SWMF thought it had had no need to be so generous; after the ballot the Industrial Union was allowed to bow out, in its own manner, by merging with its enemy. Indeed, at the SWMIU victory banquet (contributed to, in part, by Captain Lionel Lindsay) William Gregory made friendly overtures:

> If you have a Federationist working next to you, treat him as a pal. Bury the hatchet. Tonight we celebrate a release from bondage, and we still long for the peace that we have preached for eleven years.[24]

The representatives of the two unions met, for the first time, under the chairmanship of the coalowners' secretary, on 13 October, and on two other occasions during the following fortnight. George Spencer attended to advise on ways of amalgamating; the Federation agreed to certain safeguarding proposals. There were no startling moves one way or the other, since both sides were keen not to give way nor to obstruct the negotiations; so both kept their suggestions on the table until a compromise could be agreed. This was finally reached in late January of 1938 when the EC approved the terms.[25]

The SWMIU was merged with the Federation. All the Industrial Union members were taken into the Federation, without fee, for a three month period of grace; they were guaranteed equal rights which would be further safeguarded by the appointment of a commission to exist for two years (Iestyn Williams, Oliver Harris and William Gregory were to serve) that would look into any infringement of these rights. The office furniture was bought and disposed of; although the Federation refused categorically to take on any SWMIU officials they did promise (along with Spencer and Iestyn Williams) to help in the location of new jobs. In fact, Gregory and his staff were given, though not directly by the SWMF, the equivalent of a year's salary; it now emerged that money, purportedly coming from Spencer himself, had paid for wages and other expenditure, since November 1935 to the tune of £2,925, whilst their 'cash at the Bank and in Hand' was only £109. The SWMF gave Spencer £1,500 to deal with all liabilities (a sum of £5,772 15s. 0d.), a sum which covered those items other than the money from Spencer himself. In turn, Spencer undertook to dissolve the SWMIU and wind up all its affairs.[26]

Since Taff-Merthyr had never been in the sole charge of any one Federation official (S. O. Davies apart, and he had gone) the bitterness that had occurred at Bedwas between the Company and SWMF officials did not arise so that Horner did not need to act as agent. Instead the miners' agent for Area No. 5 (D. Emlyn Thomas who had succeeded Noah Ablett) was empowered to act with the chairman and secretary of the new lodge in any negotiations. There was to be a new agreement drawn up and approved by the men in work *before* the lodge committee was elected.

This agreement was almost a fascimile of the Bedwas one, that is, it maintained existing arrangements at the colliery, including day-to-day contracts, with the proviso that wages would alter in the face of any general advance or reduction. Disputes were to be referred through all levels up to an Arbitrator whose decision was to be binding, whilst the workmen were to 'undertake that no restriction of effort or strike action of any kind shall take place nor shall any stoppage of the colliery be brought about by them provided that any and every dispute which may arise is . . . settled in the manner provided'.

The Federation were bound down as firmly as the Company could manage. Not only were there to be no 'show cards' or meetings on the premises without the management's permission but the agreement, binding until September 1941, had to be signed (as with the Bedwas one) by the President, Vice-President and Secretary of the SWMF, by all its EC members and by the officials and committee of the Taff-Merthyr workmen.

There was one clause in both the agreement with the SWMIU and with the Company which was most difficult to take since it reflected directly the reality of the SWMF's defeat at the ballot and thus presented no solace to the hurt nursed by those who had looked for a victory in the ballot as a final, sweet vindication of the anguish they had undergone since 1926. The principles involved in the whole struggle were, indeed, as vital as the Federation had claimed; so much so that the EC could feel justified in making major concessions to attain their primary objectives. The losers, though, in the immediate sense, were those who had fought longest – the local men.

Clause 16 of the Agreement to Work reads:

Having been assured by the Company that it is their intention in general to take back into employment men previously employed at the Colliery, reserving the right to take into employment individuals not previously employed at Taff-Merthyr Colliery at any time, that the managerial discretion has to be exercised in favour of suitability, we agree that no seniority rule shall be countenanced in the employment or withdrawal of workmen. The management will agree to discuss with the miners' agent, from time to time, the operation of this clause.

For the immediate future, the Federation was thus resigning any attempt to control the colliery. Even worse was Clause 8 of the

Agreement to Merge which brought the new lodge committee into existence as a unique hybrid:

> The Lodge Committee at Taff-Merthyr shall be composed of nineteen persons, including the Chairman, Secretary and Treasurer, all of whom must be workmen in employment at the colliery. . . . The Chairman and Secretary, together with eight members of the Committee, shall be elected and appointed by workmen who were members on the register of the South Wales Miners' Industrial Union on the 2nd October 1937.
>
> The Treasurer, together with eight members of the committee shall be elected and appointed by workmen who were members of the Miners' Federation and who were in employment at the colliery on the 2nd day of October 1937.
>
> The committee and officials shall hold office for two years certain from the date upon which they effectively take office.
>
> The Chairman and Secretary of the Taff-Merthyr Committee shall attend all meetings of the South Wales Miners' Federation Executive Council at which any subject affecting Taff-Merthyr Colliery or the workmen employed thereat may be under discussion and shall have power to exercise one vote.[27]

That one vote, paltry as it might sound, was symbolic of the pinprick which the Industrial Union could inflict even at its demise. Rumours began to circulate about the proposed terms and their possible rejection by the men involved,[28] but, in fact, at a mass meeting of the Taff-Merthyr workmen, the Federation Lodge decided, after a long discussion, to give their unanimous approval. A Special Conference of Delegates was called to sound out opinion in the coalfield and this too was accorded by an overwhelming majority. A ballot of Industrial Union members also indicated a majority for acceptance so that a committee could now be elected at the colliery as the merger and the agreement with the Company were ratified (the latter was accepted at the earlier meeting of the men, and ratified later by the elected committee).[29]

Just as the persuasion of the Bedwas militants had been at the heart of the 1936 settlement so the Taff-Merthyr men had to be won over first before the issue was put to the coalfield as a whole. Their defeat in the ballot gave Horner his soundest argument – What else could they do? At the meeting held in the Workmen's Institute, Bedlinog, on Sunday, 6 February 1938, the three senior officials of the SWMF and two EC members (Alf and Jack Davies) addressed the SWMF Lodge

Committee to convince them to accept the terms before they were put to the general meeting.

Horner's exposition of the case[30] was, again, a masterly blend of realism and threats, sweetened by his assertion that, appearances to the contrary, a victory had been gained. He began by chiding the committee for rejecting the agreement even before it had been explained to them, even though they had been promised that they were to be consulted. The vital issue, he reminded them, was that the SWMF had agreed to a ballot, and being a responsible organisation they had to abide by its verdict whether they won or not. In the cold light of the defeat, Horner looked back not only to the unjustified certainties of the committee that the SWMF could win but also to the 1934 Agreement and its acceptance of the principle of a ballot:

> Why that agreement was entered into was because everybody thought the afternoon shift might restart and the Federation would have the majority. That agreement was justifiable if the afternoon shift would be restarted but obviously our people were tricked into believing it would restart.

Arthur Horner was rarely content to dwell on the past; the small majority achieved in the ballot ensured a stalemate (and this would have applied for both sides), so the issue of 'recognition' was still unsettled and to that end the SWMF met with the Industrial Union to try to end that organisation, despite its victory – 'These people exist and our object has been to get them to go out of existence, and in order to achieve that we have had to face certain facts.' Those 'facts', Horner was claiming, were the dictators of the unpleasant features of the proposals. He went through the clauses in the terms, commenting on each in turn, and at length on the awkward points.

Essentially his argument was that the SWMIU was finished and that all that followed from that, good and bad, were minor matters. The Federation were to have nothing to do with the SWMIU in the future:

> . . . We have no jobs for anybody. There is not one of those persons going to have a job in the Miners' Federation or anything we are connected with. . . . We are not paying the officials any money but simply taking away their jobs. The most we have promised to do is to try and use every effort to secure satisfactory employment.[31]

As for the Industrial Union members who were to join the Federation without fee and on an equal basis, the answer was that this was the only way to achieve a frictionless amalgamation whilst the commission that was set up would allow Federation members the right of appeal against local officials, as well as vice versa. The joining of Taff-Merthyr to Area No. 5 again caused him to review a past history of confusion:

> At the beginning the Dowlais District wanted you; the Taff and Cynon District wanted you, and Merthyr wanted you; but Taff-Merthyr got into such a problem that nobody wanted you, and the Executive had to to take it up. We have put it into Area 5 on geographical grounds, and in addition the Miners' Agent of Area No. 5 has had nothing to do with the trouble . . .

Similarly he was able to point out that the agreement with the Company had to await the workmen's ratification, that the Group Life Insurance Scheme in operation was not compulsory, and that the agreement was to end on 30 September 1941 which was the same date as the general Wages Agreement (or before if the Company joined the Coalowners' Association) so that nothing was irrevocable. The question of a double-headed lodge was not one that could be glided over, however. Horner chose to meet it in a direct fashion.

In his view, the MIU could have insisted on total control of the lodge, by the terms of the ballot; as it was they had agreed to have a majority of one. His rhetorical question was both a reproach and a challenge:

> Because you start off with one less do you give up the ghost and think you have a lost cause? . . . It is the minimum of sacrifice in face of the fact that we lost the ballot and that the colliery belongs to the Miners' Industrial Union.

Besides, this was only for two years, whilst the men were now in the Federation; any other arrangement would have deprived the men of Federation protection in the pit and of Federation influence in securing the re-employment of old Taff-Merthyr men. Worse, it would 'give the Industrial Union an opportunity of rising again in the coalfield'. For all these reasons, Horner concluded, the EC was unanimous in its recommendation. His final words again spelled out the brutal truth that would follow rejection.

> If you turn it down we report it to the Conference but if Conference accepts it and you turn it down the Conference cannot accept responsibility for your future. If, on the other hand, Conference turns it down we are still confronted with the possibility of the revival of the MIU and the Company could say that the ballot decided the issue. . . .
>
> Do not think the Conference is willing to come out to fight for Taff-Merthyr in face of the fact that the Taff-Merthyr workmen themselves, by a majority, were in favour of the MIU.

Horner's phrase 'in face of the fact' reverberates through his speech like a bell tolling for the hour of decision. It was to this, after some further points had been cleared up,[32] that the committee came when they adopted, unanimously, the resolution that:

> In view of the further explanations of the agreement made between the Fed and the MIU and the assurances given by the Officials of the Federation, the committee agrees to recommend this agreement to the mass meeting this afternoon.

When that mass meeting also unanimously accepted it, the SWMF had come almost to the end of one of the most debilitating struggles that it had ever faced. Oliver Harris reviewed the whole struggle in February 1938 as the end of a 'queer chapter' that had begun as a reaction to the prolonged stoppage of 1926:

> [The SWMIU] . . . was based on ideas so alien to the ideology of the South Wales Miners that it could never take root except in some specially cultivated spots where its growth was encouraged by coalowners who thought it could be used as a means to undermine the power and authority of the Federation. . . .
>
>   We hope that in those localities where the controversy has led to bitter personal feelings affecting the industrial, social and even the religious life of the community, the hatchet will be buried and that all sections will unite and work together for the good of all.[33]

These pious hopes had no chance of a quick fulfilment. Undoubtedly the SWMF had won the day; undoubtedly, too, there had been many casualties along the way. Harris's remarks did not do justice to the necessary vigour (and misery) of the earlier struggles that had allowed the Federation to hang on in certain areas despite its central weakness, nor could the overall triumph disguise the sacrifices that were still being borne at local level.

At Taff-Merthyr, the unemployed men who had worked in the pit (most of them lived in Bedlinog) formed their own separate organisation and settled down to wait for the 'President's efforts . . . to bear fruit'. By late September they were complaining that the management were appointing men who had never worked at the Colliery before on the grounds of their 'suitability' despite the fact that men starting as repairers were soon reduced to labourers because they were not able to do the work, whereas many of the ex-Taff-Merthyr men were available who had worked in those specific grades.[34] Such complaints, and the individual casualties, would not abate for a long time but a combination of effective leadership and the willingness of specific communities and particular individuals to pay a considerable price had resulted in the removal of the only outright rival the SWMF had had since 1898. There was still D. B. Jones' Colliery Enginemen, Boilermen and Craftsmen's Association, but this too, after discussions through 1938, was wound up in November 1938 by a merger, with Jones becoming one of the Federation's craftsmen's agents.[35]

For the rest, at least in a formal sense, it was now a question of conducting mopping-up operations to draw in those men who were still outside the Federation. The membership had been raised from 112,743 in 1936 to 120,280 in 1938 (with the number unemployed remaining steady) and the MIU closed down;[36] there were still around 10,000 not accounted for, and they could, it seemed, only be brought in by the hard work of Lodge Officials and the concerted action of the Combine Committees.[37] The policy adopted was that of issuing notices over non-unionism, conducting a sharp campaign and then, with success achieved or almost anyway, withdrawing notices at the last moment. There were constant threats of large-scale action by the Combine Committees throughout 1937 and 1938, whilst in July 1938 there was a one-day strike by the Ocean Combine and in January 1939 the Cory Combine had a strike involving 6,000 men for three days. In both instances, the men returned to work having created a 100 per cent membership.[38]

The last occasion on which there had been a resort to strike action over non-unionism the matter had led directly to the wave of 'stay-in' strikes of late 1935; in these later disputes, the evidence was that the owners, in contradistinction to their attitude in 1935, and now devoid of an alternative union to organise the men, wished to co-operate even to the extent of pressuring workmen in arrears to join the SWMF.[39] There were, nevertheless, no easy avenues to success, especially where the massively powerful Powell Duffryn Company was concerned, for the official attitude towards the combines was still that there should be no formal recognition of them:

> The customs and practices operating in the individual collieries vary so considerably that it is important that these customs and practices should be maintained. There is a very grave danger if Management meet Combine Committees for the extension of those customs and practices which are most advantageous to the workmen.[40]

If any evidence were still needed as to the use which management could make of weak organisation, it could be found in the three reports, each compiled by two different EC members, into conditions of work and of organisation in the Powell Duffryn Company pits, that the EC had requested in January 1938. Their reason for this lay in the vast size of the group, the consequent difficulty in organising an effective Combine Committee, and the kind of management that had full rein there. Or as one of the reports said:

> The ideal method, from the owners' point of view, is indicated in the lecture of Mr Morris Hughes, agent, Merthyr Vale, to the PD officials and Students' Association at the Britannia Mining School. A given mineral area which is to be worked by the pit concerned is panelled out right to its boundary. The size of the panel, the conveyors required, the number of men required, the material and costings are all set out before the panel is touched. The rate of advance, the daily output, is all fixed. Even the date of commencing the panel and the date of its completion form part of the plan. The plan is passed to the manager to operate. His task is predetermined. Equally, the task of each workman is predetermined. Where Price Lists exists, the conformity to a predetermined task is blurred. Where no Price Lists exist, task work and quota systems flourish in their mechanical conformity to the plan. In this situation the collier becomes even more the mechanical machine. . . . The Task Work gives the collier a higher wage than the minimum, but it must be recognised that he fills coal at less than 1s. 0d. per ton. This rate is less than a Price List would give the collier, and the collier is a mere coal-filling tool to go where and when directed. The effect of the predetermined speed upon the collier's health, and the effect of his lack of rights upon his trade union spirit can best be imagined rather than described.[41]

Altogether forty-three lodges were visited, with depressing results. In all there was a full tilt move towards intensive methods of working supervised by 'Efficiency Experts' produced from the 'company's training centre'; the operation of payment on a yardage-tonnage basis (i.e. a grossly inequitable means of paying a collier for the tonnage of coal he cut on the prearranged basis of what a particular measured panel would produce), contracting-out of heading and stall work, the employment of boys to do men's work, alleged intimidation by officials, and so on. Some lodges had a better deal than others, invariably where the organisation was stronger, others (including Mardy, that had reopened in 1936 and now had 330 men employed full-time with 95 per cent in the Federation, had no checkweigher and no Price List) were in a state of chaos, openly prevented from fulfilling lodge functions by the management, and prevented from organising proper methods of payment for colliers by the practice of management employing day-wagemen to cut coal on faces determined by management. This, as with the yardage-tonnage basis of payment, caused endless friction *between* workmen who lost any basis for united action:

> The method of individual approach adopted by the management at several collieries is undermining the influence of the lodge. Packers, fitters and other grades of workmen are being compelled to accept terms that the lodge officials and committees would reject as being contrary to all trade union principles.
>
> The Colliery Company are slowly taking out of the control of the Lodges those functions that are fundamental to the existence of the Federation.
>
> Unless this matter is taken by the EC very seriously, the future of the SWMF at PD collieries will be one of the gravest difficulty.
>
> [The] policy of the Company is calculated to break up that unity that is essential to the well-being of the Federation, and at the same time make it possible to depreciate the value of work done by the different grades of workmen.
>
> The Company must be stopped introducing individual contracts for day-wagemen. The existing contracts that have been forced upon workmen must be broken. The authority of the lodge and the principle of collective bargaining must be maintained.[42]

All of this was accentuated by a deliberate policy of recruiting labour from a wide catchment area so that 'in none of the collieries is there to be found a homogeneous body of workmen who, as in the past, had a community interest in the working conditions of the colliery. The only intimate association between workmen is in the collective working at the pit, and that, obviously, only of a limited character'. As a result combination and organisation were inordinately difficult.[43]

Formal approaches were made,[44] via the Coalowners' Association, but the crucial prerequisite was the revitalising of individual lodges. This, in turn, required financial and organising aid from the Central who, indeed, strongly supported the PD Combine Committee's decision in early 1939, after a delegate conference of all their lodges, to proceed to an 'all-in' policy over a three-month period. After initial forays groups of lodges were singled out, each in turn, being the subject of a campaign headed by EC members and, if need be, of strike action. The result was that, one by one, 100 per cent membership returns were being recorded with the EC for the first time, giving individual lodges the permission to strike with the promise of financial support.[45] This was a special case they had decided because:

For many years the PD Company had quietly and stubbornly maintained an attitude of antagonism towards the Federation and this created a mentality among the men which made it impossible to create a sound organisation at these collieries.[46]

By the late summer of 1939 even the PD collieries were fully organised, either by the threat of strikes or, as in the Aberdare Valley that saw three short non-unionist disputes that summer, by the men coming out against small minorities.[47] A greater percentage of the workmen employed now belonged to the SWMF than at any previous time other than during the First World War. The Federation had truly built itself up again. The reality of this was apparent, from 1937, with the destruction of the SWMIU and then the Craftsmen's Association, even to the owners who began to explore means of curing 'this running sore' of non-union stoppages which they felt disrupted working and so made it difficult to 'maintain and extend markets'. The SWMF, in the words of their secretary, had come to feel that it would be worth being patient 'if we can come to a satisfactory arrangement which will avoid the periodical crises at the collieries over the non-unionists'.[48]

From late 1937 and through 1938 the two sides began to meet to discuss joint action on the matter, though the owners were, at first, only prepared to listen to proposals since the concept of a 'closed shop' is one that they had vehemently opposed, so far as the SWMF was concerned anyway, throughout the history of their Association.[49] The EC therefore pressed on with its support of lodges in giving in notices over non-unionism but tempered any pleas for 'drastic widespread action' in order to pursue the hope of 'a permanent solution to this age-old problem' for which Horner said the 'only possible final solution is to establish a "closed shop"'.[50]

During the summer of 1938 the EC worked on their proposals and, having had them approved at a delegate conference, they presented them to the Coalowners' Association. Their intention was to have only Federation members employed at all collieries that came under the Conciliation Board Agreement and that men who fell into arrears would be informed by the owners that they were not fulfilling their contractual obligations. The proposals insisted that the desired peace in the coalfield could only come through a collective agreement which, in turn, could only be honoured by the SWMF if they had a 100 per cent membership. If this was achieved then agreements would be strictly honoured and industrial disputes avoided if at all possible.[51]

The owners had no real quarrel with the pacific intentions expressed, but they wished for the kind of categorical promises that the SWMF were unwilling to give, whilst their counter-proposals over the administration of the scheme which involved deduction of dues on behalf of the Federation imposed such restrictions on the traditional Federation activities in organising that, to many, they smacked of the SWMIU itself.[52]

The Federation felt unable to agree to this deduction on their behalf since it might destroy one of the purposes of a full membership, i.e. an involved rank and file, leaving instead the facsimile of one, i.e. a union organised by the owners for the sake of convenience. Horner insisted that the Federation remain in control of the machinery of collection of dues in case the owners ever chose to opt out of the scheme. What was at risk, he felt, was the complete independence of the Federation.[53]

Therefore when the Second World War began the EC were still having to sanction lodge campaigns against non-unionism. However, they also strove to have the owners accept their proposals for the duration of the war. The owners at last gave in, and offered to 'give such assistance as may be necessary' to see that all their employees met their obligations 'as members of the SWMF'. A delegate conference accepted a position that had taken more than two years of war, a coalfield-strike and Government intervention to achieve in the previous World War.[54] It was not war-time exigency alone that had caused the owners to concede, for the long-drawn-out industrial guerrilla war of the years since 1926 had laid the groundwork. The war was merely the immediate catalyst.

The procedure to be adopted was that lists of non-unionists would be periodically handed in to management for them to act on in consultation with miners' agents and lodge officials. In practice, however, there proved to be continued friction because of management recalcitrance and the EC were forced to appeal to the men not to issue notices to strike[55] against those workmen who, in the words of the PD Combine in 1941, were 'taking ... advantage of the national emergency' in order to ignore 'their trade unions'. Every non-unionist, they declared, 'is supporting a Nazi regime'.[56] There was increasing pressure on the EC to end this state of affairs by having membership of the SWMF written into a new coalfield agreement and that membership dues be deducted from the wages at the colliery office before being handed over to the lodge secretary. In this way, it was felt, friction and expenditure could be decreased whilst any apprehension about a reversion to pre-1939 difficulties after the war could be alleviated.[57] Reluctantly, the EC succumbed to these demands and it was agreed by the South Wales Conciliation Board that the 'closed shop' principle would operate to the full, with deduction of dues.[58]

The complete control of the colliery workforce that was thereby attained can rightly be seen as the end of a long road. At the same time it was only a formalisation of an industrial and social struggle for hegemony that had been established, in the face of stern opposition, since the foundation of the SWMF itself. The purpose of a complete organisation was manifold but its immediate origins, and its swiftest impact, were always in the individual pits themselves. The Federation was as strong as its weakest branch because each part had a distinct, specific existence in its own section of the coalfield. Here was where the work had to be done and maintained for 'more and more it has been impressed upon us that lodge activity and service is the basis of our organisation. Much of this service receives no financial recognition and is carried on away in the villages without any public limelight.'[59] Any 'closed shop' then was as strong or as weak as the motivation of the men who wielded the weapon, 100 per cent organisation, that had been forged.

Those who opposed the 'closed shop' did so because they feared it might encourage passivity, a relaxation of the will that had been prepared to sacrifice so much in the years since 1926.

As the 1930s ended with the predicted war the SWMF, though reorganised and, to an extent, revitalised, appeared to be set on a familiar course. The grave problems of the coal industry allied to the social devastation of the coalfield were still there, now intensified by the demands war would make on a debilitated industry. Arthur Horner's remarks to the Annual Conference in 1940 made no concession to the fact that 'the living experience of the South Wales mining community' had been changed 'by conditions of war':

> The South Wales Miners' Federation, like all trade union organisations, has as its fundamental duty the obligation to safeguard the working and living conditions of its members in all circumstances. The change from peace to war cannot lessen the obligation ... we must preserve the complete independence of our organisation and avoid being drawn into unhealthy collaboration which ignores class relations within modern capitalist society.[60]

Nevertheless the war did enforce a change in established positions.

As it progressed the SWMF, in common with the other federated bodies within the MFGB, discovered new reaches of power as against the dwindling influence of the coalowners. Once again, in wartime, the industry had come under government surveillance and direction; wages had risen at a rate unknown since the First World War whilst the long-deferred twin dreams of a national union and a nationalised industry were clearly on the agenda. In effect the war had given back to the mining unions the lever of bargaining power. They were still operating, however, and the exigencies of war apart, in a very narrow context. The loss of traditional markets overseas along with the insistent demand, after 1940, for increased production for the war effort did nothing to improve the crippled condition of the coal industry. Whatever weight should be given to the altered expectations aroused by the war and to the tangible gains, in wages and organisation, that were made, this fundamental fact of a circumscribed reality has to be kept to the forefront. W. H. B. Court, in concluding his magisterial Official History of the coal industry during the war, underlined the point by making the war years a part of a process that stretched back and forward:

> An important change of public attitude towards the coal industry took place between 1939 and 1945, largely as a result of the experiences of the nation in this matter of coal supplies. Before the war, the coal industry was a sick industry, the coal-mining community a sick society. The indifference and therefore the ignorance of the country on both points had been profound . . . By 1945, the mood of public and political opinion had begun to change . . . But while the change in public opinion must be recorded, it should also be noted that the war aggravated rather than improved the condition of the industry. No other major British industry carried so many unsolved problems into the war; none brought more out.[61]

The People's War of 1939–1945 may have begun amidst apathy, despair and confusion but it became instrumental in releasing the frustrated political and social blockages of the inter-war years, especially in the depressed areas, by its novel economic strategies. The production of coal was one of the most vital areas of the war on the Home Front whilst the siting of ordnance factories in regions like South Wales brought women into employment on a new scale. The war concentrated thinking on neglected priorities in social health and welfare, elicited promises about an end to mass unemployment and invested those who had long agitated for such changes with renewed will-power. A war whose total control over state and people was not to be gainsaid, in turn became the 'final' struggle. For Horner the war itself was transformed into 'the highest form of class struggle'. This paradox, and seeming reversal, in the President's position highlights the complexities of the war situation where so many of the difficulties experienced stemmed from a grim inheritance and much of the hope lay in a future still to be won.

The constant dilemma for the war-time government was their failure to raise the production of coal to the required level so that periodic fuel crises hit the country between 1941 and 1944, with even military preparations put at risk. The problem was rooted in the indiscriminate closure of pits during the inter-war period, the depletion of the labour force by lack of opportunities, migration, now a military call-up which further increased the age of remaining miners, as well as the inadequate technical standards of Britain's collieries. In April 1940 the Government had set up a Coal Production Council 'with a view to increasing coal exports while maintaining supplies for essential home production'.[62] Yet, within two months, the fall of France led to a crisis in the coalfield (especially in the Anthracite) with the closure of more markets, and a net loss of 30,000 from the workforce.[63] The pull of the new (and better-paid) munitions' factories was one cause for low morale, the comb-out of ex-miners for the armed forces was another, and both were compounded by the tardiness with which Government came to accept the full magnitude of the crisis of manpower in the coal industry. In 1941 the coalowners complained that a workforce of 126,597 in 1938 had shrunk to 101,526 with a short-fall of at least 5,600 men needed to meet current demand.[64] The Essential Work Order, applied under the Emergency Powers Act in spring 1941, recognised the issue but nothing solved the problem satisfactorily.

Indeed the question of manpower for coal (the irony was a bitter-sweet one) had many ramifications for it tapped a deep fund of pent-up resentment. Exhortation proved inadequate even when the Secretary for Mines in Churchill's new Government was the first ex-miner ever appointed. Dai Grenfell, MP for Gower, came down to South Wales to address a special conference in June 1940,[65] in order to stress 'the present serious situation arising from the loss of the French and Belgian coalfields and the dependence of the Allies for their supply of coal on the production of the British coalfields'. He was confident that when the colliery workers realised the gravity of the position every effort would be made by them to make up as far as possible the loss of the continental coalfields. He had examined the proposals of the

Executive Council . . . for increasing coal output, and he was satisfied that if the measures recommended were earnestly and seriously carried out in all the British coalfields a very substantial increase in the supply of coal without increase in the hours of work per shift was assured.'

None the less, despite the EC's co-operation on the Joint Coal Production Committee, absenteeism, go-slows, strikes and a continuing decline in coal production mark the war years. In part there was, in addition to long-term causes, the immediate explanation of the months between January 1940 and March 1941 when miners found themselves, by turns, accused of being unpatriotic if they did not leave the mines, thrown on to a war-created unemployment heap and then retrieved from the forces to be told they had to return to the pits. A rank-and-file miner who had been involved in some of the fiercest of interwar disputes voiced his disquiet publicly in late 1940:

> There is a serious crisis facing the South Wales coalfield with thousands of miners being thrown out of work and many thousands working short-time. A few months ago before the loss of the French and Italian markets and when an increase of about 30,000 tons p.a. were needed to meet the requirements, the miners were told by the Government that they must sacrifice by working weekends, foregoing holidays and that absenteeism must cease, while the coalowners sacrificed nothing.
>
> Today, with a crisis upon us, we see the same policy of sacrifice operating. The Government comes to the assistance of the coalowners by increasing the price of coal by 1s. 9d. a ton, which will mean more pits closing down, due to the inability of thousands of home consumers to pay the increased charges. On the other hand the thousands of miners that are, and may become unemployed are told they must again sacrifice by going to Kent and the Forest of Dean coalfields, but there are no guarantees regarding conditions of pay and lodging allowance. The sacrifices are always one-sided.[66]

Nothing seemed more inequitable than the bureaucratic rigidity of the Ministry of Food's policy which allocated supplies on the basis of pre-war consumption, so that the unnaturally low levels (and low protein content) of food in mining areas was thus perpetuated at a time when miners were being urged to work harder.[67] Attempts to provide supplementary clothing rations and an extra allowance of cheese hardly met the need or the resentment.[68] War imposed the inconvenience of black-outs which curtailed the already poor bus services in the coalfield, and this added to the travelling time of many miners with late arrivals and possible loss of shifts (and wages and production) as a consequence. Again, in South Wales this was aggravated by the redistribution of working collieries in the wake of the decline in the coal industry. Horner suggested this policy had been applied to the workforce as well:

> One of the difficulties in organising the employment of unemployed miners arises from the bad system which has grown up of giving priority to men whose homes are considerable distances away from the collieries in which they are given work.
>
> Following the 1926 stoppage, I am afraid certain coalowners drew the conclusion that they could restrain workmen if they separated them from each other socially. The view was expressed that if the men only met in their work, and did not fraternise with each other so fully in the evenings, there would be less prospect of unity in their ranks, and, therefore, less likelihood of stoppages or strikes. The result of this is, that men are passing each other going to and from their work, travelling as much as twenty miles a day, which is quite unnecessary. If workmen were permitted the right to choose for themselves, so that they might work as near their homes as possible, part of the difficulties of absorbing those now unemployed could be overcome.[69]

From July 1940 when the TUC accepted the Conditions of Employment and National Arbitration Order strikes were declared illegal: all the same, between September 1939 and October 1944 there were 514 stoppages, mostly of short duration, in the South Wales coalfield.[70] These staccato eruptions in particular pits, often across the coalfield, speak for an underlying band of grievances that refused the blandishments of trade union advances, patriotic propaganda, even threats and punishment. Horner told the coalowners whom, he felt, did not always respond readily:

> There is a terrific feeling in the coalfield which is almost 'un-get-at-able'. I find it like elastic; if you go and push against it, it has no clear justification which it can express and articulate and it gives, but immediately afterwards it comes back at the same place.[71]

Certainly there were clear advances. The national wage agreement made in October 1939 had given some small increases per shift and tied further advances to the spiralling cost of living (there were six more increases down to June 1941).[72] Much more important was the White Paper published by the government in 1942. Now the mines were to be controlled, in their operation, by the state (though ownership and finance remained in private hands) through a Controller General and his regional staff who would direct the management of the industry. The

Pit Production Committees which had been in existence since 1940 were now relieved of their task of dealing with individual cases of absenteeism though retained as joint worker–manager bodies to assist the push for higher output. Wages were to be dealt with by entirely new machinery. At the same time unrest in the coalfields over the poor rate of wages received by miners in comparison with other industries had led the MFGB to press for a minimum weekly wage of £4 5s. 0d. The coalowners refused and so it was to the new Board of Investigation under Lord Greene that the dispute went. The Greene Award did not give the miners all they wanted (£4 3s. 0d. a week as a minimum for all over twenty-one underground, £3 18s. 0d. for surface workers and a flat-rate increase of 2s. 6d. a shift with further increases related to output fixed for a pit) but it raised them from fifty-ninth to twenty-third position in the wages league and provided the vital *weekly* minimum to which no miner had ever been entitled before. It was a major step back on to the road of national wage agreements which augured well for a resurrection of a truly national union. An independent national tribunal of three members was established to pronounce on any further wage disputes.[73]

Dual control and a national wages procedure were regarded by the leadership in the SWMF as seeds to be nurtured; in other eyes they remained sops. To understand these two attitudes and why they were not always necessarily contradictory, requires analysis of the policy of the SWMF towards the more general operations of war and peace. This leads as always back to the particular case studies which, as so often before, obtruded a prickly reality against theoretical plans.

From early 1939 to the outbreak of the war the Federation pursued its established policy of opposition to the Voluntary Defence Scheme and conscription plans of a government they considered insincere in its professed anti-fascism. Active support of Bevan in his clash with the Labour Party, housing of Czech miners from the Sudetenland and demands for a defence of the country were tied to resolutions calling for an alliance with the Soviet Union.[74] This consistent Popular Frontism crashed in ruins in August when the Nazi–Soviet non-aggression pact was signed. The EC forlornly sent telegrams to Chamberlain and to Arthur Greenwood (Deputy Leader of the Labour Party) – 'convinced that Anglo-Russian Pact more urgent than ever in view of German–Russian Pact'[75] – but the painful twist of this turn-about was inescapable as, within a month, the Soviet Union pronounced the war an imperialist one in which the first duty of the Communist Party was to defeat their own ruling class. Horner recalled 'being terribly shocked' despite his belief that the Soviet Union had needed to take such a strategic step. Nor could he 'accept the thesis that it was an imperialist war like the First World War'. He did not, like Pollitt, have to drop out of the leadership because of his personal convictions though he did swallow them with some difficulty.[76]

What was quite clear was his unwillingness to adopt a straight-forward anti-war line, preferring rather to direct attention to continuing social discontent.[77] It was an uncomfortable position to maintain as the Conference called to discuss the war in early 1940 indicates. The EC, on Horner's casting vote, had decided that the two motions they had discussed would be put to the conference by two of their members, D. R. Llewellyn and Will Arthur.[78] Llewellyn argued that the war was 'being waged for imperialist aims and not for the defence of democracy against fascism', citing in its support the alleged intention of the British government to replace Hitler with a regime ready to attack the Soviet Union, French suppression of the Communist movement and war profiteering at home. He demanded an end to the war via an overthrow of Labour's political truce and the replacement of Chamberlain's government. Will Arthur's resolution also called for a new government and the push for social justice at home, but it urged support for the war, 'so long as it is fought against fascist aggression and for the achievement of permanent peace'. When the conference reassembled in March to receive the opinion of the coalfield the pro-war resolution was carried by a 3 to 1 majority.[79] At the Annual Conference Horner wrestled with the dilemma posed by Communist Party policy and resolved it by attacking the policies that led to war whilst not actively disassociating himself from his own union's declared intentions:

> So long as I am President of this Federation I will operate majority decisions. When I cannot carry out the wishes of the majority of the members I will do the only honourable thing, that is, offer my resignation.[80]

In fact after the Fall of France he became a member of the Invasion Trade Union Committee for South Wales 'which had the responsibility of deciding on measures of resistance and sabotage in the event of a German invasion. So I was able to make clear even in this period that I was ready to defend my country'. This position was not revealed to anyone, either in the SWMF or in the Communist Party.[81]

Militants (both in the Labour Party and Communists of both persuasions on the war) were able to enter most wholeheartedly into the pressure politics directed through the People's Vigilance Committee set up in July 1940, in the wake of the military setbacks in Norway and at Dunkirk, in order to press for a 'People's Government'. Although the CP was the organising force, the subsequent People's Convention in September 1940 revealed clearly the degree to which there was dissatisfaction with the government in office, if not over the war itself then over its prosecution and domestic politics.[82] The SWMF supported the movement whose proscription by the Labour Party's NEC and the TUC led to the expulsion of a number of Labour Party members in South Wales, whilst the EC received protests about its affiliation from individual lodges as well as from the Labour Party and the MFGB. Four delegates, including Horner, attended the convention held in January 1941.[83] Conditions in the coalfield seemed to match up to the harsh criticism voiced of the government as unemployment consequent upon the war was increased by rail blockages and failure to provide domestic markets for South Wales coal. The population, declared the EC, was 'being driven to ruin and destitution' though they should be 'entitled to reasonable treatment during the war and to the prospects of maintaining existence when the war is over'.[84]

As the war crisis deepened the overt intervention of the Peoples' Vigilance Movement receded[85] and then the war took on a different complexion, both objectively and in the subjective interpretation of many now destined to switch from a passive defence to a most active pro-war line. Germany on 23 June 1941 invaded the Soviet Union. The Convention followed the CP into an overnight declaration of full support for the war. Much heart-searching could now end in a joyful acceptance of that twinned demand of the 1930s – anti-fascism and Soviet alliance. Both sides in the SWMF united in assertions of support for the Soviet people, levying, as they had during the Spanish Civil War, 2s. 6d. per member as tangible proof.[86] (The irony was to be the loss of a leadership able and willing to articulate the complaints that remained insistently present and rigidly adamant.)

Horner now spelled out with a clarity born of long-deferred hopes the advantages the war was putting the way of the Labour movement, uniting, by force of circumstance, the 'progressives' who had, albeit fitfully, coalesced in South Wales even in peace. However, the ability to see long-term possibilities led him, and those who worked with him, into a playing-down of objective grounds of dissatisfaction at ground level. Down to 1944 the insistence on discipline and sacrifice that was so suddenly emphasised after June 1941 took a left-wing leadership into camps they had spurned in the past. Whatever the ultimate justification for their demands for more production, less absenteeism and no strikes (and indeed their immediate justification, too, since not all 'disputes' were clear-cut affairs), this ardent support for the war did not carry all before it. Overall, though, the line adumbrated by Horner on behalf of the EC was supported by the membership except where the general procedure adopted clashed with any of the bread-and-butter matters underground where the familiar fight was not always put aside in favour of 'higher considerations'. Slowly the EC came to take cognisance of this fact.

The pro-war policy stressed that the coal industry was not in a properly organised shape to meet the nation's demands but that the war was, inescapably, one to which 'we as mineworkers and as a Federation are fully committed'. So, notwithstanding the poor wages and conditions, the lack of timber and of steel which held back production, and the accidents and sickness which caused unavoidable absenteeism, those 'small percentage of our people' who absent themselves from work without reasonable cause . . . must be dealt with ruthlessly and be treated as enemies of the miners and a menace to the country'. Horner could put the argument he had stated in 1940, but, in 1942, draw an opposite conclusion:

> It is . . . true that we live in a capitalist country in which private ownership still permits the exploitation of our class by another class, and that we have a Government which represents a Class System. Yet, notwithstanding these two undeniable facts, I now state that we are serving the cause of Socialism by placing our full energies at the disposal of our Government which is organising the struggle against Fascism.
>
> To collaborate with our Government so long as it earnestly fights against this menace, is not to deny the class struggle. In the circumstances of the present time, the failure to fight against these forces which have despoiled the world . . . is to desert the working class and all it stands for. . . .
>
> If nursing our past grievances, which are many, militates against the maximum effort to win this war, forget them. If any sections of the community prejudices the war effort by anxiety about their vested interests, they must be ruthlessly dealt with.
>
> . . . We must see that on this occasion the great sacrifices made . . . shall not be in vain.[87]

The Pit Production Committees had not been a great success since management resented 'interference' by the men. After representation it was accepted that the men could attend meetings in the evening so that they could wear clean clothes, thus having the semblance of formal equality but there was still continual friction, with some meetings breaking down completely. Management wished to emphasise the 'control factor' by having the men deal with absenteeism; the men wished to discuss the 'objective' causes of a pit's low output. The EC's wish to stimulate these committees often came up against a blank wall – their Central Production Committee issued a questionnaire to all pits in mid-1943 with detailed queries as to the working of the PPCs. Less than 50 per cent of all lodges bothered to answer at all which the Production Committee stated 'is indicative of the interest shown in the problem back at the pits', for 'there is a wide gap between Executive Council policy and the attitude of certain lodges to the vital question of production'. It was only in 1944 that the EC were again prepared to see the issue from two sides, i.e. their own desire and the bleak actuality. The PPCs, like Dual Control, did not give any effective power to the men themselves:

> In some instances it brought to light the latent creative powers of the workmen ... in other instances it has served merely to heighten class antagonism due to an overemphasis on the Gaffer and Kaffir approach to the problem.[88]

Failure to initiate a new approach here drove the EC back on to exhorting the men and chivvying the owners. They checked on the track records of pits with output declining below the targets set per shift, urging more production even in the face of war-weariness.[89] Horner's addresses to the annual conferences were a skilful compound of a survey of the war, praise of the efforts of miners and an insistence that social justice must be won after its end, along with a grim reiteration of the sacrifices still required:

> There is probably no coalfield in the world in which memories of past class conflicts are so sharp. The bitterness arising from long years of unemployment and destitution has left its mark. Even the menace of Fascism, which is the most cruel form of class exploitation, has not proved strong enough to remove from the minds of our people memories of past depression and fears for the future. We know now that these deplorable experiences could have been avoided and we keep them in mind so as to strengthen our determination to ensure that they must never be repeated.
>
> We cannot, however, allow our present actions to be determined by our memories of the past, or our fears for the future. There is too much at stake for all of us.

We must all appreciate that the fight against Fascism now is the way to ensure that the evils of the past are ended, and that the future is one of progress and not of reaction.

Without adequate supplies of coal there can be no victory. Shortage of coal would negative all the efforts of the fighting forces. This is not a theoretical question; it is practical and immediate in view of the serious coal crisis which exists in this country at the present time. . . . The uncertainty about the future organisation of the industry (since the Coal Control Scheme of 1942) is affecting the attitude of those engaged in the industry. Supervisory grades often times pay more regard to the desires and future interests of the coalowners than to the needs of the existing situation, whilst workmen's representatives in certain cases fear to advocate or support measures which are absolutely essential in the present situation lest these measures be utilised against them in post-war days.

I have stated that the vast majority of our members deserve full credit for the manner in which they have borne the burden of coal production in these monotonous and difficult war days. I would not be doing my duty, however, unless I declared that there is still a small minority who are acting in a fashion which cannot be justified by this or any other organisation, pledged as we are to the effective conduct of this war.

It is necessary to establish in the minds of all members that this organisation is operated on the principle of Majority Rule. Those are the blacklegs who refuse to carry out the will of the majority even though they strike or hold up work in violation of the policy of this Organisation to which we all belong. To depart from this fundamental principle would bring about the early disintegration of this Federation. . . . The coming months may force all of us to a new understanding of the significance of the word 'sacrifice'. Mineworkers everywhere know too well what sacrifice means, and we are ready. Our readiness will be effective to the extent we are united. Let us close our ranks; let us set an example by what we are prepared to do in the struggle for victory; let us remove every factor which prevents the realisation of the task we are called upon to perform.

We must never forget what our comrades in the Armed Forces and the Merchant Service are expected to face and suffer; what the comrades in occupied Europe are doing, and, above all, the unprecedented sacrifices of the people of the Soviet Union in these recent months. Let us steel ourselves to intensify our work so as to justify our demand upon the Government to open a Second Front in Europe. Let us demonstrate our readiness to play our full part in the struggle to destroy the war machine of Hitlerite Germany. . . .

Once this is done we can face the future in all the indestructible confidence of the organised working-class, and go forward unitedly to conquer new fields of social advance, increasing the rate of development towards Socialism.[90]

This was the fullest statement of his interpretation of the needs and hopes elicited by war which Horner delivered. It is doubly important in that his voice had become the most important in South Wales as the war thrust coal production to the centre of the stage. Undoubtedly he saw the war not only as an opportunity to forge the new national institutions in the industry for which he had so long pressed but also as the last, and maybe worst, chapter in a bloody saga. His conviction caused him to be impatient with those who either could not see as far as he could or did not accept the idealism that fired his practicality. Either way there were times when Horner allowed his own rhetoric to blur his judgement. There were very few who would, in Britain at that time, deny the necessity of winning a war whose justness was unquestioned, and yet that did not of itself ensure a sustained spirit of obedience in the pits themselves where a long history of wariness remained alert against all outside pronouncements. The SWMF, and the miners' MP's (even former pacifists like James Griffiths) had put themselves in that 'outside' position by 1943 because of their blanket approach to issues that required a detailed analysis. At a special conference in July 1943, called to urge lodge delegates to adopt a more 'disciplined attitude towards the problem of production', Horner 'dealt . . . with the argument advanced for the solution of our local problems in this opportune time by means of strikes and ca' canny, etc., that would obviously jeopardise the chances of solving favourably the bigger international problem'; and 'stated that whatever the owners do on Pit Production Commitees, etc., our duty is clear, we must fight in the Pit Production Committees for the maximum production, not in the interests of the owners, but in the general interests of all the progressive forces of the World. . . . The calling of strikes in this situation is cowardly and a betrayal of past interests of the working class.' After D. R. Grenfell spoke in support, Jim Griffiths 'paid a glowing tribute to the President for a very fine and courageous address and impressed upon the delegates the necessity of carrying out our obligations to our comrades in the Armed Forces'.[91]

To which the retort was that they would not wish to return to see customs and practice eroded by co-operation with management they had been taught to resist. The penalties imposed in the Courts under the Essential Work Order, often for petty offences or through unavoidable causes such as late arrival of buses, did not serve to bolster the men's faith. B. L. Coombes, who called Horner 'the best President we have ever had', was also a working miner in touch with these gut reactions:

. . . We do not hear of colliery companies being prosecuted for their faults in these days. A miner loses time or does something which upsets some of our minor law dispensers. The offender is sent to prison and we lose his output for that time. Also we embitter the miner, and he is not likely to become a contented citizen, rather I expect him to become a rebel. But he never meets coalowners in gaol . . . in fact no coal controller or magistrate ever seems to speak roughly to them. . . .

Let's examine one affair, that which happened at Penrhiwceiber Colliery [August 1943]. Incensed by long sustained failure to get their proper payment, the men stopped work, other pits joined them, and the support of the working miners was spreading rapidly, whilst a large amount of coal was lost each day. Finally the controller arrived, held an inquiry and found that the men were in the right, then work was resumed. What I want to know is when are the ones responsible for that stoppage going to be prosecuted and sent to gaol? Or must we be more convinced of what we have always believed – that there is one law for the worker and another for the rich?[92]

The law had been invoked at the Tareni Colliery at the top of the Swansea Valley in June 1943 when twenty-four hauliers who had been accused of ca' canny were prosecuted by the Ministry of Labour and National Service for a breach of the EWO. They were found guilty and ordered to pay a £20 fine or be imprisoned for a month – when twenty of them chose gaol a rush of sympathetic strikes erupted, both in the Swansea and Dulais Valleys, despite the fact that a ballot at Tareni had decided not to support the hauliers and there was no official lodge support forthcoming elsewhere. This dispute reached back to May 1942 when, after a five-day stoppage, an agreement had been made which the hauliers claimed entitled them to extra remuneration as working conditions altered. Management's failure to agree led to four months of go-slows. The EC condemned this behaviour but appealed for the men's release; a 'pit-consciousness' brought 4,231 men out after the Whit Monday holiday in a week's sporadic stoppage.[93]

Even more intractable was the almost simultaneous flare-up referred to by B. L. Coombes in the Penrhiwceiber Colliery. Although there had been no major stoppage, except over non-unionism, for thirty-five years, a change of ownership in 1942 from Cory Bros to the PD Colliery Company brought a change in the manner of working the coal. The tonnage method of payment was abandoned in favour of yardage, with a consequent withdrawal of allowances that caused a number of men to fall below the minimum wage. Through April and July attempts by the local lodge, the EC and then the Regional Controller to reach a settlement foundered as men found their pay again short. On 20 August, 104 men stopped work, followed the next day by the remaining 1,100. The local men, after mass meetings and a ballot, voted 2–1 to stay out in the teeth of EC pressure (Horner said it was the first time in twenty-five years that he had been turned down by a mass meeting); a hastily convened delegate conference of the coalfield had its urgings also refused as the Penrhiwceiber men insisted on payment before they returned. The Cwmcynon, Abercynon and Albion Collieries came out in sympathy.[94] Horner warned the owners that the minor grievances in other places could well erupt if the dispute was not settled:

> We have had four years of war and the men in the valleys have had four years of the most drab and sordid existence, with nothing to do and nowhere to go except work. I tell you that if you ignore the fact that there is a certain measure of war-weariness, tiredness and frustration about at this critical time, you are making a mistake.[95]

What was at stake, as well, for the EC was its ability to obtain a settlement for their members without the latter having recourse to strike action. They were acutely conscious of lack of sympathy from the owners despite their toeing this unusual, and often unpopular, line. Sir Evan Williams dismissed coalfield grumbling and stoppages as the 'anarchy' of 'the forces of revolt'. The EC who had to wrestle with both sides since 1941 could not afford to take such a simplistic view. There was no longer any doubt that the loyalty on which they could call had worn very thin in places. Horner spelled out why Penrhiwceiber was a symptom not a cause. It was 'the opportunity to express all the grievances that existed, especially in Powell Duffryn Collieries'. This was a theme to which he would return; at the end of August 1943 it was the manner in which this minor dispute threatened the war-time structure of conciliation that concerned him:

> Now . . . we were up against a very difficult position, not only for the owners and the Government, but for the Federation itself. We have taken a stand and our stand has been that we can negotiate for a settlement. We are quite conscious that if that result is now obtained without a return to work we will have been proved to be wrong and all the people who have said 'stop the wheels to get a settlement' will be proved to be right. The consequences of that in the future is something he could not measure; but he should think it would convey to the average man that the way to get settlements is to cease production. . . . He expressed serious alarm at the situation that has developed in the coalfield which is largely due to the unreasonable and unrealistic approach made by certain owners to problems of the coalfield.

That was the case stated before the owners. Amongst themselves the EC were equally gloomy about a matter which, in origin, involved twenty-five men and money amounting to £10 18s. 8d. over a three-week period – 'A point of view was expressed that this would be the worst form of capitulation because it would be used as the one remedy for all the ills obtaining at the several collieries in the coalfield. It was suggested that the mood that had developed in this coalfield was due to lack of political convictions.' Both sides could do nothing other than agree to an Inquiry headed by the Regional Coal Controller which would pronounce its findings before the men returned.[96] Humble pie, then, was duly eaten. The cases were investigated with the PD Combine Committee about to give fourteen days' notice to terminate contracts in all their lodges; the issue was decided, swiftly, in the men's favour, with immediate payment. Horner and Iestyn Williams, for the owners, cleared up the accumulated gripes. It was with some feeling then that Horner attacked the Messrs Hann of the PD Company for their consistent policy of high-handedness. When Edmund Hann complained of this treatment points were enumerated that alleged a complete lack of consultation afforded by management in their pits on any and every issue. The list could have come from the 1930s:

5. That the Conciliation Board Agreement is carried out rigidly with no elasticity. One could almost say oppressively.

6. That their Colliery Agents have no power to arrive at settlements on any question involving principle without the prior consent of their superiors to whom the miners [and] their representatives have no access.

7. That the workmen are employed to do any job asked of them without question. The Colliery Manager being the sole judge as to the reasonality or otherwise of the task to be performed.[97]

At the same time as the EC determined to grasp the nettle of concrete grievances they still gave precedence to their overall strategy for the war. Disputes should be defused wherever possible. Just as the Penrhiwceiber strike was being settled, a special conference urging that the Second Front be opened up in Europe pledged full support in the domestic effort required for the victory which could come 'provided that all tendencies leading to complacency and slackness are ruthlessly eradicated'.[98] When the new EC came into office on 1 January 1944 the whole issue was again thrashed out. There were no fundamental alterations in policy, though a new emphasis was being given not only to the vision of post-war reconstruction but also to the demand for present redress of ills. However, 1944, too, was to reveal the fissures that could appear between men and leadership.

The Special EC Meeting called to discuss Federation policy on the war reiterated the pro-war resolution of 1940 by acknowledging there were two fights to win yet insisting on the primacy of the war effort. The original wording from the officials then made a call for a new post-war government. However, the discussion which ensued amongst the Executive (and which was subsequently incorporated into a statement for the coalfield) deepened criticism by spotlighting the dissent they had to face daily. Some of the points raised quite clearly show that the understanding now reached was as wide-ranging as it was sophisticated:

That theory and practice was in great contradiction in the coalfield at the moment. Ideologically our members supported the war but their feet did otherwise.

There was no fundamental difference between the Executive Council and the rank and file on the greater issues, but there was, seemingly, a difference on limited issues such as price lists and other contentious matters at the collieries. . . .

That we should carry out a militant policy side by side with our agitation to give full support to the war effort.

That the control of the industry should be radically improved.

That the lack of movement of man-power in the industry due to the provisions of the Essential Work Order marred the relations in the coalfield.

That we were reaping the fruits of previous agitation and propaganda that had taken deep root in this coalfield.

That the rank and file of our organisation are far ahead of the outlook of the Executive Council.

That colliery managements are irritating the men and causing unnecessary disputes.

That there should be a monthly bulletin explaining to our members what the MFGB and this Council is doing on their behalf.[99]

This was, indeed, a mixed bag. Understandably there seemed no straightforward way of sorting it out. In any case the plea for increased communication was overtaken by events. The logical step after the 1942 White Paper's development of national machinery was, in the eyes of the MFGB and its supporters, full-blooded nationalisation to meet the crisis in production. On 13 October 1943 in a full Commons debate Churchill rejected the measure as not being 'bona-fide needed for the war'. The main counter-proposal was the great lack of the manpower required after dispersal to the Forces and the concomitant urgency in making the condition in the industry more attractive.[100] One disappointment was followed by another when the national Reference Tribunal (set up after 1942) under Lord Porter delivered its findings on an increase in the minimum wage on 23 January 1944. They did not meet the full claim of £6 a week underground and £5 10s. for surface workers though their actual figures of £5 and £4 10s. were the highest ever given. The root of the ensuing trouble was the attempt to by-pass the more arcane wages structure that had developed in the separate regions over the years – there was to be no equivalent increase in piece-work rates so that skilled workers at the coalface and craftsmen would receive the same rates as those unable to do their jobs. Special allowances such as those for working in water and even the cherished privilege of cheap house-coal were to be counted in the minimum wage, with appropriate deductions made.[101] Immediately the EC, sensing it might have a typhoon by the tail, pronounced with its now accustomed mixture of sympathy and firmness:

> General opinion in the coalfield is that the award is unsatisfying. Firstly, it has failed to provide the increase which we asked for. The demand has not been conceded for a percentage increase to piece workers so that their wages would bear the same relation to the new minimum for day-wagemen as was the case previously. This is certain to discourage the actual coal-getters and we consider this a mistake.
>
> The Council considers the terms of the award as a temporary expedient which will give opportunity for the wage structure to be thoroughly received in conjunction with general conditions. This is of the greatest importance and we propose at the National Conference on Thursday to press that it should be expedited.
>
> We are aware of the discontent in the coalfield about the award, but we urge all miners to continue at work so that anomalies can be dealt with as speedily as possible. Isolated action taken without complete information as to the significance of what has been obtained can only upset the negotiations and discredit those conducting them.[102]

Although this plea was, in general, accepted output fell for two successive weeks to their lowest war-time levels, whilst acute dissatisfaction with the award brought a greater willingness to stop work if any minor issue rankled.[103] The MFGB and the owners negotiated over the anomalies being experienced in the districts, believing that the extra cost would be borne by the Coal Charges Fund (established since 1942 as a financial chest drawn from coal profits whereby solvent concerns kept weaker companies and districts going in the overall interest of coal production). Suddenly the Government responding to pressure not to increase coal prices further, either to industry or domestic consumers, announced that only the cost of implementing the original award would come from this fund. In their turn the owners were adamant that adjustment of the wage anomalies could come from no other source. Negotiations were not abandoned and the MFGB and the owners endeavoured to make the implications of the decision clear to the Government. The February strikes had just ended in some of the other coalfields when on 6 March 10,000 miners, mostly from Monmouthshire, came out in the South Wales coalfield. There was no particular cause at this time (it was six weeks after the award, three weeks after the Government had refused to finance adjustments) except that it was a day before discussions were due to begin on a complete overhaul of the wages structure, and shortly after Horner had advised a delegate conference that the decision over house coal could not be altered. This undoubtedly caused strong feelings of resentment. Its eruption in South Wales as well as the subsequent mass stoppages in Scotland and Yorkshire (where 120,000 came out between 16 March and 11 April) indicate how strong was the rejection of Porter and all it stood for.[104] B. L. Coombes saw it as the accumulation of years of resentment:

> Possibly the action was wrong in view of the circumstances [i.e. the imminent launching of the Second Front]. But it was but the climax to a series of happenings which could have been avoided. It was the outlet of a seething disgust for the continual delays and evasions, intensified by the feeling that men who knew nothing of our work or ideas were making decisions that would affect our lives and our families.[105]

There were sixty pits out on the first day. The EC's insistence that, as a decision carried by an MFGB conference, the Porter Award automatically applied in South Wales did nothing to alter the situation even when coupled with appeals to hard-won unity:

> The Council regards the Porter Award as a definite advance in the struggle of mineworkers to improve both the income and the status of mineworkers. It deplores the stoppages which have taken place during this week and the threatened extension of the stoppages, because they place in jeopardy the principle of a national minimum for mineworkers secured after long years of

struggle. They threaten the unity of the SWMF and if developed may drive a wedge between the South Wales miners and the remainder of the mineworkers of Great Britain.[106]

The Conference called for Saturday, 11 March, was 'to consider the position as it may then exist'. That phrase was wishful thinking; the call for resumption of work went unheeded despite the alacrity with which miners' agents and lodge officials harangued the men. The strike extended westwards to the Aberdare Valley (where the Abergorki pit came out after having broken its production target for forty consecutive weeks), and took in the PD pits in the Rhymney Valley and those of the Evans-Bevan Combine in the Dulais Valley. On the third day the Rhondda, Tredegar and Swansea steam coal area pits were out – a total of 150 pits and over 85,000 miners. By Thursday the figures were 90,000 men and 175 pits whilst the first pay-day under the award, Friday, served to underline the anomalies feared over reductions in concessionary house-coal and housing allowances. By the week-end the strike was almost complete in the South Wales coalfield. Once more the coalfield had, at a crucial juncture in war-time, gone against all 'official' advice.[107]

At the delegate conference, attended by 230, the miners' agents and thirteen miners' MPs spoke sharply and urged a return to work. They warned that the disruption could prolong the war and cause deaths, needlessly, in Europe. Horner emphasised that the grievances raised were being met, and would receive even more attention when the new wages structure came in. No vote was taken. The delegates were sent back to the lodges to put the case. On the Sunday, EC members visited mass meetings to urge an end to the strike. Results of a hastily taken ballot were to be phoned in.[108] When it came the EC had a majority of 60,963 to 43,248.[109] Nevertheless, on Monday the situation became confused again with a number of pits, after pit-head meetings, reversing their earlier decision to return. During the week numbers of men refused to go down the pit in some collieries – 'for a whole week the position was one of complete chaos with some men on strike and others working, some men going in and coming out like a concertina. Logically the principle of the minimum wage calculation was sound, but logic has little force in some situations, and this was one such occasion.'[110] It was a hard-working week for the EC who finally succeeded in having 90 per cent of the men back in the collieries. Some 500,000 tons of coal had been lost in the strike.[111] Undoubtedly there had been special circumstances surrounding the intense fervour of the men in Area No. 8

(Monmouthshire) to which the EC turned as it considered the unhealthy growth of 'sectionalism' in the coalfield,[112] but the Porter Award strikes were, overall, symptomatic of the pent-up frustration that had gathered during the war in all the British coalfields. Bereft of a leadership willing to give them their head, the men were blowing off steam anyway. The Government's blunder in February had simply ensured that the explosion would be a substantial one. Now rapidly backtracking they conceded almost all that had been contentious in the award. Differentials in pay were restored.

The strikes of February and March 1944 hastened action on a plan to avoid these periodical upsets by altering the absurdly complex wage agreements in the industry. The new National Agreement of April 1944 which was to last for four years was thrashed out by the Government, the MFGB and the owners. It froze the old ascertainment system established after 1921, established a National Minimum Wage that was the highest in the country and merged other additions since 1936 into the District Wage rates. Piece-workers were given considerable incentives. Miners moved from eighty-first position in the average earnings of 100 trades in 1935 to fourteenth in the league table.[113]

This was not to the full satisfaction of the SWMF EC but it was, of course, a dramatic reversal of fortune in the ten years since 1934 when the Bridgeman award reversed the downward trend in wages. In reviewing ten years of advance Horner placed wages first on his list of the achievements made possible as the SWMF rebuilt, signalling out 1944 as the first 'genuine Holidays with Pay' since in 1938 the first scheme had involved the men in conditions that often led to deductible penalty fines. In the wake of the Porter Award (and he castigated the men for striking in defiance of their own Federation) Horner was anxious to stress the gains made over the decade, particularly if they were not always obvious ones. The establishment of a Compensation Department in 1934 under Evan Willams[114] was seen in this light:

This phase of a mineworker's life has always been held by me to be equally important with wages . . . In South Wales . . . we have a greater urge in this respect than most other coalfields, as in addition to the ordinary accidents we have a higher incidence of disablement and death due to dust diseases.[115]

1944 was a crucial turning-point for the coal industry. In Horner's view the forward steps taken in wartime could be sustained if a disciplined unity was shown. The aim had to be nationalisation:

I give it as my considered opinion that the only permanent solution of the coal situation this side of Socialism is the nationalisation of the mining industry. No other demand has so consistently received the support of every section of the Labour, Trade Union and Co-operative Movement over such a long period of time. Today I am convinced that due to generations of exploitation of miners, wartime conditions and the whole general history of our industry there is deep down in the hearts of our people a firm and unassailable conviction that only when the State has taken over the mines will there be that planning, that efficiency and that human and considerate treatment of the miners which alone can guarantee that Britain will get the coal it requires both now and in the future. . . . This demand for nationalisation is not just some capricious demand on the part of miners who are alleged to be 'awkward', 'difficult to understand' and 'never satisfied', but the demand of a section of the community who from first-hand experience know that only when private enterprise and private property in the mining industry has been eliminated can there be scientific planning, introduction of new methods of production, and clearing away of obsolete methods. . . .[116]

Although that saving phrase 'this side of Socialism' did put nationalisation in perspective, Horner's rhetorical reaching for the dream of a state-controlled industry in peacetime is obviously based on the hope of permanently progressive government. Under those circumstances, as in wartime, the task of the socialist trade unionist would be to work for the men by improving the industry itself. There was, for Horner, no contradiction involved provided the basis of development was as he predicted. Of course if that basis crumbled then the dream was shattered anyway. 1944 was a year for planning the materialisation of dreams. Already, in 1943, the EC responding to the request of the Welsh Reconstruction Advisory Council had set up a sub-committee to consider the position in South Wales. They too, had emphasised planning in the coal industry and its association, wherever possible, with new industries on a long-term basis to replace any enforced pit closures because of worked-out seams. In all these pronouncements there was the constant reminder of the waste of the recent past, whilst the future was depicted in terms not only of industrial prosperity but also by reference to the special nature of the community that had been thrown together in the coalfield:

She has a population experienced in industry and very adaptable to new industrial conditioning. Every effort should be made to make use of their labour in peace time as in war. The claim made on behalf of Wales is that the great material resources of the country should be fully developed. There is a social claim which should not be ignored. A strong community has been built up in South Wales in response to the industrial demands of more than a hundred years. It has contributed greatly to the export trade and the general prosperity of the United Kingdom. It has suffered deeply from the inter-war industrial depression. Men and women have been forced to go away with their families. The district must continue to suffer unless the youth of both sexes are given work and a decent livelihood.[117]

The future had to be made if it was not just to happen. One aspect of the manpower problem in the war had been the advanced age of the workforce, another had been its youthfulness. Many of the latter had been plunged into work and into war at the same time, divorced by a generation from their older workmates and told, at a time of hardship, to keep in line by their own union. During the inter-war years the high level of unemployment and mass migration had led to a declining number of youths in the industry. The Essential Work Order blocked the escape route for those who remained; their entitlement to pay was lower than that of the men whose jobs they often did. The predictable result was a sequence of unofficial, lightning strikes by apprentice miners, with, on occasion, the support of the older men as in May and June 1942 when over 10,000 men and boys came out, as did some 7,500 in October 1943. Alleviation of pay demands went some way to meeting the problem though, as many had recognised in the 1930s, the 'disinheritance' of unemployment was a running sore that work itself could not cure overnight. B. L. Coombes, who had no wish to see his son forcibly sent down the pit, was a sensitive observer:

Inside the entrance the refuge holes are crowded by youngsters averaging about 20 years of age. They are always disputing viciously it seems. Their language is brutally profane. Girls, film stars, miners' agents, politicians are all brought inside the bawling discussion and are cast out besmirched as they pass on to condemn others of whom their knowledge and conception must be very slight. Everything and everybody outside their groups receives the same verdict of being, 'no blasted good'. They are just a section of our mining youth, not the largest section by any count, but their insolence and indifference to all discipline made them a problem in our work and in our future. They linger until the overman has reached them, they move inwards unwillingly, disputing and swearing as they go. The overman follows, knowing they will go only so far and so fast as he makes them. What mistake in environment and education has brought these growing kids into this condition. . . .

It seems to me that the years in which these lads saw their relatives idling about the street corners, or watching each hapless day recede before the misery of the next, has left an imprint on their minds which it is difficult to erase.[118]

The SWMF gave attention to this disquiet in 1944 when they resolved to call a Trade Union Conference on Youth, to be addressed by Horner and Jack Tanner of the AEU. The object of the conference was to stimulate youth into an interest and active participation in trade union work. Once more, though, this was no narrow recruitment drive, for the Federation were fully conscious of their role as a social organism within past coalfield society. This they wished to maintain by educating youth 'in the history of the struggle of the working class . . . and of socialist thought', by providing in towns and villages, 'healthy working-class entertainment, such as inter-valley sports, drama, art, eisteddfodau, literature and working-class culture'.[119]

It was an ambitious, aggressively framed, curriculum that reflects the confident determination with which the brave new world in South Wales was to be assembled. The conference heard inspired speeches by Horner and Tanner, with the latter insistent upon the need for a vigorous challenge by younger men to established patterns of thought. They set out to invoke the spirit that had, between 1909 and 1926, nurtured working-class education in the coalfield. Horner emphasised, as he had before, the power that had accrued to trade unions in two world wars. It was its dissipation that concerned him:

We have solved many problems confronting the working class . . . in a manner that will not always be open to us . . . in the post-war period when the needs of Government will not be as great as they are at present. The struggle after this war will be much sharper than it is today. The old forces will take their corners as hitherto, and it is for this task that we desire to prepare the membership of our unions so as to equip themselves with the strength, organisation, conceptions and the will necessary to achieve our aim.

Our final aim is the common ownership of all industry in this country, but prior to achieving this, many awkward corners will have to be turned . . .

To this end the workers . . . must realise that education is a great instrument of social and political power, and just as the surveyor in a mine uses his knowledge of science through instruments so as to draw his roadways through the unseen to the spot he desires, so must the workers use the instruments of political education in the social sciences in order to lead the people through the dark days of economic and political crisis to the new society they so ardently desire. Before the workers can understand and predict the kind of world that the future holds for them, they must understand the Forces operating within this Society. . . . Education in the hands of the working class . . . will enable the movement to go forward as one solid phalanx to the world the old pioneers portrayed so vividly to us during the early days. . . .[120]

Three days later the result of the ballot for one miners' union was announced. Nationally the result was 10–1 in favour, in South Wales 74,303 for and only 9,446 against. Horner, himself, was an 'old pioneer' for a 'solid phalanx'. The formation of the National Union of Mineworkers was not quite that, yet it was, apparently, another unprecedented leap forward, another fruit of that careful nurturing of strength which had been the policy of the late 1930s after the stinging setbacks of the 1920s. With the future yet to unfold and the past all too clear a memory, the aim of the later war years must have seemed alive with hope. In 1939, at the annual conference of the MFGB held in Swansea, Horner had reviewed the vacillation of the federated districts since 1932 when contiguous areas had been advised to merge. Horner, though one of the principal advocates of a dismantling of the MFGB, had urged caution, insisting that unity of agreement amongst the districts be first established.[121]

Finally the Reorganisation Sub-Committee drafted a scheme which was submitted to conference in July 1944. In essence the scheme was a compromise whereby industrial activities were centralised and funded, but the Districts, maintaining their areas and staff for the present, would still exercise considerable local powers, especially over divergent practices and benefits.[122] Horner[123] stressed the need to organise effectively for post-war developments, so that even an emasculated scheme was valuable if it delivered the form of a unitary mineworkers' union whose creation, unlike a National Wages Ascertainment, only needed agreement amongst themselves:

Twenty-five years ago I wrote a pamphlet. I made a beautiful draft with diagrams of one Mineworkers' Union. I drafted it believing I had a nice flat floor on which to build a lovely union. I have learned from bitter experience that it is not a flat floor; it has different District interests with different District conceptions, different degrees of development. This we are now proposing is an attempt to make a superstructure over what already exists, and we cannot do it independently of what exists.[124]

The report was referred to the Districts and the rules thrashed out at a special conference in October 1944 that advocated a National Union of Mineworkers. There was a 10 to 1 majority in favour on the ballot vote.[125] The EC of the SWMF met for the last time in that capacity on 28 December 1944. From 1 January 1945 the NUM was in being.

That was one step out of parochial limitations. Another, framed in a more rhetorical flourish, had occurred at the conference in October 1944 when Horner moved, on behalf of the SWMF, an amendment to the proposed Rule 3 of the NUM:

> ... We are moving that there shall be contained within the Rules what is already in the South Wales Rules – our determination to work 'for the purpose of and with the view to the complete abolition of Capitalism'. We do not think that the Executive explanation that we are out for public ownership of the mining industry is tantamount or equal to the abolition of Capitalism. . . . We cannot accept that Nationalisation of certain industries is the abolition of Capitalism.[126]

The amendment was carried. When nationalisation came in 1947 it was, again, the circumscribed reality that Horner welcomed. But, at that stage, and without the difficulties that were to come when the euphoric buoyancy that surrounded the early years of the first majority Labour Government had been dissipated, it must have seemed like another staging-point, another significant marshalling of the forces making for a socialist Britain. The burdensome reality of the complexity of societal (not just political) barriers to deep change was to reassert itself. But, after all, this was a road that had been trodden already, in South Wales and elsewhere. The events of 1926 had been the summation of that particular combination of industrial strength, economic dislocation and political inefficacy.[127] Horner recognised that as a defeat, but one whose bitterness helped swing 'a tremendous feeling for nationalisation after the Second World War'; more significantly he can stand as a spokesman for the dialectic that has been traced between a local molecular social consciousness and its translation, via institutional strength, into a weapon able to resist economic attack and then to enact social change:

> I sat gazing out of the train window on my way back to Mardy. I was returning with bitterness in my heart to my own people, to tell them that we were beaten, that the sufferings ahead were going to be far worse than those we had endured in the strike and the lock-out. But I knew there would be no personal recriminations from the men and women of Mardy. They would

never have given in. Right to the end, there was not a whisper of defeatism among . . . the members of Mardy Lodge.

If the whole coalfield had stood as firmly as Mardy we could have won. . . .

. . . The aims we set ourselves many years before in *The Miners' Next Step* were thus more imperative than ever after the 1926 strike. So I went back realising that we had to start a period of organisational rebuilding leading to the creation of one miners' union and the nationalisation of the mining industry.[128]

That was, perhaps, enough for one man's life, one generation's experience. Certainly it was not the end.

NOTES

1. *The Miners' Monthly*, April 1937.
2. There were 112,743 members for 1936 as opposed to 110,294 in 1935 (the amount of unemployed members in these figures remained almost the same, i.e. at 24,364 and 24,753 respectively). There were 126,233 employed in coalfields in South Wales in 1936. See FS.12/137. 116OT, PRO; 3rd Annual Report of the SWMF EC 1936–7.
3. *The Miners' Monthly*, November 1936.
4. There was a short 'stay-down' by fourteen men in Bedwas Colliery in 1937 over wages that the EC settled speedily; conversely, the Fernhill dispute of August 1936 had been lengthy despite all official efforts to end it. See *Western Mail*, 17 April 1937.
5. SWMF EC Minutes, 17 September 1936.
6. This was an article by Iorwerth Thomas in *Western Mail*, 29 September 1936. Will Paynter took the same line on 'stay-in's' later:

    It is . . . an action to be undertaken by a small group . . . its effect is to prevent a much larger group from working. In this sense it is undemocratic and should only be used in rare circumstances of the kind referred to and never as a method of forcing a settlement of questions and disputes capable of settlement by other means. (Paynter, *op. cit.*, p. 115.)

7. Oddly enough, in view of his earlier pronouncements, Iorrie Thomas took the opportunity of the new wages agreement to complain that the SWMF was now, under a CP President, 'like a great industrial Samson, shorn of its revolutionary locks'. This prompted replies from Alderman Sydney Jones and Idris Cox (District Secretary of the S. Wales CP), from different angles repudiating Thomas's professed dislike of 'concessions'. See Letters to the *Western Mail*, 29 April, 3, 4, 7 and 12 May 1937.

8. *The Miners' Monthly*, April 1937; *Western Mail*, 25 March, 5 April 1937; Will Paynter, *op. cit.*, p. 115 – 'Months of negotiation at the end of 1936 and into 1937 resulted in a new coalfield agreement based on one rate for the job throughout the coalfield and involving an increase in wages. It was, in fact, a coalfield wages structure that became the forerunner of a similar *national* agreement between the Union and the Coal Board in 1955.'

9. Horner, *op. cit.*, p. 154.

10. Letter from Harris to W. E. Jayne (colliery agent), 24 September 1936.

11. SWMF EC Minutes, 30 September and 19 October 1936.

12. There are eight SWMF leaflets and two SWMIU ones surviving from late 1936. SWMF files.

13. *Merthyr Express*, 18 January 1936.

14. *Ibid.*, 10 April 1937.

15. Letter from the Secretary of the Taff-Merthyr Lodge to Oliver Harris, 3 April 1937.

16. See A. R. Griffin, *op. cit.*

17. *Western Mail*, 29 May 1937.

18. *Ibid.*, 15 September 1937; EC Minutes, September 1937, *passim*.

19. SWMF EC Minutes, 27 July, 18, 21 and 29 September 1937.

20. *Western Mail*, 8 October 1937.

21. Interview with Edgar Evans, 1 April 1969; interview with D. D. Evans, 7 August 1973. Horner opposed it in a District Party meeting.

22. Thus it was a forlorn hope that the Federation could end 'this conflict on the same constitutional lines as at Bedwas' by both sides lifting the 'social boycott'. Letter from Alf Davies (organiser in Taff-Merthyr), to Oliver Harris, 21 October 1936.

23. Typescript of the proceedings of a meeting of the Taff-Merthyr Lodge Committee, addressed by Horner, on 16 February 1938. SWMF files.

24. *Western Mail*, 11 October 1937.

25. *Ibid.*, 13, 14 and 20 October 1937; SWMF EC Minutes, 12, 18 and 21 October 1937; 25 January 1938.

26. Documents of agreement and a Balance Sheet of Assets and Liabilities of the SWMIU in February 1938, dated 31 March 1938, and signed by Iestyn Williams, Spencer and Horner (SWMF files). These terms were not revealed at the time, and the monies paid out were only shown as expenses incurred over the campaign.

27. For the preceding details see the documents *Proposed Terms for Winding Up the SWMIU* and *Agreement between South Wales Miners' Federation and the Taff-Merthyr Steam Coal Co. Ltd., passim*.

28. The *Daily Herald* was the chief culprit in this. The Taff-Merthyr Federation Committee had, in fact, spoken against the terms. *Western Mail*, 3 February 1938.

29. *Western Mail*, 7 and 21 February 1938; 25 April 1938.

30. Typescript of the meeting, 6 February 1938. SWMF files.

31. This was strictly true but there is little doubt that some of the £1,500 given to Spencer must have been earmarked for Gregory. D. D. Evans thought only some of the EC knew this, and that even Oliver Harris was not aware of it because 'old Ollie wouldn't think of compensating the buggers'. Mr Evans thought it was the cheapest way to get rid of the SWMIU. Interview, 21 August 1973.

32. Rhys Davies, a long-standing militant, was concerned about the unemployed

ex-Taff-Merthyr men with respect to the Lodge Committee and their own future in the colliery. Horner thought the former issue would have to be left until matters improved (though the unemployed could and should remain Federation members), and that Clause 16 allowed the miners' agent to intercede on behalf of those men who had been employed.

33. *The Miners' Monthly*, February 1938. In an otherwise predictably orthodox piece, Harris manages to almost justify some part of the SWMIU's own history:

> It also appealed to that not inconsiderable section of the miners who question the ready and frequent use of the strike weapon as being the best way to secure improved conditions in the industry.
>
> It is now generally agreed that the prolongation of the miners' strike after the collapse of the general strike in 1926 was a colossal blunder of leadership for which the rank-and-file had to pay dearly, and in the reaction of the moment the ground was favourable for the propagation of the ideas for which the MIU professed to stand.

34. Letters from Morgan Jones (the old Secretary of the Taff-Merthyr Lodge and the new Secretary of the Taff-Merthyr Unemployed Lodge) to Oliver Harris, 25 April 1938 and 10 September 1938. Harris advised consultation with the miners' agent.

35. *Proposed Merger of the Craftsmen's Association into the SWMF; Western Mail,* 16 April, 10 August, 20 October 1938. Correspondence of Jones with Harris (SWMF files).

36. PRO, FS. 12/137. 1160.

37. The policy is clearly stated in a reply by Harris to the Secretary of the Newlands Lodge, Kenfig Hill, 28 July 1937, who requested EC approval for tendering notices against fifty men:

> I am instructed to point out that the consent of the EC is not strictly necessary for the tendering of notices on the non-unionist question as, in the event of a stoppage, the Central Executive will not provide strike pay. A large number of collieries hand in these notices regularly instead of taking show cards, and the EC is never consulted – if you require the services of members of the Executive every assistance will be provided.

38. *Western Mail,* 19 April; 6, 13, 24 and 27 September; 15 November; 15 December 1937. 25 April; 17 May; 11 and 12 July 1938; 16, 23 and 26 January; 8 May; 5 June; 22 and 28 August 1939.

39. During the Ocean Combine strike of July 1938, the owners allowed men who wanted to pay up and to draw upon their previous week's pay that had been held over by the company (*Western Mail,* 12 July 1938). And compare the letter from the Secretary of Emlyn Colliery to Harris, 24 June 1938, where he says: 'I do not anticipate any trouble [over the non-unionists], as if they do not pay up the manager will stop their lamps.'

40. *Resumé for Joint Standing Disputes Committee,* 6 April 1936, by Iestyn Williams. Monmouthshire and South Wales Coalowners' Association Papers.

41. *Inquiry into Conditions of Employment at the Powell Duffryn Collieries and the Conditions of the Federation Organisation in relation thereto.* The McVicar Group, 31 January 1938. By W. H. Crews and John Davies, SWMF files.

42. *Report of Investigation . . . within the Frank Hann Group.* 25 February 1938, by W. H. Arthur and Albert Bennett, SWMF files.
43. *Report on Investigation in D. A. Hann Group* (n.d.) by W. Paynter and W. R. Davies.
44. Letter from Oliver Harris to Iestyn Williams, 3 June 1938. Coalowners' Papers.
45. *Western Mail*, 6 January, 10 April, 13 March, 24 May 1939.
46. *The Miners' Monthly*, June 1939.
47. *Western Mail*, 29 and 30 May, 3 July, 22 and 28 August 1939.
48. Letter from Iestyn Williams to Harris, 17 September 1937; Letter from Harris to D. E. Thomas, 8 December 1937. SWMF files.
49. Minutes of the Monmouthshire and South Wales Coalowners' Association, 4 October 1937; 17 October; 31 October 1938.
50. *The Miners' Monthly*, April 1938.
51. *Western Mail*, 25 August 1938.
52. *Ibid.*, 14 and 28 November 1938; SWMF EC Minutes, 26 November 1938.
53. There was a long article on the need for 100 per cent unionism, by Horner, in the *Western Mail*, 31 May 1939.
54. SWMF EC Minutes, 5, 12, 26 and 29 September; 10 and 21 October 1939.
55. *Ibid.*, 9 and 19 January, 6 February, 13 August 1940; 14 January 1941.
56. *Aberdare Leader*, 21 June 1941.
57. See Letter from the Tredegar Combine Executive, 9 August 1941, to the secretary of the other combines (SWMF files).
58. *Western Mail*, 8 May 1942.
59. *Inquiry into the McVicar Group.* By W. H. Crews and John Davies, January 1938, SWMF files.
60. Address by Arthur L. Horner to Annual Conference of the SWMF, April 1940. For a comprehensive account of the social and economic consequences of the war on the coalfield, including the impact of evacuees, 'Bevin' boys and changing employment opportunities for women, see S. R. Broomfield 'South Wales in the Second World War: The Coal Industry and Its Community' (University of Wales Ph.D., 1979).
61. W. H. B. Court, *Coal* (1951), pp. 390–1.
62. R. P. Arnot, *The Miners in Crisis and War*, p. 299.
63. President's address to SWMF conference, 1944.
64. Monmouthshire and South Wales Coalowners' Association Papers. Memorandum, 24 February 1941.
65. SWMF EC Minutes, 15 June 1940.
66. *Merthyr Express*, 23 November 1940 (Letter from Ned Gittins, Bedlinog).
67. Page Arnot, *op. cit.*, p. 308.
68. Angus Calder, *The People's War* (1969), pp. 436–7.
69. Address by Arthur L. Horner to Annual Conference of the SWMF, April 1940.
70. *Western Mail*, 18 November 1944. Major Lloyd George (Minister of Fuel and Power) replying to questions in the House of Commons.
71. Minutes of Proceedings concerning the Conciliation Board, 2 March 1942.
72. *Western Mail*, 23 May 1941.
73. Page Arnot, *op. cit.*, pp. 334–54.
74. SWMF EC Minutes, 17 January, 21 March, 2 May, 10 June 1939.
75. *Ibid.*, 22 August 1939.

76. Horner, *op. cit.*, pp. 161–2.
77. See tape-recorded interview with Dai Francis, 21 June 1976.
78. SWMF EC Minutes, 10 February 1940; *Western Mail*, 24 February 1940.
79. SWMF EC Minutes, 17 February, 2 March 1940. On a card vote the result was 1,940 votes to 607 (or 90,000 to 30,000) in favour of prosecution of the war.
80. Address by Horner to Annual Conference, April 1940.
81. Horner, *op. cit.*, pp. 244–6.
82. Calder, *op. cit.*, p. 163.
83. SWMF EC Minutes, 3 and 10 December 1940.
84. *Ibid.*, 6 December 1940.
85. Though there were lobbies of the Regional Food Controller, *Western Mail*, 3 March 1941.
86. SWMF EC Minutes, 21, 24 June, 26 July 1941. There were some dissentients – notably Trevor James who became a miners' agent for Area No. 1 in 1943.
87. Address by Horner to Annual Conference, April 1942.
88. SWMF EC Minutes, 22 July 1941, 14 April 1942, 25 June 1943, 17 May 1944. And see below, pp. 406–16.
89. *Ibid.*, 23 March 1943.
90. Address by Horner to Annual Conference of the SWMF, April 1943.
91. SWMF EC Minutes, 5 July 1943.
92. B. L. Coombes, *Those Clouded Hills* (1944), pp. 30–1.
93. SWMF EC Minutes, 20 April, 16 and 21 June 1943; Amalgamated Anthracite Combine Committee Minutes, 17 June 1943; *South Wales Voice*, 19 June 1943. The men served their full time.
94. Conciliation Board Minutes, 27 August 1943; SWMF EC Minutes, 28 August 1943; *Western Mail*, 30 August 1943.
95. Conciliation Board Minutes, 30 August 1943.
96. SWMF EC Minutes (incorporating a Report of the Centralisation Board meeting), 30 August 1943.
97. *Ibid.*, 21 September, 11 October 1943. Dai Francis who had come on to the EC in March 1943 recalled:

We were meeting in the Executive Council that morning, and Albert Bennett was reporting on Penrhiwceiber . . . and arrangements had been made now to meet the full owners . . . and the Powell Duffryn men were there, Edmund Hann, Douglas Hann and Frank Hann. The three of them were there. And Horner goes to town on them, and he puts the responsibility entirely on their shoulders. He said, 'You must understand that the men . . . were fighting against these tyrannical measures [fascism] . . . people were losing their blood for it.' And he likened them to the fascists in that meeting. And they didn't come back – they didn't come back. But at the meeting in the morning Arthur was, . . . the Devil's Advocate, putting the case. . . . And I thought to myself, 'Well, damn, he's a queer guy, he's not the fellow that I know.' But I didn't understand his tactics, you see. But I was proud of him in the afternoon, the way he brought those men to heel, and have a promise from them that it wouldn't happen again, or South Wales would be out.

Interview with Dai Francis, 21 June 1976.
98. SWMF EC Minutes, 2 September 1943.

99. *Ibid.*, 3 and 4 January 1944.
100. Page Arnot *op. cit.*, pp. 385–92.
101. *Ibid.*, pp. 392–7, SWMF EC Minutes, 25 January 1944 (with Porter's Wages Award reproduced verbatim).
102. *Western Mail*, 26 January 1944.
103. There were twenty-two stoppages involving 5,750 men in February.
104. Page Arnot, *op. cit.*, pp. 395–6. *Western Mail*, 7 March 1944.
105. B. L. Coombes, *Miners' Day* (1945), p. 25.
106. SWMF EC Minutes, 7 March 1944.
107. *Western Mail*, 8, 9, 10, 11 March 1944.
108. SWMF EC Minutes, 11 March 1944.
109. *Ibid.*, 13 March 1944.
110. Paynter, *op. cit.*, p. 123. SWMF EC Minutes, 14 March 1944.
111. *Western Mail*, 8 April 1944.
112. SWMF EC Minutes, 3 April 1944.
113. Court, *op. cit.*, pp. 261–5; Page Arnot, *op. cit.*, pp. 397–9.
114. Evan Williams became General Secretary when Oliver Harris retired in April 1941; shortly after this he was transferred to work with the Regional Coal Controller and W. J. Saddler, the Vice-President, took over his job. Harold Finch, later MP for Bedwellty, succeeded Evan Williams in the Compensation Department.
115. President's Address to the Annual Conference, April 1944. In March 1944 the SWMF held its first conference on 'Dust Suppression and Pneumoconiosis', discussing the greater possibility for compensation, since the 1943 Compensation Act widened the definition of chest ailments to include pneumoconiosis as well as silicosis. See SWMF EC Minutes, 4 March 1944, and below Ch. 12, pp. 438–41.
116. President's Address, April 1944.
117. SWMF EC Minutes, 14 and 30 August 1943.
118. B. L. Coombes, *Those Clouded Hills*, p. 65; *Miners' Day*, p. 7.
119. SWMF EC Minutes, 26 July 1944.
120. *Ibid.*, 28 October 1944.
121. Report of MFGB Annual Conference, July 1939.
122. R. Page Arnot, *The Miners in Crisis and War* (1961), pp. 404–8.
123. He had been President on a full-time basis in 1940 when the Rules were altered so that: 'The position of the President shall be a full-time appointment, subject to election by the Annual Conference every three years, and he shall not be allowed to hold the position of Member of Parliament or any other public office during his tenure of office.' The Vice-President was to be elected every three years by Annual Conference. The Presidency became a full-time position after the formation of the NUM in 1944.
124. Report of the MFGB Annual Conference, July 1943.
125. Page Arnot, *op. cit.*, pp. 412–30.
126. MFGB Special Conference on Reorganisation, August 1944. Held, appropriately enough, in George Spencer's Nottingham.
127. See G. A. Phillips, *The General Strike* (1976), pp. 1–41.
128. Horner, *op. cit.*, pp. 90–2.

CHAPTER TWELVE

The Dawn of a New Era?[1]

Forget not the dreams of the few who dream tonight
Among the rubbish heaps of 1944! . . .
And meanwhile, Dai, with your woollen muffler,
Tight around your pit-scarred neck,
Remind us of the gratitude we owe you,
We who so easily pass you by.
Remind us of your long endurance,
Those bitter battles the sun has never seen,
And remind us of the struggles you have waged
Against the crude philosophy of greed.
And remind all who strut with noses high in the air,
How the proudest of nations would falter without you,
And remind us when we lie on fireside cushions
Of the blood that is burnt within the flame.
And remind us when we kneel to the unknown God
And turn and cry to the cold infinitive heavens,
Remind us of the toil of the blistered hands
And the courage and comradeship of men.

Idris Davies, *Tonypandy* (1945)[2]

On Saturday morning . . . at 9 a.m. we started off for Hyde Park . . . to move into our position for the Victory Parade. The sights I seen was very impressive foreign Regiments from all corners of the globe. . . . The Mall this is where the King and Queen stood at the Saluting Base we were now marching rigidly to attention and the order was given [eyes left] we all looked to the left and the King saluted. . . . As we miners marched through the streets of London the overwhelming reception which the people gave to us was terrific, and whatever the Press say or our picture shows we were the favourites of the people.

Jack Dorgan, Onllwyn miner, June 1946[3]

1945 was a year of victory for the British people and for no section more than the British miners. The year witnessed the emergence of the

National Union of Mineworkers (NUM), the Allied military victory in Europe and Asia and a resounding triumph for the Labour Party in the General Election. The South Wales miners had played a prominent role in all these changes which were to lead inevitaby to fundamental and long-overdue advances in the quality of their lives: central to all of this were the new Government's plans for the nationalisation of the coal industry and founding of the Welfare State.[4]

On 1 January 1945, the SWMF became the South Wales Area of the NUM. The miners of the coalfield had voted overwhelmingly for the change, which still gave some financial autonomy to the new areas so as to win over the more 'conservative' elements. William Brace, who had campaigned over half a century before for a national union, urged the miners in a stirring speech at a celebration dinner, to strengthen further their organisation so as to participate more effectively in the moulding of the post-war world. With the new government legislation and the evolving of a stronger more unified national union, it might have seemed logical that the comprehensive localised role consistently performed by the SWMF would not now be continued. On the contrary, as if following Brace's advice, the new union strove to unify all mineworkers within the South-Western Division and to broaden the base which it had already achieved within South Wales society.[5]

Encouraged by its success in 1938 in eliminating the company union, (the South Wales Miners' Industrial Union) and the craft union (the South Wales Colliery Enginemen, Boilermen and Craftsmen's Association) and also in securing the first coalfield-wide closed-shop in 1942, the South Wales Area proceeded to unify the workforce as provided under the new rules of the NUM.[6] The Area assisted considerably in setting up and then recruiting for the Colliery Offices and Staffs Area (COSA): from the outset COSA worked extremely closely with the Area, so much so that it shared its offices at 2 St Andrew's Crescent, Cardiff. This was considerably assisted by the close working relationship established between Dai Dan Evans, the Area's chief administrative officer, and COSA's regional officer, the former Abertridwr colliery blacksmith, Tom Mantle.[7] In 1946, overtures to the National Association of Colliery Overmen Deputies and Shotfirers (NACODS) nationally seemed to fail only narrowly.[8] In 1948, the Winding Enginemen became part of the South Wales Area and this process towards an industrial union demanded by *The Miners' Next Step*, and provided under NUM rules moved beyond the geographical bounds of South Wales in 1960 when Somerset also joined the Area.

The Forest of Dean had already merged with SWMF in 1940. Both these small coalfields maintained a measure of autonomy through their miners' agents, Ted Cooper and John Williams, respectively, who continued to serve them.[9] The South Wales Area is the only large coalfield within the NUM to succeed in eliminating both craft sectionalism and coalfield parochialism. Its experience therefore serves as an example to those smaller coalfields which in the late 1970s fear the democratic streamlining of the NUM's archaic structure. Much of this development was considerably assisted by the unifying atmosphere provided by the 1937 South Wales Wage Agreement which rationalised grades from 150 to 6 on the principle of equal pay for equal work. Such a system was not established in the rest of the British coalfields until 1956.[10]

Against this background of growing unity, the union continued to develop its wider role within the mining communities and society at large despite the fact that nationalisation, at least at first sight, might be seen to have undercut its traditional role. The union's massive presence, expressed most obviously in its numerical strength and through its dynamic political role, ensured, however, that it still initiated its own socio-political institutions. In so doing it persisted in questioning both traditional and relatively new social institutions within the coalfield.

Two of the union's major activities have been the Miners' Eisteddfod and the Miners' Gala, both conceived originally as a means of reviving cultural activities in the coalfield which had declined dramatically in the war years. They were also ways of re-focusing local initiatives as well as underpinning and developing an indigenous culture. The novelist, Gwyn Thomas, who provided the commentary for the promotional film of the 1960 South Wales miners' gala described it lucidly:

From the valleys that spread northwards from Pontypridd like dark fingers has come stupendous wealth, a wealth of coal and above all a wealth of people. . . . On the second Saturday in June they pour down into Cardiff, the miners marching behind their lodge banners, the housewives delighted for a chance to be away from the endless chores. The valleys fuse with Cardiff. The men and women of the mining villages show the capital some part of their traditions and their pride. Banners, bands, gaiety, and besides the brass bands, the colourful character bands are an interesting echo of the gazooka bands of the 1926 period. A day of explosive joy.

History marches here, these are men asking for security and peace. The names of their lodges are a fanfare of heroic conflict for the achievement of a saner social set-up, for greater happiness and peace: Mardy, Newlands,

Penallta, Penrhiwceiber, Tower, Duffryn Rhondda, Cambrian, they're all here.

We enter Sophia Gardens. This would have been a place denied to us in the long ago but now it is part of our inheritance, and we are prepared for a day in which gaiety and thought will compete for equal place in the long years of endurance, the long years of conflict. These men have listened, thought, planned, worked. Their hands have been hands that sustained a nation. Strong creative hands on which a community can always rely no matter how the community may have sometimes treated them. Men as strong as the steel of the pit head gear that takes them down into the earth and up into the light, men as ardent as the coal they bring to us, men as enduring as the hills from which they hew the stuff that keeps us all alive. . . .

Violins would not do for men like these; they need instruments of strength to blow the message they have to give the world: the message – brotherhood. . . . Everything is interfused here. . . . The day has become a great roaring carnival of pleasure. . . . With banners furled we go back to our valleys, to work, to remember the laughter of the day and to think about the future.

The Eisteddfod was begun in 1948 in Porthcawl where it has remained and prospered, growing from a one day event to three days in the late 1970s. It is a unique cultural event being the only truly bilingual Eisteddfod in Wales, the only Eisteddfod which is visibly growing and the only festival of its kind to be sponsored by a British trade union. Most significant of all, the Miners' Annual Eisteddfod has been one of the most influential factors in stimulating a range of cultural activities, particularly choral music for adults and children alike, at a time when the decline of the industry has threatened the very existence of so many Welsh mining communities.[11]

Unlike other British coalfields, there had not been a long-established gala tradition in South Wales. Communication problems had also caused delays in organising the event which was only established in June 1953 in Cardiff following the success of the massive demonstration the previous October against a change in unemployment insurance regulations, relating particularly to some disabled miners. Since 1953, the Gala has continued to grow so that by the 1970s it had become the most important social and political gathering in the calendar of the Welsh Labour movement. It is one day in the year when the capital city, built on coal, is given over to the miners. From the early days, when it was essentially a political occasion with Aneurin Bevan verbally slaying the Tory class enemy, it has diversified into being a family outing with bands (brass and jazz), folk-dancing, soccer, rugby, art and craft exhibitions all adding to the occasion. One special characteristic of the Gala has been its consistent internationalist flavour. As if expressing the universality of its socialism, emblazoned so vividly and so often on their crimson banners, honoured guests at the Gala have frequently been representatives of peoples struggling against fascism and imperialism overseas, including notably the Greek seamen's leader, Tony Ambatielos in 1964, and the South Vietnamese National Liberation Front in 1970.

Such internationalism, whilst appearing most evident at its Galas and on its banners, also permeated the day-to-day activities of the miners' union in South Wales, particularly, and understandably, on the Spanish question. Activities included involvement in vigorous campaigns against fascism and reactionary regimes from post-war Greece to Chile in the 1970s; against German Rearmament (notably the Castlemartin NATO base in the early 1960s); and constant financial support for striking Spanish miners, even in the midst of their own strike in 1970. Such an outlook did not seem to waver even in the difficult Cold War period (although there was a breakdown of the old internal unity with some bitter left-right election battles within the coalfield in the 1950s). Even the Soviet invasion of Hungary in 1956 (which the Area did not condemn, and yet 'welcomed' refugee miners) and that of Czecho-slovakia (which the Area did condemn) did not cause the traumas experienced elsewhere. Typical of this long, unusual, internation-alist approach was the successful campaign (with other organisations) on behalf of the Negro singer Paul Robeson who had had his passport withdrawn during the American McCarthyite period.[12]

Both the Gala and the Eisteddfod were initially sponsored solely by the union, but have subsequently relied on the support of the Coal Industry Social Welfare Organisation, the jointly administered NCB-NUM scheme which owed so much to the long educational, recreational and cultural traditions of the miners' institutes and miners' welfare schemes in the valleys. CISWO had been established in 1952 to succeed the Miners' Welfare Commission which had in turn been founded in 1920 following the recommendations of the Sankey Commission to provide indoor and outdoor recreational facilities in the British coalfields and this to be financed by contributions from coalowners and miners alike.[13]

It was only after the Second World War that the Welfare Movement was able to begin to satisfy the needs of the valley communities. The optimism of the post-war world was expressed most tangibly in the

The First Annual

CHAIR EISTEDDFOD

(In connection with the above). WILL BE HELD ON

SATURDAY, 21st JANUARY, 1933

In the Wesley Hall, Blackwood

Musical Adjudicators—MATTHEW DAVIES, Esq., B.A., Mus.Bac. (Neath);
GEO. A. JAMES, Esq., A.R.C.O. Mus.Bac. (Leicester)
Literary and Poems—E. PHILLIPS, Esq. (Trefinog), Blackwood

	Prize—£	s	d
1.—**Male Voice** Own Selection	15	0	0
2.—**Chief Choral** Own Selection	10	0	0
3.—**Juvenile Choir** "The Lily" T. Price ...1st: 4	0	0
(1st and 3rd verses) If 4 or more Choirs compete, 2nd: 2	0	0
4.—**Party** of 12 voices **(Juvenile)**			
(a) "Hen Aelwyd Cymru" Alawon Gwerion Cymru II			
(b) "Wrth fynd efo Deio i Dywyn" Allan o		Silver Cup
"Ten Welsh Songs," tr. Hubert Davies			
Adopted from Programme of the Urdd Eisteddfod,Caerphilly—May 25th, 26th and 27th, 1933			
5.—**Chair Poems:** Entrance Fee, 1/-		Chair
(a) Cywydd Byr (24 llin) : 'Y Talcen Glo '—"The Heading"		solid
(b) Soned : "Shift y Nos "—"The Night Shift "		6s'.
(c) Telyneg : "Gadael Gwaith" Leaving Work "		and Bide
(Chairing of the Bard at Eisteddfod)			
Chair given by Baber's, Modern Furnisher, Blackwood—Call and inspect Showroom.			
6.—**Open Champion Solo** Own Selection	2	0	0
7.—**Open Soprano Solo** "Parting" David E Williams (key Eb)	1	1	0
8.— " **Contralto Solo** "Spring Serenade" Angelo Mascheroni	1	1	0
9.— " **Tenor Solo** "Lover's Thoughts"			
Alberto I. Randegger (key Eb)	1	1	0
10.— " **Bass or Baritone Solo** "Blow, Winds, Blow "			
Kennerly Ronway	1	1	0
11.—**Novice Soprano Solo** "The Long Ago' Mary Nightingale(key D)	0	10	6
12.— " **Contralto Solo** " Dear Heart O' Mine' Pax, Elliott	0	10	6
13.— " **Tenor Solo** "Fallen Roses" Arthur F. Tate (key Eb)	0	10	6
14.— " **Bass or Baritone Solo** "A Huguenot " W. J. Meatyard	0	10	6
(No one to compete in Novice Class who has won a prize of more than 10/6)			
15.—**Open Recitation** " The Passing of Arthur " Tennyson	1	1	0
Commence at line :—" The old order changeth yielding			
place to new."			
16.—**Recitation**, Boy or Girl under 14 years	1st : 0	7	6
" Dewi Gwared " E. Phillips ...2nd : 0	3	6
17.—**Recitation**, Boy or Girl under 10 years	1st: 0	5	0
" The Land of Story Books R. L. Stevenson	2nd: 0	2	6
No. 16 and 17 printed on Official Programme			
18.—**Essay Competition**, for Blackwood Elementary School	1st : 0	5	0
Children " Blackwood in the year of 2032 "	2nd : 0	2	6
19.—**Prize Bag Competition**	0	5	0
20.—**Boy's Solo**, under 14 years			
" Within the Gates of Light " Theo. Bonheur	0	5	0
21.—**Girl's Solo**, under 14 years "Holyland" Theo. Bonheur	0	5	0
22.—**Solo**, Boy or Girl under 12 years			
"Only an Armour Bearer" Sankey's Songs	0	5	0
23.—**Duet**, under 16 years Own Selection 1st : 7/6	2nd ; 3/-
24.—**Pianoforte Solo**, under 10 years			
" Forest Flowers" Sydney H. Gambrell	0	5	0
25.— " " under 12 years " On the Pier" Allan Neville	0	5	0
*26.— " " 14 years and under " Confetti " Rene Morel	0	7	6
*27.— " " under 14 years " Ricordanza in F"			
W. Millward	0	7	6
28.— " " under 16 years "Sincerite" S. H. Gambrell	0	7	6
*Competitions Nos. 26 and 27 open to those only			
who have never won a prize.			

To ensure correct editions, all Musical Copies should be obtained
from Mr. G. PAUL, High St., Llanhilleth, Mon. 2/- post free

Official Programmes may be obtained from the Secretaries at
"Fairfield," Blackwood; or 6 Park View, Cefn Road, Blackwood;
Price 2d., per post 2½d. (ready shortly)

Roberts, Typ., Blackwood.   Sydney Jones (Gen. Sec.), Blackwood, Mon

An early Eisteddfod at a Monmouthshire Institute.

gaiety of the D-Day Celebration Carnivals, invariably organised by the local welfare committees often under the strong influence of the miners' lodges. Several welfare schemes in 1945–6 celebrated their twenty-first birthdays, having had little to celebrate in the intervening period. The small isolated community of Gilfach Goch in the Ogwr Fach Valley organised a week of entertainments to mark their painstaking achievement of establishing, since 1924, a hall containing a library, reading and billiard rooms as well as an impressive range of outdoor recreational facilities. The occasion was used to reflect upon the missed opportunities of war and depression and to urge greater efforts in the new world opening up before them:

> We still have some of our pioneers with us. They are the living witnesses of the Seed in Bloom, the foundation stones that had to go down almost into the mire of despair. . . . The call for unity among the working classes is heralded from the four winds, and yet we have to appeal to our inhabitants to lend a hand and help build this wonderful oasis in our desert by subscribing a few coppers a week.[14]

The Welfare Movement tapped the socialist enthusiasm of the mining valleys which Horner, presumably, hoped to channel industrially when he urged in September 1945 that miners become Stakhanovites.[15] The Movement experienced an all too brief golden era up to the mid-fifties when a recharging of the old ideals inspired workmen's institutes and welfare halls, as at Tredegar in the Sirhowy Valley where the institute provided a focus and support for the silver band, choral and operatic societies, cinema and a splendid library. Elsewhere, at Onllwyn in the Dulais Valley, two generations of striving for a village hall was accomplished as late as 1955.[16]

From the outset, the South Wales Area of the NUM continued the deep concern of the SWMF for the medical care of its members. The Talygarn Convalescent Home in the Vale of Glamorgan was established by the Miners' Welfare Commission in 1923 and then subsequently became a Miners' Rehabilitation Centre in 1943. In the immediate post-war years it achieved a world-wide reputation for its treatment of injured miners. In 1951, the Centre was taken over by the Ministry of Health with a Management Committee made up of representatives from the Union, National Coal Board and the Welsh Hospital Board. Throughout the whole period of its existence, either as a Convalescent Home or Rehabilitation Centre, Talygarn has benefited from the decisive involvement of the miners' union, and during most of

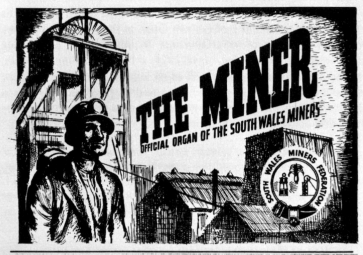

VOL. II.   AUGUST, 1946.   No. 10.

TALYGARN
MINERS' REHABILITATION CENTRE

FOREWORD

THIS issue of "The Miner" is entirely devoted to the work done at Talygarn to rehabilitate the miner who has been unfortunate enough to have been seriously injured at the colliery.

Although the Home is full and doing a grand job of work, it is felt that it is necessary to publicise the work done at this Centre. The Mining Industry is a hazardous and exacting one. The incidence of fracture cases in the industry is far higher than in any other. Indeed, the number of cases reported by the Colliery Companies shows us that there is a great need for a second Centre to be set up in South Wales. More than half of the fracture cases occuring in the South Wales Coalfield fail to get the proper treatment to restore them back to their normal lives. This failure is generally due to the lack of co-operation on the part of local Hospital Authorities in notifying the Rehabilitation Centre at Talygarn of the cases they treat.

The staff at the Centre is getting the distressing experience every day of cases too long delayed in reaching them, and making it almost impossible to restore the proper function of the limb, so as to allow the invalid to go back to his normal employment. A stitch in time saves nine, and the man goes back to his work quicker and better able to get about.

the post-war period, the long and devoted service of Margaret Urwin and Connie Thomas known throughout the South Wales coalfield simply as 'matron' and 'sister'.[17]

The Court Royal Hotel, Bournemouth, was purchased by the Miners' Welfare Commission in July 1947 and was converted into a Convalescent Home for South Wales miners. This again illustrated the breadth of the union's activities in that it was largely the South Wales Area of the NUM, guided by its former vice-president and acting general secretary Alderman W. J. Saddler which had taken the initiative in the matter. 'Court Royal' has also been fortunate in having the distinguished commitment of Mrs E. M. Candler, matron from its opening until 1976. 'Court Royal' and Talygarn have both made remarkable contributions to the quality of life of injured and ailing miners. Unfortunately, another worthy experiment, the Millendraeth Holiday Village in Cornwall, proved to be a failure and a fiasco: had it been undertaken in the mid-1940s and not the mid-1960s, it might have shared the successes of the earlier ventures.[18]

The union also gave its enthusiastic support to the Pneumoconiosis Research Unit at Llandough Hospital, near Penarth. The Unit was established in June 1946 under the aegis of the Medical Research Council. For over thirty years, the Unit has been acknowledged as a leading research establishment for the study of several types of dust diseases. As a token of appreciation of the work undertaken in attempting to solve the scourge of pneumoconiosis, the union presented a mural to the Unit depicting life in a mining community.[19]

The union's broadening post-war role was an integral part then of the confidence and hope generated by Labour's victory at the General Election. All thirteen South Wales miners' sponsored MPs were returned with resounding majorities with the exception of W. H. Mainwaring, who only narrowly held his Rhondda East seat following a strong challenge from Communist Harry Pollitt, who was particularly popular amongst many of the constituency's miners.[20]

There was an unmistakable determination pervading the whole organisation, from its lodges, executive council, full-time officials and its Members of Parliament that the union was at last having an opportunity to create a socialist society.[21] At the core of this expression was the support for the new Government's nationalisation and social policy legislation. The influence of the South Wales miners was indeed profound: three of their MPs were now cabinet ministers. Aneurin Bevan became Minister of Health and Housing, James Griffiths

Minister of National Insurance, and Ness Edwards ultimately became Post-Master General. In addition to these appointments, Arthur Horner was elected General Secretary of the National Union of Mineworkers in 1946 and in this capacity played a crucial role in the nationalisation of the coal industry.[22]

As the architect of the National Health Service, Bevan used to advantage the experiences he had amassed whilst working with the Tredegar Medical Aid Society and, more importantly, as a Member of Parliament for one of the most socially deprived areas in Britain. Central to his notion of socialism was the freedom from 'preventable poverty' and 'preventable pain'. His riveting, passionate championing of the new Health Service was but an extension of the collective and accumulated concerns of the South Wales miners, their communities and their own, often sophisticated, local medical schemes. Despite the enormous opposition organised by various vested interests and perennial financial problems, the National Health Service remains, despite its blemishes, *the* greatest achievement of the 1945–50 Labour Government and the central pillar of Britain's Welfare State.[23]

The importance of the National Insurance Act and the Industrial Injuries Act introduced by James Griffiths in 1948 was that they removed the obligation demanded by the old Workmen's Compensation Act to prove damage to the earning capacity of an injured miner. The new law paid compensation according to the loss of faculty to enjoy life and also allowed for a quinquennial (five year) review of the whole administration of the law.[24]

But the most dramatic changes to occur in the post-war years in the mining valleys was coal nationalisation which promised to effect a complete revolution in the social relationships within the industry. The NUM's major concern during the 1945 General Election was public ownership. It declared in its own Election Manifesto:

> Labour stands for a nationally owned and controlled mining industry. The Churchill Tory Government is against all forms of effective control and national ownership. . . . It prefers to put private interests before national needs. . . . Give Labour the mandate to make the coal mines public property.[25]

The South Wales Area of the union in its Manifesto was more forthright:

> Britain owes a debt to the miners – IT IS TIME THAT DEBT WAS PAID. . . . The future of . . . Welsh towns and villages depends upon the prosperity of the

coalmining industry in these areas. We beg the electors to ensure the return of the Labour Candidates so as to guarantee a prosperous and efficient mining industry. We do this because only a strong Labour majority, in charge of the Government of this nation, can ensure that resources shall be available and be used to fulfil the needs of the people in peace as they were made available to organise victory over the fascist powers in war.[26]

The feeling amongst the miners in the pits was even more anxious, determined and at times bitterly aggressive. The defiance of pre-war days had been transformed by war:

... I came back from the war in 1947. . . . I could have come back in 1944. . . . I was in a regiment that had quite a number of miners but not one of them opted for release . . . you knew the type of life you were leading . . . that was even better than going to work under the PD's (Powell Duffryn). . . . The only thing we felt when we came back from the forces was that some of the old trade union leaders at the time, particularly in the Aberdare Valley, were more inclined to eulogise nationalisation, instead of getting down to the fundamental reasons why we were nationalised. That was to do away with the exploitation that was there prior to us going into the forces because when I went back to Bwllfa, we were working on the same price list: they hadn't been revised . . . it was the same management, with the same aptitudes for carrying out Powell Duffryn policy and not a socialist policy . . . after nationalisation. Because the one thing that hit you was the boys coming back from the forces at that time (it was optional whether you wore safety helmets and they used to wear their berets. You could see boys from the Parachute Division, the Tank Corps and anywhere: they had their different berets and it indicated that there was this influx of miners coming back from the armed forces. And I believe it did a lot to strengthen the role of the NUM after nationalisation. Because a lot of these lads then became active, they were not going to go back to the old systems. . . . I was elected lodge chairman in 1947 covering the Bwllfa Pit and the Nantmelin. . . . I made it a point then of course of recruiting into the lodge committee people I knew were dedicated socialists and were prepared to be activists as well.[27]

Nevertheless, the principle of nationalisation was universally welcomed in the coalfield and heralded as 'the dawn of a new era'. Two prominent union officials, Gomer Evans and W. J. Saddler, accepted the posts of Divisional Labour Director and Deputy Labour Director respectively. From its inception the NUM had been closely associated with the shaping of the Coal Industry Nationalisation Bill indicated graphically by Horner's appointment as National Coal Production Officer in 1945 and his intimate working relationship with Emmanuel

Shinwell, the Minister of Fuel and Power.[28] Vesting Day, 1 January 1947, was greeted in every pit with splendid long-overdue well-rehearsed speeches delivered with dignity and burning sincerity. One such ceremony occurred at Lady Windsor Colliery, Ynysybwl, near Pontypridd:

> To J. E. Morgan, as being the oldest workman present as well as the oldest local Federation official, was given the privilege of hoisting the flag of the National Board to signalise the taking over of the colliery.
>
> Before doing so he reminded the audience that 50 years previously nationalisation of the mines had been the dream of a few visionaries who were then considered cranks. However, today the vision had become a reality, fraught with tremendous possibilities for those engaged in the industry and for the prosperity of the nation as a whole.[29]

Similar events occurred everywhere. Evan John recalled the ceremony at Clydach Merthyr and Abergelli collieries in the Swansea Valley:

> I remember the opening ceremony of course: raising the flag, the oldest member of the Lodge, Isaac Hill, a compressor man, he was eighty-two, and we had the youngest boy, working on the screen, and they were hauling it up together. . . . Oh the feeling was good, you know, that we were entering a new era.[30]

The coming of nationalisation, given the history of the industry between 1918 and 1939, was inevitable, made more so by wartime Government control and by the critical need for coal in the post-war economy. There was only token resistance from the coalowners who, by 1947, were morally and politically bankrupt. They had outlived their social usefulness particularly after 1926 when they plumbed new depths of social and economic irresponsibility.

The Reid Report of 1945 put them where they should have been following the Sankey Royal Commission of 1919, in the dustbin of history:

> The employers as a body have been prepared neither to accept the principle of the survival of the fittest nor fully to abandon their traditional individualism. In relation to their own undertakings the short view has too often prevailed. . . . We have come to the conclusion that it is not enough simply to recommend technical changes which we believe to be fully practicable, when it is evident to us as mining engineers that they cannot be satisfactorily carried through by the industry organised as it is today.[31]

What was surprising, and received with some measure of justifiable disbelief amongst many South Wales miners, was the way in which the changeover occurred. It soon became evident that the necessary break had not happened and that there were quite clear elements of continuity, particularly in management, policy and personnel. The first chairman of the Board was the Rt Hon. Lord Hyndley of Meads who had been Managing Director of the Powell Duffryn Group for fifteen years and a Director of both Guest, Keen and Nettlefolds and the Bank of England.[32] In South Wales, 'PD' influence continued and even extended octopus-like across the coalfield. 'PD men', notably the Hanns, were offered most of the key positions: in the Anthracite coalfield, never their patch under private enterprise, most of the old hands within the management of the Amalgamated Anthracite Combine seemed to be swept out and replaced by 'PD' and, to a lesser extent, 'Ocean men'.[33] The first Area Director was Lieutenant-General Sir A. Goodwin-Austen who had no previous link with the industry in South Wales and G. E. Aeron-Thomas, formerly a small Anthracite operator, was appointed his Deputy. When all the appointments were announced in the autumn of 1946 there was some disquiet. The South Wales Area Executive of the NUM declared its 'no confidence' in Goodwin-Austin and Aeron-Thomas in December, although this decision was reversed following pressure from the NUM leadership.[34] As if deliberately underlining these grave misgivings, Goodwin-Austen, in true officer-style at a Powell Duffryn Sports Committee Dinner in April 1947, called for everyone in the mining industry to be 'butties' and at the same time deplored anyone who attacked some 'very fine masters in the coalfield before the Board came'.[35]

A more serious and enduring criticism from the miners was the growth in bureaucracy. Eleven South Wales lodges in May 1947 complained that the industry was being overloaded with appointments. Such criticisms were still being voiced in 1952 in the form of a successful protest resolution at the 1952 Area Annual Conference.[36] The decision to allow private enterprise to dominate the more lucrative aspects of the industry, particularly distribution and the manufacture of machinery and equipment, also led to bitter comment. Nationalisation had come like manna from heaven for Powell Duffryn and their like. Another cause for great bitterness from the outset was the compensation to the former coalowners, totalling £375 million nationally on which interest had to be paid, and the £260 million loans necessary to modernise the industry. Added to these burdens, the fixed low price of coal led to misuse of a valuable energy source by the rest of the British industry, particularly the private sector, and in turn this policy retarded the proper reconstruction of the industry. Above all, the refusal of successive Governments to accept the NUM's demand for an integrated fuel policy only exacerbated the whole situation.[37]

Nevertheless, although miners soon became sceptical of the motives of Board management and the wisdom of the Labour Government of the time, a great fund of goodwill and even enthusiasm continued to exist for some time for *their* industry. It was undeniable that there was a new atmosphere. The long-awaited five-day week followed Vesting Day, wages and conditions improved steadily and a training programme for new entrants was devised which became the envy of the rest of British industry. By the early 1950s the British miner was at the top of the industrial wages league. Much of these early improvements were based on the Miners' Charter of 1946 which the NCB accepted in principle although, revealingly, less was achieved by negotiation with the Board than was won by ultimatum to the Government at the end of the 1972 strike. Horner, who drafted the Charter, believed that the most critical problem facing the industry in the immediate post-war period was manpower which had fallen, nationally, despite government controls and 'Bevin' boys, from 766,000 (1939) to 696,000 (1945). The Charter's purpose was to save the industry for the nation: this was not to be the last time the NUM took its *national* responsibilities seriously.[38]

The crisis in the industry after the war was probably more critical in South Wales than anywhere and nowhere was the commitment greater than in South Wales on the part of the miners, through their union, to rescue it. Manpower had fallen from 135,901 (1937) to 107,624 (1946) and output in this period from 37,773,000 tons to 20,950,000 tons.[39] But the traditional nineteenth-century industries of coal and steel still reigned supreme in the South Wales economy so that an ailing coalfield, particularly in isolated single-industry mining valleys, had a very severe effect on a narrowly based local economy. It was also an ageing coalfield, in pits and manpower. Young men were not being attracted to the three hundred or so mines which were taken over, of which all but one were over twenty-five years old, many were small and obsolescent and only 36 per cent of the output was cut by machines. There was also a subsequent tendency to solve the manpower problem by importing Italian and Polish labour rather than by trying to make the industry more attractive.[40]

The most harrowing problem of the time related to pneumoconiosis, known more familiarly in the mining villages as 'pneumo', 'the dust' or 'diffug-anal' (short of breath). It appeared to be more extensive in South Wales, especially in parts of the Anthracite coalfield, than elsewhere in Britain and partly accounts for the decline in manpower during this period. From 1931 to the middle of 1948, over 22,000 British miners were required to leave their work because they had pneumoconiosis and 85 per cent of them lived in South Wales. After a prolonged campaign by the MFGB, silicosis had become compensatable in 1929. Parliament restricted the applicability of the Order, although this was partly removed in 1931. Obtaining compensation remained difficult until the 1934 Silicosis Orders provided compensation for any workman who was certified as suffering from silicosis and had been working underground within three years of certification. The struggle for compensation continued to be a problem, owing to the legalistic resistance by coalowners (notably that of Tirbach Colliery in the Swansea Valley, a case which the SWMF lost in the House of Lords in 1934). To highlight this a 'Silicosis Pageant' was organised by the SWMF in the Amman Valley on May Day 1939. In 1942, the Industrial Pulmonary Disease Committee of the Medical Research Council concluded that the disease commonly found in coalminers could be caused by coal-dust and rock-dust and suggested calling both 'coalworkers' pneumoconiosis'. From 1943, all miners certified with pneumoconiosis were suspended from employment within the industry and as compensation they received a lump sum or a weekly payment (the latter was reduced if alternative work was obtained). The effect on individuals, families and communities was devastating. With little or no alternative work, particularly in such Anthracite mining villages as Brynamman, Gwaun-cae-Gurwen and Tumble, life became a nightmare for the disabled pneumoconiotic miner. The situation became even more desperate after the war with the rundown of Royal Ordinance Factories. Plans to alleviate the problem with 'Grenfell' factories (named after the miners' Labour MP for Gower whose Board of Trade Report established them) at Brynamman, Ystradgynlais, Tonypandy, Treorchy, Merthyr, Hengoed and Blackwood proved ineffective, with 30 per cent (about 5,000) still unemployed in 1949. Virtually all pneumoconiotic miners were financially worse off after their suspension from 1943 onwards.[41] One Brynamman pneumo-coniotic miner was certified in 1945 when he was thirty-five years old. (About 240 other miners were forced to finish within four months at Gwaun-cae-Gurwen. Such were the employment difficulties, un-employed committees were set up in every village in the area.) He only had work from time to time as a casual labourer and was forced to finish when he was fifty years old. He recalled his plight and that of the locality:

In the ten houses here and across the road about twenty of us had to leave Gwaun-cae-Gurwen collieries in 1945 . . . and only five of us are left [in 1974]. . . . Eventually, it came now, you couldn't get work. . . . As you had no trade, it was difficult you see. And then around about 1950, I was getting browned off. There was a scheme came out now where you could go before a Board and settle off and go back to the colliery. I know boys who went before these Boards and they were certified as being 10 per cent disabled, given £1,000 and went back to the colliery. Well, I went back to that Board . . . but because . . . my father died of TB and my brother had died of TB I wasn't considered at all. I wouldn't be allowed to be employed in or about the colliery ever. So I had to make the best of it.[42]

The findings of a survey of a typical mining valley, the Rhondda Fach, were first published in 1952. 89 per cent of the entire adult population were X-rayed by the Llandough Pneumoconiosis Unit. It was found that half the working miners (about three thousand) had pneumoconiosis. Nearly one in five had it in its severest and most deadly form, progressive massive fibrosis. This form was believed to be due to tuberculous infection of lungs already damaged by dust. Six in every thousand males and seven in every thousand females had such a severe form of tuberculosis of the lungs as to be infectious to others.[43]

The South Wales Area of the NUM undertook a considerable amount of educational work, especially in the 1950s, on the question of dust. It published books by Lyndon R. James, the head of its Safety Department, on the control of dust in mines, and by Archie James, head of its Compensation Department, on industrial injuries, as well as a comprehensive survey of pneumoconiosis by Dai Dan Evans, its general secretary. This survey covering the period 1948 until 1961, revealed the progression of the disease between the date of initial certification and the reassessment of disability. Collieries were chosen at random across the coalfield to examine this progression. The results were 'startling': the percentages were uniformly high with the worst returns at Elliot (New Tredegar, Rhymney Valley) with 40 per cent and Great Mountain (Tumble, Gwendraeth Valley) and Ferndale (Rhondda Fach) both with 38 per cent. Another disturbing revelation was that 2,619 were certified in the period, of whom 1,044 were reassessed as having greater disability. Deep Duffryn Colliery (Mountain Ash) was not unusual. There were 213 miners certified, of whom 93 were subsequently reassessed upwards, and 47 of these were still at work. 35 per cent had died from the disease during the period of study. The most disturbing feature of all was that the methods of dust suppression were entirely inadequate and that record keeping of dust counts was unsatisfactory.[44]

Whilst the NUM continued to campaign on behalf of these disabled miners, it did, nevertheless, in 1951 decide to co-operate with the Government and the NCB in allowing back into the industry, because of the manpower shortage, all those with pneumoconiosis who satisfied two medical examinations: such an arrangement, known as the Re-employment Scheme, was never subsequently revoked. Never was there a more startling example of NUM goodwill in helping the NCB through its most difficult early years.[45] Charles Fletcher, the Director of the Llandough Unit, ended a radio broadcast in 1950 on pneumoconiosis in this way:

> When I am an old man I hope to go around the mines in South Wales and not find a single young man coughing, spitting and panting with nothing to do but 'wait for the undertaker', as their fathers have grimly said to me. I know no reason why, within a generation, this modern Black Death – coalminers' pneumoconiosis – should not be as much a piece of history as the plague itself.[46]

If such a hope has not been realised, then the NCB, the Government *and* the NUM should reflect on that early goodwill.

A further illustration of the sacrifices the NUM and its members were prepared to make in order to give the nationalised industry every possible help in the post-war years was the partial suspension, in the summer of 1947, of the five-day week agreement so as to allow voluntary Saturday working. This was in addition to the herculean efforts already made by the miners during the coldest recorded winter in Britain's history following the fuel crisis earlier in the year. But perhaps the most obvious example of goodwill came in July 1947. The Parc and Dare miners in the Rhondda, who had set an example to 'the nation' on Sunday work during the fuel crisis and who had recently broken production targets, decided, following a dispute over changes in their price list, to 'continue to work and not play the game of the Tories who are inciting them to come out on strike and sabotage the nationalisation of the mines'.[47]

When the new Minister of Fuel and Power, Hugh Gaitskell, announced that the 'honeymoon' in the mining industry was over, he was merely confirming the misgivings of many miners. 'NC bloody B' soon became a common expression within mining communities. One discerning novelist of the period expressed this feeling in sharper language:

> Class distinction had reared out its fat belly among higher officials of the Coal Board, who wore wedding rings and drank whisky and hoped to buy a drink for the General Manager. . . .[48]

By the 1950s this renewed antagonism resolved itself into an uneasy truce which frequently broke down due to localised piecework disputes, friction over customs and, ominously, over pit closures. The most serious disruption in the coalfield since nationalisation occurred between May and July 1951 over the threatened partial closure of Wern Tarw Colliery, at Pencoed near Bridgend. NCB policy since 1947 had been one of rationalising into bigger production units: there had been thirty-four closures in South Wales alone up to 1950, many of which had been resisted.[49] The dispute brought to a head rank-and-file frustrations with the NCB *and* the NUM which were to boil over from time to time throughout the decade. Although there had been very many unofficial disputes in the coalfield, the strike by about 15,000 miners led mainly by D. C. Davies, Penry Jones and Frank Hayward (all of Wern Tarw), but also including the whole of the Dulais Valley in the Anthracite area, was the first concerted joint action since nationalisation. The NCB wanted to transfer eighty-seven miners to Llanharan Colliery because of a manpower shortage but this was seen by the Wern Tarw miners as one step towards closure. Although an official coalfield conference decided not to support the lodge, and the transfer went ahead, the incident proved catalytic in bringing together, in an unofficial movement, militant elements within the coalfield who were dissatisfied with the relatively passive role played by the rank-and-file Executive Council on a range of inter-related issues, most notably pit closures, the five-day week and wages.[50] Ironically, Wern Tarw outlived Llanharan Colliery which, despite millions of pounds of investment and expert forecasts of reserves for 150 years, closed in 1962.[51]

In February 1952, Parc and Dare, the biggest lodge in the coalfield, decided to ban Saturday working as a protest against the Conservative Government's economy measures, commonly known as the 'Butler cuts'. The lodge, which had been so disciplined in 1947, also took it upon itself 'to give a lead to the South Wales coalfield' by calling on

WERN · TARW

WHERE NEXT ?

Last week, we the miners of Wern Tarw, came out on strike against the Policy of the National Coal Board in transferring 87 men to another colliery.   In fact they gave notices to 10 more than the Executive was informed of.

Rather than provide the pay and other conditions in the industry to attract sufficient Welsh lads, the Board is trying to solve its man power problem by closing collieries (Cilely), by transfering miners, and by introducing Italian labour.

In our opinion Districts in our colliery have been systematically "murdered" in order to establish a case for the Board.

This is a threat to the whole of S. Wales

What is happening to us at Wern Tarw can be arranged in most pits.

Is this to continue ?   Who is NEXT on the list ?
IT MAY BE YOU. We say that NOW is the time to PUT A STOP TO THIS PRACTICE OF THE BOARD

This is what the miners of Coedely, Newlands, Pentre and Aberbaiden say, too, as they have come out on strike on Tuesday in our support. We miners of Wern Tarw are grateful for this support, and feel confident that other pits will follow.

Only a stand can halt the N.C.B. There can be no repitition of Cilely. We say – **NO Transference.**
The 87 men can be, and want to be kept in the pit.

We ask for your FULL SUPPORT

Although resolutions to the E.C. are useful, our whole history shows that only **ACTION** can solve these problems.

UNITED WE STAND, DIVIDED—TRANSFERENCE AND CLOSURE WILL CONTINUE

Published by Wern Tarw Lodge Committee 12/6/51

Baileys, Printers, Tonyrefail.

Wern Tarw leaflet warning against pit closures, 1951.

other lodges to follow its unoficial action. The lodge had a rather remarkable leadership in two Communists: Tom Evans, a quiet resourceful chairman and Eddie Lloyd, a flamboyant, charismatic secretary, known throughout the coalfield as 'the uncrowned king of Parc and Dare'. The lodge's acceptance of this combative, vanguard role, in the same way that Cambrian, Mardy and Seven Sisters had assumed the lead in other periods, was unmistakable. In their coalfield circular, there were perhaps echoes of *The Miners' Next Step*:

> The miners have power in their hands, United Action by the Miners can force the Government of War and Cuts to change its policy or get out. Churchill of Tonypandy Fame doesn't listen to reason, the Warmonger is only impressed by ACTION. Let the Miners of Wales lead the people of the country into action, and show him that we are not prepared to have our living standards attacked to serve the interests of the Tories.[52]

An unofficial movement, based on the resurrected pre-nationalisation combine committees and the recent experiences over the Wern Tarw issue, were now clearly in operation. Representatives of as many as forty-one lodges (this rose to sixty-eight at a later meeting) met unofficially at a Neath pub, 'The Shakespeare', and succeeded in banning Saturday overtime for 40,000 out of a total of 100,000 miners. Continued sporadic industrial action through until May seemed to co-ordinate a variety of grievances from water money in the Aberdare Valley to bus fares in the Dulais Valley.[53] A specially convened conference in May 'outlawed' the unofficial bodies. A prominent figure in this movement was Evan John, chairman of Clydach Merthyr lodge and chairman of the unofficial Swansea Valley Joint Lodges. He recalled the electrifying speech of the new president and fellow Communist, Will Paynter:

> He wanted to know who was running the union. Was it the Executive or was it the boys from The Shakespeare?

Paynter's concern, and that of the majority within the coalfield, was that such actions were divisive in that they undermined the democratic leadership of the union: a biennially elected area executive council made up of working miners.[54] The division between the desire of the area leadership to contain all action within a constitutional framework so as to achieve maximum unity, and the championing of local, sectional or even political grievances by abrasive unofficial action resulted in a synthesis which ultimately made for a very dynamic organisation:

without consciously being aware of it, the one side relied upon the other. Similar apparent contradictions had occurred in 1951 and were again to reappear in another 'unofficial movement' from 1969 onwards. Indeed, many of those who had been prominent in 1951–2 were to lead the movement in 1969.[55]

Although 1951–2 saw the high-water mark of this movement, a form of unofficial action continued to be a serious problem into the mid-1950s and related particularly to minority action by groups of pieceworkers. Elected leadership, according to Paynter, was ignored and the unifying philosophy of industrial unionism undermined by 'the selfish interests of the few being regarded as paramount'.[56]

The most serious of these local problems occurred in 1956 at Gwaun-cae-Gurwen in the heart of the Anthracite coalfield where the changeover to nationalisation had probably proved most difficult. The responses of the Anthracite miner at this time were also much sharper, indeed more confident, even brazen, partly because he had not suffered the same deprivations as his brothers in the rest of the South Wales coalfield. 'Hidden' customs and agreements between management and men, outside printed price lists, had to come to light after 1947. The coming of mechanisation to the coalfield was also very largely a post-nationalisation phenomenon with all its accompanying difficulties precipitated, from time to time, by conflict between independent-minded, dry-humoured, 'custom-conscious' Welsh-speaking colliers and the abrasive, alien 'PD trained managers and agents'.[57]

The dispute was national news. One old miner, John 'Saer' Davies, recalled that the BBC programme *Panorama* angered the locality by referring to it as a 'straggling village' and as being 'as safe on the streets of Nicosia as it is in Gwaun-cae-Gurwen' (there was an emergency in Cyprus at the time). The commentator, Christopher Chataway, had been unusually snubbed because the lodge committee, meeting in its office known locally as 'The Kremlin', had ensured that the whole community did not speak to him. It was not the first time, nor the last, for the outside world to fail to understand the Anthracite miner.[58]

The NCB gave notices on 11 May to all workmen at East and Steer pits, Gwaun-cae-Gurwen, with the intention of closing both pits from 26 May onwards. It was claimed by the Board that there had been a 'long history of trouble', with 238 unofficial stoppages since nationalisation. In 1948, both pits were closed for a time because of 'restrictive practices' and in 1949–50 Steer was closed for eighteen months. An unofficial strike began on 24–25 April 1956 because two shacklers at the bottom of Steer pit had been discharged for a 'go-slow'. It was alleged that the miners at the pits had not honoured agreements made on their behalf and did not make use of the conciliation machinery. Eight other neighbouring pits struck in sympathy. The whole dispute had been precipitated by the implementation of the new Day Wage Structure Agreement in place of a 'very anarchic' local system: the NCB maintained that the shacklers were not task-workers but day wagemen and such a difference meant a fall in earnings. After complicated, even confusing, negotiations lasting nearly a year the GCG men were still dissatisfied and therefore struck in April. Similar 'go-slow' allegations by the NCB had been made against the neighbouring collieries of Pwllbach, Cwmllynfell and Brynhenllys. Will Haydn Thomas, the GCG lodge chairman, claimed that the situation had been worsened because of the actions of one of the NCB colliery agents. Repairs had been allowed to deteriorate and for these inconveniences men were paid extra allowances which were often conceded behind the back of the lodge committee. The two pits were eventually reopened, but only a proportion of the men were taken back and only on the NCB terms of ending sectional action including 'go-slow', improving production and the acceptance of demotion to day-wage grades if unofficial action were taken.[59]

The major preoccupation of the area leadership was to achieve industrial unity: between day wagemen and pieceworkers within the collieries, unity within the coalfield and between coalfields. Sporadic localised industrial action, however justified, did not assist this. With this in view, the Day Wage Structure Agreement in 1956 created coalfield unity by rationalising further the job descriptions and payments under power loading, a process which had started in principle with the 1937 Wages Agreement. A house-coal pooling scheme which made haulage charges uniform, also had the intention of creating greater unity.[60] But most important of all, the union embarked on an ambitious policy of educating its membership. Under the dynamic leadership of Will Paynter and Dai Dan Evans, there was an attempt to mould a more politically conscious lodge and area leadership at a time when interest in the union amongst younger miners seemed to be declining. To this end, a Youth Advisory Committee was established in 1951 and in 1953 the union's journal, *The Miner*, was revived.[61] *The Miner* proved a most effective link with individual members in that it dealt not only with industrial and political questions but also cultural and sporting activities within the coalfield. The magazine later became a tabloid and was wound up in 1968 so as to give every support to the NUM's new journal of the same name covering all the British coalfields.[62]

The union also reorganised its educational scheme in 1956. It severed its long link with the National Council of Labour Colleges, an association which had existed since 1936 and had helped produce a militant Marxist lodge leadership in several parts of the coalfield, particularly those areas where Noah Ablett and Nun Nicholas were tutors.[63] This tradition of independent working-class education in South Wales reached back to the founding of the Labour College following the Ruskin College strike of 1909. The Labour College, owned by the National Union of Railwaymen and the SWMF, in its short, turbulent life up to 1929 had a remarkable achievement in producing a series of sometimes brilliant union officials and Members of Parliament not simply for miners but for the whole Labour movement. Such a tradition was strengthened by the magnificent workmen's institute and welfare hall libraries in every village and town throughout the coalfield.[64] It was in this context that the new scheme was devised to equip lodge officers with expertise on a range of subjects including political economy, social history, safety, social insurance and union administration. In discussing the Workers' Educational Association, Coleg Harlech (with which the union had been briefly associated), the NCLC and the whole state educational system, the union's most effective education officer, Dr Ronald Frankenberg, outlined the background and aims of the scheme:

The fact that sons of miners, and South Wales miners in particular, have reached the highest positions in the State is an achievement of the Central Labour College and not of orthodox Universities. . . . The problems of wages, housing, health, social services, war and peace are problems to which there is more than one answer. The working class members of trade unions, going daily to pit or factory, to earn their bread, have a different outlook to those who receive their income as a reward for occasional attendance at the Stock Exchange or the Directors' Board Room. . . . I think that it is essential that the young and the experienced should be in class together in order that the young may learn from the older men and that the latter may gain insight into the minds and ideas of a generation as yet untempered by serious struggle. . . . The final test, however, is in the lodges and amongst the men in the coalfield. With your co-operation and support we can hope to restore independent working class education to its lost historical position in the South Wales coalfield. When this is achieved, we may hope to receive the sincerest form of flattery, the imitation of our scheme by other Areas, and indeed, other Unions throughout the world.[65]

One test of success is that half of the rank-and-file executive in 1979 have, at some time, been students on the union's educational scheme.[66]

For the South Wales valleys, in which the union and its lodges were so often the big pulsating heart, the 1950s was still that faraway era before mass pit closures, bingo, social drinking and a television in every home. It was the golden era of the Miners' Welfare Movement when many mining communities believed they were building little socialist islands by their own enthusiastic voluntary labour: a time of carefully tended bowling-greens, sparkling dance halls, shining new pit-head baths and Welfare Halls with cinema-scope screens showing such delights as *Three Coins in a Fountain*, *Quo Vadis*, *The Robe*, and *River of No Return*.[67]

As late as 1957, James Bowman, the chairman of the National Coal Board was reflecting and confidently anticipating:

> Coal has provided the nation with the resources to weather the first critical decade of the post-war world. Even in an age of oil and atomic energy, it will continue to be the mainstay of Britain's prosperity.[68]

Such obvious truisms were soon scattered to the winds by the expert decision-makers whose follies dominated the coming, unhappy, demoralising and dishonourable decade.

Even before the NCB announcement on 3 December 1958 of mass pit closures in the British coalfields, anxiety had been expressed over the disturbing policies of the Conservative Government and the growing number of closures which had occurred throughout the 1950s. As early as March 1958, Will Paynter was anticipating that the world economic recession could affect the South Wales coalfield. Stocks were already ominously rising with the fall in domestic demand and there was a buyer's market for the first time since the war. The Conservative Government's policy had been one of allowing oil to replace coal in British industry even though the 1956 Suez Crisis had revealed the insecurity of supply. The Government was also pursuing a policy of slowing down economic growth and so creating a pool of unemployment. The oil monopolies had stepped up their essentially unfair aggressive penetration of the domestic market by making significant price cuts at a time when coal was still burdened with interest charges, compensation to old coalowners and fixed prices. The adaptation of domestic heating, of steel, rail, gas and electricity industries to new alternative sources was another worrying factor.[69]

When the announcement was made by the NCB that thirty-six

British collieries were to close at the beginning of 1959, whilst not unexpected, its extent was received with numb disbelief in South Wales. Scotland, South Wales and Cumberland were to be the worst affected areas. Mount, Steer, Cwmllynfell and Cefn Coed (partially) were to close in the Anthracite area, affecting a total of 1,400 men. As there were only ninety-six vacancies in neighbouring pits, the others would become unemployed. The closure of Aberbaiden and Pentre at Kenfig Hill meant displacement for 720 men of whom only 221 could be accommodated in neighbouring pits. The end of mining at Tydraw Colliery meant 360 men being displaced but all these could obtain work in other Rhondda collieries. Possibly the most desperate situation was in the Forest of Dean where the closure of Eastern United Colliery resulted in all but 79 of the 450 men would be unemployed.

The union concluded that over half the men displaced would be unemployed, that the mining villages affected would become derelict, or at best, dormitory centres and what embittered the communities most of all, a familiar contrast in the unexpected setting of nationalisation:

> For the displaced miners, dole and poverty; but for the old owners of these mines, compensation and interest beyond the value of the pits they owned, which the Coal Board will continue to pay although the pits may be closed.[70]

There was also bitterness from the union for the apparent shabby, off-hand, even callous, manner with which the National Coal Board took its decisions: an institution which would not have existed but for the sacrifices of the miners and their families over generations. Within eight weeks of the announcement, the pits had been closed without any opportunity of negotiation. D. M. Rees, chairman of the South-Western Division, wrote a letter to Will Paynter on 1 January 1959, the last paragraph of which could not have been better penned by a nineteenth-century coalowner:

> I fully understand your anxiety, and that of your Executive Council, to safeguard now the well-being and security of your present members and I must emphasise that we, too, suffer the same anxieties. We must look, however, to future security for the majority of the personnel now employed in the industry throughout the Division. I must, therefore, point out that if precipitate action of any kind is taken, instead of accepting the fullest co-operation which we are extending to your Union at the present time, the results of such action can be only disastrous to the Division as a whole and to the greater number of the personnel whom we employ at present. Our decisions, difficult as they were, are final.

The venom in the tail betrayed a state of mind which seemed oblivious of other dictated terms in 1926, the intervening depression and war, the wider philosophical implications of public ownership and, above all, the economic and political forces which had made coal nationalisation possible. Even more disturbing was the apparent blissful ignorance of what was to befall the industry in the coming decade whose manpower was to be cut to one-third *and* what was to befall the 'personnel' for whom such great 'anxieties' had been expressed.[71]

The response of the NUM in South Wales was predictable enough and set a pattern for most of the 1960s. Having sounded out the coalfield, the Executive Council, supported by a delegate conference, decided against any industrial action. Only in the Anthracite area was there a call for a strike and even there it was qualified and muted. With the failure of the national leadership of the NUM to mount realistic opposition, the Areas were thrown back on their own resources. But this was not before over two hundred South Wales miners, organised by a re-emerged, although now familiar, 'unofficial movement', had lobbied the National Executive Committee. Whilst not opposed to industrial action in principle, the Area's main concern was unity at a time when opposition to the NCB's policy was uneven inside and outside the coalfield, and at a time when there were growing coal stock-piles. It was therefore decided to mount a campaign of demonstrations, public meetings and a lobby of Parliament by eight hundred miners. The Area's case was one of 'the right to work' and believed that although it failed to halt the closures, its Parliamentary lobby, in particular, alerted the Labour Movement to the danger of growing unemployment. The lobby was an action replay of the Thirties, except that the marchers came by bus: even the slogans were the same with the poet Elfed's 'Nid cardod i ddyn ond gwaith' ('Not charity to man but work') making an unwelcome return.[72] Will Paynter, in leading a delegation from the lobby to the Minister of Fuel and Power on 29 January, called for a national fuel policy and demanded that the cut-back in coal production should be borne entirely by open-cast mining (an undertaking which had been made previously but was not honoured). The Minister, with the fumbling of a Pontius Pilate, said it was out of his hands: the NCB was going to do the Tory Government's dirty work of crucifying the coal industry. In his last message to the South Wales miners, before he became national secretary of the union, Will Paynter called on them 'to keep up the pressure to prevent further closures and change Government policy towards this industry and industry generally'. It was a problem that dominated his whole period of office and transformed the industry beyond recognition.[73]

For such abandoned communities as Cwmllynfell, high above the Swansea Valley, these clarion calls were rather academic and were to be so later for very many villages across the coalfield from Abercrave to Clydach Vale and Cwmfelinfach. Much suffering could have been avoided had the NCB kept Cwmllynfell Colliery open until the nearby new 'super pit' of Abernant needed its full complement of miners. As it was, one of the most cultured and talented villages in South Wales was left to die, for there was no alternative work: a village which produced the poet Watcyn Wyn and Rhys Williams, one of Wales's greatest rugby forwards, who captained his country the following year; a village in which a thriving university extra-mural class had existed since the early 1920s and which was made up entirely of unemployed miners in 1959. It was a colliery community in which such seasoned characters as the dry-humoured Joe Brickman, earnest Will Post, champion collier Dai Daff and Tom Dan (who had lost only three shifts in forty-eight years) and many others, had given a lifetime's service.[74] As a young Mountain Ash miner was to say nearly twenty years later, on the eve of another round of possible pit closures:

> We've taken a hundred years to build these communities; you can't kill them overnight.[75]

Therein lay the key to Cwmllynfell's survival, a community which had seen the sinking of its first shaft in 1825. For the stranger struggling up the Berrington Hill into the village in 1979, he would not, on the face of it, be met by the air of despondency which had prevailed in 1959. He would still hear old men telling ironic stories of 'commandos' (special heavy work miners) being paid only Boy Scouts' wages. Doubtless it is an ageing community and there are plenty of empty shops, but its village pride is still there with well-kept chapels and clubs, still stolid, tidy houses, a newly painted welfare hall and a much respected West Wales rugby team which almost toppled mighty Pontypool in 1978.[76]

Following the shock of 1958–9, the social and economic consequences of closures began to be realised. One miner from Coedely Colliery, on the edge of the Rhondda Fawr, recalled:

> I know in 1950 Cilely closed . . . , they had a stay-in strike for a week, they took the case to London and lost. . . . But in those days . . . we never took notice of pit closures . . . because there was always plenty of work in the mines . . . without travelling long distances. . . . But after 1959 . . . it means

now that men are travelling about 20 miles each way to get to work. . . . But
you know it never hit us until after '59, and I think Llanbradach was one of
the first to close. . . . I remember they'd spent a million pounds on getting a
new winder and everything in, and after they'd put it in they closed the
bloody place.[77]

The changed fortunes of the coal industry in South Wales are clearly
seen in the following statistics:[78]

Year	No. of collieries (at start of year)	Manpower (at year end)	Saleable output (including licensed mines)
1949	194	106,000	24,209,000
1959	141	93,000	21,192,000
1969	55	40,000	12,788,223
1979	37	28,500*	8,046,000†

* At start of year.   † For year up to March 1979.

Rather than halting the decline, the much awaited return of a Labour
Government in 1964, and then in 1966, merely accelerated the trend.
Despite Prime Minister Harold Wilson's earlier support of the industry
in his book *New Deal for Coal* and at the 1960 national study
conference on energy, coal no longer seemed to fit into his vision of
white-hot technological/scientific revolution.[79] The Labour Government almost immediately reneged on its Party's Home Policy Committee commitment to a minimum of 200 million tons of coal. Its
1965 *Coal Plan* calculated that national production would fall to
170–180 million tons by 1970. In November 1967, these estimates were
revised, not upwards because of the lessons of the Arab-Israeli War of
that year, but downwards because of the discovery of North Sea gas.
The new estimates were 120 million tons for 1975. Quite apart from the
wildly inaccurate forecasts, the most obvious and heart-rending
conclusion drawn by the NUM was that the Labour Government and
their 'experts' had succumbed completely to the oil lobby. Caught in the
middle was Lord Robens in his *Ten Year Stint*, who, whilst accepting
contraction, was highly critical of the superficiality and short-
sightedness of Government policy. It was he who apparently favoured
the Welsh miner who had said, 'Do you think the Arabs are going for
ever to live in tents?' against the 'expensively briefed' and 'disastrously
wrong' civil servants.[80]

The social, economic and political repercussions of this policy were
far-reaching. Realising the inherent divisive nature of pit closures,

where lodges were always looking over their own shoulders, the South Wales Area was loathe to take localised industrial action, although increasingly a minority of other areas did (as in 1967) favour a national strike and guerrilla tactics (as in 1968). It put all its energies into more militant and unified national representations for the *political* solution entailed in a changed governmental policy towards an integrated fuel policy which emphasised the advantages of indigenous fuels over imported oil. Simultaneously, it campaigned for the bringing of alternative light industries into the valleys if pits were closed, even though there was always a feeling that 'miners did not fit easily into pop factories'. Admittedly, Labour's policies, particularly as outlined in its *National Plan*, wrote off a £400 m. debt, did bring in a redundancy scheme, banned imported coal, continued the fuel oil tax and did set up advanced factories. But the effect of all this was, at best, minimal.[81] Its proposals set out in *Wales, The Way Ahead* merely accentuated the crisis by implicitly accepting the rundown of the 'dying' valleys in putting so much emphasis on the importance of Llantrisant Newtown sited outside the coalfield.[82]

The most immediate and obvious backlash for the Government came with the Carmarthen by-election in July 1966, four months after the General Election. In a constituency with a substantial mining community in the Gwendraeth Valley and the Ammanford area, Plaid Cymru's first-ever Parliamentary victory had much to do with the rundown of the coal industry. The holding, by very small majorities against the Nationalist challenge, of the formerly impregnable mining seats of Rhondda West and Caerphilly, in 1967 and 1968 respectively, was further evidence of the depth of disillusionment. The failure of the NUM to get its two candidates adopted for 'their' seats was part of a continuing pattern, but in the atmosphere of 1967–8, it was particularly galling. By 1970 only two NUM sponsored MPs remained (S. O. Davies for Merthyr Tydfil and Elfed Davies for Rhondda East) and by 1974 there was none.[83]

The miners also voted with their feet. Despite constant warnings by the NUM, the insecurity, low morale and relatively low wages coupled with good job opportunities elsewhere, led to an increasing drift out of the industry, particularly by craftsmen. Projected transfers to more profitable pits were not materialising: the younger, more mobile, skilled miners, once their pits were closed, tended to opt out of the industry and take up more lucrative, secure employment. Amongst the most popular choices were Fords (Swansea), Morris Motors (Llanelli), the steel industry at Llanwern (Newport) and Port Talbot, BP Llandarcy, British Nylon Spinners (Pontypool), Metal Box (Neath) and Hoovers (Merthyr).[84] There was also an underlying, often underestimated, psychological factor. Mining communities in South Wales, as elsewhere, had understandably mixed feelings about pit closures. The entertainer Max Boyce epitomised such an attitude: having worked in the industry for nearly eight years, he left in the 1960s for a cleaner, healthier, safer, better paid job in a factory. He put his all-too-familiar experience and feelings to music in the song 'Duw It's Hard':

> They came down here from England
> Because our output's low,
> Briefcases full of bank clerks
> That had never been below.
> And they closed the valley's oldest mine
> Pretending that they're sad.
> But don't you worry buttie bach
> We're really very glad.[85]

The social and economic consequences of the rundown of the industry were as dramatic as the political repercussions. The effects were not as devastating as in parts of the Durham and Scottish coalfields whose miners often became 'industrial gypsies' in NCB-provided caravans and could certainly not be compared with the plight of the Appalachian coalfields in the USA.[86] Nevertheless, very serious problems were experienced. The most obvious immediate effect following a colliery closure was the virtual collapse of a welfare scheme so that by the end of the 1960s the whole philosophy of 'miners' welfare' with its emphasis on educational, sporting and cultural pursuits had for the most part given way to bingo and drinking. As a means of survival, welfare halls became clubs and during this strange metamorphosis, they seemed to lose their way. But such a change is only fully comprehensible against the background of greater British emphasis on leisure and pleasure during the decade.[87] A miner, turned school-teacher and poet, reflected on the passing of an age, whose proudest and most representative symbol was the 'miners' library':

> The literary silence of the rooms
> Still prevails. The ghosts
> have multiplied and their miseries
> Occasionally invade the conscience

of a nation. Here, long ago,
Around polished tables, hungry eyes
Probed under scarred brows.[88]

The elimination of mining from certain localities also meant of course that the leadership, authority and cohesion provided within the community by the miners' lodge and its officials similarly disappeared. The lodge chairman and secretary, in particular, had continued to perform the social role hitherto held by the workmen's checkweigher who apart from his industrial duties was counsellor to the needy, letter-writer, conscience of the community, and as much of a respected figure as the minister, if not more so in latter years.[89]

But there were also more tangible effects on the daily lives of the miners and their families. The period of uncertainty when a colliery was threatened with closure, followed by the inevitable closure itself and then transfer elsewhere led to a sullen bitterness not experienced since the thirties. Older miners were moved from colliery to colliery after having worked all their lives in the village pit, whilst some young miners, having worked in as many as four pits, could not take seriously an employer who promised that the next transfer would be the last.[90] The initial transfer itself could often be traumatic enough, especially if it was from a drift mine to a colliery. The old comradeship and customs, the sheltered employment for the disabled and the familiarity of the old pit were threatened or lost with a transfer. Sometimes the difficulties manifested themselves in psychological problems:

The first six months at Cefn Coed were terrible, every night I used to pray that I would get badly injured so that I wouldn't have to go down again. Injury seemed the only way out. It was terrible, I was working with people I didn't know. None of my old butties were working with me. You get used to a colliery, you know which parts are dangerous and what to look out for, you can feel when something is going to happen. At Cefn Coed it was strange, I didn't know anything.[91]

Perhaps the harshest social effect was the considerable distance many miners now had to travel to work. This meant less time at home and less time for recreational pursuits. Family and community life inevitably suffered. This was not new: it had been a feature of the inter-war period when mass unemployment had existed in the steam coalfield. But in the western part of the Anthracite coalfield, this was a relatively new phenomenon, which had other repercussions as one social survey of the Amman Valley revealed:

. . . the bus for the Cynheidre day shift leaves Garnant at 5.00 a.m. and does not return until after 4.00 p.m. extending what might have been little more than an eight hour day for a man working in a local colliery to one of over 11 hours; the strain which this sort of travelling produces has been suggested as part of the explanation for high absenteeism in the area, in that a man is said to need a longer rest at times.[92]

Transfers and closures also meant a drop in earnings despite the operation of the redundancy scheme after 1967 for those over fifty-five. Very often transfers in the 1960s were from unmechanised to mechanised pits where a different set of skills were needed with craftsmen becoming relatively more important than colliers. The problems were compounded for those who left the industry if their skills were peculiar to mining, although Government Training Schemes did assist some.[93] A Risca Colliery pipe-turner, aged forty-three, with three dependent children, earned £24 a week, but when the colliery closed his wage at South Wales Switchgear at Blackwood was £11 12s. 0d. He recalled bitterly:

> . . . It was only after being involved in two pit closures, namely Nine Mile Point, where I was employed for 25 years, then at Risca for the past two years that I decided to make the break. The National Coal Board transferred me to Bedwas but I did not start there. After being a skilled worker all these years and earning a good wage, to work outside your mining skill means nothing – its only labouring jobs offered . . . I received my first pay from Switchgear which amounted to £10 16s. 0d. after stoppages – this amount to keep my family, I could get more if I was unemployed.[94]

But probably the most important effect of pit closures was the impact it had on the workforce. For the young, skilled miner with a craft apprenticeship, he could conceivably escape to other industries particularly if he did not have strong family or social ties. For the middle-aged and those approaching retirement they were trapped and a sense of resignation tended to prevail. More than this, pit closures were divisive within the colliery and within the coalfield, far more so than the iniquitous piecework system with which the miners had learnt to live and finally conquer (for a while). When a pit was threatened it was extremely difficult to get coalfield-wide sympathy, for others were looking over their shoulders and industrial action might only hasten their own demise at a time when demand for coal was falling. Furthermore, whilst the pit was under threat pressure was exerted downwards through 'investigation' and 'jeopardy lists' and those who felt it most were those who had the most physically arduous tasks: the face workers. Absenteeism and output levels were scrutinised to a point where often the only sane response was 'shut the damn pit!' After a transfer, there was also rivalry between different sections of the workforce, sometimes friendly but on other occasions not so. Old pit loyalties and parochial attitudes re-emerged so that in the Dulais Valley 'bobl ochr draw' ('people from the other side') that is, the Swansea Valley, became simply, in more anglicised times 'ODs' and rival factions in one pit were 'Blaenanties and Cefncoedies'.[95]

Generally speaking, however, such differences tended to disappear with the coming of more optimistic signs in the industry. Furthermore, these experiences during the 1960s, for the few who remained in the industry, ultimately had a hardening, sobering effect which was to be one of the major contributory factors towards the remarkable transformation to occur in the 1970s. One of the South Wales miners' leaders of the period recalled:

> [The turning point which made the miners see the NCB as just another employer was] pit closures, unquestionably. In some parts of the British coalfields . . . they dealt with the men ruthlessly. There was no difference between the old . . . coalowners and the National Coal Board. They were now turning it into state capitalism . . . and they had the best man they could have had at that time, to operate the acceleration of pit closures and that was Robens.[96]

The decline of mining had its wider repercussions. Constant references to 'dying valleys' and 'dying villages' in themselves implied a certain inevitability. It became not only difficult to encourage young men into the industry but also to keep them in the valleys. It also proved difficult to encourage light industries into the region. The infrastructure rotted. Railway lines were pulled up, health-care problems increased, chapels closed, youth clubs became derelict and the young left. One of the worst affected areas was the upper Afan Valley which had seen all its collieries close and whose socio-economic problems, continuing as they did into the 1970s, were scrutinised minutely by a Government supported Community Development Project. One of the research papers reported poignantly:

> Special Development Area Status has attracted firms to the area. However, apart from a footwear factory which has since closed down and a book-binding company, which began a redundancy programme eighteen months

ago, they have mostly been light engineering or manufacturing firms employing small numbers of women. For many months the sole employees of an advance factory were two security guards. . . . The population of the Upper Afan [8,360] receive approximately £23,000 a week in social security, a situation which has existed for several years, and would surely be higher still, but for the high figure of net migration losses the area has suffered since the mid sixties. It would appear, therefore, that at least for this type of community regional policy is less than successful.[97]

But the most harrowing feature of an already depressing decade were the three major disasters associated with the industry. The explosions at Six Bells (near Abertillery) in 1960 and Cambrian (at Clydach Vale, Rhondda) in 1965 claiming forty-five and thirty-one lives respectively were the worst in post-war South Wales mining history. The Aberfan disaster in 1966 was a human calamity of a different kind. All were reminders that in an age and a society which did not seem to put great value on the miner and his work, mining communities were still having to endure the most heart-rending experiences. All these disasters attracted massive press coverage, often bordering on melodrama. By contrast, rarely was there a mention of the miners who died in ones and twos at the coalface or slowly and painfully of dust diseases, at home, mourned only by their families and friends.

On 28 June 1960, at Six Bells Colliery, there occurred the worst explosion in South Wales since 1927 (in that year, fifty lives were lost at Marine Colliery, Cwm, near Ebbw Vale. In 1934, Gresford Colliery, North Wales, exploded, claiming 265 lives.) At the Public Inquiry which sat for eight days in September 1960, it was revealed that following the explosion in the 'W' District under the Arrael Mountain, twenty-eight had succumbed to carbon monoxide poisoning and seventeen to 'violence'. Only three miners came out alive from the District. The Court concluded that the likely cause was falling quartzitic rock although the union maintained that 'hanging flame' from shotfiring was a more probable reason. Lyndon James, the head of the union's safety department in South Wales, reported that the explosion focused attention on many safety problems: (1) the dust hazard on conveyor roads; (2) the potential incendive properties of certain rocks; (3) the danger of gases in wastes and remote places; (4) the need for effective and regular gas detection in waste areas near workings; (5) the need to support and ventilate or properly fill cavities; (6) the dangers associated with firing explosives in places where breaks containing methane were certain to exist; (7) the need to control the use of air blowers; (8) more careful attention to shotfiring procedure; (9) more meticulous attention to support requirements; (10) an extension of the benefits that arise from the use of methane drainage.

In a forthright review of the Inquiry, Lyndon James concluded:

> The road head was not properly supported; had it been, the fall that caused the explosion, if fall it was, should not have happened. . . . The investigation and subsequent Inquiry were exhaustive and costly; many lessons and pointers to increased safety emerged. If they will be learned and followed, then, and only then, will our duty be done by those whose lives were so tragically lost.[98]

Nearly five years later, on 17 May 1965, thirty-one miners were killed in a blast that rushed through the P26 power loading face at Cambrian Colliery. Fifty-eight witnesses gave evidence at a four day public enquiry. In a long and complex report, it was revealed that an air bridge was not as air-tight or as strong as required by the NCB training manual on pit ventilation: this caused a short-circuit of the ventilation which allowed a build-up of firedamp. As there was no witness to the events prior to the explosion, the report could only suggest what two electricians were doing to rectify electrical trouble on the tail end plough drive electrical panel before the explosion occurred. They opened the switch by removing the ten cover bolts which they did not replace. The report concluded that the explosion was probably caused when 'gas was ignited within the switch and the cover not being secured permitted the flame to pass to the outside atmosphere'. The report's main recommendations were that there should be statutory provision requiring firedamp determinations at the end of the face return roadways, a greater development of instruments for testing firedamp and more rigorous testing systems of electrical faults where firedamp is a hazard. The union's safety department in reviewing the year 1965–6 reflected on the explosions at Six Bells and Cambrian, as well as that at Tower which claimed nine lives in 1962:

> . . . these grim statistics . . . are an indictment on all persons responsible in any way for the ventilation of mineworkings and for the detection and rendering harmless of firedamp.

Apart from the NCB's own Safety Campaign with which the NUM co-operated, the union had also formulated its own Safety Plan: this involved lodge '123' inspectors (so-called because of the section in the Mines and Quarries Act) receiving preparatory tuition, refresher talks and guidance in actual inspections. Whilst explosions appeared to attract greatest attention particularly at their regular Safety Schools, deaths or injuries were also caused daily by other hazards and these too were the subject of the union's deep concern.[99]

On the morning of Friday, 21 October 1966, a 'mining' disaster occurred, the like of which had never before been experienced. At about 9.15 a.m., a large part of one of the waste tips above the small mining village of Aberfan, south of Merthyr Tydfil, suddenly started to slide. Within minutes it had engulfed Pantglas Junior School, two farm cottages and a number of houses. The school half-term was due to start at noon: had the avalanche come three hours later many of the children would have been spared. As it was, 144 perished, of whom 111 were children. The first miners, from nearby Merthyr Vale Colliery, were on the scene within twenty minutes and were able to direct digging operations immediately. A major rescue operation followed, involving a wide range of services and organisations. The Tribunal of Inquiry which was set up by Parliament heard 136 witnesses over a period of seventy-six days and found that the National Coal Board was responsible, a verdict which it accepted fully. The Board, it was revealed, had lacked any policy regarding tipping and was indifferent to the need for safety measures. The author of the most authoritative study of the disaster assessed the impact beyond the coalfields:

> The world reacted to the disaster with shock, horror and perhaps a guilty conscience for a hundred years of cheap coal. Money poured into the Disaster Fund. Aberfan became a household word all round the world, and has never since escaped the limelight . . .[100]

The NUM in South Wales felt it ought to accept its share of the responsibility and was criticised for its lack of action over an earlier slide in 1963, but was exonerated from blame because the Board had falsely reassured them. The union stated in a pamphlet on spoil tip stability:

> At the time of the disaster our technical staff, like other parties involved, were forced to admit a lamentable lack of information on the applied science involved in the preparation, construction and stabilisation of spoil heaps.[101]

The effect the disaster had on the world's conscience was measurable. But its impact on the community of Aberfan was another matter. The grief of parents and surviving children were 'things that cannot be measured and perhaps can only be fully understood by those who underwent the experience'. The resulting Disaster Fund which realised £1.75 million became a focus for considerable controversy and was an outlet for the anger of a grieving community. The failure of the Government to comprehend the natural anxiety of the village in its desire to remove the rest of the tips was a source of continuing bitterness. When the Government did finally succumb, it succeeded in extracting £150,000 from the Disaster Fund to assist the operation. This act of brutal insensitivity denied the village the opportunity of fully developing its new community centre, giving more endowment or accommodation. One of the tribunal's recommendations was that a standard code of practice be prepared and that a National Tip Safety Committee be set up. It was savagely ironic that a disaster of this magnitude was needed to begin the systematic removal and landscaping of the ugly waste-tips which had for so long scarred the mining valleys of South Wales.[102]

The 1960s cannot be dismissed as entirely unhappy or wasted years. The butchering of the industry was indefensible: however much closures might have been 'justified', and however much the union swallowed narrow notions of individual pit 'viability', the social and economic losses were considerable and inescapable. Throughout, the miners and their union in South Wales believed that the short-sightedness of the NCB and of governments was unforgivable.[103] Nevertheless, some worthwhile reorganisation and new development did occur with even greater emphasis on mechanisation. It was the 1960s that saw the emergence of the master or super pits, notably Abernant, Brynlliw and Cynheidre in the west; sizeable investment in such existing collieries as Deep Navigation (£500,000) and Merthyr Vale (£2 million) in the Merthyr Valley, at Coegnant (Maesteg) and Blaenant (Dulais Valley); and a £1.5 million investment in the new drift mine of Treforgan (also in the Dulais Valley).[104]

One of the achievements, which almost passed unheralded because of the all-embracing gloom created by the pit closure programme was the coming of the National Power Loading Agreement in 1966. The agreement, which eliminated piecework and all that it represented, was welcomed both by the NCB and the NUM, although the former could never have envisaged its long-term significance in forging greater unity between the coalfields. There was also understandable annoyance and even bitterness among some face-workers who saw a substantial fall in their real wages as a result of the agreement, although undoubtedly accepting the positive features enshrined in its principles. It seemed, all

too briefly, that the idiot 'ianto fullpelts' of the coalfield who lived only
for work, were gone for ever.[105]

It was widely felt that pit closures had seriously eroded morale
and militancy within South Wales and elsewhere. But a remarkable
resilience did from time to time shine through, albeit sometimes in the
strangest ways. Most bizarre, perhaps, was the 'swear-word strike' in
May 1965, sparked off by a confrontation between a young miner and
an official at Deep Duffryn Colliery (Mountain Ash). This seemingly
minor issue led to a coalfield strike by the colliery officials' union, the
National Association of Colliery Overmen, Deputies and Shotfirers
(NACODS) because the spontaneous solidarity in support of the
dismissed young miner by unofficial NUM strikes had resulted in his
reinstatement. The episode revealed not only the continuing antipathy
towards the officials but also that a surprisingly combative spirit still
existed in the coalfield.[106]

A more reliable clue of what was soon to come occurred in October
1968. A group of South Wales miners, who had minutes earlier
been passively picketing over pit closures, dramatically and
unceremoniously stormed into the Labour Party's Annual Conference
and held up the proceedings during the Opening Address by the
President, Jenny Lee. The stunned delegates were being reminded that,
remarkably, there were still miners left in South Wales. It was later
claimed that this unorthodox demonstration had contributed to the
delegates' decision to oppose the Government's Fuel Policy.[107] The
action encapsulated a growing feeling : the loyalty of the miners was not
inexhaustible. They had consistently not pressed for higher wage
increases because they genuinely wished to assist *their* ailing
nationalised industry. But as one perceptive observer was to write of the
South Wales Miners' Gala nearly three years later:

. . . something is stirring: a new order is being born. Anyone who meddles
with the people who came to Sophia Gardens will live to regret it.[108]

In the meantime, there had been more than stirrings. Some young
miners were even moved to refer to the dramatic events of the autumn of
1969 as 'the October Revolution'. The 'surfaceman's strike', as it
became known, can be viewed as the most important single event in the
history of the NUM in South Wales. A firm commitment to rectify the
deteriorating wages and conditions of surfacemen, so many of whom
were incapacitated through mining diseases or accidents and who found

difficulty in getting alternative work elsewhere, had been made at the 1968 NUM National Conference.

There had already been a marked shift in the Area's leadership at the beginning of the year, when six new members were elected to the rank-and-file Executive Council: this was the biggest single change since the council had been reformed in 1933. Amongst the newcomers from West Wales was Evan John who had served a brief period on the EC during the war and who had been prominent ever since in agitating for a more militant policy on pit closures. Also elected were Emlyn Jenkins and George Rees, both of whom represented a younger generation in the traditionally militant central part of the coalfield where a radical revival was underway. All three were Communists.

At the Area Conference in April–May 1969, frustration with the failure to remedy the situation was clearly evident. Although it was explained that a Rest Days Agreement had been accepted in place of a reduction in surface working to $36\frac{1}{2}$ hours, a resolution calling for strike action if the demand were not met, was carried. What was remarkable about the debate was that no one from the floor spoke against what became known as the 'Cwm resolution' and those who spoke in support were mainly the 'minority' voices who had called for more militant action over wages and pit closures in the 1960s. Bryn 'Bara' Williams (Cwm) referred to the surfacemen as the 'Cinderellas of our industry' and in a telling speech Ron Saint, from the neighbouring Coedely lodge, said, '. . . If we don't fight on this issue we won't fight on any.' But the most significant statement came from a surfaceman, Brin Daniel of Pantyffynnon lodge, whose words had a defiant ring:

> . . . Seventy of the 110 men employed at the Wernos Washery either suffer from the effects of industrial disease or industrial accident. The hours of work are scandalously high and the payment scandalously low. It is only by strike action that we will get the Board to move on this issue, and if the Executive Council are not prepared to use this weapon, we ought to tell them that we will.

The union was now on a collision course which had been precipitated by an unexpected issue: as the year was to unfold the wider significance of its decision became ever more apparent. However, the Area leadership misinterpreted the clearly discernible and growing unease within the coalfield. In August, and for the first time in its history, the EC recommended strike action over a pit closure. The Avon Ocean Colliery at Abergwynfi in the Afan Valley was to be closed although its productivity had improved dramatically. The union argued, as it had throughout the decade, that its very young workforce was unlikely to accept transfer to neighbouring collieries and that there would be dire social consequences. Yet an Area Conference on 20 August rejected industrial action by 49 to 32. Although the unconstitutional nature of such a strike did influence some delegates, the more probable reason for the rejection was their continuing fears for their own individual collieries.

Within seven weeks, however, unofficial industrial action had closed down half the coalfield over surfacemen's hours. The solidarity which had been so elusive over the Avon closure, now expressed itself, albeit in a fragmented way, with underground workers marching out in support of the surfacemen. This represented an unmistakable shift in attitude within the membership so that anxiety over pit closures clearly appears to diminish. This has to be understood against a background of a slow-down in closures, a recession in neighbouring industries which staved off some of the manpower drift from the pits and a revival of industrial militancy within the British trade union movement, most significantly in the Yorkshire coalfield, whose total stoppage on the issue was an example to other Areas. As Cliff True (Fernhill) unsuccessfully urged a Special Area Conference on 14 October:

> I think delegates should recognise that for the first time in many decades the Yorkshire Area of this Union, which is a powerful section of this Union, is prepared to fight and are fighting.
>
> If Yorkshire remain on their own for another week then they will fail and we will have lost our cause for another twenty years. . . . I am certain that there is enough feeling in each lodge if a proper and objective report is made by the Lodge officials, for immediate strike action in support of the Yorkshire Area.

But the Avon closure and the surfacemen's hours were not inseparable. It was essentially the same lodges (those within and near the Rhondda) which forced the pace for a more militant action on both issues. A psychological barrier was broken for the leadership and the membership when the EC called for industrial action on the first issue: given the history of pit closures, it was almost inevitable that they were defeated. But the experiences on the two issues deepened the age-old debate about unity, sectional action and unofficial movements. In the midst of the unofficial stoppage a turbulent conference was held at Porthcawl on 22 October in which the President, Glyn Williams, was barracked from the visitors' gallery for not allowing a vote. A Coedely delegate recalled later: 'That was the day we nearly threw Dai and Glyn into the sea!'

It was undoubtedly a process which could not have been resolved in one struggle. Those who argued against sectional action were led by full-time officials whose bitter struggle for unity stretched back over half a century. Their views were crystallised in the profound words of Trevor James, the miners' agent for West Wales, who was about to retire:

> I was privileged to attend the Conference at Nottingham in 1944 when this National Union was formed. At this Conference many of the older delegates reminded us of the dangers of federation and the need to unite as a National Organisation. I am not here as a critic of struggle but as a defender of it, but we must appreciate that in any struggle with the Coal Board we are also fighting against the State and don't anyone under-estimate the importance of this. There is only a thin veil between the Board and the State. . . . What we are saying is that any action that is taken must be a National action . . . and I support the call for a return to work to all Lodges that are now on strike.

In the aftermath of the strike, the unofficial leaders continued to justify their sectional actions and were undoubtedly influenced not only by similar contemporary strikes but also by heroic examples from the past. At an Area Conference on 18 November, Ron Saint (Coedely) claimed:

> This Unofficial Committee is no frivolity. The reason why we supported Yorkshire in their struggle was because there was not a call from any other quarter. We knew that apart from the Avon issue, the Executive Council would not call for action . . . the dustmen, dockers, blast furnacemen and others . . . had taken part in strikes and this had strengthened not weakened their Union. . . . The Cambrian strike of 1910–11 was an unofficial action, but this achieved the minimum wage. The unofficial movement was never at any time a dual leadership but a ginger group. The struggle will continue providing this is what the rank and file want. We will decide when to disband and this Union will never quite be the same as it was prior to the strike.

But the dominant tendency within the union in South Wales in 1969 remained one of following the constitutional path of seeking approval of the National Executive Committee and a membership ballot before embarking on industrial action. Such an approach was typified by Dannie Canniff of the Oakdale lodge in Monmouthshire, probably the most constitution-conscious part of the coalfield:

The trouble with the so-called militants is that they are prepared to accept majority decisions, but only when it suits them. If this unofficial movement is allowed to continue we might as well disband the structure of this trade union and the union itself.

Events in the period from 1968 to 1970 on university campuses and on the streets of many of the world's major cities represented the questioning of an old order. Symbolically, comparable changes in the South Wales coalfield coincided with the miners' union moving its Area offices from Cardiff, a city which owed its existence to coal, to Pontypridd, in the heart of the coalfield, whose Rocking Stone was the meeting place for the Miners' Federation in its earliest days.

It was left to the President, Glyn Williams, who had borne the militants' anger with equanimity, to reflect on the positive features of these traumatic events:

... The year now drawing to a close had been a tough one. There had been many deep differences of opinion but, as always, there was a strong bond of comradeship within this Union and the respect for each others' point of view was sincerely held.

The significance of 1969 was that it revealed a rising tide of militancy which was harnessed temporarily by an unofficial movement (embracing Communists, Labour Party members and miners with no party affiliation) and whose sympathisers existed at every level of the union. It was a resurgence which, at least to the outsider, was totally unexpected for it sprang from a coalfield (unlike Yorkshire) which had been butchered, and seemingly demoralised, by a decade of closures.[109]

The Conservative Party's victory in the General Election of June 1970 did not, at the time, seem to alter significantly the process towards greater militancy within the British coalfields: much more important was the continued fall in the miners' wages relative to other industrial workers, the greater unity between coalfields provided by the NPLA, the levelling off in the industry's contraction and the general industrial unrest which had commenced in earnest the previous year and was to grow during the life of the Conservative Government to proportions at least comparable with the 'Great Unrest' of 1910–14. The approach of the Government, however, to the economic crises of the 1970–4 period undeniably contributed to the sharpening of this unrest: the vanguard and extra-parliamentary role played by the miners, particularly those from South Wales, in this confrontation was, on the face of it, a throw-back to the inter-war period, except that the miners had the sweet taste

ROBENS GETS AN **EXTRA** £50 PER WEEK FROM THE TORIES FOR REFUSING THE MINERS £5

VOTE **NO** ON FRIDAY

South Wales Area poster prior to the 1970 strike.

of revenge in 1972 and 1974 for the humiliations of 1921, 1926 and thereafter. But the build-up to this vindication was not as straightforward as is sometimes portrayed.[110]

The unofficial strikes in several coalfields in November 1970, led in large part by the South Wales Area, whose 'strike' resolution had been narrowly carried at the NUM Annual Conference, can be seen (in common with the 1969 action) as an aberration: it was contrary to the historical development of the British miners. The National Union, by definition, had always striven for *national* unity. Had those who wished to spread the sectional action been more successful in persuading more coalfields to strike and to hold out for a longer period, the long-term result could have been to deepen divisions. As it was, 1969 and 1970 undeniably contributed in at least two ways to the essence of the 1972 and 1974 victories: the maximum national and local unity of the miners *and* the solidarity of other industrial workers. Firstly, they provided the groundswell which forced through, by constitutional means, the South Wales resolution at the 1971 NUM Annual Conference, allowing the sanctioning of industrial action by a 55 per cent poll in favour by the membership in place of the archaic two-thirds majority. It was this Rule 43 which had caused so much anger in 1970 when 55·5 per cent had voted for strike action (South Wales with 83 per cent in favour, recorded the highest poll). Secondly, the smearing of the miners by the chairman of the NCB, Lord Robens, only served ultimately to close ranks within the union. At every level in the union, Communists had been agitating for a more vigorous implementation of the National Conference decision on wages, but they were not by any means alone in this agitation and their pleas could not have carried much weight had they not reflected accurately the views of the majority of the membership. Robens' allegations that miners were being manipulated by a handful of conspiring Communists were given full coverage by a hysterical mass media which also headlined the 'Coal Shortage [as] a death threat to old'. The *Western Mail*, revealing once again in times of crisis its true historical role, implied that '. . . the men have to stay out, with pickets at some collieries to make sure they do'. Such claims were deliberately misleading. Charlie Blewett, secretary of the Penallta Lodge and later a Parliamentary Labour candidate, described the situation more accurately:

Everyone who voted [for strike action] at the delegate conference at Porthcawl last week was mandated to do so. . . . Most of those who voted

are members of the Labour Party. There is no question of a small handful of
bogeymen influencing events.[111]

The Area leaders had their work cut out to contain the militancy.
Following an Area conference decision on 4 November to take
unilateral strike action, the coalfield was at a standstill for the first time
since 1926. By 10 November, nearly half the British miners (a total of
about 125,000) were on strike. Against Area conference instructions,
five West Wales lodges (Caerau, Cwmgwili, Cynheidre, St John's and
Garw), prevented safety men working and other pits in West Wales
were without winding enginemen, banksmen, ventilation fanmen and
pumpsmen.

Dai Francis, the Communist general secretary of the South Wales
miners, was in the invidious position of having voted against the NEC
acceptance of the improved NCB offer but then had to urge its
acceptance to a coalfield conference which overwhelmingly rejected it.
His dismissal of Robens' simplistic distortions was brief:

> Lord Robens is talking a load of rubbish. His main purpose is to divert
> attention from the real issue – the reasonable wage demands of the
> miners.[112]

The 1970 dispute in South Wales embraced a much broader
geographical and political spectrum than that of the previous year. The
over-enthusiasm of some lodges in bitterly criticising other lodges,
notably Penrhiwceiber and South Celynen (who called for a return to
work since it was clear the strike was not spreading in other coalfields
and since, if continued, unconstitutional action could undermine the
national union) was something only time and events could curb. For
those local, area and national leaders who had the patience and,
because of the career of Horner, a scientific approach, the events
of 1969 and 1970 led inexorably to the possibility of the miners'
greatest victory if the twin lessons of national unity and discipline could
be learnt from the earlier skirmishes. Whilst they could not be described
as victories, they did secure the most substantial wage advances since
nationalisation and in that sense alone provided a practical and
inspirational platform for a further offensive. The 1969 increases were
27s. 6d. virtually across the board and those for 1970 were £3 (day
wagemen), £2 16s. 0d. (craftsmen) and £2 7s. 6d. (those on power
loading coalfaces). The union had also obtained payment for
surfacemen's meal-breaks which was the spark that started the dispute
the previous year.[113]

The momentous victory of the British miners in 1972 and the role played by the South Wales miners in that struggle cannot be adequately dealt with in a history of this kind.[114] A brief outline of the strike, particularly as it affected South Wales, will, however, give some understanding of its development and significance:[115]

July 1971	NUM Annual Conference carries Yorkshire resolution demanding minimum rates of £26 (surface workers), £28 (underground) and £35 (men on Power Loading Agreement) and for the NEC to consult members on industrial action in the event of an unsatisfactory response from the NCB. This represented a 43 per cent wage demand when the Conservative Government's 'norm' was 7–8 per cent.
31 October 1971	Overtime ban in all coalfields, supervised by liaison committees, had the effect (if that were necessary) of revealing the miners' bare earnings and of conditioning and disciplining the membership at local level for the struggle ahead.
2 December 1971	Result of NUM ballot on strike action for their conference wage demand announced:

> 145,482 vote for strike action
> 101,910 vote against strike action

In South Wales, 65·5 per cent of 29,249 voted for strike action.

9 December 1971	NUM NEC accept the ballot result and unanimously decide to commence first national coal strike since 1926 on 9 January 1972.
5 January 1972	NUM NEC rejects, by 23 to 2, marginally improved pay offer from NCB.
6 January 1972	S. Wales Area EC supports unanimously the rejection of the latest NCB offer. South Wales District, National union of Railwaymen, decide that they will refuse to handle any coal in the event of a miners' strike, a decision which was fully endorsed by the train-drivers' union (ASLEF). South Wales Electricity Board announces that its coal-fired power stations have stocks sufficient to last fourteen weeks, but South Wales merchants say they only have a two-week stockpile.
7 January 1972	NCB's withdrawal of all pay offers over the previous three months and that backdating would not apply to any eventual settlement, only serves to strengthen further

the miners' resolve. At South Wales Area Conference, 100 delegates unanimously support call for strike to begin as planned. All lodges to meet over the week-end to consider their situation and findings to be reported Area EC on 11 January. It is decided that only safety men should continue to work during the strike and that miners' agents can call area or strike committees: by the middle of the first week twelve such committees cover the coalfield and beyond: their main functions are picketing and the supervision of essential coal distribution but they also deal with social security problems and present their case to the 'public'. South Wales members of transport unions volunteer information to NUM on coal movements.

9 January 1972   National coalfield strike begins. In South Wales all fifty collieries and eighty-five private mines are at a standstill.

10 January 1972   TUC calls on all its members not to cross NUM picket lines. Miners begin picketing opencast coal sites in South Wales where contractors are bringing out coal: nearly all twenty opencast sites working but no movement of coal. At seven pits (Blaenavon, Caerau, Coegnant, Cwmgwili, Fernhill, Garw and St John's) safety men have been withdrawn contrary to union instructions. Only partial safety cover at five pits in the coalfield. A hundred coal merchants in the South Wales valleys report that they are completely out of coal.

11 January 1972   South Wales Area NUM lift picket lines to allow coal supplies to be delivered to hospitals in the area.

12 January 1972   South Wales Area NUM announces intensification of picketing. Twenty-four hour picketing of coal-powered power stations to begin. 3,000 schoolchildren in Glamorganshire and Monmouthshire unable to go to school because of lack of coal supplies.

13 January 1972   NUM instruction on non-colliery picketing announced. All power stations, steelworks, ports, coal depots and other major coal users to be picketed. Responsibilities for picketing in non-mining areas are allocated. South Wales miners are given the South and South-West. COSA in South Wales decides to join strike from 15 January (1,200 members, mostly clerks in Area and colliery offices). Mass meetings of Newport dockers vote to support the miners and refuse to unload two coal-laden ships. At Cardiff Docks, miners from Cwm,

Nantgarw and Fernhill lodges protest at plans to unload a French coal ship, the *Alain L. D.*, and appeal to Cardiff dockers not to supervise the unloading.

14 January 1972   Cardiff dockers refuse to supervise unloading of the *Alain L. D.*, which is forced to leave the port. Similar decisions to black imported coal at Swansea, Bristol, Avonmouth and Portishead.

16 January 1972   Welsh Old Age Pensioners' Association decides to back the miners.

17 January 1972   Pickets stop coke movements in and out of Ebbw Vale and Port Talbot steelworks. Two more pits (Ffaldau and Wyndham-Western) without safety cover. South Wales Area EC reaffirms its decision that safety men should work. Pickets persuade members of the Clerical and Administrative Workers' Union (CAWU) at seven collieries to go home, but other members at the NCB Area offices (Ystradmynach, Tondu and Llanishen) go to work.

18 January 1972   Pickets at Aberthaw and Llynfi power stations. Coal operations virtually ceased on opencast sites because TGWU lorry drivers refuse to deliver fuel oil. At Ystradmynach NCB offices, 400 CAWU members turn back after speaking to pickets. At Pontarddulais, pickets prevent ninety clerks from entering NCB West Wales Area Wages Office. Twenty-four pickets at Llanwern and Port Talbolt steelworks. 6,500 children away from Glamorganshire schools owing to coal shortage.

19 January 1972   400 CAWU members at Ystradmynach cross picket lines.

20 January 1972   TGWU shop stewards at Port Talbot Steelworks 'black' all coal to and from Ebbw steelworks.

21 January 1972   NUM decides to try to stop the movement of all fuel supplies. 400 CAWU members turned back by pickets at Ystradmynach.

22 January 1972   At the Baglan Bay petro-chemicals site, shop stewards agree to black all lorries of any contractor whose vehicles cross NUM picket lines anywhere in Britain.

24 January 1972   Police intervene to allow 500 clerks through a picket of fifty miners at Llanishen. 900 clerks do not report for work at Pontarddulais, Tondu and Ystradmynach.

25 January 1972   CAWU members at Tondu, Pontarddulais and Ystradmynach return home after angry scenes with pickets.

26 January 1972   South Wales Area EC rejects call for withdrawal of safety men and instructs its members not to picket clerks

at NCB offices. Deputation of coal merchants from South Wales visits Commons to inform Welsh MPs that coal stocks now non-existent and that they had been misled by the NCB on coal supplies.

27 January 1972　20,000 South Wales miners and their families along with other sections of the Labour Movement, march through Cardiff to a rally at Sophia Gardens addressed by national secretary Lawrence Daly. 1,000 workers (many of whom ex-miners) from Baglan Bay petrochemicals site, down tools to join the march and present miners with £365 cheque. 140 schools in South Wales now affected by coal shortages.

28 January 1972　Pickets begin to stop all oil and machinery supplies reaching opencast sites. The TGWU (the union on the sites) gives full support even though this would lead to redundancies.

29 January 1972　NCB claims that a critical safety situation exists in eleven South Wales collieries where there is no safety cover.

30 January 1972　Central Electricity Generating Board appeals to industrial and domestic consumers to economise on usage. Llynfi and Upper Boat power stations close for the day to conserve supplies.

31 January 1972　Voltage reductions throughout South Wales as pickets stop all supplies to the seven coal-burning power stations.

1 February 1972　260 schools in Wales affected: 33,000 children in Glamorganshire home from school.

2 February 1972　Two blast furnaces close down at Ebbw Vale steel works. Angry scenes between pickets and safety men at Penrhiwceiber Colliery. Electricity voltage reduced up to 6 per cent for $2\frac{1}{2}$ hours in South Wales.

3 February 1972　Fred Matthews of Hatfield Main Colliery, Doncaster, killed by a lorry whilst on a picket line at Scunthorpe. NCB claim that pickets preventing safety men entering Penrhiwceiber Colliery are causing flooding. Lodge replies that it is letting in the number of men NACODS consider necessary.

4 February 1972　300 pickets clash with police at Penrhiwceiber when they halt NCB van carrying safety men. NACODS members decide that they will not now work under any conditions. Miners in Merthyr area (as elsewhere) bagging coal at NCB yards to deliver to needy cases.

5 February 1972	Large South Wales contingent on NUM National Demonstration in London. South Wales miners amongst those arriving in Birmingham to reinforce picket at Saltley Marsh Coal Depot of West Midlands Gas Board.
7 February 1972	Lay-offs at a Landore (Swansea) foundry and Cardiff paper mills because of coal shortages. No safety men at Deep Duffryn and Penrhiwceiber Collieries. 81,000 children in 307 South Wales schools affected by the strike.
8 February 1972	200 South Wales miners amongst those picketing Saltley, four of whom are among the twenty-four miners arrested following scuffles with the police. Gelligaer UDC first local council in Wales to start miners' hardship fund.
9 February 1972	Government declares State of Emergency owing to serious power shortages consequent on the coal strike. Power cuts for domestic and industrial consumers to begin on 10 February. Pickets at Lewis Merthyr prevent safety men entering the colliery. 7,000 at Fred Matthews' funeral.
10 February 1972	Almost 40,000 workers down tools in scores of Birmingham factories and 10,000, mainly engineers, march to Saltley to join 2,000 miners and the 1,000 police. The gates are closed at 10.42 a.m. and *Labour Research* calls it 'one of the finest days in British trade union history'. Left wingers on the NEC of the NUM stand to applaud the victory. After new national talks between NUM and NCB break down, Government decides to set up Court of Inquiry.
11 February 1972	Government announces plans for three-day week in industry and total ban on electric heating in shops, offices and public buildings. NUM rejects Government's demand that Lord Wilberforce's Court of Inquiry should be binding or that miners should return to work whilst it is in session but agrees to give evidence.
14 February 1972	Government announces that at present rate of consumption coal stocks at power stations will only last another two weeks unless picketing ends. Three-day week begins with about 800,000 laid off, rising to 1·6 million by the end of the week. BSC lay off 1,000 in Wales, also lay-offs at Mettoys and Fords. The Trelewis Drift without safety cover because of picketing. Windows of three colliery officials at Lewis Merthyr

broken and NACODS members banned from Lewis Merthyr Club whilst strike is on.

15 February 1972   5,000 Welsh miners amongst those in a mass lobby of Parliament. Further 50 per cent increases in power cuts announced for following day. Two Welsh miners (Alan Carter, a Mardy surface worker, and Gerald Thorne, a Coedely underground rope changer) amongst those giving evidence on first day of Wilberforce Inquiry.

16 February 1972   South Wales Area NUM Conference: call for removal of safetymen sent to lodges for consideration. 40,000 workers laid off in Wales.

17 February 1972   Government announces that from February 23 restrictions on power consumption to be increased by further 50 per cent, leading to one-day working or total shutdown in industry. Merthyr miners delivering coal to 1,400 old age pensioners affected by power cuts.

18 February 1972   Report of Wilberforce Court of Inquiry recommends increases of £6 for underground workers, £5 for surface workers and £4.50 for face workers, but is rejected by NUM NEC (13 to 12). The two South Wales members formally move and second rejection which instructs its negotiators to seek more from NCB. Negotiations transfer to Downing Street,

19 February 1972   Downing Street negotiations end at 1 a.m. The improvements to Wilberforce included an extra 80p for winding men; the full basic increases to be applied to piece and contract workers, to eighteen-year-olds, and to coke and clerical staff; consequential increases for canteen workers from 1 November; adult rate to be paid at eighteen over a two-year period; an extra five days' holiday a year; the bonus shift payment to be consolidated to give a five-shift basic week; no redundancies on return to work; rent arrears to be cleared up over a 12-month period; talks on a subsidised transport scheme, to operate from 1 May; talks on a productivity bonus scheme from the autumn. NEC recommends settlement to members and picketing is called off. South Wales Area EC unanimously recommends acceptance.

21 February 1972   South Wales Area Conference: only 2 out of 80 delegates vote against acceptance.

23 February 1972   South Wales Miners ballot on settlement. NCB announces that seven faces in South Wales pits seriously damaged.

24 February 1972	Two miners killed and one seriously injured at Cynheidre Colliery whilst preparing the pit for return to work.
25 February 1972	Result of national ballot: 210,039 for, 7,581 against; in South Wales 22,332 for, 1,078 against.
28 February 1972	Return to work.

The miners' victory cannot be seen in isolation. It had everything to do with a widespread hostility to the Conservative Government's pay and employment policy and its anti-trade union legislation. The solidarity with the miners' cause throughout the Labour Movement and beyond sprung from an admiration of their determination, sympathy for their case as well as a desire not to see the NUM defeated by the most hard-faced Government since the war. Although it is undeniable that the miners could not have won without such support, it was only their confidence in their own resolve which launched the strike and their understanding of their own history which resulted in the TUC being excluded from all negotiations. At the outset, the notion that coal was a dying industry was still widely prevalent. To the outsider, particularly the Conservative Government and virtually the whole of the mass media, the miners' stubbornness was interpreted at best as mass suicide: the industry could not recover from a crippling strike. 'Why not accept the initial offer, after all, we're doing you a favour by keeping you in work', was the patronising argument which had countered the wage claims and opposition to pit closures in the 1960s. Undoubtedly, a new apocalyptic attitude surfaced within mining communities: why should miners risk their lives for starvation wages to save an industry which experts said was dying anyway. As it happens, the seven-week strike did more to save the industry (by revealing the continued importance of coal and by making employment in it more attractive), than a decade of NCB rationalisation, pit closures and low pay. But this new outlook was underpinned by the double-edged unity achieved by the NPLA. The agreement drew miners from different coalfields closer together but also embittered the more productive areas (such as Nottingham) whose wage rates had been held back for the benefit of other areas.

What shook everyone, including some miners, was the critical role of coal in the British economy and the depth of sympathy for the miners' struggle. The rapid contraction of the coalfield in the 1960s had led to an army of ex-miners throughout the other industries in South Wales who responded almost spontaneously. More than this, sons, daughters and widows of miners and ex-miners in South Wales and elsewhere provided a further network of solidarity which, in the euphoria of the time, seemed unconquerable.

For the older miners, the tradition of struggle, the collective and individual memory of defeats, the depression and the dashed hopes of nationalisation were now interwoven with a younger generation whose experiences were confined largely to the failure of the NCB to solve the problems of coal through pit closures and low pay. Certainly in South Wales, the whole atmosphere of 1972 was cloaked as much in retribution for 1926 and all that followed, as with a conviction that there must be a decent future for miners and their families in the British coalfields. The stories that old miners cried when their grandsons had vindicated them may be apocryphal, but a close analysis of the family and community background of those young 'shock-troops' at Saltley would reveal a blinding shaft of light on the miners' cause over three generations. Class and community converged in 1972, as it had in 1926 and in all other moments of crisis in the intervening period:

> 'What do you think you are doing, getting into trouble like this?' said the 'responsible' NUM official to his twenty-year-old son who was languishing in a police cell near the Saltley picket line.
> 'I've spent all my life listening to my grandfather telling me about how he went to prison in 1926; I had to do something,' came the deafening reply.[116]

Yet within two years, the miners and their families were once again forced into a position of having to make substantial sacrifices so as to win back the wages position which they had gained in 1972. Having slipped from first to eighteenth in the industrial wages league, the NUM now embarked on another struggle fortified with the knowledge that Arab oil prices had quadrupled in the autumn of 1973. Following a total overtime ban from November onwards, the British miners balloted 80·99 per cent in favour of strike action (South Wales polled the highest with 93·15 per cent). The claim was £35 for surface workers, £40 for underground workers and £45 for those under the NPLA (with appropriate differentials for craftsmen and other grades). The four-week strike which commenced on 9 February had many of the features of the 1972 confrontation, although at least one South Wales leader, Dai Francis, believed that, by comparison, '1974 was a picnic'. Having refused to compromise on Phase Three of its 'counter-inflation' Price and Pay Code (£2.25 a week or 7 per cent), Edward Heath's Conservative Government announced a State of Emergency, a three-day week and finally a General Election, for 28 February. Even though the

WANTED

1,600 UNDERGROUND WORKERS TO FILL VACANCIES IN
SOUTH WALES COALFIELD

FREE
- ★ DUST MASKS
- ★ GOGGLES
- ★ EAR MUFFS (for excessive noise)
- ★ OIL SKINS (when working in water)
- ★ RESPIRATOR MASKS (for emergencies)
- ★ CHEST X-RAYS (monitoring Pneumoconiosis)

Good Bus Services to neighbouring pits from nearby towns and villages—commencing at 5 a.m.

Hours of Work — 7¼ plus winding time (you will be on the colliery premises approximately 8¼ hours.)

Good Canteen facilities before and after your shift.

Death benefits if you die in service.

Present Basic Gross Wage (for 5-day week)		Basic Gross Wage from 1st March, 1974 for 5-day week (if offer accepted)	
Coal Face — £36.79		*Coal Face — £39.29	
Grades A — £36.79		Grades A — £39.29	
B — £31.71		B — £34.21	
C — £29.99		C — £32.49	
Grades 1 — £28.16		Grades 1 — £30.66	
2 — £27.66		2 — £30.16	
3 — £27.29		3 — £29.79	

*IF YOU ARE PREPARED TO WORK NIGHTS REGULARLY ON COAL FACE YOU CAN EARN
£46 PER WEEK GROSS

Note :—For the majority of miners the MINIMUM Wage Rates are also the MAXIMUM

SORRY — NO SURFACE VACANCIES AVAILABLE   THESE ARE USUALLY RESERVED FOR
INJURED AND DISABLED UNDERGROUND WORKERS!

THE NATION NEEDS COAL — JOIN THE DWINDLING BAND OF THOSE PREPARED TO DIG IT !

Issued by the National Union of Mineworkers (South Wales Area) and printed by the Cymric Federation Press, Neville Street, Cardiff.

South Wales Area leaflet during 1974 strike, which the *Western Mail* refused to publish.

Election and the Industrial Relations Act meant that picketing and other campaigning activities were low-key affairs compared with 1972, the miners' resolve did not diminish. The return of a minority Labour Government led to an early settlement. In Britain's long and turbulent social history, never had a government fallen directly as a result of an industrial dispute. Sporting a 1972 South Wales miners' victory badge on his jacket, the new Secretary of State for Employment, Michael Foot, implemented the Pay Board Report which showed that the miners' average weekly earnings had been seriously eroded since 1972. The settlement, which was overwhelmingly accepted by the NUM membership, gave £32, £36 and £45 to surface workers, underground workers and those on NPLA respectively. There were additional increases for underground craftsmen and improvements in night allowance, holiday pay and retirement pensions as well as new death-in-service benefits. Two other important consequences of the strike were the implementation of a scheme for compensation for pneumoconiosis sufferers, which cost the new Government £110 million, and a new superannuation scheme commencing in 1975 which cost a further £60 million.[117]

As we have seen, the period from the 1969 'surfacemen's strike' to the fall of the Conservative Government in 1974 was one characterised by gigantic industrial and political confrontations during which the British miners reclaimed their place in the forefront of the British Labour movement. It was an era when new forms of political and industrial struggle emerged, notably mass and flying picketing and factory occupations. In South Wales, the period had special, perhaps unique, features in which the miners revived their earlier extra-parliamentary role. Two seemingly contradictory omens were provided by the 1970 General Election when the veteran miners' leader S. O. Davies defeated the official Labour candidate at Merthyr Tydfil and the Conservatives lost their deposits in eight coalfield constituencies.[118] The miners increasingly came to the fore in localised community-based struggles, whether it was the Merthyr Borough Council's opposition to school milk cuts, the non-implementation of the Housing Finance Act by the Bedwas and Machen UDC or the mobilisation of the Cynon Valley against the siting of gas tanks in the village of Hirwaun. Throughout the period, the NUM in South Wales seemed to be constantly involved in Parliamentary lobbies, demonstrations or other actions on a wide variety of causes including opposition to the 1970 Springbok tour, unemployment, the Industrial Relations Act, improvements in pensions, support for the Upper Clyde Shipbuilders' Work-In and perhaps most effectively a coalfield-wide strike against the imprisonment of the 'Pentonville Five' dockers in July 1972.[119]

Arguably, the most rewarding change occurred in 1973–4 when the Wales TUC was established. It was widely believed that it had its origins on the 1972 picket lines when grass-roots solidarity for the miners, especially among transport workers, exposed the TUC's archaic regional structure. The main impetus undoubtedly came from the TGWU (Wales Region) and the NUM (South Wales Area) and the regard with which the miners were now held within the trade union movement was fully expressed when delegates at its inaugural conference elected Dai Francis as its chairman in April 1974.[120]

The return of the Labour Government in 1974 seemed to herald that elusive *dawn of a new era*. The NCB's new *Plan for Coal* was endorsed by the Government. It included an investment programme with a capital cost of £600 million. The Department of Energy's 'tripartite examination' into the future of the industry also appeared to be a worthwhile and refreshingly new departure. The eventual lowering of the retirement age to sixty-two (albeit initially on a voluntary basis) was a further indication of an improved atmosphere in the industry.[121]

Yet fears for the very survival of the South Wales coalfield have grown since the 1975 Common Market fuel and energy plans which proposed the contraction of production to a European profitable market level: by implication this meant the phasing out of such 'peripheral' coalfields as South Wales and Scotland.[122] The subsequent and ominous arrival of a 'disturbance' allowance (a financial payment to miners in the event of a closure) and an incentive bonus scheme were not without their wider significance. Pit closures and piecework have been the most divisive issues in the history of the miners and their re-emergence alongside each other in South Wales in the late 1970s poses very serious social and political questions for the miners. Hostility to the new incentive bonus scheme was widespread, particularly in South Wales, partly because of the very difficult geological conditions in the coalfield, partly because of safety factors, but also because of the long-standing belief that it undermined unity at every level of the miners' organisation. It was small comfort for South Wales, in January 1978, to know that the Area was the last to succumb to the scheme: the means by which it was foisted on the British miners is something that history will judge tomorrow but the miners of today have to endure. The problem of improving miners' basic wages was aggravated rather than solved by the scheme in that it undermined the importance of NPLA. As one miners' leader in South Wales caustically remarked: 'It's the law of the jungle and we haven't even got spears.'[123]

Furthermore, the Labour Government's policy of wage restraint encapsulated in its 'Social Contract' seriously strained the traditional loyalty of the British miners. The South Wales miners (at least until the spectre of mass pit closures reappeared in 1979) along with other left-wing Areas within the NUM had been less inclined to follow blindly a Labour Government's incomes policy. Typical of this rather un-orthodox *British* trade union perspective was the occasion when Emlyn Williams, president of the South Wales miners, rocked the Stock Exchange in May 1976 with some clear echoes of A. J. Cook's straightforward syndicalist views. In calling for £100 for face-workers (a 33 per cent increase) he argued:

> Why should we demand this sort of wage? My answer is 'Why shouldn't we?' At some point some workers have got to challenge the grossly unequal distribution of wages in British society. . . . The Government clearly is not intent on altering the distribution of income significantly. So we have to tackle the job ourselves. . . . Why should men who risk their lives through injuries and disease, who work physically hard, who produce a commodity which is essential to British industry not be paid accordingly? And if the answer is that society cannot afford it, then my reply is that society must be changed so that it can afford it.[124]

There was also a healthy scepticism about the reasons for the sudden refloating of notions of industrial democracy in the mining industry. Genuine fears that the traditional demands for a democratically-run industry would be coupled with the reintroduction of piece-work were widespread in South Wales. That uncompromising tribune of the Penrhiwceiber miners, Mike Griffin, posed some disturbing questions which could not be solved by isolated utopian blueprints:

> . . . to think we are gathered here [NUM forum on industrial democracy] listening to this subject that I have heard now for the last thirty years, at a time when the wages of mineworkers are in one of the lowest states they have been for the last five years, where we have had a ballot, proper industrial democracy, on incentive schemes, etc., I was up for a considerable time last night arguing with people who want to ignore the ballot. . . .
>
> All we have ever had is what we have fought for, and the Coal Board as a nationalised concern have never given us anything. . . . If they want

production committees let them say so. Don't dress it up in fancy clothes and call it participation and democracy. . . .

Get the chap on the shovel even now in the tailend, in the bite . . . , and you talk to him about workers' participation. It is a load of rubbish. . . .

The [NCB] are trying to run an industry, and if we could get in there and find out the fiddles like [the] . . . £6,000 given . . . by the National Coal Board to take delegates up and down the Rhine to propagate . . . central heating, . . . the fiddles in the private contractors . . . robbing us, and our men filling are being robbed by giving money to contractors . . . [enabling] coal to be sold at twice the pit-head price. Those are fit subjects for discussion in an industrial democracy. . . .[125]

The other ever-present problems of the South Wales miners including the classification of emphysema and bronchitis as industrial diseases; widows' house-coal and the neglect of pneumoconiotic miners (or their widows) who commuted their claims; the role of craftsmen; the rundown of public transport and social services; the internal unity and democracy of the NUM; demands for an integrated fuel policy; all are now overshadowed by the anxieties for the future of the coalfield itself. With short-time working, factory closures and redundancies in other industries throughout the valleys, the very social survival of many communities is now in doubt.[126] Speculation about the imminent end of mining in ten or even eighteen collieries by the early 1980s has been heightened by the immediate threat to Deep Duffryn Colliery at Mountain Ash in the Cynon Valley. But there are signs of hope. Whilst the NUM's mobilisation of communities through the Cynon Valley Action Committee Against Colliery Closures has a familiar ring, there are significant departures. The nature of the resistance, including unofficial strike action by four lodges and a COSA branch, on 19 April 1979, is *new*. Even more important, the NCB's 'stewardship of the mines' has been scrutinised and called into question, as is its heavy social responsibility 'because of the sacrifices made by the population of the Valley to the Coal Industry and because of the Profit made by the National Coal Board since nationalisation, from the Valley'.[127] This seemingly controlled offensive from below may well be the means by which the town of Mountain Ash whose community 'has taken over a hundred years of class struggle to build' will set an example to the rest of the coalfield.[128]

Hard-faced Treasury notions of short-term profitability, divorced from past investment patterns, are now being challenged. Whether the South Wales mining community, synonymous, even in the late 1970s,

The BOARD'S NEXT STEP—or
THE CASE FOR DEEP DUFFRYN

When the first results of the productivity scheme were totted up, Deep Duffryn was held up as an example to follow. Eight months later, the Board are demanding the closure of the pit!

THE BOARD SAY—

THEY MUST CLOSE THE PIT BECAUSE IT IS UNECONOMICAL.

But is it economic to lose 500 jobs in the Valley?

To keep young men out of work when 1 in 12 in the Valley are on the dole?

Is it economic when the world faces an energy crisis—now and in the future—to throw away coal reserves that will then be gone forever?

THE BOARD SAY—

THERE ARE NO WORKABLE RESERVES.

This is nonsense! There are 5 years work in the present seam, and for a cost of 4 million pounds, 20 years of prime Welsh dry steam coal can be worked through a major fault to the west of the pit.

SINCE THE BOARD HAVE HACKED OUR INDUSTRY SO VICIOUSLY IN THE PAST, THERE ARE NO OTHER PITS LEFT TO WORK THIS COAL.

COAL IS BRITAIN'S LIFEBLOOD—North Sea oil will run out before very long. Then every scrap of coal will be required.

WHY are nationalised industries (e.g. C.E.G.B.) allowed to import coal from West German **privately owned mines** while the N.C.B. say our pits must close?

EVERY PIT CAN BE RUN DOWN TO CLOSURE.

If the Board wish to close a pit today, they do it in **a** very subtle manner, by

(1) **Stopping Recruitment** and using the Early Retirement Scheme **we** fought for, against us.

(2) **Stopping Investment.** Belting structure, drive heads, have to be salvaged from old workings.

(3) **Stopping Repairs**—roadway conditions can easily be run down

IT IS OBVIOUS TO THE LODGE—

That the only reserves required by the N.C.B. are our experienced miners in other pits. If the Board require miners—give us

the right pay, good conditions, and **security of work in our pits** and then they **will get all the miners they need!**

Recruitment of miners, production of coal, and good industrial relations cannot be separated from these reasonable demands.

WE KNOW THIS—WHEN WILL THEY LEARN?

77 pits were closed in the 1960's. We kidded ourselves that the next pit in line was always the best one to defend.

Surely we have learned our lessons by now—Governments respond when WE act!

ACT TOGETHER AND THERE WILL BE NO CLOSURES!

DEEP DUFFRYN LODGE COMMITTEE.

Published by the Deep Duffryn Lodge Committee, and printed by the Cymric Federation Press, Neville Street, Cardiff.

Deep Duffryn leaflet warning against pit closures, 1979.

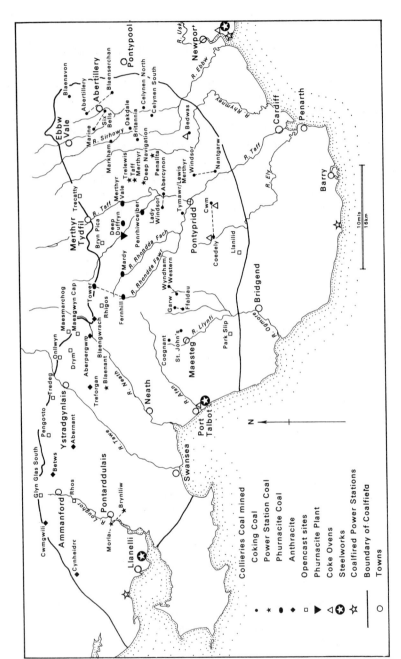

Fig. 2. The Coal Industry in South Wales, 1979.

with comradeship, community spirit, choral music, universally acclaimed opera singers, rugby, darts, bowls and snooker players, can transform its economy for the benefit of its people is, as it has always been, *the* political question. The history of the miners' union shows that it *alone* cannot do it.[129]

The next decade could be the most testing period in the long and turbulent history of the South Wales miners. The way they confront their problems will depend on whether they fully comprehend the lessons of the past and whether they can apply those lessons imaginatively to a new situation. The new Area banner encapsulates matters neatly but perhaps ambiguously: 'The past we inherit, the future we build through socialism.' If the fire kindled by the miners at Deep Duffryn in 1978–9 is any indication, then their comrades throughout the coalfield will continue to play their traditionally dynamic role in British society. Let us hope that the poet's pessimistic reflections are not prophetic:

> Men lunched on a book a day
> And broken promises and nursed
> A fading pride in jobless hours.
> Dressed in blue serge they sang
> Martyrs of the Arena
> For a supper of prizes . . .
> Their history is now a spiritual concession
> Recorded in new books on the same shelves
> That once bordered their besmirched lives.
> The aged ones, who remain, recite
> Their stories on park benches . . .[130]

NOTES

1. 'The Dawn of a New Era: Nationalisation 1947' was the slogan of the Risca miners banner which is now housed at the South Wales Miners' Library.
2. Idris Davies, *Tonypandy and Other Poems* (1945), p. 12.
3. UCS, David Francis (Onllwyn) collection, Jack Dorgan to DF, 8 June 1946.
4. For a full account of this period, see L. C. B. Seaman, *Post-Victorian Britain* (1967), pp. 415–502; also D. N. Pritt, *The Labour Government 1945–51* (1964)).

5. R. Page Arnot, *The Miners in Crisis and War* (1961), pp. 428–30; *The Miner* (official organ of the South Wales Area Council, NUM) Vol. 1, No. 7/8, April/May 1945, p. 8.
6. See above, pp. 382–9.
7. Information from D. D. Evans and Tom Mantle.
8. At the time it was known as the National Federation of Colliery Officials and Staffs, which did not seem to have any presence in South Wales. For details of the merger discussions see MFGB, minutes of organisation sub-committee 19 June, 20 August 1946.
9. SWMF minutes, 1940 *passim*; NUM (S. Wales Area) minutes, 1960 *passim*.
10. See D. I. Gidwell, 'Philosophy and Geology in Conflict: The Evolution of Wages Structures in the South Wales Coalfield. 1926–74', *Llafur*, Vol. 1, No. 4, Summer 1975, pp. 44–57.
11. A set of the Gala and Eisteddfod programmes are preserved at the South Wales Miners' Library. As a recognition of the contribution of the Miners' Eisteddfod towards the cultural life of Wales, Dai Francis (the general secretary of the NUM in South Wales) taking the name 'Dai o'r Onllwyn' was made a member of the National Eisteddfod's Gorsedd of Bards in 1976.
12. Full accounts of galas and eisteddfodau are to be found in the union journal *The Miner*. A short film, with a commentary by the writer, Gwyn Thomas, was made of the Gala by the South Wales Area, so as to propagate more effectively the idea in the mining valleys. For further details of this internationalism, see NUM (S. Wales Area) minutes, 1945–79 *passim*.
13. For an account of the early work of the Commission see *After Ten Years: A Report of Miners' Welfare Work in the South Wales Coalfield 1921–31* (n.d.). See also A. Horner, *Incorrigible Rebel, op. cit.*, pp. 202–4.
14. *Souvenir Celebrating the Twenty-first Birthday of the Workmen's Welfare Hall Gilfach Goch* (1945).
15. *Colliery Guardian*, 7 September 1945.
16. For a fuller account of these developments see Hywel Francis, 'The Origins of the South Wales Miners' Library' in *History Workshop*, No. 2, Autumn 1976, pp. 183–205; CISWO *Annual Reports, passim*; Chris Evans, *History of Blaencwm-dulais* (1977), pp. 118–20.
17. SWML, 'Talygarn' (unpublished draft of pamphlet 1959); W. Paynter, *My Generation, op. cit.*, p. 128.
18. NUM (S. Wales Area) *Annual Reports, 1947–48, 1966*; also information provided by David Francis, retired general secretary (S. Wales Area NUM), 21 January 1979. One of the most 'dramatic' events associated with the Home was the occasion convalescing miners disturbed the serenity and gentility of Bournemouth cricket ground when they invaded the pitch in 1948 to congratulate the Glamorgan team on defeating Hampshire and so winning the County Championship for the first time. Much less well known but no less important, is the 'Rest' Home at Porthcawl. Following a £75,000 boost in 1979, its role has been broadened and extended with the provision of a special wing for paraplegics. Over 2,000 patients use the Home every year. Having been used by the South Wales miners for a hundred years, in recent times it has survived through the assistance of the union, the NCB, CISWO, its League of Friends, Government grants and a very active management board; see *Coal News*, March 1979.

19. NUM (S. Wales Area) *Annual Report, 1946–7*; NUM (S. Wales Area) EC minutes, 1959, *passim*. The mural was unveiled on 4 May 1959 by a miner in the pneumoconiosis ward of the hospital.

20 The thirteen sponsored MPs were Aneurin Bevan (Ebbw Vale), George Daggar (Abertillery), S. O. Davies (Merthyr), Sir Charles Edwards (Bedwellty), Ness Edwards (Caerphilly), D. R. Grenfell (Gower), James Griffiths (Llanelli), George Hall (Aberdare), Arthur Jenkins (Pontypool), Will John (Rhondda West), W. H. Mainwaring (Rhondda East), D. J. Williams (Neath), and Ted Willams (Ogmore and Garw). Almost all of them had previously been miners' agents, one was a former SWMF president, three were former vice-presidents, seven had attended the Labour College and two had been to prison. For an account of the Rhondda East contest, see John Mahon, *Harry Pollitt* (1976), pp. 305–10. Another former miner, Tudor Watkins of Abercrave, won Brecon and Radnor for Labour but he was not NUM sponsored.

21. NUM (S. Wales Area) *Annual Report, 1946–7*, pp. 33–64; *The Miner* (official organ of the SWMF and subsequently S. Wales Area NUM), 1945–7 *passim*.

22. D. N. Pritt, *The Labour Government, 1945–51* (1963), p. 31; Horner, *op. cit.*, pp. 179–80, 190.

23. For a full account, see Aneurin Bevan, *In Place of Fear* (1978 edition), pp. 21–32; 98–121; David Stark Murray, 'Bevan and the NHS' in Socialist Medical Association, *Aneurin Bevan: An Appreciation of his Services to the Health of the People* (pamphlet, n.d.), pp. 7–9.

24. SWML Interview with D. C. Davies, Social Insurance Officer, S. Wales Area NUM, 19 June 1976.

25. *Manifesto of the National Union of Mineworkers* (leaflet, 1945).

26. *General Election: To the Electors of South Wales and Monmouthshire* (Manifesto issued by the NUM, South Wales Area Council, 22 June 1945).

27. SWML Interview with Emlyn Williams, President, S. Wales Area NUM, 19 June 1976, who believed that nationalisation was inadequate: it should have been socialisation. Such a view was shared by another miners' leader, Dai Dan Evans, who saw it only as a change of ownership and not a fundamental change in social relationships. But such observations were very much in the minority and the dominant view was that most effectively expressed by Horner, SWML interview with D. D. Evans, former general secretary S. Wales Area NUM, 7 August 1973.

28. *Guide to the Coalfields* (1948), pp. 287–8; A. Horner, *Incorrigible Rebel* (1960), pp. 176–80. The NUM, however, was determined from the outset of nationalisation to maintain its identity by not getting involved in the administration of the industry.

29. J. E. Morgan, *A Village Workers' Council: A Short History of the Lady Windsor Lodge* (SWMF) (n.d.), p. 72.

30. SWML Interview with Evan John (Clydach), *op. cit*. For another account see C. Evans, *Industrial and Social History of Seven Sisters* (1964), p. 167.

31. Quoted in the Manifesto of the NUM (1945), *op. cit.*

32. Israel Berkovitch, *Coal on the Switchback: The Coal Industry since Nationalisation* (1977), pp. 73–4; *The Colliery Year Book and Coal Trades Directory* (1943), p. 635.

33. This continuity is revealed and explored fully by Kim Howells, 'The South Wales Miners, 1937–57: A View from Below' (Warwick, Ph.D., 1979). It is also

confirmed by the experiences of retired Anthracite miners attending extra-mural classes conducted by one of the authors in 1978–9. More detailed research work on the nature of nationalisation in the South Wales coalfield will be undertaken at the South Wales Miners' Library in 1979–82.

34. *Colliery Guardian*, 13, 23 December 1946.
35. *Colliery Guardian*, 25 April 1947.
36. *Colliery Guardian*, 22 May 1952.
37. Michael Barratt Brown, *The Background to the Miners' Strike: What Really Happened to the Coal Industry* (Institute of Workers' Control pamphlet, 1972), pp. 6–11 *passim*.
38. *Ibid.*, p. 5; A. Horner, *op. cit.*, p. 176. Horner, as usual, put it succinctly: 'I was not setting down the minimum conditions which would enable the industry to go on functioning. We were not presenting an ultimatum; we were simply setting on record the conditions which must obtain in the mines, if the men were to be there to dig the coal.' Miners often referred to Horner's catch-phrase of the time, 'We could have asked for the moon!', to which the reply of the young miners of the 1970s invariably was 'You should have!' (This is a constant retort heard by the authors on the South Wales Area Educational Scheme since 1974.) But the NUM at the time was saddled with the problem of compulsory arbitration.
39. Statistics provided by the Public Relations Department, National Coal Board (South Wales Area).
40. Graham Humphreys, *Industrial Britain: South Wales* (1972), pp. 36–50 *passim*. 'Foreign labour' was an issue as late as 1955–6, see *The Miner* (organ of the South Wales Area NUM), Vol. 3, No. 5, Sept./Oct. 1955.
41. P. Hugh Jones and C. M. Fletcher, *The Social Consequences of Pneumoconiosis among Coalminers in South Wales* (HMSO, 1951) *passim*; *South Wales Outline Plan* (HMSO, 1949), p. 23; D. C. Davies interview *op. cit.*; SWML, Jack Evans (Gwaun-cae-Gurwen), Notes and Papers re Silicosis Pageant, 1939.
42. SWML, tape no. 168, 22 May 1974. A Gwendraeth Valley miners' banner at a 1952 miners' demonstration read:

> Mountain of Despair   Valley of Gloom
> Hundreds of Miners from one Village disabled by
> PNEUMOCONIOSIS
> THE DEADLY DUST
> (see photograph section)

43. Socialist Medical Association, *Challenge of the Rhondda Fach Survey* (reprint from *Medicine Today and Tomorrow*, January–February 1953); see also Socialist Medical Association, *Danger, Dust at Work* (pamphlet, n.d.)
44. Archie James, *The Industrial Injuries Act, Damages at Common Law and other Legislation* (1957); Lyndon R. James, *The Control of Dust in Mines* (1959); D. D. Evans, *A Survey of the Incidence and Progression of Pneumoconiosis Related to the Environmental Conditions* (2 part pamphlet 1963).
45. NUM (S. Wales Area) EC minutes, 17 April 1951; D. C. Davies interview, *op. cit.*
46. Charles Fletcher, 'Fighting the Modern Black Death', *The Listener*, 18 September 1950.
47. A. Horner, *op. cit.*, pp. 179–81; *Colliery Guardian*, 25 July 1947.
48. Menna Gallie, *The Small Mine* (1962), pp. 26–7. This reference to the 'N.C.

bloody B' was an expression the authors frequently heard in their childhood and is immortalised in Menna Gallie's novel (p. 39). One of the authors also recalls a children's joke in the Dulais Valley about the time of the 1956 Suez Crisis:

Question: What does NCB stand for?
Answer: Nasser's Cream Buns!

His Communist father reprimanded him for repeating it.

49. Statistics provided by the Public Relations Department, National Coal Board (South Wales Area). See also Appendix V, pp. 509–11.

50. *Colliery Guardian*, 5 July 1951; D. C. Davies interview, *op. cit.*; SWML interview with Don Hayward, chief administrative officer, NUM (S. Wales Area), 19 June 1976; SWML, *Wern Tarw Where Next?* (leaflet published by the Wern Tarw Lodge, 12 June 1951).

51. *The Miner* (magazine of the South Wales Area NUM) Vol. 10, No. 5, Sept.–Oct. 1962, reproduces a poignant cartoon.

52. SWML, 'To All Lodges – The South Wales Coalfield' (circular issued on behalf of the Parc and Dare Lodge, February 1952).

53. *Colliery Guardian*, 7, 14, 21 February, 8, 15 May 1952; E. Williams interview, *op. cit.*

54. Evan John interview, *op. cit.*; W. Paynter, *My Generation, op. cit.*, p. 131. Despite their differences, the two men remained on friendly terms throughout and according to Evan John, Paynter bought him a pint of beer immediately following the Special Conference.

55. Interview with D. C. Davies, Evan John, Don Hayward and Emlyn Williams, *op. cit.* One interesting feature in this situation was that, along with Will Paynter, Alun Thomas, the secretary of the Communist Party in Wales by 1952, had played a prominent role in the 1931 dispute. Thomas agitated for more unofficial action, but Paynter ultimately won the day by appealing direct to Harry Pollitt, general secretary of the CPGB.

56. W. Paynter, *My Generation, op. cit.*, pp. 131–2.

57. For a full account of the distinctiveness of the rural Anthracite coalfield see Lynn Davies, *Aspects of Mining Folklore in Wales* (reprinted from Folk Life 9); Lynn Davies, *Geirfa'r Glöwr* (1976); George Ewart Evans, *From Mouths of Men*, pp. 121–4; Edgar ap Lewys, *Hiwmor y Glöwr* (1977).

58. SWML interview with John Davies (Gwaun-cae-Gurwen), 24 January 1974.

59. NUM (S. Wales Area) minutes, 1956 *passim*.

60. W. Paynter, *My Generation*, p. 126; *The Miner*, Vol. 1, No. 1, January/February 1953.

61. NUM (S. Wales Area) EC minutes, 22 December 1951. The decline in interest in the union is revealed in the columns of *The Miner*, see, for example, Vol. 4, No. 4, July/August 1956, pp. 17–18.

62. A file of *The Miner* (magazine of the South Wales Area, NUM) exists in the South Wales Miners' Library. The new national organ had been, in effect, the brainchild of Will Paynter while he was general secretary of the national union: it had taken over six years to publish and was his last achievement before he retired. *The Miner* was to have a vigorous role during the 1972 and 1974 strikes and, as intended by Paynter, it was to play its part in breaking down the artificial barriers that existed between coalfields and forge a greater national unity.

63. *Miners' Monthly* (official organ of the SWMF), May 1936; D. D. Evans interview, *op. cit.*; Richard Lewis, 'Leaders and Teachers: The Origins and Development of the Workers' Education Movement in South Wales, 1906–40' (University of Wales, Ph.D., 1980).

64. W. W. Craik, *Central Labour College* (1964) *passim*; H. Francis, 'Origins of the South Wales Miners' Library' in *History Workshop Journal*, issue 2, Autumn 1976; R. Lewis, 'The South Wales Miners and the Ruskin College Strike of 1909' in *Llafur*, Vol. 2, No. 1, Spring 1976.

65. NUM (S. Wales Area) Education Department, *The Year's Work* (n.d., report compiled by Ronald Frankenberg, Education Officer). Frankenberg is now Professor of Social Anthropology at Keele University.

66. The scheme was temporarily abandoned in 1971 owing to declining numbers of young miners, caused by the contraction of the industry. The scheme was restarted in the autumn of 1974 largely due to the revival of interest in the union of young miners during the 1972 and 1974 strikes. Many of these miners had joined or rejoined the industry following improvements in wages and conditions after the two big strikes. The revived scheme, which is different in some respects from the original scheme, is now organised in association with the Department of Extra-Mural Studies, University College Swansea, is centred at the South Wales Miners' Library and involves about thirty young lodge officers every year.

67. For a literary portrayal of the period see Menna Gallie's *Strike for a Kingdom* (1959), *Man's Desiring* (1960), *The Small Mine* (1962) and Aldryd Haines, *The Drift* (1974): all four deal with the Anthracite mining village of Crynant in the 1950s.

68. National Coal Board, *British Coal: The Rebirth of an Industry* (1957).

69. Will Paynter, 'A Recession Must Not Come Here' in *The Miner*, Vol. 6, No. 2, March/April 1958, pp. 18–20.

70. NUM (S. Wales Area), *The Miners' Case Against Pit Closures: An Indictment of Tory Government Policy* (pamphlet, n.d.), p. 4. The NCB claimed the situation would be eased if those miners over sixty-five were pressed to retire in the affected pits. The union argued that pensions were still inadequate. Compulsory retirement of all mineworkers aged sixty-five came in the summer of 1959.

71. Reproduced in NUM (S. Wales Area) bound minutes 1959, Vol. 1, pp. 13–14. It was also alleged that the NCB had deceived the NUM into conceding Saturday working in the summer of 1957 and had thus contributed to over-production, see D. C. Davies 'The NCB Deceived Our Leaders' in *The Miner*, Vol. 6, No. 5, Sept./Oct. 1958, p. 11.

72. NUM (S. Wales Area) EC minutes, January 1959 *passim*. A vivid account of this lobby is given in *Wales* (ed. Keidrych Rhys), January 1959, pp. 6–9. The ever-present Evan John is described as: 'Big Evan John, again, green bow-tie, silk foulard pattern scarf, the "un-official" Chairman from Clydach, near Swansea rested his pint to argue whether "Abertawe" was the correct Welsh for Swansea. He thought Mor Alarch it should be and displayed a knowledge of local history by saying it was the spot where King Swain landed from Norway. Their localities obviously mean a good deal to these men . . . towns and villages steeped with lore, legend and traditions which they are not prepared to leave easily. Evan John then said he must have a bath at Waterloo but would be back at 3 p.m. One or two of his buddies said they didn't want to be mentioned because of their relatives . . . didn't want 'em to know they'd been in a pub!'

73. Will Paynter, 'The President Reviews Recent Events' in *The Miner*, Vol. 7, No. 1, Jan./Feb. 1959; NUM (S. Wales Area), *Vice-President's Address by Glyn Williams* (1959), pp. 2–4.
74. Lyn Evans, 'Death of a Village', in *The Miner*, Vol. 7, No. 5, Sept./Oct. 1959, pp. 8–9. This section is also based on the personal recollections of one of the authors.
75. Statement made by Peter Evans, chairman of Deep Duffryn NUM Lodge at a public meeting against the proposed closure of Deep Duffryn Colliery, 10 December 1978.
76. Lyn Evans, *op. cit.*, personal recollections, *op. cit.*
77. Don Hayward interview, *op. cit.*
78. Information from NCB (S. Wales Area), Public Relations Department.
79. Harold Wilson, *New Deal for Coal* (1944); W. Paynter, *My Generation* (1972). Rather revealingly, given the importance of the miners in the development of the Labour party, Wilson made very few direct references to the coal industry in his mammoth account of the period, *The Labour Government 1964–1970: A Personal Record* (1971).
80. Lord Robens, *Ten Year Stint* (1972), pp. 221–2; *Fuel Policy* (HMSO, Cmnd 3438, November 1967).
81. NUM (S. Wales Area) EC minutes, 1959–68; W. Paynter, *My Generation, op. cit.*; Peter Evans *op. cit.*
82. For a development of this argument, see David Reynolds, 'Planning a Future for Rhondda's People' in K. S. Hopkins (ed.), *Rhondda Past and Future* (1975), pp. 254–6.
83. C. Cook and J. Ramsden, *By-Elections in British Politics* (1973), pp. 230–57.
84. For a fuller account of the changing employment pattern in the economy in this period, see G. Humphreys, *op. cit. passim*; G. Humphreys, 'Industrial Change: Lessons from South Wales', in *Geography*, Vol. 61, part 4, November 1976, pp. 246–54.
85. 'Duw It's Hard' from the EMI long-playing record of Max Boyce, *'Live' at Treorchy* (1974).
86. For an interesting comparison, see Martin Bulmer (ed.), *Mining and Social Change: Durham County in the Twentieth Century* (1978), pp. 235–84; H. M. Lewis, L. Johnson and D. Askins (eds), *Colonialism in Modern America: The Appalachian Case* (1978).
87. For a fuller account of the demise of Welfare Halls, see Hywel Francis, 'Survey of Miners' Institute and Welfare Hall Libraries' in *Llafur*, Vol. 1, No. 2, May 1973, pp. 35–61.
88. Robert Morgan, 'Miners' Library, South Wales' in *On the Banks of the Cynon* (1975), p. 8.
89. W. Paynter, *The 'Fed', op. cit. passim*; John Sewel, *Colliery Closure and Social Change* (1975), pp. 74–81.
90. Sewel, *ibid. passim*; a friend of one of the authors had worked at Onllwyn No. 1, Abercrave, Dillwyn, Cefn Coed and Blaenant by the time he was twenty-two years of age.
91. Sewel, *ibid.*, p. 25.
92. Stephen W. Town, *After The Mines: Changing Employment Opportunities in a South Wales Mining Valley* (1975), pp. 91–2.
93. *Ibid.*, pp. 93–4.
94. Graham Gardner, 'The Changing Pattern of Industry and the Problems Caused'

(with particular reference to Abercarn and Risca, n.d.), p. 12 (copy at the SWML).

95. SWML interview with Del Davies (Abercrave), 9 May 1974. Much of this information is also based on the personal recollections of the authors and our discussions with miners at all levels of the union in South Wales during the 1960s and 1970s.

96. David Francis interview, *op. cit.*

97. See Julian Hart, 'The Forgotten War – Health in the Valleys' in *Medicine in Society*, Vol. 3, No. 3, pp. 3–6; Teresa L. Rees, 'Population and Industrial Decline in the South Wales Coalfield' in *Regional Studies*, Vol. 12, pp. 69–77.

98. Lyndon James, 'The Six Bells Inquiry' in *The Miner*, Vol. 9, No. 2, of March/April 1961, pp. 14–20; for a history of mining disasters, see Helen and Baron Duckham, *Great Pit Disasters: Great Britain to the Present Day* (1973).

99. David Francis, 'The Disaster at Cambrian Colliery' in *The Miner*, May/June 1965, pp. 1–6; NUM (South Wales Area) EC *Annual Report, 1965–6*, bound minutes, pp. 85–162 *passim*.

100. Joan Miller, *Aberfan: A Disaster and its Aftermath* (1974), p. 17; Duckham, *op. cit.*, p. 208.

101. NUM (South Wales Area), *Spoil Tip Stability*, a Lecture by Mr L. R. James (pamphlet, May 1967), p. 3; Miller, *ibid.*, p. 36.

102. Miller, *ibid.*, p. 28, pp. 53–62.

103. One academic claimed in his study of the closure of National Colliery, Wattstown, 'The result of the cost/benefit analysis can only be tentative, but seems to indicate that society benefits from this particular pit closure, and perhaps from pit closures in general. Many of the miners interviewed were, surprisingly perhaps, glad that the pit had closed.' As far as the Lower Rhondda is concerned (where the colliery was located), the harmful effects of the closure on 'society' became increasingly evident with the passing of time. (A. V. Galt, 'Closing a Colliery' in *Planet*, No. 3, December 1970/January 1971, pp. 20–4).

104. Information from NCB (South Wales Area) Public Relations Department. Investment policies, however, require closer examination. It has been argued that Deep Duffryn's crisis in 1978–9 was caused by lack of investment in the 1960s.

105. D. Gidwell, *op. cit.*, pp. 44–57.

106. NUM (South Wales Area) minutes, 1965–6 *passim*. Even amongst many young miners in the late 1970s, 'taking a lamp' (becoming a colliery official) meant 'that you have gone over to the other side'.

107. NUM (South Wales Area) EC *Annual Report, 1968–9*, bound minutes, p. 5. When George Thomas, MP, Minister of State of Welsh Affairs, met the South Wales EC, on 10 September 1966, he was reminded of the history of the miners: 'Had it not been for the mining areas, the Labour Party in 1931 would have passed into oblivion. Surely we had the right to better treatment than this.' Only Brynlliw and Penallta survived closure threats but these victories occurred when the energy situation had changed.

108. Illtyd Harrington, 'The Generation Gap at the Miners' Gala' in *Tribune*, 18 June 1971.

109. This account of events in 1969 is largely based on the NUM (South Wales Area) bound minutes, *passim*, and discussions with those involved in the strike, notably Don Hayward (Coedely), Emlyn Jenkins (Lady Windsor), Ron Saint (Coedely)

and Dane Hartwell (Tower), now secretary of Blaengwrach Lodge who told one of the authors about the second 'October Revolution'. One of the authors was tape-recording International Brigaders in Bedlinog on the day the 'surfacemen's' strike began. The talk in the village was full of references to the struggle against 'scab' unionism in the 1930s at the nearby Taff-Merthyr Colliery in 'the last strike': this was one of the main reasons given by older miners for militancy at 'Taff' over surfacemen's hours in 1969. The nine lodges which led the unofficial action were Coedely, Cwm, Deep Navigation, Fernhill, Lady Windsor, Mardy, Taff-Merthyr, Tower and Wern Tarw.

110. For a thought-provoking discussion of the historical significance of 1970–4, see Royden Harrison's Introduction to *Independent Collier* (1978).

111. *Western Mail*, 10 November 1970.

112. *Morning Star*, 10 November 1970. For a fuller account of Lord Robens's attitude, see his *Ten Year Stint, op. cit.*, pp. 14–39.

113. For a comprehensive description of the 1969–70 period, see the NUM (S. Wales Area) bound minutes, 1969–71 *passim*.

114. The strike is so important that one working miner, Malcolm Pitt, has written a book entirely on the role of the Kent miners in the dispute. Entitled *The World on Our Backs: The Kent Miners and the 1972 Miners' Strike* (1979), it graphically reveals the critical part played by one of the smallest coalfields.

115. This account is based upon a press chronology compiled by David Egan for the South Wales Coalfield History Project; 'The Story of the Miners' Strike' in *Labour Research*, Vol. 61, No. 4, April 1972, pp. 66–75; John Hughes and Roy Moore (eds), *A Special Case?: Social Justice and the Miners* (1972); Minutes of the South Wales Area NUM; and interviews and conversations with several South Wales miners.

116. Accounts of such conversations could be repeated many times over. This particular exchange is said to have occurred between Haydn Matthews, lodge secretary at Mardy, and his son Wayne, a youth representative on the lodge. So appalled was the colliery manager with the treatment 'his' miners had received at Saltley at the feet of the police, he offered them the keys to their lockers so that they could return to the picket line properly shod. The 'comfortable' synthesis of class and community (brought about mainly by the action of the miners' union) in South Wales coalfield society is an enduring theme which deserves greater exploration than provided in this book.

117. NUM (S. Wales Area) minutes, 1974, *passim*; L. Berkovitch, *op. cit.*, pp. 175–83; D. Francis interview, *op. cit.*

118. Alun Morgan, 'The 1970 Parliamentary Election at Merthyr Tydfil' in *Morgannwg*, 1979, pp. 61–81. Only one other Conservative lost his deposit outside South Wales.

119. See NUM (S. Wales Area) minutes, 1970–4 *passim*.

120. The subsequent development of the Wales TUC has not been without its critics, but it is undeniable that it is potentially the most important forum for the working class in Wales.

121. I. Berkovitch, *op. cit.*, pp. 184–5; see also the Department of Energy's *Coal for the Future: Progress with 'Plan for Coal' and Prospects to the Year 2000* (n.d.) and *Coal Technology: Future Developments in Conversion, Utilisation and Unconventional Mining in the United Kingdom* (n.d.).

122. For a review of this, see Bert Pearce, 'Why the Miners must Fight', *Morning Star*, 30 March 1979.

123. This was said by Emlyn Williams, president of the South Wales miners, in opening the NUM residential course at the South Wales Miners' Library, 11 September 1978.

124. NUM (S. Wales Area), *Annual Conference President's Address* (1976), pp. 5–6.

125. NUM, *Report of a Discussion Forum . . . [on] Industrial Democracy* (6–7 December 1977), pp. 851–3. For the historical background, see Ken Coates (ed.), *Democracy in the Mines* (1974).

126. For evidence of these concerns, see NUM (S. Wales Area) minutes, 1974–9 *passim*; in particular, see *Coal Workers Pneumoconiosis, Emphysema and Bronchitis* (n.d.) being a Report to the NUM by a panel of five medical doctors. The first craftsman to be elected as a central official of the union came in 1976: George Rees' election as general secretary marked an important point of departure reflecting the changing nature of the industry, but there was also an element of continuity in that he was the third successive Communist to hold the position.

127. Quoted from the resolution passed by a public meeting called by Cynon Valley NUM lodges, 25 March 1979. The resolution was part of one of the documents presented to the NEC of the NUM on 12 April 1979 by Arfon Evans, Mike Griffin and Peter Evans, officers of the Aberdare and Rhondda Joint NUM lodges. See *Morning Star*, 26 March 1979; *Western Mail*, 11 April 1979.

128. From a lecture given by Peter Evans, chairman Deep Duffryn NUM Lodge. Entitled 'Communities in Crisis Today: Deep Duffryn Colliery and Mountain Ash', it was delivered at the annual Wales TUC *Llafur* week-end school at University College Swansea on 6–8 April 1979. The Deep Duffryn miners have been offered alternative work at other collieries located within ten miles. There is no alternative local work in other industries. Jobs lost through redundancies and closures in the Cynon Valley totalled almost 1,500 in 1978, four to five times greater than 1975 and 1977 (see Cynon Valley Action Committee against Colliery Closures file deposited at the SWML).

129. For accounts of the reactions to the report of the Coal Industry Tripartite Group Sub-Committee on the South Wales coalfield which provoked the fears, see *Coal News*, April 1979; *Guardian*, 31 March 1979. The report, whilst it did not specify any closures, put great emphasis on reasonable viability by 1983–4. The announcement of the proposed investment plan of £200 million (including £80 million for the Margam 'super mine') in no way diminished the anxieties for the coalfield.

130. Robert Morgan, *op. cit.*, pp. 8–9.

APPENDICES

APPENDIX I

SWMF Lodges in January 1926

Anthracite District

Pontyberem, Great Mountain, Seven Sisters, Onllwyn, Emlyn, Trimsaran, Pentremawr, Rhos, Ammanford No. 2, Park, Crynant, Hendreladis, Brynhenllys, Gellyceidrim, Pwllbach, Ponthenry, Blaenywaun, International, Cross Hands, Dillwyn, Cawdor, Abercrave, Caerbryn, Gwaunclawdd, Gwauncaegurwen, Tirydail, Tirbach, Gwendraeth, New Cwmgors, Llwynon, Gurnos, Gilwen, New Cwmmawr, Ystradfawr, Carway, Diamond, Black Mountain, Pantyffynnon, Brynteg, Llandebie, Wernos, Maesmarchog, Tarreni, Amman Valley, Lamb, Ynysgeinon, Dulais, Cwmllynfell, Raven, Ynysdawela, New Dynant, Gwys, Rhosamman, Blaenhirwaun, Saundersfoot, Coedamman, Pontyclerc, Rock, Hook, Sylen, New Brook, Duke, Ystalyfera, Rhiw, Cwmnantmoel, Brynderi, Cwmtawe, Lower Cwmtawe, Mynydd Bach, Glantwrch, Gorsgoch.

Aberdare District

Aberaman, Blaenant, Blaengwawr, Bwllfa, British Rhondda, Bwllfa No. 3, Cwmaman, Cwmneol, Dyllas, Enginemen, Stokers and Craftsmen, Fforchaman, Lower Duffryn, Llwynhelyg, Nantmelyn, River Level, Tower, Tirherbert, Windber, Werfa Dare.

Afan Valley District

Corrwg Vale, Cwmmawr, Merthyr Llantwit, Duffryn Rhondda Pits, Glenavon, North Rhondda, Glyncymmer, Glyncorrwg, Abergwynfi, Argoed, Oakwood, North End, Oakland, Nantewlaeth, Blaenmawr, Ynyslas, Craiglyn, Maesmelyn, Llwynffynnon, Glyncastle, Court Herbert, Aberpergwm, Gored Merthyr, Brynderwen, Empire, Villiers, Glyn Merthyr, Bryncoch, Cilfrew, Neath E. and S., Craignedd, Clyne Merthyr, Premier Merthyr, Rhydygau, Dulais Mountain, Glyn Neath Enginemen, Blaengwrach.

Blaina District

Beynon Lodge, Clydach Lodge, Red Ash, Dyffryn Lodge, Lion Slope, East Red Ash.

Dowlais District

Taff-Merthyr, Nantwen (Dowlais), Nantwen (Bedlinog), Brithdir Levels.

East Glamorgan District

Llanbradach, Senghenydd, Abertridwr, Penallta, Bedwas, Blackbrook, Bedwas Mechanical.

Eastern Valleys District

Varteg United, Rose of Cwmsychan, Llanerch, Tirpentwys, Blaendare, Cwmbran, Glyn Pontypool, Elled, Blaenserchan, Gwenallt, Oldside Blaenavon, New Side Blaenavon, Pwlldu, Lanelly Hill, Talywain Red Ash, Crumlin Valley, Eastern Valley, Baldwins, Glyn Tillery, Llanerch Craftsmen, Blaenavon Craftsmen, Blaenavon By-Product.

Ebbw Vale District

Red Ash, No. 1 Marine, No. 2 Marine, Marine Surface, Cwm Enginemen, Ebbw Vale Enginemen, Clay Level, Prince of Wales, No. 1 Waun Lwyd, No. 2 Waun Lwyd, By-Product, Tradesmen's.

Garw District

International, Garw Ocean, Ffaldau, Ton Phillip, Aberbaiden, Cribbwr Fawr, Coytrahen, Nanthir, Raglan, Meiros, Llanelay, Llest No. 1, Wern Tarw, Tynywaun, Maendy, Bryncae.

Maesteg District

Avon Ocean, Caerau, Coegnant, Maesteg Deep, Maesteg Merthyr, Garth, Llangynwyd, Bryn, Cefn-y-Bryn, Cwmdu, Tondu Artizans, Bryn Mercantile, Cwmduffryn, Cwmgwynen, Glenhafod, Llynfi Sundries.

Merthyr District

South Pit No. 2, South Pit No. 1, Graig Pit and Levels, Castle Pit and Levels, Thomas Merthyr, Mechanical, Dowlais Paying Station.

Monmouth Western Valleys District

Celynen South, Llanhilleth, Cwmtillery, Abercarn, Rose Heyworth, Arrail Griffin Joint, Vivian, Tillery, Gray, Crumlin Navigation, North Celynen, Cwmcarn, Aberbeeg, Cwm, Aberbeeg South, Kendon, Arail, Twyn Gwyn, Llandawel, Penyfan, Llanhilleth H. C., New Havod Van.

Ogmore and Gilfach District

Nantymoel, Dinas Main, Britannic, Wyndham, Lower Gilfach, Penllwyngwent, Rhondda Main, Trane, South Rhondda, Mechanical Section, G. Mechanical Section, Brynniau Gwynion, R. M. Mechanical Section.

Pontypridd District

Pentre, Maritime, Lady Windsor, Rockwood, Abercynon, Hafod, Coedcae, Great Western, Mynachdy, Llanharry, Nantgarw, Cwm Llantwit, Pwllgwaun, Abercynon Mechanical, Darranddu.

Rhondda No. 1 District

Hendrewen, Bute Merthyr, Cilely, Mardy, Fernhill, Naval, Tylorstown, Coedely, Gelli, Parc and Dare, National, Tynybedw, Maindy and Eastern, Abergorky, Ferndale, Llwynypia, Albion, Ynysfaio, Standard, Blaenclydach, Cymmer, Lewis Merthyr, Cambrian, Tydraw, Lady Lewis.

Rhymney Valley District

Elliots, Bedwas, New Tredegar, Gilfach, Abertysswg, Bargoed Steam, Bargoed H.C., Pengam, Maesycwmmer, Groesfaen, Britannia, Mardy, Ogilvie, Barracks Level, Rhymney Engine, Gelly Haf, Rhymney Convenience.

Taff and Cynon District

Deep Dyffryn, Navigation, Cwm Cynon, Mechanical Workers, Penrhiwceiber, Merthyr Vale, Troedyrhiw, Aberfan, Treharris, Trelewis, Graig, Nelson, Bedlinog.

Tredegar Valley District

Tredegar Combine, Markham, Abernant, Llanover, Oakdale, Rock, Gelli, Nine Mile Point, Risca, St David's, Argoed, Sirhowy.

Western District

Primrose, Clydach Merthyr, Cae Duke, Killan, Mynydd Newydd, Broadoak, Birchrock, Copper Pit, Birchgrove, Glynea, Morlais, Trebanos, Burry Port, Tirdonkin, Berthlwyd, Torygraig, Mountain, Garngoch No. 3, Hills, Bryn Lliw, New Pool, Acorn, Samlet, Pentre, Garngoch No. 1, Mooretown, Glais, Beili Glas, Marchhywel, Western, Llan Morlais, Ashburnam, Lon Lâs, Moody, Elms, Cefn Caeau, Talyclun.

Source: SWMF, *Directory for 1926.*

'Dictated Terms', 1926

Mr E. Morrell:	. . . Am I to gather from what you have said that you have made up your mind on the question of hours, and that it is not a matter for discussion?
Mr Evan Williams:	I have not said that that is not a matter of discussion, but what I do want to convey to you is this, that there is no possibility of any discussion changing our attitude in regard to the question of hours. . . . Upon no other foundation [i.e. increasing hours], to my mind, is it possible for us to get conditions anything like those of prosperity in the industry, or which will enable work to be given regularly to the men.
Mr E. Morrell:	May I say, Mr Evan Williams, that I congratulate you upon your ability to force this Government to give you a permissive Act of Parliament – an Act of Parliament permitting eight hours to be worked; but the inference largely which would be drawn by anyone reading that Act is that the necessity for it had to be more or less demonstrated. . . .
Mr Evan Williams:	The welfare argument does not appeal to me very much, although if we were asking you to work twelve hours a day, it might. There has been a tendency growing in this country, and in this country only, I think, to treat work as the least important thing in the day, and pleasure as the most important thing.
Mr T. Richards:	You are speaking for your own class.
Mr Evan Williams:	The tendency in this country is to look upon work as something to be got through as quickly as possible.
Mr T. Richards:	We agree that.
Mr E. Morrell:	You are now putting your finger on the spot, Mr Evan Williams.
Mr Evan Williams:	Yes, I am, and I can assure you that if it applies to what you call my class, it applies with greater force to your class, because there are so many of you. . . . I can tell you that if it does not apply to me I should be glad to get off

with an eight hours day, as a good many others on this side of the table would. . . . I do not think we should be occupying ourselves usefully if we went on discussing this question. You may say that we are presenting you with a proposition which is not to be discussed, but we do not present it in that form. . . .

Mr E. Morrell: . . . Are you prepared to put the hours question to arbitration?

Mr Evan Williams: No.

Mr E. Morrell: Definitely no?

Mr Evan Williams: Definitely no.

Mr Oliver Harris: That is because they have no case, Mr Morrell.

Mr T. Richards: What you want is your full pound of flesh. That is the impression we have got, and if that is wrong, we want you to try and remove that impression from our minds.

Mr Evan Williams: If that reproach is made to us, I am sorry, but I am not prepared to attempt to remove it by doing the whole district the gravest injustice it could ever have done to it.

Mr T. Richards: Then you have no regard for some permanent, or, at any rate, *some* period of peace.

Mr Evan Williams: *This* is the only basis upon which a permanent peace is possible.

Mr S. O. Davies: You will not get a permanent peace if you talk like you have been doing this afternoon.

Mr. E. Morrell: It seems to me my task this afternoon is a very hopeless one – it seems to me to be hopeless to attempt to get any measure of mutuality as between the two sides of the Board. I have attempted to put one other view to you, and that is in regard to the men working a short shift on Saturdays – a five hours' shift.

Mr Evan Williams: Mr Morrell, as I have said, we have considered this matter very carefully, and our offer is based upon a full eight hours shift every day of the week, and any reduction from that must be compensated for in some other way.

Mr John Thomas: Do you realise your offer means that from Monday morning until Saturday night many men will be away from their home for twelve hours each day owing to the economic conditions under which we are labouring at the present time, which are caused by the shortage of houses, and so forth? There are men working in my district who start from Merthyr at six o'clock every morning, and start back to Merthyr from Glyn-Neath every day at half-past three. Under your proposal it means that for six days every week they will be away from their homes twelve

502   THE FED

hours a day. Surely there is some kind of humanity on your side. Some of you in the past have intimated that you would be willing to consider this phase of the matter so far as a short shift on Saturdays is concerned.

Mr T. Richards: The same thing as Mr John Thomas has mentioned obtains in several of the Monmouthshire valleys.

Mr John Thomas: That is so.

Mr Hubert Jenkins: The men go right over the coalfield, more or less, to their work, and back again to their homes.

Mr Evan Williams: We have made no provision in the offer we have put to you for anything less than a full eight hours' work on each day of the week.

Mr A. L. Horner: Are you not prepared to let us have the figures and the calculations which have determined you in your actions, which Mr Ted Williams has asked for twice this afternoon? You say you have come to certain conclusions on your figures; cannot we see those figures?

Mr Evan Williams: We have not them this afternoon.

Mr A. L. Horner: Can we have them?

Mr Evan Williams: I think there is no difficulty in your getting all the information in that regard which you want from the evidence which was given to the Royal Commission; it is all there.

Mr A. L. Horner: That brings us to an entirely different conclusion to the conclusion it brings you to.

Mr Evan Williams: Then I am afraid any figures I might put to you today might have no better effect.

Mr S. O. Davies: You could not produce them.

Mr James Griffiths: Speaking as a practical miner, I am sure that if the suggestion of a short day on Saturdays was put to the managers in the coalfield, there would be a unanimous vote for it by them.

Mr Evan Williams: We are in a position to know the feeling of the managers in regard to this matter better than you are.

Mr E. Morrell: I think I ought to tell you, Mr Evan Williams, that in regard to the Agreement we are not likely to consider your suggestion of five years. It will have to be of a considerable shorter duration than that in any case. I join with you that you do want stability and you do want a measure of security, but, as I have told you before, and as I tell you again, there must be two parties to carrying on this industry, and unless they can come to something like a reasonable understanding, I do not think the industry can be prosperous.

Mr Evan Williams:	I quite agree with you, Mr Morrell. I do not think it is possible for the industry to be prosperous unless the terms of employment in it are such as are likely to give regular work to the men.
Mr T. Richards:	You remind me of Mabon's old Dowlais man who worked at Dowlais for four days a week, and then went to the Rhondda because he got work every day and was satisfied, although his wages were less!
Mr E. Morrell:	Will you reconsider your attitude, if we separate for an hour or two, Mr Evan Williams?
Mr Evan Williams:	No, Mr Morrell.
Mr E. Morrell:	Very well.
Mr Evan Williams:	I indicated to you last week, when we dealt with the Customs Clause, there might be something else which we should have to put before you. We do not want to alter what we consider is the position in the coalfield at all –
Mr T. Richards:	We must see your suggested alteration before it is made. We cannot promise to agree now to any such alteration. You seem to have the most rapacious appetites.
Mr Evan Williams:	There is no rapacity about us at all.
Mr T. Richards:	The Customs Clause has not in the past given us what it ought to have given us many times, but we are prepared for it to remain without there being any attempt to meddle with it – and that applies to everything we have not discussed here.
Mr S. O. Davies:	What you really want is a new Customs Clause in the Agreement, Mr Evan Williams. The old Customs Clause is very simple and you cannot possibly qualify it if it is your intention to observe the old customs in regard to the men's conditions of employment.
Mr T. Richards:	I do not think we had better discuss this further. We cannot discuss any further changes. We have agreed to the changes you wanted made, and we cannot discuss anything further now. If these things are to be sprung on us, we shall soon be in the same position as Lloyd George was in 1915 when I met him at twelve o'clock at night at the Park Hotel with his coat collar turned up to his ears marching backwards and forwards. I said to him: 'What is the matter?' and he said: 'Another damned point.'
Mr E. Morrell:	What I had in my mind was this. The afternoon shift men if they want to go away from home for Christmas would not be able to do so in very many cases if they have to work that shift, and it would be rather a pity for them to be penalised –

Mr Evan Williams:	That has always been the position – and it may be a great deal more necessary now for the afternoon shift to work than it has been on previous occasions.
Mr E. Morrell:	Well, I cannot say more than I have said in regard to the matter.
Mr Evan Williams:	Neither can I.
Mr E. Morrell:	I have told you exactly what I feel. I am jolly well ashamed of signing *this* Agreement, but I am prepared to sign it.

Source: Extracted from *Minutes of Proceedings* at meetings of representatives of the Monmouthshire and South Wales Coalowners' Association (MSWCA) and the South Wales Miners' Federation (SWMF), 23 November 1926–18 January 1927 (Revision of Conciliation Board Agreement, 1926) *passim*. Those in the extracted text are Evan Williams, secretary of the MSWCA; Enoch Morrell, president of the SWMF; Tom Richards, general secretary of the SWMF; Oliver Harris, treasurer of the SWMF; A. L. Horner, EC member of the SWMF and the MFGB; John Thomas, Hubert Jenkins, James Griffiths, all miners' agents; S. O. Davies, vice-president of the SWMF and miners' agent.

SWMF Report on Conditions in their Various Districts following the 1926 Lock-out

District	Colliery	Synopsis of conditions
Anthracite	Gelliceidrim	Owners refuse to start work until Price List has been settled. This has been in hands of conciliators up to April 30th 1926.
	Emlyn	Refuse reinstatement until a revised List on Conveyor system is agreed to.
	Blaencaegurwen	Men presented themselves for work but they would not be reinstated until they accept a list of concessions in wages and other conditions.
	Hook	Forty to forty-five men idle in consequence of other men filling their places.
Garw	Ocean	Lodge Officials not reinstated.
	Ton Philip	Company refuse to meet Lodge Secretary or allow him on premises.
	Cribbwr Fawr	Committee-men who have not resumed their employment not recognised by Company.
	Newlands	Company only recognise Lodge Officials who have resumed work.
	Meiros	This Colliery is full up, and has been for quite two months before the settlement. Hundreds of strangers have been employed, and at least 300 of the old workmen are still out. The Co. refuse to recognise the Lodge Officials, none of whom have secured work. It is reported that the men have set up some kind of an Union which has no connection whatever with the SWMF.
	Raglan	This colliery is full up, and the same state of affairs exist as at Meiros, but it is definite that

District	Colliery	Synopsis of conditions
		at this colliery men have formed an Organisation of some kind, and one of the declared objects is to work in harmony with the Co. and to look upon them as their friends, and not their enemies as they have done in the past. The Co. have given every facility to the men and the Lodge Secretary is ignored both by the men employed and by the Co.
	Wern Tarw	The colliery is full, mostly strangers. The Co. refuse to recognise the full time Secretary and contend that he does not represent the men at present employed at the coliery.
	Lanelay	The colliery is full, mostly strangers. None of the Lodge Officials are recognised, and they have been told that their services will not be needed any longer.
	Bryncae	This colliery is full up, mostly strangers, of whom a large number started some time prior to the settlement. Lodge Officials are recognised, but have not yet been able to resume their employment.
Ogmore and Gilfach	Gilfach Goch Joint Committee	Ask for Conference for purpose of protesting against method of reinstating the workmen, and several other complaints.
Rhondda No. 1		The management of the collieries within this District seem to be pursuing a common policy based upon a desire to insist upon a distinction between re-employment and re-instatement, and to give weight and emphasis to their authority to take either course. In doing so, at the majority of the collieries men who might have resumed in their own working places have been prevented and others put in their stead. The men thus discriminated have been either Lodge Officials, or have been active during the Lock-out, and this is interpreted as evidence of spite and revenge on the part of the management. Feeling in the District running very high.
Western	Mountain	Committee-men and Lodge Officials not reinstated. Active members kept idle and their places filled with men who had never seen a colliery before. Demand for Conference.

District	*Colliery*	*Synopsis of conditions*
Ogmore and Gilfach		General victimisation of men who have been active during the stoppage; told definitely that there is no work for them at any time. No member of Communist Party has been employed up to the present time. At most collieries men are not employed in their former working places as they become available. Management exercise their right to re-employ them as they think fit. Serious interference with old customs and practices.

Source: UCS, SWMF bound circulars, 13 December 1926.

Annual Manpower and Saleable Output of the South Wales Coalfield, 1890–1978

Year	Manpower	Tons		Year	Manpower	Tons
1890	109,935	29,415,000		1935	131,697	35,025,000
1891	116,624	29,993,000		1936	126,233	33,886,000
1892	117,713	31,207,000		1937	135,901	37,773,000
1893	117,989	30,155,000		1938	134,824	35,293,000
1894	124,655	33,418,000		1939	128,774	35,269,000
1895	126,199	33,040,000		1940	128,470	32,352,000
1896	125,205	33,868,000		1941	111,647	27,426,000
1897	126,802	35,806,000		1942	114,181	26,723,000
1898	128,813	26,724,000		1943	114,274	25,116,000
1899	132,682	39,870,000		1944	112,343	22,393,000
1900	147,652	39,328,000		1945	110,057	20,470,000
1901	150,412	39,209,000		1946	107,624	20,950,000
1902	154,571	41,306,000		1947	108,000	22,712,000
1903	159,161	42,154,000		1948	108,000	23,913,000
1904	163,034	43,730,000		1949	106,000	24,209,000
1905	165,609	43,203,000		1950	102,000	24,314,000
1906	174,660	47,056,000		1951	102,000	24,669,000
1907	190,263	49,978,000		1952	104,000	25,012,000
1908	201,752	50,227,000		1953	104,000	24,963,000
1909	204,984	50,364,000		1954	103,000	25,059,000
1910	213,252	48,700,000		1955	101,000	24,227,000
1911	220,593	50,201,000		1956	100,000	24,140,000
1912	225,213	50,116,000		1957	101,000	24,269,000
1913	232,800	56,830,000		1958	99,000	22,822,000
1914	221,545	53,880,000		1959	93,000	21,192,000
1915	202,147	50,453,000	FD	1960	84,000	19,537,792
1916	213,674	52,081,000		1961	81,000	18,398,540
1917	219,225	48,508,000		1962	79,000	19,349,697
1918	218,554	46,717,000		1963	77,000	19,367,201
1919	257,002	47,552,000		1964	72,000	18,827,020
1920	271,161	46,249,000		1965	64,000	16,771,135
1921	232,043	30,572,000		1966	58,000	16,384,535
1922	243,015	50,325,000		1967	53,000	15,746,000
1923	252,617	54,252,000		1968	48,000	14,505,748
1924	250,065	51,085,000		1969	40,000	12,788,223
1925	217,809	44,630,000		1970	38,000	11,685,478
1926	156,381	20,273,000		1971	36,000	9,665,305
1927	194,100	46,256,000		1972	34,000	10,808,839
1928	168,269	43,312,000	S	1973	31,000	7,349,729
1929	178,315	48,150,000		1974	31,455	8,631,767
1930	172,870	45,108,000		1975	30,483	8,437,237
1931	158,162	37,085,000		1976	29,997	7,785,000
1932	145,709	34,874,000		1977	28,965	7,445,560
1933	142,900	34,355,000		1978	27,384	7,624,876
1934	139,806	35,173,000				

From 1963–4 onwards figures are shown for fiscal years (April to March).
FD = Final closure Forest of Dean coalfield.
 S = Final closure Somerset coalfield.

Source: National Coal Board, South Wales Public Relations Department.

Colliery Closures – South Wales, Forest of Dean and Somerset Coalfields, 1947–79

1947

Blaenclydach, Charmborough, Cynon, Erskine, Llanerch, Llanmarch, North Rhondda No. 2, Penrhys, Rhiwcolbren No. 3   9

1948

Broad Oak, Cwmhneol, Glanamman, Hook, Islwyn, Mardy, Maindy, Nantewlaeth, New Gellihir, Pwllgwaun, West Blaina   11

1949

Blaendare, Brithdir, Coalpit Heath, Cwm Cynon, Eryl Bryn, Glynogwr, Marsh Lane, Pontyberem, Tareni, Werfa Dare, Wen Fawr   11

1950

Camerton, Cilely, Rhiw Colbren No. 2   3

1951

NIL   –

1952

Garngoch No. 1, Talyclun   2

1953

Oaklands, Pidwellt, Pwll, Rhas   4

1954

Brynteg, Radstock, Trimsaran   3

1955

Brynhenllys, Lucy Thomas, Mynydd Maen, Ynysarwed, Mynydd Newydd   5

1956

Bedlinog, Crynant, Deakins Red Ash, Pengam, Saron   5

1957

Deakins Slope, Gelliceidrim, Rock (Mon.), Ystalyfera   4

1958

Glenhafod, Llandybie, Naval, Pensford, Tirherbert   5

1959

Aberbaiden, Arthur and Edward, Cwmllynfell, Eastern United, Ferndale
No. 5, Garth Merthyr, Glengarw, Mount, Pentre, Steer, Ty Trist, Tydraw   12

1960

Britannic, Cannop, Hendy Merthyr, North Rhondda, Tylorstown No. 9,
Carway, Rock (Glam.)   7

1961

Clydach Merthyr, Graig Fawr, Llanbradach, Maritime   4

1962–3

Aberaman, Blaenhirwaun, East, Gelli, Great Mountain, Llanharan, New
Cross Hands, Onllwyn No. 3, Princess Royal   9

1963–4

Cwmgwrach, Bryn, Ffaldydre, Harry Stoke, New Rockwood, Seven
Sisters   6

1964–5

Cwmgorse, Daren, Garth Tonmawr, Nine Mile Point, Norchard,
Onllwyn No. 1, Pochin, Rhigos, Varteg, Wern Tarw   10

1965–6

Glyncastle, Fforchaman, Felinfran, Wernos, Aberbeeg South, Northern
United, Garngoch No. 3, Parc, Pwllbach, Norton Hill   10

1966–7

Dillwyn, Old Mills, Cambrian, Glenrhondda, Albion, Risca, Duffryn
Rhondda, Abercrave   8

1967–8

Elliot, Abergorki, Crumlin, Wyllie, Pentreclwydau, International,
Newlands, Ynyscedwyn   8

1968–9

Cwmcarn, Groesfaen, Llanhilleth, New Rock, Cefn Coed, National,
Pantyffynon, Penllwyngwent   8

1969–70

Tirpentwys, Waterloo, Avon, Mountain   4

1970–1

Glyncorrwg   1

1971–2

NIL   –

1972–3

NIL   –

1973–4

Coed Cae, Kilmersdon   2

1974–5

Ogilvie   1

1975–6

Beynon, Glyntillery   2

1976–7

Ammanford No. 2   1

1977–8

Bargoed   1

1978–9

Graig Merthyr, Caerau   2

Source: National Coal Board, South Wales Public Relations Department.

Chief Officials of the South Wales Miners 1898–1979

Presidents

William Abraham	1898 to 1912
William Brace	1912 to 1915
James Winstone	1915 to 1922
Vernon Hartshorn	1922 to 1924
Enoch Morrell	1924 to 1934
James Griffiths	1934 to 1936
Arthur L. Horner	1936 to 1946
Alf Davies	1946 to 1951
William Paynter	1951 to 1959
William Whitehead	1959 to 1966
Glyn Williams	1966 to 1973
Emlyn Williams	1973 to date

General Secretaries

Thomas Richards	1898 to 1931
Oliver Harris	1931 to 1941
Evan Williams	1941 to 1943
W. J. Saddler*	1943 to 1946
Evan Williams	1946 to 1947
William Arthur	1947 to 1951
W. H. Crews	1951 to 1958
D. D. Evans	1958 to 1963
David Francis	1963 to 1976
George Rees	1976 to date

* Acting General Secretary (appointed by the EC during Evan Williams' absence)

APPENDIX VII

NUM (South Wales Area) Lodges in January 1979

Swansea District

Abernant, Amman Valley and Rhiwfawr (licensed mine), Betws, Blaenant, Blaengwrach, Brynlliw, Cwmgwili, Cynheidre, Dulais (licensed mine), Graig Merthyr, Morlais, Pantyffynnon, Resolven (licensed mine), Swansea Valley (licensed mine), Treforgan, Vale of Neath (Aberpergwm), Winding Enginemen (West Wales).

Maesteg District

Coedely, Coegnant, Cwm, Garw Valley, Lynfi Sundries, Ogmore Valley, St John's, Tondu Artisans.

Aberdare, Rhondda and Merthyr District

Abercynon, Bedlinog (Trelewis Drift), Deep Duffryn, Deep Navigation, Fernhill, Lady Windsor, Lewis Merthyr, Mardy, Merthyr Vale, Mountain Ash Mechanical, Nantgarw, Penrhiwceiber, Taff Merthyr, Tower, Tymawr, Winding Enginemen (East Wales).

Rhymney District

Bargoed Surface, Bedwas, Britannia, Markham, Oakdale, Penallta, Tredegar Combine.

Monmouthshire District

Six Bells (Arrael Griffin), Blaenavon, Blaenserchan, Celynen North, Celynen South, Cwmtillery, Marine, Roseheyworth, Crumlin (licensed mine).

Source: NUM (South Wales Area) Directory, 1979.

A Note on Sources

We provided detailed notes on sources at the end of each chapter because much of the material we used had only recently been collected and made available. Whilst useful collections exist at the National Library of Wales and at the South Wales record offices, the main Archive of the South Wales miners is at the library of University of Wales Swansea: comprehensive printed guides to the collection are now available at the Archive. Similarly, details of the holdings of the South Wales Miners' Library (including books, pamphlets, journals, newspapers, leaflets, posters and maps) can be obtained from the librarian at Hendrefoelan House, Hendrefoelan, Gower Road, Swansea, SA2 7NB.

A number of valuable bibliographies on the coalfield have been published. In particular, one compiled by John Benson and Robert G. Neville entitled 'A Bibliography of the Coal Industry in Wales' is to be found in *Llafur*, Vol. 2 No. 4, Spring 1979. Also available are:

T. Baggs, P. H. Ballard and P. Vining, *The South Wales Valleys: A Contemporary Socio-Economic Bibliography* (1974)

A. Morgan, *The South Wales Valleys in History: A Guide to Literature* (1975).

Supplements to both, by Elaine Mahoney, were published in 1978 and 1977 respectively.

For those readers who wish to pursue more detailed research into some of the subjects dealt with in this book or require further bibliographical information, we would suggest consultation of our Ph.D. theses:

David Smith, 'The Rebuilding of the South Wales Miners' Federation, 1926–39' (University of Wales, 1976)

Hywel Francis, 'The South Wales Miners and the Spanish Civil War: A Study in Internationalism' (University of Wales, 1977).

Further Reading

Since the first publication of *The Fed* in 1980, a number of important general histories of Wales and the British coalfields as well as histories of the South Wales coalfield and its Valleys have been published.

General histories

Jane Aaron, Theresa Rees, Sandra Betts and Moira Vincentelli (eds.), *Our Sisters' Land: The Changing Identities of Women in Wales* (Cardiff, 1994).

Martin Adeney and John Lloyd, *The Miners' Strike* (London, 1988).

William Ashworth with Mark Pegg, *The History of the British Coal Industry 1946–1982, Volume 5, The Nationalised Industry* (Oxford, 1986).

Huw Beynon (ed.), *Digging Deeper: Issues in the Miners' Strike* (London, 1985).

Alan Campell, Nina Fishman and David Howell (eds.), *Miners, Unions and Politics 1910–1947* (Manchester, 1996).

Tony Curtis, *Wales: The Imagined Nation: Studies in Cultural and National Identity* (Bridgend, 1986).

John Davies, *Hanes Cymru* (London, 1990) (subsequently published in English as *A History of Wales* in 1993).

Paul Davies, *A. J. Cook* (Manchester, 1987).

Roger Fagge, *Power, Culture and Conflict in the Coalfield: West Virginia and South Wales 1900–1922* (Manchester, 1996).

David Gilbert, *Class, Community and Collective Action: Social Change in Two British Coalfields, 1850–1926* (Oxford, 1992).

Trevor Herbert and Gareth Elwyn Jones (eds.), *Wales 1880–1914* (Cardiff, 1988).

Trevor Herbert and Gareth Elwyn Jones (eds.) *Wales Between the Wars* (Cardiff, 1988).

Trevor Herbert and Gareth Elwyn Jones (eds.), *Post-war Wales* (Cardiff, 1995).

Philip Jenkins, *A History of Modern Wales 1536–1990* (London, 1992).

Angela V. John (ed.), *Our Mothers' Land: Chapters in Welsh Women's History* (Cardiff, 1991).

Ieuan Gwynedd Jones, *Communities: Essays in the Social History of Victorian Wales* (Llandysul, 1987).

K. O. Morgan, *Rebirth of a Nation: Wales 1880–1980* (Cardiff/ Oxford, 1981).

Dai Smith, *Wales! Wales?* (London, 1980) (to be republished in 1998 as *Wales: A Question for History*).

Gwyn A. Williams, *The Welsh in their History* (London, 1982).

Gwyn A. Williams, *When Was Wales?* (London, 1985).

South Wales, the Coalfield and the Valleys

Colin Baber and L. J. Williams, *Modern South Wales: Essays in Economic History* (Cardiff, 1986).

Phil Cope, Pat Hill, Simon Jones and Jenny Turner (eds.), *Chasing the Dragon: Creative Community Responses to the Crisis in the South Wales Coalfield* (Ebbw Vale, 1996).

Tony Curtis (ed.), *Coal: An Anthology of Mining* (Bridgend, 1997).

John Davies and Mike Jenkins (eds.), *The Valleys* (Bridgend, 1984).

Arwel Edwards and Richard Jenkins (eds.), *One Step Forward?: South and West Wales Towards 2000* (Llandysul/Swansea, 1990).

Hywel Francis, *Miners Against Fascism: Wales and the Spanish Civil War* (London, 1984).

Hywel Francis, *The Tower Story: Lessons in Vigilance and Freedom* (Hirwaun, 1996).

Colin Hughes, *Lime, Lemon and Sarsaparilla: The Italian Community in South Wales, 1881–1945* (Cardiff, 1991).

Richard Lewis, *Leaders and Teachers: Adult Education and the Challenge of Labour in South Wales, 1906–1940* (Cardiff, 1993).

Mike Lieven, *Senghennydd: The Universal Pit Village, 1890–1930* (Llandysul, 1994).

Dai Smith, *Aneurin Bevan and the World of South Wales* (Cardiff, 1994).

Chris Williams, *Democratic Rhondda: Politics and Society, 1885–1951* (Cardiff, 1996).

Chris Williams, *The South Wales Coalfield: Industry and Society, 1898–1947* (forthcoming 1998).

John Williams, *Was Wales Industrialised? Essays in Modern Welsh History* (Llandysul, 1995).

Journals and Articles

A number of articles have appeared in the journals *Contemporary Wales, Llafur, New Socialist and the Welsh History Review* in the interim period. These articles are particularly relevant:

Hywel Francis and Gareth Rees, 'No Surrender in the Valleys: The 1984–85 Miners' Strike in South Wales', *Llafur*, Vol. 5 No. 2 (1989).

Marilyn Thomas, 'Colliery Closure and the Miner's Experience of Redundancy', *Contemporary Wales*, Vol. 4 (1991).

N. Wass and L. Mainwaring, 'Economic and Social Consequences of Rationalisation in the South Wales Coal Industry', *Contemporary Wales*, Vol. 3 (1989).

Chris Williams, 'The South Wales Miners' Federation', *Llafur*, Vol. 5 No. 3 (1990).

Raymond Williams, 'Mining the Meaning: Key Words in the Miners' Strike', *New Socialist*, 25 (1985) and subsequently in Raymond Williams, *Resources of Hope* (London, 1989).

I. M. Zweiniger-Bargielowska, 'Miners' Militancy: A Study of Four South Wales Collieries during the Middle of the Twentieth Century', *Welsh History Review*, Vol. 16 No. 3 (1993).

Name Index

General Index

524   THE FED